The Public and
Its Possibilities

IN THE SERIES *Urban Life, Landscape, and Policy*
EDITED BY ZANE L. MILLER, DAVID STRADLING, AND LARRY BENNETT

ALSO IN THIS SERIES:

William Issel, *For Both Cross and Flag: Catholic Action, Anti-Catholicism, and National Security Politics in World War II San Francisco*

Lisa Hoffman, *Patriotic Professionalism in Urban China: Fostering Talent*

Andrew Hurley, *Beyond Preservation: Using Public History to Revitalize Inner-Cities*

THE PUBLIC AND ITS POSSIBILITIES

Triumphs and Tragedies in the American City

JOHN D. FAIRFIELD

TEMPLE UNIVERSITY PRESS
PHILADELPHIA

For MARY MCPARTLAND

and in Memory of

CHRISTOPHER LASCH

"Produce great Persons, the rest follows."
—Walt Whitman, "By Blue Ontario's Shore," 1860

Temple University Press
Philadelphia, Pennsylvania 19122
www.temple.edu/tempress

Copyright © 2010 by Temple University
All rights reserved
Published 2010

Library of Congress Cataloging-in-Publication Data

Fairfield, John D., 1955–

 The public and its possibilities : triumphs and tragedies in the American City / John D. Fairfield.
    p. cm.—(Urban life, landscape, and policy)

 Includes bibliographical references and index.

 ISBN 978-1-4399-0210-3 (hardcover : alk. paper)

 1. City and town life—United States—History. 2. Community life—United States—History. 3. Civic improvement—United States—History. 4. Popular culture—United States—History. 5. Political culture—United States—History. 6. Political participation—United States—History. 7. United States—Social conditions. 8. United States—Intellectual life. 9. United States—Politics and government. 10. United States—Social policy. I. Title.

HT123.F28 2010

307.760973—dc22   2009038150

∞ The paper used in this publication meets the requirements of the American National Standard for Information Sciences—Permanence of Paper for Printed Library Materials, ANSI Z39.48-1992

Printed in the United States of America

2 4 6 8 9 7 5 3 1

CONTENTS

Preface: *The Public and Its Possibilities* — ix

Introduction: *Liberalism and the Civic Strand in the American Past* — 1
Civic Aspirations and Liberal Values — 1
An Urban Thesis — 2

PART I CIVIC ASPIRATIONS AND MARKET DEVELOPMENT IN A LONG AGE OF REVOLUTION

1 Democratizing the Republican Ideal of Citizenship: *Virtue, Interests, and the Citizen-Proprietor in the Revolutionary Era* — 9
   Seaport Cities: Crucibles of Market and Public — 10
   The People Out of Doors and the Imperial Crisis — 13
   A More Democratic Public: Consumer Boycotts Politicize the Household — 15
   The Threat of Enslavement and the Need for Virtue: The Unifying Myth of the American Revolution — 17
   Virtue and Vice in an Overheated Market — 20
   Redeeming the Revolution: Virtues or Mechanisms? — 22
   Citizen-Proprietors and the Democratization of Competence — 25
   Revolutionary Legacies, Democratic Futures — 29

2 Creating Citizens in a Commercial Republic: *Market Transformation and the Free Labor Ideal, 1812–1873* — 33
   The Origins of the Free Labor Ideal — 34
   The Market Revolution and the Public Purpose — 35
   Labor Politics in the Jacksonian City: Unjust Government and a Conspiracy to Enslave — 37
   A Crippled Democracy: Jacksonian Fears and Whig Paternalism — 40

The Free Labor Ideology and the Transformation of Northern Whiggery	43
Positive Liberty: Turning Slaves into Citizens	45
The Limits of Radical Republicanism	48

3 The Short, Strange Career of Laissez-Faire: *Liberal Reformers and Genteel Culture in the Gilded Age* — 53

Big Business and Small Politics in the Gilded Age	55
Liberal Reformers and Genteel Culture	57
The Liberal Reformers' Encounter with the City	59
Civic Murder: Liberal Reformers and Public Opinion	61
"This Word Culture": An Industrial Tragedy at Pullman	64

PART II POPULAR CULTURE, POLITICAL CULTURE: BUILDING A DEMOCRATIC PUBLIC

4 The Democratic Public in City and Nation: *The Jacksonian City and the Limits of Antislavery* — 71

Constructing a Public Realm	72
In the Streets: Law and the Public Realm	74
To the Park: The Strengths and Weaknesses of the Jacksonian Public	76
Popular Culture, Political Culture	79
Young America and Democratic Culture	81
The Republic of the Streets and Fields	83
The Astor Place Riot	85
Fatal Flaw: Young America and Negrophobia	88
Cultural Laissez-Faire versus the Evangelical United Front	89
Antislavery: Passion and Rationality in the Antebellum Public	92
Lincoln's Rhetorical Revolution	95

5 The Democratic Public Discredited: *The New York City Draft Riots and Urban Reconstruction, 1850–1872* — 98

"The Most Radical City in America"	100
Nativism and the Erosion of Municipal Autonomy	101
The New York City Draft Riots	103
Draconian Justice: Reconstructing New York City	107
The Spectacular Rise and Precipitous Fall of Boss Tweed	110
Postwar Republicanism: Labor Revolt and Metropolitan Capital	114
Retrenchment and Reform	116

6 Cultural Hierarchy and Good Government: *The Democratic Public in Eclipse* — 120

Highbrow/Lowbrow and an Incompetent Citizenry	121
Don't Get Out the Vote	124
Municipal Counterrevolution: Dillon's Rule and the Benevolent Expert	127

Domesticating the City   130
Civic Vertigo: The City Biological and Pathological   133
The Degeneration of Popular Politics   136
Mob Mind, Befuddled Public   139

PART III THE PUBLIC IN PROGRESSIVISM AND WAR

7 The Republican Moment: *The Rediscovery of the Public in the Progressive Era*   147
    The City Beautiful and Intelligent   149
    The Georgists and the City Republic   151
    Democracy as Cooperative Inquiry: The Social Centers Movement   154
    Mass Media and the Socialization of Intelligence   157
    Nickel Madness or the Academy of the Working Man?   159
    The National Board of Review of Motion Pictures and the Mutual *Decision*   163
    The Rise of Hollywood and the Incorporation of Movie Culture   167

8 The Public Goes to War but Does Not Come Back: *Requiem for a Participatory Democracy*   170
    The War Intellectuals and The New Republic   173
    The War for the American Mind   176
    From Mastery to Drift   178
    Trusting the Public Too Much or Too Little?   181
    A Democrat on the Defensive   183
    Participatory Democracy and Urban Culture: From Public Opinion to Public Relations   186

PART IV A DEMOCRACY OF CONSUMERS

9 From Economic Democracy to Social Security: *The Labor Movement and the Rise of the Welfare/Warfare State*   193
    Industrial Democracy, Industrial Discipline   194
    The Syndicalist Moment   195
    From the New Freedom to the New Nationalism: War and the Triumph of the Corporate State   198
    Labor's War   201
    From Welfare Capitalism to Moral Capitalism   203
    Democratic Unions, Labor Party   205
    The Second New Deal: Consumerist Democracy and the End of Antimonopoly   207
    From New Deal to New War: Liberals and Labor Abandon Reform   209
    Taming Labor in the Welfare/Warfare State   212

10 **Constructing a Consumer Culture:** *Redirecting Leisure from Civic Engagement to Insatiable Desire* ... 215
   The Popular Demand for Leisure and the Rise of the Saloon ... 216
   The Leisure Question and Cheap Amusements ... 218
   The Discovery of Play ... 221
   Captains of Consciousness, Land of Desire ... 223
   Exit the Saloon, Enter the Bijou ... 225
   Shaping Character, Inculcating Values ... 228
   The Incorporation of the Consumer Culture ... 230
   Mass Culture, Mass Media, and the Consumerization of Politics ... 234

11 **Private Vision, Public Resources:** *Mass Suburbanization and the Decline of the City* ... 238
   New Deal Urban Policy and the Suburban-Industrial Complex ... 241
   The Origins of the Urban Crisis I: Eroding the Tax and Employment Base ... 245
   The Origins of the Urban Crisis II: Homeowner Populism and the Fragmentation of Metropolitan Government ... 247
   Central City Housing: The Racial Time Bomb ... 250
   Dispossession: Urban Redevelopment and Urban Renewal ... 253
   Confronting the Reverse Welfare State: From Civil Rights to Black Power ... 256
   Two Societies, Separate and Unequal ... 261
   Suburban Secession and Farewell to the Public Realm ... 264

Conclusion: The Future of the City: *Civic Renewal and Environmental Politics* ... 268
   The Great Unfinished Tasks of American Civilization ... 270
   Private City, Public Crisis ... 271
   Visions of Fear and Hope ... 273
   Toward an Ecology of the City ... 275

Acknowledgments ... 281
Notes ... 283
Index ... 343

PREFACE

The Public and Its Possibilities

Half a century ago, the consensus school of historians argued that the values of the market always reigned supreme in the United States. "Capitalism came in the first ships," announced a 1959 survey of "the forces which shaped modern America." Challenging the progressive historians who placed economic conflict between the people and the interests at the center of American history, consensus historians saw basic agreement on the pace and direction of economic development. All Americans agreed on "the economic virtues of capitalist culture as necessary qualities of man" and "shared a belief in the rights of property, the philosophy of economic individualism, the value of competition." The "business of politics" had been to protect "this competitive world," not "to cripple it with a plan for common collective action."[1]

Although the consensus interpretation once seemed unassailable, two generations of historians have since challenged it by recovering a rich history of "collective action for the public good." The rethinking began with the rediscovery of civic republicanism in the ideological origins of the American Revolution, but there is hardly a field that has not been transformed. We now know that nineteenth-century political leaders who spoke only the idiom of self-interest risked losing contact with the citizenry. Radical artisans claimed the mantle of civic virtue and invoked the commonwealth to defend their crafts and communities against innovators pursuing economic self-interest. African Americans appropriated republican concepts of virtue and benevolence to indict slavery and racism and reshape American public life and politics. Women created a public culture of sociability, solidarity, and neighborhood attachments that provided an alternative to privacy and domesticity and challenged the exclusion of women from the public realm. In the revisions most pertinent to this study, the successes and failures of American cities, once seen as functions of a capitalist culture of privatism, also hinged on struggles over the uses of public power.[2]

Yet even as the consensus interpretation faded in our historiography, it materialized in our politics. We entered the twenty-first century in the grips of a "golden straitjacket" in which private self-interest defined the limits of respectable thought. The market answered to all difficulties: voucher systems to supplant public education, for-profit hospitals in place of universal health insurance, and pollution credits in place of environmental regulations. Meanwhile, public institutions decayed. We inherited a legacy of city parks, transit and library systems, tunnels and bridges, and facilities for public health and safety from previous generations, but we have failed to preserve this legacy, much less add to it. The balance between our private and public lives has skewed too far toward the private, as is reflected in the technologies of our everyday lives—from cars, computers, and cell phones to TVs, VCRs, and iPods.[3]

The deterioration of the public realm generated an explosion of scholarship on civic life, public space, and democratic theory. But this work exerted only limited influence on public debate and policy because too few scholars write for a general audience. In the neglect of public things, public intellectuals disappeared as well. The city has become inhospitable to those who think most creatively about its future. Store-lined sidewalks, cheap bars, cafes, restaurants, and affordable apartments—the urban habitats of independent scholars like Jane Jacobs, William H. Whyte, and Paul Goodman—disappeared under interstate highways or upscale urban renewal projects. As big-city newspapers, journals, and bookstores gave way to university presses and academic conferences, the monograph and the lecture supplanted more urban forms of intelligence like the essay and the conversation.[4]

But over the past thirty years, the academic investigation of the idea of the public has reconnected scholars with popular experience. A shared frustration with the loss of self-government and the erosion of community unites scholars and citizens in search of a public philosophy. We "can hardly offer a meaning for the word public," a democrat theorist warned in 1984. But since that time, the translation or rediscovery of theorists and historians of the public (such as Jurgen Habermas, Hannah Arendt, John Dewey, and J.G.A. Pocock) has stimulated creative work across disciplines. Rich but ponderous, this is not the sort of scholarship one might expect to find reshaping public debate. Nevertheless, it has found its way into mainstream journals of opinion and public debates because it speaks to the desire for a politics that transcends self-interest.[5]

The remarkable variety of uses that we make of the word "public" in everyday speech reveals the popular aspirations that inform scholarship. We use public as an adjective to refer to formal government (public office, public servant), openness and accessibility (public utilities, public meetings), or political expression (public opinion, public good). Combining these meanings, we use the public as a noun to envision an ideal world in which political convictions and policies arise out of ongoing arguments in open and accessible settings that, in turn, direct formal political action. Athens's agora, Rome's forum, Paris's cafes, London's pubs, New England's town squares, and Beijing's Tiananmen Square all suggest the potential of this ideal. Both scholars and citizens are drawn to the public because it makes it possible for us to imagine democracy as something other than the bureaucratic state.

No one has done more to explore the public in the past thirty years than historians. Keenly aware that their craft once shaped public debate, historians have also lamented their declining public role more than most scholars. Writing in the profession's flagship journal in 1986, an eminent historian explored the possibilities of using public life as a focus for a new narrative that could recapture a general audience. Yet despite the production of hundreds of exemplary monographs over the past two generations, no new historical narratives have synthesized this work for general readers.[6]

Recent historical writing does, however, contain the elements of a new narrative. In exploring previous efforts to cultivate a responsible citizenry and create an economy and culture that support our democratic aspirations, historians have recovered not just the roots of the present in the past but the roads not taken as well. They have used the public to rediscover the possibilities obscured in our excessively privatized world. A "sense of possibilities that are unrealized and that might be realized," the philosopher John Dewey observed, "are when they are put in contrast with actual conditions, the most penetrating 'criticism' of the latter that can be made." In showing that our past contained multiple possibilities and that our choices shaped which of those possibilities would be realized, historians provide us a fuller understanding of our past and underscore the importance of the choices we make.[7]

Despite Dewey's emphasis on possibility, his canonical work on the public is entitled *The Public and Its Problems* (1927). By "problems," Dewey meant to draw our attention to the broken character of the modern public and to the public as a form of association that identified problems and created political agencies to deal with them. Ordinarily, Dewey defined democracy as a moral ideal infusing work, culture, and social life, as well as formal political structures. But he narrowed his conception of democracy in his single work of formal political philosophy. In defining the public, Dewey excluded associations "for scientific inquiry, for religious worship, for artistic production and enjoyment, for sport, for giving and receiving instruction, for industrial and commercial undertakings." Just as this narrative includes much of what Dewey excluded, its title respectfully invokes his fuller democratic philosophy. To provide each individual ample opportunity "to be socially useful and to develop personal powers in the only way they can be developed, through some form of creative activity," democracy requires a public that creates possibilities even as it solves problems.[8]

The following narrative, rather than tapping new documentary sources or employing new methods, synthesizes much of the vast monographic literature of the past two generations. In the middle of William Gaddis's great novel on the nature of originality, *The Recognitions*, a minor character named Otto writes down the words of one of the main characters for later quotation in his perennially unfinished novel: "Orignlty not inventn bt snse of recall, recgntion, pattrns alrdy thr, q." I have long identified with poor Otto—whose talent never matched his ambition—more than I would like. But through the seemingly endless process of completing this manuscript, I have taken heart that Gaddis saw fit to allow Otto to utter, even if only through the words of another, the central message of his novel. In that spirit, this narrative brings into greater clarity patterns and themes already present in recent historical writing. In reexamining our history in light of public life and experience, it hopes to rekindle our political imagination and contribute to a coming and necessary debate about the future of our democratic civilization.[9]

INTRODUCTION

Liberalism and the Civic Strand in the American Past

We find civic aspirations everywhere we turn in the American past, even in the most unlikely places. Civic aspirations arose from conservative and radical perspectives, from theological and secular foundations, from a bleak view of human nature and a hopeful one, and from the determination to either overcome the depravity of human nature or to unlock its potential. They appeared in times of war and times of peace, in periods of economic depression and economic expansion, and in debates concerning work and leisure as well as politics. Americans have recognized civic affairs as the measure of their civilization, from the Puritan effort in 1630 to "seek out a place of cohabitation and consortship under a due form of government civil and ecclesiastical" through President Dwight Eisenhower's warning in 1961 that "security and liberty may prosper together" only if "an alert and knowledgeable citizenry can compel the proper meshing of the huge industrial and military machinery of defense with our peaceful methods and goals." An integral and ubiquitous aspect of American experience, our unrealized civic aspirations provide the essential counterpoint to an excessive focus on private and individual interests. They speak to our better selves.[1]

CIVIC ASPIRATIONS AND LIBERAL VALUES

Liberalism in both its classical and modern forms treats private interest as the essential business of life and thereby obscures our civic aspirations. It leaves public matters to representatives of the people, who are thus freed to pursue their private happiness. American liberalism in its great historical innovation, the United States Constitution, asserted that a republic might dispense with civic virtue and minimize the influence of citizens in public affairs. Rather than count on the civic virtue of citizens, the Founding Fathers relied on a system of checks and balances to "make it advantageous even for bad men to act for the public good." Vice would check vice and ambition check ambition, making virtue unnecessary.[2]

It has never been that simple. The liberal tradition for two centuries lived off the borrowed capital from civic and religious traditions that tempered and enriched its vision of private freedom. But in the recent past, liberals lost touch with those traditions and gave rein to license. Liberalism now lacks the moral resources to chasten the self-seeking that returns nothing to the society it exploits. Its vision of the liberated individual is no longer leavened with a recognition of the obligations and opportunities that bind us together. This leaves an unalloyed liberalism ill-equipped to satisfy aspirations for self-government at a time when people believe they have lost control of the institutions that shape their lives and that their communities have fallen into disarray.[3]

In this crisis, Americans have exhibited a renewed interest in the virtues missing from the liberal tradition. Liberal values, they discovered, gave an excessively private cast to our civilization, focusing it on capitalist enterprise, individual rights, and domestic ideology. Market expansion, driven first by individual entrepreneurs and later by corporate enterprise, made material abundance a central part of the American dream. The United States embraced the cult of domesticity and the single-family dwelling more completely than any other society. In the last half of the twentieth century, Americans' fear of intrusive government gave rise to an expansive conception of privacy, placing a long list of private choices beyond the reach of democratic majorities.[4]

Immersed in our private lives, we abandoned the responsibilities and satisfactions of self-government. Rather than face up to internal tensions and injustices, Americans exported their conflicts to an ever-expanding frontier, which now includes the Middle East and the militarized reaches of outer space. The elaboration of our imperial infrastructure in the national security state and military-industrial complex of the post–World War II period created the most imperial of presidencies in the first years of the twenty-first century. The Founding Fathers' nagging fear that an unfettered executive, in collaboration with the military and secret services, might lead to catastrophic consequences has never been timelier.[5]

An Urban Thesis

But there is also a civic strand in the American past, one associated with cities rather than frontiers. From colonial times, the city "forced attention to matters of common concern which could not be ignored even by a people individualistically inclined," wrote Arthur Schlesinger in his 1940 essay from which urban historians trace their origins. City life promoted a "necessary concern with the general welfare" that "contravened the doctrine of individualism and nourished a sense of social responsibility." Cities promoted a "civic spirit," Schlesinger concluded, fueling voluntary efforts that provided "training in collective action, constantly reenforced by the everyday contact of the citizens in less formal undertakings."[6]

Schlesinger's essay came at the culmination of a hundred years of American thought centered on the ideal of the great city that provided people with stimulation, beauty, and communion. Ralph Waldo Emerson wrote that "we can ill spare the commanding social benefits of cities." They must be reorganized to suit "an intellectual purpose," while public sponsorship of art, music, and intellectual life should insure universal "access to the masterpieces of art and nature." Cities played a special role in shaping our civilization, an 1843 study of American life added, because they afforded "a wider field both for virtue and vice and they are more prone to innovation, whether for good or evil." A powerful religious impulse reinforced civic concerns. The city "reveals the moral ends of being," a midcentury minister put it, and "sets the awful problems of life."[7]

The recognition of the city's role in American life came to a head at the turn of the nineteenth century. Having gone through a period of political upheaval and cultural anxiety, Americans explored their urban future in a national literature of the city (Crane, Norris, Dreiser), a school of urban painting (Sloan, Henri, the Ashcan artists), and utopian visions and programs of action. Given national prominence through the White City at the center of the 1893 Chicago World's Fair, the new civic architecture of the City Beautiful movement envisioned a city organized to meet the needs and interests of its people.[8]

Neither frontiers nor rugged individuals, markets nor self-interest, but the city and civic life stood at the center of Progressive Era ideals. "Make no little plans, they have no magic to stir's men's blood," wrote Daniel Burnham, whose *Plan of Chicago* (1909) exemplified the civic aspirations of the era. We forgot how "intensely interesting civic affairs are," another progressive argued, "and how admirably adapted to the beautiful and happy use of leisure are the common services of thought and action." Let us emulate Athens, a settlement house leader added, and "use leisure time to create great ideals, great loyalties, great power" rather than imitate Rome and "dissipate our leisure time and corrupt not only ourselves but the whole world." As late as the Great Depression, the usually staid pages of *The Encyclopedia of the Social Sciences* still described the city as "the vital concern of all who desire high national aspirations."[9]

The civic strand thus leads us inevitably to cities. The city is etymologically and historically the foundation of civilization, often defined as the ability to live harmoniously in cities. For at least two thousand years, cities have been cradles of civilization where the full richness and potential of human life unfolds. Cities must cultivate citizens who create, sustain, and organize civilized life. As part of that process, cities have long nurtured experiments in face-to-face politics and self-government, an irrepressible demand that reemerges every time it is suppressed. The unique promise of American cities has always been the aspiration to build a democratic civilization that involves each individual in civic life and thereby encourages the highest development of the mind and character of all. An active, articulate, and responsible citizenry represents democracy's most demanding ideal and the ultimate achievement of a democratic civilization.[10]

As the organizing force in the rise of our democratic and capitalistic civilization, American cities have been the crucial arena for the cultivation of an active citizenry attentive to the public good and suspicious of those who put self-interest above the welfare of the whole. Cities therefore shaped national debates over the competing demands of civic and market, public and private. These national debates, in turn, often focused on cities. Thus, the following narrative develops an overlapping analysis of national and urban experience, placing cities at the center of our national history and urban issues in a broader political, cultural, and economic context. The story returns always to cities, where the tensions between civic and market and between public and private have been most pronounced.[11]

The narrative also develops an overlapping analysis of economic and cultural matters. The prospects for a democratic civilization in the United States have always depended on the construction of an economy and a culture that complement our civic aspirations. The triumphs and the tragedies of our history thus reveal themselves only through these overlapping stories. Therefore, while the general thrust of the narrative is chronological, its thematic orientation requires some moving back and forth in time. Finally, the narrative invites other narratives to overlap this one. This book, that is, offers *a* civic history, not *the* civic history of the United States, for no single study can possibly comprehend the richness and complexity of our civic history.[12]

Part I examines the search for economic arrangements that would produce a responsible citizenry from the Revolution through Reconstruction. At the height of this long age of revolution, just as Americans embarked on a breathtaking experiment in transforming slaves into citizens, a genteel culture of manners and morals undercut the faith in democracy and helped to bring Reconstruction to an end. Part II picks up this theme of culture, retracing our steps through the nineteenth century, focusing on the rise and fall of a democratic culture, and ending with the eclipse of the public in the Gilded Age. Part III begins with the rediscovery of the public as a counterweight to corporate power in the Progressive Era. It then explores the transformation of the Progressive Era faith in public opinion into the techniques of public relations during the pivotal period just before and after the American intervention into World War I. Part IV analyzes the role of the corporate economy and consumer culture in transforming civic values in the twentieth century and ends with a discussion of the role of postwar suburbanization in the decline of the city. The conclusion considers the future role of the city in American civilization.

PART I

Civic Aspirations and Market Development in a Long Age of Revolution

Two powerful revolutions remade Western societies in the eighteenth and mid-nineteenth centuries. Economic revolution expanded the range of the market, quickened the pace of commerce, laid the foundation for industrialization, and introduced capitalist methods and attitudes. Political revolution weakened or destroyed monarchical and aristocratic forms of power and introduced republican or democratic regimes. In Europe, the age of revolution began with the French Revolution in 1789 and ended with the failed revolutions of 1848. An age of capital followed in which a triumphant bourgeoisie remade the world in its image.[1]

Although deeply intertwined, economic revolution tended to precede political revolution in Europe. But the most dramatic period of economic transformation in the United States came only after its political revolution. As a consequence, Americans experienced economic revolution as citizens. David Ramsay, a South Carolinian delegate to the Continental Congress, understood the "immense" difference the shift from "subjects to citizens" entailed. "Subjects look up to a master," the Charleston physician explained in 1789, "but citizens are so far equal, that none have hereditary rights superior to others." European visitors in the early nineteenth century noted that the new republic differed from Europe in not having "permanent and distinct classes." Europeans expected the "laboring man" to be "patient over his toils, from the settled conviction that he can never go beyond his circle and can never change the laws that govern him." But in the United States, citizenship gave rise to a "universal spirit of improvement in the humblest as well as in the highest classes."[2]

Capitalism and democracy, in other words, grew up together in the United States, sometimes in support but often in opposition. Even as Americans *feverishly pursued economic interests, they measured economic arrangements against civic concerns and held politics responsible for shaping society. Yet the first one hundred years of the American republic have long been interpreted in terms of an irresistible triumph of competitive individualism and capitalist culture. Alexis de Tocqueville's analysis of democracy in America has often been deployed in such interpretations, without mention of the thing that amazed Tocqueville above all else, a civic culture he thought likely to "produce wonders."*[3]

Reporting back to curious Europeans after his visit in 1831, Tocqueville felt confident of his ability to describe the liberties and equality that Americans enjoyed. But "the political activity that pervades the United States," he demurred, "must be seen in order to be understood." No "sooner do you set foot upon American ground, than you are stunned by a kind of tumult; a confused clamor is heard on every side; and a thousand simultaneous voices demand the satisfaction of their social wants."

The "great political agitation of American legislative bodies," Tocqueville observed, "is a mere episode, or a sort of continuation, of that universal movement which originates in the lowest classes of the people and extends successively to all ranks of society." Almost "the only pleasure which an American knows is to take part in the government." Deprived of political outlets, the American would "feel an immense void" and "his wretchedness would be unbearable." It was "impossible to spend more effort in the pursuit of happiness."

Americans "frequently conduct public business very ill," Tocqueville conceded, but the democratic process generated "an all-pervading and restless activity, a superabundant force, and an energy which is inseparable from it." The "ceaseless agitation" of democratic politics enabled the "lower orders" to extend the "circle of their ideas" and gain a "certain degree of self-respect." By virtue of his vote, the citizen commanded "the services of minds more enlightened than his own. He is canvassed by a multitude of applicants, and, in seeking to deceive him in a thousand ways, they really enlighten him."

In Europe, Tocqueville feared, the "source of public virtues is dried up." But in the United States, no one "easily allows himself to be reduced to the mere material cares of life and the humblest artisan casts at times an eager and a furtive glance into the higher regions of the intellect." The "multitude begin to take an interest in the labors of the mind" and the "number of those who cultivate science, letters, and the arts, becomes immense." American citizens are "better informed and more active" than Europeans. "In no country in the world," Tocqueville concluded, "do the citizens make such exertions for the common weal."

The democratic energy that amazed Tocqueville claimed the American Revolution as its own. Civic pride and an obligation to perpetuate the republic remained powerful and ineffaceable legacies of the Revolution. Citizens found in political debate the same "public happiness" and pursued the same "passion for distinction" that fired patriot elites like Thomas Jefferson and John Adams. A revolutionary citizenry, lacking any model of where it inevitably should be heading, remained uncertain about everything in the future except that its own decisions would shape it. An intense interest in public affairs and the joy of being "a participator in the government of affairs," in Jefferson's phrase, shaped the early history of the new republic.[4]

The age of revolution thus began earlier and lasted longer in the North American colonies and in the United States than it did in Europe. In the 1760s and 1770s, colonial rebellion sparked a utopian effort to preserve political liberty and "prepare in time an asylum for mankind." The age of revolution continued through the Jacksonian and antebellum years when Americans attempted to square their commitment to civic virtue with the acquisitive opportunities of an expanding market economy. It climaxed during the 1860s with the stupendous bloodletting of a civil war to preserve the "last, best hope of earth" and ensure that "government by the people, for the people, and of the people shall not perish from the earth." The United States' long age of revolution ended only with the collapse of Reconstruction and the abandonment of the effort to turn slaves into citizens. When Gilded Age Americans accepted the inevitability of corporate hierarchy and economic inequality, an unfinished revolution came to an end.[5]

Part I tells the story of this long age of revolution and emphasizes the centrality of civic aspirations from the American Revolution through the early years of Reconstruction. The public and the market first emerged alongside each other in the colonial seaports and, over the course of the American Revolution, gave rise to a new civic ideal of the citizen-proprietor. An amalgam of liberal, republican, and Protestant values, the ideal of the citizen-proprietor subsequently shaped various civic responses to the market revolution that transformed the United States in the half century after the end of the War of 1812. The ideal of the citizen-proprietor underwrote a fuller free labor ideology as Americans linked economic independence to political freedom and ultimately applied that logic to the destruction of slavery. But in the face of mounting demands from former slaves, women, and workers at the height of Reconstruction, the free labor ideal gave way. A dissident group of Liberal Republicans bolted their party in revolt against active government and the effort to reconstruct the nation along free labor lines. Liberal Republicanism both depended upon and strengthened the influence of a genteel culture that legitimized the growing inequalities of the Gilded Age, obscured political and economic realities, and brought the age of revolution to an end.

CHAPTER 1

Democratizing the Republican Ideal of Citizenship

Virtue, Interests, and the Citizen-Proprietor in the Revolutionary Era

The market and the public grew in tandem during the colonial era, generating the tension between liberal rights and republican virtue that shaped Anglo-American debate in the revolutionary era. In protesting Britain's new imperial regulations imposed after the Seven Years' War (1756–1763), American patriots invoked a liberal vision of the emerging market society alongside civic republican warnings about the corrupting influence of commerce. The new regulations violated the liberal rights of life, liberty, and property. But they also gave rise to republican fears of a British conspiracy to corrupt American virtue, ensnare the colonies in an economic system that produced extremes of luxury and misery, and replace liberty with slavery. Colonists resolved to "forego the elegancies and luxuries of life" if that proved the only means of protecting their liberty. Writing in 1773, "A Consistent Patriot" warned that when "the importation is connected with the ruin of government, . . . when it is designed for that purpose and will infallibly have that effect, we ought to consider and treat it as we would THE PLAGUE."[1]

As they expanded outward from Britain, the market and the public took more democratic form in the colonies. The availability of land led American patriots to hope they might avoid the economic inequality and political corruption they saw threatening liberty in England. Even before the Revolution, the wider distribution of property encouraged broader participation in public affairs. Consumer boycotts and other revolutionary actions then brought new voices into politics, as did the struggles over the new constitutions and the foreign and domestic policies of the new republic. By the 1790s, new commercial opportunities encouraged independent farmers and urban artisans to abandon the traditional republican suspicion of commerce. Engaged in what Benjamin

Franklin called "the necessary and useful kinds" of trades, small proprietors proclaimed themselves the most virtuous of citizens.[2]

The American Revolution thus democratized the republican ideal of citizenship. Before the Revolution, a small elite claimed exclusive possession of civic virtue, insisting that only those aloof from the daily struggle for existence could perceive and pursue the public good. That view did not survive the Revolution. During the Pennsylvania Assembly's debate over the rechartering of the Bank of North America in 1786, backcountry legislator William Findley refused to allow merchant Robert Morris and other directors of the bank to pose as disinterested gentlemen. Advocates of recharter, Findley charged, "feel interested in it personally, and therefore by promoting it they were acting as judges in their own cause." Findley wished not to discredit self-interest, but to expose the false pose of disinterestedness and to assert the right of small proprietors to pursue their interests too. "Any others in their situation," Findley concluded, should "do as they did."[3]

Findley's defense of self-interest did not preclude seeing small proprietors as more virtuous than idle aristocrats. Small proprietors claimed that their common sense and limited wants, their habits of honesty and frugality, their thorough acquaintance with the needs and abilities of the people and the productive capacity of the country made them the most competent and virtuous citizens. During the Constitutional ratification debates, New York City's leading Antifederalist insisted that small proprietors "are more temperate, of better morals and less ambition than the great." They "have less temptation," Melancton Smith continued, "they are inclined by habit and the company with which they associate, to set bounds to their passions and appetites." When "the interest of this part of the community is pursued," he concluded, "the public good is pursued." Smith later helped create New York City's Democratic Society in 1794, one of many city-based political clubs that identified the virtues and the interests of urban artisans and mechanics with the health of the republic.[4]

SEAPORT CITIES: CRUCIBLES OF MARKET AND PUBLIC

As crucibles of market and public, colonial seaports first experienced the tension between economic interest and civic aspiration that shaped the age of revolution. As centers of commerce, the seaports required more intensive government to police the boundary between individual right and public good. As the focus of British policy and the locus of British officialdom, they tested the extent of imperial power and the limits of popular protest. Their dense populations and crowded streets, taverns and churches, public buildings and print shops made the seaports the centers of political mobilization and ideological ferment.[5]

As the colonies became integrated into the empire and the Atlantic market, government policy and prerogative came under greater scrutiny. As representative assemblies and contested elections became a regular feature of colonial life, seaport elites complained that the "rabble" no longer took their political cues from their social betters. But the growing disposition to criticize political authority depended on places and spaces in which to do so. The first American newspaper came out in the 1690s, although the colonial government silenced it after one issue. An intercolonial postal system also emerged in the 1690s. In 1704, Boston's postmaster started a more cautious and long-lived newspaper. In the following decades, seaport printing presses churned out almanacs and magazines as well as newspapers.[6]

Coffeehouses, out of which the first newspapers came, provided a new forum for discussion among the seaport's commercial and professional classes. Taverns provided similar opportunities for a broader spectrum of urbanites. In the 1750s, New York City's *Independent Reflector* carried on the conversations and advanced the political ambitions of what royalists disparaged as a "republican cabal." Admiring the network of coffeehouses and newspapers of London's republican opposition, the independent New Yorkers proposed to "extend their chearful Influence" throughout the colonies. Setting in motion plans for a library and a college, they promoted "a spirit of inquiry among the people" and dismissed learning that could not be "exerted for the Benefit of Mankind" as a "specious Kind of Ignorance."[7]

The urban press spread both literacy and a new style of politics. In 1715, the Massachusetts House of Representatives began printing its journals to win popular support in its conflict with the royal governor. By 1750 newspapers and pamphlets became an essential part of electioneering and legislating. Read aloud and discussed in taverns, coffeehouses, and open-air meetings, newspapers and pamphlets generated arguments that turned government from a private to a public matter.[8]

By the time of the Revolution, more than half of all white, adult males in the colonies could read. While the rate for women lagged behind, both rates exceeded those in Europe. Elites railed against literary efforts "to inflame the minds of the common people," to "breed and nourish discontent, and to foment Faction and Sedition." Worried that "scribbling" led to "leveling," elites nevertheless responded in kind, conducting their political disputes in print, often with passion. "When all Order and Government is endeavored to be Trampled on," and "Reflections are cast upon Persons of all Degrees," they feared, "must not these things end in Sedition?" If abandoning deference for participation meant sedition, colonists made the most of it. In eroding the equation of social position and public authority, the impersonal world of print undermined hierarchical relations rooted in face-to-face encounters. Reading and writing, disputation and controversy became important means of civic engagement.[9]

Neither political operatives nor professional news gatherers, entrepreneurial printers supplied commercial news for an urban market. But they were also public figures, attached to post offices, serving as clerks, and printing the laws. A "walking public sphere," Benjamin Franklin pursued civic endeavors even as he described his press as a private business rather than a public institution. With the rise of political contentiousness and the pamphleteering that accompanied it, political news crept into the press. Printers' professions of neutrality and their pecuniary interests encouraged them to give voice to contrary opinions. Printers saw themselves as providing a forum for opinions, not endorsing them. When men "differ in opinion," Franklin put it, "both Sides ought equally to have the Advantage of being heard by the Publick."[10]

The more political rivals clashed in public, the more they invited plebeian voices to join in. "We all know it is neither the Great, the Rich, nor the Learned, that compose the Body of the People," Pennsylvania's colonial governor announced in defense of debtor relief in 1722, "and that Civil Government ought carefully to protect the poor laborious and industrious Part of Mankind." Philadelphia elites disagreed. "Sobriety, Industry and Frugality" alone made one rich, while "luxury, Idleness and Folly" made one poor. Joining the fray, the plebeian pamphleteer "Roger Plowman" judged the rich man's wealth nothing more than the poor man's debt. "It is an old saying with us," Plowman wrote, "that we must never grease the fat Sow in the Arse, and starve the pigs."[11]

By midcentury, colonial seaports joined an Atlantic market of vast opportunities and perilous vulnerabilities. Particularly in times of war, these outposts of the British Empire generated great wealth (from contracting, privateering, piracy, and smuggling) and dire hardship (from unemployment, impressment, death, and abandonment). Expanding opportunity spread the idea that one person's advance did not come at another's expense. But hardship meant that traditional ideas of the commonwealth remained potent. "For men to overreach others," Boston's Cotton Mather preached in 1710, "because they find them ignorant, or screw grievously upon them, only because they are poor and low. . . .'tis an abomination."[12]

In the Great Awakening of the 1740s, in the midst of the boom and bust of imperial war, evangelical preachers looked askance at great riches. He who was "governed by regard to his own private interest," the evangelical leader Jonathan Edwards warned, acted "the part of the enemy to the public." Fiery pamphleteers criticized the rich as "carnal wretches, hypocrites, fighters against God, children of the devil, cursed Pharisees," while radical evangelists called on the poor to "Pull them down, turn them out, and put others in their Place." But as market values spread, the established clergy sanctified wealth. In 1748, Congregational minister Jonathan Mayhew spoke for the wealthy when he argued that "public happiness is nothing but the happiness of a number of individuals united in society."[13]

The market and the public created an unstable mix as visions of abundance clashed with nightmares of poverty and degradation. In Boston, where only the new structures to incarcerate the poor rivaled in size the mansions of wealthy merchants, elites expressed a combination of political and economic ideas difficult to square. Claiming a monopoly of political power on the basis of their stewardship of the public good, they chafed under any restriction of their pursuit of self-interest. When the few piled up riches, an editor instructed in 1748, the people "ought to make a strict Enquiry, how they came by them." Is "it a crime to be rich?" he asked. "Yes, certainly, At the Publick Expense." Even without a new and onerous British policy in the wake of the Seven Years' War (1754–1763), tensions were bound to rise.[14]

THE PEOPLE OUT OF DOORS AND THE IMPERIAL CRISIS

In 1765, the Stamp Act imposed a new tax on all written documents, and the seaports erupted in protest. Building on a tradition of the people "out of doors" (outside legal representative assemblies), angry crowds directed their wrath at British authority and symbols of colonial wealth, smashing in the doors of elegant houses with axes, reducing furniture to splinters, even ripping through partitions, leaving hollow shells. Mobs acted "with a rage scarce to be exemplified by the most savage people," wrote the Massachusetts colonial governor, in "a War of Plunder, of general levelling and taking away the Distinction of Rich and Poor." In New York City, a crowd burned the governor in effigy and gutted the house of a military leader who vowed to "cram the Stamps down their Throats with the End of my Sword." Enraged Philadelphians demanded that the houses of supporters of the Stamp Act "be level'd with the Street."[15]

In the ensuing revolutionary crisis that led to independence in 1776, radicals organized colonial anger to challenge the formal institutions of royal power. In the colonial seaports, constricted size and the intermingling of commercial, residential, and productive spaces made it relatively easy for citizens to gain a knowledge of city life. Cramped interiors encouraged merchants and laborers, proprietors and porters, to live out of doors. Coffeehouses and taverns, even those that merchants made into their specialized meeting places, opened onto the life of the street. The public, gossipy style of life of these walking cities facilitated the mobilization and organization of popular energies during the Revolution.[16]

The Boston waterfront, the "grand engine" of the city's market economy, also provided the public spaces—coffeehouses, taverns, streets, and wharves—where all ranks came together to air their differences and confront British power. Merchants and laborers, artisans and sailors, servants and slaves battled custom and naval officials over new taxes, smuggled goods, and the press gangs that seized Bostonians for the British navy. Unequal sacrifices and hardships sometimes led the poor to steal or destroy property and servants and slaves to run away. But most Bostonians united in a community of interest, judging nonimportation and smuggling as "public virtue and Patriotism." Under the direction of elites, gangs of toughs took control of the waterfront and forced British officials to the safety of Castle Island in the harbor. Meanwhile, the waterfront's newspapers and shipping lines provided the networks of communication that spread revolution throughout the colonies.[17]

Radicals used taverns to assemble crowds; exhort, persuade, and recruit followers; create extralegal committees; and establish communication with other radicals across the colonies. New York City supported one drink seller for every thirteen adult white males, ranging from refined taverns that hosted clubs of respectable men devoted to self-improvement and the public good to unlicensed grog shops that encouraged prostitution, gambling, theft, and the buying of votes. Some New Yorkers questioned the propriety of mixing liquor and politics. But taverns, long the sites of formal political meetings and spirited conversation about civic improvements and the public good, as well as the sharing of gossip, mail, and newspapers, irresistibly became centers of revolutionary mobilization. "It is indeed possible to be *merry* and *wise*," a wag concluded.[18]

The tavern's egalitarian and leveling spirit, the absence of authority, and emboldening effects of strong drink aided radicals in fomenting revolution. The intercolonial Stamp Act Congress, meeting in New York City, spent much of its time in Burn's City Arms Tavern. Leaders of the local resistance to the Stamp Act convened meetings in the same tavern, inviting "Persons of all Ages, Ranks, and Conditions" to attend. Taverns became the focus of the assertion and rejection of royal authority and flashpoints for violent clashes between colonists and British troops. Moderates might wish "the People would be Sober," but in disavowing the disorderly disruptions of taverns, they conceded to radicals a key site of orderly resistance.

In Philadelphia, the people out of doors faced an entrenched oligarchy in the Pennsylvania Assembly anxious to placate Parliament and curry royal favor. Before 1735, the assembly met in various locations surrounding the courthouse, where "turbulent spirits" with "very little at stake, and scarce any Thing but their Noise and Clamour to distinguish them" dared to "insult and menace the Members of this House." The external stairs of the courthouse, which voters ascended on election day, linked formal political space to the city. Not so the new State House, into which the assembly moved in 1735. Designed to be intimidating and awe-inspiring, the State House arose on the outskirts of the city far from the markets and wharves where working people congregated. A brick wall (seven feet high after 1770) surrounded the State House and its expansive yard in an effort to keep the people at bay. The assembly generally closed its galleries, jealously guarded reports of its proceedings, and heard few petitions.[19]

But in the 1770s, Philadelphia radicals broke the assembly's power. Rather than discouraging popular mobilization, the expansion of the State House yard and the completion of its wall encouraged larger crowds and lent an air of orderliness and legitimacy to the people out of doors. Frequent meetings in the yard led to demands "That the Doors of the Assembly Room be set open" and the people be allowed "to hear the Debates of the House." When merchants eager to abandon nonimportation lectured the "Rabble" who had "no Right to give their sentiments respecting an importation," defiant radicals formed a Mechanicks Committee that condemned the "absurd and Tyrannical custom of shutting the Assembly doors during debate." On June 18, 1774, twelve hundred people met in the State House yard and resolved to establish a committee of correspondence with radicals in other cities. The new committee—not the assembly—would "determine what is the proper mode of collecting the sense of this province" and select delegates for the newly formed Continental Congress.[20]

The Continental Congress arrived in Philadelphia in September 1774, taking the future of the Revolution into its own hands. While keeping their deliberations secret, congressmen mixed with radicals and listened to opinions "out of doors among citizens, gentlemen, and persons of all denominations." Over the next two years, Philadelphians met frequently in the State House yard to organize revolutionary committees and militias. In 1775, Congress began meeting in the State House, arguing and scheming with the crowds in the yard as it moved toward independence. In January 1776, Thomas Paine published *Common Sense*, lumping the assembly with Parliament as tyrannical oligarchies. "Some convenient tree," Paine wrote, could serve as "a State House, under the branches of which the whole colony may assemble to deliberate on public matters." On May 20, 1776, in a meeting in the yard to "take the sense of the People," four thousand Philadelphians resolved to establish a new government to replace the assembly.[21]

On July 8, jubilant radicals heard Congress's Declaration of Independence read in the State House yard. Over the next three months, Pennsylvania's Constitutional Convention confirmed the victory of the radicals. Asserting that all power derived from the people, the new constitution established that "the People have a right to Assemble together to consult for their Common good" and to petition the legislature. It also stipulated that the "Doors of the . . . General Assembly, shall be and remain open for the Admission of all persons." The new assembly would publish bills *before* debate and subsequently publish its votes and proceedings. Benjamin Rush, an opponent of the new state constitution, nevertheless conceded that the "majority of the people . . . will determine questions out of doors, and wherever we go contrary to their sentiments they will resent it—perhaps with arms."

A More Democratic Public: Consumer Boycotts Politicize the Household

Pennsylvania's new constitution guaranteed the vote to all taxpayers, but the revolutionary process created an even more democratic public. In the wake of the Townshend duties (which Parliament passed in 1767 to establish its right to tax the colonies and raise revenues to support a colonial administration independent of local assemblies), patriots called for a consumer boycott in protest. When merchants proved insufficiently zealous to halt the importation of British goods, patriots appealed to "the public" by listing the names of recalcitrant merchants and providing news of successful boycotts across the colonies in the "public prints" (newspapers and journals). The circulation of subscription lists, pledging citizens to nonconsumption, and the extralegal associations and committees that orchestrated the boycotts gave the public a palpable existence and turned colonists into Americans who trusted one another to make sacrifices for the cause.[22]

Nonconsumption transformed private market choices into public matters, allowing women as well as men, the poor as well as the wealthy to act politically. Anyone could now demonstrate "virtuous self-denial" in defense of liberty. In relying on merchants, nonimportation "stood on a rotten and unsolid basis," but noncomsumption demanded that the people take responsibility for their own liberty. In the wake of the Boston Tea Party in 1773, nonconsumption agreements spread rapidly through the colonies. In 1774, Congress created a Continental Association to enforce these agreements. In voicing their opinions in open forums, signing nonconsumption agreements, joining voluntary associations and organized protests, destroying goods, and penning invectives in newspapers and pamphlets, those excluded from formal elections joined the Revolution.[23]

Consumer boycotts politicized the household, destabilizing patriarchal power and bringing women out of domestic seclusion and into public life. In enforcing boycotts, women pledged to "save this abused Country from Ruin and Slavery" and proclaimed women's duty to do "every thing as far as lies in our power" to protect the "publick good." As "Daughters of Liberty," women organized spinning bees to produce the homespun that replaced British imports. Public events covered in the daily press, spinning bees allowed women to "vie with the men in contributing to the preservation and prosperity of their country and equally share in the honor of it." "Yes, Ladies," a patriot leader acknowledged in 1774, "You have it in your power more than all your committees and Congresses, to strike the stroke, and make the Hills and Plains of America clap their hands."[24]

Women found direct participation in public debates more difficult, but not impossible. Male opposition caused many women to fear that political debate remained outside their "province." But others found political conversation "so very interesting" that they insisted on speaking their minds. It seemed that "every body has something to say" on "the most animating Subject" that "Concerns us all." As one female patriot explained of her opinions, "I cannot help them, nor can I by any means think them seditious." Women took pride in noting that all "trifling discourse of fashions, and such low chat was thrown by, and we commenced perfect statesmen." Female participation increased up and down the social scale, both inside and outside of marriage. Political convictions later brought some women to the front lines of the military conflict.[25]

The politicization of the household especially threatened the patriarchal powers of the Charleston, South Carolina, slaveholding elite. Patriarchal households promised security and protection for their families, black and white, while facilitating supervision of slave labor and affording a display of finery, hospitality, and culture. But the revolutionary process disrupted these arrangements. During the Stamp Act crisis, the wealthy slaveholder Henry Laurens heard at midnight "a most violent thumping and confus'd Noise at my Western door and Chamber Window, and soon distinguish'd the sound of *Liberty, Liberty and Stamp'd Paper, Open your doors* and let us search your House & *Cellars*." Forced to allow a drunken and armed crowd of sailors and townsmen to search his house for stamps, Laurens learned to align himself with the popular will.[26]

The nonimportation struggles complicated life for Charleston's elite, who enjoyed British finery and used it to uphold their status and authority. Laurens might decry imports that "tend to impoverish the community, by promoting Luxury, Idleness and Debauchery," but radicals saw an elite becoming "fond of British manners even to excess." The management of household consumption often fell to women, who heard frequent appeals to their patriotism and offered stinging rebukes to their profligate husbands. A patriot urged Charleston's women to prove wrong those British officials who judged they would "suffer this empire to be enslaved and your husbands throats to be cut" rather than give up the "darling tea-dish ceremony." Challenging patriarchal dominance of the household, women enlisted it in the revolutionary cause.

Charleston's households suffered a more dire threat of domestic insurrection. The largest colonial center of slave trading and slaveholding, Charleston contained more slaves than Boston, New York, and Philadelphia combined, as well as a large population of free blacks and the countless runaways who hid among them. Urban slaveholders attempted to re-create the order of their rural plantations, but they found that city life provided their slaves with time and space for freedom. Hiring out their time, buying and selling, haggling over prices, and acquiring goods that raised their self-esteem and asserted their independence, urban slaves also mingled with free blacks and acquired "a peculiar kind of pride and bearing."

A long history of insurrection rumors troubled Charlestonians. As antislavery sentiments and black assertiveness spread outward from the Northern seaports, nervous elites reported "some Negroes had mimick'd their betters in crying out '*Liberty*' " in the streets. Patrols and councils of safety intensified their vigilance as the Revolution gathered strength. In the summer of 1775, whites accused a free black man of spreading news of a "great war coming" that would "help the poor Negroes." Although prominent whites doubted his guilt, the man's conviction and execution signaled the strategy of uniting whites, rich and poor, behind the suppression of slaves. On this central question, white artisans and mechanics and backcountry farmers stood behind Charleston's elite, denying slaves the full fruits of the Revolution and maintaining elite power in household and polity.

The Threat of Enslavement and the Need for Virtue: The Unifying Myth of the American Revolution

The printing presses, coffeehouses, taverns, and public protests of the colonial seaports generated a ferment of ideas during the American Revolution. Successful revolution required unifying ideas to mobilize energies, close divisions, ease strains, justify sacrifices, and inspire commitment to something larger than the individual interests of the participants. Had the colonies experienced little social conflict or Britain represented an oppressive ancien régime, the demand for individual rights might have been sufficient to mobilize and sustain a revolutionary opposition. But patriots needed something stronger than individual self-interest to unify cities riven by economic conflicts and lead them in revolt against the most powerful and progressive society in the world.[27]

The need for American virtue to resist a corrupt British conspiracy to enslave the colonies provided the unifying myth of the Revolution. Americans crafted these ideas from the tradition of civic republicanism. Derived from classical and Renaissance sources and coming to the colonists via the eighteenth-century British "country" opposition to the royal court, civic republicanism held that only the constant vigilance of virtuous citizens frustrated the normal tendency of power to infringe upon liberty. Prophets without honor in monarchical Britain, the country spokesmen represented a counterculture confined to a rural gentry. But civic republicanism thrived in the colonies, where it shaped the response to the new British taxes and regulations beginning in 1765.[28]

Civic republicanism made sense of life in colonial seaports, where slavery haunted the streets and wharves and more egalitarian and spartan conditions encouraged Americans to fancy themselves a virtuous lot. Civic republican warnings about tyrannical power encroaching upon liberty resonated with the residents of colonial seaports—not just Charleston, but Boston, Newport, New York City, and Philadelphia—who knew slavery and its degrading effects firsthand. The imagery of slavery filled colonial rhetoric, as in an assertion by Charleston's Christopher Gadsden that virtuous Americans refused "the abject Slavery intended for us and our posterity." Moreover, as economic inequality began to grow, civic republicanism supplied a revolutionary doctrine that condemned luxury and called for the suppression of individual self-interest in favor of the public good. Leavened with the Puritan ethic, civic republicanism answered colonial anxieties about the growth of British corruption and the decline of American virtue in its call for moral regeneration.[29]

In its traditional emphasis on a virtuous elite and a deferential politics, civic republicanism gave the Revolution a conservative cast, discouraging wholesale redistribution of property or power. The nonimportation agreements following the Stamp Act proved a perfect vehicle for sacrifice at home and deference in the face of an external enemy. Events in Boston, with its explosive economic tensions, illustrate the conservative implications of civic republicanism. Nonimportation vented frustrations against the dissolute rich, promising, as Samuel Adams put it, to "mow down luxury and high living in New England." But nonimportation also demanded a spartan, virtuous citizenry that set aside its own demands in favor of the greater good. Let "our burthens be ever so heavy, or our grievances ever so great," James Otis told Bostonians, "no possible circumstances, tho' ever so oppressive, could be supposed sufficient to justify private tumults and disorders."[30]

Civic republicanism muted the revolutionary implications of economic frustration, but it demanded its own version of social revolution. In articulating and defending a political liberty already existing and newly threatened by British actions, revolutionary theorists proposed no dramatic transformation of the existing order. The literature of the Revolution tended to be didactic, rational, and instructive rather than imaginative. Yet it advanced a powerful and potentially democratic civic myth, for it placed the colonial revolt in a world historical context of progress and decay.[31]

Civic republicans argued that while liberty wavered in Britain, a sturdy and undefiled branch of the British nation took root in the egalitarian and spartan setting of the New World. The victory over France in the Seven Years' War promised a new empire for liberty with virtuous cities "rising on every hill." Republican liberty included natural rights, but above all it meant the liberty to participate in public affairs. As one colonist put it, liberty was "a power of acting agreeable to the laws which are made and enacted by the consent of the PEOPLE, and in no ways inconsistent with the natural rights of a single person, or the good of the society."[32]

The Puritan ethic added a cosmic meaning to civic republicanism's secular warnings. Colonized as part of God's grand plan and standing "at a critical junction on the map of mankind's destiny," Puritan America suffered no insignificant crises. A Calvinist clergy bemoaned colonial covetousness, envy, ostentation, and greed; interpreted British depravations as just punishment; and called for a renewal of virtue. Republican revolution and moral regeneration blended together, particularly in the spartan sacrifices demanded by the nonimportation agreements. As the Puritan suspicion of luxury and its emphasis on frugality energized a citizenry resisting British corruption and tyranny, the Puritan city on a hill took on a republican cast.[33]

When corruption threatened to spread to the colonies, Americans understood their duty. When tyranny is loose, Boston's Andrew Eliot wrote in 1765, "submission is a crime." Such convictions shaped the seaports' response to British taxes and impositions. Parliament's repeal of most of the Townshend duties in 1770 quieted the colonial seaports. But with the passage of the Tea Act in late 1773, they erupted again. Although the law exempted the East India Company from the duty on tea, colonists saw it as an attempt to legitimize the tax in the very act of providing an exemption from it. As virtuous citizens, they rejected the seduction of cheap tea, clung to their liberties, and dumped the tea into their harbors—most famously in Boston. In response, Parliament passed the Coercive Acts of 1774, closing Boston Harbor, suppressing self-government in Massachusetts, quartering troops in the city, and providing for royal officials charged with crimes to be tried outside the colonies.[34]

The Coercive Acts, dubbed the "Intolerable Acts" in the colonies, provided radicals with proof of what Thomas Jefferson called "a deliberate and systematic plan of reducing us to slavery." Colonists feared that corrupt courtiers, desperate for new wealth to maintain their luxurious living, would stop at nothing to deprive virtuous Americans of their rights and their property. The one success story in a sorry history of liberty giving way to tyranny, even Britain now succumbed to corruption. Liberty and virtue could not be expected to survive in Britain, Boston's John Adams proclaimed, where "luxury, effeminacy, and venality are arrived at such a shocking pitch." Only the colonies remained to defend liberty. No narrow "cause of a mob, of a party, or a faction," the patriot struggle became "the cause of *self-defense*, of *public faith*, and of the *liberties of mankind*."[35]

The American defense of liberty now became "a world regenerative creed." Previous republicans believed only a small elite capable of civic virtue. But now the fate of liberty across the world hinged on the character and spirit of the American people, particularly at its seaports where the Revolution began. John Adams opposed the Stamp Act as a threat to an intelligent urban culture. It seemed "very manifest" that the Stamp Act would have stripped the colonists "of the means of knowledge, by loading the press, the colleges, and even an almanac and a newspaper with restraints and duties," while "taking from the poorer sort of people all their little subsistence, and conferring it on a set of stamp officers, distributors, and their deputies." Adams embraced popular resistance to the Stamp Act as "the opening of a grand scene and design in providence for the illumination of the ignorant and the emancipation of the slavish part of mankind all over the earth."[36]

The need for virtue raised the fear that Americans might not be equal to the task, but it also encouraged grand hopes for a whole world of heroes. A republican revolution "introduces knowledge among the people, and inspires them with a conscious dignity," argued John Adams, who had seen something of this in Boston. The "elevation of sentiment" inspired by republican government would "make the common people brave and enterprising." The tendency of "ignorance, vanity, excessive ambition and venality" to "creep into government" reinforced the necessity for "every subject . . . to be in some degree a statesman."[37]

VIRTUE AND VICE IN AN OVERHEATED MARKET

But Americans saw ambiguous signs as to whether there was virtue enough to sustain the republic. Many thought the popular refusal to use tea in the wake of the Coercive Acts, and the bonfires of tea that lit village greens across the colonies, boded well for the future of the republic. But others saw an unseemly scramble for social position in an overheated market. The cities particularly inflamed patriot fears that "extravagance, love of gaieties, the taste for modish pleasures, are in a chain of imitation carried down to the lowest orders." To "increase in numbers, in wealth, in elegance and refinements, and at the same time to increase in luxury, profaneness, impiety, and a disesteem of things sacred," many thought, "is to go backward and not forward."[38]

A broad range of Americans embraced republican revolution as the means of halting moral decay. A desire to "banish the syren LUXURY with all her train of fascinating pleasures, idle dissipation, and expensive amusements" coincided with the call for "honest industry, sober frugality, simplicity of manners, plain honesty and christian benevolence." The clergy joined in the enthusiasm for republican revolution as the Calvinist litany of sins—luxury, intemperance, pretension, ostentation—matched the vices of republican strictures. The city upon the hill now aspired to be, in the words of Boston's Samuel Adams, "the Christian Sparta."[39]

In the early years of the crisis, Americans appeared to be rising to the challenge. Consumer boycotts, the decision for independence, and the organization of the revolutionary armies all called forth sacrifice and unity and generated "a joy unutterable and an exaltation never felt before." The clergy rejoiced that "no threatening quarrels, or animosities have subsisted; but harmony and internal peace have ever reigned, and one soul has inspired the body politic." Without coercion, the people proved "that a spirit of public virtue may transcend every private consideration."

But the strains of war tested republican virtue. The Continental Congress pumped four to five hundred million paper dollars into local economies, while the British and the French armies spent two hundred million more. The reliance on domestic manufacturing for war materiel provided abundant opportunities for profit, while the military struggle disrupted the economy through physical destruction, the drain of manpower, and the British navy's attack on coastal shipping. Some citizens accepted economic problems as the sacrifices necessary to war, but others seized the opportunity to hoard or withhold goods, or sell for British gold rather than suspect Continental paper.[40]

While George Washington's army starved at Valley Forge over the winter of 1777–1778, Pennsylvanian farmers and millers sold foodstuffs to the occupying army in Philadelphia. Others supplied the army with defective goods, including the food and gunpowder on which lives depended. Pennsylvania's chief executive complained that graft and fraud and trading with the enemy financed the importation of "sugar, wines, spirits, and gewgaws of every kind." The gratification of "pride, intemperance and folly" squandered resources "that would give us great relief, if applied to the service of the country." Even Congress, an incredulous Franklin learned, spent great sums for "superfluities," while failing to "find remittances to pay for the arms and ammunition necessary for our defense." So great was "the Spirit to trade," a patriot charged, "that if Belzebub was to appear with a Cargoe—the people would deal with him." A French commissary officer offered a more blunt assessment of Americans: "They love money."[41]

Tensions peaked in colonial seaports where a flood of paper money raised the prices of foodstuffs and other essentials, while advocates of price controls squared off against defenders of a free market. Food rioters, often women, took to the streets to demand "just prices" and a "moral economy." Merchants and entrepreneurial craftsmen countered with market logic. "It is not from the benevolence of the butcher, the brewer, or the baker that we expect our dinner, but from their regard to their own interest," the British economist Adam Smith taught. "We have more to expect from the Enterprise, Activity and Industry of private Adventurers," John Jay told the Continental Congress in a Smithian vein, "than from the Lukewarmness of Assemblies.... Public Virtue is not so active as private Love of Gain. Shall We shutt the Door vs. private Enterprise?"[42]

By 1779 political and economic tensions in Philadelphia reached a crisis when radicals accused merchants Silas Deane and Robert Morris of manipulating markets and using information about public needs to garner private profits. The Deane affair ended inconclusively, but inflamed ongoing debates about virtue and vice. The doubling and redoubling of food prices produced ominous conflicts in the streets. Hard-pressed Philadelphians averred that only traitors "harangued upon the doctrine, of private vices being public benefits."[43]

Sailors and soldiers took to the streets of Philadelphia in January 1779. Condemning the "monied men" who were "basking in the sunshine of monopoly ... and withal pampering their vile natures in ease, superfluities and luxury," they demanded redress. "We had arms in our hands, and knew the use of them," they remonstrated, but "instead of avenging ourselves," we "patiently waited the interference of the Legislative Authority." For "every man to do what he pleases," they charged, was "repugnant to the very principles of which society and civil government are founded." Meanwhile, the Boston press printed warnings that violence would "burst on the heads of monopolizers, as it did on the odious stamp-masters."[44]

Nothing focused anxiety about the future more than the military struggle itself. A virtuous militia, republican logic dictated, would defeat a standing army of conscripts and mercenaries. The "spirit of 75" saw Americans enthusiastically enlisting in local militias. A Philadelphian explained that the "Rage Militaire, as the French call the passion for arms, has taken possession of the whole Continent." But the spirit was one of anticipation, "the convulsive Labors of Enthusiasm" and "the empty Bubbles of Hope." The "times that try men's souls," in Thomas Paine's famous phrase, followed when quick victory eluded the patriots. Militiamen sometimes fought hard, and sometimes did not, but always proved unreliable, returning home at inopportune moments to protect their families and repair their fortunes. While Washington believed he would have won the war sooner with adequate support for a conscript army, most revolutionaries refused to admit that they needed a standing army—the very thing that threatened their liberty—to win their independence.[45]

REDEEMING THE REVOLUTION: VIRTUES OR MECHANISMS?

Notwithstanding the anxiety about virtue, the people asserted their sovereignty and showed little interest in handing power back to their betters. The revolutionary doctrine of popular sovereignty held that all power derived from the consent of the people. Consequently, the people took political power into their own hands "at any time, or any cause, or for no cause, but their own sovereign pleasure," an astonished orator observed, "to alter or annihilate both the mode and essence of any former government, and adopt a new one in its stead." Every man out of doors, New York City mechanics added, "is, or ought to be by inadmissible right, a co-legislator with all the other members of that community."[46]

Rethinking their revolutionary enthusiasms, some patriot leaders came to see popular sovereignty as an invitation to democratic despotism. Elites ridiculed the idea that "every silly clown and illiterate mechanic" could decide political questions. To "collect and assemble together the tailors and the cobblers and the ploughmen and the shepherds" and expect them to "treat and resolve about matters of the highest importance of state" courted anarchy. But the people could no longer be intimidated. "Notwithstanding the mystery with which the science of government has been enveloped, for the purpose of enslaving, plundering and imposing on mankind," Paine argued, "it is of all things the least mysterious and the most easy to be understood."[47]

Popular sovereignty made government authority an autonomous public power, rather than an extension of the private resources of kings and aristocrats, and placed it in the hands of the people. Democracy once seemed a recipe for tumult. But in the new republics, "tumultuous proceedings are as unnecessary as they would be improper and ineffectual," a Charleston pamphleteer wrote. "Other means are in our hands, as much preferable as good order is to confusion." But the old fear of tyranny could intensify where public authority seemed so dramatically extended as to obliterate private rights when they conflicted with the public will. Protecting private property and minority rights without destroying popular sovereignty became the central dilemma of American politics.[48]

In the mid-1780s, public powers did infringe on private rights. The postwar economic slump generated popular demands for paper money, inflation, and the easing of debts in every state. Elites chalked up the economic troubles to *"an immoderate desire of high and expensive living"* and concluded that the new republics faced a crisis in character. "LUXURY, LUXURY, the great source of dissolution and distress, has here taken up her dismal abode," complained one orator, destroying "that simplicity of manners, native manliness of soul, and equality of station, which is the spring and peculiar excellence of a free government." When duly elected legislatures confiscated property, manipulated the currency, and suspended the payment of private debts, popular sovereignty appeared indistinguishable from democratic despotism. The people, elites feared, "do not exhibit the virtue that is necessary to support a republican government."[49]

The presumed failure of virtue haunted the Constitutional Convention in 1787. We entertained "too good an opinion of human nature in forming our confederation," Washington wrote privately in 1786 (in the year of Shays's Rebellion, when debt-ridden farmers closed the Massachusetts courts at gunpoint to prevent foreclosures). The "commotions and temper of numerous bodies in the eastern States," Washington concluded, "exhibit a melancholy proof . . . that mankind, when left to themselves, are unfit for their own government." Some continued to hope for the redemption of the people through education or religion. But a new strategy of devising mechanical remedies for republican ills took hold. Initial attention focused on the state constitutions, where executive powers were strengthened, senates made less directly accountable to the voters, and judges appointed for life. Attention soon focused on the central government. "Firm union," Alexander Hamilton explained, would serve "as a barrier against domestic faction and insurrection."[50]

The Founding Fathers, who wrote and secured ratification of the Constitution, worried more about private rights than popular participation. Their Constitutional mechanisms relied less on civic virtue than the rational calculation of interest. The people needed only to "study and pursue merely their own interest and happiness" and vote accordingly. Even leaders did not need to be virtuous. "Enlightened statesmen will not always be at the helm," James Madison warned, but when virtue failed, the Republic could still rely on "the machinery of government." The "auxiliary precautions" of the separation and balancing of powers, he concluded, implemented the "policy of supplying, by opposite and rival interests, the defect of better motives."[51]

The Founding Fathers prided themselves on their realism. If the people would just have "virtue and intelligence enough to select men of virtue and wisdom," Madison wrote, representative machinery would "refine and enlarge the public views." Even so, the people should not "place unlimited confidence" in their leaders or "expect nothing but the most exalted integrity and sublime virtue." Faction was "sown in the nature of man," Madison continued, making people "much more disposed to vex and oppress each other than to co-operate for their common good." Regulating the clash of interests thus formed "the principle task of modern legislation." Take "in a greater variety of parties and interests," Madison concluded, and we make it "less probable that a majority of the whole will have a common motive to invade the rights of others" and "more difficult for all who feel it to discover their own strength."[52]

Interest would not be transcended by virtue but frustrated by balance. But the Founding Fathers also recognized their own wishful thinking. "Is there no virtue among us?" Madison asked. "If there be not we are in a wretched situation. No theoretical checks, no form of government can render us secure." Even a society of self-interested individuals required some minimal virtues—self-restraint, an enlightened capacity for sober calculation of one's rational interests, and a respect for the rights of others. John Adams continued to insist that "public virtue is the only foundation of republics."[53]

The Founding Fathers also knew they could not count on the people to defer to their betters. The Revolution taught Americans that tyranny meant the exclusion from public affairs as much as the destruction of private well-being. What John Adams called the universal desire of the individual "to be seen, heard, talked of, approved and respected by the people about him" meant that the people, in Jefferson's words, wanted a polity "where every man is a sharer in the direction of his ward-republic, ... and feels that he is a participator in the government of affairs, not merely at an election one day in the year, but every day." Yet the founders discounted their hopes and gave in to their fears. Reducing the citizen's role to choosing enlightened representatives, they gave little thought to cultivating the virtues of citizenship.[54]

The founders created a durable republic. But for those who kept faith with the revolutionary experience, virtue retained its relevance. Doubting "that private vices are public benefits," the Antifederalists who opposed the Constitution insisted that whatever "the refinement of modern politics may inculcate, it still is certain that some degree of virtue must exist, or freedom cannot live." Antifederalists saw in the new Constitution all the old threats once emanating from Britain—standing armies, oppressive taxes, and proliferating customs officials. Acknowledging that a consolidated government might place commerce on a firmer foundation, they calculated the cost as too high. "You are not to inquire how your trade may be increased," Patrick Henry insisted, "nor how you are to become a great and powerful people, but how your liberties can be secured."[55]

The Antifederalists accepted the reality of interests but denied that any virtuous elite could speak for the interests of the people. "Farmers, traders and mechanics," Pennsylvania's Antifederalists insisted, "all ought to have a competent number of their best informed members in the legislature." The common sense of the people should be the focus of politics, New York City's Melancton Smith added, rather than "extensive political and commercial information" or an "acquaintance with the abstruse part of the system of finance." If people of "sense and discernment" joined elites in the offices of government, Smith concluded, you "will then combine the abilities and honesty of the community—a proper degree of information, and a disposition to pursue the public good."[56]

CITIZEN-PROPRIETORS AND THE DEMOCRATIZATION OF COMPETENCE

The Antifederalists lost the Constitutional debate. But they preserved a democratic vision that reemerged when urban artisans and mechanics opposed the resurgence of aristocracy in the new Federalist Party in the 1790s. Uniting in Jefferson's Republican Party, artisans, mechanics, and small farmers defeated Federalist efforts to restrict political participation and thus secured the democratic future of the United States when it remained in doubt.[57]

The struggle between Republicans and Federalists first emerged in the differing approaches to the market between Jefferson and Hamilton in the 1790s. According to the Jeffersonian persuasion, the modest growth of the market promised economic independence for small producers who could be relied upon to be the backbone of the republic. In food-growing regions, farmers and ancillary urban trades and crafts flourished in the 1790s, vindicating Paine's prediction that American producers would prosper "as long as eating is the custom in Europe." Economic stability and security allowed small producers to claim that same independence from "the fickleness and inconstancy" of the marketplace that underlay the elite claim to civic virtue. Instead of drudgery, work became a badge of the virtuous prosperity of small proprietors, who needed no tariffs, taxes, or other government favors to secure their well-being. The leisure once secured by "proprietary wealth" now appeared more likely to corrupt government than provide its virtuous basis.[58]

Republicans idealized the market as self-directed and impartial yet orderly, but feared that government might be corrupted to secure economic privileges for favored groups. For civic reasons of his own, Hamilton set out to do just that in his financial plans. Hamilton believed that the assumption and funding of the revolutionary debt; the creation of a national bank, army, and navy; and the granting of bounties to manufacturers would tie commercial interests to the new republic. Motivated more by civic glory than economic interest, Hamilton wanted a mighty fiscal-military apparatus that would turn a tiny republic into a world power. Republicans saw the Hamiltonian program as corruption, pure and simple. It raised the old republican fear of a corrupt alliance of finance, centralized government, and standing army. Worse, the fiscal-military state required taxes that fell hardest on small producers.[59]

Corrupting government and depriving honest labor of its just reward, the Hamiltonian program offended both republican and liberal values. It is ironic that the most democratic forces in the early Republic embraced the free market and expressed a deep suspicion of government. But the Jeffersonians recognized the potential of the state to serve the interests of the rich, even to hand out privileges that created new classes of the rich, allying them with a powerful state. The Jeffersonians' critique of the fiscal-military state became a staple of democratic and populist politics.[60]

While the financial debate remained within the confines and decorum of Congress, an explosive debate over the people's fundamental right to participate erupted in the mid-1790s. Republican revolution in France and denunciations of the pro-British policies of the Washington administration led to the formation of political clubs among urban artisans and mechanics across the new republic. The Democratic Society of New York City announced in 1794 that in a republic, "it becomes a duty" for citizens to "acquire a perfect knowledge of the government and political institutions of their country." Neither the "check which a constitution affords" nor the "periodical return to elections" sufficiently protected liberty. Only "a zealous examination of all the proceedings of administration" could do that. But when the political clubs criticized his policies, President Washington thought nothing "more absurd, more arrogant, or more pernicious" than for "a self created permanent body . . . to declare that this act is unconstitutional and that act is pregnant of mischief."[61]

As Americans engaged in passionate debate over the fundamental basis of government for the third time in thirty years, Jeffersonians claimed the mantle of republicanism and redefined it in democratic terms. "Purely and simply," Jefferson later explained, a republic "means a government by its citizens in mass, acting directly and personally." The political clubs agreed. "If the laws of our Country are the echo of the sentiments of the people is it not of importance that those sentiments be generally known?" asked the Democratic Society of Philadelphia. "How can they be better understood than by a free discussion, publication, and communication of them by means of political societies?"[62]

In 1794, frontier farmers rebelled against an excise tax on whiskey, a source of Hamiltonian revenues that fell on Jeffersonian producers. When President Washington led an army of thirteen thousand (larger than any he commanded during the Revolution) to crush the Whiskey Rebellion and then denied legitimacy to any criticism of his act, the political clubs refused to be intimidated. "It has ever been a favorite and important pursuit with aristocracy to stifle free inquiry," the Democratic Society of Philadelphia charged, "to envelop its proceedings in mystery, and as much as possible, to impede the progress of political knowledge." The clubs ridiculed the view that elections and representation eliminated the need for popular assembly.[63]

The Republican clubs articulated an ideal of a classless society composed of intelligent and virtuous citizen-proprietors. The doctrine that "all men were not equally fitted to be Philosophers, Legislators, and Statesmen but that some were intended for working with their hands," a Republican lectured a Federalist, "did not suit this side of the Atlantic." As if to prove the point, hundreds of obscure citizens penned tracts, essays, and pamphlets over the course of the turbulent 1790s. Neither "genius, nor exquisite subtlety of refinement," Republicans insisted, "is necessary to the ordinary disquisition of politics." Representatives should be chosen "not only of ourselves," a Republican newspaper added, "but as much as possibly as ourselves, Men who have the same kind of interests to protect and the same dangers to avert."[64]

The Federalists, hoping to check popular majorities at the local level with a vigorous government at the center, created the national forum that brought the Jeffersonian Republicans to power. Republicans and their city-based political clubs used the mails, post roads, and national press that arose with the new federal government to mobilize and inform the public beyond the seaboard and into the interior. In their brief and last moment of ascendancy, when tensions with France escalated in 1798, the Federalists prosecuted every major publisher and many minor journalists under the Alien and Sedition Acts. But the voices were too many to silence. The election of 1800 provided yet another national forum, this one on the wisdom of sedition prosecutions, in which the Republicans triumphed and Jefferson gained the presidency.

The Republicans took on a national administration in the hands of their opponents and won with nothing more than words. Attributing humanity's failings to the workings of autocratic government, Republicans insisted that human nature would develop more positively with political freedom. Those "who think that men are naturally vicious and degraded," declaimed a New York City Republican, "will of consequence become attached to that form of government which embraces the greatest proportion of coercion and restraint." Federalists thought just so and asked whether the "free and independent man will voluntarily submit to the restraints which the good of the community requires of him." Republicans responded that a new day had dawned. The extraordinary political deliberations of the past thirty years and the peaceful, democratic revolution in 1800 supported their case.

The dramatic political transformation during the revolutionary era, along with the self-directed system they saw emerging in the market, supported the Republicans' hopes for a more democratic future. To be sure, they feared intrusive government. An "excessive energy in government," Republicans argued, produced "all those rigid codes of law that have subverted the natural liberties of mankind." Republicans saw no need for a fiscal-military state. The taxes to support it, wrote a Republican victim of the Federalist sedition prosecutions, would inevitably fall upon "the farmer, the mechanic, and the labourer. They and they alone pay." But limited government did not mean no government. This same Republican argued that government might "improve your roads, clear your rivers, cut your canals, erect your bridges, facilitate intercourse, establish schools and colleges, diffuse knowledge of all kinds." A government close to the people could be trusted to act for the public benefit.

Republicans and Federalists argued not simply over economic development, but about the relationship between economic development and civic life. Republicans embraced a future in which competent producers might live in comfort. By competence, they meant both a modest holding of property and the skill and intelligence to manage it. A New England mechanic described "competency" as an independent "condition below the dissipation of wealth and above the solicitude of necessity." A competency, Philadelphia artisans added, meant the ability "to live decently without acquiring wealth." Comfort implied a genial middle ground between the luxury of elite consumption and the scarcity of necessities that afflicted the poor. Republicans described the new Republic as "this land of comfort where, blessed with health, and being industrious, no one needs despair of a comfortable livelihood at least."[65]

Freed from unrelenting, mindless labor and cultivating the democratic traits of intelligence and initiative, self-reliance and responsibility, small proprietors made good citizens and established self-governing communities. The Republican vision saddled the emerging democracy with an exaggerated fear of active government and gave the market a moral force it did not deserve. But the Republican vision also energized democracy by defending the competence of working people and insisting that a leisured elite could no longer monopolize political intelligence. Republicans encouraged the democratization of competence, giving citizens the opportunity to participate in political as well as economic and cultural affairs.[66]

REVOLUTIONARY LEGACIES, DEMOCRATIC FUTURES

The democratization of the republican ideal of citizenship obliged future generations to live up to its demands. "Our fathers have purchased for us political rights and an equality of privileges, which we have not yet had the intelligence to appreciate, nor the courage to protect, nor the wisdom to employ," a trade unionist chastised his colleagues in 1834. How "would it profit us," the labor leader William Sylvis asked in 1865, "were we to preserve our institutions and destroy the morals of the people; save our Constitution, and sink the masses into hopeless degradation, poverty and crime; all the forms of our republican institutions to remain on the statue books, and the great body of the people sunk so low as to be incapable of comprehending their most simple and essential principles." The "stability and success" of the republic, Sylvis concluded, depended upon "the virtue and intelligence of the masses."[67]

But even as it empowered small producers, the ideal of the citizen-proprietor excluded others from full participation. In the long run, revolutionary ideals of equality underwrote the liberation of women and slaves. But in the short run, proprietorship meshed all too easily with patriarchal power, leaving most women and African Americans trapped in domestic service or chattel slavery, more property than proprietor. When revolutionaries allowed slavery to linger in the Northern states and to flourish in the postrevolutionary Southern states, slaveholders successfully wrapped the mantle of proprietorship around themselves. Rallying small farmers and urban workers to their side, they dominated the new national government and blunted the democratic implications of the Revolution.[68]

But the Revolution also left a legacy of democratic experiences and ideas. There could have been no Revolution without the contribution of women. Aside from their role in consumer boycotts, women joined crowd actions, organized petition campaigns, aided soldiers and widows, and maintained farms and businesses. Women who took on greater economic roles during the Revolution or whose urban residence immersed them most fully in the revolutionary process were especially assertive. Tending to her husband's business affairs while he was serving the republic, Abigail Adams famously urged him to "remember the ladies" in writing republican constitutions. Many more wives must have asked their husbands, "Why should I not have liberty whilst you strive for liberty?"[69]

But assumptions about women's domestic and dependent roles nevertheless proved difficult to overcome. Writing soon after the Revolution, Mercy Otis Warren anticipated the ideology of republican motherhood that submerged women's public claim to civic virtue within the private realm of domestic duties. "I think it very immaterial," Warren wrote, whether political ideas "flow from a female lip in the soft whispers of private friendship or are thundered in the Senate in the bolder language of the other sex." From a secure and exalted place in the domestic realm, republican mothers could exert an indirect civic influence—if not a direct civic power—by raising and educating patriotic children.[70]

Through the ideal of republican motherhood, women gained a foothold in public life. As the family became an essential agency of political socialization, women laid claim to educational opportunities that prepared them for their patriotic duties. "A woman of virtue and prudence is a public good—a public benefactor," an early nineteenth-century orator explained, as she made "public decency...a fashion—and public virtue the only example." But republican motherhood also reinforced women's association with a restricted domestic realm and threatened to freeze their political consciousness at the level of deference.[71]

With the upsurge in democratic attitudes after 1830, the women's rights movement rejected the idea of separate spheres undergirding republican motherhood. "We deny the right of any portion of the species to decide for another portion... what is and what is not their 'proper sphere,'" the 1851 women's rights convention resolved. The "proper sphere for all human beings is the largest and highest to which they are able to attain." The women's rights movement based its demands on the principles of the Revolution. "We hold these truths to be self-evident," the first Women's Rights Convention declared in 1848, "that all men and women are created equal."[72]

Radical women recognized that civic participation presented the most fundamental challenge to women's confinement to the domestic sphere. In writing their resolutions, Elizabeth Cady Stanton recalled, the women felt "as helpless and hopeless as if they had been suddenly asked to construct a steam engine." Barely audible in their earliest efforts, speaking with "trembling frames and faltering tongues," women's right activists learned how their lack of civic skills bred psychological insecurity. Unsupportive husbands and fathers and the "domestic bondage" of marriage and children also frustrated political consciousness.[73]

The Revolution excited the political consciousness of African Americans as well, especially in cities. In taverns and coffeehouses, on street corners and docksides, free and enslaved African Americans heard and interpreted for themselves the arguments for revolution. Thousands of slaves fled to the British side, seizing the offer of freedom for those who would fight against the Revolution. Others petitioned legislatures to recognize their right to freedom, resulting in thousands of manumissions. In the wake of the Founding Fathers' failure to move against slavery, the boldest plotted and sometimes launched politicized insurrections. Despite losing many of its most physically able and politically assertive members to the British cause, the newly enlarged free African American community laid an institutional groundwork of urban churches and associations from which to launch a demand for civic equality. A cadre of self-made leaders emerged, a tough and adaptable group who took pride in their competence and challenged the nation's conscience to adhere to its best principles.[74]

The stimulation of city life on the intellect of slaves led slaveholders to limit the growth of urban slavery in the South. As in revolutionary Charleston, urban slaves often hired out their time, lived away from their masters, accumulated small sums of cash, and mingled with free blacks and whites in a public and associational life ranging from churches to grog shops. "The city, with its intelligence and enterprise," a slaveholder wrote, "is a dangerous place for the slave." By 1860, white leaders moved to limit the black urban population and to impose new forms of segregation. The decision robbed the slave population of civic experience and condemned most of it to "the intellectual stagnation and gloom of the plantation." Slaveholders recognized "the march of intellect" as the force that could ignite general insurrection.[75]

The decline of slavery in the cities left civic agitation to free African Americans in Northern cities who, like the advocates of women's rights, recognized the principles of the Revolution as the essential basis for their demands. "We hold this truth to be self-evident, that God created all men equal," the free Philadelphian James Forten wrote in 1813, and that "whatever measures are adopted subversive of this inestimable principle, are in direct violation of the letter and spirit of our Constitution." The free artisan David Walker similarly evoked the Declaration of Independence in his ringing call for militant resistance to slavery. Even the former slave Frederick Douglass, who bitterly complained that "the great principles of political freedom and natural justice" became "mere bombast, fraud, deception, impiety and hypocrisy" when they were denied to African Americans, recognized their power. Douglass paid homage to "great deeds" of the revolutionary generation and drew "encouragement from 'the Declaration of Independence'" and "the great principles it contains."[76]

Douglass embodied the promise of the American Revolution. He never lost sight of civic participation in the equality that African Americans sought. A self-made man of unusual distinction and talent, Douglass recognized that his political writing and speaking provided "the best possible school for me." It obliged him "to think and read, it taught me to express my thoughts clearly." Participation changed everything. "If nothing is expected of a people," Douglass explained in 1865, "that people will find it difficult to contradict that expectation. By depriving us of suffrage, you affirm our incapacity to form an intelligent judgment respecting public men and public measures; you declare before the world that we are unfit to exercise the elective franchise, and by this means lead us to undervalue ourselves, and to feel that we have no possibilities."[77]

Elizabeth Cady Stanton and Frederick Douglass demanded the same opportunities for others that the Revolution opened for white men. But for better or worse, the immediate future of democracy depended on those who could claim the revolutionary ideal of the citizen-proprietor. The health of the republic, a New York City artisan proclaimed in 1797, depended upon "tradesmen, mechanics and industrious classes of society," who for far too long thought "themselves of TOO LITTLE CONSEQUENCE to the body politic." As a market revolution transformed the crafts in the next century, urban artisans and mechanics held the future of democracy in their hands.[78]

CHAPTER 2

Creating Citizens in a Commercial Republic

Market Transformation and the Free Labor Ideal, 1812–1873

Defying the lessons of history, Americans built a commercial republic of continental proportions in sixty years after the War of 1812. But even as they pursued their interests, Americans expected economic development to support their republican institutions. Alexis de Tocqueville found the tension between material interest and civic aspiration to be central to the emerging democracy of the United States and coined the term "individualism" to describe the civic dangers arising in the commercial republic. As individuals acquired the means "to satisfy their own wants," they developed the conviction that they "owe nothing to any man, they expect nothing from any man." The tendency of each individual "to sever himself from the mass of his fellows," he warned, immediately "saps the virtues of public life." A "people passionately bent on physical pleasures" regarded political rights and responsibilities as "a tiresome inconvenience."[1]

Tocqueville recommended civic engagement as the means of raising the sights of the commercially minded above "the petty and paltry pleasures with which they glut their lives." Tocqueville cited city politics as the most likely setting for the citizen to develop "clear practical notions on the nature of his duties and the extent of his rights." Attending to "the interests of the public, first by necessity, afterwards by choice," citizens developed "the habit and the taste" for public affairs. The resulting public feeling was not "wholly insincere," Tocqueville concluded, as Americans "make great and real sacrifices to the public welfare." Just as Tocqueville recommended, Americans became the most active and intelligent citizenry in the world by making public judgments about the civic implications of economic development.[2]

The Origins of the Free Labor Ideal

The Erie Canal, linking the Great Lakes to the Atlantic Ocean, demonstrated the audacity and assured the triumph of the commercial republic. At Lockport, New York, near Buffalo, the canal required a herculean three-mile cut through a mountainside that allowed boats to pass thirty feet below the surface. The capstone placed upon completion of the locks in 1825 read: "Erie Canal: Let posterity be excited to perpetuate our free institutions, and to make still greater efforts than our ancestors, to promote public prosperity, by the recollection that these works of internal improvements were achieved by the *spirit and perseverance* of REPUBLICAN FREE MEN." This combination of economic dynamism and political freedom became the foundation of a free labor ideal that sought to reconcile market transformation and republican values.[3]

But the canal did not materialize wholly through the work of republican free men. Irish immigrants dug much of the canal. Like the slaves and convicts with whom they shared an occupation, immigrant canal diggers found that their propertyless status, unskilled labor, and degradation disqualified them as citizens. The hard work of the towpath demanded a similar group of workers and raised concerns about the Republic's future. "A despotic government can exist where people are degraded," declared the American Bethel Society (dedicated to uplifting canal workers), "but free institutions will be sustained only by an intelligent and moral people—Make then this people ignorant and immoral, and you will destroy our prosperity, peace, and republic."[4]

A work of ingenuity, craftsmanship, and heroic labor, the Erie Canal invited tributes to the triumph of art over nature. To the business classes, art meant technological sophistication and entrepreneurial vision. Proud of their artificial river, they gave little credit to the work of craft and brawn. At the Grand Celebration in New York City in 1825, the business classes toasted to "Genius and Enterprize.... They command mountains to move, and rivers to flow in dry places. The word is spoken, and it is done!" The stonemasons, blacksmiths, and mechanics who built the canal knew it took more than words. For them, art meant skilled labor. "Gigantic genius led the van," they toasted, "while sturdy toil fulfilled the plan." As for the canal diggers, no one thought to raise a toast to them. With the canal completed, unskilled laborers moved on, some of them to the Republic's largest cities where the concentration of degraded labor raised the civic issue in acute form.[5]

As honest producers and competent citizens, urban artisans and mechanics saw themselves as the true heirs of the Revolution. In mechanics' institutes, grand parades, and civic projects, they made themselves central to civic life: "Less respect to the consuming speculator, who wallows in luxury," New York City artisans toasted themselves, "than to the productive mechanic, who struggles with indigence." The city's printers praised their craft as "one of the most deadly engines of destruction that can possibly be arrayed against the encroachments of despotic power." The "mechanics are the bone and sinew of the nation," a Cincinnati artisan added, without which "society would sink into savage barbarism."[6]

But even as they celebrated the opening of canals, artisans divided over the civic implications of market transformation. Entrepreneurs defended the transformation of the crafts with a vision of progress centered on new opportunities for energetic producers, steady work for journeymen, and cheaper necessities for working families. They played down the growing importance of machines, describing them as the servants of skilled labor that eased its burdens. Securing the independence of small producers, teaching self-discipline to a rising generation, and uniting skilled labor with the principles of art and science, market transformation provided "an essential element in the continued happiness and progressive elevation of the human mind."[7]

As entrepreneurs subdivided work to lower prices and capture larger markets, the new regime of wholesalers, sweatshops, piece rates, and driving foremen undermined the artisans' ideals of independence and equality. Radical artisans endorsed "small but universal ownership" as the "true foundation of a stable and firm republic" and saw anything else as slavery. As a New York City journeyman argued in 1826, a system where men are "compelled to labour, while the proceeds" are "taken and enjoyed by another," is "the very essence of slavery." Labor created all value, he concluded, but in New York City, the "products of labour belong to almost any other than the producer," who receives nothing more than "a bare subsistence."[8]

Many artisans, both masters and journeymen, resisted market transformation in defense of the self-governing workshop and the independent craftsman. American masters were "all alike" in resisting the division of labor, an English journeyman complained, having "never read Adam Smith." His master replied: "This, sir, is a free country.... We want no one person over another which would be the case if you divided the labor." But the rapid reorganization of the crafts testified to the numbers of entrepreneurial masters who answered the call of market opportunity. A Cincinnati artisan judged his employer "a very shrewd man," but disdainfully added that he was "contented with nothing but a continual stream of money flowing into his pockets." Entrepreneurs and radicals divided over the meaning of market transformation, but each evaluated economic change with reference to civic values. The free labor ideal came out of their struggle.[9]

The Market Revolution and the Public Purpose

Over the course of the nineteenth century, the construction of roads, canals, and railroads linked ever-larger majorities of Americans to regional, national, and international markets. Huge undertakings beyond the capacities of private capital, new transportation arteries depended on public enterprise and shaped urban rivalries. Completed in 1825, the Erie Canal created an empire for New

York City, spurring Philadelphia and Baltimore to action. By the 1840s, public funds accounted for nearly $100 million of the $113 million spent on canal construction. Canals extending outward from Cincinnati, Chicago, and other interior cities connected midwestern producers to Atlantic ports and formed the beginnings of a national market.[10]

Public munificence accelerated private enterprise not only in providing a transportation network but also in granting corporate charters. In limiting the liability of investors to the money actually invested in the enterprise, incorporation facilitated the mobilization of capital from multiple sources. A British invention, the corporation did not recommend itself to most postrevolutionary Americans whose experience with the Bank of England, the East Indies Company, and other "moneyed companies" underscored the threat of monopoly, favoritism, and the corruption of government. But economic elites in Philadelphia and other cities recognized the corporation as a means of insulating economic power and policy from the postrevolutionary popular politics they mistrusted. Faced with the need for banking, transportation, and municipal services beyond the capacity of individual proprietors or partnerships, states began granting corporate charters in the 1780s. The pace accelerated during and after the War of 1812.[11]

As a grant of a sovereign legislature to serve a public purpose, corporate charters invited public oversight. But the states increasingly incorporated all sorts of profit-oriented enterprises. In 1819, the United States Supreme Court declared corporate charters to be contracts, protected by the Constitutional ban against the states "impairing the obligations of contracts." Describing the corporation as an "artificial being," Chief Justice John Marshall argued in *Trustees of Dartmouth College v. Woodward* that the law endowed it with "immortality and, if the expression be allowed, individuality." The decision, Justice Joseph Story explained, protected corporate charters against "any undue encroachments . . . which the passions or the popular doctrines of the day may stimulate our State Legislatures to adopt."[12]

Setting policy and distributing profits in the private meetings of boards of directors, corporate leaders shielded much of their economic power from the public sphere. But the severing of incorporation from public accountability did not win universal acclaim, particularly during financial downturns. During the financial panic of 1819, the Pennsylvania Senate regretted the powers granted to Philadelphia bankers. Blaming the panic on the banks, the frustrated senators complained that "incorporation of the monied interest already sufficiently powerful of itself, was but the creation of odious aristocracies, hostile to the spirit of free government, and subversive of the rights and liberties of the people."[13]

But banking and transportation created new opportunities for smaller enterprises, and corporate promoters overcame skepticism with the promise of equal opportunity. Thanks to Republican legislatures, more than two hundred state-chartered banks opened their doors by 1815. Charters for canal, bridge, and turnpike companies proliferated as well. The courts added fuel to the market revolution by favoring commercial over subsistence uses of property, limiting suits by property owners damaged by abutting developments, expanding the power of eminent domain and conferring it on private corporations, charging unions with criminal conspiracy and outlawing strikes, limiting employers' liability for accidents at work, and introducing the doctrine of "buyer beware" to contractual law.[14]

An expansive definition of the public purpose justified governmental assistance in the form of loans and tax exemptions, as well as bounties and monopolies for manufacturing enterprises. "Works of public importance," a Pennsylvania act loaning money to an iron works put it, "deserve public encouragement." A New York grant to a manufacturer declared that "the establishment of useful manufactures is clearly connected with the public weal." The courts again joined in, accepting any "reasonable reference to public convenience and general good," broadening "the definition of public purpose almost to meaninglessness."[15]

Although public oversight declined, corporate enterprisers still addressed the public purpose. The Boston merchants who incorporated the textile mills of Lowell, Massachusetts, in 1826 promised to show the compatibility of manufacturing and republicanism. Employing farmers' daughters who would presumably marry after a few years of work, the Lowell mills imposed a strict moral order. In 1830, Lowell's congressional representative, Edward Everett, proclaimed the town "a peculiar triumph of our political independence" and the "complement of the revolution."[16]

In 1825, President John Quincy Adams enlisted the federal government in promotion of the public purpose. As part of a program of national and individual improvement, Adams advocated federal support for canals and roads, tariff protection for emerging industries, and the rechartering of the Bank of the United States. The president also called for the establishment of a national university and naval academy, subsidies for exploration, patent protection for inventors, a national astronomical observatory, and a program of compensated emancipation and colonization. The "progressive improvement of the condition of the governed," Adams insisted, is the "great object of the institution of civil government."[17]

Labor Politics in the Jacksonian City: Unjust Government and a Conspiracy to Enslave

Controversies over the role of government in promoting market development provided the foundation for labor politics in the Jacksonian city. Finding much of economic policy outside their reach despite their status as citizens, radical artisans criticized activist government as a source of privilege and economic inequality. As the spread of wage labor undermined the independence of small producers, the Philadelphia shoemaker William Heighton blamed "aristocratic legislation" and a conspiracy of nonproducers to keep labor "in ignorance and mental blindness." He spearheaded the creation of a citywide labor federation, a Mechanics' Free Library, and an independent Working Men's Party in 1827. In New York City, journeyman printer Thomas Skidmore also traced unjust accumulations to privileges created and perpetuated by government. Are "the great mass of mankind to be hirelings to those who undertake to set up a claim, as government is now constructed, that the world was made for them?" he asked. "Why not sell the winds of heaven, that man might not breathe without price? Why not sell the light of the sun, that a man should not see without making another rich?"[18]

The workingmen's movement that grew up around these charges opposed chartered banks and corporations as examples of government-bestowed privileges. But they also advocated public support for "necessary and useful public works, such as Roads, Bridges, Canals" and called on the people to seize the reins of government and enact a civic revolution to provide all with the necessities of life. In 1829, radical artisans in New York City ran a slate of candidates for the local legislature and won nearly a third of all votes in the city. After the election, professional politicians infiltrated the movement and the established parties split the workingmen's movement between them. The Democratic Party took up, in milder form, the workingmen's attack upon government as a source of privilege, but abandoned any positive role for government in promoting equality. The emerging Whig Party took the workingmen's vision of positive government, purged it of its radicalism, and tailored it to entrepreneurial ambitions.[19]

With the collapse of their independent political movement, artisans turned their energies to organizing trade unions. The rejection of political action limited their power. But freed from the compromises of party politics, the General Trades Union of New York (GTU) became one of the most democratic organizations in Jacksonian America. Organized in 1833, the GTU represented two-thirds of the city's white male workers by 1836 and provided a model for trade unionists across the country. The GTU encouraged wide participation in both debate and office holding, kept officeholders accountable to the membership, and demanded strong self-discipline from its members. Resolving internal debates in accordance with the principle that "in all governments and communities, every person is obliged to yield a little to the other," the GTU denounced violence and severed all connection with members who did not act "with that propriety becoming good citizens."[20]

A self-described "phalanx of honest worth that the aristocrat and speculator does not dare attack," the General Trades Union linked its democratic structure and program of economic reform to the health of the republic. The great danger "which threatens the stability of our government, and the liberty of the people," the first president of the GTU warned, "is an undue accumulation and distribution of wealth." Augmented by privilege and unequal laws, organized capital made "the independent character of an American citizen" impossible to maintain, turning honest citizens into "the willing tools of other men." The "time has arrived when the people of the United States must decide," a union newspaper concluded, "whether they will be a Republic in fact, or only a Republic in name."[21]

Trade unionists understood their movement as an extension of the Revolution. When the courts prosecuted trade unions as conspiracies in restraint of trade (even as manufacturers' associations proliferated), unionists warned of the rise of a new aristocracy. In the wake of the conviction of union tailors in 1836, thirty thousand workers gathered at New York's City Hall to denounce judges, employers, and the major parties as "at variance with the spirit and genius of Republican government." In handbills depicting "the Coffin of Equality," unionists charged that "these Freemen are to receive their sentence, to satisfy the hellish appetites of the Aristocracy" determined "to convert the working men of this country to slaves."[22]

As heirs of the Revolution, trade unionists believed the spread of wage labor resulted from a corrupt conspiracy to introduce new forms of slavery. The shoemakers of Lynn, Massachusetts, denounced the effort to "reduce them to degradation and the loss of that self-respect which had made the mechanics and laborers the pride of the world." The female workers of Lowell complained of being "imposed upon egregiously by the aristocratic and offensive employers, assuming to be their lords and masters." As "daughters of freemen," they refused to become "Factory slaves." Our "workingmen and women will not long suffer this gradual system of republican encroachment," a labor newspaper reported in the 1840s, "which is fast reducing them to dependence, vassalage, and slavery." The National Trades Union charged the factory system with being "subversive of liberty" and "calculated to change the character of a people" from "bold and free, to enervated, dependent, and slavish."[23]

Radical artisans condemned wage labor for undermining the independence of workers and eroding their capacity for citizenship. "Liberty is incompatible with ignorance," they insisted during the struggle for the ten-hour day in the 1830s, and long hours constituted "a slavery of the mind." It proved difficult, however, to sustain the slavery comparison. White workers hesitated to associate themselves with the degraded condition of black slaves. The "Freemen of the North are now on a level with the slaves of the South," the tailors handbill read. Hedging the comparison with the honorific "freeman," the handbill also undercut its condemnation of "tyrant masters" with the phrase "would-be masters."[24]

If white workers traced their status as slaves to the wage system, and remained under that system, they risked the traditional republican condemnation of a weak and degraded people whose acceptance of slavery left them "unworthy of the name FREEMAN." Radical artisans thus avoided the term *wage slavery*. Instead they used the term *white slavery*, emphasizing the contrast with black slaves and free blacks of the Northern cities, who lacked almost all political and civil rights. Tradition denied political rights even to those free blacks who approached the status of freemen. Violent mobs often destroyed their property to reinforce the equation of freeman and whiteness. What W.E.B. Dubois later called the "public and psychological" wages of whiteness encouraged radical artisans to abandon the troubling critique of wage dependency. Instead, they focused on the level of material deprivation that temporarily made slaves of white workers, but that might also be speedily ended.[25]

But dropping the critique of wage slavery led to the acceptance of wage dependency. In the mid-1830s, even radical artisans began to accept the wage relationship, just as long as employers recognized their labor "as any other species of property." All "we ask," artisans implored, "is to set the price of labor," since "we know its value best." The argument allowed workers to assert their status as proprietors, but it left the wages system unindicted. The critique of white slavery also left slavery itself unindicted, at least for blacks. Many labor leaders endorsed chattel slavery and even pioneered the proslavery defense, while workers joined slaveholders in a Democratic Party that lumped incorporation and abolition as equally evil expressions of intrusive government. When President Andrew Jackson's war on the federally chartered Bank of the United States in 1832 brought the artisans' indictment of privilege and unjust government to national politics, it lacked any hint of a positive role for government in promoting equality.[26]

In defense of small producers and the rough republican equality that he believed would result from limited government, Jackson vetoed the bill to recharter the bank in 1832. While Jackson defended property gained by the "fruits of superior industry, economy, and virtue," he argued that the "rich and powerful too often bend the acts of government to their selfish purposes" and "have besought us to make them richer by act of Congress." If government "would confine itself to equal protection," Jackson concluded, "it would be an unqualified blessing."[27]

Jackson left office hopeful that his assault upon the bank would leave honest producers "uncorrupted and incorruptible." But he warned his followers that "enough yet remains to require all your energy and perseverance" and "you must not hope the conflict will be a short one nor success easy." Jackson's fears proved more prescient than his hopes. Jackson's destruction of the bank's regulatory power and his distribution of federal funds to his pet banks fueled the resulting boom of the mid-1830s. Riding the boom, even radical urban Democrats abandoned their opposition to banking corporations. Instead, they passed general incorporation laws that offered limited liability to any and all who met minimum state requirements. The financial Panic of 1837 that followed left small producers destitute, destroyed unions, and inflamed ethnic and racial tensions.[28]

A Crippled Democracy: Jacksonian Fears and Whig Paternalism

The Jacksonian struggle against privilege, and the resulting fear of activist government, crippled the emerging democracy. "The majority is to govern," Jackson proclaimed in his first annual message, represents "the first principle of our system." But the other "great principle," he added, is "a government of limited and specific, and not general, powers." The government's "true strength consists in leaving individuals and States as much as possible to themselves." For years, the *Washington Globe* rallied Democrats beneath the masthead "The World Is Governed Too Much."[29]

Fearful of government-granted privileges, Jacksonian Democrats entrusted the public good to competitive enterprise. In *Charles River Bridge v. Warren Bridge* (1837), the Supreme Court denied that the state of Massachusetts awarded an implied right of monopoly in bestowing a corporate charter for a Boston bridge. The court thereby cleared the way for new investors to build a competing bridge. While the rights of property should be "sacredly guarded," Chief Justice Roger Taney wrote for the majority, "we must not forget that the community also have rights." A Jacksonian appointee, Taney severed the connection between incorporation and public responsibility, leaving unleashed enterprise to secure the rights of the community. "All communities are apt to look to government for too much," Jackson's handpicked successor President Martin Van Buren announced when the financial panic struck, and he promised only "to enact and enforce" an even field for "private interest, enterprise, and competition."[30]

The Democrats' reliance on the slaveholders of the South, deathly afraid of an activist government's potential assault upon their peculiar institution, reinforced the laissez-faire approach. So did the immigrants' and laboring Democrats' fear of intrusive moral reformers. Opposition to the Whig program of capitalist and moral improvement drove urban Democrats closer to the slavocracy, its power swelled by the Constitution's three-fifth compromise (counting slaves as three-fifths of a person in apportioning representation in Congress). But above all, Democrats embraced laissez-faire because of their fear of government as a source of privilege. "The agricultural, the mechanical, and the laboring classes," Jackson said in his Farewell Address, "from their habits and the nature of their pursuits . . . are incapable of forming extensive combinations to act together." Activist government therefore benefited only "corporations," "wealthy individuals," and "designing politicians" prepared to "move together with undivided force."[31]

Democratic voters rarely thought of using government for their own ends. They "did not want government to touch them too closely," explained Illinois governor Thomas Ford. Just as long as it "made no encroachment upon liberty," they "asked nothing and claimed nothing but to be let alone." Taking advantage of this "lethargic state of indifference of the people," Ford continued, entrepreneurial Democrats followed Whigs in passing "special laws of all kinds of individual, not general benefit." With even Democrats fanning the flames of speculative enterprise, honest producers did not know where to turn. The Whigs "were sent to make the rich richer and the poor poorer, and they obeyed the will of their constituents," a member of the Workingman's Party wrote during the Bank War. "But the Democrats what shall we say of them?" Ralph Waldo Emerson offered one answer. "I supposed once the Democrats might be right. I see that they are aimless," he wrote in his diary. The Democrats "are destructive, not constructive. What hope, what end have they?"[32]

Democrats rightly saw the existing policy of improvement as privilege. But their antipathy to privilege blinded Democrats to the need for responsible public action. "A strong and active democratic government . . . is an evil," the *Democratic Review* opined in the year of financial panic, "differing only in degree and mode of operation, and not in nature, from a strong despotism." But despotism arose as easily from private as public offices. While state governments engaged in a "competition in laxity" (gutting regulations and offering subsidies to attract business), liberal laws of incorporation allowed private interests to define and appropriate the public interest. When private interests needed public authority, they generally secured it by corrupt means from compliant municipal governments. The reign of corporate corruption that "now menace[s] the permanency of our popular government," the Interstate Commerce Commission concluded at the end of the century, arose on the "ruins" of federal and state planning in the Jacksonian era.[33]

The Whigs, to recall Emerson's lament, at least articulated a hope and pursued an end. They wanted "to improve the mind and heart of America" as much as to develop its material resources, to build schools as well as railroads, and to promote manners and morals as well as tariffs and bank notes. Notwithstanding its abuses, the Whigs' policy of improvement pursued civic ends. Through the American system, its tireless advocate Senator Henry Clay explained, the Union would enjoy "the benefits of moral and intellectual improvement of the people." Whigs believed that "a great increase in the amount of both accumulated wealth and of annual products is absolutely essential" to the effort to "redeem the mass of the people from poverty and its incidents." But they also recognized that "no mere redistribution of the existing mass of wealth could effectively answer the proposed purpose of elevating the people."[34]

Whigs believed that citizens had to be made, and they set out to do so through a host of benevolent institutions designed to shape character. The Whigs thus placed human potential at the center of Jacksonian debate. But they failed to embrace participation as the best means of developing it. Tocqueville's nightmarish vision of a future despotism in the United States derived from the urban Whigs who were his primary contacts. Tocqueville doubted that Americans would "meet with tyrants in their rulers, but rather with guardians." Submitting to an "immense and tutelary power, which takes upon itself alone to secure their gratifications and to watch over their fate," Americans would succumb to a soft despotism.[35]

The Democrats at least committed themselves to popular participation in decision making. They struggled to broaden the suffrage, equalize representation, and increase the number of elected offices. In contrast, the Whigs in Emerson's satire resembled overprotective physicians whose "social frame is a hospital," dressing everyone in "slippers and flannels, with bib and pap-spoon," prescribing "pills and herb tea, whig preaching, whig poetry, whig philosophy, [and] whig marriages." Disciplinarians who took responsibility for others, Whigs emphasized morality and duty over equality and rights. The textile mills of Lowell, Massachusetts, and plantations such as Henry Clay's Ashland in Kentucky, where workers and slaves were treated as children, exemplified Whig paternalism. The degeneration of the factory system and plantation slavery into undisguised forms of exploitation exposed the limits of paternalism.[36]

The comparison of Lowell and Ashland also suggests how the affinity between Whig paternalism and planter paternalism could obscure the difference between free and slave labor. Mouthing the proslavery indictment of naked market exploitation, radical New York City Democrat Mike Walsh found the only difference between free and slave labor to be that free labor must "beg for the privilege" of gaining a master. But under the pressure of the struggle over slavery in the 1850s, a new antislavery Republican Party articulated a free labor ideology built on the civic ideals of urban artisans.[37]

The Free Labor Ideology and the Transformation of Northern Whiggery

When artisans spoke of free labor, they meant labor that prepared them to perform the civic duties of free men. The working people of the United States, their publications insisted, "are not untaught operatives, but an enlightened, reflective people, who not only know how to use their hands, but are familiar with principles." Curious, opinionated, skeptical, resourceful, and self-reliant, the laboring classes of the new Republic were learning classes as well. The "great discoveries of science and art," visiting Europeans marveled, are "exposed to the vulgar gaze and placed within reach of all." In Europe, what was called "the populace, a compost heap, whence germinate mobs, beggars, and tyrants," could not be found in the United States, where the people were "initiated" into the "conquests of the human mind."[38]

In wedding the artisan ideal of the citizen-proprietor to a belief in energetic government, the Republican Party combined a Jacksonian faith in the competence of the people with the Whig sense of purpose. The Whig and Republican economist Henry Carey argued that federal improvements united labor and learning in a program of economic and moral development. "Highest . . . among the tests of civilization," Carey wrote, was whether society "enables all to find demand for their whole physical and mental powers." A diversified economy helped citizens develop their abilities and prepared them for "the higher enjoyments of life." The greater a person's development through useful work, Carey concluded, "the greater is his desire for knowledge, the greater his love for literature and art, the greater his desire to see for himself the movements of the world, and to learn from those who are capable of affording him instruction."[39]

Carey envisioned a republican form of industrialization that multiplied the opportunities for citizen-proprietors. In the hope of reconciliation with Southern Whigs, Carey never pressed the distinction between his vision of free labor and the reality of slavery. But Abraham Lincoln did. In response to the proslavery argument that all societies necessarily rested on the exploitation of a "mudsill class" of menial laborers, Lincoln insisted that no "such thing, as the free hired laborer being fixed in that condition for life" existed in the North. Only slaveholders believed that "labor and education are incompatible" and the education of laboring people "useless" and "dangerous." While slaveholders treated it as a "misfortune" that workers "should have heads at all," the free labor ideal held that "heads and hands should cooperate as friends; and that [each] particular head, should direct and control that particular pair of hands."[40]

Embracing the Jeffersonian legacy, Republicans celebrated the independence and intelligence of the Republic's citizen-proprietors. They championed the "middling class ... equally far removed from the temptations of great wealth and of extreme destitution" as "the main support of every free government." Small proprietors formed "the very heart of the nation, as opposed to the two extremes of aristocracy and ignorance." Republicans boasted that free labor created "that intelligent power in the masses alone to be relied on as the bulwark of free institutions."[41]

Like urban artisans, Republicans defined free labor not as a simple matter of voluntary contracts but as an economic system capable of producing a responsible citizenry. Drawing on the artisans' civic critique of inequality, Republicans held out economic independence and political responsibility, rather than great wealth, as the goal of free labor. When "a man has his property in his own hands," a Republican economist argued, "and manages it himself, he is responsible for the manner in which he does it." In contrast, an economic "system of corporations is nothing more nor less than a moneyed feudalism.... It concentrates masses of wealth, it places immense power in a few hands," establishing "absolute control over all persons connected with that corporation." But when Republicans looked to the artisans' own cities, they saw only economic inequality and political corruption and Democrats rising to power on the votes of the very rich and "the least intelligent of the population."[42]

Strongest in the small towns and rural areas of the north, the Republican Party retained the Whig temptation to reform others, particularly those in the great cities. In Lincoln, however, the Republicans found a spokesman who came closest to jettisoning Whig paternalism in favor of a Jacksonian faith in the people. Labor, he always insisted, was the "superior—greatly the superior—of capital." "Whatever is calculated to advance the condition of the honest, struggling laboring man," Lincoln told a group of immigrants in 1861, "I am for that thing." Thus, he favored the tariff because the tax burden "falls almost entirely on the wealthy and luxurious few" and their imported "fine cloths, fine silks, rich wines, golden chains, and diamond rings." The "laboring many" would thus not be "perpetually haunted and harassed by the tax gatherer."[43]

The antislavery cause brought Lincoln's democratic convictions to the fore. In the "right to eat the bread, without the leave of anybody else, which his own hand earns," Lincoln declared during the Lincoln-Douglas debates in 1858, the Negro "is my equal . . . and the equal of every living man." But the civic definition of free labor demanded more, the transformation of slaves into citizens. Labor reformers urged abolitionists and Republicans to denounce wage labor and to "prepare a better state for the slaves when emancipated, than the servitude to capital, to which they now seem destined." But most abolitionists defended wage labor and gave little thought to the political status of emancipated slaves. Most Republicans, including Lincoln, only gradually and partially came to accept the possibility of ex-slaves as full citizens, even though their civic definition of free labor demanded it. "Working men are the basis of all governments," Lincoln argued, which meant that the "relation of masters to slaves" is a "total violation" of our "ancient faith."[44]

Positive Liberty: Turning Slaves into Citizens

After Lincoln won the presidency in 1860, the secession of eleven slave states and their successful resistance to the Union efforts to subdue their armies turned a limited war into a revolution. Continually prodded by the Radical Republicans, the Lincoln administration employed what Horace Greeley called the "cardinal" Whig principle, the idea that "government need not and should not be an institution of purely negative, repressive usefulness and value, but that it should exert a beneficent, paternal, fostering element upon the Industry and Prosperity of the People."[45]

The most stupendous example of government activism, the Emancipation Proclamation in 1863, gave the war a moral dimension and grafted a reforming mission onto the nation-state, newly baptized in blood. In his fullest synthesis of Whiggery and Jacksonian democracy, Lincoln described the egalitarian principles of the Declaration of Independence as a collective duty rather than an individual right, something to be "constantly looked to, constantly labored for, and even though never perfectly attained, constantly approximated." Treating equality as the goal rather than the precondition of democracy, Lincoln's Gettysburg Address (1863) called for "a new birth of freedom," a devotion to the Republic's "unfinished work" and "the great task remaining before us."[46]

The "world has never had a good definition of the word liberty," Lincoln explained in 1864, "and the American people, just now, are in want of one." The "shepherd drives the wolf from the sheep's throat for which the sheep thanks the shepherd as a liberator, while the wolf denounces him for the same act as the destroyer of liberty, especially as the sheep is a black one." Lincoln and the Radical Republicans rejected the wolf's negative liberty in favor of the shepherd's positive liberty. The first eleven amendments to the Constitution limited the powers of the federal government by defining what it "shall not" do. The three Reconstruction amendments, including the Thirteenth Amendment, which abolished slavery, concluded with the words "Congress shall have the power to enforce this article by appropriate legislation."[47]

After Lincoln's assassination, Radical Republicans recognized the power of the federal government as the only means of protecting liberty in the Southern states. Citing Article IV, Section 4 of the Constitution ("the United States shall guarantee to every State in this Union a Republican form of government"), they extended citizenship and voting rights to African American males in the Fourteenth and Fifteenth Amendments to the Constitution (adopted in 1868 and 1870, respectively). Republican leader Thaddeus Stevens argued that no "class is safe, no freedom is real . . . which does not place in the hands of the man himself the power to protect his own rights." When "twenty-five million of a privileged class exclude five million from all participation in the rights of government," Stevens added, "government is a tyranny." Without the vote, the abolitionist Wendell Phillips concurred, "freedom, so called, is a sham."[48]

African Americans understood the difference between positive and negative liberty. "Emancipation is one fact, and effective liberty another," free African Americans in New Orleans argued. "We demand therefore . . . the right to vote and the right to be judged, treated, and governed according to equal laws." Without "political liberty," Frederick Douglass added, our "personal liberty . . . and all other rights, become mere privileges held at the option of others." In countless mass meetings, parades, and petitions at the end of the war, African Americans demanded the vote and full civic equality. Securing the vote and treating it as much a community resource as an individual right, they became the most energetic and creative citizens during Reconstruction.[49]

The Fourteenth and Fifteenth Amendments inaugurated the world's first great experiment in interracial democracy. President Ulysses Grant justly called the Fifteenth Amendment "a measure of grander importance than any other act of the kind from the foundation of our free government to the present day." As segregation in social and cultural institutions increased, politics and government became the most integrated sectors of Southern life. More American than African, the four million manumitted slaves descended from the 427,000 Africans imported to the colonies in the seventeenth and eighteenth centuries. Highly acculturated, they were as prepared for citizenship as a long-enslaved people could be. The freed people also recognized their need for allies and worked to identify their interests with those of whites.[50]

In demanding the vote and land, the freed people appealed to free labor's civic and economic values. They reminded the heirs of the American Revolution that "all free governments derive their just powers from the consent of the governed" and asked to be relieved of "the burden of onerous taxation, without a just representation." In order to prepare themselves for the great tasks of citizenship, they asked that "the three great agents of civilized society—the school, the pulpit, the press—be as secure in South Carolina as in Massachusetts." Uneducated field hands cogently argued that "the land ought to belong to the man who (alone) could work it," not to those who "sit in the house." The "property which they hold," ex-slaves said of the planters, "was nearly all earned by the sweat of our brows."[51]

Hoping for the proverbial forty acres and a mule that they had glimpsed in scattered wartime experiments and the federal Freedmen's Bureau, the freed people embraced free labor's association of proprietorship and citizenship. As they returned to reclaim their property after the war, planters complained of the difficulty of managing laborers "stuffed with the idea of proprietorship." The redistribution of land "puts people to work, it gives homesteads," a leader of South Carolina's freed people argued in 1868, and "relieves the Government and takes away its responsibility of feeding the people; it inspires every man with a noble manfulness, and by the thought that he is a possessor of something in the State." When white Southerners mocked the desire for autonomy as "wild notions of right and freedom," the freed people responded "that if they are hirelings they will still be slaves." Without a "democratization" of the plantation, a New Orleans newspaper added, emancipation became "a mockery and a sham."[52]

Radical Republicans used the civic conception of free labor to build a powerful coalition in favor of Reconstruction. "Nothing is so likely to make a man a good citizen as to make him a freeholder," Stevens argued in defense of a policy of confiscating the rebels' plantations and redistributing them among the black and white masses of the South. "No people will ever be republican in spirit and practice where a few own immense manors and the masses are landless." The "whole fabric of southern society must be changed, and never can it be done if this opportunity is lost. If the South is ever to be made a safe republic," Stevens concluded, "let her lands be cultivated by the toil of the owners or the free labor of intelligent citizens." Land "dictates government," Phillips added. "If you hold land, every man his own farm, it is a democracy; you need not curiously ask of the statute book. If a few men own the territory it is an oligarchy; you need not carefully scan its laws."[53]

The vision of a free-labor South inspired the Radical Republicans. "Instead of large estates, widely scattered settlements, wasteful agriculture, popular ignorance, social degradation, the decline of manufactures, contempt for honest labor, and a pampered oligarchy," Senator George Julian explained, "you want small farms, thrifty tillage, free schools, social independence, flourishing manufactures and the arts, respect for honest labor and equality of political rights." Convinced that landless peasants could never challenge the political power of the planters, Thaddeus Stevens concluded that "homesteads to them are far more valuable than the immediate right of suffrage, though both are their due."[54]

The radical policy of confiscation gained force from the widely held conviction that only a new class of citizen-proprietors could transform the Southern states into free labor republics. Stevens failed to get a confiscation amendment attached to Julian's 1866 bill opening public lands in the South to black homesteaders, but confiscation remained a live issue through 1867. Since the beginning of the war, Stevens and other Radicals staked out positions and waited for their party to catch up. Even moderate Republicans held out confiscation as a threat against defiant planters in the spring and summer of 1867. Southern Republicans enthusiastically endorsed the policy.[55]

But confiscation offended merchants, bankers, and industrialists, in and out of the Republican Party, eager to restore the cotton trade and rightly convinced that small proprietors would not grow cotton. Conservative Republicans also worried about the precedent of confiscation. "An attempt to justify the confiscation of Southern land under the pretense of doing justice to the freedmen," the *New York Times* argued, "strikes at the root of all property rights in both sections. It concerns Massachusetts quite as much as Mississippi." With the revolutionary crisis of war over, the Republican Party never caught up to its Radical wing on confiscation. "The only land you will get, any of you," a Union officer prophetically told striking laborers on one plantation in the summer of 1865, "will be 6 x 3 feet in that lot, and if you do not behave yourselves properly you will get your share very quickly."[56]

By 1868, confiscation was dead. But black male suffrage proved harder to dismiss. "If I were a black man, with the chains just stricken from my limbs," one Republican remarked, "and you should offer me the ballot, or a cabin and forty acres of cotton land, I would take the ballot." Senator Charles Sumner hammered home that absolute "equality before the law, and the consent of the governed are essential elements of republican government." A government that restricts the franchise on the basis of race, Republicans agreed, is "an aristocracy, it is an oligarchy; it is not republican." Having rejected confiscation, Republicans settled on the Fifteenth Amendment as the best guarantee of black freedom in the South.[57]

As long as the freed held onto the vote, African Americans used it to foster the citizen-proprietors of the free labor vision. In the black codes of the immediate postwar period and again in the Jim Crow era after the collapse of Reconstruction, planter-dominated, lily-white governments used state power as a surrogate for the master in controlling the labor of the freed. But Radical Reconstruction provided a respite from such measures and helped a small number of former slaves become independent proprietors and many more to become active citizens. Addressing daunting tasks of rebuilding a devastated land and providing the infrastructure of schools, roads, and public services that the slave regime neglected, the interracial governments of the Reconstruction South also promoted the interests of small producers on such issues as land redistribution, homesteads, consumer leagues, regulation of retailers, labor organization, progressive taxation, and lien and fence laws.[58]

The Limits of Radical Republicanism

Combining the Jacksonian faith in the will of the people and the Whig conception of an activist state, Radical Republicans endorsed an unlimited democracy. Having defanged the planter aristocracy and established "one man, one vote," Radicals saw no reason to artificially restrict governmental action. But unlimited democracy could mean many things. For Thaddeus Stevens, it meant not just confiscation, but the chance for "intelligent, pure, and just men of this Republic" to remodel "all our institutions," freeing them from "every vestige of human oppression, of inequality of rights, of the recognized degradation of the poor, and the superior caste of the rich." For Senator Ben Wade of Ohio, unlimited democracy meant the redistribution of wealth. "Property," Wade charged, "is not equally divided, and a more equal distribution of capital must be wrought out." For William Sylvis's National Labor Union, it meant the dismantling of any "system, social or political, which tends to keep the masses in ignorance, whether by unjust or oppressive laws, or by overmanual labor."[59]

The destruction of slavery encouraged these and other visions of dramatic social change. "Out of this struggle we must come with higher ideas of liberty," Elizabeth Cady Stanton rejoiced upon emancipation, "the masses quickened with thought, and a rotten aristocracy crushed forever." With abolitionists enjoying national influence and black male suffrage at the center of public debate, women's rights activists hoped to secure female suffrage as well. But the Radicals disappointed them. Instead of enfranchising women, the Fourteenth Amendment inserted the word "male" into the Constitution for the first time. Even though women collected ten thousand signatures to protest their exclusion from the Fourteenth Amendment, the Fifteenth Amendment also excluded them from the expansion of the suffrage.[60]

In failing to extend the vote to women, Radical Republicans refused to honor the just demands of their longtime allies. Antebellum women found in abolitionism an egalitarian ideology and a route from the realm of benevolent moral reform into politics. Although William Lloyd Garrison's wing of abolitionism rejected politics, its anticlericalism provided feminists with an alternative to a pietistic alliance with the clergy. Attacked by the clergy for speaking in public, feminists met them on their own religious ground, disputing the meaning of scripture. "The Lord Jesus defines the duties of his followers . . . without any reference to sex or condition," Sarah Grimke proclaimed. "Men and women are CREATED EQUAL! They are both moral and accountable beings and whatever is right for man to do is right for woman."[61]

In demanding the suffrage, the women's rights movement transcended Garrisonian abolition. Garrison's assertion of the moral equality of blacks failed to grapple with the historical fact of their degradation, leaving many to embrace a covert belief in biological inequality. Similarly, the abstract belief in the equality of the sexes failed to account for the history of women's domestic confinement and therefore left many to believe in separate spheres for women and men. The most controversial of women's demands (barely passing at the 1848 Women's Rights Convention), suffrage rejected women's confinement to the private sphere. In providing access to the public sphere, suffrage challenged women's legal dependence and civil inferiority. Radical feminists linked suffrage to economic independence, demanding that married women have the right to control their own earnings and property. "The fundamental principle of democracy," the 1853 Women's Rights Convention asserted, is "that taxation and representation should go together." If "the principle is denied, all our institutions must fall with it."[62]

The demand for suffrage underscored women's lack of proprietary rights in themselves. "Whence arises the right of men to govern the women without their consent?" John Adams asked during the Revolution. Men's economic support of women, came the answer. When women's demand for political equality called forth overt defenses of the unthinking exclusion of women, women's economic dependence remained the preferred argument. Without control of one's labor, property, or even physical person (husbands enjoyed sexual rights within marriage), women lacked the proprietary independence associated with citizenship. The emergence of women out of the paternalistic care of men and into public life depended on securing the same independence that other proprietors enjoyed.[63]

In failing to support women's suffrage demands, Radical Republicans bowed to the widespread fear that women's entrance into the public sphere would transform the private sphere as well. Already challenging racial assumptions, Radicals judged gender assumptions too strong to overcome. The costs of the Radicals' abandonment of women's suffrage included the alienation of key partners in the struggle for equality and social justice (women secured four hundred thousand signatures in favor of emancipation in 1863). "If I were to give free vent to all my pent-up wrath concerning the subordination of women," Lydia Maria Child wrote to Charles Sumner, "I might frighten you.... Suffice it, therefore, to say, either the theory of our government is false, or women have a right to vote."[64]

In refusing to address the link between the economic dependence and the civic disability of women, Radical Republicans abandoned the civic conception of free labor and moved closer to the abolitionists' contractual view of free labor. "Set your miscalled free laborers actually free, by giving them enough property or capital to live on," the proslavery theorist George Fitzhugh taunted abolitionists before the war, "and then call on us at the South to free our negroes." Abolitionists said then about wage laborers what Republicans soon said about the freed people. Every class "must owe its elevation and improvement ... to economy, self-denial, temperance, education, and moral and religious character."[65]

Only the Radical Republicans' association with labor reform kept alive the civic conception of free labor. Some antebellum labor reformers urged abolitionists to endorse the distribution of homesteads on public lands as the solution to both slavery and wage labor. But at the end of the war, Garrison announced that the antislavery struggle ended with abolition and the institution of voluntary contracts. Wendell Phillips, the abolitionist most closely associated with the labor movement, still insisted that emancipation required full political rights and an economic foundation for those rights. In May 1865, the American

Anti-Slavery Society voted to endorse black suffrage, with Garrison resigning and Phillips ascending to the presidency. Phillips continued to insist on land as essential to making former slaves into citizens.[66]

In undercutting the association of blackness and servility and depriving white workers of the comforting comparison with slaves, emancipation made possible a frontal assault on wage slavery. The labor leader Ira Steward described the eight-hour day as "an indispensable *first step*" for labor "to wholly emancipate itself." But the assault also strained labor's alliance with the Republican Party and sped the abandonment of the civic conception of free labor. The demand for the eight-hour day, the growth of trade unions, and a wave of postwar strikes signaled a new antagonism between capital and labor, with even Radical Republicans embracing the views of the business classes. An 1867 pamphlet issued by a Chicago bank argued that wage labor "implies a certain amount of deference" with the worker "surrendering their individual freedom to the extent which is necessary for enabling him to fulfill the responsibility of the position." Trade unions were "bad, bad, bad," a Republican businessman concluded.[67]

In counseling against strikes, Republicans assured labor leaders that "in the eyes of the State," labor "is a moral, social, and public interest." It "is to the State that the rights of each should be referred . . . with absolute certainty of protection." Yet when labor reformers secured passage of eight-hour laws in nine states, manufacturers appealed to the ten-hour day as natural law. Republicans decided that "too much leisure is a detriment" to the worker's welfare, as it led to debauchery—particularly among the foreign-born, not much given to "liberal education and general improvement."[68]

In their defense of the eight-hour day, labor leaders appealed to the civic conception of free labor. Working people needed time to "comply with the public duties which we are having thrust upon us." Time for self-improvement created an active and enlightened citizenry "full of life and enjoyment" because "the man is no longer a Slave, but a man." Without a limit on the hours of labor, a labor editor explained, "property is a tyrant, and the people are its slaves." At least one Radical Republican agreed. Having resolved the slavery issue, Senator Wade argued, "that of labor and capital must pass through the ordeal."[69]

But the assault upon the rights of property troubled most Radical Republicans. Abandoning labor quicker than most, Edwin L. Godkin, editor of the newly formed Radical Republican weekly *The Nation*, pointed the way. He regretted that "when a man agrees to sell his labor, he agrees by implication to surrender his moral and social independence." But Godkin was not prepared to interfere with the freedom of contracts, much less to redistribute property to remedy the situation. To "force men to restrict their working to eight hours a day . . . on the ground that he needs the rest of his time for reading, society, and music," Godkin wrote in *The Nation* in 1865, would "nullify one of the natural economic laws by a law of the state."[70]

"The anti-slavery idea was that every man had the right to come and go at will," replied Ira Steward, the Boston machinist who built New England's eight-hour movement. "The labor movement asks how much this abstract right is actually worth, without the power to exercise it." Poverty and dependence undercut the wage worker's role as citizen and the wage worker "instinctively feels that something of slavery remains." But the struggle against slavery showed "the omnipotent power of the People when acting in their collective capacity, which is legislating." Eight-hour legislation would raise the wages and the condition of working people, for those "who labor excessively are robbed of all ambition to ask for anything more than will satisfy their bodily necessities," Steward concluded, "while those who labor moderately have time to cultivate tastes and create wants in addition to mere physical comforts."[71]

Steward defined poverty in terms of civic inequality. "The charm of the eight hour system," he explained, was that it gave the poor time to "become ashamed of themselves and their standing in society." The wisest would "study political economy, social science" and "ten thousand schemes . . . for the amelioration of the condition of man." As working people developed higher aspirations and demanded higher wages, the "republicanization of labor" would erode profits and eliminate the entrepreneurial class, ushering in a cooperative organization of the economy. Skilled workers struggled to build cooperatives to protect their "competence and independence." The effort, Sylvis argued, helped to maintain "that lofty elevation attained by a free and enlightened people capable of governing their own affairs" and "all the high and noble qualities which fit us for self-government."[72]

Neither the free labor ideal nor the cooperatives survived the Depression years following 1873, years that also sped corporate consolidation. During the Depression, Walt Whitman described his shock at seeing "three quite goodlooking American men, of respectable personal presence" rummaging for scraps. If the United States grew "vast crops of poor, desperate, dissatisfied, nomadic, miserably-waged populations," Whitman feared, our "republican experiment, notwithstanding its surface-successes, is at heart an unhealthy failure." With mass unemployment and destitution stalking the Republic's largest cities, market imperatives and civic aspirations could no longer be reconciled. It remained to be seen which would give way.[73]

CHAPTER 3

The Short, Strange Career of Laissez-Faire

*Liberal Reformers and Genteel Culture
in the Gilded Age*

Through the first two-thirds of the nineteenth century, Americans believed they could build an economy that supported their civic aspirations. But in the Gilded Age, even as the economy reached astounding heights of productivity, powerful elites rejected all political efforts to guide economic and social development as "by nature wasteful, corrupt, and dangerous." The steel magnate Andrew Carnegie asserted in 1885 that the hierarchical organization of industry "sets the limits of our social relations, determines our conceptions of good and evil, suggests our life philosophy, molds our inherited political institutions." Nine years later, the social Darwinist William Graham Sumner wrote the epitaph for the long age of revolution in describing the idea of "reconstructing the industrial system on the principles of democracy" as an "absurd effort to make the world over."[1]

The new deterministic attitude crystallized during the passage of the Ku Klux Klan Act in 1871. "There are many disorders," Republican Carl Schurz declared on the floor of the Senate, "which it is very difficult to cure by laws." Ironically, the Ku Klux Klan Act did cure the disorders that prompted its passage. In response to the horrific violence against black voters and their families across the South, the law established federal jurisdiction over individual violations of civil rights. Federal marshals and prosecutors soon broke the back of the Klan in states across the South, halted the violence, and protected African Americans in the exercise of their civil rights.[2]

But the Ku Klux Klan Act led to a breach in the Republican Party. At first alarmed by the federal threat to local self-government, a dissident group of Liberal Republicans soon opposed any legislation that upset a presumed natural order. In 1872, the Liberal Republicans mounted a third-party challenge to the reelection of President Ulysses Grant and denounced the Reconstruction experiment as a misguided attempt to place "the control of affairs in hands of the more ignorant classes." Identifying with the men of "intelligence and culture" among the former slaveholders, Liberal Republicans concluded that the "South can only be governed through the part of the community that embodies the intelligence and the capital."[3]

The campaign of 1872 brought to the fore a latent Republican skepticism about the culture of the former slaves and their capacity for citizenship. As early as 1867, Radical Republicans questioned whether legislation could ever remove from the black race its "great burden," its "want of all the ordinary claims to social respectability." Since the end of the war, Horace Greeley, the Liberal Republicans' presidential candidate, appealed to "gentlemen" in the North and the South to bring Reconstruction to a magnanimous end on the basis of manhood suffrage, universal pardon, and energetic forgetting. In 1872, candidate Greeley called on the former antagonists to "clasp hands across the bloody chasm." Privately judging African Americans as "an easy, worthless race, taking no thought for the morrow," Greeley publicly enjoined them to "Root, Hog, or Die!"[4]

Although Liberal Republicans lost the election of 1872, they hastened the postwar transformation of the Republican Party. Adopting a tone of apology and embarrassment in their defense of Reconstruction, Republicans embraced restraint and respectability. In the campaign of 1876, they advocated limited federal authority, sound money, and Protestant sobriety against immigrant excess. The former Liberal Republicans, a talented and energetic group of reformers, went on to leadership positions in both major parties and to editorships of the nation's most influential newspapers and journals. Determined to enhance the role of gentlemen in politics and limit the influence of the ignorant, they transformed the meaning of reform. Once focused on the democratic reshaping of economic and political institutions, reform now meant the frustration of the popular will and a defense of the natural order.[5]

Partisan imperatives and economic interests sped the abandonment of Reconstruction and the embrace of determinism. But a profound change in cultural attitudes also played an underestimated role in the transition from Reconstruction to the Gilded Age. Citing the freed people's "apparent want of mental, moral and physical vigor," and finding their "moral perceptions ... deficient," liberal reformers demanded the return of power to the "natural leaders" of the South, the "most active and intelligent people." They also embraced a romanticized vision of the plantation as a harmonious, paternalistic world, finding in it a version of the genteel domesticity they admired in the North. In the sentimental fictions of "the lost cause," the plantation house served as the setting for national reconciliation, with faithful and contented slaves presiding over the marriage of the genteel of North and South.[6]

Genteel culture served to justify and disguise the brutality of the Gilded Age. It is essential "for the progress of the race," Carnegie believed, "that the houses of some should be homes for all that is highest and best in literature and the arts, and for all the refinements of civilization, rather than that none should be so. Much better this great irregularity than universal squalor." Those who disliked the survival of the fittest, Sumner added, could look to "only one possible alternative, and this is the survival of the unfittest. The former is the law of civilization; the latter is the law of anti-civilization."[7]

Beneath genteel culture lay greed and avarice. "There has hardly ever before been a community in which the weak have been so pitilessly pushed to the wall," a British conservative wrote admiringly of the Gilded Age, "in which those who have succeeded have so uniformly been the strong, and in which in so short a time there has arisen so great an inequality of private fortune and domestic luxury." But the celebration of genteel manners and morals disguised the survival of the fittest (or most unscrupulous) as the rise of a cultural aristocracy.[8]

By segregating the discourse of politics from that of economics and submerging both in discourse about culture, liberal reformers constricted public debate and shielded the economic order from political challenge. They created a politics in which consideration of divisive questions "became bad taste at best, and bad politics at worst." In the face of the insistent demands of democracy, the reformers defined culture as something higher and more refined than everyday life, something vulnerable that they defended. Elevating the private over the public, the self-styled "best men" offered their own mannered gentility as the source of their authority in public life.[9]

BIG BUSINESS AND SMALL POLITICS IN THE GILDED AGE

The Gilded Age of big business produced only small politics. Compliant politicos supplied corporate leaders with promotional subsidies, protective tariffs, freedom from regulation, and strikebreaking troops. Serving special interests, a generation of corrupt spoilsmen thought only of maximizing their price. "Before business learned to buy statesmen at wholesale," a historian later quipped, "it had to buy privileges at retail." The "House of Representatives was like an auction room," an embittered congressman recalled, "where more valuable considerations were disposed of under the speaker's hammer than in any other place on earth."[10]

Liberal reformers defined themselves in opposition to the new professional leadership of the Republican Party, the "Stalwarts." Using federal patronage and policy to manage the competing demands of economic and ethnic groups, the Stalwarts abandoned ideological politics for a devotion to the Republican Party as an organization and a career. In an era defined by "the desire for office and for office as a means of gain," the liberal reformers promised to "bring back that better era of the republic in which, when men consecrated themselves to the public service, they utterly abnegated all selfish purpose."[11]

The liberal reformers pledged to replace corrupt dealing with a politics of moral purpose. But their "determined moral purpose" did not cut very deep, seldom rising above a complacent self-satisfaction. They congratulated each other, for example, in not having seen "one drunk man in the convention or on the streets" during the Liberal Republican National Convention in 1872. Meanwhile, they ignored a mounting labor and agrarian crisis, as falling prices and soaring interest rates bankrupted small producers. Conflating financial and moral probity, the liberal reformers insisted that an inflated currency meant "dishonesty, corruption, repudiation." In insisting on the gold standard as an "honest dollar," the only route to "honor" and "public virtue," the liberal reformers sanctified the status quo. "To have said and done nothing is a tremendous power," a muckraking historian later wrote of them, "but it should not be abused."[12]

The liberal reformers' agenda consisted of laissez-faire economic policy (free trade, the gold standard, strict market determination of wages), a professional civil service, and blind obedience to natural law. Even as the British liberals they admired backed away from laissez-faire and acknowledged the need for governmental intervention, the liberal reformers kept the faith. They embraced the conviction that "harmonious self-regulation required that the individual respect economic law even if it happened to destroy him." Rejecting all discussion of economic alternatives to laissez-faire capitalism, the liberal reformers denounced dangerous legislation that violated the "eternal laws of political economy."[13]

Claiming the authority of science and morality, liberal reformers ridiculed democracy. "Universal suffrage," they complained, "can only mean in plain English the government of ignorance and vice—it means a European, especially Celtic [Irish] proletariat on the Atlantic coast, an African proletariat on the shores of the Gulf, and a Chinese proletariat on the Pacific." Democracy amounted to "the transfer of power to the ignorant and the poor, and the use of Government to carry out the poor and ignorant man's view of the nature of society." Industrialization, they warned, produced a wage-earning class "different in tone and mind and mode of life" from anything the Founding Fathers envisioned. Like "southern negroes," urban workers in the North tended to "take the short view of things."[14]

The corporate order barely needed the liberal reformers. Where reform principles served powerful interests, as in upholding the gold standard, they were superfluous. Where their principles interfered with powerful interests, as in the free-trade critique of tariffs, they were ignored. But liberal reformers did serve the corporate order in minimizing the purview of politics and discrediting democratic efforts to redress the injustices of the market. They condemned the eight-hour day, for example, as an effort to "nullify one of the natural economic laws by the laws of the state," akin to trying to legislate "against the attraction of gravity."[15]

But the liberal reformers' defense of the natural order of the market poorly described the character of the emerging corporate order. Beginning with the construction of the transcontinental railroads (dependent on federal loans, land grants, and the engineering skill and military protection of the U.S. Army), corporate development relied upon public policy and governmental largesse. Protected by limited liability, using other people's money, and purchasing government favors, corporate leaders were anything but risk-taking entrepreneurs responding to the market laws of supply and demand. Seeking predictability in order to manage huge fixed costs, corporations sought to control and stabilize the market with pools, cartels, trusts, and monopolies. Risk and competition was what they tried to avoid. Corporate capitalism operated not through "the invisible hand of the market," but through the "visible hand" of management in which engineers, accountants, salesmen, engineers, efficiency experts, and lobbyists minimized uncertainty.[16]

Lacking a coherent account of public affairs, liberal reformers ultimately fell back on a defense of the domestic culture of the middle class. They attributed the "decline in public morality" to a "loss of feeling, even among our women, for the fine nature of gentlemanliness." Making equality the "highest political good," they cautioned, led "down into barbarism" and would "prove fatal to art, to science, to literature, and to law." Plutocracy threatened civilization as much as equality. The raw industrial city of Chicago, "a huge monster, gorged with pork and grain" and lacking "homes of refinement," illustrated the danger. In calling for accumulation of "the best works, the best thoughts and the best pictures of the world" to redeem Chicago's commercial crudeness, a reformer insisted the city needed "less of steers and less of pork and more of culture." But their strictures against plutocracy and their enthusiasm for a redeeming culture came to little.[17]

LIBERAL REFORMERS AND GENTEEL CULTURE

Liberal reformers spoke for and from a suffocating genteel culture sealed off from politics and the life of the city. Finding "the gutter governing the sidewalk, the slums pouring out their vice and ignorance to masquerade in seats of honor . . . , the saloons posing as the temples of liberty," they envisioned a moral reformation proceeding outward from the domestic realm, with themselves in the lead. Rejecting external, political restraints, they relied upon internal, moral restraints cultivated in the domestic realm. The "most perfect state," they held, "is that in which moral self-control is substituted for the sanction of government."[18]

Genteel culture, while protected from the market, also lacked the means to confront it. Laissez-faire policy subordinated everything to the needs of the market, forcing human values and practices other than pecuniary calculation to retreat into a secluded domestic realm. The domestic realm would become the repository of sympathy and fellow feeling, to soften the acquisitive urge or at least redirect it to the "higher selfishness of marriage and parenthood." But it did not turn out that way. Gilded Age Americans grew up "in a sort of orgy of lofty examples, moralized poems, national anthems, and baccalaureate sermons" that did nothing to shape practical affairs. Enveloped in "fine potentialities, remote, vaporous, and evanescent as a rainbow," the American was simultaneously "encouraged to assume that the world is a stamping-ground for every untrained, greedy, and aggressive impulse."[19]

As representatives of a refined domestic realm, the liberal reformers treated corruption as a case of bad manners and delighted in depicting their antagonists, high and low, as lacking gentility. Beginning with Thomas Nast's skewering of New York City's Boss Tweed and his gargantuan belly, images of voracious politicos as well as engorged plutocrats and obese moneybags filled the reform press. Only the refined gentlemen of the middle class could be trusted to control their own appetites and moderate those of others.[20]

The politicos acknowledged the liberal reformers' domestic credentials and took delight in deriding them as "man-milliners" and "miss-Nancys." The genteel reformer was a "political hermaphrodite," they chortled, a "third sex," the "neutral gender not popular either in nature or society." Stressing the reformers' ineffectuality, the politicos described them as "effeminate without being either masculine or feminine, unable to beget or to bear; possessing neither fecundity nor virility; endowed with the contempt of men and the derision of women, and doomed to sterility, isolation, and extinction."[21]

Liberal reformers found domestic refinements more promising than political reforms. Disturbed by the Malthusian pessimism of classical economic theory, the businessman-reformer Edward Atkinson investigated the culinary arts of preparing palatable meals out of cheap foodstuffs. Atkinson insisted that his cookbook would do more to improve the lot of working people than any eight-hour bill. He imagined his epitaph as: "He taught the American people how to stew." The labor leader Eugene V. Debs derided Atkinson's cookbook as the "science of the shinbone diet." Making casual references to "my summer place by the sea-side" while assuming that the workers' lot would always be a scramble for necessary calories, Atkinson epitomized liberal reformers' inability to empathize with those outside their domestic culture.[22]

Viewing politics as "a series of little morality plays," the liberal reformers "instinctively stepped forward to play the role of Virtue." But they wielded an attenuated concept of virtue, a combination of conventional morality and genteel manners that capitulated to the market. The civic republican conception of virtue once meant the aggressive assertion of self in public affairs, the obligation to engage in debate, deliberation, and decision. But as economic transactions involving things supplanted political speech among citizens as the central focus of public life, civic virtue gave way to genteel manners dedicated to ingratiation and avoiding offense. The businessman's *"smiles and manners"* were his "business capital," a scornful observer wrote, obliging him to "appear pleas'd, anxious, indifferent, or sad according to his customer's humor." An explosion of etiquette books and manuals of gentility over the course of the nineteenth century provided "plain and simple instructions in the art of appearing to the best advantage on all occasions." Facilitating the scramble for position and status in a fluid urban society, the manuals promised that, "You may be whatever you will resolve to be."[23]

Genteel manners and the law worked in tandem to brand challenges to the authority of the wealthy as challenges to a moral order, violations of propriety and good taste. Manners were laws, etiquette writers explained, the "laws of good society" and, like "the laws concerning life and property," they were to "be obeyed without question." The difference between the laws of manners and those of property sometimes disappeared. "We must watch people who know what good manners are, and try to make our manners like theirs," a catechism on manners put it. "What kind of people are polite?" the catechism asked. "The best people." The catechism left unstated what made them the best people. In obscuring the connection between wealth and gentility, the code of manners suggested that the market obeyed moral as well as iron laws.[24]

Gentility discouraged conflict, turning it back on the individual in terms of civility and self-restraint. As a means of avoiding emotional outbursts in public, etiquette books advised the genteel to avoid all controversial topics, most especially politics. Emotion expressed toward social inferiors represented a serious breach of good manners, for it brought the genteel down to the level of the rudest commoner. Anger undermined social status and authority and left the antagonists on a dangerously equal footing. The proper response to an inferior's impertinence, one etiquette writer advised, was to "summon the agents of the law to rid you of the nuisance."[25]

In recommending a strategy of moving through the city with as little interaction as possible, genteel manners limited civic interaction. The golden rule of manners boiled down to the following injunction: "All rights, and the essence of true politeness, are contained in the homely maxim, 'Mind Your Own Business'; which means, by a pretty evident implication, that you are to let your neighbor's business alone." City life reduced itself to crowds of strangers, each individual "taking no notice of his fellows, pushing and jostling them, and each with [a] weary, jaded, anxious look upon his face." A "man walks his tedious miles through the same interminable street every day," Mark Twain wrote of New York City. He "rushes, rushes, rushes, and never has time to be companionable." "I find everywhere the same expression," recalled a European diplomat of the streets of Chicago. "Everyone is in a hurry, if only to get home as fast as possible.... Everyone seems to suspect a competitor in his neighbor."[26]

THE LIBERAL REFORMERS' ENCOUNTER WITH THE CITY

Both liberal reformers and genteel culture shied away from the rough-and-tumble politics and public life of the city. For many of the liberal reformers, their encounter with Boss Tweed of New York City provided a formative experience. William Tweed, the boss of Tammany Hall's Democratic machine, ruled the city by negotiating compromises between popular conceptions of justice and elite prerogatives. Tweed's prominence and Tammany's success at the ballot box drove liberal reformers to develop new means of exerting the influence of the cultivated, from parks and museums to universities and journals of opinion. E. L. Godkin in *The Nation* and George William Curtis in *Harper's Weekly* became powerful publicists, policing public opinion at the intersection of manners and politics.[27]

As *The Nation*'s first editor, Godkin thought of it as an experiment to "see whether the best writers in America can get a fair hearing from the American public on questions of politics, art and literature." The quintessential literary man in politics, Curtis described the scholar's calling as a "public conscience by which public measures may be tested." Just as Godkin edited the organ of the Radical Republicans, Curtis's editorials and Thomas Nast's drawings in *Harper's Weekly* staunchly defended the Radicals' efforts to protect black citizenship. By 1870, however, Godkin, Curtis, and Nast turned away from the fate of the freed people to confront the challenge of Tweed, who "subverted" democracy and ruled by "plebiscite." Deploring the rise of a Democratic "machine" that served "no public purpose," they also lamented the decline of the principled Republican Party.[28]

Liberal reformers sought to depoliticize social and economic conflicts, shifting the decision-making process from freewheeling debate in public spaces, where their power was limited, to the domesticated spaces of the respectable, where they wielded considerable influence. Proposals to limit the urban electorate served their larger purpose of establishing the authority of a cultivated elite. Rather than the promiscuous crowds of the "democratic plan," Godkin preferred to exert influence on a small circle of cultivated intellects and writers. Public opinion, in his view, was not really public but the possession of a cultivated minority, the "thoughtful, educated, high-minded men—gentlemen in short." Within that narrow but powerful circle, Godkin became a force, "an authority with authorities."[29]

The Great Chicago Fire of 1871 provided another formative experience for liberal reformers, illuminating the awful threat the city posed for civilization. The fire, *Harper's Weekly* reported, unleashed "as vile a set of scoundrels as ever picked a pocket or cut a throat" who instituted a "new reign of terror." Other observers spread lurid rumors of "the awful democracy of that hour," which threw together "young girls, whose artless lives were unfamiliar with even the name of crime" with "brutes in human form, who were not only ready to do acts of crime, but whose polluting wickedness was rank and cast off prison-fumes upon the air." Released prisoners supposedly seized a wagon full of genteel clothing "and fled to remote alleys and dark passages to don their plunder and disguise themselves." Such tales juxtaposed the domestic proprieties of Chicago's better classes to the urban underworld of immigrants and criminals where "the spirit of infernal revelry prevailed."[30]

The great conflagration encouraged Chicago's business and professional elite to seize the reins of power from a city government dominated by immigrant and working-class voters. Welcoming federal troops into the city to provide order, respectable opinion also applauded the convening of an extralegal grand jury to enforce the law. The Relief and Aid Society, a private association of Chicago's elite, wrested control of the postfire rebuilding effort from a "foul brood of city politicians" who aspired to create their own Tammany.[31]

While liberal reformers tried to short-circuit the political process, popular conceptions of justice did not disappear. Working people paraded to Chicago's Common Council in 1872 to protest postfire restrictions on wood construction that limited their access to home ownership. In 1873, Irish and German immigrants united to elect the "People's Party's" candidate as mayor. In the following year, the unemployed rallied in support of public works and demanded the distribution of the Relief and Aid Society's remaining funds. In cities across the republic, working people politicized rather than obscured social and economic divisions. In rallying for public works and the eight-hour day, they demanded a redistribution of the benefits of industrial society.[32]

CIVIC MURDER: LIBERAL REFORMERS AND PUBLIC OPINION

For liberal reformers, however, certain questions were simply not open for debate. In "A Saturday Sermon" on the eight-hour day in 1865, Curtis worried that long hours and lack of education "hopelessly debarred" laboring people "from intellectual expansion, the delights of art, and of intelligent leisure." But he sternly reminded workers that "there are no short cuts to happiness." Godkin also instructed working people on the importance of self-denial and sounded an alarm over the eagerness of politicians to respond to popular demands. Courting the labor vote, Republicans even praised the valor of the Paris Communards in 1871 and held their cause "entitled to the respect of Americans everywhere." Godkin found such demagoguery appalling.[33]

But things began to turn with the onset of depression in 1873. As unemployment spread and corporate consolidation accelerated, a series of violent strikes punctuated the spread of factory conditions to 80 percent of manufacturing workers by 1880. In the great cities, class lines hardened and vagrancy laws made unemployment a crime. When the unemployed gathered in New York City's Tompkins Square in 1874 to demand bread or public work, the police violently broke up the peaceful assembly. *Harper's Weekly* thanked the police for suppressing a dangerous protest so similar to the Paris Commune. "Every lamp-post in Chicago," the *Tribune* added in 1875, "will be decorated with a communistic carcass if necessary to prevent wholesale incendiarism or prevent any attempt at it." The nationwide railroad strikes in 1877 escalated tensions. While working people refused to be "content with a bowl of rice and a rat a week apiece," wealthy Chicagoans organized a Law and Order League, dreaming of a "Gatling quick-firing gun which could sweep a street from side to side and mow down a thousand men in a few seconds."[34]

Repression did not end efforts to inject divisive issues into political campaigns. Henry George's 1886 campaign for the mayoralty of New York City particularly galled "the best men," not least because George agreed with the liberal reformers in their allegiance to the natural law but contested their definition. Properly stated, George argued, the natural law included the right of access to land and the opportunity to labor (secured through a tax on speculative land values). George's platform defined the "true purpose of government" as "the maintenance of that sacred right of property which gives to everyone opportunity to employ his labor and security that he shall enjoy its fruits." The George campaign, Godkin fumed, threatened "to undo what has been done for law and order." Liberal reformers joined regular Republicans in uniting behind the Democratic candidate Abram Hewitt to defeat "these enemies of civilization and social order."[35]

But in the Chicago anarchists, the liberal reformers met their nemesis. Like George, the anarchists shared the reformers' faith in the natural law, substituting a cooperative communism for the iron laws of the market. A "free system, with science for its guide and necessity for its impelling force," the anarchists held, would allow "the laws of nature to have full sway." Liberal reformers blamed anarchists for fomenting revolution. But anarchists hurled back the charge. "Revolutions are no more made than earthquakes and cyclones," the anarchists responded, arising only because the ruling class tried "to dictate a stand-still to eternal forces." When liberal reformers accused the anarchists of trying to destroy civilization, the anarchists again reversed the indictment. "You, in your blindness," the anarchists taunted the forces of law and order, "think you can stop the tidal wave of civilization and human emancipation by placing a few policemen, a few gatling guns, and some regiments of militia on the shore."[36]

At the extremes, neither liberal reformers nor anarchists saw much point in the give-and-take of politics. In 1873, the young Albert Parsons arrived in Chicago from Texas where, as a Radical Republican, he fought for the rights of the freedmen. Parsons soon became a regular speaker at open-air demonstrations and led marches through the city to dramatize inequality and injustice. Initially, he preached against violence and advocated working through the political system. But as Parsons watched Chicago workers brutally beaten at peaceful protests and listened to the violent rhetoric of immigrant anarchists, he acquired a fascination with violence that matched that of his antagonists. "If we would achieve our liberation from economic bondage and acquire our natural right to life and liberty," Parsons told a crowd in 1885, "every man must lay by a part of his wages, buy a Colt's navy revolver, . . . a Winchester rifle, and learn how to make and use dynamite."[37]

Most anarchists, including Parsons, used rhetorical violence only to attract attention, build confidence, and secure concessions. But their fiery speeches made them notorious. Even the respectable and mild-mannered appearance of most anarchists only marked them as the sort of confidence men that haunted the genteel. They thus shared one more thing with their antagonists, a sense of the thinness and precariousness of civilization. Parsons quoted a military report to the president and Congress that described how "the commerce of entire cities [can be] destroyed by an infuriated people with means carried with perfect safety to themselves *in the pockets* of their clothing." When tens of thousands of workers in Chicago joined a nationwide wave of strikes for the eight-hour day at the beginning of May in 1886, a city newspaper urged readers to hold Parsons and his anarchist associates "responsible for any trouble that occurs. Make an example of them if trouble does occur."[38]

On May 4, 1886, two thousand people gathered near Chicago's Haymarket to protest the killing of two strikers by the police the day before. What followed represented the climax of escalating tensions dating back to 1873. After a series of tame speeches, the crowd began to disperse. But with about 200–300 people filtering away from the scene, 170 policemen arrived. As the police gruffly commanded the crowd to disperse, a bomb went off. The police fired their guns into the crowd and clubbed indiscriminately. "Goaded to madness," the *Chicago Tribune* reported, "the police were in the condition of mind which permitted no resistance, and in a measure they are as dangerous as any mob." Of the seven deaths and sixty injuries among the police, the vast majority resulted from police bullets.[39]

The police arrested eight prominent anarchists and charged them with murder. Although no evidence tied the eight to the bomb and several played no role in the planning of the protest, the national press rushed to judgment in support of a grossly unfair trial. In the face of these "brutal ruffians," Curtis wrote, the "merciful" thing was to employ the "most complete and summary methods of repression." The executions served as a "solemn declaration" in defense of "every precious right of civilized man." Godkin agreed. He complained of the "disgusting spectacle" that delayed the executions and allowed the weak-kneed to "lash themselves into sympathy." Rejecting the argument that it was "bad policy" to punish the men for their opinions, Godkin judged it "historically absurd" to tolerate speech that questioned private property.[40]

The execution of four of the convicted men satisfied Curtis and Godkin. But the executions shattered one of the leading exponents of the genteel tradition. William Dean Howells, a protégé of Curtis and Godkin, had recently called for a literature that focused on "the smiling aspects of life, which are more American." An apolitical man, Howells "was perhaps as astonished that there were Anarchists in America as he was that legal machinery and public opinion could be mobilized to kill them." But he now believed that in silencing debate and prohibiting the expression of certain ideas, a complacent, genteel civilization committed "civic murder." The *"freest Republic the world has ever known,"* Howells despaired, "has killed five men for their opinions" (the fifth committed suicide in prison). After "fifty years of optimistic content with 'civilization' and its ability to come out all right in the end," Howells concluded, "I now abhor it, and feel that is it coming out all wrong in the end, unless it bases itself anew on a real equality."[41]

At the cost of his reputation, Howells overcame the genteel separation of culture and city life. A newcomer to New York City, Howells came to know its streets and its people in ways the suburbanized Curtis and the cloistered Godkin never did. In *A Hazard of New Fortunes* (1890), Howells dramatized the public life of the city in an effort "to do justice" to the "irreparably wronged men" of Chicago's Haymarket. Organized around the launching of a literary magazine financed by a great capitalist, the novel exposed genteel culture's complicity with the established order and its machinery of repression. Once the domestic novelist par excellence, Howells centered his story around a violent streetcar strike. Howells forced Basil March, his fictional editor, as he forced himself, to engage the city "as life" rather than "spectacle."[42]

"This Word Culture": An Industrial Tragedy at Pullman

On his visit to the famous Chautauqua grounds in 1896, the philosopher William James encountered the same complacent, genteel civilization that angered Howells. He found in that "middle-class paradise" a stifling and effeminate culture, a gentility in manners, speech, and dress that represented the opposite of the raw and practical everyday world. James decided that "culture and refinement all alone are not enough," they needed contact with the "sterner stuff of manly virtue." He left Chautauqua "wishing for heroism and the spectacle of human nature on the rack." He recalled catching a glimpse of it from his speeding train, a "workman doing something on the dizzy edge of a sky-scaling iron construction."[43]

A triumph of genteel culture, Chautauqua offered a redemptive answer to greed and exploitation. But despite its vision of art and learning in the service of political harmony and social equality, Chautauqua could secure neither. Developed in response to the chaos and conflicts of industrialization, its isolation obscured the conditions it promised to ameliorate. Rejecting both the luxury of the wealthy and the deprivation of the poor, Chautauqua might have offered a genteel version of the ethic of the citizen-proprietor. But it provided no perspective on the political and economic foundations of society.[44]

Walt Whitman recognized the danger a genteel conception of culture held for democracy. "We find ourselves," he wrote, "in close quarters with the enemy, this word Culture." Whitman held out for a different meaning of culture, one "drawn out, not for a single class alone, or for the parlors or lecture rooms, but with an eye to practical life also of the middle and working strata." While acknowledging the importance of "a few first-class poets, philosophs, and authors," Whitman's cultural ideal centered on "the formation of the typical personality" and was "not restricted by conditions ineligible to the masses."[45]

But in the wake of the Haymarket incident, many still looked to genteel culture to rescue the industrial city from anarchy. Settling in Chicago in 1859, the industrialist George Pullman served in the Relief and Aid Society in 1871 and headed the Law and Order League in 1877. But he sought a more comprehensive answer to the ills of industrial society. Between 1880 and 1884, Pullman built a model industrial community south of Chicago. The model community would "carry the world, so far as such men can reach it, to a higher level of civilization," proving the worth of genteel culture "as a force in the production of results, just as is the force of the steam engine itself." Just as his famous Pullman dining cars tamed railway passengers by invoking "the same instincts" that made people "conform their habits to elegant surroundings in homes," so the town of Pullman would transform the working class.[46]

Like Chautauqua, the town of Pullman left the disorderly city behind. Neither part of Chicago nor even a municipality in the conventional sense, the model community belonged to a single man who feared his plan would fail "if a single lot had been sold." Lacking any public space, the town also employed "no policemen or constables, no justice's court, no aldermen, no public functionaries of any description." Governed by a trusteeship of the best men, Pullman promised "to be an exact counterpart in miniature of the great cities, except that in its appointments it is a vast improvement, and by virtue of its regulations is free from many city temptations and vices." The model town excluded saloons, cheap theaters, and other forms of popular culture.[47]

Although few disputed the improved living conditions in the model town, not everyone praised Pullman. "What is Pullman," Parsons asked in 1884, "but a plantation, a penitentiary, a slave-pen, where 4,000 men come and go at the beck and call of one man?" The Progressive economist Richard Ely visited the town in the same year. Although Ely praised the town's recognition of "the *commercial value of beauty*," he also described the "sad spectacle" of a town "where not one single person dare speak out openly his opinion about the town in which he lives." Without competing political and moral voices, neither newspaper nor independent pulpit, Pullman resembled a "benevolent, well-wishing feudalism." The paternalistic order, Ely concluded, "degrades the dependent, corrupts the morals of the superior" and is responsible for much of "the degeneracy of manners and morals in public and private life."[48]

Pullman rejected the charge of paternalism and regarded his model town as a business investment. The town did become "a source of pride" for Pullman, particularly when "it gave him the glow of benevolence," as Jane Addams observed. But he expected everything in the town from the bank to the church to return a 6 percent profit to the Pullman Company. When faced with a precipitous decline in orders during the depression of 1893, Pullman slashed wages and laid off workers. But he did not reduce rents in company-owned housing and continued to pay handsome dividends to his stockholders. "Great destitution and suffering prevails in Pullman," the *Chicago Times* reported, and great "bitterness and a feeling of resentment at what is openly called slavery, imposed by the conditions of employment by the Pullman company."[49]

When workers went on strike in May 1894, Pullman fired those who remained and closed the plant. The Pullman strikers appealed to the fledgling

American Railway Union (ARU) for support. Although ARU president Eugene Debs cautioned against the sympathy strike, the ARU decided to refuse to switch Pullman cars onto trains. In response, the General Managers Association, controlling some twenty railroads, shut down the entire railroad system west of Chicago. The United States attorney general Richard Olney, a former railroad lawyer, secured a court injunction against the strike and then persuaded President Grover Cleveland to send federal troops to Chicago to protect interstate commerce and mail delivery. When Debs refused to obey the injunction, he twice suffered arrest—first for conspiracy and then for violating the injunction. The strike collapsed in mid-July. Convicted on the second charge, Debs spent six months in jail.[50]

The scale of the strike shocked the nation. Disturbances such as the Pullman strike, an editorial in the *Chautauquan* soothed, are the "natural accompaniment of the march of civilization." But platitudes no longer served and laissez-faire no longer sufficed. In intervening to end the massive strike, Federal Judge William Howard Taft wrote that the "gigantic character of the conspiracy staggers the imagination." The "starvation of a nation cannot be a lawful purpose of a combination." While labor bore the brunt of federal intervention in the name of the public welfare, such arguments could and would later be used to rein in corporations as well.[51]

Thus, even as Professor Sumner decried "The Absurd Effort to Make the World Over," the era of laissez-faire began to fade. As early as 1884, Ely argued that the Pullman experiment deserved attention precisely because the "pretty dream of a perfect, natural order of things brought about by the free play of unrestrained social forces has vanished." A year later, Ely founded the American Economic Association to "combat the influence of the Sumner crowd." Modern social science developed in reaction against laissez-faire thinking. The Pullman strike, John Dewey observed, served "to get the social organism thinking," to move beyond the individualistic calculus that pitted George Pullman against Eugene Debs and brought the nation to a standstill. Once again, Americans considered the possibility that we might see beyond self-interest and pursue the public good.[52]

No one understood the new thinking better than Chicago's Jane Addams. From a prosperous, middle-class family, Addams founded Hull House in 1889. A social settlement in a poor Chicago neighborhood, Hull House operated originally on the principle that in providing cultural uplift to the poor, middle-class "settlers" also did good for their own souls. An admirer of Pullman and his town, Addams perhaps shared Ely's assessment that the model town "offers to the majority of its residents quite as much as they are in a position to enjoy, and in many cases even more." But Addams quickly shed her genteel assumptions, learned that her neighbors knew better than she how their lives might be improved, and turned Hull House into an agency of political advocacy. We cannot simply extend the good to all classes, she later explained, because until "all men and all classes contribute to a good, we cannot even be sure that it is worth having."[53]

In "A Modern Lear," Addams described the Pullman strike as an industrial tragedy because Pullman and the railroad workers failed to recognize their common interests. Addams's democratic faith taught her that only mutual interests were worth securing. Pullman wished to do good, Addams argued, but the powerful too often believed they could do good "by pursuing their own ideals, leaving those ideals unconnected with the consent of their fellow-men." The workers, too, failed to understand that the "new claim on the part of the toiling multitude, the new sense of responsibility on the part of the well-to-do, arise in reality from the same source" and "logically converge into the same movement."[54]

Hindsight deepens the tragedy. Neither the established journals of liberal reform nor the new muckraking journals published "A Modern Lear" until 1912. In 1897, Pullman's family buried him in a concrete-reinforced vault of his own design, for fear his workers would exhume and desecrate his body. Most tragically, the Pullman strike capped two decades of defeats for the labor movement at the hands of local, state, and federal authorities. Losing faith in politics and abandoning as unrealistic its vision for a cooperative commonwealth, the labor movement lost the chance to graft its hopes onto the new period of public action about to emerge.[55]

Nevertheless, working people came closest to building the democratic culture that Addams and Whitman envisioned, a culture of participation and solidarity engaged with the world of work and politics. "If it were not for some conservative influences in the community and a certain fraternity in suffering and neighborliness in bonds which promote deeds of genuine charity and benevolence," reported the *Chicago Times* in the months before the strike, "the town would be ripe for violence." Once the strike began, Debs described the "fellowship for the woes of others" as "at once the hope of civilization and the supreme glory of mankind." The federal commission that investigated the strike added its praise. "In the midst of excitement and threatened starvation," the strikers' "dignified, manly, and conservative conduct" made them "worthy of the highest type of American citizenship." Culture, it turns out, mattered after all.[56]

PART II

Popular Culture, Political Culture: Building a Democratic Public

In 1863, the editor George William Curtis took a friend to New York City's plebeian Niblo's Gardens to see the American actor Edwin Forrest. Curtis described Forrest's acting as of "the muscular school; the brawny art; the biceps aesthetics; the tragic calves; the bovine drama; rant, roar and rigamarole," a "boundless exaggeration of all the traditional conventions of the stage." Curtis conceded that Forrest could "move his audience." Observing the young women in the audience, he remarked that they "were not refined nor intellectual. They were perhaps, rather coarse. But they cried good hearty tears." The display unnerved Curtis's companion and the men repaired to the genteel Winter Garden. "The difference of the spectacle was striking," Curtis reported, the "air of the audience was that of refined attention rather than of eager interest. Plainly it was a more cultivated and intellectual audience."[1]

Curtis and his companion took in one other entertainment that night in 1863. Asked by his "rustic friend" to show him the sights of the great city, Curtis first took him to the "great political assemblage" at Cooper Union where the vice president of the United States appeared. Founded by a self-described "mechanic of New York" for the education of other mechanics, Cooper Union encouraged working people's participation in the cultural and political life of the republic. The political meeting, one of dozens in which the citizenry deliberated on the union's war aims, supported Curtis's boast that while New York City might not have "the external signs of ancient and lofty civilization," it triumphed in promoting "the general intelligence" of the people.[2]

Squeezing into the crowd in Cooper Union's great hall, the two friends saw upon the stage something not unlike what they later saw at Niblo's Gardens. An orator was "vehemently declaiming and gesticulating," Curtis recalled, and his words were "greeted with hearty cheers." The "intense interest of the meeting was most pleasant to see," for this "before us was the government of the country." It "is by talk, by argument, by comparison, by enlightenment, by every means incessantly brought to bear upon public opinion that we are governed." The "talk of today," Curtis concluded, "is the policy of tomorrow."[3]

The evening on the town in 1863 illustrated the intersection of popular and political culture. The new headquarters of the Tammany machine which opened in 1868, to take another example, hosted both political meetings and popular entertainments. In generating the conversations that formed public opinion, popular entertainments and public meetings created a democratic public. But the merging of popular culture and political culture also meant that the transformation of the one entailed the transformation of the other. If the people fully shared in cultural affairs as participants, critics, and creators, that justified and reinforced their role in political affairs. If, however, elites judged the people incapable of enjoying, understanding, or participating in the best cultural productions, that could not fail to undercut their political standing.[4]

In 1870, just seven years after his evening on the town, Curtis reflected on the disappearance of the popular theater. He lamented the passing of the old days of mingling with the plebeians, of "familiar conversation with a seedy friend in the pit." But he judged the change for the better. "Where the noisy crowd of men were massed, upon hard, backless benches," a "luminous cloud" of perfume and fashionable dress now arose. The pit "with its noise and unhandsomeness" was gone; so too the "unspeakable third tier." The "whole house seems to be a family circle."[5]

A democratic culture that began to take shape in the first half of the nineteenth century disintegrated in the century's last decades. It left behind a cultural hierarchy that discriminated between sacred cultural forms for the elite and unredeemed, mindless entertainments for plebeians. The growing cultural gap between rich and poor in the late nineteenth century paralleled and justified a growing gap in economic and political power. In defining truth and justice, beauty and propriety, cultural authority and political authority went hand in hand.[6]

Part II traces the rise and fall of a democratic culture and a democratic public over the course of the nineteenth century, a story that overlaps and intersects with the struggle to create a more democratic economy, examined in Part I. The cultural, physical, and legal infrastructure for a democratic public took shape in the Jacksonian city, but the opponents of slavery used parts of that infrastructure to build an antislavery majority that bypassed the cities. The two forces of urban democracy and antislavery clashed violently in the New York City draft riots. A product of the failure of the antislavery movement to win over working people in the nation's largest city, the riots discredited democratic politics. Veterans of New York City's traumatic experience subsequently took a leading role in the national process of urban reconstruction that eclipsed the democratic public. The emergence of a cultural hierarchy of highbrow and lowbrow reinforced and underwrote a series of good government campaigns that questioned democratic competence.

CHAPTER 4

The Democratic Public in City and Nation

The Jacksonian City and the Limits of Antislavery

As the cultural, physical, and legal infrastructure for a democratic public took shape in the first third of the nineteenth century, the republic's largest cities produced an engaged, intelligent citizenry. City parks, civic spaces, and public meetings provided the places and occasions for political discussion and debate, while post offices, telegraph systems, and newspapers distributed it outward to every corner of the republic. Meanwhile the courts provided cities with considerable powers to plan for the public welfare and circumscribed the rights of private property.

In the thirty years preceding the Civil War, the focus of the democratic public shifted from the city to slavery. Alerting citizens to the threat posed to the free labor republic, slavery's opponents used the infrastructure of a democratic public to mobilize an antislavery majority in the small towns and rural areas of the North. But the antislavery movement never captured the cities. The same entrepreneurial and evangelical logic that condemned slavery for denying economic opportunity and religious salvation demanded the imposition of market discipline and middle-class morality on working people. As Whigs and evangelicals tried to suppress popular culture, a thirty years' war between moral reformers and plebeian democrats raged in the cities. Tragically, working people saw in the antislavery movement not a version of their own free labor values, but an intrusive, elite effort to reform them.

Constructing a Public Realm

Although they spoke for "We the People of the United States," the Founding Fathers gave little thought to creating a democratic public. But as the people refused to retire into silence, the Founding Fathers recognized the construction of a public realm as a logical and necessary response to the democratization of the republican ideal of citizenship. In order to shape the "principles, morals, and manners of our citizens to our republican forms of government," Benjamin Rush wrote in 1787, we must develop the means to circulate "knowledge of every kind . . . through every part of the United States."[1]

As an object of national policy, the construction of a public realm began with the Post Office Act of 1792. Creating a network of post offices that connected every part of the expanding republic, the law established the largest enterprise, public or private, in the country. By the 1830s, nearly nine thousand postmasters represented three-fourths of the federal civilian workforce, a staff almost half again as large as the federal army. Delivering nearly fourteen million letters a year over a 116,000 square mile territory, the postal service also circulated 16,000 newspapers a year for a modest fee and an average of 4,300 newspapers to every newspaper publisher in the country, free of charge.[2]

The postal system facilitated participation in public affairs. A public space where citizens came to learn about and discuss public affairs, the local post office served as an adjunct to campaigns and elections. Attached reading rooms made newspapers, government documents, and religious tracts widely available. Considered public resources, newspapers were "as free to all comers, as to the person to whom they rightfully belong." The postal service also facilitated the emergence of political parties. The administration of President John Quincy Adams transformed the post office into a headquarters of a federal program of internal improvements, providing a foundation for the later Whig Party. The Jacksonian Democrats began as little more than a coterie of publicists circulating their newspapers through the mails. As Andrew Jackson assumed the presidency in 1829, he seized upon the republican principle of rotation in office to justify a purge of officeholders. Distributing thousands of postmasterships to their supporters, the Jacksonians secured the loyal cadre and political influence that created an organized party.[3]

New public spaces complemented the postal system and brought some coherence to the Jacksonian city. Massive immigration, rapid economic growth, and periodic recession, as well as physical expansion and the proliferation and specialization of interior spaces made the Jacksonian city less legible than the compact walking cities of the revolutionary era. A baffling array of strangers confronted one another in "the great metropolis," a New Yorker observed, where "beggars and millionaires, shoulder-hitters and thinkers, burghers and scholars, fine women and fortune tellers, journalists and pawn brokers, gamblers and mechanics, here as everywhere else crowd and jostle each other, and all had and fill their places in some mysterious way."[4]

Neither face-to-face community nor segregated metropolis, the Jacksonian city employed public spaces to provide visual order, encourage sociability, and promote democratic association. The largest public spaces—New York's City Hall Park, San Francisco's Portsmouth Square, New Orleans' Lafayette Square—provided a setting for civic buildings and, with their grand assembly halls, an expression of popular sovereignty. Smaller parks and squares and public markets multiplied the opportunities for interaction. The public hall, a distinctive innovation of the Jacksonian city, provided a setting for formal assemblies geared to civic rather than religious or ethnic identities. Hotels, theaters, museums, and dance halls also accommodated a diverse public.[5]

The Jacksonian city celebrated a life lived in public and enjoyed a network of public avenues and streets that created identifiable sectors. A "noble street," New York City's Broadway projected "a thoroughly bustling, lively, and somewhat democratic air." New Orleans' Canal Street, ornamented with fountains and statues, served as promenade and meeting place. Eating oysters or pralines, hot corn or wild duck, drinking hot chocolate or cold liquor from public vendors, people filled the streets. In the Jacksonian city, people took delight in one another in theaters, parks, parades, and marches.[6]

Public encounters could be contentious, but people accepted it as part of city life. While men were the most visible actors, women also frequented public streets and spaces. An Irish woman told a nativist male who ordered her to "Get out of the way there, you old Paddy" that "I won't get out of your way, I'll get right in your way." The middle-class woman who witnessed this exchange wished she could "walk abroad without having misery forced upon my notice where I have no power to relieve it," but she concluded that sweeping away the poor would be worse. The demand for more aggressive policing of the streets intensified as the century wore on, but order still depended upon the citizenry. "The nature of our institutions," wrote New York City's Common Council in rejecting a proposal for police reorganization in 1836, is "such that more reliance may be placed upon the people for aid, in case of any emergency, than in despotic governments."[7]

Civic ceremonies provided occasions for citizens to take pride in and possession of the public realm. Beginning in central squares and proceeding along major arteries, processions anointed everyday spaces with civic importance. In the first quarter of the century, a patrician elite organized civic ceremonies, using public funds to provide food and drink, drama and decoration, in a ritual of communal bonding. But by midcentury, popular committees and voluntary associations joined in the organization of civic ceremonies and staged parades of social, ethnic, and occupational differences. Patrician leaders posing as a natural aristocracy faced competition from humbler citizens organized as a self-governing public.[8]

In the Streets: Law and the Public Realm

The physical infrastructure of the early nineteenth-century public realm, from the post office to massive local projects such as water systems and city halls, still depended upon elite efforts. Into the 1830s, the formal political system in New York City and other cities remained restricted, with the vote reserved for propertied white men. City governments operated as private corporations and local legislatures resembled private assemblies more than public conventions. Paternalistic elites tried to monopolize the definition of the public good. Charity illustrated this best, as elite benefactors dined and danced in splendor to raise money for the destitute, presenting themselves as "fathers of the people" and "guardians of Virtue."[9]

The legal infrastructure for the public realm also depended on elite efforts. The same jurists who created the legal framework for a capitalist market also built the legal foundation for a public realm of health, safety, and convenience. Definitions of both private rights and public responsibilities arose from city streets as courts tried to balance the rights of individuals with social duties. Invoking the legal maxim *salus populi suprema lex est* (the people's welfare is the supreme law), city governments regulated building practices and demolished buildings in the name of public safety; licensed merchants and tradesmen in defense of public economy; removed obstructions from ports, roadways and rivers, and city squares to protect public space; and controlled taverns, brothels, and offensive trades to promote public health.[10]

Relying upon and extending English common law, city governments regulated property in hundreds of ways, determining the price of necessities, dictating the use of construction materials, and controlling the location of nuisances. Blackstone's *Commentaries on the Laws of England* (1765) held that civil society created property and therefore the legislature could compel a property owner "to alienate his possessions for a reasonable price." But in the colonial and early national periods, cities rarely invoked eminent domain (an American coinage, referring to the government's power to take private property for public use).[11]

As cities grew in the nineteenth century, however, the construction of turnpikes, canals, and railroads and the deterioration of the physical quality of the urban environment encouraged municipal governments to make use of eminent domain. A daily flood of goods, people, and animals filled the streets with mud and wastes, as well as crime and vice, threatening the health, safety, and well-being of city residents. Raw sewage created "one mass of reeking, disgusting filth" from which "a frightful odor was emitted in summer, causing fevers and other diseases." Swine scavenged on the streets, transforming garbage into manure and threatening unattended infants. Tens of thousands of horses dropped hundreds of tons of manure daily, their dead carcasses left to rot for days or weeks. Endemic disease took a daily toll. Epidemics sent death rates soaring.[12]

As municipalities responded to these threats, they seized property through eminent domain. Struggles over the definition of "public use" quickly followed.

On one side stood those with vested interests, who feared eminent domain would combine with Jacksonian egalitarianism to undermine all property rights. As Daniel Webster argued, if eminent domain made the legislature and its agents "the sole judges of what is to be taken, and to what public use it is to be appropriated, the most leveling ultraisms ... may be successfully advanced." On the other side, public officials and reformers hoped to bring order to urban growth. By the 1850s, many state legislatures solidified the power of eminent domain with just compensation. The courts widened the meaning of public use to include public purpose and narrowed the situations that required compensation.[13]

The same expansion of the public purpose that privileged developmental over subsistence property and unleashed ambitious entrepreneurs also addressed the social and environmental damages arising from rapid growth. Improved conditions relied upon the courts' use of the law of private and public nuisance, based upon the legal maxim *sic utere tuo, ut alienum non laedas* (use your own property in such a way as not to injure that of another). Even as the courts denied private nuisance claims against public works that promoted economic development, they broadened the application of public nuisance law to close private cemeteries, tear down decaying buildings to discourage the spread of disease, and regulate the hauling of garbage through the city streets.[14]

The courts protected and expanded the public nuisance doctrine to create new powers of public planning. In 1828, the New York Supreme Court ruled that property loss resulting from government action in the public interest "is to be borne as part of the price to be paid for the advantages of the social condition." The court based its ruling "upon the principle that the general good is to prevail over partial individual convenience." In such cases, eminent domain and just compensation did not apply. In the Massachusetts case *Commonwealth v. Tewksbury* (1846), Justice Lemuel Shaw declared it proper for the legislature "to interpose, and by positive enactment to prohibit a use of property which would be injurious to the public."[15]

The police power also extended the potential for public planning. Beginning in the 1820s, sanitarians and physicians, landscape architects and engineers, business leaders and individual citizens all clamored for new municipal services. The provision of water, sewer, and street systems and professional fire and police departments depended on the legal power to police the public order in the interest of safety, health, and convenience. An elastic and imprecise authority, the police power gave municipalities broad leeway in taking and regulating property. Relying on the seventeenth-century English natural law concept of "overwhelming necessity," the courts expanded the power of municipalities to take property in the public interest during economic and social crises. When municipalities seized upon fire and epidemic as occasions to take property without compensation, the courts generally ruled that in such cases, "the rights of private property must be made subservient to the public welfare."[16]

Jurists made their decisive contribution to public planning where the law of public nuisance and the police power intersected. Economic development and the expansion of public services disrupted city streets and multiplied the occasions for public nuisance suits. Retrospective application of the law discouraged public improvements. From the 1820s into the 1850s, the courts therefore decided public nuisance suits with reference to the police power, making compensation unnecessary. The courts also denied legal standing to private citizens who sued government over nuisances resulting from public works. By subsuming public nuisance law under the police power, the courts gave municipalities extensive powers to promote the health, safety, and convenience of their citizens.[17]

The expansion of the police power created a distinctive public interest that transcended a defense of specific property rights. In a frequently cited Massachusetts case, *Commonwealth v. Alger* (1851), Justice Shaw distanced the police power from nuisance law's reliance on the *sic utere* doctrine. Every "holder of property," Shaw wrote, "holds it under the implied liability that his use of it may be so regulated," not only to protect other property owners from injury but also to protect "the rights of the community." Building on decades of jurisprudence, Shaw provided a ringing defense of regulation based on "the common good and general welfare," rather than competing property rights. In doing so, Shaw established regulation of the city's growth as an appropriate use of the police power.[18]

To the Park: The Strengths and Weaknesses of the Jacksonian Public

Before the Civil War, cities began to construct the water, sewer, transit, and park systems that reduced mortality rates and, by 1900, provided Americans with the finest public services in the world. But in the Jacksonian era, popular challenges to elite definitions of the public good limited the growth and use of the new public powers. The proliferation of labor, ethnic, and religious associations, skeptical of a unitary public good, increased the diversity and contentiousness of public life. As immigrant communities forced their way into public life, nativist associations promoted anti-immigrant, particularly anti-Irish and anti-Catholic, attitudes.[19]

Gender inequality also fractured the Jacksonian public. Before the 1830s, civic ceremonies employed female images of justice and liberty to illustrate a unitary public good. Female images, as abstract expressions of civic virtue, also invoked the sensuality and passion that supposedly disqualified women for civic life. In the Jacksonian era, civic imagery changed, deploying femininity to invoke the biological markers of ethnicity and the domestic virtues of purity, chastity, and sobriety. The new imagery deemphasized the passion that once disqualified women, but women moved little closer to civic equality. Despite the proliferation of women's associations after 1825, they participated in few civic ceremonies.[20]

African Americans joined women at the periphery of the Jacksonian public. They did parade through the streets of New York City in 1827 to celebrate the end of slavery in the state. But African Americans more often experienced exclusion, subordination, or cruelty. Like civic ceremonies, the post office remained the exclusive reserve of white men. Unwelcome and threatened inside the post office, women and African Americans were also excluded from its civil service jobs. Frederick Douglass complained bitterly that African Americans were "not trusted even to carry a mail bag twenty yards across the street."[21]

Despite its ethnic, gender, and racial prejudices, Jacksonian democracy created a broad public realm that could not be limited to males of Anglo-Saxon descent. The Jacksonian agenda emerged from hundreds of gatherings in parks, streets, and public halls, some convened by officials but others arising spontaneously. What radical democrats called the public process of "speechifying and resolutions at political meetings" empowered new voices that challenged elite conceptions of the public good. Securing the public good also depended more on vigilant citizens than professionalized civil servants. The volunteer fireman, rather than the paid bureaucrat, typified the Jacksonian public servant.[22]

Broadening the suffrage and increasing the number and frequency of elections democratized the public. So did the transformation of the relationship between officeholder and constituent in countless political meetings in public spaces accessible to all. Political meetings allowed those assembled to instruct their representatives on the public good. In 1835, Tammany Hall leaders tried to end an indoor meeting of New York Democrats by turning off the gaslights. Radical Democrats frustrated the ploy by producing candles and lighting them with the newfangled "Loco-Foco" matches. In Resolution No. 6, the radical Loco-Focos asserted that "the people have the right and duty at all times ... to assemble together to consult for the common good." Resistance to democratic pretension remained ("Men must be herded as cattle are herded," a Whig leader contemptuously asserted), but democrats drove it underground.[23]

The cutting edge of democratization, the Loco-Focos put class and ethnic distinctions on the defensive. The Loco-Focos stood for equal rights, asserting that "'all men are created equal'—that these United States are a nation—and that national rights of every citizen are equal and indivisible." All distinctions save those of "merit," the Loco-Focos held, are "odious and offensive." Attempts to limit the participation of recent immigrants and Catholics failed in the face of equal rights doctrine. Even racial exclusion, though widely practiced, felt the pressure of equal rights rhetoric. Only the unthinking exclusion of women remained unchallenged.[24]

Greater participation coincided, however, with a decline in the substantive stakes of public life. Even as they distributed public jobs and contracts to build their party, Jacksonians professed opposition to active government. Jacksonian laissez-faire threatened to privatize the post office and did undercut the civic potential of the telegraph. Samuel Morse, who attended lectures on electromagnetism at New York City's Atheneum and conducted his experiments at the University of the City of New York, recognized his telegraph as a product and potential extension of the public realm. He also secured a public subsidy to help pay for the first line between Washington and Baltimore. The telegraph supported the republic, a Democratic editor wrote, in generating a "lightning-like affinity of intelligence and sympathy, that renders us emphatically 'ONE PEOPLE' everywhere."[25]

Morse offered to sell his telegraph patent to the federal government, creating a public network to complement the postal system. Congress endorsed Morse's proposal for public ownership, hailing the telegraph as a promoter of "universal intelligence ... so necessary to the people living under a common representative republic." The postmaster general warned that if the public did not control the telegraph, "the evils which the community may suffer or the benefits which individuals may derive from the possession of such an instrument ... cannot be overestimated." But the Democratic administration of President James Polk refused to purchase Morse's patents or build a postal telegraph network. When Morse sold his patents to private interests, the private exploitation of the telegraph led to what critics called "the most exacting, the most extortionate, the most corrupt monopoly" in the nation, the Western Union Company.[26]

In multiplying the interests vying for recognition, democratization fractured civic unity and paralyzed civic agencies. Although some giant public projects, like New York City's Croton Aqueduct, reached completion under Jacksonian auspices, democratization discredited projects underwritten by elites. The same Loco-Foco meeting that embraced equal rights also condemned the whole panoply of public initiatives promoted by President Adams. The Jacksonian assault on activist government led to the delegation of public responsibilities to private agencies all too eager to profit by them. It also opened lucrative avenues for corrupt politicians to sell off valuable public assets and franchises.[27]

While the public good remained elusive, it also came under popular scrutiny. Democratic participation in public debates sometimes took on a pugilistic, although only occasionally deadly demeanor. Often coinciding with elections, mobs and riots provided more forceful extensions of democratic politics. Like public meetings, they brought political conflicts into public space. New York City's bread riot during the Panic of 1837 began with the Loco-Focos' call for a public meeting: "Again to the Park—To the Park. The People are Sovereign." The right of public assembly ranked higher for many Jacksonians than the need for public order. Has "it come to this?" a citizen asked during the disorderly election of 1834. "Has a democrat no right to speak his honest opinion in the public street?" The tendency to "array the police or order out the uniformed militia for the purpose of intimidation"—as a Loco-Foco resolution put it—generated more apprehension than pugnacious citizens did.[28]

Popular Culture, Political Culture

While the infrastructure for a democratic public took shape, its success still depended upon the character of the people. The people should consider it "a kind of public duty," the Protestant divine Horace Bushnell argued at midcentury, to acquaint themselves with the means "by which the completest and most attractive city may be built." The spread of literacy and education, in concert with new techniques of production, communication, and distribution of popular culture, helped produce this sort of intelligent engagement in the life of the city. Circulated by urban-industrial technologies, but interpreted, transformed, and utilized by the people for their own purposes, popular culture provided the "folklore of industrial society." In contrast to an elite culture of scarce materials and rare talent that projected the authority of its patrons, popular culture was the possession and, in large measure, the product of the people.[29]

A profusion of almanacs, magazines, chapbooks, novels, and newspapers spread the reading habit and stimulated political discussions. Novels also nurtured cultural assertiveness. Focused on ordinary people and emphasizing individual choice and contingency in the unfolding of events, novels allowed readers, many of them women, to examine social and political assumptions. At her Hall of Science (opened in 1829 on New York City's Bowery with a book store and circulating library), the radical feminist Fanny Wright examined everything from chemistry to natural history and encouraged people to think, speak, and legislate for themselves.[30]

The penny press emerged in the major eastern cities in the 1830s. Avoiding formal political ties, the penny press nevertheless broadened and politicized the reading public. Sold by newsboys on the streets, cheap newspapers provided a new public space that paralleled and illuminated the life of the city. Along with commercial signs, billboards, banners, and paper money, newspapers made reading—addressing an anonymous public without reference to status—a central part of city life. By 1835, the United States supported twelve hundred newspapers that dissected political debates, spread an accessible civil rhetoric, and sent literacy rates soaring to 95 percent of white adults in the North and 80 percent in the South. The "daily circulation of the penny papers is nearly sufficient to place a newspaper in the hand of every man," boasted the Philadelphia *Public Ledger*; in "every street, lane, and alley" the "porter or dray-man . . . may be seen with a paper in his hands."[31]

Employing new technologies and seeking out local news, the penny press widened its circulation. In 1835, the *New York Sun* first employed a steam-powered press, flooding the streets with 55,000 copies daily. Just two years before, using a hand-powered press, the *Sun* struggled to print 2,000 copies a day. Making the first private investments in the telegraph, the penny press also used the latest forms of transportation and communication (steamboats and railroads, horse expresses, even carrier pigeons) to speed production and delivery of an increasingly perishable commodity, the "news." By 1860, the United States supported more than four thousand newspapers with a combined annual circulation of almost one billion.[32]

The development of popular culture coincided with the emergence of the partisan political culture of the Jacksonian era, raising the stakes in both. The election of 1828, which pitted the nation's foremost representative of the European intellectual tradition against the champion of the people, hinged on the issue of popular culture. Widely seen as a victory of the plowman over the professor, Jackson's defeat of Adams promoted cultural as well as political egalitarianism. The victory, Ralph Waldo Emerson enthused, promised to "root out the hollow dilettantism of our cultivation in the coarsest way." A torrent of coarse, sentimental, and salacious novels and scandal-mongering newspapers followed Jackson's victory, along with dime novels depicting lurid crime and Wild West exploits, and bawdy humor in almanacs and on stages.[33]

The popular reception accorded cheap productions reflected a militant, hostile opposition to elite culture. Critics complained of a social disease called "newspaperism." "Breathed into the lungs of society" daily, the newspaper's "flippancy and triviality are weakening to the mind that feeds upon it," resulting in "a debauch of the intellect." Sensational accounts of crime, vice, and disaster did lower taste, harden hearts, and provide a distorted view of society. The coarseness of popular culture vented a hostility born of the failure of the democratic challenge to economic inequality, but it also reflected the cultural costs of Jacksonian laissez-faire.[34]

Some hoped the newspaper and the telegraph would enhance civic life. "The public mind will be stimulated to greater activity by the circulation of news," an editor predicted. "The swift communication of tidings of great events will invoke in the masses ... still keener interest in public affairs." But in the 1840s, the Associated Press and Western Union partnered to monopolize and control access to the new means of communication. As commercial purposes superseded civic goals, Henry Thoreau complained that the telegraph provided "an improved means to an unimproved end." Despite the "great haste" to connect Maine to Texas, he concluded, Maine and Texas "have nothing important to communicate."[35]

In the late 1830s, however, the democratic wing of the Democratic Party took up the challenge of elevating popular culture. A fearless critic of the powerful, the New York City journalist and Jacksonian Democrat William Leggett saw in newspapers a "glorious opportunity" of "effectually advancing the interests of mankind." Naturally democratic, newspapers found their way into "the mansions of the rich, and the hovels of the indigent." They held the power to bring "knowledge to those who had no means of acquiring it" and to activate "minds that before rusted unused."[36]

Leggett inspired John O'Sullivan, the young Irish immigrant who founded *The United States Magazine and Democratic Review* in 1837. With the patronage of the administration of President Martin Van Buren, O'Sullivan launched the *Review* in Washington "for the advocacy of that high and holy DEMO-

CRATIC PRINCIPLE which was designed to be the fundamental element of the new social and political system created by the 'American Experiment.'" The editors professed "abiding confidence in the virtue, intelligence and full capacity for self-government, of the great mass of our people."[37]

Combining political and cultural commentary with poetry and short stories, the *Review* published the best democratic writers in the country and broke the monopoly on cultured opinion once held by the well-financed journals of the Whig elite. "There is no more pernicious error than that the whole people should be instructed alike," sniffed a Whig leader, expressing the attitude the *Review* challenged. Vigorous writing (Hawthorne, Melville, Whitman, Bancroft, Thoreau, Brownson, and Poe all appeared in the journal) made the *Democratic Review* a popular success and a political force. Seeking a bipartisan tone, the editors asked John Quincy Adams to contribute. Adams's reply ("literature was, and its nature must always be, aristocratic; that democracy of numbers and literature were self-contradictory") illustrated the importance of the journal.[38]

The *Democratic Review* helped make the presidential campaign of 1840 an intellectually serious affair on all sides. Supposedly all log cabin and cider hoopla, the campaign did strengthen the ties between popular and political culture. The campaign featured sheet music and minstrel shows, penny newspapers and cartoons, theatrical speeches and souvenir bric-a-brac. But the emotional appeals that increased voter turnout by 54 percent did not preclude rational analysis. Campaign literature included memorable essays by Leggett, Orestes Brownson, William Ellery Channing, and Henry Carey. More than "the carnivalization of American elective politics," the intensity of the campaign revealed the vitality of popular culture.[39]

YOUNG AMERICA AND DEMOCRATIC CULTURE

O'Sullivan moved the *Democratic Review* to New York City in 1840, where the literary venture blossomed into a broader cultural movement known as Young America. A Democratic stronghold and publishing center, New York City also nurtured the militantly egalitarian Loco-Focos and the republic's most aggressive Democratic (and democratic) thinkers and writers. Drawn to the republican movements of Young Europe, O'Sullivan and his associates shared the Europeans' dissatisfaction with aristocratic politics and culture and the desire to build an oppositional culture based on popular energies.[40]

Whitman's poetry best exemplified the Young American impulse. But Young America also championed a group of genre painters who examined public issues from a democratic perspective. Their paintings expressed reverence for revolutionary forefathers and contempt for a postrevolutionary generation of moneylenders, explored the intersection of popular and political culture, and brought the marginalized into focus. The more famous Hudson River school of painters produced romantic landscapes that disguised the industrial exploitation of the valley. In contrast, the genre painters depicted the commercial transaction as an anxious and ambiguous encounter between folk culture and expanding market.[41]

In the 1840s, Young America's American Art-Union enrolled thousands of citizens from every state of the Union. Purchasing paintings, circulating prints, and maintaining a public gallery, the Art-Union encouraged native artists and a national appreciation for a distinctively American art. Priding itself on the number of "citizens of the laboring class" that toured its gallery, the Art-Union advocated government funding of "free lectures, free concerts, free admission to galleries of paintings and sculptures, to libraries and reading-rooms" as an essential component of political democracy. If Americans renounced their cultural enslavement to aristocratic forms, an Art-Union speaker proclaimed, and "dare and love to be ourselves, we should soon have an American literature, an American school of art, as well as a peculiar form of self-government."[42]

Legal reform also engaged Young America. Rejecting the "prolixities, uncertainties, and confusions" of English common law, Young America called for a law "perfectly intelligible to the commonest of the common people." The "primal, vital radical error" of relying on the feudal remnant of common law, the *Review* opined, allowed conservative "judge-made law" to usurp populist "legislature-made law." Young American David Dudley Field attempted to remove "all the jargon" from New York State law in favor of "the simplest and clearest language" to encourage participation in public affairs.[43]

Even as they created their own distinctly democratic art, Americans also democratized the best of European culture. William Shakespeare became a staple in popular theaters, featured alongside farce and comic opera, magicians and acrobats, singers and dancers. Frequenting theaters that catered to all classes, Whitman liked to look up to the boxes to see "the faces of the leading authors, poets, editors." But he preferred to surround himself with the "slang, wit . . . freedom of looks and manners" of the mechanics and artisans in the pit.[44]

Popular culture also included opera and symphonic music. The tour of operatic singer Jenny Lind won praise as "a very republican operation," reflecting "the quiet ease with which the luxury of the exclusives—Italian music—has passed into the hands of the people." With three thousand bands containing sixty thousand musicians and frequent festivals that involved thousands more amateur singers and musicians, American music provided a model of a democratic culture. One Boston festival featured ten thousand singers, a thousand-member orchestra, and a performance of the Anvil Chorus from *Il Trovatore* enlivened with a hundred sledge-hammering fireman and a hundred cannons.[45]

Americans shaped European cultural forms to their own expectations, treating Shakespeare not as an imposing, sacred figure, but as a model of democratic humility. They found in Shakespeare a "true gentleness and lowliness of heart." In Shakespeare's portraits of flawed human beings who accepted responsibility for their own fates, Americans found "a far better school of virtuous discipline than half the moral and religious books" of the day: "Brace up, pay for what you have, do good if you wish to get good; good or bad, shoulder the burden of your moral responsibility, and never forget that cowardice is the most fatal and most futile crime." With so many of Shakespeare's characters political actors, bold architects of their own fate, Shakespearean oratory became an integral part of political rhetoric.[46]

The cultural confidence of the people impressed observers. While some found nothing but poor manners in the "music of cracking peanuts" among theater crowds, others lauded democracy's "entire contempt for the 'polite company' in the boxes." Whitman reveled in "those long-kept-up tempests of hand clapping peculiar to the Bowery—no dainty kid-glove business, but electric force and muscle from perhaps two thousand ful-sinew'd men." The journeymen editors of Philadelphia's *The Mechanics' Free Press* railed against those who "declare that the operative part of the community, particularly the mechanics, are not capable of supporting or conducting a newspaper; that they are fit for nothing but manual and mechanical labour, having little more intellect than the brute creation."[47]

Sometimes violent in its judgments and ugly in its prejudices, popular culture could not be divorced from the emergence of an assertive citizenry that took joy in learning. Even P. T. Barnum's celebrated peddling of humbug played on the delight people took in understanding how things (including hoaxes) worked. In the United States, a Frenchman remarked, "the great discoveries of science and art" were "exposed to the vulgar gaze and placed within the reach of all." Culture became "common property in the United States." One of the "initiated," the American citizen therefore "has in himself the principle of self-government in a much higher degree and is more fit to take a part in public affairs" than the average European. The "art of government," an English visitor added, "is no mystery here."[48]

The Republic of the Streets and Fields

Popular culture became a political issue in its own right. In working-class neighborhoods like New York City's Bowery, an autonomous and belligerent popular culture thrived. The Bowery bisected a vast plebeian city of petty entrepreneurs, skilled and semiskilled workers, day and sweated labor, and servants. Hosting at least 240 different trades, the Bowery provided blocks and blocks of saloons and cheap theaters, dime museums, music halls, and restaurants, sidewalks crowded with oyster stands and vendors of candy and ice cream. As a supplement to cheap amusements, the joys of loitering under a lamppost or promenading with the crowd, of watching and being watched, cost nothing.[49]

The Bowery b'hoy and his g'hal strutted through a culture that gave free rein to physicality and emotion, providing an antithesis to the emerging culture of domesticity. Dressed in flamboyant costumes of blazing color, the b'hoy and the g'hal sported a defiant swagger when in motion and an insouciance when at rest. On the rowdy periphery of the Bowery, clashes between rival firefighting companies, the manly arts of brawling, gambling, and blood sports, and the occasional riot held sway. On the Bowery itself, sexuality and flirtation predominated. The misogynic b'hoys aggressively defended "their" women from the genteel interlopers, engaging in, while setting limits to, sexual exploitation. The high-spirited g'hal, translating wages into a measure of independence, rejected the genteel ideal of womanhood in her clothes, her searching gaze, and her dedication to pleasure.[50]

Alternatively clashing with and reinforcing the trade union movement, the republic of the streets expressed the cultural autonomy of the city's workers. Civic virtue came in a rough-and-ready form on the Bowery. It could be heard in "the clink of glasses in the taverns and porter houses punctuating arguments over 'free trade' . . . 'foreigners,' and 'native Americans' (with now and then a fight)." Serving as informal constabularies, monitoring (and accosting) strangers, and providing election day muscle, youth gangs piled public duties onto their private vendettas. The fire laddies, sacrificing a day's wages to fight a fire and battling rival companies for the privilege, performed (unreliably) an essential public service. If the use of fists sometimes flourished to the neglect of firefighting, each added to the quest for public glory that launched more than one political career.[51]

The republic of the Bowery gave popular politics some of the qualities of sport. A "gloomy, churlish, money-worshiping" spirit "swept nearly all the poetry out of the poor man's sphere," New York City's plebeian Democrat Mike Walsh complained. "Ballad-singing, street dancing, tumbling, public games, all are either prohibited or discountenanced, so that Fourth of July and election sports alone remain." While professionals turned politics into a calculating process of compromise among interests, popular politics retained some of the qualities of play, transcending purely instrumental and pecuniary matters. Glory and honor, risk and daring remained central virtues in the overlapping worlds of sports and popular politics. As an arena for playfulness in dress and demeanor, the republic of the Bowery also kept alive the sense that politics could fundamentally alter social relations. In the street gangs and political clubs, as well as in theater and sporting events, Walsh argued, working people found "a taste of the equality which they hear so much preached, but never, save there, see even partially practiced."[52]

At the same time, sport absorbed some of the energies and ambitions once invested in politics. As the cult of domesticity and innovations in construction and communication took more activities indoors, working people refused to surrender the joys of public and outdoor life. The "two most grievous misfortunes of a city life," elite reformers recognized, "are the privations of pure air and of sufficient room and accommodation for bodily exercise." With elite parks closed to active recreations, plebeians appropriated the "outlying common" of undeveloped land for their own use. In the 1850s, as artisans and clerks wrested the new sport of baseball from the genteel clubs with which it originated, every vacant lot "within ten miles of [New York City] was being used as a playing field." In 1858, all-star teams from Brooklyn and New York City met for a three-game match at a horse racing track on Long Island, providing an occasion of public festivity.[53]

Through baseball, artisans asserted a central role in public life. Baseball clubs, fraternal organizations organized on a cooperative basis for the mutual benefit of the members, taught and demonstrated the skills of self-government. Like the turnverein (the gymnastic clubs of German immigrants that emphasized "the duty of each and every association to instruct its members in . . . the various political questions" and to promote "earnest political agitation"), baseball clubs flourished among the most politically active elements of the working classes. When volunteer fire companies (also wrested from a genteel elite) gave way to professionalized departments, they metamorphosed into baseball teams and expressed the same "pride and ambition" that inspired the fire laddies. Baseball players modeled their embroidered shirts, as well as their team names and elaborate postgame dinners, on the culture of the fire laddies. The proceeds from the fifty cent admission to 1858 all-star games went to a fund for firemen's widows and orphans.[54]

The republic of the streets and fields became a backdrop for an ongoing battle between "government" and "politics," with the autonomy of popular culture at stake. Just as republican values spurred the effort to create an intelligent popular culture, the coarseness of much of popular culture inflamed elite anxieties about a people unfit for self-government. For elite reformers, organized around the Whig Party, "government" created schools, asylums, benevolent agencies, and tract societies designed to reshape the culture of the lower classes. For working people, Democratic "politics" vented frustrations and asserted plebeian prerogatives.[55]

THE ASTOR PLACE RIOT

The political conflict over popular culture exploded in a riot outside New York City's Astor Place Opera House in 1849. In the early nineteenth century theater, traditional spatial distinctions between the pit, boxes, and gallery sorted socioeconomic groups. In the pit, directly in front of the stage, middling- and working-class men mingled. Genteel men and women filled the first two tiers of boxes, the largest and most expensive section of seating. A third (or "guilty") tier of boxes added liquor and prostitution to the theater's attractions. Above the boxes, the gallery provided the cheapest seats of all for the unwashed, who honored the social order of the theater in the breach and, often enough, in the fusillade. The mingling of various classes thus served to vent resentments rather than establish hierarchy.[56]

On the stage, as well as in front of it, the theater relaxed restraints and provided an arena in which social tensions could be dramatized and redirected. The genteel Washington Irving recalled being "saluted aside [his] head with a rotten pippin" in one theater. When Irving rose to shake his cane at the "gallery gods," a man sitting behind cautioned him to "sit down quietly and bend your back to it." Crowds reeking "of onions and whiskey," the genteel Englishwoman Frances Trollope complained, indulged in "a patriotic fit" during which "every man seemed to think his reputation as a citizen depended on the noise he made."[57]

Theater audiences conducted themselves as a public. Unpatriotic statements, unpopular programs, faulty stage equipment, and, above all, aristocratic pretensions on the part of actors or patrons provoked angry responses. Hissing and throwing rotten fruit sometimes escalated into the destruction of property and wholesale rioting. No wonder theater managers and actors generally complied with the judgments of the theater public. One manager, faced with an audience that was angered at an English actor reputed to be anti-American, convened an impromptu town meeting to determine his patrons' desires. Hearing cries of "send him home!" the manager bowed "in token of compliance" and removed the offending actor from the play. In more serious disturbances, civil authorities intervened, but they, too, generally acted with restraint. "The public," a critic lamented, "in the final resort, govern the stage."[58]

The more aggressive audiences became, the more the genteel found the spatial distinctions of pit, gallery, and boxes inadequate. Worried about the corrosive impact of popular culture on social authority and personal character, the genteel desired new public spaces in which their social authority might be reestablished and working-class character disciplined. A reformed theater, Protestant leader Henry Bellows explained, provided a means of exposing the lower classes to "higher, purer and less superficial tastes." It might also counteract the genteel's own excessive materialism, their "headlong sobriety and mad earnestness of business." The designer of Central Park, Frederick Law Olmsted, recommended "parks, gardens, music, dancing schools, reunions . . . so attractive as to force into contact the good and the bad, the gentlemanly and the rowdy."[59]

The impulse to instruct and uplift often yielded, however, to the desire to retreat and exclude. In 1847, 150 members of New York City's social elite paid subscriptions to build an exclusive Astor Place Opera House for a refined clientele. The new theater featured an "aristocratized" pit of red damask seats fixed to a parquet floor and sold by subscription (replacing the traditional pit's promiscuous open seating on hard benches). Luxurious boxes, also sold by subscription, rose above the parquet. Renamed the "amphitheater," the gallery provided only a limited number of general admission seats (with views obscured by a grand chandelier). A dress code specifying "freshly shaven faces, evening dress, fresh waistcoats, and kid gloves" made the theater a preserve of gentility. A "generally diffused air of good breeding pervaded the entire atmosphere" of opening night, all shaved whiskers and pomaded hair.[60]

Resentment of the Astor Place Opera House and its genteel pretensions intensified a controversy over acting styles. William Macready, an English actor whose cerebral acting and aristocratic bearing made him a favorite of the genteel, ridiculed what George William Curtis called the "biceps aesthetics" of the American actor Edwin Forrest. Forrest possessed talent, Macready conceded, but it remained undeveloped because of the "extravagant applause" of his "vulgar" and "ignorant" audience. Forrest offered a less-decorous judgment of Macready's style, hissing at Macready's "desecration" of *Hamlet* in a theater in Edinburgh, Scotland. Forrest then publicly defended his right to "manifest his pleasure or displeasure," as well as the habit of his "constituency" (American audiences) to make their democratic judgments.[61]

While Macready ended his poorly received American tour with a performance of *Macbeth* at the Astor Theater in May 1849, Forrest played the same role at the Broadway Theater to his adoring Bowery faithful. Forrest's performance came off without a hitch, approved by a standing ovation. Macready's did not, as Forrest's partisans infiltrated the Astor Theater and greeted Macready with "three groans for the codfish aristocracy." Hurling eggs, fruits, vegetables, and finally chairs, they chased him from the stage in the third act. "This cannot end here," the genteel Philip Hone wrote in his diary, "the respectable part of our citizens will never consent to be put down by a mob." Prevailed upon by elite New Yorkers who promised "that the good sense and respect for order prevailing in this community will sustain you," Macready performed again three days later. Prodded by a petition from forty-nine prominent New Yorkers, the mayor provided three hundred police and two hundred state militiamen for the event. Assisted by the arrest of the rowdies inside the theater, Macready completed his role. But outside, a crowd of ten thousand shouted, "Burn the damned den of the aristocracy," complaining that "You can't go in there without . . . kid gloves and a white vest, damn 'em."[62]

When the crowd stoned the theater and stormed the entrances, the militia first fired into the air. Then it fired point blank into the crowd, killing 22 and injuring 150. The next day, a rally at City Hall Park protested the militia's attack. "There was evidently a strong feeling excited," a journalist reported, "but it was not so much against the military whom all parties exonerate from blame, as against the committee of the Opera House, and those who signed the requisition to Mr. Macready to appear again." Forgetting the two actors, the crowd condemned "the d——d aristocracy." The rich, another journalist warned, must "be mindful where its luxuries offend."[63]

For the first time in the history of the United States, a militia fired into a crowd of citizens. Remarkably, that first blood spilled not as a result of economic or electoral conflict, but in a deadly struggle over cultural prerogatives. In what newspapers called "thirty-six hours of civic warfare," the rioters rejected an aristocratic elite's idea of culture as a private realm that sanctified the social order and placed genteel values beyond criticism. Gathering outside City Hall the night after the Astor Place Riot, protesters asserted that "citizens have a perfect and indisputable right to express their approbation or disapprobation in all places of public amusement." Defending an egalitarian public realm that encompassed culture and politics, they demanded a share of the power to define beauty and propriety, goodness and truth.[64]

Fatal Flaw: Young America and Negrophobia

The Astor Place Riot marked a major battle in "a thirty-years' war" between plebeian democrats and evangelical reformers that culminated in the struggle over slavery. Its opening battles, pitting Jacksonian defenders of cultural laissez-faire against reformers eager to impose Christian uplift and market discipline, inoculated urban workers against the antislavery virus. The inoculation sickened democracy. In the 1830s and 1840s, the Jacksonian impulse behind Young America promoted a cultural democracy of high standards and generous instincts. But in the 1850s, Young America degenerated into an ugly, racist opposition to the emerging antislavery majority in the Northern states.[65]

Young America's fatal flaw, its racist refusal to recognize the incompatibility of democracy and slavery, led to its self-immolation in the aggressively proslavery Democratic Party of the 1850s. In its first incarnation, Young America desired to spread democratic ideals peacefully through the example of the republic's cultural excellence. In its reincarnation in the 1850s, Young America promoted racism at home and called for aggressive, forceful expansion abroad. Championing the "manifest destiny" of the United States, Young America now stood for white supremacy and the dismantling of the "imbecile" and "distracted" regimes of Latin America.[66]

Still based in New York City, Young America became a vehicle for the expansionist policies of Southern slaveholders in the 1850s. Offering imperialism as a remedy for encroaching urban inequality, Young America professed not to care whether a Northern yeomanry or a Southern slavocracy peopled the new territories. Although Young America embraced the small farmers of the North as their social ideal, they also spoke admiringly of the "liberal and refined hospitality" and "high standard of public and private integrity" they found in the slaveholding "gentlemen of culture."[67]

Proslavery principles became the essential test for ambitious Democratic leaders. The bolt of antislavery politicians and intellectuals, beginning with the Free Soil Party of 1848, left the Democratic Party all the more proslavery. Support for the Mexican War and maximum annexations, intrigue over Cuba, and wild plans for world domination spewed forth from the now jingoistic Young Americans. "East by sunrise, West by sunset, North by the Arctic expedition, and South *as far as we darn please*" became their rallying cry.[68]

Nationally, Senator Stephen Douglas of Illinois spoke for the unholy alliance of the expansionist Young America and the proslavery Democratic Party. Some thought the Young American "conceited, and arrogant," Abraham Lincoln observed in 1859, "but has he not reason to entertain a rather extensive opinion of himself?" Douglas's great antagonist continued:

Is he not the inventor and owner of the *present*, and sole hope of the *future*? . . . He owns a large part of the world, by right of possessing it; and all the rest by right of *wanting* it, and *intending* to have it. . . . He is very anxious to fight for the liberation of enslaved nations and colonies, provided, always, they *have* land, and have *not* any liking for his interference. As to those who have no land, and would be glad of help from any quarter, he considers they can afford to wait a few hundred years longer.

"History repeats itself, first time as tragedy, second time as farce," Karl Marx remarked on the failure of Young Europe's democratic revolutions and the rise of the empire of Louis Napoleon in the 1850s. Marx's epitaph serves equally well for Young America.[69]

Farce characterized Young America's second incarnation in more ways than one. The minstrel show cemented the unlikely alliance of Southern slaveholders and Northern workers in the Democratic Party. Born on the Bowery in the 1820s, the minstrel show became a mainstay of popular culture in the hard times after the Panic of 1837. Performed by white actors in blackface for white audiences, the minstrel show celebrated the joys of plantation life (Jim Crow, a lazy and stupid but contented slave) and lampooned the social ambitions of citified African Americans (Zip Coon, a ludicrously pretentious and immoral petty criminal). Fearful of competition from emancipated slaves and uneasy about their place in the social scale, many workers welcomed these messages. Laughing at the minstrels united workers across ethnic lines in a shared "whiteness."[70]

The minstrel shows also lampooned antagonists nearer to home, elite Northern Whigs. Pretentious but confused speeches by black minstrels ("Transcendentalism is dat spiritual cognoscence ob pyschological irrefragibility") skewered genteel intellectuals as much as "uppity" blacks. "Get thee to a brewery," Hamlet told Ophelia, undercutting the solemnity of temperance reformers. When Crow and Coon indulged in sensual pleasures, white workers could share in the Whig demand for self-discipline while simultaneously relishing the unbuttoning of restraint. Such moments strengthened the racist alliance of worker and planter against the meddlesome Whig reformer-abolitionist.[71]

Cultural Laissez-Faire versus the Evangelical United Front

The proslavery Democratic machine flourished in neighborhoods like the Bowery by protecting it from the "government" of reforming elites. The ideal political boss felt equally comfortable in rough taverns and the parlors of the genteel. But often the "gentleman-democrat" provided an essential complement in bridging the social divide for a boss lacking in the social graces. The champion of the common man and scourge of (at least some of) his enemies, the gentleman-democrat's athletic image, rough-and-ready manner, and sporting style marked him as a man of the streets. He soothed the machine's constituents with an image of benevolent authority, always willing to use municipal funds to ease suffering.[72]

In New York City, the Wall Street financier August Belmont served as the Democratic machine's gentleman-democrat. Newly arrived in the city in 1837, the German immigrant fell in with "a crowd of wild young knickerbockers," the sons of the city's Old Dutch and English aristocracy. Bored with the genteel, Belmont and his band admired the plebeian style of the Bowery. Escaping stuffy parlors, they snuck out to fire company dances at Tammany Hall and flirted with dressmakers and milliners at the Apollo Ball Room. Something of a dandy with a reputation for the reckless use of horseflesh, Belmont joined in the drinking and gambling at "clandestine cockfights, rat-baiting contests, and boxing matches."[73]

The Democratic king maker in the 1850s and 1860s, Belmont served as the party's national chairman and behind-the-scenes power broker. A merchant-financier untroubled by the need for a disciplined working class, Belmont tolerated—indeed enjoyed—popular culture. Successful in the rough-and-tumble world of partisan politics, Belmont saw no threat in it. He used popular entertainments as a convenient means of facilitating cross-class coalitions. At the American Jockey Club that Belmont helped create in 1865, he socialized with Tammany leaders William Tweed and Peter Sweeny.[74]

Evangelical reformers did not treat popular culture with the same equanimity. The gambling, drinking, blood sports, and promiscuity of the sporting crowd violated injunctions to prudence, temperance, emotional control, and domesticity. Making ample time for amusements and carrying its enthusiasms into the workplace, the sporting crowd also undercut market discipline. More was at stake, however, than proper public deportment. The struggle over the character of working-class culture intersected with the crusade against slavery, for both became elements of evangelical reform. When African Americans, free and slave, forced the issue of abolition onto the public agenda, they found influential allies among white evangelicals.[75]

David Walker's militant *Appeal to the Colored Citizens of the World* (1829) invoked evangelical language in condemning slaveholders for denying slaves moral and economic free agency. The black Bostonian condemned slaveholders for having "kept us ignorant of Him and His divine worship." "I know well," Walker continued, "that there are some talents and learning among the coloured people of this country, which we have not had a chance to develop, in consequence of oppression." Walker's *Appeal* and Nat Turner's rebellion in tidewater Virginia in the summer of 1831 encouraged black abolitionists to create the American Anti-Slavery Society in Philadelphia in 1833. Radicalizing white evangelicals, beginning with William Lloyd Garrison, black abolitionists forced the issue of slavery onto the public agenda.[76]

Voluntary associations of like-minded reformers proved the most effective and controversial agencies of evangelical reform. Uncomfortable in the promiscuous and contentious street-level politics of the machine, evangelical reformers needed other means of mobilizing supporters and shaping public opinion. The physical and social mobility of the expanding market as well as the decline of established church, patriarchal family, and systems of apprenticeship eroded the importance of personal example. Although evangelical reformers continued to place some hope in face-to-face persuasion, they secured their greatest triumphs in the new impersonal world of mass publishing.[77]

Dedicated to transforming society in accordance with Christian ethics, the Second Great Awakening furnished much of evangelical reform's energy. As early as the 1770s in Newport, Rhode Island, the Protestant divine Samuel Hopkins channeled abolitionist, missionary, and benevolent energies through voluntary associations. Hopkins dreamed of high-speed presses to spread messages of disinterested benevolence by the hundreds of thousands. In the 1820s, the evangelical Lyman Beecher enlisted the wealth, commitment, and organizing skills of well-heeled laymen to realize Hopkins's dream of a benevolent empire. "By voluntary efforts, societies, missions, and revivals," Beecher argued, evangelicalism could "exert a deeper influence" than the established church and visible saints.[78]

Beecher envisioned a united front of all evangelical denominations, and mass printings of religious and reformist tracts, in the service of cultural imperialism. "The integrity of the Union," Beecher explained, depended upon "institutions of homogeneous influence" to "produce a sameness of views, and feelings, and interests." Founded in 1825, the American Tract Society employed the latest steam presses to circulate thirty million tracts and three million other religious publications over the next ten years. Liberal Protestant William Ellery Channing worried that this "gigantic religious power, systematized, compact in its organization, with a polity and a government entirely its own" would overwhelm the civil authorities.[79]

But others saw in the evangelical united front a means of bringing social order to ungodly cities and self-control to undisciplined workers. This "city must be converted," New York City's evangelical merchants Arthur and Lewis Tappan warned, "or the nation is lost." Looking for "ardent and practical men" rather than abstract theologians, the Tappans found the revivalist Charles Finney. Purchasing New York City's largest and most disreputable theater in 1832, the Tappans turned it into the Second Free Presbyterian Church, opened it to the poor of the neighborhood without the usual pew rents, and installed Finney as pastor.[80]

Finney became the most influential revivalist in the nation, turning religion into a form of entertainment to compete with popular culture. He believed that revivalists need not fear to be "theatrical" or to address "animal feelings." If religion offered only "sanctimonious starch," the secular "theaters will be thronged every night." One way or the other, the "common-sense people *will be* entertained." In 1834, Finney helped design the Tappan-financed Broadway Tabernacle, a religious theater featuring a grand rotunda surrounded by rising tiers of pews. Finney urged revivalists to become like politicians who "get up meetings, circulate handbills and pamphlets, blaze away in the newspapers," using the best means to persuade people to "vote in the Lord Jesus Christ as governor of the Universe." Mass printings of the weekly New York City *Evangelist* and Finney's *Lectures on Revivals of Religion* inspired imitators in other cities.[81]

By 1835, however, Finney regretted that he turned revivalism into a form of entertainment. His efforts made religion "a sort of trade," premised on the "practical skill in the art of bringing about an excitement." With "so much policy and machinery, so much dependence upon means and measures, so much of man and so little of God," Finney feared he "erred in manner and spirit." The failure of Christian businessmen (other than the Tappans) to follow him into a crusade against slavery fueled Finney's doubts. New York City's "gentlemen of property and standing" not only refused to enlist in the antislavery cause. They led angry mobs to stone Tappan's house, invade Finney's evangelical outpost in the Bowery, and burn the Broadway Tabernacle.[82]

Finney's abolitionist hopes may have been disappointed, but he inspired reform initiatives on abolition, temperance, sexual restraint, and Protestant instruction in the public schools that polarized opinion in the city. All these reforms stemmed from the same logic that drove antislavery, an evangelical emphasis on free moral agency and the parallel market logic of free economic agency. Combining religious and economic values, antebellum reformers sought to inculcate a Protestant work ethic in religiously and ethically diverse working classes that resisted those values.[83]

ANTISLAVERY: PASSION AND RATIONALITY IN THE ANTEBELLUM PUBLIC

Reform methods proved almost as explosive as reform goals. The peak period of Jacksonian-era rioting coincided with the abolitionists' postal campaign of 1835. Using the technology pioneered by the penny press, the American Anti-Slavery Society distributed more than one million pieces of literature in 1835, nearly ten times the number distributed in 1834. Studying postal rates and regulations to minimize costs and avoid seizures, abolitionists sent twenty thousand tracts to leading citizens of the South. During the debate over the Post Office Act of 1792, James Madison warned that in facilitating the organization of factions, improved communications in the Republic might "hasten its violent death." Through the "immense facility" of improved communications, a Protestant minister added in 1829, "men of one mind, through a whole country, easily understand one another, and easily act together."[84]

Antiabolitionist elites recognized the danger and objected to the form as well as the content of abolitionist material. Fearing both its appeal to emotional passion and its reliance on efficient business methods, traditional elites feared the new "machinery" of "increased energy" and "enormous exertions" geared toward "systematic agitation." The wealth, power, and organization of New York City's reformers, they feared, created an irresistible propaganda machine of lecture circuits, petition campaigns, pamphlets and newspapers. Low prices and the use of "images and pictures" to create "visual impressions" that were "powerful and permanent" inflamed the opinions of women, children, and uneducated men.[85]

But antiabolitionists also ignited emotional passions for their own purposes. The "gentlemen of property and standing" who led antiabolitionist mobs that rocked northern cities in the mid-1830s simply used different means. "How are they to be met and overthrown?" they asked of the abolitionists, and answered with the orchestration of mob violence. In 1836, Cincinnati's antiabolitionists demanded that Tappan agent James G. Birney cease local publication of his antislavery newspaper, *The Philanthropist*. A series of public meetings ended in a resolution that "nothing short of the absolute discontinuance" of Birney's paper could "prevent a resort to violence." A week later, mobs staged a three-day riot, destroying the shop of Birney's printer and assaulting abolitionists and African Americans.[86]

Mindless vigilantes, manipulated by hidebound conservatives into enforcing the status quo and punishing those of independent mind, the mob provided the reactionary opposition to the spread of a rational public. That, at least, was how abolitionists saw their tormentors. But federal officials sided with the mobs. President Andrew Jackson denounced organized antislavery and called for "severe penalties" for its "unconstitutional and wicked" actions. He privately looked forward to hanging its leaders. Slaveholders responded with an aggressive proslavery defense and by placing prices on the heads of prominent abolitionists. Where their power could not reach, slaveholders demanded that nonslaveholding states suppress the agitation by whatever means necessary.[87]

The controversy over the postal campaign helped turn the Democratic Party and the federal government into proslavery agencies. It thereby raised questions about slavery's threat to civil liberties. "There is no other topick but slavery," Leggett complained, "in relation to which the propriety of free discussion is not universally acknowledged in this country." In undermining the "shield of the palladium of public liberty," a postal clerk recalled, the denial of free use of the mails "stirred thousands to action who had never sympathized with the abolitionists and who were even opposed to their movements."[88]

The proslavery assault on civil liberties helped create an antislavery majority, first in the Northern wing of the Whig Party and ultimately in the North as a whole. But in the short run, rioters held sway. Rioting, a Jacksonian publicist argued, "is not properly speaking an opposition to the established laws of the country . . . , but rather . . . a supplement to them—as a species of *common law*." Rejecting the Jacksonian view of rioting as an expression of popular sovereignty, a young Whig politician from Illinois maintained that "this mobocratic spirit" imperiled the republic. Whenever "the vicious portion of [our] population shall be permitted to gather in bands of hundreds and thousands, and burn churches, ravage and rob provision stores, throw printing presses into rivers, shoot editors, and hang and burn obnoxious persons at pleasure and with impunity," the twenty-eight-year-old Abraham Lincoln concluded, "depend on it, this government cannot last."[89]

Lincoln treated the events of the 1830s as a struggle between passion and rationality. The "ruling passion" of the revolutionary generation, Lincoln explained, directed ambition toward "celebrity and fame and distinction" in support of the republic. But passion was now "our enemy." The thirst for glory could never be satisfied "in supporting and maintaining an edifice that has been erected by others," Lincoln warned. The ambitious "would set boldly to the task of pulling down." Only "cold, calculating, unimpassioned reason" could "furnish all the materials for our future support and defense." "Let reverence for the laws," Lincoln concluded, "be breathed by every American mother to the lisping babe that prattles on her lap—let it be taught in schools, in seminaries, and in colleges—let it be written in primers, spelling books, and in almanacs—let it be preached from the pulpit, proclaimed in legislative halls, and enforced in courts of justice."[90]

True to his Whig roots, Lincoln believed in rhetoric as the art of logical persuasion and found in the temperance movement a model of the triumph of rationality over passion. "Happy day," Lincoln proclaimed in 1842, "when, all appetites controlled, all passions subdued, all manners subjected, mind, all-conquering mind, shall live and move the monarch of the world." But Lincoln purged Whig reform of its paternalism and linked the Democratic concern for the common person to a high cultural standard. Joining the lofty style of classical rhetoric to the rude vitality of common speech, Lincoln gave literary power to democratic aspirations. Lincoln recalled that as a youth he bristled "when anyone talked to me in a way I could not understand." Plain language became "a kind of passion with me." Lincoln's subsequent life as lawyer and politician turned on his power over words.[91]

In the 1850s, Lincoln turned the rational shaping of public opinion away from the conservative goal of preaching obedience to law toward the revolutionary goal of destroying slavery. In doing so, Lincoln harnessed his own passionate ambition and a lifetime of self-disciplined reading, writing, and speaking to a great public cause. "There is scarce any one of the passions but what is truly laudable, when it centers in the public, and makes that its object," eighteenth-century English republicans wrote of civic virtue. Possessed of "good political judgment, open-mindedness, forgiveness, dedication, and irrepressible good humor," Lincoln devoted his civic virtues to the antislavery cause.[92]

The Kansas-Nebraska Act of 1854, which opened the territories to slavery, elevated the revolutionary Lincoln over the Whig conservative. The act, forced through Congress with executive patronage and setting in motion a violent struggle in Kansas, represented everything that Lincoln condemned. "I look upon that enactment not as a law," Lincoln wrote, "but as violence from the beginning. It was conceived in violence, passed in violence, is maintained in violence, and is being executed in violence." Lincoln countered violence with rationality. "Our government rests in public opinion," Lincoln reminded Republicans in 1856. "Whoever can change public opinion can change the government."

Lincoln brought about a revolution in public opinion, convincing a majority of Northerners who already recognized slavery as wrong that its spread presented an immediate threat to the Union.[93]

LINCOLN'S RHETORICAL REVOLUTION

Like the Founding Fathers, Lincoln warned the people of a conspiracy to deprive them of their liberties. While "we cannot absolutely know," Lincoln explained in 1858, "we find it impossible not to believe" that recent events revealed a conspiracy to make slavery a national institution. Lincoln charged that when Douglas "declares that all he wants is a fair vote for the people, and that he cares not whether slavery be voted down or voted up," this is "to educate and mold public opinion, at least Northern public opinion, to not care whether slavery is voted down or voted up." Lincoln saw the *Dred Scott* decision of 1857, denying Congress the authority to exclude slavery from the territories, as the penultimate step of the conspiracy.[94]

In 1858, the Lincoln-Douglas debates focused national attention on an issue that could no longer be ignored. As incumbent senator and the Republican nominee, respectively, Douglas and Lincoln took the unusual step of campaigning for state legislative candidates pledged to vote for one or the other as the next senator. Douglas and the Democrats won, but only at the cost of widening a split between Southern and Northern Democrats. Douglas forfeited the support of slaveholders in saying that territorial governments could exclude slavery by simply failing to pass regulations protecting it. Lincoln won national recognition and a shot at the Republican presidential nomination in 1860 for his forthright stand against the expansion of slavery. It "would be difficult to find in all of history a precise instance in which rhetoric played a more important role in human destiny," concludes a distinguished Lincoln scholar.[95]

An exceptional rather than a typical event, the Lincoln-Douglas debates nevertheless cannot be dismissed as irrelevant to judgments about the antebellum public. "The debates were an explosion into a political campaign of an issue that politicians did their best to shun," writes one skeptic, making the rise of Lincoln "a powerful sign of the deep failure" of antebellum politics. The rise of Lincoln and the Republicans did reflect the failure of the second party system to contain the political energies it helped generate. But that should caution against too narrow a view that equates politics with the parties' efforts to channel political energies into predictable patterns of electoral behavior. Lincoln acted on the belief that Douglas offered "a false statesmanship that undertakes to build up a system of policy upon the basis of caring nothing about the very thing that every body does care the most about."[96]

In February 1860, Lincoln gave a major address to an overflow crowd at New York City's Cooper Union, hoping to demonstrate that a westerner could win the votes of eastern Republicans. In preparation for this encounter between the antislavery movement and the democratic culture of the republic's largest city, Lincoln carefully researched his speech. Taking as his subject Douglas's claim that the founders intentionally wrote a Constitution that forbade Congress from restricting slavery in the territories, Lincoln examined the records of the Constitutional Convention and early Congresses at the New York State library for evidence of the founders' views on the issue. Escorted to the podium by Young America's legal reformer David Field, Lincoln delivered a forceful and precise speech demonstrating that at least twenty-one of the thirty-nine framers of the Constitution voted in favor of legislation excluding slavery from the territories.[97]

Lincoln's address marked the culmination of his rhetorical revolution. "Even though much provoked," Lincoln explained, "let us do nothing through passion or ill temper. Even though the Southern people will not listen to us, let us calmly consider their demands, and yield to them, if, in our deliberate view of duty we possibly can." The slaveholders insisted that we suppress "all declarations that slavery is wrong, whether made in politics, in presses, in pulpits, or in private," even in the free-state constitutions that "declare the wrong of slavery with more solemn emphasis than do all other sayings against it." But in "view of our moral, social, and political responsibilities," Republicans could not allow slavery to expand. "Let us have faith that right makes might," Lincoln concluded, "and in that faith let us to the end dare to do our duty as we understand it."[98]

Lincoln and the Republicans derived their duty from the civic ideals of the Revolution. "What is America, and who are the Americans?" Parke Godwin asked his fellow Republicans in 1855. More than "two or three million square miles of dirt," the real America centered on the "complex idea" of civic equality that "dates from the last few years of the eighteenth century." A former member of Young America, Godwin took direct aim at the racist and nativist attitudes of Young America and the anti-immigrant Know-Nothing movement. The "real American," he concluded, is one who "gives his mind and heart to the grand constituent ideas of the republic, no matter whether his corporeal chemistry was first ignited in Kamschatka or the moon."[99]

The Republicans' defense of civic equality over ethnic, racial, or religious prejudices represented the finest expression of the antebellum mingling of popular and political culture. Godwin developed his ideas in a series of essays in *Putnam's Monthly*, a politically independent New York City magazine that took up Young America's quest for a democratic culture. "A popular magazine," its editor wrote in the inaugural issue in 1853, "must amuse, interest, and instruct." Some may wonder, Godwin wrote, why *Putman's* mingled "with our lighter entertainments grave and thoughtful considerations of the leading political, social, scientific, and religious topics of the day." We believed that "literature is the full and free expression of the nation's mind," he answered, "not in *belles-lettres* alone, nor in art alone, nor in science alone, but in all of these, combined with politics and religion." Carrying on the mission of the *Democratic Review*, without the burden of the Democratic Party's jingoism or its cultural laissez-faire, *Putnam's* offered national standards around which to forge a democratic culture.[100]

The ideas and language of Godwin's *Putnam's* articles formed the basis of the Republican Party platform of 1856, which Godwin took a leading role in drafting. The demand that slavery be "the one supreme and universal interest and that it might go everywhere and determine every question," Godwin wrote in *Putman's*, produced "an almost universal demoralization" in civic life, the "sway of the mob," and "the ascendancy of the bowie-knife and the rifle over the ballot-box and the law." But the "great question" remained whether the "just and magnanimous recognition of the worth of every human being" would again "touch our hearts, and kindle them into a fine enthusiasm." If "we would not dwindle into drawfs," Godwin concluded, we must not abandon the great republican principles "which made us giants in our youth."[101]

By 1860, Lincoln and the Republicans transformed a vague if pervasive Northern sentiment against slavery into an ideological conviction that its expansion must be stopped as a first step toward its extinction. "The anti-slavery sentiment," a Republican leader explained in 1854, "is inborn, and almost universal at the North . . . but it is only as a *sentiment* that it generally pervades; it has not and cannot be inspired with the activity that even a very slight interest excites." Just three years later, the *New York Times* observed that "the feeling is growing deeper in the northern heart with every passing year, that our character, our prosperity, and our destiny are most seriously involved in the question of the perpetuation or extinction of slavery in those States."[102]

But the Republicans' revolution in public opinion remained incomplete in the depth of its convictions and in the breadth of its acceptance. Racism, Frederick Douglass knew, remained "the greatest of all obstacles in the way of the anti-slavery cause." There is "very little moral mixture in the 'Anti-Slavery' feeling of this country," George William Curtis feared as the war began. Working people in the nation's largest cities remained immune to the antislavery appeal. Seeing it only as an intrusive moral crusade, they clung to their racial prejudices. When secession turned the electoral victory of an antislavery majority into bloody war, violent opposition to Republican rule could not be confined to the Southern states. The city's leading Unitarian minister, Henry Bellows, worried about the "possible insecurity of life and property, if secession and revolution should occur, driving our populace into panic for bread and violence toward capital and order."[103]

The draft riots that broke out in New York City and elsewhere in 1863 confirmed these fears. After the Astor Place Riot of 1849, Bellows proclaimed that the "Christian Patriot feels a greater obligation to the Constitution and to the Law, than to the caprices of a fickle public, and to the Gospel than to either." Bellows's appeal to divine authority sounded extreme at the time. But by the end of the Civil War, the dismissal of the consent of the governed as mere cant and the veneration of the state as "a kind of Providential creation" gained a more respectful hearing.[104]

CHAPTER 5

The Democratic Public Discredited

◈

*The New York City Draft Riots and
Urban Reconstruction, 1850–1872*

In 1852, Walt Whitman wrote an antislavery leader about the prospects of converting New York City's workers to the cause. "In all of them burns," Whitman wrote, "almost with a fierceness, the divine fire which more or less, during all the ages, has only waited a chance to leap forth and confound the calculations of tyrants, hunkers, and all their tribe. At this moment, New York is the most radical city in America." Whitman correctly gauged the fierceness of democratic aspiration in the city. But most of the city's workers remained immune to the antislavery virus.[1]

The chaos of a competitive market, not slavery, provided the focus of debate in New York City during the 1850s. As "dishonorable competition" and "uninterrupted individualism" threatened to tear society apart, the established parties ignored the issue. Creating dozens of new organizations, working people filled the vacuum. Through cooperatives and trade unions, congresses and conventions, they politicized social conflicts, secured a hearing for popular conceptions of justice, and produced a blueprint for participatory democracy. A mechanic "can do anything, if he will try," a New York City artisan proclaimed in 1850. "He can change the law by political action, and he can make new laws as well as any lawyer."[2]

Even as the city's workers mobilized, the antislavery Republican majority arose in the small towns and rural areas of the Northern states. Two great manifestations of nineteenth-century democracy advanced on a collision course. The Republican Party represented the most powerful organized expression of the democratic public. New York City enjoyed the most fully developed public realm, a dense infrastructure of political groups, public meetings, journals and newspapers, voluntary associations, ethnic organizations, and trade unions. But most Republicans saw in New York City the concentrated wealth, degrading poverty, and proslavery politics that undercut everything they stood for. The city's workers saw in the Republican Party, including its small contingent in the city, only an intrusive elite determined to transform their culture and control their lives.[3]

The Republican Party's confrontation with urban disloyalty, as well as Southern rebellion, called into question the virtue and viability of democratic government. Even as President Abraham Lincoln and the Republican Party mobilized Northern energy in defense of popular government, a long and brutal war threatened to destroy what they fought for. Offering persuasion as an alternative to violence in building an antislavery majority and winning the election of 1860, Lincoln and the Republicans reaped stupendous violence, not only on the battlefield but behind Union lines in the Republic's largest cities.[4]

The Union survived and, in putting down rebellion and emancipating slaves, the formal powers of the state strengthened. But violence tragically derailed the development of the democratic public. As the war approached, however, abolitionists still staked their hopes on the democratic public rather than the state. A month before Lincoln's election, the Boston abolitionist and editor James Russell Lowell warned that only constant agitation could keep alive the "vital and formative principle" behind the Republican Party. In May 1863, the abolitionist Wendell Phillips agreed that only the public could push the Lincoln administration to make emancipation a reality. Our "government is not at Washington," Phillips insisted, and we can rely on "neither the brains nor the vigor of Washington." Only the public could "save the Union by doing justice and securing liberty to all."[5]

Those skeptical of democracy, however, greeted the war as an opportunity to overturn the faith in the public and instill greater respect for established institutions and authorities. Secession brought forth a conservative demand for "strong government" through which "democracy and equality and various other phantoms will be dispersed and dissipated and will disappear forever." In the dark days following disastrous Union defeats at Fredericksburg and Chancellorsville in the winter of 1862–1863, conservatives ridiculed popular sovereignty and demanded "unconditional loyalty" to "the sacred cause of government" on the basis of "divine right."[6]

Rebellion and the horrors of war secured a respectful hearing for such views. Lincoln's defense of emancipation on the limited grounds of military necessity confronted antislavery radicals with the choice of endorsing a halfhearted measure or continuing to defend their vital and formative principle. In supporting Lincoln, one-time radicals pushed aside moral and humanitarian discussions of slavery and endorsed something close to the conservatives' view of the state. We "would not have our thought and purpose diverted from their true object—the maintenance of the idea of Government," Lowell wrote. "We are not merely suppressing an enormous riot, but contending for the possibility of permanent order coexisting with democratical fickleness."[7]

By "enormous riot," Lowell meant the Confederate rebellion. But just months later, in the midst of the great battle at Gettysburg, draft riots erupted in New York and other Northern cities in response to the Lincoln administration's determination to fill out the Union armies with draftees. In a week of violence and destruction in July 1863, New York City's draft riots exposed the Republican Party as an embattled minority in the Union's largest city. More than any other city, "the great Copperhead metropolis" convinced Republicans that the "incapacity for self-government arises out of, and is coextensive with, sham Democracy."[8]

The New York City draft riots sped the transformation of Republicans into a conservative party determined to insulate politics from the influence of urban workers. Already in the 1850s, New York City Republicans created a state-controlled police force and other extramunicipal agencies to wrest local government away from the Democratic machine and transform the culture of a refractory population. Secession redoubled their fears of internal rebellion. Even as the city mobilized to support the war in 1861, a New York City financier worried that "the moment hostilities shall break out at the front, we will be in danger of *insurrection at New York*." A young patrician saw a parallel in secession and urban disorder, remarking that the North "must hold the South as the Metropolitan police hold New York."[9]

After the war, New York City Republicans convinced their party that the reconstruction of Northern cities represented a task no less important—perhaps more important—than the reconstruction of the South. For a time, the frightening explosiveness of the city's working classes divided elites on how to respond to the draft riots and left Republicans content to rule New York City with the aid of the Democratic machine of Boss William Tweed. Tweed presided over an attenuated version of democratic rule by making concessions to popular conceptions of justice. But the fall of the corrupt Tweed regime and a series of militant labor strikes in 1872 brought to an end an era in which working people explored the potential for authentic popular rule. After 1872, New York's merchants, manufacturers, and industrialists coalesced into a self-conscious group of metropolitan capitalists determined to limit the power of working people to shape the city's and the nation's affairs.[10]

"The Most Radical City in America"

As the 1850s opened, New York City's workers battled competitive individualism with cooperative associations and trade unions. In June 1850, more than ninety trade unions and labor reform organizations united in the Industrial Congress. Rising above ethnic and religious strife, the Industrial Congress created a powerful working-class presence in public life. Meeting at City Hall and setting the terms of urban debate, the Industrial Congress called for a minimum wage and an eight-hour day on public work projects, improved housing and public health standards, municipal support for cooperatives and labor exchanges, and public baths and reading rooms.[11]

The Industrial Congress also orchestrated support for strikes. When police clubbed and arrested striking tailors, thousands rallied in City Hall Park. "We did not expect to find in this free country a Russian police," unionists protested, while the Industrial Congress organized a boycott in support of the strike. In August, police killed two strikers and severely wounded dozens. The deaths strengthened support for the strikers. By September, almost all employers gave in. Meanwhile, three thousand German and Irish tailors started their own cooperative.[12]

Fired by a vision of "the people turning their own lawyers," radicals within the Industrial Congress called for the expulsion of doctors, lawyers, and politicians demanded that every delegate be a "practical laboring man." But in May 1851, when Tammany Hall Democrats invited members of the Industrial Congress to a mass meeting "of all those in favor of land and other industrial reform, to be made elements in a presidential election of 1852," radicals failed to secure the Congress's independence. Tammany captured and then narrowed the broad agenda of the Industrial Congress, subordinating it to the electoral strategy of the Democratic Party. By the end of 1852, the Industrial Congress disappeared.[13]

The demise of the Industrial Congress ushered in a new period of defensiveness in the labor movement. The Industrial Congress's demand for positive action to prevent the accumulation of "immense wealth regardless of the misery and distress thereby entailed upon hundreds and thousands" gave way to opposition to intrusive government. Criticizing the Industrial Congress for focusing "on the minds of the public *without* rather than on those *within*," the Amalgamated Trades Conference of 1853 met in secluded halls and avoided public debate. By 1853, working people felt they "had lost that political equality which they were primarily presumed to possess." Some skilled artisans still took to streets on their own account. But workers in the sweated trades stayed home and looked to prominent Democrats for protection.[14]

Even New York City's most politicized artisans showed little interest in the rise of the Republican Party after 1854. They dismissed the new party for failing "to excite the interest and attention of the working people." Labor "is now asserting its right," a unionist put it, and "Nebraska and Anti-Nebraska are nothing compared to it." But as the Republican Party empowered moral reformers eager to intrude on the workers' domain, artisans remained on the defensive. In the depression winter of 1854–1855, when attention shifted back to labor issues, Mayor Fernando Wood replaced working-class organizations as the preeminent "friend of labor." Having little interest in proposals for redirecting industrial development, Mayor Wood promised public welfare and put the unemployed to work rebuilding City Hall.[15]

Nativism and the Erosion of Municipal Autonomy

While radical artisans tried to focus attention on the excesses of competitive individualism, nativists blamed urban disorder on the city's immigrants. The nativist Know-Nothing Party (or the American Party) burst on the national scene in 1853. Amid massive immigration (between 1845 and 1852, three hundred thousand immigrants a year entered the United States), the Know-Nothings blamed the immigrant poor for political corruption and declining status of native-born workers and small producers. Largely unskilled and Catholic, the immigrants depressed wages, taxed city services, overcrowded housing, and flocked into the Democratic machines. To protect the city from this plague of strangers, the nativist Know-Nothings promised to minimize the political participation of immigrants while cleaning up the messes they made.[16]

Nativists transformed politics in cities across the republic. Pledging to restore civic purity, they nevertheless displayed a deep distrust of democratic procedures. Secretive political movements and avenging vigilantes used clandestine and violent means to advance nativist goals. Nativists also created state agencies to bypass city governments dominated by immigrant voters, eroding municipal autonomy. New York City nativists launched a local chapter of the Know-Nothing movement in 1853. The immigrant-based Democratic machine provided nativists with an inviting target. Dubbed the "Forty Thieves," Democratic aldermen mouthed laissez-faire principles while selling public assets and contracts to the highest bribe. As legislators lined their pockets, police and fire protection, sanitation, and public health deteriorated.[17]

The growing public presence of immigrants at the ballot box, as well as in marches, festivals, and militias, produced violent clashes that convulsed politics in New York City. Repulsed by the "brutish" and "simian" character of the Irish with their "prehensile paws," elite nativists considered schemes for disfranchising immigrants. Securing a new city charter in 1853, they curtailed the power of the legislature and professionalized the police force. Elected in 1854 under the new charter, Democratic Mayor Fernando Wood promised law and order and improved city services. But his solicitude for immigrants, selective enforcement of antiviceordinances, and expensive public works programs during the depression winter of 1854–1855 offended nativist, evangelical, and business values.[18]

In 1855, nativists found a new vehicle for their ambitions in the Republican Party that swept statewide elections and now cast its eyes on the metropolis. Employing recent New York Court of Appeals decisions that declared the municipal corporation a creature of the state without independent authority, the state legislature declared its power to intervene in municipal affairs at will. The state legislature revised the city's charter again in 1857, this time without submitting the revisions to popular approval. Again weakening the city legislature, the new charter placed three-fourths of the city's budget in the hands of state-appointed agencies.[19]

The most controversial of the new state agencies, the Metropolitan Police Commission created a new police force responsible to state rather than municipal officials. The state instructed the commission to maintain order, supervise elections, and enforce a new liquor excise law aimed at the eradication of saloons. The *Irish News* predictably called the new laws "specimens of despotic legislation which Louis Napoleon, with his legion of spies, a garroted press and an army of mercenary bayonets at his back, would hardly attempt in Paris." But even the respectable *Harper's* thought the laws resembled those imposed "on revolted districts or conquered places."[20]

When Mayor Wood refused to disband the local police force, fifty Metropolitans arrived at City Hall to arrest him in June 1857. They confronted eight hundred loyal members of the municipal police force and a crowd of perhaps ten thousand "Burly ruffians." The Metropolitans got the worst of it. "The scene was a terrible one," the *New York Times* reported, "blows upon naked heads fell thick and fast, and men rolled helpless down the steps, to be leaped upon and beaten till life seemed extinct." Only the timely appearance of the state militia prevented further violence. On July 3, the Court of Appeals disbanded the Municipals. But during Fourth of July celebrations, the inexperience of the Metropolitans led to bloody violence that left twelve dead and scores injured in immigrant wards. Assaulted by Irish gangs, the Metropolitans broke and ran, rescued only by nativist gangs. The rest of the month, the Metropolitans kept the peace only with the aid of the National Guard.[21]

These violent clashes over intrusive Republican authority culminated in the draft riots of 1863. Allied locally with nativists and evangelical reformers and nationally with antislavery, Republicans brought divisive means as well as ends to the forefront of city politics. Lacking popular support, New York City Republicans adopted the secretive meetings and exclusive associations pioneered by the nativists. Meanwhile, they attacked the mass and ward-level meetings of the Democratic machine as the work of morally suspect, corrupt politicos. Republicans promised a leadership of the respectable businessmen and professionals presumed to be above partisanship and self-interest. But most New Yorkers did not see it that way. "There is in the Legislature at Albany a great preponderating power over us," Mayor Wood complained in his reelection campaign in 1861. "We have been deprived of the right to appoint our own police; to build our own court houses; to lay out our public parks, or to say what shall be the legal observance of the Sabbath."[22]

The disunion crisis and war cemented the defensive, anti-Republican position of the city's working people. Indifference on the slavery issue gave way to aggressive racism, antiabolitionism, and charges that the Republicans conspired to "reduce white men to a forbidden level with negroes." The outbreak of war brought a burst of patriotism, but also economic hardship for which Republican policies were quickly blamed.[23]

THE NEW YORK CITY DRAFT RIOTS

The aggressive Republican prosecution of the Civil War never won a following among New York City's workers. As Wood's Peace Democracy emerged as the voice of labor, the mayor charged that Republicans "will get Irishmen and Germans to fill up the regiments and go forth to defend the country under the idea that they will themselves remain at home to divide the amount of plunder."

Immigrant as well as native workers did enlist and die in extraordinary numbers during the war. While inflation eroded the income of working families, employers recruited European immigrants and Southern blacks to undercut unionization efforts.[24]

By the end of 1862, taxes and other war measures made Republican power ever more intrusive. The announcement of the preliminary Emancipation Proclamation in September 1862 inflamed popular fears of an effort "to bring hoards of Blacks from the South, as well as Whites from Europe, to fill the shops . . . and by that means compel us to compete with them for support of our families." Peace Democrats swept the fall elections in the city and stepped up the pressure for an end of the war with slavery intact. Financier and Democratic kingmaker August Belmont underwrote the Society for the Diffusion of Political Knowledge and its antiwar, antiemancipation tracts. Republican elites countered with the Union League Club and the Loyal Publication League. Over the next two years, the competing organizations circulated more than a million pamphlets, sparking a debate that continued in the city's newspapers.[25]

In the face of military reversals and declining enrollments, the Republican-dominated Congress passed the National Conscription Act in March 1863. Bypassing local and state authority, the Conscription Act created federal provost marshals in each congressional district with extraordinary powers to enforce the law and arrest evaders and resisters, deserters and spies. The federal law also provided for a $300 commutation fee for draftees, a sum far beyond the means of working people. The draft commenced in New York City in July, just as the Confederate invasion of Pennsylvania stripped the city of most of its defenses. Pledging to challenge the law's constitutionality, Democratic governor Horatio Seymour addressed a mass protest meeting in New York City on July 4. The "bloody and treasonable and revolutionary doctrine of public necessity," Seymour injudiciously proclaimed, "can be proclaimed by a mob as well as by a government."[26]

On Saturday, July 11, federal authorities chose twelve hundred names by lottery at the Ninth District Headquarters on the outskirts of the city. All day Sunday, working people poured over the names in the newspapers, planning their response. Early Monday morning, hundreds of workers began marching north to the site of the draft, calling out others to join them. At 10:30 a.m., the draft recommenced, surrounded by thousands of angry protestors and guarded by sixty police. Volunteer firemen, determined to destroy evidence of the draft list that included some of their members, drove off the police and set fire to the building. The crowd beat policemen and looted and burned mansions and institutions associated with the Republican elite. By late afternoon, the crowds sacked an armory for its carbines (burning the structure and killing ten rioters trapped inside) and savagely attacked African Americans. Later that evening, rioters put the Colored Orphan Asylum to the torch and laid siege to Republican newspaper offices.[27]

Thousands of New Yorkers, high and low, put aside other activities to discuss the "all-absorbing subject" of the draft. On Tuesday morning, crowds continued their targeted attacks on symbols of federal and Republican authority, including workplaces and Protestant missions. Only the heavily defended Wall Street district escaped harm. Engaging in torture and lynching, the crowds beat policemen and soldiers, hunted down and murdered African Americans, and destroyed their residences and shops. Erecting barricades and cutting telegraph wires, destroying the furniture, crockery, and other domestic effects of wealthy residents, the crowds tried to purge their neighborhoods of the Republican elite.[28]

As the violence escalated, skilled workers, trade unionists, volunteer fire companies, and ethnic associations joined the forces of order. Having endorsed a one-day political protest, they rejected the violent assault on persons and property. After the first day, the crowds consisted of unskilled and largely Irish workers. Authorities divided as well. Democratic leaders met with crowds, engaging in face-to-face negotiations that gave the protests legitimacy. Flanked by Tweed and other Tammanyites, Governor Seymour addressed a crowd outside City Hall as "My Friends," pleading for calm and promising to secure relief from the draft. Republicans preferred to "Crush the mob!" Calling for "an immediate and terrible" exercise of federal authority, Republicans welcomed the five regiments from Gettysburg that arrived Wednesday night. All day Thursday, bitter fighting proceeded in the "infected" districts. Artillery poured grapeshot and canister into the streets while troops fought building to building. By evening, the six thousand troops restored order.[29]

Elite divisions over how to respond to the violence turned massive civil disturbance into political crisis. Republican merchants, professionals, and intellectuals, organized around the Union League Club, demanded martial law. "It is the beginning of a new era of violence, resistance to law, contempt of the government," one Republican wrote, "and disregard of all public and private good." Troubled as much by Democratic appeasers as by the rioters themselves, he was certain that "the civil authorities here will but smoulder and strengthen the fire and not subdue it." Republicans looked to federal troops, not only to quell the riots but also to arrest and even execute Democratic notables.[30]

Union League Republicans seized upon the riots as an opportunity to establish their authority as a national elite tied to an activist federal government. Appalled by the violence, they defended the city's blacks and praised them as a model of a loyal working class. Offering alms and then arms to the black poor, the Union League first extended paternalist protection to a threatened minority, distributing $40,000 to the deferential black community. The following spring, Union Leaguers paraded the thousand-man Twentieth Regiment United States Colored Troops—flanked by elite white women—through Union Square as an answer to the rioters' atrocities.[31]

Facing wholesale insurrection among their workers, Republican industrialists favored martial law as well. But they could not write off the white working class so easily. Dependent on a variety of skilled workers, they still dreamed of a pliant, respectable working class. They long encouraged an individualistic rather than cooperative ethos among their workers with differential wages, profit sharing, personal interviews, company-sponsored evening schools, and mutual aid societies and, when the war came, draft insurance and factory brigades. In the Association for Improving the Condition of the Poor (AICP), industrialists joined with evangelical reformers to reach into working-class neighborhoods and promote middle-class virtues. "Our mechanics and laborers form not only the broad granite base of society, but they are a great conservative power," AICP leaders argued during the secession crisis. "We have too few of the dangerous classes, for any well-founded apprehension of violence and social disorders."[32]

The industrialists' programs made them the prime symbol of intrusive Republican and evangelical authority, invading neighborhood and household. The enormous scale and fierceness of the riots confounded the industrialists' hopes. While continuing their efforts to create a disciplined, upward-striving workforce, industrialists now embraced more coercive means to supervise and police a disloyal and insurrectionary poor. In the riots' aftermath, the AICP mapped out a comprehensive strategy to reach the "semi-brutalized masses" who lay beyond the reach of moral reform. The strategy centered on the "training and discipline of the children of the poor" in public schools backed by strict enforcement of truancy laws. "The debasing effect of tenement house life" demanded aggressive municipal programs in housing and public health. An activist Republican state and bipartisan reform associations became key vehicles for imposing moral reform and social order.[33]

In contrast, Democratic leaders defended home rule for New York City and negotiation with the rioters. Long practiced in diverting and moderating the "perilous process of agitation," the Democratic gentry fanned out across the city to calm angry crowds by promising to challenge the draft in the courts. Closest to the line of fire, the petty entrepreneurs behind the Tammany machine called for a municipal subsidy to purchase draft exemptions for those without means. Securing a municipal appropriation to purchase substitutes for those drafted while at the same time prosecuting rioters, the Tammany machine emerged as the loyal face of Democratic New York City. With the Lincoln administration eager to avoid further disorder and willing to administer the draft through prominent Democrats, Governor Seymour negotiated a reduction of the state's draft quota.[34]

The responses to the riots reflected conflicting conceptions of the future of democratic politics in New York City. The Union League Club proposed an odd combination of authoritarian politics and democratic aspiration, in which a new national elite, not constitutionally responsible to the people, provided a model of democratic excellence to which all could aspire. Although initially interested in uplifting white workers, the Union League Club seized upon the grateful black poor as its ideal constituency in the wake of the riots. The industrialists and evangelicals organized around the AICP practiced a more forthright and intrusive paternalism. Advancing the most controversial policy, they wanted private and public agencies to reshape the cultural habits and values of a respectable white working class.[35]

Democrats offered two additional models of how democracy might work in New York City. The merchant elite associated with the Democratic Party conducted a plebiscitary politics, asking the people to assent to paternalist policies and programs. The Tammany machine offered a brokerage model, a politics less about policy than the exchange of jobs and services for votes. Tammany found its constituency among the unskilled Irish laborers, sweated workers, and small contractors who looked to the machine for protection, employment, and contracts.[36]

Draconian Justice: Reconstructing New York City

Postwar politics in the metropolis revolved around these various models of democracy. But the violence of the draft riots obscured and discredited the participatory model of democratic politics long advanced by the city's workers. In his 1866 poem "The House-Top," Herman Melville captured the disillusionment of democratic-minded elites who once had embraced popular participation. "All civil charms," Melville wrote, "like a dream dissolve, / And man rebounds whole aeons back in nature." Invoking the harsh Athenian lawgiver (Draco) and the theologian of human depravity (Calvin), Melville's poem concludes:[37]

> Wise Draco comes, deep in the midnight roll
> Of black artillery; he comes, though late;
> In code corroborating Calvin's creed
> And cynic tyrannies of honest Kings;
> He comes, nor parlies; and the Town redeemed,
> Give thanks devout; nor being thankful, heeds
> The grimy slur on the Republic's faith implied,
> Which holds that Man is naturally good,
> And—more—is Nature's Roman, never to be scourged.

The persecuted black New Yorkers who left the city, tramping north on the railroad tracks along the Hudson River all summer long, testified to the "grimy slur upon the Republic's faith." But the artisans who quit the riots after the first day and joined the forces of order continued a long history of civic responsibility among working people. Rather than reacting to the initiatives of others, they had crafted a broad program for municipal and economic reform. Taking pride in and responsibility for the city their skills built, craftsmen condemned the shoddy work of those "who have never learned the trade, usurping the places of legitimate mechanics, manufacturing herds of unfinished workmen, piling brick together unsightly to the eye and disgraceful to the trade."[38]

Convinced of their own political importance and believing they could shape the city's agenda, artisans shaped the first day's protests against the draft. Their march on the draft office stopped the city's business, bringing a "concourse of over twelve thousand" citizens from all walks of life into the streets to discuss the draft. The artisans' vision of a participatory politics arose from the Republic's most fully developed public realm and owed little to the most proletarianized workers in the city, the unskilled Irish laborers who committed most of the violence. Meanwhile, those in the sweated consumer trades, loyal Tammany voters, sat out the disturbance altogether.[39]

The industrial workers and common laborers who joined artisans in the antidraft protests and shared their willingness to take independent political action. They lacked the citywide influence of artisans, but retained considerable power within their workplaces and neighborhoods. The rise of a Republican majority in the nation and New York State, however, undercut their local friends and empowered their local enemies. The fears and frustrations of industrial workers and common laborers turned political protest into horrific violence, leaving artisans to try to restore order. The artisan-dominated fire companies declared the draft "unnecessary and illegal," but added that "in the present exciting times, we deem it our duty" to protect the lives and property of the city's residents. When their efforts proved inadequate, the savagery that followed obscured all else.[40]

Amid a bloody civil war, workingmen and workingwomen perpetrated unspeakable violence, leaving more than one hundred people dead in the largest incident of civil disorder in the history of the United States. But working people also helped restore law and order. One thousand German turnverein members joined a predominantly Irish police force in clearing the streets. Fire companies of workers braved bricks and stones to fight fires. An all-Irish unit returned from Gettysburg to quell the riot as vigorously as it stopped Confederate General Robert E. Lee. Draft riots of lesser intensity occurred in cities from Boston to Chicago and across the North. But neither in New York City nor other cities did the riots signal a mass defection to the Copperheads (Northern Democrats sympathetic to the South). Although Republicans remained a minority in the city, a majority of urban workers remained loyal to the war. Subsequent elections in New York City went to the War Democrats organized around Tammany Hall, not to the discredited Peace Democrats.[41]

For most working people, the draft riots represented not an embrace of slavery but a protest of the burdens the war placed on them. The violence only served as a distraction from their legitimate demands. "The people have too much at stake to tolerate any action beyond the pale of the law," the labor press editorialized. "Every mob has been put down." A year later, with the great (Confederate) "antagonist to free labor" all but dead, the labor press returned to the "emerging question" of the day: "Have the laboring men of the country any rights which capital is bound to respect?"[42]

Appalled by the riots, New York City Republicans made no such distinctions. The draft riots added treason to venality and immorality in the Republican indictment of Democratic politics. Just as the Southern states needed the tutelage of the national state, so too did Northern cities need the tutelage of Republican state governments. Elites also crossed partisan lines and joined with "thinking men of various schools and political ideas" to limit popular democracy and reform the working classes. They resolved to end the "dynasty of dirt and the sovereignty of sots." The professionalization of health, police, and fire services, tenement reform and truancy laws, and public health all offered promising avenues for transforming the culture of the unwashed.[43]

Republicans continued to transfer municipal powers to state-controlled agencies, undercutting Democratic power and placing the city under the tutelage of responsible state authorities. The emerging social science professions provided surveys and statistics that promised to place urban reform under "the control of scientific thought." Between 1865 and 1867, the state legislature created a new thousand-man professional fire department and a Metropolitan Board of Health (with power over liquor licenses), passed a Tenement House Law, and secured new taxes and teacher training for the public schools.[44]

In the nonpartisan Citizens' Association, created in response to the draft riots in December 1863, Republicans established a brief alliance with artisans and trade unionists. Introduced in the state legislature by a former president of the Painters' Union, the Tenement House Law of 1867 united workers and employers in opposition to slum landlords. But beneath the cooperation with artisans an anxious, riot-intensified determination to transform working-class culture remained. In the "overcrowded neglected districts," the Citizens' Association argued, the "closely-packed houses where mobs originated seemed to be literally hives of sickness and vice."[45]

Many Republicans looked instead to African Americans for a loyal workforce and an electoral base of support. Universal manhood suffrage promised to add eleven thousand voters to the city's rolls, enough to tip statewide elections. Speaking in churches, newspapers, and conventions, African Americans themselves demanded the vote as just reward for wartime service. Republicans opened a state constitutional convention in June 1867 with high hopes for an elimination of the $250 property requirement for black voters first placed in the state constitution in 1821. But in the fall elections of 1868, Tammany Democrats promised that "WHITE MEN SHALL RULE AMERICA!" and crushed the Republicans, taking control of the state assembly. When the Republicans' proposed amendment finally came up for a vote in November 1869, it went down to decisive defeat.[46]

As black suffrage failed, Republicans began to rethink their commitment to universal manhood suffrage. Perhaps only a restriction of the suffrage to the city's largest taxpayers could secure Republican rule and scientific reform. But in the meantime, the 1869 election gave Tammany control of both state and local government, from the governor (Tweed's protégé, John Hoffman) on down. The victorious Tweed machine proposed a new home rule charter for the city, abolishing the state commissions, strengthening the mayor, and granting the city virtually unlimited borrowing power. Caught off guard, reformers saw in the charter a simplified, centralized, and fiscally responsible city government and gave it enthusiastic support. The new charter became law in April 1870.[47]

Prospects for a Republican administration under the new charter brightened with the ratification of the Fifteenth Amendment to the federal Constitution early in 1870, establishing universal manhood suffrage. Again with prodding from New York's African American community, New York Republicans looked to Washington for federal legislation to enforce the new voting rights. After a congressional investigation established a pattern of voter fraud in the city's 1868 elections, Congress passed the first Enforcement Act in May 1870, making voter fraud in congressional elections a federal crime. In July, Congress passed a second enforcement act, tightening procedures for the naturalization of immigrants. With these acts, the reconstruction of New York City and other Northern cities displaced the reconstruction of the South at the center of the national agenda of the Republican Party.[48]

The enforcement acts applied only to cities with populations over twenty thousand, less than one-sixth of which were in the South. For the next twenty-five years, thousands of federal officials supervised elections in every major city in the North. Although the enforcement acts are associated with Southern Reconstruction, the vast majority of federal expenditures went to Northern cities, 25 percent to New York City alone. In 1870, federal officials in New York City appointed an interracial force of nearly eight hundred supervisors and twelve hundred marshals to oversee the fall elections. When the Tammany-controlled police harassed the resurgent black community, federal marshals and municipal police engaged in clashes and traded arrests in late October. As fears of wholesale violence mounted, Tweed ended his fall campaign by condemning the Republican "invasion" of New York City and warning that "the oppressor's hand ... is upon our throat."[49]

The Spectacular Rise and Precipitous Fall of Boss tweed

On election day 1870, 6,000 deputy marshals and 2,500 local police guarded the city's ballot boxes. The militarized election—a Tammany sweep—came off with only scattered violence. Even Republicans admitted it had been fair. Now Tweed controlled the newly empowered municipal government in addition to enjoying a dominant influence in state government. Under Tweed, Tammany restored order and its ebullient, flag-waving patriotism softened memories of the draft riots. Meanwhile, the dapper mayor, A. Oakley Hall, presided over the rehabilitation of a loyal, Americanized Irish presence in the city.[50]

As reformers feared, many of their initiatives fell away. Tammany turned the Board of Health into a do-nothing patronage mill and used the Tenement House Law mainly as a source of bribes for lax enforcement. But in one area, the Tweed machine embraced the Republicans' program as it own. In 1866, state Republicans expanded the powers of the Central Park Commission, encouraging it to devise a plan for undeveloped portions of the city. The Republicans' vision of city building became the blueprint for Tammany rule. As commissioner of the Department of Public Works, Tweed assigned professionals to supervise the laying of miles of sewer, water, and gas pipelines and the paving of broad avenues on Manhattan's East Side. Sparing no expense and providing land for parks and public institutions, Tammany envisioned working-class tenements along the avenues, middle-class row houses along the side streets, and elite mansions on Fifth Avenue facing Central Park.[51]

Private contractors followed in wake of public munificence. The *Real Estate Record and Builder's Guide*, the voice of the construction industry, praised Tammany's public improvements. The East Side had been "laid out and improved in the highest style of Tammany Art—opened, regulated, curbed, guttered and sewered, gas and water mains laid, with miles and miles of Telford-McAdam pavement, streets and avenues brilliantly lighted by fancy lamp posts." Padded contracts and patronage jobs drove the work forward, supported an economic boom, and cemented Tammany's power in the city. Inside information made Tweed and his close associates big winners in the real estate boom. Lavish expenditures sent municipal debt soaring, tripling from 1867 to 1871. But the wartime profits of local capitalists flowed into municipal bonds while Belmont and other Democratic bankers sold the remaining bonds in international credit markets.[52]

Other private interests added to explosive urban growth. The Wall Street financial center expanded uptown and skyward, telegraph and newspaper giants built new skyscrapers, railroad corporations erected new passenger and freight terminals, and retailers constructed new fashionable shopping and entertainment districts. Public enterprise struggled to keep pace with private development. Traffic snarled, garbage and filth reached as high as knee level, and docks deteriorated. "NO PIECEMEAL IMPROVEMENT WANTED," the developers' *Real Estate Record and Builders' Guide* announced in 1870. "What is wanted is one, general, comprehensive plan . . . for the thoroughfares of the whole city."[53]

In response, Tweed proposed even more grandiose public works. In 1867, New York City agreed to contribute $1.5 million in public funds to the state-chartered New York Bridge Company for construction of the Brooklyn Bridge. Tweed's 1870 charter included a new Department of Docks, which developed a plan for a grand waterfront highway and massive masonry bulkhead encircling Manhattan Island, absorbing private piers and wharves into an efficient, public waterfront. In 1871, state Democrats also authorized Tweed's chartering of the New York Railway Company to build two colossal elevated railroads. Mounted on masonry arches forty feet high, the Viaduct Railway would plow through the

East and West Sides at midblock (leaving the long avenues to handle other traffic) and encircle the island.[54]

Although Tweed opposed the expansion of federal power that Radical Republicans advanced in the early years of Reconstruction, he conducted his own local experiments in unlimited democracy. Mobilizing democratic aspiration and entrepreneurial interest in favor of a dramatic expansion of the public realm, Tweed wielded Napoleonic powers of public planning. Tammany's city building strengthened the position of small building contractors who had mediated between Republican elites and insurrectionary workers during the draft riots. Now those contractors again played a pivotal role as agents of Tammany Hall who maintained peace between elite real estate developers and the powerful building trade unions. On "the avowed ground . . . that the great public works on this Island would be vigorously pushed forward," New York City's leading citizens supported Tammany and its uses of the new home-rule city charter.[55]

With a protracted and largely successful bricklayers' strike in 1868, however, the fault lines in Tweed's coalition began to appear. Just as the spring building season began, two thousand bricklayers went on strike with support from other building trade unions. Hoping to enforce the state eight-hour-day law passed in 1867, the bricklayers also defended craft rules and regulations and even tried to control the pace and quality of building in the metropolitan boom. While investors and developers fumed, Tammany remained aloof and waited in vain for public opinion to turn against the strike.[56]

Over the next three years, the same independent labor movement that sapped the courage of the Radical Republicans nationally bedeviled the Tweed machine locally. During the electoral campaign in the fall of 1869, labor leaders charged that "both of the existing parties are corrupt, serving capital instead of labor." Although Tammany swept the 1869 elections, organized workers concluded that only an independent labor party could secure labor's right to control conditions within their own trades. Tammanyites warned of the "danger of the labor movement being wrecked by being converted into a political machine." But organized workers scoffed at the idea that a labor party already existed in the Democrats.[57]

The bad news continued to pile up for Tweed in the summer of 1871. Just as Tammany lost control of the organized working class, its loyal Irish following became a liability in the Orange Riot of July. Responding to protests from its Irish Catholic constituents, Tammany officials forbade Irish Protestants from parading in commemoration of the Battle of the Boyne. The previous year, a small group of Orange marchers taunted Irish Catholic laborers, resulting in violence and eight deaths. Tammany hoped to avoid a similar incident. But Democratic governor John Hoffman, prompted by complaints of the city's Protestant elites about Irish Catholic violence, rescinded the Tammany order. Protected by 800 police and 2,200 soldiers, 160 Orangemen marched through Catholic neighborhoods in an act of provocation. With Irish Catholic toughs ready and waiting, bitter street fighting followed. Troops fired directly into crowds of Irish Catholics. Sixty people died and 125 were wounded, leaving the sidewalks "thickly coated with a red mud."[58]

Following hard on the heels of a violent May strike of Irish quarrymen, the Orange Riot merged in elite minds with both the draft riots of 1863 and the 1871 Commune in Paris. Only "once in the history of the city did this terrible proletaire class show its revolutionary head," the *New York Times* observed in June. "For a few days in 1863 New York seemed like Paris, under the Reds." Only the "spirited assistance of the United States soldiery" prevented "a communistic explosion . . . which would probably have left this city in ashes and blood." In the wake of the Orange Riot, the *Times* concluded that the "Dangerous Classes" cared little for "our liberty or civilization" but would "come forth in the darkness and in times of disturbance, to plunder and prey on the good things which surround them."[59]

The Orange Riot hardened elite opinion against any sort of popular rule. The "ruling classes had the 'Commune' on the brains," a radical wrote, and resolved to teach the "dangerous classes" that order "could and would be saved." The *New York Times* reveled in "the sight of women and children in the throes of death at their own doorsteps." The sidewalks became a "panorama of blood, a vista of gore, an arena of agony," with "women making the night hideous with their cries." The "deaths of so many comparatively innocent beings is an event at which humanity shudders," the *New York Herald* added, "but the responsibility rests not on those who defended themselves and the cause of law at once, but on the reckless imbroglio." After describing a child's head being blown off, the *Herald* concluded that the authorities had been "mercifully cruel."[60]

Repeating their role in the draft riots, Tammany officials appeared before the crowds during the Orange Riot, asking for calm and urging the soldiers to retire. But elite New Yorkers saw in the Orange Riot only evidence that "again, as in 1863, the criminal weakness and vacillation of the authorities have caused the peace of the city to be broken and its streets sprinkled with blood." In September, a racially and ethnically diverse group of workers paraded to City Hall in support of an interracial stonecutters' strike. When the assembled workers voted unanimously to "throw off all allegiance to the Democratic party in the Fall elections," the Tweed machine had outlived its usefulness. Fearing "a fraternization of the laboring classes of this city with the great Internationale of Europe," elites concluded that if "the higher classes will not govern, the lower classes will."[61]

As elites mobilized to take back the city, the final blow to Tweed came from revelations of corruption that threatened to bankrupt the city and topple its leading banks. As late as the fall of 1870, a blue ribbon panel of local business leaders examined and endorsed municipal finances. But in July 1871, a disgruntled insider's damning evidence appeared in the *Times*. Surcharges of from 10 to 85 percent on all contracts fueled the Tweed machine and undermined faith in city bonds. A September meeting at Cooper Union, uniting a wide range of interests, demanded that the "wisest and best citizens" take control of city government. While some called for lynchings, cooler heads organized an elite Committee of Seventy and resolved to withhold taxes and bar public spending. Starved of funds and abandoned at the polls, the machine disintegrated in November. The new administration under Mayor William Havermayer laid off workers, cut salaries, and canceled Tweed's more expansive transit and waterfront projects. The city threatened to renege on its contributions for the Brooklyn Bridge. Even street construction ceased.[62]

Postwar Republicanism: Labor Revolt and Metropolitan Capital

The destruction of the Tweed machine coincided with and reinforced the Liberal Republican abandonment of Radical Reconstruction. The emergence of a powerful, independent labor movement drove both developments. Nationally, organized labor seized upon Radical Republican activism to demand federal eight-hour legislation. In New York State, organized labor secured eight-hour legislation as a logical extension of the Republicans' health and housing legislation. Republicans welcomed neither effort. Abandoning activism for laissez-faire, the Gilded Age's plutocratic Republican Party took shape.[63]

Events in the spring of 1872 solidified the new Republican outlook. New York City's building trades struck to demand enforcement of state and federal eight-hour legislation. Initially, things went well for the strikers, as President Ulysses Grant invoked the 1868 federal eight-hour law entitling workers building a new federal post office to overtime pay. Masons and carpenters also won an eight-hour day from their employers. Emboldened by this success, more and more workers joined what became a general strike. Eventually, two-thirds of the city's manufacturing workforce (100,000 workers from 52 crafts) went on strike.[64]

The success of the eight-hour strikes mobilized employers. Some small proprietors gave in to and perhaps even sympathized with the eight-hour demand. But, as iron and metal workers joined the strike, the city's largest employers took charge and demanded that the police step up efforts to scatter pickets and open the way for strikebreakers. Eighty police arrived at one strike site, a manufacturer recalled, and "charged on the strikers and clubbed them on the arms and legs, they running as fast as their legs can carry them." On June 18, a meeting of four hundred employers resolved to crush the eight-hour movement. "I see behind all this the specter of Communism," one manufacturer warned. "Our duty is to take it by the throat and say it has no business here." By the end of the summer, the ten-hour day returned to New York City.[65]

The eight-hour strikes brought to an end a long struggle over popular conceptions of justice and working-class culture. Distancing themselves from the violent and insurrectionary poor of the draft riots, organized workers seized upon the eight-hour movement as an expression of discipline and responsibility. Workers had "two enemies with which to contend," one activist put it, "whiskey and the oppression of heartless capitalists." The eight-hour movement intended to attack both, with job actions to enforce the law and the creation of a working-class world of lyceums, reading rooms, and cooperative stores. Such workers offered a popular but respectable alternative to the Committee of Seventy's definition of civic reform.[66]

The early successes of the 1872 strikes depended on employers' embrace of an ideal of intelligent workmen. "I am for the eight-hour rule," one employer put it at a May meeting that conceded the eight-hour day to carpenters. "It's better for the bosses. The plasterers, the bricklayers and the painters—men who do not require anything like the brains the journeyman carpenter requires—are working at eight hours; and it's not to our interest to make intelligent workmen serve at harder service than men of those other trades." But other employers disagreed. "The men who are getting up this strike are the rag, tag and bobtail of the trade," one argued. "Talk about brains into carpenters. I have been in quest of brains into carpenters for a long time. There ain't any very intelligent or trusting men among those strikers."[67]

The first employer credited the workers' claims to respectability and good citizenship. The second treated strikers as simply bad workmen. Beneath these views lay a more complicated reality. The eight-hour strikers were often sober, respectable, and intelligent men prepared to use coercion and perhaps even violence to enforce work rules that limited the property rights of employers. If, for a time, the intelligent, respectable face of eight-hour men invoked the sympathy of small employers (who also felt the keenest pressure to get strikers back to work), the radical face of the eight-hour movement became more apparent as the strikes wore on.[68]

At the height of the building trades strike, the Furniture Workers' League joined the eight-hour struggle. Among the most militant workers, the heavily German furniture workers confronted some of the best organized and most powerful employers. In calling out workers in the most mechanized and subdivided workplaces, they employed physical intimidation where necessary. Amid sporadic violence between strikers and strikebreakers and threat of arson, the furniture workers staged an eight-hour parade on June 10. Although thousands of building trades workers abandoned the march, the furniture workers paraded beneath the banner: "Eight Hours—Peacefully If We Can, Forcibly If We Must."[69]

Militant expressions of the eight-hour principle appeared only occasionally and divided the ranks of organized workers. But they made divisions among employers disappear. At a June 17 meeting dominated by the city's largest builders, employers in the construction industry rejected the eight-hour movement's conception of good workmen. Employers complained that "although the eight hours has been granted, some of the men do not really do six hours' work," so that "while all men are paid the same wages, there are some workmen who are almost worthless, and this class are rapidly superseding the good mechanic." The next evening, the decisive June 18 meeting created an Employers' Central Executive Committee determined to hire only ten-hour men.[70]

The militant eight-hour strikes united New York City's merchants, manufacturers, and industrialists into a bipartisan, self-conscious group of metropolitan capitalists, who rejected the legitimacy and respectability of working-class culture. In October 1872, the annual report of the Association for the Improvement of the Condition of the Poor announced the new orthodoxy. The AICP dismissed the "pleasant theory" that "four hours a day for self-improvement" would result in "elevating effects on the character and condition of the workingman." Instead the AICP thought the shorter work day would result in the worker "lounging about street corners, gossiping and drinking at liquor-shops, neither [of which] tends to his own elevation nor to the happiness of his household, but rather to thriftless, dissipated habits and domestic wretchedness." The eight-hour movement's violation of "individual rights," the AICP concluded, "should be resisted, if necessary by the entire power of the State."[71]

The eight-hour strikes of 1872 brought an era to an end. For a generation, New Yorkers of all classes pursued political means of bringing order to the chaos of their expanding city. In 1872, as organized workers once again took the lead, the elites who had divided during the draft riots came together to demand an end to popular rule. In "a commercial and manufacturing community, it is not possible to prevent the union of wealth and political power," a Republican editor editorialized. Property shall rule, whether it is "property honestly earned in commerce and manufactures and lawful speculation, or property accumulated in cheating, stealing, and corruption." The editor reduced the question of "rich men in politics" to whether property "shall weigh openly, legitimately, and by fair and moral means, or secretly, illicitly, and through bribery and corruption." Reform now meant cutting out the middleman.[72]

RETRENCHMENT AND REFORM

The onset of depression in 1873 confirmed the new order and brought laissez-faire principles to the fore. When the suffering of the unemployed overwhelmed the efforts of private charities, New York City's Workers' Central Council organized a mass meeting to demand "Work or Bread" in December 1873. Creating a Committee of Safety to organize the unemployed, labor leaders sent a delegation to City Hall. Mayor William Havermayer, the successful candidate of anti-Tammany reformers and former chair of the Committee of Seventy, commiserated, but advised "that workingmen should lay up something for a rainy day." The *New York Graphic* put it bluntly: "Whining and whimpering are as useless as they are disgusting." The "natural laws of trade" were "working themselves out," the *New York Times* explained. Governments could "only watch the process" as "things must regulate themselves."[73]

When the Committee of Safety called another meeting in Tompkins Square for January 1874, the respectable press recommended suppression. At the last minute, the Police Board rescinded the permit to rally in the square, too late to prevent seven thousand people from arriving. Just before eleven in the morning, thousands of police waded into the crowd, clubbing protesters in "an orgy of brutality." In the aftermath, workers complained that "every protest, petition, or demand of labor is met with the cry of 'Commune.'" Labor's right to protest had been canceled. "Nothing better could have happened," Mayor Havermayer rejoiced. "It was the most glorious sight I ever saw the way the police broke and drove that crowd," the police commissioner added. "Their order was perfect as they charged with their clubs uplifted."[74]

As New York City's municipal government cut taxes and slashed spending despite mounting unemployment, the city's elite played a leading role in formulating new attitudes across the nation. Working people clung to a positive conception of liberty that included economic and political participation; elites looked to a negative liberty that promised them freedom from popular demands. "Free soup must be prohibited," *The Nation* editorialized, and "all classes must learn that soup of any kind, beef or turtle, can be had only by being paid for." Warning of the danger of a "proletariat" as different "from the population by which the Republic was founded, as if they belonged to a foreign nation," such editorials united respectable opinion behind fiscal conservatism, property rights, and a restriction of popular rule.[75]

Silk-stocking Democrats joined Republicans in demanding retrenchment and reform. Samuel Tilden, corporation lawyer and Committee of Seventy member who prosecuted Tweed, emerged as the preeminent Democratic reformer. Elected governor of New York in 1874 with promises of austerity in government, Tilden cut taxes in half in his first year, slashed public works programs, and linked financial probity to a frustration of the popular will. In a victory celebration after his election, Tilden warned of the "consequences in a republican community of the disregard of the duties of citizenship" and scolded his fellow elites for the "pretty general neglect of these duties" on the part of the "best class of men."[76]

In his initial address in January 1875, Governor Tilden called for the creation of a commission to explore property qualifications for suffrage in the cities of New York State. Announced in November, Tilden's twelve-member Commission to Devise a Plan for the Government of Cities represented a bipartisan who's who of elite reformers. Uniting retrenchment and reform, the new figure of "taxpayer" replaced "citizen" in the thinking of the Tilden Commission. In March 1877, the commission recommended a constitutional amendment to create a board of finance with complete control over municipal taxing and spending in every city in the state. The electorate for the board of finance would be restricted to those who paid taxes on property assessed at more than $500 or who paid an annual rent over $250.[77]

Even supporters of the commission, including Tilden himself, doubted the wisdom and viability of such drastic measures. The disputed presidential election of 1876, whose resolution by an Electoral Commission dragged into 1877, dampened enthusiasm for unelected commissions. But the link between the restriction of the suffrage and the defeat of popular demands for public works and welfare soon won over the skeptical. Believing that city governments should serve primarily to "protect the industrious citizen" from municipal profligacy, the commission argued that the "general failure especially in the larger cities, to secure the election or appointment of fit and competent officials" demanded a restriction of the franchise. "Taxpayer" provided a durable identity that brought together opponents of popular rule who found it "preposterous" that "a mere majority should direct how the public expenses, paid by the minority, should be regulated."[78]

Two successive legislatures had to pass the amendment before it could be submitted to popular vote. When the legislature in Albany approved the amendment just weeks after its announcement, the fate of the recommendations hinged on the November election of a new legislature in 1877. Initially, working people showed little interest in the issue. But by the summer, they recognized the connection between their own demands for public works and the effort to restrict the suffrage. The "public thought is gradually losing sight of the equal dignified position given to all our citizens by the Fathers of the Republic," observed one worker, while the "proud name of 'citizen' has sunk, or is fast sinking, into the far less proud name of employee."[79]

The nationwide wave of railroad strikes in the summer of 1877 raised the stakes in the fall election. In July, New York City workers held a series of public meetings in support of the strike and in defense of universal manhood suffrage. "I speak to you," labor journalist John Swinton told a crowd of more than twenty thousand in Tompkins Square on July 28, "not less than to the 4,000 rifles that here cover you and the 1,200 clubs now drawn against you." Linking a defense of the suffrage to the violently suppressed demand for public works, Swinton called for "nothing short of a political revolution through the ballot box on the part of the working classes." As respectable opinion lined up solidly behind the amendment and *Harper's* recommended its extension to national affairs, labor leaders insisted that "the elective franchise is a privilege and a power that must be retained by the wage labor class even at the cost of bloody revolution."[80]

The November elections produced a defeat for the restriction of the franchise. With newly elected Democrats pledged to oppose the amendment and in control of the state legislature, the Tilden Commission's proposals failed in the winter of 1878. But the struggle for suffrage restriction placed democracy on the defensive, while mounting labor troubles made military occupation a frequent occurrence in cities across the nation. "All the great cities seem to be united to make all law ridiculous," national elites fumed, as city life reduced to "a seething mass of smells, stale beer, and bad language." In this context, veterans of the battle in New York City spread the word that "the most serious question which faces the modern world today is the question of great cities under universal suffrage." New York's reformers took the lead in a national battle to reshape urban politics, employing a cultural hierarchy that demonized working-class culture to justify the ascendancy of the elite.[81]

CHAPTER 6

Cultural Hierarchy and Good Government

◆

The Democratic Public in Eclipse

As a cultural hierarchy of highbrow and lowbrow emerged in the Gilded Age, elite skepticism about the cultural competence of the people reinforced the discrediting of the democratic public. Genteel critics defined popular culture as lowbrow—lacking in intellectual or artistic distinction and exerting a corrosive force that threatened to tear down civilization—and simultaneously set off certain cultural forms as highbrow, work of demanding complexity and transcendent value. Isolating highbrow culture in a sacred realm cut off from the everyday life of the city, the new cultural hierarchy eclipsed both the democratic culture and the public spaces of the antebellum city.[1]

Cultural hierarchy undercut the earlier commitment to a competent citizenry, equally adept at judging political and cultural matters. In 1858, the *Democratic Review* proclaimed art as no longer the exclusive preserve of "opulence and wealth" and pledged "to republicanize art—to impart to its exquisite language an intonation whose lulling melodies are heard in the cottage as well as in the palace." At midcentury, professional artists addressed a democratic citizenry educated in the ways and means of art. "Anyone who can learn to write, can learn to draw," one of their drawing manuals put it. Yet, by the 1870s, leaders in the world of art ridiculed the idea of a democratic art and insisted that artists be educated in studios "divorced from everyday affairs."[2]

The transformation of the women's suffrage movement reflected the intersection of cultural hierarchy and skepticism about popular government. Allied to abolition and briefly linked to the labor movement, the demand for women's suffrage had long reinforced the general trend toward democracy. African Americans, women, and labor would unite, Elizabeth Cady Stanton told the National Labor Union in 1868, in "a triple power that shall speedily wrest the scepter of government from the non-producers." But frustration over the defeat of women's suffrage in the debate over the Fifteenth Amendment generated an elitist backlash. One of the suffragists' more dubious allies argued that giving black males the vote while denying it to elite women favored "Muscle, and Color and Ignorance" against "Beauty, Virtue and Intelligence."[3]

In the Gilded Age, the National Women's Suffrage Association promised to enhance the power of a cultured elite while counterbalancing a democratic electorate of ignorant blacks, immigrants, and workers. Stanton condemned the "open, deliberate insult to American womanhood" that placed them "under the iron-heeled peasantry of the Old World and the slaves of the New." She warned women of "wealth, education, virtue and refinement" of the threat that "the lower orders of Chinese, Africans, Germans and Irish, with their low ideas of womanhood" might "make laws for you and your daughters."[4]

Forcing the popular and political cultures of working people to the margins, the cultural hierarchy of highbrow and lowbrow worked in tandem with good-government campaigns to limit the influence of the ignorant and unwashed. Frustrated in their efforts to restrict the franchise, good-government reformers focused on civil service reform, greater use of unelected commissions, and strict limits on municipal debt. Cultural hierarchy and good government culminated in a new educational style of campaigning that targeted the educated voter with rational, printed appeals. "Instead of attempting to restrict suffrage," a New York Democrat put it, "let us try to educate the voters." In truth, reformers who prescribed what a New York City editor called "the dry diet of public education" discouraged voting among those they saw as uneducable.[5]

Highbrow/Lowbrow and an Incompetent Citizenry

The fate of Shakespearean drama, once a staple of popular and political culture, epitomized the view of culture as standing above and beyond the life of the city. Convinced that Shakespeare's plays were "so deep that the depth of them lies out of the reach of most of us," cultural elites looked for ways to shield the bard from ignorant audiences. "Shakespeare off the stage is far superior to Shakespeare on the stage," a genteel critic observed. But only the educated possessed the "rigid mechanical training" that reading Shakespeare required. When staged, Shakespeare and other "legitimate" drama required its own exclusive settings because "the more ignorant spectators, who formerly followed the lead of the educated, now read, have opinions and enforce them." Not surprisingly, galleries "packed with a proletarian audience" disappeared as working people came to see highbrow culture "as something that belonged to the other class—and they will not go near it."[6]

Opera occupied a similar place to Shakespeare in mid-nineteenth-century culture. When the operatic soprano Jenny Lind toured the United States in 1850, the "very republican operation" revealed that "this great people, so intent on acquisition, so bewildered at times by the rapidity of their own progress, have not forfeited the capacity of appreciating excellence." But by the end of the century, opera fell under the control of "a few rich men" and exuded "an exotic atmosphere in which the normal person finds difficulty in breathing."[7]

Opera became the preeminent symbol of a museum culture set off from the city in its own exclusive settings. But symphonic music also underwent the transformation into highbrow culture. The German immigrant Theodore Thomas proved a pivotal figure. A member of the pit orchestras at New York City's Park, Bowery, and Niblo's theaters before the Civil War, Thomas developed the ambition to bring great music to the public. As director of his own orchestra after 1862, Thomas staged summer concerts in New York, Chicago, Cincinnati, St. Louis, and other cities, adding "little extravagances" to attract and hold audiences (stationing piccolo players in trees or tuba players behind scrubs). I "have only done the public justice," he explained in 1872, in believing "that the people would enjoy and support the best in art when continually set before them in a clear and intelligent manner."[8]

But Thomas came to believe that the demands of popularity forced him "to prostitute my art and my talents." As his wife recalled, Thomas decided that neither children nor wage workers "were sufficiently advanced intellectually to be able to appreciate" great music. The "highest flower of art," Thomas wrote, appealed only to "the most cultivated persons." Invited to form a permanent orchestra in Chicago in 1889, Thomas seized the chance to present symphonic music in a proper way. Insisting that the wealthy directors subsidize large deficits, Thomas made no more concessions to popular taste.[9]

Thomas took as his model the Boston Symphony Orchestra, established through the efforts of the critic John Sullivan Dwight and businessman Henry Lee Higginson. Like Higginson, financial titans with cultural ambitions funded highbrow orchestras in other cities. In 1908, the Philharmonic Society of New York—for sixty-five years a cooperative controlled by the musicians—handed over financial and artistic control to a group of patrons that included Andrew Carnegie, J. P. Morgan, and Joseph Pulitzer.[10]

With the proliferation of orchestras, concert halls, theaters, universities, museums, and libraries organized and funded by the elite, culture came to be equated with private wealth. Housed in imposing buildings with marble columns and stained glass windows, sweeping stairways, and frescoed ceilings, the new institutions set culture off in an exclusive realm. A later generation of democratic critics derided museum culture as hermetically sealed off from the life of the city. But the museum had itself once been a part of popular culture, bringing painting and sculpture to a democratic citizenry. Early in the twentieth century, however, a controversy over the Boston Museum's collection of plaster cast models of classical sculpture reflected a new conception of the highbrow museum's mission. Curators relegated the plaster models, despite their effectiveness as means of education, to the basement as cheap artifacts that profaned the museum's highbrow purpose.[11]

Public libraries also underwent transformation. "Every person in the community, however humble, or lacking in literary culture," the original mandate of Chicago's Public Library stated, "has a right to be supplied with books adapted to his taste and mental capacity." An official of Newark's Public Library added: "Better a shallow mind than an empty one. It is a proper function of a library to amuse." But backhanded defenses of the people did not prevent the shortening of hours, closing of branches, and emphasis on reference collections in the last decades of the nineteenth century.[12]

In sharpening rather than bridging cultural divides, elites legitimized their privileges and power and justified the submersion of the masses. Paralleling the racial thinking of social Darwinists, the phrenological terms "highbrow" and "lowbrow" entered cultural criticism around the turn of the century. Making invidious distinctions about the level of civilization and evolutionary progress attained by various racial groups, highbrow and lowbrow placed all cultures along a continuum beginning with the subhuman and culminating in the Caucasian of northern and western Europe. By 1918, the New Orleans' *Times-Picayune* banished popular musical forms to "a kind of servants' hall of rhythm," where one could find "the hum of the Indian dance, the throb of the Oriental tambourines and kettledrums, the clatter of the clogs, the click of Slavic heels, the thumpty-tumpty of the negro banjo." Civic honor, the paper concluded, demanded the suppression of the "basement" in the "mansion of the muses."[13]

Most reformers demanded segregation rather than suppression. Imposing structures, imperious staffs, high prices, and obscure fare warned off the unwashed. Some of the unenlightened stubbornly insisted on access to the higher realms of culture. New York City's Metropolitan Museum of Art long resisted the demand to open on Sunday when working people might visit. In 1891, the museum relented. As the staff prepared for a crowd of twelve thousand, the *New York Times* warned that "Kodak camera fiends" would be denied admission. All patrons would have to check canes and umbrellas "so that no chance should be given for anyone to prod a hole through a valuable painting." The museum's director complained that Sunday patrons "brought with them peculiar habits which are repulsive and unclean."[14]

Reformers who worried about cultural incompetence sought docile audiences. "This masterpiece deserves your attention," the *Dial* lectured the unwashed, "for it has the power to raise you to a higher spiritual level. If you do not like it now, pray that you may learn to like it, for the defect is yours." An unbridgeable barrier between stage and audience turned theater audiences from a public into passive spectators. Not only hisses, but applause, bravos, and encores fell under the ban.[15]

The injunction to silence and deference to expert judgment transformed art from a public to a private experience. Defenders of highbrow culture served as conservators not proselytizers, guarding a private reserve not a public resource. No doubt many still saw culture as "a civilizing institution," as an elite New Yorker said of Thomas's concerts, keeping "a good many young clerks and others out of mischief." Henry Lee Higginson called for "education in all ways and on all sides" to "save ourselves and our families and our money from mobs." But the imposing and exclusive edifices of highbrow culture were so effectively isolated from working-class life that William Dean Howells feared they appeared "as causes and symbols of the laborer's poverty and degradation, and therefore as things to be hated." Genteel critics confirmed such suspicions in arguing that culture "is not a democratic achievement, because culture is inherently snobbish."[16]

Like the genteel home, highbrow culture offered a refined sphere of domestic values. Vaudeville borrowed the genteel decor and etiquette of legitimate theater and concert halls to cater to a respectable middle and working class priced out of elite venues. B. F. Keith's and Edward F. Albee's vaudeville circuit operated on the principle of "cleanliness and order," keeping the show free from "vulgarisms and coarseness of any kind." Their "Sunday-school Circuit" provided theaters as "homelike" as possible. Keith and Albee employed police and bouncers to tame the rowdiest, while ushers discreetly handed cards to patrons who made excessive noise or laughed too loudly. In 1890, Thomas Edison predicted that the movies would become part of highbrow culture, bringing refined entertainment into the homes of the wealthy, where they could enjoy it free from lowbrow crowds.[17]

Don't Get Out the Vote

Good-government reformers translated cultural hierarchy into political terms. "No matter what the majority is in intellect and morals," a reformer lamented, "fifty-one ignorant men have a natural right to legislate for the one hundred, as against forty-nine intelligent men." Reformers floated all sorts of schemes for reducing the influence of the "barbarians," including literary tests and educational requirements for voters and weighted voting on the basis of education or wealth. The people must understand, the *New York Times* instructed in 1878, that "the pursuit of happiness involves, to be sure, the right to good government, but not the right to take part, either immediately or indirectly, in the management of the state."[18]

Good-government reformers particularly feared urban electorates. The "cities are to be dreaded in modern times," they argued, for they take "the lead in all commotions." In cities, "the dangerous classes are most strong, and the effects of flinging the suffrage to the mob are most disastrous." Reformers argued that since the city was a corporation, only shareholders should vote. That logic underwrote the recommendation by the New York Commission to Devise a Plan for the Government of Cities for a board of finance chosen by an electorate restricted to the propertied.[19]

Although franchise restriction spread quickly in the Southern states in the 1880s, it proved less successful in the North. But reformers maximized the power of educated, independent voters by undermining the intense partisanship that encouraged high rates of political participation. Subjective, aggressive, demonstrative, and contentious, partisanship provided a worldview that politicized everyday life. The parades, marches, serenades, and orations of spectacular campaigns drew people into public affairs, while the partisan press encouraged their engagement with the issues of the day. Voting became a public act, with one's allegiances openly announced through participation in the rituals of the campaign.[20]

Reformers saw partisanship as only irrational emotion, fueling corrupt political machines that herded ignorant voters to the polls. Partisanship did sometimes simplify politics, but in the press and on the stump, partisanship also included detailed discussion of issues. Excitement lured men into consideration of complex political questions. One reformer admitted that the "activity of mind produced throughout all classes of society by an exciting election, the habit of considering public affairs, the occupation of mind with matters of great scope, not having a merely selfish or local interest—these are educatory powers of immense value to the community."[21]

But good-government reformers nevertheless tried to wrest political leadership from partisans by forging educated, independent voters into "an organized class." Since reformers rarely advocated an expansion of educational opportunities and resolutely opposed federal aid for public education, their efforts necessarily focused on those already educated. In lectures and pamphlets on "The Public Duty of Educated Men" and *Politics as a Duty, and as a Career*, they hoped to rejuvenate a cultured elite, alerting them to their responsibilities. Running reform candidates and engaging in bipartisan efforts, reformers rejected strict party loyalty. Reformers asserted their right to "bolt" the party or to vote a split ticket. In 1884, reformers refused to endorse the Republican candidate, the notorious spoilsman James Blaine. The mugwump revolt put Grover Cleveland in the White House and established the independents as a crucial swing vote. "The position of the independents is a recognized one," *Harper's Weekly* announced in 1892, "for they constitute the very element to which . . . both parties address their appeals."[22]

Independent voters leveraged their power in good-government associations aimed at educating the rest of the voting public. Through a stream of pamphlets, lectures, press releases, and books, good-government advocates disseminated conclusions already arrived at while minimizing opportunities for argument and debate. Placing "a good, efficient journal into the hands of every voter who will read it is the true mode of prosecuting a political canvass," Horace Greeley observed, "meetings and speeches are well enough, but this is indispensable."[23]

On the surface, good-government associations did not appear successful. Membership remained small, money scarce, and electoral results meager. But in concert with their assault on blind partisanship, reformers transformed political culture. The major parties spent less on spectacular campaigns and more on educational efforts. In addition, civil service reform eliminated many of the patronage jobs that fueled partisan organizations and brought the educated into government service. And by the 1890s, adoption of the Australian ballot (government-printed ballots that replaced the ballots printed by each party listing only their candidates) made it easier to split tickets and harder to control how party workers (or the bribed) voted. An alternative political style symbolized by the "vest pocket" voter, who eschewed public displays of partisanship for the secrecy of the Australian ballot, made voting a private rather than a public act.[24]

The educational campaign epitomized the new political culture. Instead of locally organized and staged spectacles and a partisan press, the educational campaign relied on the centralized production and distribution of pamphlets and other didactic literature. The corporate lawyer Samuel Tilden pioneered the educational campaign, reshaping the Democratic Party along the lines of the centralized and hierarchical railroad corporations he knew so well. Preferring "the quiet of his study to the give-and-take of the stump," Tilden introduced "cold business methods" to political campaigning. Reformers did their work "*carefully* and *silently*," compiling names of voters and sending out millions of pieces of literature. While spectacular campaigning retained its devotees, Tilden's presidential campaign of 1876 established the power of educational techniques. Although deprived of the presidency, Tilden left behind a cohort of experienced veterans who converted the party to educational politics over the next twenty years.[25]

In the wake of the Democrats' election of the good-government reformer Grover Cleveland in 1884, Iowa editor and businessman James Clarkson demanded the conversion of the Republicans to educational campaigning. The campaign of 1884, Clarkson recalled, began the shift of "political discussion from the open field, as in Lincoln's day, to the private home," where discussion focused on "which party promised the most for the elevation and comfort of that special home." Clarkson subsequently domesticated Republican campaigning, creating an educational bureau to deliver "literature of attractive and efficient kind" directly "into the intelligent homes of the land."[26]

Hard-pressed workers and farmers took little interest in most educational campaigns. When educational politics addressed vital issues, working people could be attentive. But New York City workers, a Cleveland campaigner reported in 1888, showed little interest in the reformers' gyrations over the tariff. Such arcane discussions targeted what reformers described as the "active and intelligent voters." But most voters had "neither time nor inclination to read long, dry articles upon the tariff question," a Democrat complained in 1892. Reports piled up that "a ringing campaign speech is considered to be worth two tons of literature," that voters ached to "listen to a rattling speaker" and wanted torchlight parades, "especially if there is a corking stump speaker on hand." Both parties found "astonishing lethargy" among the voters in 1892, "a great lack of enthusiasm or even of interest," a "most unexpected and discouraging apathy."[27]

Yet reform politics succeeded in failure. Despite the higher costs and apparent ineffectiveness of educational politics, the parties denied funds for local spectacles while raising large sums from business leaders to finance the educational campaigns. Educational campaigns increased the power of national political leaders and their business backers, not least in allowing them to define the issues of the campaign. The declining turnouts that began in the 1890s also enhanced the importance of the educated voter "who decides the battle" and is best "reached through the mails and by personal approach."[28]

If the demise of spectacular campaigns meant fewer voters, reformers who once flirted with disfranchisement could not be expected to care. "Banners are fine," Whitelaw Reid's *New York Tribune* put it, "but the man who votes for the best-looking face on the costliest banner is not fit to vote at all." We are told that the "brass band and the sky-rocket have their effect and are necessary to secure a certain class of voters," another reformer complained, "to which the proper answer is, that it would be better to let such votes go where they will." Reformers did not ask whether discussions amid the skyrockets might contribute something to public debate.[29]

Municipal Counterrevolution: Dillon's Rule and the Benevolent Expert

Good-government reformers took a special interest in municipal affairs, which they insisted bore no legitimate connection to partisanship. "Party divisions . . . properly arise, only when men differ in respect to some general principles or methods of state policy," the Tilden Commission reported. "Good men cannot and do not differ as to whether municipal debt ought to be restricted, extravagance checked, and municipal affairs lodged in the hands of competent and faithful officers." The Tweed machine, of course, differed on the first two issues, expanding municipal debt to fund a lavish municipal agenda. Other municipal governments did too, even using tax revenues to finance railroads that—while judged crucial to the city's future—did not come within 350 miles of city limits.[30]

Reformers thus looked to state legislatures and the courts to restrict expansive uses of the planning powers that municipal corporations acquired before the Civil War. Although the grant of all corporation privileges rested on a presumption of serving public purposes, the proliferation of privately controlled corporations encouraged courts to distinguish between private and public corporations beginning in the 1820s. Public corporations served political purposes, New York City jurist Chancellor Kent wrote, and thus "are invested with subordinate legislative powers to be exercised for local purposes connected with the public good, and such powers are subject to the control of the legislature of the state." Kent's definition gave municipal corporations considerable flexibility in promoting public works, but it also established state legislatures as the ultimate arbiters of appropriate municipal action.[31]

A dissenting opinion in the Pennsylvania case *Sharpless v. The Mayor of Philadelphia* (1852), involving municipal investment in a distant railroad, provided the groundwork for restricting the scope of municipal governance. Recognizing that the "fate of many most important public improvements hang on our decision," the majority held that municipal corporations could engage in mixed private-public endeavors that ranged far beyond city limits to promote the health, safety, welfare, and prosperity of their citizens. The minority agreed that the "paving and lighting of streets of a large city, and supplying it with wholesome water" represented legitimate municipal actions. But the dissenting minority added that municipal corporations must confine themselves to "*local and governmental objects*." If the law allowed municipal corporations to compete with private enterprise, it would be "impossible to assign any limits to their powers." They might "take control of every branch of industry," the minority concluded, and "swallow up all private enterprises."[32]

The majority and the minority agreed on one other thing in the *Sharpless* decision. Municipal corporations enjoyed none of the attributes of sovereignty, no existence apart from the state legislature. As "mere creatures of the government," municipal corporations "may be established without the consent of the inhabitants within their limits" and "abolished at the pleasure of the power that created them. They have no permanent existence for a single day." *Sharpless* anticipated "Dillon's Rule," which established state sovereignty over municipal corporations. Named after an 1868 decision of the chief justice of the Iowa Supreme Court, Dillon's Rule dominated legal thought in the last three decades of the nineteenth century and enabled state legislatures and courts to restrict the police power and to require compensation for property owners damaged by new public works or public regulations. An expansive definition of the police power, the U.S. Supreme Court declared in 1870, "would place every house, every business, and all the property of the city, at the uncontrolled will of the temporary local authorities."[33]

Dillon's Rule crippled the planning powers of the municipality by circumscribing its ability to construct public works and regulate the use of private property. John F. Dillon spread the gospel of municipal restraint as a U.S. circuit court judge, a professor of law at Columbia University, and a lawyer for the nation's largest private corporations. Between 1872 and 1911, Dillon's everexpanding *Treatise on the Law of Municipal Corporations* (reaching five thick volumes) encouraged the aggressive enforcement of eminent domain and the constriction of the police power.[34]

In his effort to deny power to what the courts called "temporary local authorities," Dillon turned the reformers' distrust of the political machines and their constituents into black letter law. "The usefulness of our municipal corporations has been impaired," Dillon argued, because the voters seldom choose the men "best fitted by their intelligence, business experience, capacity and moral character" to govern. Dillon shared the reformers' faith that benevolent experts could protect society from both private greed and public excess. "It is a duty of perpetual obligation," Dillon concluded, "on the part of the strong to take care of the weak, of the rich to take care of the poor."[35]

Where public health and public morals appeared to be at stake, the courts and state legislatures continued to support an expanded police power. Water and sewer systems, street lighting and street railways, and health and building codes won legal approval. "The streets of a city are never deserted at any hour of the night," wrote a conservative jurist otherwise eager to limit municipal powers, "and the presence in the city of evil designing persons, together with the difficulty of locomotion in the dark, makes it highly essential to the safety and comfort of the inhabitants of a city that its streets be properly lighted at nights." If the "protection of the health of the community" demanded action, he added, the municipal corporation may "construct sewers, drains and culverts ... not only without compensation being made to the adjacent owners, but at their expense."[36]

By 1900, new water, sewer, transit, fire prevention, police, park, and library systems provided Americans with public services unsurpassed anywhere in the world. Public enterprise reduced mortality rates and created a more orderly and humane city. A frontier outpost in 1830, Chicago pumped 500 million gallons of water every day to its 1.5 million residents by 1900. In that year, the city enjoyed 1,400 miles of paved roads, 38,000 street lamps, 925 miles of streetcar lines, 129 fire engines, a public library of 300,000 volumes, and 2,200 acres of parkland. To properly drain the swampy city, municipal authorities raised Chicago's buildings ten feet and, later, reversed the flow of the Chicago River. Other cities accomplished similar, if not quite as spectacular, feats of engineering and administration. This unheralded triumph hinged on the efforts of thousands of highly trained and dedicated public servants. Municipal activism nurtured the growth of professions from civil engineering and landscape architecture to the library and medical sciences.[37]

The celebrated American standard of living owed as much to these public services as to market agencies. But public enterprise eclipsed rather than empowered the democratic public. Neither citizens nor their elected representatives played a role in determining municipal policy. An alliance of metropolitan elites and benevolent experts took control of municipal affairs through strengthened executive offices and autonomous boards. In 1885, the *New York Times* observed that appeals "to the Board of Aldermen are all a solemn farce, intended to give the Aldermen the appearance without the reality of having something to do with the matter." Across the nation, appointed boards transacted most of municipal business, leaving city councils "more ornamental than useful."[38]

While the good-government ethos veered back and forth between laissez-faire and scientific governance, both strategies denied a significant role for the citizenry in public affairs. Washington Roebling, the engineer who oversaw the construction of the Brooklyn Bridge, captured the new division of labor: "When it comes to planning, one mind can in a few hours think out enough work to keep a thousand men employed for years." Through associations such as the

American Bar Association, American Institute of Architects, American Public Health Association, and the American Society of Civil Engineers, professionals sealed off their expertise from elected officials and the voters.[39]

Despite the quality of public services, Americans expressed intense frustration over character of their city politics. Although municipal indebtedness and taxation remained within reasonable limits, citizens complained about a low moral tone in municipal affairs. Aldermen accepted petty bribes, while the business community perjured itself to evade taxes. A lingering attachment to the civic virtue lauded in schoolbooks left people dissatisfied with an efficient municipality that ignored citizens. In turn, reformers complained about an apathetic citizenry uninterested in reform. Even Bird Coler, the hardheaded banker who served as New York City's comptroller from 1898 to 1901, described the withdrawal of "civic pride and public spirit" as the major weakness in municipal politics.[40]

Domesticating the City

The expansion of public services did more to promote middle-class domesticity than civic pride and public spirit. The antebellum drive for municipal water systems focused on public uses, for firefighting, street cleaning, fountains in public parks, and public bathhouses. But after midcentury, municipal water systems focused on bringing running water into domestic households. Horrified by the tenement districts, reformers practiced a moral environmentalism that linked physical deterioration and moral disease. "This depressed physical condition, and bad moral and social habits and propensities," wrote a leading sanitarian, "stand clearly in the attitudes of cause and effect." But indoor plumbing rarely reached the tenement districts. Washbasins, bathtubs, and water closets became marks of gentility, a privilege enjoyed by only one-fourth of all urban households in 1880.[41]

In turn, new standards of hygiene reshaped the language of good government. The "slimy, oozy soil of Tammany Hall," Reverend Charles Parkhurst complained in 1895, turned the city into an "open cesspool." Parkhurst demanded an exercise in "municipal sewerage" to "drain that political quagmire, and ... get rid of the odor, the mire, and the fever germs." Municipal housekeepers pledged to extend the benefits of cleanliness to the entire city, offering "the outside neatness, cleanliness and freshness, which are the natural complement and completion of inside order and daintiness and which are to the feminine taste and perception, simply indispensable, not only to comfort but to self-respect." Condemning the Chicago anarchists and other agitators as dirty, reformers sarcastically offered soap and water as the most potent weapon in cleaning up city politics. George Pullman's model town prided itself on its sanitized cleanliness. "Where the sewage water leaves the drains it is as clear and sparkling as spring water," an effusive reformer wrote, "and laborers often drink it."[42]

Compared to Europe, the United States' network of public services allowed more of its residents to enjoy suburban, single-family residences. The flush toilet and bathtub became standard in middle-class housing by 1900. Suburban jurisdictions provided sufficient water for maintaining lawns. Access to city services encouraged suburban electorates to vote for annexation to the central city. But suburban expansion necessitated a much larger acreage of paved streets and more track mileage than in European cities. Although cities generally rejected municipal ownership, they eagerly granted private franchises for public transit and encouraged the adoption of new technologies. Municipalities also financed and constructed subways, leasing them to private operating companies.[43]

American cities led the world in public health and fire prevention, two areas in which the costs of neglect could be felt across the metropolis. But other public services betrayed a bias in favor of the suburban middle class. The uniform five-cent fare for public transit subsidized the longer rides of suburban commuters. Improved pavements and faster public transit turned city streets from public spaces into traffic arteries. Inadequate street cleaning, rotting buildings and wharves, and polluting industries made for fetid tenement districts. Poorly designed sewers spewed wastes into city streets. While pumping hundreds of millions of gallons of water to affluent neighborhoods, American cities lagged far behind European cities in the provision of public baths, leaving poorer residents with "the most meager bathing facilities" in the civilized world.[44]

The earlier reform impulse to improve conditions for the poor gave way to a determination to demolish the "unhealthy" districts in the city. In *How the Other Half Lives*, his 1890 exposé on "the foul core of New York's slums," Jacob Riis described tenement dwellers as "shiftless, destructive and stupid," just "what the tenements have made them." "Once already our city . . . has felt the swell of its resistless flood. If it rises once more, no human power may avail to check it," Riis wrote in reference to the draft riots. "Who can estimate the extent of the physical and moral disorder thus created by this one building," a housing reformer asked in 1903, "the loathsome diseases, the death, the pauperism, the vice, the crime, the debasement of civic life." Yet municipal governments failed to do much about the tenement districts. Earmarked for demolition, the tenement districts settled for neglect.[45]

Even the greatest civic accomplishments of the period reflected the eclipse of the democratic public. The most famous public building of the late nineteenth century, Tweed's courthouse, functioned as a symbol of civic corruption rather than civic pride. The public funds that made the Brooklyn Bridge possible remained under private control (and manipulation) until rumors of gross mismanagement led to a transfer of authority to municipal officials in 1875. The great urban parks, the most spectacular public works of the Gilded Age, served as vehicles for denigrating democracy and promoting a new professionalized and restricted public authority.[46]

The last great achievement of the antebellum public, New York City's Central Park anticipated postwar developments. The park's designer, Frederick Law Olmsted, complained of the "wanton defacement" of park property and the "filthy practices" of park goers. The people "are ignorant of a park," Olmsted warned. "They will need to be trained to the proper use of it." An evangelist for the public servant as expert, Olmsted deferred to neither aldermen, commissioners, nor the public. Insisting that venal politicians could not be trusted with the park, Olmsted demanded professional administration and regulation to insure that "none of the great army of small persecutors who torment the outside world, can enter into this pleasant place to make us miserable in it."[47]

The creation of great urban parks accelerated in the last three decades of the century. Designed as domestic rather than civic spaces, the parks welcomed women and children as their ideal inhabitants and the family picnic as their ideal event. The urban park served as an "outdoor parlor," Protestant minister Horace Bushnell observed, promoting "the cultivation of good manners and a right social feeling." Bushnell's theory of the moral influence of domestic environments shaped the profession of park planning through his parishioner Olmsted. Planners conceived of parks as domestic havens from the "rush and turmoil of urban life" that would exercise a "potent influence upon the moral condition of the society." They provided a "green oasis in the arid deserts of business and dissipation for the refreshment of the city's body and soul."[48]

Too distant from the poorer districts for easy access, the great parks mainly served an affluent population. During the debate over Central Park, New York City's Industrial Congress called for new parks to be built in "vacant squares in the more thickly populated districts." But by the 1850s, cities no longer punctuated the urban grid with small public spaces. For the well-to-do who promenaded through them, the great parks extended the polite intercourse of the domestic realm. Central Park became "the great rendezvous of the polite world," allowing the genteel to escape the indignities of the street in their carriages. The "full oceanic tide of New York's wealth and 'gentility,'" Walt Whitman observed in 1879, promenaded through Central Park.[49]

In contrast to the small parks and squares of the antebellum city, the great postwar parks substituted seeing and being seen for ruling and being ruled. They forbade political discussion. "No public meeting, and no public discussion or debates shall be held within the limits of the said parks, avenues or grounds," read the regulations governing San Francisco's Golden Gate Park. Central Park's regulations prohibited speechifying, as well as the drinking, dancing, and games that accompanied popular politics. Although Central Park sometimes accommodated ceremonial and patriotic assemblies, supervisors refused permits for political protests.[50]

The great parks promised social harmony rather than civic debate. Counteracting the dangers of the tenement districts, the great parks provided "innocent amusement" to "weaken the dangerous inclinations" and exert "a distinctly harmonizing and refining influence upon the most unfortunate and most lawless classes of the city." Parks, Olmsted continued, broke up the "young men in knots of perhaps half a dozen in lounging attitudes rudely obstructing the sidewalks," always ready to descend to some "brilliantly lighted basement, where they find others of their sort, see, hear, smell, drink and eat all manner of vile things." The parks also provided a space where the personal example of the genteel might have a refining effect, encouraging "courtesy, self-control, and temperance" among the less fortunate.[51]

CIVIC VERTIGO: THE CITY BIOLOGICAL AND PATHOLOGICAL

The neglect of civic and public spaces turned the cities of the late nineteenth century into disorienting landscapes crowded with people and goods. In 1877, the photographer Eadweard Muybridge ascended millionaire railroad baron Mark Hopkins's mansion atop San Francisco's Nob Hill to capture a coherent image of the city. Muybridge's photographs, positioned side by side, provided a 360-degree panoramic view of San Francisco. But his "boudoir view of San Francisco" (taken from a millionaire's bedroom) revealed only block after block of close-packed private residences and commercial structures, a city bereft of legible public and civic spaces.[52]

Muybridge's failed effort at perceptual clarity underscored the "civic vertigo" overtaking the late nineteenth-century city. Only the statistical methods of the social sciences could apprehend the "motley multitude." In two comprehensive volumes in 1880, the U.S. Bureau of the Census employed new biological distinctions to classify urban populations. To account for increasing numbers of African American migrants and Asian immigrants, the census replaced the civic distinction of "free" and "slave" with new racial classifications. Gender and domestic arrangements also figured prominently in its statistical portrait, as they did throughout the emerging social sciences.[53]

The social sciences' search for statistically predictable patterns of behavior also gave rise to the concept of the "slum." Defined as concentrated pockets of poverty, the slum encouraged acceptance of economic inequality as a natural, timeless fact of city life, akin to smoke, bricks, or saloons. Behind the antiseptic social scientific descriptions stood lurid journalistic accounts of slums as places where "vice and abomination, the filth and misery, are not prominently visible but are hid from public gaze." The slum's deviant domesticity nevertheless came under public scrutiny. In slums like San Francisco's Chinatown, the respectable learned, a single eighty-square-foot room sufficed for a family of six.[54]

At the opposite end of the social scale, granite-faced mansions housed the elite. Fenced and fortified, mansions accommodated affluent families in the same square footage that housed hundreds in the slums. In the 1870s, apartment houses became popular among the respectable classes and reinforced the culture of privacy. Limiting the size of lobbies and entries, providing separate stairways for servants and services, and focused inward on a private courtyard, apartment houses promised their residents "the moral effect of housekeeping." Rising six to ten stories, flush to the sidewalk, they lorded over a shrinking public space and cultivated an "excessive exclusiveness, to guard their dearly cherished state of exaltation."[55]

Skyscraping office districts and new residential districts left antebellum public spaces overwhelmed or stranded in declining neighborhoods. Lost in snarls of traffic and electric wires or overrun with vice or poverty, public spaces became symbols of civic disorder. "The grass has disappeared, the iron fence is broken, the wall promenade near the sea gone to decay," wrote a New Yorker of the battery. Filled with "ragged, tattered and drunken men and women," it became "as unsafe a place at night as can be found in the city." The paraded differences of the antebellum city gave way to moralistic contrasts. A New Yorker described Broadway's passing throng as "saints and sinners, mendicants and missionaries, priests and poets, courtesans and chiffoniers, burglars and bootblacks." Commercial attractions rather than public spaces became the city's landmarks. Grand department stores provided safety zones for genteel women and enshrined shopping as the essential public act.[56]

Skyscrapers offered a partial antidote to civic vertigo. "How shall we impart to this sterile pile," Chicago architect Louis Sullivan asked of the skyscraper, "the graciousness of those higher forms of sensibility and culture that rest on the lower and fiercer passions?" Chicago architects lavished attention on the skyscraper's semipublic spaces—its entrances, lobbies, ground-floor walls—to provide a pleasing face for what Sullivan called "the crude, harsh brutal agglomeration, this stark, staring exclamation of external strife." What white-collar workers actually did in these skyscrapers "will be a source of wonder to the visitor," a Chicago guidebook explained, undoubtedly "something to coax the almighty dollar in their direction." But ensconced in their "place above the clouds," in gracefully ornamented skyscrapers, office workers enjoyed status as "people of culture." Natural lighting, fresh air (via mechanical ventilation), clean hands, and clean collars further elevated the status of white-collar workers.[57]

But skyscrapers also added to the chaos and confusion on city streets. Elevation separated office workers from the newsboys and peddlers, shoe shines and ditch diggers, street toughs and preachers who appeared "like pigmies" from office windows. Yet skyscrapers nevertheless multiplied the crush of crowds and the rush of activities on city streets. While their long shadows darkened the streets and stagnated the air, the soft coal that powered the buildings covered downtown with soot. Meanwhile, few architects were paid to add ornamentation or redeeming touches to factories, stockyards, and other industrial workplaces.[58]

In neighborhood markets, on stoops and roofs, and in the streets themselves, people still joined in conversations. Civic responsibility survived too, in citizens like the San Francisco fruit dealer who sheltered stranded children. But many worried about the collapse of the public world where each person became "a link in a chain of association which runs through the whole community." Now "the links are all nearly separated, and where they are connected it is generally by open links which can be slipped at pleasure." In William Dean Howells's novels, disagreeable encounters in streetcars and on city streets revealed "our weakness as a public." Henry James's fictional characters rarely ventured into the streets and then for secretive or nefarious purposes, engaging in those "close dealings with other minds without any friendly flowing toward them" that Olmsted designed his parks to combat.[59]

Providing an even less forgiving vision of public life, an expanding literature depicted the city as a tangle of pathology. Vast hordes of immigrants from southern and eastern Europe who failed to appreciate "the new civilization into which they have come" made "foreign" the most telling of accusations. Focused on the perversion of domestic instincts among poor immigrant women, the literature of urban pathology "shuddered at the thought that such a creature bears the name of woman." The children of the poor, "strange little creatures who flaunt their rags," filled the streets in their "semi-savage independence." Biological metaphors proliferated in calls for a quarantine of the "herds" of poor "cattle" who violated domestic purity in their "putrid mass" and "stagnant pool," their whole "cauldron of offensive rottenness."[60]

Juxtaposing filthy inner-city gutters and genteel suburban toilets, the unequal distribution of municipal services encouraged the use of biological metaphors to describe the dangers of the slum. Poisoning and ulcerated, curdled and stinking, the neighborhoods of the poor threatened social decay and contamination. Like other leaders of the settlement house movement, Chicago's Jane Addams recognized that the failures of municipal government fell heaviest on her neighbors. She struggled to redirect municipal priorities, urging the city to provide garbage boxes to clean up the streets and wholesome amusements to supplant salacious ones. But the genteel continued to associate the city with filth. The children of the poor "are absolutely brought up in the gutter," a moralist complained. "Whenever we get beneath the shining mask of the city's public face," a French visitor shuddered, "we discover what is squirming about in the depths of the sewers."[61]

As social scientists classified the voiceless multitude, the tramp topped the hierarchy of negative connotations of the streets. The antithesis to the taxpayer, the tramp represented the greatest social menace. A "lazy, incorrigible, cowardly, utterly depraved savage," a "vicious and idle" carrier of moral infection, the tramp moved restlessly in search of charity. A socially defective product of damaged heredity, the tramp forfeited the rights of procreation. In the confines of the metropolis, the tramp metamorphosed into the hoodlum or street-corner tough. Until "we kill him outright, until the metropolis is purified," went one warning, "he may awake us at midnight with his mingled hiss and roar and strike and strangle us in the arms of Love, and in the very breast of Peace."[62]

With increasing labor unrest and unemployment, the tramp menace enveloped all working people. In the wake of the 1877 railroad strikes, the *New York Times* condemned the strikers not only as tramps and hoodlums, but as roughs, rioters, mobs, blacklegs, looters, communists, agitators, a dangerous class of people, bummers, ruffians, bands of worthless fellows, incendiaries, enemies of society, malcontents, riffraff, and idiots. When the unemployed filled public parks, the respectable saw only "dirty unkempt people," "bums," and "idlers." The threat led some authorities to remove park benches.[63]

Other terms used to describe the people—"the mass," the "multitude," the "tide"— suggested an irrational, uncontrollable force rather than a collection of citizens, more biological than civic. The police department, with its accumulation of statistics measuring criminal and immoral behavior, replaced city hall as nerve center of the city. A professionalized police force blanketed the city with precinct houses and call boxes, ordinances and licensing regulations. The police arrested tens of thousands annually in the largest cities, far more than in European cities (three times London's rate). Although the absolute numbers of violent crimes rose to newsworthy levels, they did not grow disproportionately to expanding populations. While the poor suffered most from violent crime, arrests delivered up a pathetic assortment of drunks, deformed beggars, and prostitutes that inflamed elite fears.[64]

The police represented only the first line of defense against urban pathology. New armories arose in major cities, housing the National Guard behind concrete walls, iron gates, and thick oak doors. Addressing New York City's Seventh Regiment during the dedication of its new East Side armory in 1879, President Rutherford Hayes praised the troops and remarked that "behind the policeman's club glistens your bayonet worthy of an imperial state and the imperial city." Labor strife made military occupation a regular feature of city life. Even charity required a militarized approach in response to the "heavy expense and great evils resulting . . . from the large numbers of able-bodied vagrants and tramps." Founded in 1882, the Charity Organization Society (COS) eliminated sentimentality from the provision of alms. Distinguishing between the worthy and unworthy poor, the COS treated the city as a war zone in which mass suffering must be stoically accepted for the greater good.[65]

The Degeneration of Popular Politics

Good-government reformers called for the disfranchisement of tramps and loafers, a category in which they lumped nearly half the population. But when disfranchisement proved impossible, elections remained to be won. Aware of the limitations of educational politics, the established political parties became pioneers in the techniques of mass persuasion. Taking on the characteristics of giant corporate enterprises, the parties mass-produced not only buttons, playing cards, and other novelties stamped with candidates' names, but fluff and deceit as well.[66]

The educational campaigns first introduced industrial methods into campaigning. In 1892, the parties "established foundries and are turning out education in great hunks and wads—by the yard, mile or ton, in any quantity that may be desired." But party leaders came to recognize "the uselessness and the waste of the old form of campaign documents, branded as partisan on the face ... not read by one in a thousand to whom they were sent." The parties shifted to "a lot of lighter and more catchy cards, dodgers, circulars, and the like, printed in bright colors ... designed to attract the eye." Partisan materials "disguised as news matter" went out under misleading headings such as the Ben Franklin Publishing Company.[67]

Although devoted first and foremost to private profit, metropolitan newspapers helped the parties reshape political culture. In 1879, the editor of the *New York Tribune* described the metropolitan daily as "a great business enterprise, as legitimate as a railroad or a line of steamships, and as rigidly demanding the best business management." Neither publishers nor the growing numbers of professional journalists understood their newspapers as partisan or political undertakings. Boasts about circulation replaced ideological slogans on mastheads. Readers' growing hunger for news, dating from the Civil War, further undercut the partisan nature of journalism. Newspapers served readers in "the dissemination of fact rather than in the advocacy of policy," a prominent editor explained.[68]

Market opportunities, professional development, and readers' expectations all undermined the newspapers' partisan affiliations. But the new independent journalism stemmed most of all from the ambitions of reforming editors in the nation's largest cities. Sharing the good-government faith in an objective and empirical social science, independent journalists championed impartiality and accuracy in the presentation of the news. Partisanship "commands its newspaper to equivocate, to pervert, to deny the truth," George William Curtis told a convention of editors in 1881, leading to "the abdication of that moral leadership of opinion which is the great function of the political press."[69]

While discrediting partisanship, independent journalism did not always supply objectivity or a faithful expression of public opinion. Freed from political pressures, editors bowed to market dictates. Advertisers shaped the independent journals in their own interest, demanding neutrality and the avoidance of controversy in order to attract affluent readers and add an aura of authority to advertisements. Consequently, the "editor of the great metropolitan daily," reported one investigator, gazes down upon his readership "from an elevation of reserve and self-esteem." The editor "will not consider what [his readership] thinks when he finds he has only to consider what it will buy." This "attitude of superiority," the investigator concluded, "does not recommend our 'great newspapers' as echoes of the public voice."[70]

Reforming editors eschewed the banner headlines and explosive prose that made politics more accessible and engaging. "Of course this printing of all the news and giving both sides a fair hearing is apt at times to bewilder the reader," one editor conceded. Unimpressed with the "passionless ether" of the independent press in 1900, a journalist praised the disappearing partisan press for producing "radical differences of opinion," the "discussion of which is a contribution to popular education." The partisan press provided (as Greeley put it in 1841) a viewpoint "removed alike from servile partisanship on the one hand and from gagged, mincing neutrality on the other." Partisan editors provided a distinct point of view and sharp criticism of other points of view, while reforming editors avoided the controversies that promoted "a wide public intelligence."[71]

By the turn of the century, politics lost much of its popular appeal. "Many political meetings are occurring nightly," the New York City papers reported in 1892, "yet the theaters are crowded as if there were no such distraction." Never before had the pursuit of pleasure been "so little disturbed as it is now by political excitement." When they blamed sporting events and commercial amusements for political apathy, critics stumbled over the deeper cause in the divorce of political and popular culture. Earlier forms of popular culture (newspapers, theaters, and sports) enriched political culture. But political and popular culture now parted ways.[72]

Just as the independent press emptied politics of its popular appeal, the new sensational journalism emptied popular culture of its political import. Pioneered by Joseph Pulitzer's *New York World*, the sensational press provided an emotional substitute for intense partisanship. Trivializing politics, the *World* buried political news amid an avalanche of gossip, scandal, and crime or refashioned it as a human interest story. Gossipy features on candidates' personalities or personal lives addressed a public of consumers rather than partisans (a development pioneered by the independent press in its new "interview" format). Diluting the news with sex, crime, sports, fashion, and cooking, Pulitzer made use of multiple illustrations, photographs, and comics (including "the Yellow Kid," from which came the term "yellow journalism") to reach a poor, immigrant, semiliterate readership.[73]

William Randolph Hearst's *New York Journal* took sensationalism to a new level. Lurid, dishonest, and simplistic, the *Journal* spoke to "that class least infused with the modern intellectual spirit of inquiry, least apt to study their facts before forming their theories." Faked or flimsy stories, huge headlines, cartoons and comics strips, and copious illustrations filled its pages. Ostensibly the crusading voice of the people, making war on both "class privilege" and "the foolishness of the crowd," the *Journal* actually discouraged political activism. Often ignoring political news even during elections, the *Journal* trivialized what little it covered. But the *Journal* remained "important to the peaceful stability of society, BECAUSE IT ACTS AS A SAFETY VALVE FOR PUBLIC INDIGNATION," or so claimed its editor, Arthur Brisbane. Venting frustrations in bombast, the *Journal* crusaded only as long as crusading sold papers. It then moved on, leaving the public to bear the consequences, most infamously its jingoistic demand for war with Spain.[74]

Sensational journalism banked on a low assessment of popular capabilities, a self-fulfilling conviction about the people's weak and transitory interest in public affairs. "Care must be exercised not to overdo one subject," the muckraker Lincoln Steffens explained, "for the theory of sensationalism includes the belief that the average newspaper reader's mind is as fickle as it is shallow." But the muckraking magazines that flourished after 1900 also flitted from topic to topic, discouraging sustained attention to politics and leaving behind a pervasive cynicism. The muckrakers, Walter Lippmann complained, produced a public with "an alert and tingling sense of labyrinthine evil" all too ready to embrace a "sense of conspiracy and secret scheming." But you "cannot go very far by reiterating that public officials are corrupt, that business men break the law," Lippmann concluded, for the charge lacked a "vivid sense of what politics and business might become."[75]

Just as partisan journalism supported the spectacular campaign and independent journalism promoted the educational campaign, sensational journalism brought forth the advertising campaign. Focused on personalities and negative in its content, advertised politics became the dominant style in the twentieth century, discouraging anything but a fitful and superficial interest in public affairs. First glimpsed side by side with spectacular and educational politics in the election of 1896, advertised politics depended on clever slogans and compelling images to package the candidate in emotional wrapping. Orchestrated by Mark Hanna, William McKinley's campaign revolved around simplistic images and slogans, casting the candidate as "The Advanced Agent of Prosperity" and promising "The Full Dinner Pail." Hanna "advertised McKinley," Theodore Roosevelt recognized, "as if he were a patent medicine."[76]

Ironically, the voters responded as never before to the simultaneous educational campaign in 1896. "The people display an amount of interest in pending questions which is astonishing," a Kansan reported of a campaign shaped by the populist critique of the gold standard. "They listen to long and tedious discussion with extraordinary patience. They even bear the reading of coinage acts and quantities of dry statistics." Critics dismissed the populist agitation as "the silver craze," but it rose upon a foundation of popular education far more democratic and effective than that of the good-government reformers. Populists educated voters through cooperatives, lecture bureaus, and the national journals and local weeklies organized in the National Reform Press Association, just the sort of popular and political culture cities once enjoyed.[77]

Mob Mind, Befuddled Public

The dumbing down of popular journalism and the degeneration of popular politics led to different conclusions. One might conclude that institutions and habits crucial to cultivating an active, intelligent citizenry had broken down and that new institutions might create new habits more conducive to democratic politics. Or one might conclude that people's inherent irrationality made it imperative to place strict limits on popular participation in politics. The popular literature on the mob mind that proliferated in the 1890s supported the second conclusion. But populists initially made a reasonable case for the first.[78]

Populists charged that economic concentration stifled the free expression of public opinion, pointing to the emergence of the Western Union Telegraph Company as the nation's largest corporation and first great industrial monopoly. Allied with the Associated Press (AP), Western Union betrayed the telegraph's potential as a common carrier of information. An 1872 congressional investigation concluded that collusion between the AP and Western Union endangered a democracy where "the perpetuation of the Government must have its ultimate guarantee in the intelligence of the people." Monopoly power meant that "no new or projected journal can have the use of the telegraph at rates not absolutely ruinous, and many journals, long established ... are in the absolute power of the telegraph companies."[79]

The Associated Press and Western Union claimed information as private property over which they exerted complete control. In 1879, populist editor Henry George felt this corporate power when the AP refused to sell news dispatches to him and then Western Union cut his access to the telegraph lines. "I claim that there is a property in news," argued an AP spokesman, "and that property is created by the fact of our collecting it and concentrating it." An angry senator replied that this ignored the difference between a business "which affects public affairs and the general interest of the people, and that which merely affects the private affairs of the citizens." Between 1866 and 1900, seventy bills and twenty congressional investigations looked to the reform of the telegraph industry. The Populist Party, the Knights of Labor, the American Federation of Labor, and an 1890 petition of two million signatures all called for a public telegraph system. Western Union lobbyists defeated all these efforts, leaving the telegraph in the hands of a "wicked monopoly" and its "most miserly and despicable greed."[80]

Rejecting the populist critique of monopoly power, respectable opinion insisted that the irrational mob mind represented the greatest threat to democracy. In a decade punctuated by the Homestead Strike of 1892, the start of a economic depression in 1893, the nationwide strike in sympathy with the Pullman workers in 1894, the populist insurgency in 1896, and the sensational press's agitation for war with Spain in 1898, the mob mind became an obsession of elite opinion. Fearing "the ragged edge of anarchy," nervous elites poured over the academic studies of European mobs that filled American journals. A reprint of a British article condemning the "imbecility" of mob violence demanded that the "right to assemble in large numbers in the heart of a busy and populous metropolis" be curtailed. With "startling suddenness impunity begets audacity, till what began as a common riot may end in an attempted revolution." Another article observed with admiration that the "Russian government, knowing well by experience the conditions that favor the formation of mobs, prohibits all kinds of public gatherings," even "an assembly of four or five men."[81]

In 1895, the French conservative Gustave Le Bon examined the mob mind in the pages of the *Popular Science Monthly*. Le Bon argued that a handful of ruling ideas—paradise, hell, socialism—shaped history. Such ideas worked not through rational, conscious deliberation but by seeping into the "unconscious regions of the feelings" where they "cease then to be influenced by the reason." Truth or value had nothing to do with it. Only ideas that produced "striking images" became fixed and exerted a power "so great that no person is able to arrest their progress." Through repetition and affirmation, an idea acquired prestige and "a kind of domination exercised over our minds which paralyzes all our critical faculties."[82]

Le Bon denied the existence of rational public opinion. Since ruling ideas possessed "immunity from discussion," everyone suffered from a crowd mentality. As long as ideas did their work within the sober "upper ranks of the nation," however, no danger existed. But when ideas began to "influence the mob," trouble ensued. Certain "nervous, excitable persons who live on the borders of madness" stirred up a faith among the masses that could "move mountains." If "the future threatens to belong to the socialists," Le Bon warned, "notwithstanding the annoying absurdity of their doctrines, it is because they are today the only persons who are really convinced. The modern directing classes have lost faith in everything. They do not believe in anything."[83]

Writing in the *Popular Science Monthly* two years after Le Bon, American sociologist Edward A. Ross proved no less flattering to popular abilities. The product of a "mental contagion" that set off a collective demoralization, Ross explained, the mob resembled an animal herd. The "reiteration of a single idea from all sides" made for a situation of high suggestibility, producing "unanimity, impulsiveness, exaggeration of feeling, excessive credulity, fickleness, inability to reason, and sudden alterations of boldness and cowardice." The mob mind did not depend on physical proximity, for "the behavior of city populations under excitement shows the familiar characteristics of the mob quite apart from any thronging." The "space-annihilating devices" of mass communications assailed "the individual with a mass of suggestion almost as vivid as if he actually stood in the midst of an immense crowd."[84]

Although the prevalence of the mob mind had discredited city democracies since classical times, Ross continued, modern city conditions exacerbated the problem. The "nervous strains of great cities" and the "continual bombardment of the attention by innumerable sense impressions," led to a mass hysteria indistinguishable from the mob mind. Impulsive and ill-considered actions destroyed "that wholesome deliberateness which has distinguished indirect from direct democracy."[85]

Ross saw the mob mind everywhere, in war fevers and political landslides, sympathy strikes and financial panics, fads and crazes. Democratization, as much as urbanization, explained its prevalence. The mob mind resulted from the raising of "the common folk . . . from the slough of custom to the plane of choice and self-direction." A "half-education" provided the masses with ideas, but "without developing the ability to choose among them." If a "touching credulity" proved to be the final "outcome of the attempt to emancipate the common man and fit him to be helmsman of society, we might well despair." But if we would "cultivate a habit of doubt and review," Ross concluded, we might yet "brace men to stand against the rush of the mass."[86]

At the end of the century, the final verdict came down against the democratic public. A best-selling account of the mob mind declared the United States a "crowd civilization," where we "live in crowds," "get our living in crowds," and are "amused in herds." The problem with modern man was "not that he does not think, but that it takes ten thousand men to make him think." With "the infinite value of the individual" a thing of the past, the popular study concluded, every "new and fresh human being that comes upon the earth is manufactured into a coward or crowded into a machine as soon as we get at him." John Q. Public, the cartoon character created by the Hearst syndicate's Fred Opper, provided an enduring image of the democratic public in eclipse. A befuddled figure, balding with a hat several sizes too small, John Q. Public dimly perceived, through his thick glasses, dangers on all sides.[87]

PART III

The Public in Progressivism and War

In 1901, the investment banker J. P. Morgan created U.S. Steel, the world's first billion-dollar corporation. In the great merger wave between 1895 and 1904, compliant legislatures and courts facilitated the creation of similar corporate giants. Combining production with distribution, eliminating competitors and disciplining suppliers, corporations accounted for three-quarters of industrial production in the United States by 1904. Two-thirds of all manufacturing workers labored for corporations that employed at least one hundred. One-third worked for firms employing more than five hundred. In capital-intensive, technologically advanced industries, three hundred firms a year disappeared as corporate oligopoly took shape.[1]

Exerting enormous influence over individuals and communities, the visible hand of corporate management organized natural and human resources, developed national and international markets, directed the process of technological development, and streamlined production and distribution. The largest corporations planned entire cities, most dramatically at Gary, Indiana. Beginning in 1906, U.S. Steel turned a barren site on Lake Michigan, strategically located between Minnesota iron ore and Pennsylvania coal, into a "magic city" of 55,000 by 1920. Leveling sand dunes, filling in swamps, and moving three railroads and the Grand Calumet River, U.S. Steel deemed its creation "the eighth wonder of the world." Dozens of other satellite cities arose across the nation under the guiding hand of corporate enterprise. Meanwhile, privately owned utilities like Bell Telephone envisioned "an absolutely new type of city." Bell's "foresight department" boasted of employing "the first real corps of practical sociologists" who would "prepare a 'fundamental' plan of the whole United States."[2]

Corporations also corrupted the political process. Few disputed Theodore Roosevelt's assertion in 1910 that "the great special interests too often control and corrupt the men and methods of government for their own profit." But corporate power went deeper. Usurping citizens and their elected representatives, corporate leaders sought to short-circuit civic life. George W. Perkins, Morgan's partner and a director of U.S. Steel, celebrated the transformation of the corporate executive "into the public official" who acted "the part of the statesman." Situated at the "commanding heights" of industrial life, Perkins concluded, corporate statesmen "instinctively lose sight of the interest of any one individual and work for what is the broadest, and most enduring interest of the many."[3]

The National Civic Federation advanced the ambitions of corporate statesmen. Nominally composed of representatives of business, the public, and labor, the National Civic Federation became the voice of corporate leaders like Perkins. Politicians with close corporate ties, such as Grover Cleveland and William H. Taft, represented the public. Organized labor served as a junior partner, charged less with representing its membership than with securing labor's acquiescence to corporate priorities. Meanwhile, merchants and corporate executives, investment bankers and retailers, advertisers and marketing experts constructed a new culture that offered the pleasures of consumption as a substitute for the satisfactions of civic participation and self-directed work.[4]

But just as corporate initiatives threatened to supplant all others, Americans rediscovered the public and made it the central focus of the Progressive Era. "Every thinking man and woman must be convinced that the nation to-day is passing through a severe political crisis," explained civic reformer Benjamin DeWitt. "After a period of unprecedented industrial and commercial expansion, during which time little or no attention has been given to the problems of government, the people have suddenly realized that government is not functioning properly and that radical changes are needed." The presidential election of 1912 confirmed popular recognition of the political crisis. While the leading candidates, Roosevelt and Woodrow Wilson, offered competing programs of civic renewal, the Socialist Party's indictment of corporate dominance polled a million votes.[5]

What DeWitt called the "new political era" hinged on a cultivation of the mind and character of the citizen. We "are awakening," the black civil rights activist W.E.B. Dubois observed, "to the fact that the perpetuity of republican institutions on this continent depends on the purification of the ballot, the civic training of voters" and "striving for a renaissance of civic virtue." The influential journalist Walter Lippmann also saw the desire for a renaissance of virtue. The same graft that provided a "reason for opening a bottle of champagne" in private life, Lippmann observed, when practiced in public life now landed many an alderman in jail. We finally had come "to expect more of the politician," to "regard some of the interests of life as too important for the intrusion of commercial ethics." A "public willing to recognize as corrupt an incredibly varied assortment of conventional acts," Lippmann concluded, provided one of the "hopeful signs of the age."[6]

Progressive Era Americans recognized that the widest possible distribution of political and economic responsibility still offered the best recipe for the creation of a democratic citizenry. "Good citizenship in a democracy," a national civic leader argued, "is the consciousness of responsibility, not only for obeying the government but for participation in being the government." The right of voting carried the responsibility of deliberating with others, articulating one's own views and engaging those of others. Industrial democracy followed the same logic. What "kind of a citizen-sovereign can a man be," industrial democrats asked, who "becomes a mere machine and does what he is told, asking no questions and incurring no risks?"[7]

Experiments in direct democracy and industrial self-government cultivated new competencies and inspired new ambitions. Once "timid and torpid," democracy now took "a searching look at its own meaning and responsibilities," The New Republic editor Herbert Croly wrote in the months before the outbreak of war in Europe in 1914. Although much remained to be done, democracy had "no reason for discouragement." "What the situation calls for is faith," Croly concluded, democracy's "primary virtue." But just as the new democratic experiments began to take root, the American intervention into World War I tested and then shattered the faith in democracy.[8]

Part III focuses on a pivotal period in American history when the prospects for a revitalization of republican values and institutions hung in the balance. Seizing on the city as the most hopeful setting for an engaged and intelligent citizenry, civic reformers used public spaces, university extensions, social settlements, civic forums, social centers, and even movie theaters to promote a democratic public. The eruption of war in Europe in 1914 provided a stressful test of the deliberative capacity of the democratic public. The administration of President Woodrow Wilson might have used the city-based experiments to encourage a grassroots debate over what role the United States should take in World War I. Instead, Wilson's administration enlisted them in a top-down, federal effort to mobilize public opinion behind a predetermined policy of intervention. When Wilson's war to make the world safe for democracy turned out badly, and a manufactured public opinion erupted in ugly violence during and after the war, the Progressive Era faith in a democratic public collapsed.

CHAPTER 7

The Republican Moment

The Rediscovery of the Public in the Progressive Era

As the Progressive Era began, the civic values and republican institutions of the United States suffered from thirty years of decay. Now the growing centralization of power in economic and political institutions threatened to eradicate them completely. Unless Americans reformulated a participatory conception of democracy and reasserted the necessity of an active citizenry, their republican experiment in self-government could not survive. Returning to first principles, Americans revived a republican idiom and applied it to the reform of political, economic, and cultural affairs.[1]

The call for civic renewal reached the highest levels of politics. This "great republic means nothing unless it means the triumph of a real democracy, the triumph of popular government," thundered Theodore Roosevelt in 1910, as he began his campaign to regain the presidency. Citizens lacked "free access" to government, answered Woodrow Wilson in his successful battle with Roosevelt for the presidency in 1912. The "machinery of political control must be put in the hands of the people," Wilson concluded, restoring "their right to exercise a free and constant choice in the management of their own affairs."[2]

Roosevelt and Wilson expressed the widespread conviction that governmental powers must be expanded to balance corporate power. Under their leadership, the federal government dramatically extended its responsibilities. During the American intervention into World War I alone, the federal government created five thousand new agencies. But rather than dismantle the corporate order, Roosevelt and Wilson strengthened it by using federal power to stabilize corporate capitalism and guide it toward greater social responsibility. They proved less attuned, beyond a rhetorical commitment, to the need to reactivate citizens.[3]

If democracy meant material well-being and the equitable distribution of wealth, then the regulated corporation and the welfare state served reasonably well. But if democracy meant participation in the decisions that shaped one's life and required the fullest development of the mind and character of the citizen, then the corporation and the state had to be democratized. The "need of imposing more exacting standards of behavior upon the citizens of an industrial democratic state," Herbert Croly of *The New Republic* put it, "applies to the citizen as citizen no less than to the citizen as worker." But corporate interests placed "many stumbling blocks ... in the way of a free formation of public opinion and a free expression of the public will," a civic reformer explained, demanding new efforts to revitalize the public. By restoring popular government at the grassroots, civic reformers cultivated an active citizenry as a counterweight to corporate power.[4]

The city provided the essential battleground for those committed to civic renewal. As they competed with one another to attract business enterprise, cities became the most active and the most corrupt of polities. With national and state planning in abeyance, private enterprise looked to municipal government for public subsidies and employed corrupt means to secure them. Ironically, public service corporations, securing franchises from city governments to supply essential utilities, provided "the chief, if not the only source, of corruption" in municipal affairs.[5]

The escalation of labor violence and the deepening of poverty also focused civic reform on the city. A vast literature of urban disorder depicted the destruction of the city in lurid terms. But the turn of the century also produced a literature of urban utopia, imagining cities reborn in civic splendor. "At my feet lay a great city," Edward Bellamy's Julian West recalled his reawakening in the renewed Boston of 2000. "Every quarter contained large open squares filled with trees, along which statues glistened and fountains flashed in the late-afternoon sun. Public buildings of a colossal size and architectural grandeur unparalleled in my day raised their stately piles on every side."[6]

In cities, the forces of concentrated power and technological interdependence converged in ways that could intimidate and overwhelm the citizen. But the city also generated an inescapable public life. On sidewalks and streetcars, in neighborhoods and newspapers, around soapboxes and lecture halls, city people met and mingled, struggled and cooperated, addressed problems and discovered possibilities. Shortly after his arrival in Chicago in 1894, philosopher John Dewey wrote that the city "seems filled with problems holding out their hands and asking somebody to please solve them—or else dump them in the lake." Things "simply stick themselves at you, instead of leaving you to think about them. The first effect is pretty paralyzing, the after effect is stimulating." Dewey could not escape the feeling "that there is a 'method' and if one could only get hold of it things could be so tremendously straightened out."[7]

In offering "the improvement of the methods and conditions of debate, discussion, and persuasion" as an alternative to plutocracy, Dewey provided many

Progressive Era activists with a philosophical basis for their faith in a democratic public. As in previous periods of civic crisis, a faith in the essential goodness of the people underlay fears of a conspiracy to corrupt the political process. But a recognition of the atrophy of civic skills lent a new anxiety to the struggle to redeem the Republic. Many civic reformers who embraced the New England town meeting as their model wondered whether face-to-face politics could develop in gritty, industrial cities with few public spaces. But they resolved to try, in part through the city beautiful movement, which built parks, squares, gardens, and monuments as a focus for civic pride and engagement.[8]

The City Beautiful and Intelligent

With roots going back to the 1880s, the city beautiful movement united citizen activists and professional city planners in such organizations as the American Civic Association (1904). "The making of the city will mean the making of a new citizen," explained Charles Zueblin, an activist and veteran of Jane Addams's settlement house. Chicago planner Daniel Burnham agreed that "good citizenship is the prime object of good city planning." But producing good citizenship could mean a variety of things. Charles Mulford Robinson, theorist and publicist for the movement, thought public buildings should be grouped at a high, visible point in the city, where "the community would look up, seeing them lording over it at every turn, as, in fact, the government ought to do." Parks in the city, a city beautiful report of 1897 added, would help "soothe . . . popular discontent." Others promoted monumental civic art to advertise the culture of a philanthropic elite, turning citizens into passive consumers of pleasing prospects.[9]

Others saw the city beautiful as a means of creating an active citizenry. Beautiful and generous civic spaces invited a critique of the dreary commercialism of urban life and encouraged citizens to develop a "sense of ownership" in their city. "Magnificent public buildings, beautiful parks, artistic boulevards, sightly streets arouse in the individual a keen sense of proprietary pride." The "spirit of liberalism and equality" of civic spaces also promoted interaction among different sorts of people. Spaces and halls designed specifically for public meetings produced a "civic conscience" and "virtue which is born of a community of interest."[10]

The civic potential of the city beautiful intersected with that of the social settlement. Jane Addams defined the settlements' goal as nothing less than "the complete participation of the working classes in the spiritual, intellectual and material inheritance of the human race." Hull House and other social settlements brought middle-class reformers into the city to share the lives of their poorer neighbors and encouraged civic engagement through forums and lectures on public issues. In "a democratic country nothing can be permanently achieved save through the masses of people," Addams explained of the objective necessity for settlements, making it "impossible to establish a higher political life than the people themselves crave." But she also acknowledged the subjective necessity for settlements in the "fast-growing number of cultivated young people who have no recognized outlet for their active faculties." Feeling "the need of putting theory into action," of reuniting culture with the life of the city, the settlers rejected genteel culture and devoted themselves "to the duties of good citizenship and to the arousing of the social energies."[11]

At its best, the city beautiful reunited popular and political culture in a richer American civilization. An activist inspired by classical Greece described city beautiful spaces as "open-air clubs at which political affairs and questions of art and literature were discussed from varied, individual points of view." Zueblin saw the city beautiful as a "laboratory of applied democracy" in which the public engaged in ongoing deliberation and self-education. "The city is symbolically, as well as etymologically, the basis of civilization," Zueblin argued, and he tried to fill civic spaces with active citizens dedicated to civic improvement. "One can be a citizen only by participation," Zueblin concluded, "and that not merely in the annual casting of the ballot, but in daily citizenship."[12]

Zueblin seized upon the university to extend the city beautiful's effort to create a new civic culture. He believed that university extensions might become leaders in popular education, sponsoring the sort of political forums found at the social settlements. "Nowhere else is there a forum where the public questions are discussed as freely, the verdict given as fairly, and the multitudinous voice of the people registered as effectively as in the meetings of the People's Institute," Zueblin wrote of one of New York City's most important settlements. But the greater intellectual and financial resources of urban universities could enrich and extend such forums. Indeed, Columbia University, under the leadership of Seth Low, pursued a dialogue with the city and its people. Low explained that he "should be glad to have it known by the workingmen of America that at Columbia College ... the disposition exists to teach the truth ... without fear or favor, and we ask their aid to enable us to see the truth as it appears to them." By establishing links with museums and other cultural institutions, sponsoring public lectures on academic and political issues, and bringing nonacademic thinkers onto the faculty, Low sought to make Columbia a civic institution that gave "a distinctly intellectual tone to life in the great city."[13]

Other universities shared Low's ambition. The University of Wisconsin and the University of Chicago became leaders of university extension in the 1890s. William Rainey Harper, University of Chicago's president, endorsed university extension programs to create "in the community at large that demand for the best of everything in the intellectual, aesthetic and moral world which is at once evidence of, and the surest means toward, the higher civic life." As a public lecturer for the University of Chicago, Zueblin spoke to groups across the city and the nation. He battled "the degrading, yet ever-extending grasp of the octopus of commercialism" to wean people away from mindless entertainment and struggled against his own elitism in order to "learn from the workingmen and workingwomen" while maintaining the ability to criticize and inform popular attitudes.[14]

The surest measure of the potential of university extension came in the trouble it caused for its practitioners. University officials questioned the wisdom of criticizing the powerful capitalists who funded the university's operations. These officials reprimanded or fired controversial lecturers, reduced funding for extension programs, and promoted an objective, value-free conception of knowledge against "partisan, unscientific methods." It "is all very well to sympathize with the working man," Harper remarked candidly, "but we get our money from those on the other side, and we can't afford to offend them." In disgust, Zueblin quit the university in 1908 and continued to lecture in forums outside of academia.[15]

THE GEORGISTS AND THE CITY REPUBLIC

Like Zueblin, Frederick Howe also turned from the university to the wider city in his quest for civic renewal. Trained as a political scientist, Howe joined Cleveland's city beautiful movement and Tom L. Johnson's 1901 mayoral campaign. Howe valued the city beautiful's encouragement of "more intelligent interest in . . . common things" and admired Johnson's effort to turn Cleveland into a model "city on a hill." A former street-railway magnate who became a follower of the antimonopolist Henry George, Johnson supported the municipal ownership of public utilities as a means of eliminating corruption and expanding the public realm. Johnson also championed home rule, adopted by Ohio and twelve other states by 1920. Home rule overturned Dillon's Rule (see Chapter 6), granting municipalities control over their charters and legislative agendas without interference from state legislatures.[16]

Johnson and Howe saw home rule and municipal ownership as the keys to civic renewal. Home rule and municipal ownership created "a city republic with full powers within itself," Johnson argued, and taught urbanites the skills of "self-government." Howe provided Johnson's efforts with a broader intellectual vision. "Home rule would create a city republic," Howe wrote, "a new sort of sovereignty, a republic like unto those of Athens, Rome, and the medieval city states," re-creating in the modern world the "local love and patriotism" of these historic cities. Home rule and municipal ownership also counteracted the tendency toward political centralization and the growth of public apathy. As owners of streetcar and other public systems, citizens would take an active interest in them. "The real test of municipal ownership," Howe concluded, "is not a monetary one; not the relief of taxation; not a profit or loss account; not even cheap water, gas, or electricity. It is rather one of higher civic life."[17]

Howe also hoped to turn city planning into a vehicle for civic renewal. "A much better phrase to describe city planning," Howe wrote in 1912, "is city building." German city planning provided a model. Addressing questions of transportation, public utilities, architecture, and, above all, ground rents, German municipalities became "great landlords" and refused to allow rent to become "a social burden imposed on people." People became "in large measure what the city makes them," so German cities spent lavishly on public spaces and public utilities with an eye to making "better citizens, better artisans." Howe believed American cities should similarly "awaken love, affection, interest" and serve as a "socializing agency" for the creation of good citizens. But the ideal of "public service," Howe concluded, must first replace the scourge of "monopoly."[18]

Howe, Johnson, and others saw themselves as carrying on the legacy of Henry George. Rejecting the belief in automatic progress, the view that "improvement tends to go on unceasingly, to a higher and higher civilization," George had warned in the 1880s that unless Americans closed the growing gap between the rulers and those ruled, the Republic would collapse from "internal decay." The growing complexity of society demanded greater "social intelligence," that "consensus of individual intelligence which forms a public opinion, a public conscience, a public will." Acknowledging the "selfishness and greed and vice and crime" that burdened the Republic, George insisted that "there is even now among men patriotism and virtue enough to secure us the best possible management of public affairs." If we committed ourselves to the "moral and intellectual" development of the people, he concluded, the Republic might still enjoy "a higher conscience, a keener sense of justice, a warmer brotherhood, a wider, loftier, truer public spirit."[19]

George recognized the city, its wealth and attractions, as a social product. The "increased powers of co-operation and exchange which come with increased population" made a "wider, fuller, more varied life" possible in the city. People flocked to the city, not only for economic opportunity but also to share in gratifications of a "social and intellectual nature." The city concentrated "that stimulus which is born of the collision of mind with mind," enlarging "the realms of the imagination." George and his followers argued that socially created forms of wealth, including speculative land values and profitable opportunities to deliver water, transit, light, and energy to residents, resulted from the growth of the city and should be used to enhance city life. By appropriating socially created wealth for public purposes, George argued, we could fill the city with "public baths, museums, libraries, gardens, lecture halls, music and dancing halls, theaters, universities . . . playgrounds, gymnasiums, etc. Heat, light and motive power, as well as water, might be conducted through our streets at public expense; our roads be lined with fruit trees."[20]

For the Georgists, the city also provided the best setting for engaging people in politics and developing the civic virtues essential to democracy. *The Public*, a weekly newspaper founded in 1898 and edited by George's longtime associate Louis F. Post, advanced the Georgist agenda. *The Public* promised a "lucid" and "continuous narrative" of current affairs that enabled its readers to make "themselves intelligent." The weekly encouraged its readers to recognize the interdependence of the world and to "see it whole," and did so by paying particular attention to urban affairs. *The Public* kept its eye on the efforts of Georgists (like Cleveland's Johnson and Howe, Detroit's Hazen Pingree, Toledo's "Golden

Rule" Jones and Brand Whitlock, and Cincinnati's Herbert Bigelow) to mobilize democratic constituencies in favor of municipal ownership, progressive taxation, and the expansion of public revenues and responsibilities.[21]

Like the movement it represented, *The Public* linked the effort to create an educated citizenry to an enlargement of the public realm. Celebrating the opening of subway extensions, the creation of municipal dance halls, schools, and hospitals, *The Public* argued that municipalities "fare better by performing their own public functions than by farming them out." Countless articles on street improvements and other public projects demonstrated "the amazing power of a city to create wealth," which the city should claim for itself and reinvest. Civic art should be the "natural outgrowth of all efforts to meet the essential needs of the city dweller" rather than an "external scheme of decoration." Like everything else in the public realm, art should awaken in the citizen "civic pride and a feeling of personal responsibility." *The Public* emphasized the relationship between democracy and public space, criticizing cities for failing to provide meeting places and lambasting the frequent prohibition of public meetings (including one planned for Philadelphia's Independence Square).[22]

The Georgists thrived in public spaces. Tom Johnson held tent meetings across Cleveland, inviting the public to address political issues. Rejecting the idea that newspapers could adequately express public opinion, Johnson encouraged an active, deliberating public constantly educating itself as it made up its mind. In his tent meetings, Johnson recognized "a freedom from restraint that is seldom present in halls." He understood that "heckling is the most valuable form of political education." The give-and-take of argument educated the people "as no amount of reading, even of the fairest newspaper accounts, could do." Providing equal time for uninterrupted speeches from opposing sides and ample time for questions, Johnson's tent meetings generated lively discussions that people found both serious and enjoyable.[23]

City people saw themselves experimenting with democratic forms in these meetings, embracing the necessity as well as the pleasures of public life. Johnson did not always respect the public's right to embrace ideas and make decisions he disagreed with. While he allowed radicals to speak freely in Cleveland, he tried to block a popular referendum that defeated his plans for municipal ownership of street railways. But Johnson ultimately accepted defeat and embraced the democratic public he helped revive. Recognizing that his greatest victory came in overcoming "the indifference of the public," he concluded that people "learn by their mistakes and the good effects that have and will come from the referendum will largely outweigh any temporary disadvantage."[24]

Howe shared Johnson's faith in democracy as the most educational form of politics. There "is no training school comparable to politics for the promotion of social and political ideas," Howe wrote. Endorsing the initiative, referendum, and recall, Howe argued that they led "to constant discussion, to a deeper interest in government, and to a psychological conviction that a government is in effect the people themselves." His move to the People's Institute of New York City in 1913 reflected these convictions. Charles Sprague Smith, a professor dissatisfied with university life, founded the People's Institute in 1897 in the belief that "there is no greater educational need within a democracy than training for participation in public life."[25]

The People's Institute sponsored a People's Forum that met at Cooper Union, bringing together politicians, intellectuals, activists, and citizens to deliberate on public issues. The forum sent resolutions to the city council reflecting its judgments. Jacob Riis recalled that whoever spoke at the forum must "be well fortified in argument, for his questioners are in touch with them in their practical working out, and some of them are . . . masters in debate." Howe also recognized that audiences of "workingmen of the most intelligent type" who "asked many shrewd questions" encouraged speakers to avoid jargon, clarify ideas, and address practical considerations.[26]

By 1916, one hundred people's forums met across the country. At Boston's Ford Hall where he regularly spoke, Zueblin found "an eager, restless desire to compass knowledge and human welfare" that surpassed anything else in the city. The forums provided "an intellectual and emotional power-house, sending out currents to vitalize the wireless service of the municipality." The forum movement complemented the initiative and referendum. "If the people are to assume the responsibility of voting upon measures, as well as men," wrote one supporter, "it is obvious that some effective means of public discussion must be devised." Indeed, Herbert Croly feared that without "that thorough ventilation and discussion which tends to inform and illuminate popular opinion," the initiative and referendum became the tools of powerful minorities. The forum movement answered Croly's injunction "to stimulate the liveliest possible political interest over the widest practicable political area."[27]

The forums provided a two-way political education. "We are a press-reading and lecture-hearing people, but our genius for debate has gone long unused," an advocate of "the parliament of the people" explained. "We are a chronic audience, and the *audience habit is death to the creativeness of a people.*" But as people became articulate and learned how to listen, argue, and deliberate, audiences became publics. When people challenged and debated speakers, moreover, a new sort of intellectual began to emerge, one who understood that political knowledge came out of public deliberations. Uniting experts and citizens in cooperative inquiry, the forums pointed the way to a reconciliation of efficiency and democracy and dissolved the specialized language of experts in the medium of public debate.[28]

Democracy as Cooperative Inquiry: The Social Centers Movement

Writing to a trustee of the People's Institute, Howe described the forum movement as something "that we can build in any way we want as a democratic agency for a lot of things." Just as organizers chose the lecturers, and the lecturers led the discussions, civic activists too often expected the public to follow their lead. But in the most important democratic experiment of the Progressive Era, the social centers movement enabled citizens across the United States to meet in public school buildings and determine for themselves the topics for open-ended discussions. Asserting the people's right to use public buildings for their own deliberations, the social centers movement challenged the idea that policy could be entrusted to experts and elites. In linking neighborhood issues to metropolitan and national debates, the movement demonstrated that democratic participation in local settings could provide the foundation for a greater public.[29]

The social centers movement took off in 1907 when civic groups in Rochester, New York, petitioned the Board of Education to open the public schools in the evenings. Arising out of Rochester's active civic culture, including university extension and privately funded forums, the social centers movement embodied what the Board of Education called a faith "in free discussion as a means of forming intelligent opinion." From the beginning, the movement relied on popular initiative. Citizens determined topics and speakers and the board provided funds only on the basis of local petitions and a minimum level of attendance. The board hired activist Edward Ward, an admirer of Addams and Dewey, to administer the program. But neighborhood civic clubs ran the actual forums. The civic clubs embraced the tasks of becoming "well informed upon the economic, industrial and political questions of today" and cultivating "the powers of clear thinking and good expression by means of debates, essays, orations, public readings and discussions."

In Rochester's social centers, the public became a force capable of counteracting corruption and enriching political debate. "If every member of the common council and every other public servant had frequently such opportunities as this to come before the people whom he is supposed to represent, and discuss with them the things in which he is supposed to represent them," an alderman confessed at one meeting, "it would mean that we would have a better representation of the people's interest and a more intelligent government." Over the course of 1909, three hundred meetings occurred across the city. In a single week in 1910, Rochesterians met to discuss a range of issues from economic conditions and social organization to health, art, and prohibition.

Fearing the open debate that made backroom deals difficult, Rochester's power brokers turned against the social centers and shut them down in 1911. Charging the social centers with having an undue "influence" on "the ignorant and unthinking," the city's political machine found the pretext for shutting off public funds and closing the schools in an inflammatory speech by a radical professor. Rochesterians protested to no avail, but the idea of "small parliaments which created civic intelligence" nevertheless caught on nationally. In 1909, New York's governor Charles Evans Hughes lauded social center activists for "buttressing the foundations of democracy." Others, including Zueblin and Steffens, came to witness Rochester's experiment and spread it to more than one hundred cities by 1912.

Ward left Rochester in 1910 for the University of Wisconsin, where he linked social centers to university extension. Senator Robert La Follette of Wisconsin believed that the social centers movement "would unquestionably result in the establishment of a foundation of intelligent democracy," making "civic progress not only rapid, but conservative and sure." In the presidential campaign of 1912, Wilson lauded the movement for regenerating "the constructive and creative genius of the American people," while Roosevelt endorsed social centers as "the Senate of the People." In 1915, Ward joined the Wilson administration to promote the movement from within the Federal Bureau of Education.

As the movement spread across the country, social centers activists used their practical experience to recast political thought. The ideal of community associated with the New England town, of organic, unconscious social solidarity leading to consensus, did not work in the modern city where democracy could only arise from conscious and contentious interaction that produced the skills of public judgment. Public judgment relied upon debate and deliberation to produce a contingent knowledge that, while providing a basis for immediate decision and action, remained open to ongoing challenge.

Although respect and civility remained crucial to the success of the social centers, tolerance for the opinions of others mattered less than the development of better, more public opinions through vigorous debate. Simultaneously conservative and radical, public judgment promoted "cautious, all-considering procedure . . . and the prevention of hasty and impulsive action." But it also put every issue up for discussion, allowing nothing to be considered permanently settled. In requiring justification and informed consent for every decision, public judgment rejected dogma for cooperative inquiry and deliberation.

The most important thinker to grapple with the social centers experience, Radcliffe-trained Mary Parker Follett published a dull work of mainstream political science in 1896. Arguing that "the consolidation of power has been an inevitable development," Follett recommended the merging of the executive and legislative branches as the key to a more efficient government. But in 1908, as a member of the Women's Municipal League, Follett began organizing social centers in Boston. The experience transformed her personally and intellectually. She discovered in Boston's social centers a new faith in people's ability to deliberate intelligently. She also experienced the excitement of public interaction. "My gospel is not for a moment of citizenship as mere duty," she wrote in this new vein. "We must bring to politics passion and joy."

The social centers experience led Follett to reject a liberal conception of politics that treated government as a necessary evil to protect private interests. She embraced instead the republican emphasis on civic virtue as essential to political order and the fulfillment of human potential. Active and articulate, passionate and engaged, the citizen represented democracy's most challenging and inspiring ideal. Follett joined other Progressive Era thinkers in believing that people made up their minds—and developed their characters—only in interaction with others. In social centers, this intersubjectivity took the form of argument and deliberation, an "experiment in cooperation." Follett added to the widely shared belief in intersubjectivity, her own idea of interpenetration, whereby citizens did not so much compromise their opinions as release them into an ongoing debate that preserved and transformed them. Through interpenetration, differences were "not annihilated, nor absorbed" but "integrated" into a higher synthesis.[30]

But like other civic activists, Follett understood that the skills of debate and deliberation must be cultivated. She thought the city neighborhood provided the ideal starting point because its diversity provided the "stimulus and the bracing effect of many different experiences and ideals." In creating occasions for cooperative inquiry, the neighborhood created similar possibilities for the polity as a whole if local deliberations could be connected to debates at the metropolitan and national levels. Without concern for public affairs and the public good outside the neighborhood, even neighborhood politics degenerated into selfishness. Judgments formed at the local level had to be integrated into a higher unity rather than ignored or negated. A new conception of federalism, beginning at the ward level as Thomas Jefferson once urged, made possible both autonomy at the local level and unity at the national level.[31]

Follett joined others who saw that the growing power of the state made democratic participation all the more essential. A benevolent and paternalistic government, Croly cautioned, "will do nothing to make the people worthy." It can only produce "popular servility or organized popular resistance or both." The public had "to think as well as to act for itself." Attitudes that originated when "the popular will had no effective means of expression," Croly continued, must be cast aside. The rise of mass media provided "abundant opportunities of communication and consultation." If we turned our attention from administrative efficiency to the cultivation of citizenship, Croly concluded, we would recognize that direct democracy "has again become not merely possible, but natural and appropriate."[32]

Mass Media and the Socialization of Intelligence

The emergence of the mass media created new possibilities for developing a democratic public opinion and a democratic culture. The mass media captured a wide range of ideas and experiences, sociologist Charles Cooley argued, and spread them across barriers of space, time, and class. The mass media also made it possible "for society to be organized more and more on the higher faculties of man, on intelligence and sympathy, rather than on authority, caste, and routine. They mean freedom, outlook, indefinite possibility." Cooley could not imagine any "broad and rich growth of democracy without a corresponding development of popular art."[33]

Dewey shared Cooley's interest in the democratic potential of mass communications. In 1892, Dewey joined financial reporter Franklin Ford and muckraking journalist (and future urban sociologist) Robert Park in a venture called *Thought News*. Ford explained that in substituting factual reporting and sober analysis for opinion and bombast, *Thought News* would "out sensationalize" the mainstream press by showing that the "social fact is the sensational thing." The newspaper, Park added, would be "able and willing to report political and social events with the same accuracy that it was then reporting the stock market and ball games." Dewey saw *Thought News* as an experiment in the socialization of intelligence, developing in each individual an understanding of society and his or her role in it. In assuring that knowledge "extends and distributes itself to all so that it becomes the Common-wealth," Dewey wrote, we democratized competence. If we failed to socialize intelligence, he concluded, the "dead weight of intrenched class interest" ruled and "democracy is still untried."[34]

The *Thought News* experiment collapsed, however, and the spread of sensational journalism tempered enthusiasm for the democratic potential of mass communications. In substituting manipulation and suggestion for debate and deliberation, sensational journalism tarred all the mass media with the specter of emotionalism, impulsiveness, and the mob mind. The "more rapid and multitudinous flow of personal images, sentiments and impulses," Cooley concluded, produced "an over-excitation which weakens or breaks down character."[35]

Theorists of mass communications also found little to praise in the popular culture emanating from the mass media. Although he tried not to dismiss the "poor taste of the masses," Cooley could only see "superficial thought and feeling in the cheap press, moving pictures, radio and the like." Park's dismissal of popular culture derived from a distinction between "expressive" and "referential" communications. Expressive communications conveyed emotions, sentiments, and unexamined attitudes, while the referential delivered ideas and facts. Choosing the rational public over the emotional crowd, Park saw in the mass media "demoralizing" forces, "subversive" cultural influences, and sources of "social disorganization."[36]

In neglecting the world of ragtime and jazz, of Charlie Chaplin and Mary Pickford, the theorists of mass communications missed how radio and the movies allowed marginalized groups to acquire a national voice that served as a foundation for civic inclusion. Breaking with the theorists, a small group of civic activists refused to reject popular culture entirely and hoped to redirect the mass media toward civic aims. "I am entirely a socialist when it comes to the municipal ownership and operation of amusement places," John Collier of the People's Institute proclaimed in 1912. "There is no more reason why moving pictures ... should be the property of commerce to exploit, than there is in the case of the public libraries." We foolishly allowed "irresponsible, money-making agencies" to exploit our need for emotional, aesthetic, and social gratifications.

When developed "merely as a form of entertainment giving the people thrills, with no output of effort on the part of the audience, and with no definite constructive object, then the theater becomes a method of disorganizing the public." But as a part of civic culture, Collier concluded, the movies might "aid the public in carrying out the great primary social function of public discussion."[37]

Having watched the explosive spread of nickelodeons through immigrant and working-class neighborhoods, Collier recognized municipally sponsored movie theaters as a logical extension of the social centers movement. Municipal theaters could become part of a new system of public education "which has learned from commercialized amusement how to be interesting, and which has, as its guiding star, the conception of spontaneous citizenship and of a developing spirit of sociability and of enthusiastic citizenship." Others joined in the call for cities to "supply municipal moving-picture theaters where there may be exhibited films that will have all the attractiveness and none of the dangers" inherent in the "tawdry, cheap moving-picture shows catering to a taste for the sensational."[38]

With the rise of the movies, the mass media irresistibly became a civic issue. Mechanically reproduced commodities, movies reached a mass audience that transcended divisions of class and region, language and political affiliation. By communicating complex political ideas more accessibly and immediately than books, newspapers, or speeches, the movies intensified the presentation of public issues and broadened participation in the formation of public opinion. Undeniably popular but also staking a claim to artistic quality, the movies also challenged the cultural hierarchy of highbrow and lowbrow that helped eclipse the democratic public.[39]

Nickel Madness or the Academy of the Working Man?

Although Thomas Edison's Motion Picture Patents Company attempted to monopolize the industry, control of the early movie industry remained in the hands of hundreds of independent producers and thousands of independent exhibitors. Before the appeal of movies spread up the social scale, working people shaped early movie culture as audiences, subjects, employees, and producers. The shortening of hours and the increase in wages provided time and money, while work that had "none of the joy of responsibility, none of the sense of achievement, only the dull monotony of grinding toil" generated a powerful demand for cheap entertainment. In 1905, two Pittsburgh entrepreneurs opened a storefront theater devoted exclusively to showing movies and coined the term "nickelodeon." By 1907, five thousand nickelodeons operated in cities and towns across the nation. Seven years later, eighteen thousand movie theaters attracted a daily audience of seven million. In some cities, weekly attendance approached twice the total population.[40]

The guardians of genteel culture, ensconced in suburban enclaves, only belatedly noticed the spread of nickelodeons. In 1907, when *Harper's Weekly* warned of the "nickel madness... sweeping the country coast to coast," anxious elites condemned the movies as the latest expression of the mob mind. Beginning with the lurid posters outside the nickelodeon's gaudy architecture, the "nickel delirium" delivered "a psychological blow in the face." Darkened theaters and silent images supposedly relaxed the active part of the mind, opening the subconscious to mass-produced fantasies. "Intense ocular and cerebral weariness," advised a physician, produced "a sort of dazed 'good-for-nothing' feeling." The films themselves offered "a cruel realism which at once dulls the imagination and destroys the illusive romance of the art. They are utterly incapable of intellectual content."[41]

The "biggest attraction of the nickelodeon," *Harper's Weekly* observed in 1913, "is that it makes no demands on the audience." But Harvard professor Hugo Munsterberg offered a more balanced account of the psychology of the movies in 1916. The movies demanded an active mind, Munsterberg explained, that transformed two-dimensional, still images into an experience of depth and motion. Indeed, the power of movies stemmed from their ability to mimic "the laws of the mind." Allowing for the coexistence of a variety of temporal and spatial settings, the movies fused events distant in time and place "in our field of vision, just as they are brought together in our consciousness." The "soul longs for the whole interplay" of experiences in various times and spaces, Munsterberg concluded, and the movies "alone give us our chance for such omnipresence."[42]

Munsterberg argued that the movies heightened mental powers rather than dulled them. In adjusting the space, time, and causation of the outer world to the emotion, memory, and imagination of the inner world, the movies enhanced the mind's capacity to apprehend reality. Munsterberg agreed that the movies served "to intensify the personal feeling of life and to stir the depths of the human mind." The "high degree of suggestibility during those hours in the dark house," he added, "may be taken for granted." But he saw nothing necessarily irrational or pathological about the psychology of movies. If an "enthusiasm for the noble and uplifting, a belief in duty and discipline of the mind, a faith in ideals and eternal values" were made to "permeate the world of the screen," then movie culture might exert "an incomparable power for the remolding and upbuilding of the national soul."[43]

Munsterberg's analysis of the movies as a powerful cultural force pointed to a major source of elite concern. "It seems as if we who have this education, this culture have had something taken from us," a reporter mused in 1913. "I wonder if we will ever get it back." Serving as a "Workingman's Theater" and "the academy of the working man," the nickelodeon became a center of communication and a crucial cultural resource for working people. In inner-city neighborhoods that lacked other public spaces, the nickelodeon served as a community center for working people. As a locale for entertainment, dating, and flirtation and as an informal day-care facility, the nickelodeon particularly expanded working women's access to public life.[44]

To be sure, nickelodeons also offered frivolous excitement. Garish placards, barkers with megaphones, salacious and titillating films gave movies an illicit appeal. Their "twinkling, tungsten facades, the apotheosis of pressed tin and light bulb," seemed "effulgent, wild, and imaginative." But movie culture also contained more constructive possibilities. Working people found their struggles with employers, landlords, politicians, and reformers dramatized on screens. Once hidden or ignored, their hopes and dreams became the visible subjects of public life. "For a mere nickel, the wasted man, whose life hereto has been toil and sleep is kindled with wonder," a reporter explained. "He sees alien people and begins to understand how like they are to him; he sees courage and aspirations and agony and begins to understand himself." Working people saw their enemies vanquished or ridiculed, stirring hopes for broader victories. While women saw their sexuality commodified, they also saw their competence celebrated and their emancipation advanced. The movies, Collier recognized, functioned as "an agent of challenge, of conflict, even of revolution."[45]

The movies recreated the participatory public of the nineteenth-century theater and reconnected popular and political culture. Enjoying its "atmosphere of independence," working people felt "a kind of proprietorship" in the nickelodeon. Early moviegoers commented on the films, conversed with fellow patrons, and even mounted the stage on amateur nights. Intertitles (cards of written dialogue that punctuated silent films, sometimes read aloud and translated by spielers) enticed the illiterate or immigrant into learning the language of political life. Twelve years before women won the vote, a New York City exhibitor made "voting by women in his [seven theater] lobbies a permanent feature of election day performances." Suffragists found theater managers willing to screen such films as *Votes for Women* (1912) or *Eighty Million Women Want –?* (1913). Exhibitors catered to local tastes and allegiances, screening prolabor films like *From Dusk to Dawn* (1913) and *the Jungle* (1914), and allowing Socialists and suffragists to address their audiences, even allowing unionists to solicit funds for striking workers.[46]

Two horrible tragedies and the films made about them revealed the civic potential of the movies. In 1911, a fire in the Triangle Shirtwaist factory killed 146 female garment workers. Finding the doors of their workplace locked, the women either jumped ten stories to their death or succumbed to fire. Within months of the Triangle fire, the antiunion National Association of Manufacturers financed Edison's *The Crime of Carelessness* (1912), blaming the Triangle fire on worker negligence. A second movie, by an independent producer, indicted greedy employers in *The High Road* (1915).[47]

In 1914, John D. Rockefeller's Colorado Fuel and Iron Company demanded that the National Guard clear a tent village of striking miners. With the help of company guards, the National Guardsmen poured gunfire into the village and then set the tents on fire, killing twenty-four men, women, and children in what became known as the Ludlow incident. In its aftermath, the Federal Bureau of Mines, with cooperation from the coal operators, produced *The Miner's Lesson* (1914), blaming the tragedy on worker stupidity. Socialist actor-producer Joseph Weiss's *What Is to Be Done?* (1914) used a fiery female labor organizer to link the Triangle and Ludlow stories in a feature-length treatment of labor exploitation and an employer conspiracy to commit murder. In 1916, William de Mille, son-in-law of Henry George, made *The Blacklist*, a feature-length account of the "state of practical slavery" and the resulting violence at Ludlow.[48]

Much like the partisan press at its best, competing accounts engaged moviegoers in public arguments and encouraged them to form their own opinions. "Far more people today are reached by the moving picture than by the daily press," a reporter observed, "and while we read the newspaper only in parts, the moving picture we see complete." Drawing on muckraking literature, short features and newsreels addressed the issues of the day from a variety of political perspectives. Uncontested, partisan movies amounted to little more than propaganda, reflecting the emerging techniques of mass persuasion and the management of public relations. But taken together, they allowed people to judge for themselves the veracity of conflicting claims. "The crowds not only throng the shows," stated *The Nation*, "they talk about them, on the street corners, in the cars, and over the hoods of baby carriages."[49]

Rather than an opiate of the masses, early movie culture served as an arena of political struggle and public debate. The most popular filmmakers addressed the political concerns and everyday experiences of working people. Charlie Chaplin's two-reel masterpiece, *Easy Street* (1917), one of the most popular films of the period, examined the hard life of the inner-city poor. (The film's title is ironic.) In twenty engaging minutes, the film raised questions about the social gospel, charity organizations, police brutality, street crime, domestic abuse, birth control, prostitution, and drug use. Beginning with a parody of a Protestant mission, with a droning preacher and his distracted flock, the film ends with a reformed "New Mission," more attuned to the people's needs, that looks suspiciously like a nickelodeon. The final title card, "Love Backed by Force, And Forgiveness Sweet, Brings Peace and Order, To Easy Street," served as irresistible language lesson and poetic provocation to further discussion.[50]

The most innovative and influential filmmaker of the period, D. W. Griffith, also made movies that packed a powerful political wallop. Most famous for his *The Birth of a Nation* (1915), a racist account of the Civil War and Reconstruction with the Ku Klux Klan as hero, Griffith also attacked monopoly, sweatshops, hypocritical reformers, and the idle rich in dozens of popular films. His own impoverished background in the South nurtured his racism, but also stimulated his sympathy for the poor and outrage at injustice. In films dramatizing social injustice like *The Lily of the Tenements* (1911), Griffith vowed to make the movies "a moral and educational force." Notwithstanding its racist agenda, *The Birth of a Nation* offered a parable of the corruption of politics by big business in the early twentieth century and a populist call for common (white) people to unite in defense. Featuring quotations from Wilson's historical writings, *The Birth of a Nation* provided a film version of Wilson's New Freedom. Democratic publicist George Creel dreamed of making Griffith a "consulting-architect" on Wilson's 1916 campaign films. *The Birth of a Nation* also generated protest and discussion and prompted African Americans to produce their own movies in response.[51]

Between 1905 and 1917, at least six hundred films addressed struggles for power between working people and employers, landlords, the police, governmental officials, and reformers. Nearly half of these focused on organized labor. Although the profit motive accounts for much of the focus on the working classes, many filmmakers expressed political convictions ranging from radical to conservative. For example, Edison's *The Strike at the Mines* (1911), based on an actual strike in the Pennsylvania coalfields in which company guards and state police attacked strikers, depicted strikers assaulting innocent workers and destroying the property of kindhearted owners.[52]

Independent socialists and labor organizations made their own dramas and newsreels and helped launch a worker film movement. In 1911, the American Federation of Labor produced and distributed *A Martyr to His Cause*, the first worker-produced feature. Better than any other form of communication, a socialist argued in 1912, movies "could drive home . . . the insanity of capitalism and all that it entails." There "is no question but that when these scenes are portrayed on a screen in all their agony and suffering their silence will be louder and more impressive than the most eloquent orator." Worker-made newsreels focused on the daily struggles of working people, "breaking the boycott on news relating to capitalist brutality and oppression" and "making known the facts of the class struggle in this country."[53]

THE NATIONAL BOARD OF REVIEW OF MOTION PICTURES AND THE *MUTUAL* DECISION

The movies themselves became part of the class struggle, as the respectable classes awoke to their power. On December 23, 1908, a public meeting in New York City led to the closing of the city's 550 nickelodeons for violations of public morality. Movie producers, distributors, and exhibitors quickly united to secure an injunction against the closing. The nickelodeons reopened, but with higher license fees and tighter regulations. In order to protect their investment, industry leaders asked the People's Institute of New York City to take the lead in forming a National Board of Censorship in March 1909. Reviewing films and providing a seal of approval for those that passed muster, the National Board of Censorship provided a nationwide, voluntary form of self-censorship for the industry.[54]

A coalition of civic activists, moral reformers, and industry insiders, the National Board of Censorship contained a strange amalgam of interests. The board declared in 1913 that the movies have "become a public power and a moral and cultural influence which must be brought under social control." But social control meant different things to different interests. Moral reformers hoped to eliminate salacious and radical material from the movies and promote morally uplifting films. The leaders of Edison's trust saw the National Board of Censorship as a means to forestall governmental censorship, scour the movies' image, secure a broader audience, and eliminate independent filmmakers. Finally, he National Board of Censorship also included activists who hoped to turn the movies into a force for civic renewal.[55]

John Collier, Frederick Howe, and other members of the People's Institute (the settlement whose forums inspired the social centers movement) helped shift the National Board's emphasis from censorship to civic renewal. As a cofounder (with Charles Sprague Smith) of the National Board, Collier applied the logic of the social centers movement to the movies. The nickelodeon served the "simple instinct of sociability," Collier wrote, and promoted civic engagement through "consciousness of one's own fellow kind, the desire to mix with one's fellows, to interchange views, to compete with them, to realize one's own nature through the reflection that we get from others." Collier committed the organization, renamed the National Board of Review of Motion Pictures after 1915, to "the civic theater movement" and "the development of sundry co-operative methods for the taking over of the theater by the people."[56]

Not everyone shared Collier's enthusiasm for the civic potential of movies. With socialists in Chicago and Los Angeles opening theaters, labor organizations producing feature films, and working-class audiences boycotting antilabor films, some warned that from "the Syndicalist's point of view . . . the movies should be regarded as a blessing, as an aid in the growth of class consciousness." What economist Simon Patten called "the conserving moral agencies" of culture appeared overwhelmed by the movies. Finding library, church, and school darkened on his visit to a New England town, Patten worried about the bright lights and excited activity surrounding the town's nickelodeon. Between commercial amusements and the traditional agencies of cultural uplift, sociologist Edward Ross also saw a battle between "warring sides of human nature—appetite and will, impulse and reason, inclination and ideal."[57]

Activists on the National Board of Review of Motion Pictures knew that poor ventilation and lighting, dangerous overcrowding, inadequate sanitation, salacious films, and live acts obscured the civic potential of nickelodeons. But this only strengthened their determination to wrest the movies from commercial agencies. Condemning the laissez-faire policy that left recreation to "the commercial enterprise which ministers to pleasure in order to drag it into excess because excess is more profitable," Jane Addams and other settlement leaders also called for municipal provision of recreational opportunities. The Russell Sage Foundation agreed that "recreation within the modern city has become a matter of public concern." A study of working women in Pittsburgh confirmed that a reformed nickelodeon offered the "possibility for constructive diversion" and "social expression."[58]

Frederic Howe, who chaired the National Board of Censorship from 1910 to 1915, shared Collier's vision. Although at first alarmed by the rise of the movies, Howe came to embrace their civic potential. The demand for censorship would intensify, Howe predicted, as "the movies begin to portray labor struggles, conditions in mine and factory; when it becomes the daily press of industrial groups or classes, of Socialism, syndicalism, and radical opinion." But Howe resisted the urge to censor. "Shall pictures which honestly and with reasonable accuracy portray any or all of these questions be suppressed, because they deal with unconventional or forbidden topics?" Let the state assume "the right of regulating this most important avenue of expression," Howe warned, and "only the safe and sane, the purely conventional, the uncontroversial film would be produced."[59]

Collier and Howe defended the free flow of information as the best means of securing an intelligent democracy. Rejecting the paternalism that would protect "the youngest and most ignorant" from a form of communication that "made no demand of punctuality, or patience or of intelligence," they saw the civic theater as the best "proof that we have evolved beyond the caste system which had land-locked the thoughts of men since the beginning of history." Much of the board's early activity focused on driving overt sexuality and immorality out of the movies. But after 1914, the National Board became much more proactive, encouraging the production of better-quality films, establishing links between the movies and other civic movements including the city beautiful, promoting closer ties between movie theaters and public libraries, attaching reading rooms to nickelodeons, and securing cheap projectors for schools.[60]

Despite the efforts of the National Board of Review, the demand for censorship intensified. Critics warned that the board "must expect to see its extra-legal and therefore imperfectly performed functions undertaken by duly authorized and legally equipped government agencies." Many cities and states created censorship boards, including one that operated under the auspices of the Industrial Commission of Ohio beginning in 1913. The Mutual Film Corporation challenged the Industrial Commission in federal court, charging that movie censorship constituted a prior restraint of free speech. In 1915, the Supreme Court issued a unanimous decision upholding the legality of movie censorship. Until overturned in 1952, *Mutual Film Corporation v. Industrial Commission of Ohio* (1915) enabled censors to serve not only as "guardians of the public's morality" but also as the "guardian of its social and political thought."[61]

The *Mutual* decision denied the connection between popular and political culture that civic reformers sought to restore. The Supreme Court acknowledged that movies served "many useful purposes as graphic expression of opinion and sentiments, as exponents of policies, as teachers of science and history, as useful, interesting, amusing, educational, and moral." "We may concede the praise," the *Mutual* decision continued, as "all films of a moral, educational or amusing and harmless character shall be passed and approved." But in many films, "a prurient interest may be excited or appealed to," making it "in the interest of public morals and welfare to supervise moving picture exhibition." Describing movies as a form of entertainment like the circus and other "spectacles," the Court insisted that the "argument is wrong or strained which extends the guaranties of free opinion and speech to the multitudinous shows which are advertised on the bill-boards of our cities and towns." The "exhibition of moving pictures is a business, pure and simple," the Court concluded, "originated and conducted for profit, like other spectacles, not to be regarded . . . as part of the press of the country or as organs of public opinion."[62]

The National Board of Review supported Mutual's suit and, after the decision, sought its reversal. The *Mutual* decision, Collier argued, violated the central principle of a democratic society—the "guaranty of freedom in the intercourse of ideas." Warning against a radical breach of the "constitutional guaranties" of free speech and "an unlimited star-chambered censorship of this delicate potent art," Collier hoped the Supreme Court might "fundamentally modify or reverse its decision." Shortly after the *Mutual* decision, the Ohio censors banned the exhibition of *The Strike of Coaldale* (1916). The film, Collier protested, "did not incite to riot, but definitely the contrary. It did not depict crime, it did not even indict a class of society; while showing the haughtiness of capital, it dwelt likewise on the impulsiveness of labor. Its sole offense was that it dramatized the victory of labor and mildly sided with the cause of labor."[63]

The *Mutual* decision emboldened censorship around the country. Censors banned prolabor newsreels, films on tenant farmers, poverty, and school integration, as well as allegedly socialist or pro-Soviet films. The expenses and uncertainties associated with such bans weakened financially strapped independent and labor filmmakers. Even the most powerful filmmaker of the period felt the impact of the new mood. Enraged by the "malignant pygmies" who condemned the racist and populist elements of *The Birth of a Nation*, Griffith resolved to rally the people to his side with his four-hour extravaganza, *Intolerance* (1916). The film's four interweaved stories from different historical periods all depicted greedy men who tyrannized the people. Maintaining Los Angeles's only fully unionized studio during the filming, Griffith felt himself branded a communist.[64]

Griffith's modern story in *Intolerance* featured an "autocratic industrial overlord" and the "vestal virgins of uplift," transparent stand-ins for the movie industry leaders and moral reformers and settlement leaders who protested *The Birth of a Nation*. As sexually frustrated matrons, Griffith's fictional reformers ally with the mill owner's sister, who taps her brother for charitable donations. Denying the people their innocent amusements, the mill owner orders a 10 percent wage cut to finance his sister's charities. An intertitle expressed the workers' rage: "They squeeze the money out of us and use it to advertise themselves by reforming us." A violent strike follows. In sprawling scenes modeled on the 1912 strike in Lawrence, Massachusetts, the mill owner instructs his gun-toting private police to "clear the yard."[65]

The National Board of Review divided in response. The prominent businessmen and moral crusaders who graced the board's executive committee saw little of value in Griffith's *Intolerance*. But board staffers defended it, arguing that the attack on films "which present problems and facts ... which only the people at large have a right to decide upon as to the ethical and moral value" provided the "greatest argument" against censorship. Censorship destroyed the movies' ability to promote "free discussion" of the "vital forces in society." While censors concerned themselves with "morals," staffers concluded, the National Board of Review must concern itself with "art and vision and genius and enthusiasm."[66]

THE RISE OF HOLLYWOOD AND THE INCORPORATION OF MOVIE CULTURE

In the decade following the American intervention into World War I, the diversity of early movie culture declined. Films on labor conflict continued to flood movie theaters, but in the five years beginning in 1917, less than a quarter of all these films depicted labor positively. In concert with greater censorship, the rise of a consolidated corporate movie industry facilitated the change in tone. Combining production, distribution, and exhibition, Adolph Zukor's Paramount studio took shape during the war and grew to become "the United States Steel Corporation of the motion picture industry." Zukor's rivals built their own integrated studios so that by 1940, eight major corporations—known collectively as Hollywood—controlled 95 percent of the movie industry. Wall Street financiers became essential to the movie industry, financing the construction of theater chains and, in the late 1920s, the shift to sound.[67]

The rise of Hollywood increased the ante, ideologically and financially, for independent filmmakers. Labor filmmakers launched a series of corporate ventures of their own, hoping to turn out a steady stream of films and newsreels covering the workplace and political conflicts. As several labor ventures struggled to find funding and book theaters, some local labor organizations opened their own theaters. Rivaling the technical proficiency of Hollywood films and weaving political messages around melodrama, four major prolabor feature films appeared before record-setting crowds in the 1920s. *The Passaic Textile Strike* (International Workers Aid 1926) combined dramatic acting and documentary footage to reveal the police rather than the strikers as the source of violence and lawlessness. *Labor's Reward* (American Federation of Labor 1925) toured the country with its own lecturer who led postscreening discussions of trade unionism.[68]

But the difficulty of breaking Hollywood's monopoly over showcase urban theaters led to chronic shortages of operating funds for the worker film movement. The reluctance of local censors to pass prolabor films reinforced the refusal of Wall Street financiers to invest in films depicting class conflict. The limited means of working people and their unwillingness to invest in a risky venture closed off another potential source of capital. Between 1918 and 1921, four worker film companies approached the American Federation of Labor (AFL) for financial assistance. Despite the AFL's decade-long concern with antilabor films, AFL president Samuel Gompers and other union leaders feared to associate with the socialists and radicals who launched the companies. In 1921, the AFL convention voted to investigate the creation of a labor studio and chain of theaters to support "the true principles, objects, and activities of organized labor." A year later, the Executive Council vetoed the plan as too expensive.[69]

In November 1927, the Hollywood electricians' union made one final effort to enlist organized labor in the cause of the worker film movement. Writing in the union's journal, the secretary of the International Brotherhood of Electricians argued that fifteen hundred union halls might be cheaply outfitted with movie projectors and screens, providing organized labor with the largest chain of theaters in the country. Profits from distribution and exhibition could be used to finance the production of prolabor films, while a captive market of fifteen hundred theaters would make organized labor a force in the movie industry. But despite early enthusiasm in the labor press, William Green (who replaced Gompers as president of the AFL) and other union leaders refused to divert funds from direct organizing efforts. An older generation of labor leaders who had not been raised on movie culture failed to see how profoundly the new mass media shaped political attitudes.[70]

Even the limited success of the worker film movement prompted more censorship and harassment from federal agencies. But Hollywood provided the more formidable challenge. Offering luxury for the masses in its lavish new theaters, the studios screened stories of upward mobility and cross-class romance, reshaping political attitudes in a period when old allegiances and ideologies had worn thin. Screening out economic and political conflicts, movie culture encouraged acceptance of the individualized pleasures of the emerging consumer culture and spread what one survey called "that insidious disease know as 'sit-itis' alias 'spectatoritis.'" Even labor activists found the air-conditioned, sumptuous picture palaces more alluring than the neighborhood theaters where they might still see prolabor films.[71]

Moviegoers did not suddenly become mindless and passive consumers of movie culture in the 1920s. Neighborhood audiences and the labor press still encouraged different readings of Hollywood productions. But the spread of Hollywood fantasies and the increasing role that images played in political discourse placed movies at the heart of the debate over democratic participation. The proliferation of images lowered barriers to civic participation and stirred up irrational emotions and prejudices. The "moving picture is steadily building up imagery which is then evoked by the words people read in their newspapers," journalist Walter Lippmann explained in 1922. In the movies, "the whole process of observing, describing, reporting, and then imagining, has been accomplished for you."[72]

The movies figured in Lippmann's conception of democratic politics as little more than a distracting circus, a spectacle that kept the masses content while organized experts made the tough decisions. Citizens formed their opinions from "unchallenged pictures in the heads," Lippmann wrote, images gathered without "more trouble than is needed to stay awake." Collier and Howe would have agreed that unexamined images generated a befuddled citizenry, but they argued all the more that a political culture dominated by images intensified the need to develop the skills and habits of debate and deliberation. They also recognized that movie images could be used to engage people in civic debate.[73]

In and of itself, the worker film movement might have done little more than replace one class ideology for another. But in conjunction with competing visions, it encouraged an open-ended debate that pulled people into the political process. When the movies became part of the emerging consumer culture, they produced something of the bland conventionality of which Collier and Howe warned. With the disappearance of "a field of contending interests," Collier wrote of the *Mutual* decision, democratic "minorities would cease to grow to majorities; stagnation or retrogression would be inevitable." In 1926, the executive secretary of the National Board of Review still rejected the impulse to censor as "repugnant to the genius of democracy." But in the wake of the transforming experience of World War I, it carried little weight.[74]

CHAPTER 8

The Public Goes to War but Does Not Come Back

Requiem for a Participatory Democracy

On the eve of the American intervention into World War I, promising experiments in creating a deliberative public raised democratic hopes. Reviewing the latest study of the mob mind in 1915, Walter Weyl, editor of *The New Republic*, admitted that "the crowd-like actions of ignorant and irresponsible constituencies" cast doubts on democracy. But such doubts only "compel us to justify our faith" in "a people capable of clumsily looking out for its own interests in politics." As more and more citizens gained "a measure of political independence and of political skepticism," Weyl concluded, the "'sovereign crowd' is becoming a public."[1]

The emerging faith in a deliberative public did not survive the American intervention into World War I. "Can democracy be efficient?" a civic reformer impatiently asked just weeks after the American declaration of war in April 1917. Are "the democratic masses capable of intelligent self-direction, or must they in self-defense surrender the control of government to the superior ability of the trained and exceptionally gifted few?" Perhaps in "the long run laws cannot be enforced without the convinced support of public opinion," but in the present emergency, what "reason is there for supposing that the mass mind can be permeated by the light of science?" The time had come, he suggested, for "public opinion . . . to humble itself in voluntary subjection to the scientific expert and expert opinion."[2]

Sophisticated techniques of propaganda flourished on all sides in World War I, as the belligerents struggled to maintain popular support for continued slaughter. In the United States, President Woodrow Wilson assigned the leading role in mobilizing public opinion in support of the war to the federal Committee on Public Information (CPI). The CPI promised to inform the public rather than censor or repress dissent. But once caught up in the war spirit, the CPI churned out propaganda and discouraged open debate. Eventually, federal repression of dissent supplemented propaganda in maintaining support for the war. As the passions aroused spilled out across the United States, vigilantes assaulted dissenters and labor radicals as well as ethnic and racial minorities.[3]

In 1919, American cities exploded in violence due to labor conflicts combined with ethnic and racial tensions. With news arriving of revolutionary ferment in Europe and four million American workers engaged in strikes and lockouts, industrialists inflamed the public with dire warnings of foreign radicals while importing black strikebreakers from the South. A red summer of violence against labor radicals and African Americans followed in dozens of cities. Mobs beat and mutilated radicals in New York and Cleveland. In Chicago, gangs terrorized African Americans for thirteen days, killing or injuring scores and burning thousands out of their housing. Nationwide, a series of bomb scares led to mass arrests and deportations of suspected foreign radicals. So recently the site of an emerging democratic public, the cities now appeared as cauldrons of irrational hatreds.[4]

The ease with which propaganda swayed the public and the intolerance and violence it unleashed shattered the faith in public opinion. A 1919 survey of "The Crowd in Action" found the danger of the mob mind "far more pressing than ever before." Even a once-ardent democrat, a director of New York City's most successful civic forum, feared that "society is becoming a veritable babel of gibbering crowds." With "mob outbreaks and riots increasing in number," he lamented, public opinion fell "into a confusion of propagandist tongues," forcing all to "speak as the crowd, think as the crowd, understand as the crowd."[5]

In its effort to win public opinion over to the war effort, the Wilson administration and the CPI enlisted and compromised all the Progressive Era urban experiments in deliberative democracy, from university extensions and social settlements to social centers and movie theaters. None of those civic experiments survived the war intact. The mobilization of public opinion compromised many one-time civic reformers as well. A group known as the "war intellectuals" turned away from a city-based democratic public to court federal power and implement their vision of national planning and international order from above. The war intellectuals gained little, becoming glorified public relations agents for policies determined by the Wilson administration.[6]

After the war, disillusioned war intellectuals argued that the public could not be trusted to act wisely or responsibly. These self-styled realistic democrats blamed the city, with its stresses, strains, and distractions, for the weaknesses of the public. The preservation of democratic forms and civil liberties, the realists insisted, depended upon leaving public affairs to an enlightened elite. Journalist Walter Lippmann, a leading war intellectual and the most influential of the democratic realists, ridiculed the idea of a participatory democracy and recommended the creation of intelligence bureaus, staffed by experts, who would make policy with as little input from the public as possible. Modern urban society, Lippmann wrote, had become "too big, too complex, and too fleeting" for the average citizen to comprehend. Effective knowledge remained "out of reach, out of sight, out of mind" for the majority "whose experience has comprehended no factor in the problem under discussion."[7]

The excesses of wartime propaganda and postwar intolerance also disillusioned philosopher John Dewey. Unless "war can be shown to be the most economical method of securing the results which are desirable with a minimum of undesirable results," Dewey wrote a year before the American intervention, "it marks waste and loss." But like Lippmann, Dewey threw his support behind American intervention into the war, gambling that intellectuals could direct the war effort toward the democratic reconstruction of society. It fell to the young journalist Randolph Bourne, Dewey's former student, to expose his teacher's misplaced hope. Bourne rejected the idea that the "war-technique can be used without trailing along with it the mob-fanaticisms, the injustices and hatreds, that are organically bound up with it."[8]

After the war, a chastened Dewey tried to pick up the pieces of the shattered faith in the democratic public. Dewey accepted Lippmann's account of "the failure of self-governing people to transcend their casual experience and their prejudice, by inventing, creating, and organizing a machinery of knowledge." He believed, however, that such a machinery of knowledge might still be invented. But in the wake of the destruction of the Progressive Era experiments in creating a deliberative public, Dewey left participatory democrats little more than a theoretical approach to the public and its problems. The war cast a long, pessimistic shadow over the prospects for reviving a participatory democracy.[9]

Lippmann also ignored Progressive Era experiments in creating a more deliberative public, but his decision is not surprising. Although a Boston tenement fire in 1908 drew him into social activism while still an undergraduate at Harvard University, Lippmann quickly lost patience with big-city politics. Apprenticed to the urban muckraker Lincoln Steffens, Lippmann learned that the people were no better than the bosses and monopolists. Corruption was endemic in the system, Steffens taught Lippmann, and the grafters faced it more honestly than the reformers. Steffens encouraged Lippmann's growing criticism of the "cult of democracy," the tendency "to assume that the people have all the virtues and then pretend, when they don't exhibit them, that it is somebody else's fault."[10]

Four months work for the Socialist mayor of Schenectady, New York, in 1912 deepened Lippmann's skepticism about urban democracy. Impatient with the "petty vexations" and "distracting details" of practical politics, Lippmann translated his personal frustrations into an indictment of the "great dull mass of people who just don't care." Public apathy and ignorance, more than vested interests, blocked responsible reform. No longer the muckraker or the Socialist eager to arouse the people, he conceded that you "can't build a nation out of Georgia crackers, poverty-stricken negroes, the homeless and helpless of the great cities." Instead, Lippmann decided to shape the thinking of the powerful.[11]

But Dewey's postwar neglect of the prewar experiments is more surprising. His democratic philosophy came out of his encounter with a series of industrial cities, including his birthplace in Burlington, Vermont; his first place of employment in Oil City, Pennsylvania; and his most intellectually formative period in turn-of-the-century Chicago. "Chicago is the place to make you appreciate at every turn the absolute opportunity which chaos affords," he wrote his wife two weeks after arriving in Chicago amid the Pullman strike. Dewey's philosophy reflected his engagement with Chicago's reformers, particularly Jane Addams's Hull House settlement. Dewey's call for "a socialism of the intelligence and of the spirit" also owed much to his encounter with the labor movement's demand for a more participatory role in the life of Chicago.[12]

Dewey's engagement with the city put him at the center of a variety of civic experiments. Aside from sponsoring many forums and lectures at Hull House, Addams became active in Chicago politics, urging the expansion of municipal responsibilities to help her neighbors escape the degraded conditions they suffered as a result of their poverty and the city's inadequate public services. Dewey himself designed the laboratory school at the University of Chicago and provided the philosophical rationale for the social centers movement in arguing that "every public school" might do "the same sort of work that is now done by a settlement." Dewey also understood that democrats could not rely solely on the school. They needed to engage "all the agencies and influences that shape disposition," because "every place in which men habitually meet—shop, club, factory, saloon, church, political caucus—is perforce a school house, even though not so labeled."[13]

In 1905, however, Dewey left the University of Chicago for Columbia University in New York City. He continued to develop his democratic philosophy, reached a wider audience as a public intellectual, and remained intermittently active in politics on a national scale. But his practical engagement with the problems and possibilities of the modern city virtually ended. Like Lippmann, Dewey looked to a national stage for the realization of his ideas. Their quests brought them together at *The New Republic* on the eve of World War I.[14]

The War Intellectuals and *The New Republic*

As Americans debated the appropriate response to the European war that broke out in August 1914, the Progressive Era experiments in deliberative democracy lay ready to help the nation make up its mind. But the influence of Lippmann, Dewey, and the other war intellectuals who supported American intervention came through the pages of *The New Republic*. With a Wall Street financier absorbing the costs, the new journal first appeared three months after Europe went to war. Launched with the political resurrection of Theodore Roosevelt in mind, *The New Republic* nurtured an intelligentsia linked to a policy-making elite rather than the deliberative public.[15]

The original impulse behind *The New Republic* came, ironically, out of the effort to build a democratic public in Progressive Era New York City. Herbert Croly, who later became the chief editor of *The New Republic*, began his career as an architectural critic who embraced the city beautiful as a means of reshaping civic life. Croly hoped that an "inclusive and democratic social ideal" for the entire nation might come out of the intellectual ferment of New York City. Croly's vision attracted cultural radicals like Dewey and Randolph Bourne, eager to reach a wider public. But the war, as Bourne observed, "brought an immense and terrifying inflation to the political sphere." Privileging technique over vision, the war crisis empowered technocrats like Croly's coeditor, Lippmann, who wanted to advise policy-making elites.[16]

In the debate over the war, those who favored intervention long remained in the minority. Into 1916, most Americans opposed intervention. Hoping for a "peace without victory," pacifists urged the United States to remain neutral, forestalling a decisive victory for either side and standing ready to broker a just peace. Progressives saw the war as a distraction from the task of domestic reform. Pacifists and progressives both feared that intervention would strengthen financial and industrial monopoly and open the way for imperial adventures aboard and repression at home. War "is usually identified with reaction at home," argued Frederick Howe, who bridged the two groups, and "checks social legislation."[17]

As Congress approved a doubling of the size of the regular army and a dramatic buildup of naval forces in 1916, antiwar forces secured tax legislation that shifted the burden toward the financial and industrial interests most eager for war. The victory suggested the reform possibilities that intervention might bring. President Wilson was "associating with preparedness many different plans for domestic reorganization," Croly editorialized, "which only yesterday would have been dismissed as centralized paternalism." Even as Wilson campaigned for reelection with the slogan "He kept us out of war," the editors of *The New Republic* moved steadily toward war.[18]

Lippmann led the way. In February 1916, he lashed out against the "vices of the American character, its trust in the magic of words, its collective irresponsibility, its shirking of facts and the harder realities of life." As Lippmann despaired of the public rising to the crisis, he twice met with Wilson, who won him over with a confidential admission that neutrality would be impossible in the face of the expected resumption of submarine warfare after the election. "Now we'll have to face it," Lippmann explained to his colleagues at *The New Republic*. "What we're electing is a war President—not the man who kept us out of war."[19]

Lippmann threw himself into the 1916 presidential campaign, but did not divulge the core reason for his support of Wilson. "We never believed Wilson when he said he would keep us out of war," Lippmann later recalled. "We were convinced we were going to get into the war." Although he increasingly thought about the war in geopolitical terms, Lippmann continued to deploy progressive justifications. When Wilson asked Congress for a declaration of war in April 1917, Lippmann praised Wilson's "Great Decision" as "unmistakably the cause of liberalism and the hope of an enduring peace." Rallying progressives behind the war, Lippmann predicted that the destruction of foreign tyrannies would mean "we shall turn with fresh interest to our own tyrannies—to our Colorado mines, our autocratic steel industries, our sweatshops and our slums."[20]

A similar vision of democratic reconstruction guided Dewey's route to intervention. But as the war in Europe began, Dewey initially warned of the dangers of ideological absolutism. Germany's "talk of Duty, Will and Ultimate Ideas" and Wilson's invocation of "'immutable principles,' waiting ready-made to be fastened upon the situation," distracted attention from a pragmatic analysis of the probable consequences of any action. A democracy that "faces the consequences of its activities and accepts responsibility for them," Dewey argued, must avoid any activity "which disguises its nature to the collective consciousness by appeal to eternal principles . . . of pure idealism."[21]

The need for a pragmatic analysis of consequences applied particularly to the use of force. All action required force, Dewey argued, but force became violence when it undercut the ends for which it was employed. A democratic public engaged in a critical analysis of means and ends, purposes and consequences, must reject undemocratic means as inappropriate, particularly in a war to make the world safe for democracy. As a microcosm of the challenge of cultural, ethnic, and racial pluralism facing the world, the United States could best aid the belligerents not by going to war, Dewey concluded, but by providing a vision of a democratic "future in which freedom and fullness of human companionship is the aim, and intelligent cooperative experimentation the method."[22]

Dewey thus entered the war crisis with an ideal of participatory democracy foremost in mind. Recognizing that "the depth and width of human intercourse is the measure of civilization," he envisioned American foreign policy as opening the door to "the fruitful processes of cooperation in the great experiment of living together." But in the spring of 1917, Dewey lost sight of his ideal. Swayed by Wilson's rhetoric about a "people's war" to make the world safe for democracy, he embraced the potential for top-down reform. Bringing with him many other progressives, socialists, and pacifists who "sensed the possibilities of planning and communal effort," Dewey enlisted in Wilson's war.[23]

Convinced that war held great possibilities for democratic transformation, Dewey chided those who dissented. He criticized pacifists for forfeiting a great opportunity when they "turned so vigorously to opposing entrance into a war which was already all but universal, instead of using their energies to form at a plastic juncture, the conditions and objects of our entrance." Dewey believed war mobilization would underscore the need for intelligent social control. "Failure to recognize the immense impetus to reorganization afforded by this war; failure to recognize the closeness and extent of true international combinations which it necessitates," Dewey charged, "is a stupidity equaled only by the militarist's conception of war as a noble blessing in disguise."[24]

But wishful thinking rather than pragmatic analysis marked Dewey's embrace of war. He dreamed of sweeping away the laissez-faire principles and natural laws of conservative social science in favor of a democratic social science based on "competency of inquiry, discussion, reflection and invention organized to take effect in action in directing affairs." He predicted that Americans would resist the "glamour and impetuous rush of traditional war psychology." But the corporate management of the war effort and the wave of official and unofficial repression that silenced dissent, even at his own university, soon tempered Dewey's optimism. He later admitted that he banked too much on "the community of emotional consciousness generated by the war," which proved "the sandiest of foundations" for democratic reform.[25]

THE WAR FOR THE AMERICAN MIND

Madness enveloped Europe with the outbreak of World War I in August 1914 and during the murderous stalemate that ensued. A desperate quest for the total victory that alone could justify the enormous sacrifice left little time for debate about the costs and benefits of war. But the United States, an ocean away from the fighting, experienced the war first and foremost as an affair of the mind. Having committed themselves during the Progressive Era to a central role for public opinion in political affairs, Americans vigorously debated the issues of preparedness and intervention. But no consensus emerged and antiwar sentiment remained powerful. When Wilson opted for intervention, he also launched a war for the American mind to rally an ideologically and ethnically divided nation behind a distant and brutal conflict. "It is not an army we must shape and train for war," Wilson explained, "it is a nation."[26]

A lifelong educator and political outsider who approached politics as a moralizing evangelist, Wilson exemplified the Progressive Era faith in public opinion. With the crucial exception of its eventual repression of dissent, the Wilson administration relied on the techniques of publicity and persuasion rather than coercion in financing the war, retooling industry, mobilizing labor, and rationing scare goods. "What we had to have was no mere surface unity," the head of the CPI later explained, "but a passionate belief in the justice of America's cause that should weld the people of the United States into one white-hot mass instinct with fraternity, devotion, courage, and deathless determination." Yet, Wilson and his advisers prevented the grassroots, open-ended debate that alone could generate that belief and determination.[27]

An executive agency created to publicize the war, the CPI became a propaganda mill, mobilizing emotions to manufacture consent for Wilson's policies. The war intellectuals hoped to use the patriotic war spirit to promote a new social idealism. But the war technique, Bourne charged, relied upon "coercion from above . . . rather than patriotism from below." The war intellectuals confused education, Bourne continued, the most "malleable" and rationally motived of activities, with "an absolute, coercive social situation." As the war machine kicked into gear, even Dewey admitted that "the appeal is no longer to reason; it is to the event."[28]

Bourne might have added that even education itself took on a coercive edge during the war. The nation's schools became a major focus of the effort to define the meaning of the war. Local school districts ended the teaching of German, imposed loyalty oaths, and banned "seditious" schoolbooks. The Wilson administration developed "war study courses" for the nation's primary and secondary schools. Urging educators to appeal "primarily to the imagination and to the emotions," the Wilson administration provided distorted and one-sided accounts of the conflict. In the nation's colleges and universities, a "War Issues Course" spread cultural stereotypes, hate-filled propaganda, simplified historical accounts, and reactionary political attitudes.[29]

The appointment of the former muckraking journalist George Creel to head the CPI reinforced the relationship between the prewar faith in public opinion and the wartime effort to build support for Wilson's policies. Staffing the agency with prominent muckrakers, Creel adopted the credo of "faith in democracy . . . faith in the fact." Priding himself on the CPI's lack of coercive powers, Creel engaged in "the fight for the *minds* of men, for the 'conquest of their convictions.'" Instructing its speakers to stick to the facts and avoid hate-filled diatribes, the CPI distributed 75 million copies of its thirty pamphlets explaining the aims of the war.[30]

But the CPI soon adopted more aggressive means of persuasion. Following Wilson's injunction to use the mass media to "sell the war to the American public," Creel (a former screenwriter) promised "to bring the motion picture industry into the fullest and most effective contact with the nation's needs." With the help of industry leaders, the CPI made its own newsreels, shorts, and features designed to encourage patriotism, and promoted sensational commercial movies like *The Kaiser: Beast of Berlin* (1918) and *The Prussian Cur* (1918). The CPI also placed illustrated advertisements in mass-circulation magazines urging readers to inform on "the man who spreads pessimistic war stories . . . , cries for peace, or belittles our efforts to win the war." Early in 1918, CPI speakers received instructions to use atrocity stories. Participation in "Four-Minute Singing," the CPI advised, kept patriotic feeling at "white heat."[31]

The CPI substituted an uncritical war spirit for open debate and deliberation. But the Wilson administration made every effort to place a veneer of grass-roots support over policies predetermined in federal agencies. Working through local agents whenever possible, the Wilson administration recognized the social centers movement as a valuable resource. Under the slogan "Every School District a Community Council for National Service," the federal government absorbed the social centers movement and turned it into what a progressive journal called "a new piece of democratic machinery for the conduct of the war."

Eager to win legitimacy for their movement, and feeling that they were in no position to refuse support to the national war effort, social centers activists enlisted in the war for the American mind.[32]

Social centers activists believed that the stress of war required an engaged citizenry, something "much more powerful than a people cowering behind mere external fortifications." But the activists found themselves part of a top-down effort that showed little interest in democratic deliberation. "Educational propaganda necessary for the proper emphasis of war measures essential to victory was prepared in Washington," federal officials explained, and then sent to community councils "where immediate decentralization of the message to be conveyed or of the work to be done took place." The "keynote of efficient decentralization," federal officials instructed, "is promptness and accuracy by the local agents in carrying out the requests from a central source."[33]

The CPI also enlisted settlement houses in its drive for unity, initially endorsing the settlements' policy of securing loyalty through education and the protection of immigrants. But as the war ground on, that policy gave way to an emphasis on patriotism and "100-percent Americanism." The demand for a submissive loyalty produced violence against those out of step with national priorities. German Americans suffered the worst. As for labor, the CPI initially defined its "most important task" as "that of convincing the great mass of workers that our interest in democracy and justice begins at home." But by the end of the war, the CPI secretly bankrolled an effort to keep labor "industrious, patriotic and quiet."[34]

Anti-immigrant and antilabor attitudes reinforced one another. The *New York Times* asserted that labor "agitators are in effect, and perhaps in fact, agents of Germany." The leader of the National Security League associated the immigrant with the "proletarian . . . who is devoid of thrift, industry or any accumulation by reason therefore." The specter of a propertyless, disloyal industrial proletariat fed the vigilante spirit, branding any deviation from a homogenized Americanism as treason.[35]

The war to make the world safe for democracy thus dispensed with democracy at home. The Wilson administration suppressed radical publications and organizations, supported the Espionage and Sedition Acts, and acquiesced in and even fostered vigilante actions. The Espionage and Sedition Acts made virtually all criticism of the war illegal and resulted in more than eleven thousand arrests. Civil libertarians hoped that with the end of the war the Espionage and Sedition Acts would be declared unconstitutional. But in a series of cases in 1919, the Supreme Court upheld both laws. At the end of 1919, Wilson called for the passage of a peacetime sedition act.[36]

From Mastery to Drift

In *Drift and Mastery* (1914), Lippmann argued that an educated elite could replace repression and violence with education and scientific technique and master the process of social change. But in the summer of 1917, as Wilson called for

"Force, Force to the utmost, Force without stint or limit," Dewey chided pacifists for unrealistically opposing a war "which was already all but universal." Embracing war as if succumbing to the inevitable, the war intellectuals fell back on the justification that—in Bourne's words—"only on the craft, in the stream" would they have any chance of "controlling the current forces for liberal purposes." How soon, Bourne concluded, "their 'mastery' becomes 'drift.'"[37]

That same summer, Lippmann left *The New Republic* and headed to Washington as special assistant to the secretary of war, Newton Baker. In the fall of 1917, when Wilson began to draw up peace proposals through a top-secret task force known only as "The Inquiry," he appointed Lippmann director. "Unity of purpose and control" among the Allies, Lippmann reported, was essential "to that general purification of aims which must precede a fine peace." But in October 1917, the Bolsheviks seized power in Russia, sued for a separate peace, and revealed the Allies' secret treaties (dividing the spoils of war) that the Tsar had signed.[38]

To discredit the Bolshevik calls for peace, Wilson promised to repudiate the secret treaties in December 1917. The Inquiry rushed to compile an eight-point document delineating postwar borders. Adding six general principles of his own, Wilson aimed his Fourteen Points address of January 8, 1918, over the heads of state, directly at the peoples of Europe. Calling for a new diplomacy of open covenants, Wilson championed freedom of the seas, removal of economic barriers between nations, a reduction of armaments, a dismantling of empire and ethnic self-determination, and a league of nations to guarantee the peace. The peoples of Europe responded enthusiastically, but their governments remained silent. The Fourteen Points did nothing to change the Allies' territorial ambitions.[39]

Lippmann remained enthusiastic about Wilson's new diplomacy, and in June 1918, he joined the Military Intelligence Branch, a small propaganda unit focused on the German population. Pledging to get "away from propaganda in the sinister sense, and substituting for it a frank campaign of education," Lippmann prepared to explain "as simply and persuasively as possible the unselfish character of the war, the generosity of our aims, and the great hope of mankind which we are trying to realize." But the CPI asserted its authority over the military unit and Wilson declined to take advice from the upstart propagandist.[40]

When Wilson arrived in Europe to head the U.S. peace delegation in December 1918, Lippmann found himself on the outside. Struggling to make sense of the tangle of rumors and innuendos surrounding the conference, he no longer saw propaganda as a positive force and began to formulate his postwar critique of public opinion. The peacemakers' "pathetically limited education," he wrote a few months later, prohibited them from "seeing or understanding the strange world that lay before them." In panic, they exchanged "gossip and frantic exclamation." Every "dinner table, every lobby, almost every special interview, every subordinate delegate, every expert adviser" became a "focus of intrigue and bluster and manufactured rumor."[41]

While Lippmann's hopes for mastery over the postwar world ended in drift, Dewey also drifted as the war went in unexpected directions. In the face of a federal program of propaganda and repression, Dewey confessed that his earlier hopes for rational deliberation appeared "strangely remote and pallid." But into 1918, he still insisted that the war provided opportunities for the democratic reconstruction of society. In "every warring country, there had been the same demand that in time of great national stress production for profit be subordinated to production for use." Industrial reorganization brought a "greater ability on the part of the workers in any particular trade or occupation to control that industry." With workers no longer subject to "external control where they have no interest, no insight into what they are doing, and no social outlook upon the consequences and meaning of what they are doing," Dewey concluded, participatory democracy might thrive.[42]

Even as these more expansive hopes faded, Dewey argued that democratic gains might emerge as the unintended results of an undemocratic war. The hierarchical agencies that directed war mobilization at least demonstrated the potential for social planning. The complexity of large-scale institutions and the invisible webs of interdependence that stretched across the world seemed "too big to be got in hand" until the war "put the immensity of things into a new light." A top-down, centralized war effort might seem an unlikely route to participatory democracy in politics and industry. But by embracing the potential "for human beings to take hold of human affairs and manage them," democrats could advocate a different means of social planning for different ends.[43]

In his critique of the war intellectuals, Bourne both deployed Dewey's pragmatic philosophy and called it into question. Pragmatism treated ideas as tools, useful for analyzing the probable consequences of action. But Dewey's use of "democracy" in defense of the war, Bourne argued, served as "an unanalyzed term, useful as a call to battle, but not an intellectual tool." "Industrial democracy is on the way," Dewey told a reporter, the "rule of the Workmen and the Soldiers will not be confined to Russia." But Bourne countered that Dewey failed to explain how industrial democracy could arise from an alliance of federal bureaucrats and corporate leaders, "the least democratic forces in American life." Part of the trouble, Bourne added, lay in pragmatism itself. In its "unhappy ambiguity ... as to just how values were created," pragmatism subordinated values to technique, the ideal to the actual. "Vision must constantly outshoot technique," Bourne concluded, otherwise thought "becomes an easy rationalization of what is actually going on or what is to happen inevitably tomorrow."[44]

If Dewey's supreme value remained participatory democracy, he lost sight of it. Skeptical of the war intellectuals' desire to be close to the action, Bourne observed "a peculiar congeniality between the war and these men. It is as if the war and they had been waiting for each other." The war exposed their exaggerated faith in the pragmatic ability to adjust, adapt, and redirect all social forces.

"If the war is too strong for you to prevent," Bourne asked the war intellectuals, "how is it going to be weak enough for you to control and mold to your liberal purposes?" Having its own purposes, war would not be guided in democratic directions.[45]

Trusting the Public Too Much or Too Little?

With the end of the war, Lippmann and Dewey began to make sense of their experience. In January 1919, Lippmann returned to the United States, determined to shape public opinion on the peace settlement. In a March essay that marked his return to *The New Republic*, Lippmann warned the Europeans that "if you make a peace that can be maintained only by the bayonet, we shall leave you to the consequences and find our own security in this hemisphere." In May, *The New Republic* made good on Lippmann's threat, urging rejection of the treaty. With a sense of personal betrayal that disguised his own complicity in the failed effort, Lippmann blamed Wilson for not having secured a revision of Allied war aims before intervention (though Lippmann failed to urge this at the time).[46]

The defeat of the treaty did not ease Lippmann's sense that he aided an undertaking that now appeared tainted. Nor did it dampen the antiradical hysteria that gripped the country. Part of a shrinking liberal minority, Lippmann despaired over "the blackest reaction our generation has known." Guilty of "shrinking from intellectual effort," Lippmann wrote, liberals lost to conservatives who "manipulated better" and knew "how to go past the fragile reason of men to their passions." Making liberalism "seem incredibly naive," Wilsonian idealism generated "apathy and disillusionment in the general public, and cynicism in most of my friends."[47]

Resigned to having little influence in the coming decade, Lippmann decided to "use that time well to reexamine our ideas." Modern politics revolved around the interaction between the executive and public opinion, Lippmann argued in 1920, putting a "premium on the manufacture of what is called consent" and making protection of the sources of opinion "the basic problem of democracy." Democracy depended upon a "steady supply of trustworthy and relevant news," something modern journalism—distorted by the hopes and fears of reporters—appeared ill-prepared to provide. But Lippmann thought a better organization of the news might improve the quality of public opinion.[48]

In *Public Opinion* (1922) and *The Phantom Public* (1925), Lippmann's pessimism about democracy deepened as he turned his attention from the press to the public itself. The citizen knew his environment only indirectly, Lippmann argued, relying on a "picture inside his head of the world beyond his reach." We needed such maps of reality, but Lippmann asked "why the picture inside so often misleads men in their dealings with the world outside." Most people lacked access to reliable information, he answered, while censorship, lack of time, the vagaries of language and media, and a fear of disruptive information all added their distortions.[49]

Once we received information, Lippmann continued, a second distortion occurred in our minds. We "tend to perceive that which we have picked out in the form stereotyped for us by our culture." Like maps, these stereotypes were essential. But only the scientifically trained developed the habit of treating stereotypes as tentative hypotheses open to revision. Most people took them for granted. Political leaders recognized the role of stereotypes and used them to manufacture consent. Stereotypes mobilized "the common bond of common feelings, even though those feelings were originally attached to disparate ideas," Lippmann explained, allowing political leaders to bypass rational consent to their policies.[50]

Democratic theorists refused to acknowledge the citizen's limited understanding or shifted the burden of providing reliable information onto the newspaper. But even at their best, newspapers provided news rather than truth. News operated "like the beam of a searchlight that moves restlessly about, bringing one episode and then another out of the darkness into vision," following the whims of a distracted public. Truth arose from disinterested scientific inquiry, bringing "to light the hidden facts" and setting "them into relations with each other." A reliable source of truth would eliminate the need for public debate, which occurred only in the absence of reliable information. Rather than a "remedy for the incompetence of democracy," debate represented democracy's "primary defect."[51]

Biding farewell to virtue, Lippmann rejected the possibility that the challenges of self-government might bring out unsuspected capacities in the minds and characters of citizens. "A political theory based on the expectation of self-denial and sacrifice by the run of men in any community," he wrote, "would not be worth considering." Lippmann dismissed the idea that political arguments helped citizens make up their minds, made them avid seekers of information, and transformed private opinions into a broader conception of the public good. Lippmann expressed little interest in such matters, rejecting the "false ideal" that citizens were "inherently competent."[52]

In *Public Opinion*, Lippmann recommended the creation of intelligence bureaus. Staffed by experts specially trained to compile accurate information undistorted by prejudice or stereotype, the intelligence bureaus would help elected leaders make decisions that citizens could then approve or reject. In *The Phantom Public*, Lippmann went further, urging the public to surrender all its power over substantive decisions, retaining only the remnants of sovereignty on procedural questions. "The public is interested in law, not in the laws," he wrote, "in the method of law, not in the substance." The "public must be put in its place . . . so that each of us may live free of the trampling and the roar of a bewildered herd." To "support the Ins when things are going well; to support the Outs when they seem to be going badly," Lippmann concluded, "is the essence of popular government."[53]

As Dewey rethought his participation in the war, he did not abandon his faith in democracy. Instead, he blamed himself for leading the "gullible throng who swallowed the cant of idealism as a sugar coating for the bitter core of violence and greed." Without mentioning Bourne, he agreed that those who enlisted in the war for democracy should "undertake an unusually searching inquiry into the actual results in their relation to their earlier professions and belief." Dewey did not renounce the combination of idealism and force he saw in the war for democracy. But the war highlighted the need to explain how force might be used in a fashion both democratic and effective.[54]

The international movement to outlaw war provided Dewey the opportunity to develop a means of making the world safe for democracy consistent with its end. Dewey argued that the movement should abandon its reliance on international agreements and international sanctions, which included war. Instead, the movement should encourage democratic publics in each nation to outlaw war. "National plebiscites" would "insure the education and registration of public opinion." Then, each "nation should make offenses against the law of nations crimes under domestic law so that war breeders be tried and punished in their own country." The movement thus served democracy as both means and end. Dewey described his strategy as a revolt against authoritarian politics, "a movement for peace that starts from the peoples themselves, which expresses their will, and demands that the legislators and politicians and the diplomats give effect to the popular will for peace."

The movement to outlaw war reflected Dewey's conviction that he trusted the public too little rather than too much during World War I. In contrast, Lippmann traced the irrational spirit of war to the public and criticized the movement to outlaw war for having too little faith in a reformed system of elite diplomacy. But Dewey thought it unlikely the public would resort to war without elite manipulation. It made all the difference, Dewey argued, "whether you begin with the people and end with the politicians, or begin with the politicians and end by putting something over on the people." Only a democratic movement could abolish the "war system," Dewey concluded, for our foreign policy "is still being determined for us behind out backs and without our knowledge or consent, by a small clique of persons."

A Democrat on the Defensive

Lippmann and Dewey represented a fundamental division among postwar liberals. Convinced that the public responded only to emotional appeals, Lippmann joined those liberals who resolved either to master the new methods of propaganda or limit the role of public opinion and popular participation in politics.

Painfully conscious of his own failings, Dewey joined a smaller group of liberals who concluded that they entrusted too much to strong leaders and failed to win a popular following. This second group resolved to intensify their efforts to promote what Croly now called the "vitality of opinion." Liberals, Croly concluded, should commit to improving public debate through which "a nation learns to know its own mind."[55]

Now a democrat on the defensive, Dewey feared that the wartime manipulation of public opinion would continue, as business, government, and media elites prepared to "make democracy safe for the world by a careful editing and expurgation of the facts." Concerned by "the stirrings of hate and suspicion bred by war," Dewey continued to defend civil liberties and industrial democracy, linking them as "part of the struggle for freedom of mind in industry, freedom to participate in its planning and conduct." But even in these struggles, Dewey lost many of his one-time liberal allies.[56]

Liberal social science, which Dewey once hoped would lead a democratic reconstruction of society, now joined hands with government bureaucracy and corporate philanthropy to discredit the public's capacity for rational deliberation. The military's wartime intelligence tests declared 60 to 70 percent of soldiers mentally deficient, while prominent psychologists pointed to racial amalgamation as the source of cultural degeneration. Freudians warned that the people would fall prey to unconscious and irrational impulses, while behaviorists compared human behavior to that of rats in cages. Others pointed to the existence of an irrational "night mind" that democratic politics brought to the fore.[57]

Although their discipline had been founded to support the democratic polity, political scientists seized on the boss-ridden machine politics of the great cities to indict democracy. Empirical studies described the urban electorate as "indiscriminate and unintelligent," prone to "instinctive, emotional, and habit pattern-responses." "Familiarity with the ruling public," a prominent political scientist wrote, "has bred contempt." The few upon whom civilization depended must "find the good and when we have found it," he concluded, "let us find out how to make up the public mind to accept it. Inform, cajole, bamboozle and seduce in the name of the public good."[58]

The transformation of the social centers and settlement movements into the professions of community organization and social work reflected the skepticism about the city as the hope of democracy. The new professions assumed the existence of "disorganized" neighborhoods that could be organized, if at all, only from the outside. Rather than promote participatory democracy, community organizers and social workers focused on the efficient delivery of professional services to the disorganized. As the social scientific professions looked to national networks to advance their interests, they found the idea that the neighborhood might serve as the basis of a democratic revival absurd. "Most of us now," sociologist Robert Park observed, "are so busy on some minute detail of the common task that we frequently lose sight altogether of the community in which we live." Only the "incompetent" retained any interest in the neighborhood.[59]

Social scientists promoted the view of the city as a rootless mass society in which community bonds ceased to exist and civic life attracted no interest. Most people are engaged in a "restless search for excitement," Park wrote, thereby "seeking to escape a dull world instead of turning back to transform it." In 1919, a veteran of the social centers movement still thought a concerted effort might bring "into the foreground the natural community life which is too buried amidst the strain and stress of city conditions." By 1921, however, he concluded that the provincialism of the neighborhood represented a "hindrance . . . to progress."[60]

Dewey confronted the skepticism about democracy in *Human Nature and Conduct* (1922). Rather than irrational impulses, Dewey argued, habits held the key to the mind of the citizen. He described habits as acquired dispositions, predilections, and aversions, characteristic ways of responding to stimuli. Invariably social, habits redirected impulses into organized, meaningful actions. An impulse to anger became, through habit and social context, "a smoldering sullenness, an annoying interruption, a peevish irritation, a murderous revenge, a blazing indignation."[61]

The prevailing habits of a society shaped individual minds. Thus, if democracy proved dysfunctional, we must blame "the objective conditions in which habits are formed and operate" rather than individual mental deficiencies. The impulses that realists thought incapacitated most people for political participation provided Dewey with the means of making intelligence habitual. Impulses were primary, but habits gave them meaning and direction. Like smoldering sullenness or murderous revenge, "habits are formed under the influence of association with others who have habits already," and provide models of how the impulse might be discharged. The cooperative habits found in science and art, for example, might be used to reconstruct the competitive habits in political and economic life.

In constructing the case for making intelligence habitual, Dewey took on the pessimism of Freudians and behaviorists. Freudians left impulses in an isolated psychic realm untouched by socially conditioned habits. They treated the repression of impulses as the shaky foundation of civilization and sublimation as the rare, creative exception. Dewey described the sublimation of impulses as a normal and conscious process that socially conditioned habits could reinforce, as when "a gust of anger" was "converted into an abiding conviction of social justice." Criticizing the behaviorists for treating impulses as untouched by thought, Dewey described thought as an observable collection of habits that did "all the perceiving, recognizing, imagining, recalling, judging, conceiving, and reasoning that is done." Thoughtfulness, the quintessentially human habit, made possible our flexible, creative responses to new situations. It could also create responsible citizens.

Participatory Democracy and Urban Culture: From Public Opinion to Public Relations

Dewey rejected the realists' explanation for the failure of participatory democracy. But the failure demanded some explanation, and he found it in the work of a writer he deeply respected, Walter Lippmann. Dewey agreed with Lippmann's account of the failures of public judgment in complex urban society. With the growing sophistication of the social sciences, Lippmann and Dewey agreed, the social scientist should step out from behind decision making (judging decisions only afterward) and stand squarely in front of the decision-making process. Turning the social sciences into policy sciences filled the need for "some form of expertness between the private citizen and the vast environment in which he is entangled."[62]

But where Lippmann thought organized intelligence ought to be directed at policy-making elites through intelligence bureaus, Dewey thought it ought to be directed at citizens. Dewey fleshed out his differences with Lippmann in *The Public and Its Problems* (1927). He agreed that the public faced the daunting intellectual problem of understanding a vast, interdependent world and that representative democracy did not equip citizens to make sense of this world. Representative democracy failed to promote "the social and moral aspirations and ideas which underlie the political forms," therefore a participatory democracy needed its own means of preparing citizens. Given a democratic organization of knowledge, Dewey thought it a good bet that the public could make sound judgments about common concerns. Such judgments demanded not individual and innate intelligence but social and embodied intelligence, the sort of intelligence that came with participation in public affairs.[63]

A democratic organization of knowledge might be created in a variety of ways. A radical reform of education, Dewey argued, could promote "a spirit of criticism in dealing with history, politics, and economics" and sharpen public judgment. Social science might also be reformed to be practiced in society rather than on society. Such a social science might publish academic books and journals to "supply and polish tools of inquiry," but ultimately it must "manifest its reality in the daily press." The findings of a democratic social science, Dewey predicted, would "have such an enormous and widespread human bearing that its bare existence would be an irresistible invitation to a presentation of it which would have a direct popular appeal."[64]

But a democratic organization and distribution of knowledge could never be realized without face-to-face discussion and debate. No profundity of social analysis, no amount of newspaper reading, no scheme of education could ever take the place of conversation in a democratic culture. An effective public opinion did not depend on accurate pictures in our heads, as Lippmann would have it. An effective public opinion developed only in the course of arguments about appropriate courses of action. "Vision is a spectator," Dewey wrote, "hearing is a participator. Publication is partial and the public which results is partially informed and formed until the meanings it purveys pass from mouth to mouth."[65]

Everything about Dewey's defense of participatory democracy pointed back to the importance of urban culture and the prewar experiments in creating a deliberative public. The social centers movement, Dewey might have added, showed how public judgment became habitual. University extensions and civic forums, he could have pointed out, encouraged social scientists to engage and learn from popular audiences. Big-city movie theaters provided a model of what Dewey meant when he predicted that democracy "will have its consummation, when free social inquiry is indissolubly wedded to the art of full and moving communication." In linking movie theaters to discussion rooms and branch libraries, Progressive Era reformers—inspired by Dewey's democratic philosophy—had tried to unite vision and hearing in a renewal of civic culture.[66]

Neglecting his more robust understanding of democracy as a social and moral ideal, Dewey remained on the ground Lippmann chose, political philosophy and the formal political apparatus. Only his recognition of the need for a democratic public to root itself in conversations in city neighborhoods forced Dewey to address, with some reluctance, "the question of the practical reformation of social conditions." Dewey pointed to the "many signs" of "an enrichment of the experience of local communities," but he identified no such signs and said nothing about the war's destruction of the prewar experiments. The war transformed the urban social centers and settlement movements into the community organization and social work professions. It also undercut the development of the city-oriented university, compromising academic freedom, civic forums, and university extensions.[67]

The war transformed big-city movie culture most of all. When Creel took charge of the CPI, he enlisted the movie industry in the war effort and, in the process, helped give rise to the Hollywood studio system. Earning government money for making training and propaganda films, Adolph Zukor and the other architects of the studio system used the profits from federal contracts to build their empires. Creel encouraged the production of movies that "presented the wholesome life of America," using the lure of lucrative, CPI-granted licenses to export films to Europe. Creel also tied the movies' status as an "essential" industry to its production of "wholesome" films, imposing an ideological uniformity on the medium.[68]

The end of the war did not end federal intervention into the movie industry. With the wave of labor militance and the anticommunist Red Scare that followed the war, federal agencies continued to monitor Hollywood's output. Beginning in 1918, the federal government compiled secret files on Hollywood personnel suspected of radical sympathies. Movie images of manipulative radicals and corrupt union officials distorted popular perceptions of labor activism and built popular support for government suppression of labor and leftist organizations. Hollywood soon abandoned political themes altogether and produced fantasies of cross-class romance amid the luxurious settings of the city's emerging consumer culture.[69]

Dewey knew that the emerging urban culture of consumption undercut his hopes for a democratic public. "No one knows how much of the frothy excitement of life, of mania for motion, of fretful discontent, of need for artificial stimulation," he wrote, "is the expression of a frantic search for something to fill the void caused by the loosening of the bonds which hold persons together in immediate community of experience." But when Dewey demurred that it was "outside the scope of our discussion to look into the prospects of the reconstruction of face-to-face communities," he allowed Lippmann to have the last word on urban popular culture.[70]

Lippmann thought of consumer culture emanating from the big city as a useful distraction for incompetent citizens. Refusing to hang human dignity "on the one assumption about self-government," he redefined democracy as an interest "in all kinds of things, in order, in rights, in prosperity, in sights and sounds and in not being bored." Incapable of mastering complex issues, the public should leave legislation to "those who are responsibly concerned as agents of the affair." Lippmann did, however, assign one task to the public. While the public should not "obscure or censor private interest," it should "make it sail under its own colors." Citizens might not be able "to judge their merits of the arguments," Lippmann concluded, but public debate should at least "betray the partisan and the advocate."[71]

But as advertisers and public relations experts helped remake the city in the 1920s, urban culture developed in ways that maximized the influence of partisan advocates of private interests. Giant display windows and colorful, brightly lit signs with moving parts and streaming text invaded every public space. "In the city," a critic complained, "every accessible spot where the eye may wander, frantically proclaims the merits of somebody's pickles or Scotch whiskey." Department stores sponsored pageants, musical recitals, art exhibits, and fashion shows, placing themselves at the center of city life, which thus revolved around consumption. Public relations experts staged vast commercial spectacles—such as Chicago's 1926 State Street Illumination Festival—by coordinating the efforts of retailers and developers, transit authorities and park departments, mass media and entertainers, and public utility corporations. Public relations experts turned these commercial spectacles into pseudoevents designed to "compete with other news."[72]

New York City's Edward Bernays virtually invented the profession of public relations. The nephew of Sigmund Freud and inventor of the publicity stunt, Bernays studied Lippmann and the entire literature of crowds and the mob mind, stretching back to Gustave Le Bon. Bernays knew how to manipulate the public mind, in part from his service on the Committee on Public Information. The CPI, he explained, "opened the eyes of the intelligent few in all departments of life to the possibilities of regimenting the public mind." Having discovered "how readily individuals and groups will accept modifications of viewpoints or policies," Bernays wrote, the "manipulators of public opinion" could use "mental cliches and emotional habits of the public to produce mass reaction."[73]

In his postwar work for major corporations, Bernays turned public relations into a major force that shaped and ultimately supplanted public opinion. The public relations counsel, Bernays explained, simply disseminated the truth. To promote the consumption of bacon in the early 1920s, for example, Bernays surveyed physicians on whether they recommended light or hearty breakfasts, without mentioning bacon. He then disseminated their conclusion that "hearty breakfasts are dietetically sound," linking it to a breakfast of bacon and eggs. In 1929, Bernays convinced several young women's rights marchers to light up their Lucky Strike cigarettes as "Torches of Freedom." The stunt broke the taboo on women smoking and opened new markets for his clients. The public relations counsel, Bernays argued, maintained "an intense scrutiny of his actions, avoiding the propagation of unsocial or otherwise harmful movements or ideas." But this did not prevent him from increasing the consumption of cigarettes, which he thought deadly, by linking smoking to the emancipation of women.[74]

As a servant of the corporate economy, the public relations counsel buried the tattered faith in public opinion. By the end of the century, some 40 percent of "news" came from public relations bureaus. Lippmann defined the "basic problem of democracy" as "the protection of its sources of opinion. . . . Without protection against propaganda, without standards of evidence, without criteria of emphasis . . . popular decision is exposed to every prejudice and to infinite exploitation." In his review of *The Phantom Public*, Dewey pointed out that with the rise of public relations, a new "falsification has come in." "Acting for ends of their own," public relations agents "claim to be the agents of a public will . . . and to get the latter as a working force, they bamboozle the public."[75]

Bernays bristled at such criticisms. As "the purveyor of truthful, accurate and verifiable news," the public relations counsel embraced the "duty of the higher strata—the cultivated, the learned, the expert, the intellectual" to "inject moral and spiritual motives into public opinion." But Bernays manipulated rather than empowered the public. While the "basic elements of human nature are fixed," he wrote, the directions "in which these basic elements may be taken by skillful handling are infinite." The public relations counsel appealed "to the instincts and fundamental emotions of the public," taking the "headline and the cartoon," the "compact, vivid simplification of complicated issues," as his model.[76]

In asserting the dignity of the public relations counsel in *Crystallizing Public Opinion* (1923), Bernays claimed that the "highest usefulness" of the profession will come in "the creation of a public conscience." Reviewers expressed more modest hopes. If the fancy new title signaled a change in the "ethics and manners" of the old press agent, wrote one reviewer, "people will be delighted to call him a public relations counsel or sweet little butter cup or anything else he wishes." Describing Bernays's arguments as "the higher hokum," another reviewer reminded readers of the public relations counsel's function "to make people want things they don't need; to perfume the malodorous; to make the weaker appear the better cause." Are we really better off with a public that, while it "no longer tolerates being damned, guilelessly permits itself to be 'bunked'?" he asked. "Is seduction preferable to ravishment?"[77]

PART IV

A Democracy of Consumers

Progressive Era Americans recaptured the nineteenth-century ambition to create an economy and culture based on democratic participation and popular abilities. The struggle for industrial democracy, which lasted into the early 1920s, represented the last stage of that effort.

But by the end of the Progressive Era, a new consumerist conception of democracy challenged the participatory conception. Endorsing the hierarchical corporation and the welfare state as the means of producing and equitably distributing a material abundance for all, advocates of a consumerist democracy expressed little concern for civic responsibility or fear of concentrated power. Rather than a democratization of work and politics, they called for a democratization of leisure and affluence.[1]

In the 1920s, the consumer culture took hold as spending on entertainment, amusement, and recreation skyrocketed. A host of agencies located in New York City's Times Square directed the convergence and capitalization of advertising and show business. Crowded with movie palaces and Broadway theaters, restaurants and hotels, and lined with retailers' display windows, Times Square symbolized the new consumer culture. Giant, multistoried electrical signs created a carnival atmosphere of perpetual motion and excitement. Colorful calling cards of giant corporations, moving signs covering half a city block blinked and wriggled twenty-four hours a day. Seen by a million people a day, the signs made Times Square the most expensive advertising space in the world.[2]

But Times Square troubled even as it delighted. "The dazzle of white lights, the color of electric signs, the alabaster architecture of the moving-picture palaces, the aesthetic appeal of the show window," Lewis Mumford wrote in 1923, provided "the great compensatory" antidote to "the drab perspectives of the industrial city."

But it also represented a "spiritual failure," a city devoted to consumer rather than civic values. The "principal institutions of the American city," Mumford concluded, "are merely distractions that take our eyes off the environment instead of instruments which would help us mold it . . . nearer to humane hopes and desires."[3]

The English critic G. K. Chesterton also found Times Square aesthetically pleasing, but feared it threatened the democratic traditions of the United States. "Citizenship is still an ideal in America," Chesterton wrote, but the "reality of modern capitalism . . . is menacing the ideal with terrors and even splendors that might well stagger the wavering and impressionable modern spirit." He objected particularly to the consumer culture's expropriation of color, glass, and light. Once reserved for the sacred and the heroic, "the new illumination has made people weary of proclaiming great things, by perpetually using it to proclaim small things." No longer used as sources of inspiration, color, glass, and light now merely moved the goods. All "the colors of the rainbow," Chesterton concluded, now "belong to Mr. Bilge."[4]

In capturing the public imagination and crowding out alternative visions, the consumer culture exercised its most decisive power. Major retailers built bigger and bigger department stores, occupying entire city blocks. Some soared more than twenty stories, helping the skyscraper become "a symbol of force and power proclaiming aloud its costliness and solidarity of purpose" through its "massive impressiveness." In New York City, Macy's metamorphosis into "the largest department store" with "the biggest volume in the world" awed the young literary critic Dwight MacDonald. Its owners and managers, MacDonald wrote, "were so cold, so keen, so absolutely sure of themselves, and so utterly wrapt up in business that I felt like a child before them. They were so sure of their values that I began to doubt mine." The "real case" against the consumer culture, Chesterton added, was "not that it is vulgar, but rather that it is not popular." It is being "imposed on us by a mercantile minority and we are merely passive to the suggestion."[5]

Part IV examines the shift from a democracy of participation to a democracy of consumption over the course of the twentieth century, as the growing importance of the private pleasures of consumption eroded civic values and public experience. It begins with an analysis of a fundamental shift in the labor movement, from the drive for industrial democracy to a desire for social security, which helped pave the way for the consumer culture and welfare state. The abandonment of efforts to democratize the corporation and the state freed those institutions to promote consumerism as an alternative vision of democracy. As a top-down elite effort to create a culture of consumption reshaped a bottom-up popular demand for leisure in the middle decades of the century, consumer desire and self-gratification replaced civic engagement and self-development as the central purposes of leisure. In the last half of the twentieth century, a private vision of security and consumer comfort, focused on the single-family home, redirected public resources from cities to suburbs. Disinvestment in the city led to a deterioration of the public realm, while suburban development produced a metropolis rigidly segregated by race and income.

CHAPTER 9

From Economic Democracy to Social Security

The Labor Movement and the Rise of the Welfare/Warfare State

Complementing Progressive Era experiments in deliberative democracy, an antitrust movement and a drive for industrial democracy identified the hierarchical corporation as an obstacle to a participatory democracy. The antitrust movement sought to break up the great corporations and preserve an economy of citizen-proprietors. Industrial democrats urged workers to develop their civic capacities in a struggle to take responsibility for production within the factory.[1] But over the next forty years, a desire for social security replaced the struggle for economic democracy. Under the pressure of two world wars, the Great Depression, and the early cold war, a transformed labor movement supported the rise of the welfare/warfare state. As late as 1946, the president of the Congress of Industrial Organizations, Philip Murray, endorsed "a program for democratic economic planning and for participation by the people in the key decisions of the big corporations." But in the 1950s, the unions abandoned their lingering interest in industrial democracy in favor of collective bargaining over wages and benefits, while the antitrust movement refocused its attention on protecting consumers within the corporate economy.[2]

The heroic victories of the labor movement in the 1930s and 1940s made the United States a more just society and provided a countervailing power to the corporations. But the demand for security represented a diminished aspiration that left much of the labor movement's democratic potential unrealized. Claiming the mantle of nineteenth-century populism, industrial democrats defined workers as citizen-producers determined to democratize the whole of society. By the 1950s, however, organized labor pursued security through contract negotiations with private corporations rather than through politics, neglecting public needs that reached beyond their membership. In abandoning its broader agenda, the labor movement left the expanding welfare/warfare state under the control of political elites and opened itself to the charge of being a special interest. In doing so, organized labor imperiled even the material benefits gained in its heyday, which many workers lost in what Douglas Fraser, president of the United Auto Workers (UAW), called the "one-sided class war" that followed declining corporate profits after 1965.[3]

INDUSTRIAL DEMOCRACY, INDUSTRIAL DISCIPLINE

In the late nineteenth century, working people mounted a spirited challenge to the values of the emerging corporate order. Against the ethic of limited liability, they championed sympathy; against hierarchy, they asserted equality; against competitiveness, they upheld cooperation; against individualism, they practiced solidarity. But in the wake of the federal suppression of the 1894 Pullman strike, labor abandoned the hope for a cooperative commonwealth as unrealistic while the "pure and simple" unionism of the American Federation of Labor (AFL) recast labor's agenda. AFL President Samuel Gompers, John Mitchell of the United Mine Workers, and others organized skilled workers into stable "business" unions. Rationalizing relations with corporate management and joining the corporate-led National Civic Federation, business unions signed no-strike trade agreements in exchange for concessions on wages and hours.[4]

Gompers and the AFL secured wage and hour concessions from corporate employers for many skilled workers. Reviving a moribund movement in the late 1890s, Gompers doubled union membership to more than one million by 1901 and two million by 1904. Such successes helped working people retain broader ambitions. There is "nothing oppressed or submissive" about the American worker, a German economist remarked in 1906. "He carries his head high, walks with a lissom stride, and is as open and cheerful in his expression as any member of the middle class." Skilled workers still shaped local affairs, calling mass meetings, collecting strike funds, and establishing libraries and reading rooms. They also controlled many workplace decisions and enjoyed considerable political power locally. Radical labor leaders struggled for workers' control of industry and expected unions "to educate our class, to prepare it . . . to establish a cooperative industry in place of the wage system, to emancipate the workers from subjugation to the capitalists."[5]

Impatience with the cautious strategy of AFL business unionism spread during the Progressive Era. Organized in 1905 (at what Bill Haywood called the first "continental congress of the working class"), the Industrial Workers of the World (IWW) condemned the "association of misleaders of the workers with the capitalists in the National Civic Federation, where plans are made for the perpetuation of capitalism, and the permanent enslavement of workers through the wage system." When the rank-and-file shoe workers of Lynn, Massachusetts, rejected business unionism in favor of a militant policy of strikes and mass organizing in 1909, the revolt spread to other cities.[6]

The introduction of new machinery and the techniques of scientific management intensified labor's revolt in cities across the nation, pitting industrial democracy against the corporate need for industrial discipline. To wrest control of production from skilled workers, a labor journal charged, scientific managers separated "craft knowledge" from "craft skill" and reduced the labor process to minute instructions whereby "the worker is no longer a craftsman in any sense, but is an animated tool of management." Drawn to the industrial unionism of the IWW, skilled and unskilled workers united in opposition to scientific management. As the introduction of semiskilled machine tenders threatened the status of skilled workers, scientific management also intensified the workers' effort to secure control of production within the factory, a movement known as syndicalism and advocated by the IWW. Syndicalism made little headway, a union official explained to Congress in 1916, "until we heard of scientific management and new methods of production."[7]

As syndicalism gained momentum, the Socialist Party engaged in a parallel program of "agitation, education and organization." Socialists also mobilized support within the AFL against labor's participation in the National Civic Federation. When business leaders sought to extend the principles of scientific management to municipal affairs through the adoption of city manager and commission forms of government, the Socialist Party led the opposition. Committed to enhancing labor's participation in city politics and expanding the public sector, Socialists elected hundreds of officials (including seventy-nine mayors) in more than three hundred cities between 1910 and 1919.[8]

The drive for industrial democracy also led to the creation of new independent unions. The "uprising of the 20,000" in New York City in 1909 began when three-fourths of the city's female garment workers joined a general strike. After three months, victory enabled the newly powerful International Ladies' Garment Workers' Union to negotiate more than three hundred union contracts. Uniting with middle-class allies, the garment workers also demanded the vote. In Chicago, a similar strike led to the creation of the militant Amalgamated Clothing Workers of America.[9]

THE SYNDICALIST MOMENT

Rejecting both business unionism and electoral strategies in favor of direct action in the workplace, syndicalists defined slavery rather than poverty as the great issue of modern society. They argued that through disciplined struggle for control of industry, working people could acquire the independence, self-respect, and civic responsibility once associated with proprietorship. The IWW represented the most powerful American expression of syndicalism, deriving syndicalist principles from practical experience rather than theoretical tracts. "Whenever the workers are organized in the industry, whenever they have a sufficient organization in the industry," an IWW leader explained, "they will have all the government they need right there."[10]

Although the IWW fought most of its battles in the West, its greatest victory came in the industrial city of Lawrence, Massachusetts, against the giant American Woolens Company in 1912. When the Massachusetts legislature cut the maximum work week of women and children from fifty-six to fifty-four hours, employers cut wages for thirty thousand workers. Already in poor health and facing a speedup of production, a group of young Polish women organized a walkout that quickly spread across the city. IWW leaders and other radicals converged on Lawrence, imposing strict discipline on more than twenty thousand strikers, organizing relief, and uniting a dozen nationalities in an infectious spirit of solidarity.[11]

The strikers held out for more than two months, braving both militia attacks and winter cold. Mill owners conspired to plant dynamite across the city and blame the explosions on the strikers, a plan that backfired when the arrest of a company official turned public opinion against the corporation. An attempt to bring in strikebreakers led to the death of an Italian woman, the imposition of martial law, and the arrest of strike leaders. But still the strike held and strikers refrained from violence. When strikers tried to send their starving children to supporters outside the city, the police beat mothers and children indiscriminately. Nationwide sympathy for the strikers helped secure victory as the American Woolens mill granted virtually all the strikers' demands.[12]

The IWW suffered defeats in the industrial cities of Paterson, Akron, and Detroit in 1913, and lost its gains in Lawrence in 1914. But the great Lawrence strike demonstrated the potential power of militant, disciplined effort and made syndicalism a hotly contested issue in the United States. In some ways, the IWW proved an appropriate vehicle for syndicalist hopes. Just as French syndicalism arose from the rapid industrial transformation of an economy of small workshops, the IWW emerged from the clash between small mining and logging operations and predatory, ruthless corporations. Western miners and loggers experienced industrialization not simply as a decline in wages, but as an assault upon their independence and control of the workplace.[13]

But unlike European syndicalists, the IWW celebrated the wandering, rootless male rather than the small proprietor responsible to household and community. Rootlessness gave the IWW an undeniable courage and boldness, but frustrated the effort to build stable democratic unions and cultivate an ethic of civic responsibility. Bill Haywood's vision of a victorious labor movement hinged on a "beneficent, omnipotent executive board" and cadres of "brain workers" and technical experts, not self-governing, decentralized workplaces. "Our task," the *Industrial Worker* editorialized, "is to develop the conscious, intelligent minority to the point where they will be capable of carrying out the imperfectly expressed desires of the toiling millions" who remained "hopelessly stupid and stupidly hopeless."[14]

The IWW found its natural allies in the avant-garde intellectuals of Greenwich Village, who shared their sense of being outcasts, rebels with artistic flair. But syndicalist aspirations also flourished in the established, ostensibly conservative trade unions of the AFL. Skilled workers in the older craft unions recruited unskilled workers and struggled to defend and extend their control of the workplace. In 1911, six craft unions jointly struck the Illinois Central Railroad to resist the introduction of piece rates and scientific management. For four years, the bloody conflict continued until court injunctions and the federal militia finally allowed the corporation to enforce its discipline. Syndicalist actions in basic industry escalated with the economic expansion of the war years beginning in 1914, often without official union sanction.[15]

The rising level of labor conflict pushed the question of industrial democracy to the highest level of politics. Each of the main contenders in the presidential election of 1912 recruited a close adviser sympathetic to the logic of industrial democracy. Louis D. Brandeis, who met Woodrow Wilson in the summer of 1912 and shaped his campaign, criticized corporations for overwhelming local communities and governments and undercutting the civic and moral capacities of their workers. "Can any man really be free who is constantly in danger of becoming dependent for mere subsistence upon somebody and something else than his own exertion and conduct?" Brandeis asked, and concluded that political liberty could not coexist with "industrial slavery."[16]

Herbert Croly, who inspired Theodore Roosevelt's campaign in 1912, also embraced industrial democracy. Croly agreed with conservatives who argued that the welfare state could never "create a class of industrial citizens." A democratic nation, Croly wrote, "cannot provide the mass of the people with the needed opportunity of activity and life merely by distributing among them the wealth owned by the minority." Of course, he continued, the people needed "a larger share of material welfare, but they need most of all an increased opportunity of wholesome and stimulating social labor," the performance of which encouraged "the development of more eager and more responsible human beings." Croly argued that syndicalists only needed to abandon their fascination with violence and focus on the "deliberate education of wage-earners" and the creation of "self-governing communities."[17]

Croly tried to reconcile syndicalism and scientific management. The syndicalist struggle, he argued, needed "the impulse of something more than a class ideal." He found such an impulse in the "general increase in industrial and social efficiency" that would provide "the necessary economic basis of a liberal life." Unfortunately, the efficiencies promised by scientific management met "with the stubborn opposition of the unions," Croly continued, who resisted the "unprecedented severity of shop discipline" and a "regimentation not dissimilar to that required of an army." Croly insisted that workers must be "free to accept or reject" scientific management. But in "proportion as they gain their independence and are made jointly responsible instead of jointly irresponsible for the success of their work," he concluded, "they may be converted to scientific management."[18]

Others joined in Croly's effort to reconcile scientific management with syndicalism. The Taylor Society, the institutional expression of scientific management, gravitated to the political Left after the death of the pioneering efficiency engineer Frederick Winslow Taylor in 1915. Once relying on coercion and intimidation, scientific management came under the direction of a new group of mediators, managers, and consultants, who later played key roles in the New Deal. As passion for social efficiency supplanted the antimonopolist fear of concentrated economic power, Croly and other self-described "progressives" hoped that corporate employers would recognize that only with "alert, intelligent and interested workers" could industry "reach its highest efficiency."[19]

The reconciliation of democracy and efficiency, of syndicalism and scientific management, would not be easy. The logic of scientific management degraded both work and worker. By collecting traditional craft knowledge and redesigning work to separate conception from execution, scientific managers determined the pace and character of labor by controlling the decisions made in the course of work. Substituting unskilled for skilled labor, scientific management threatened to make every worker, as Gompers put it, "merely a cog or a nut or a pin in a big machine." For a time, however, experiments in workers' councils and corporate parliaments, shop delegates and profit sharing made the marriage of syndicalism and scientific management seem plausible.[20]

From the New Freedom to the New Nationalism: War and the Triumph of the Corporate State

Syndicalism represented only one part of the debate over economic democracy in the early twentieth century. The antitrust question focused on the civic consequences of concentrated economic power. But an alternative to antitrust developed during the presidency of Theodore Roosevelt. Rather than break up the great corporations, Roosevelt prodded Congress to create a Bureau of Corporations that used publicity to regulate corporations in the public interest. In concert with corporate leaders in the National Civic Federation, Roosevelt understood regulation as part of a welfare state that balanced the interests of corporations and consumers. In his 1912 campaign, Roosevelt called for a "New Nationalism" and made an even stronger commitment to curbing the power of the great corporations. The corporate form of organization, Roosevelt proclaimed, must be made "subject to the general right of the community to regulate its use to whatever degree the public welfare may require it."[21]

When Roosevelt failed to secure the Republican Party's nomination in 1912, he stayed in the race atop the Progressive Party's ticket. Stressing the need for a powerful state to make corporations socially responsible, Roosevelt ridiculed the idea of restoring a competitive economy by breaking up the trusts. Antitrusters tried "to remedy by more individualism the concentration that was the inevitable result of the already existing individualism," Roosevelt argued, an effort as plausible as unscrambling eggs. In turn, Wilson dismissed Roosevelt's New Nationalism as a paternalistic program that legalized monopoly and made the people wards of a "new and all-conquering combination between money and government."[22]

As the election approached, Wilson offered his own critique of the civic consequences of concentrated economic power. Calling for "the New Freedom," Wilson warned of corporations "vastly more centralized than the political organization of the country itself" and playing a greater role than government in "the lives and fortunes of entire communities." But Wilson saw no reason to oppose corporate power when it arose from superior efficiency rather than "illicit competition." "I am for big business," he proclaimed, "and I am against the trusts." Wilson proposed to halt the growth of monopoly by outlawing price fixing, exclusive control of raw materials, and other forms of cutthroat competition.[23]

As president, Wilson won a series of legislative victories in 1913 that reduced the tariff, initiated an income tax, and created the Federal Reserve System. But Wilson did little to curb corporate power. The passage of the Clayton Anti-Trust Act in 1914 confirmed Wilson's limited conception of economic democracy. The Clayton Act appeared to deliver on the New Freedom's promise to outlaw illicit forms of competition, but the law proved too vague and too weak in its provisions for criminal penalties for antitrust violators and remained silent on the social responsibilities of corporate enterprise. The Clayton Act, a senator charged, resembled "a tabby cat with soft gums, a plaintive mew, and an anaemic appearance." Nor did the Clayton Act, hailed by Gompers as "labor's Magna Carta," give the labor movement the stronger protections it wanted. The law appeared to exempt labor unions from antitrust prosecution and forbid court injunctions against strikes, but the courts' subsequent interpretations of the law proved otherwise.[24]

Legislative disappointments and economic developments pushed Wilson toward Roosevelt's new nationalist vision. By the time of its passage, Wilson already believed that the Clayton Act could not restore a competitive economy. Gratified by the business community's acceptance of tariff and banking reform and alarmed by the economic downturn that began at the end of 1913, Wilson moved toward a regulatory policy. Taking Roosevelt's Bureau of Corporations as their model, corporate leaders drafted the law creating the Federal Trade Commission (FTC), signed by Wilson in September 1914. The head of U.S. Steel told Congress in 1911 that corporate leaders desired a "responsible governmental authority" that might tell them "what we have the right to do and what prices we have the right to charge," while shielding them "from danger, trouble, and criticism by the public." As Wilson's secretary of commerce later explained, the FTC acted as "a counselor and friend to the business world" rather than "a policeman to wield a club over the head of the business community."[25]

The outbreak of European war in August 1914 also pushed Wilson toward Roosevelt's new nationalist vision. A powerful national state, in alliance with corporate interests, could promote social order at home and project American power abroad. "Business concerns which have the largest means at their disposal," President Roosevelt remarked in 1901, insured our success "in the strife for commercial supremacy among the nations of the world." Yet, corporate expansion offered only a means to a civic (and martial) end for Roosevelt. "No amount of commercial prosperity," he argued, "can supply the lack of the heroic virtues" found in war. All the "great masterful races have been fighting races," Roosevelt concluded, the "futile sentimentalists of the international arbitration type" could only produce "a flabby, timid type of character which eats away at the great fighting qualities of our race."[26]

Preferring to speak softly rather than carry a big stick, the preachy Wilson seemed unlikely to realize Roosevelt's dream of martial order at home and aggressive expansion abroad. Where Roosevelt reveled in the spilling of blood and territorial acquisition, Wilson defended his interventions in South America as an effort to teach those erring republics to elect good men. Yet the differences between the warrior and the priest were not that great. A defense of "civilization" overlay Roosevelt's bellicose combination of racial superiority and capitalist expansion, while Wilson's schoolmaster's moralism covered a hardheaded calculation of national self-interest. They both saw the need to project American power abroad. "Our domestic markets will no longer suffice," Wilson argued during the campaign of 1912. "We need foreign markets."[27]

In preparing the United States for international leadership, Wilson abandoned his laissez-faire and antitrust principles and pursued voluntary cooperation between representatives of private and public interests. As part of the drive for preparedness, Congress created the Council of National Defense in August 1916 to foster harmonious industrial "relations which will render possible in time of need the immediate concentration and utilization of the resources of the nation." After the declaration of war, Wilson asked Congress to create the War Industries Board that, like other federal agencies that coordinated war production, cajoled rather than coerced. Established under the direction of Wall Street financier Bernard Baruch in the spring of 1918, the War Industries Board eased public concerns about war profiteering and forestalled more radical measures. It also strengthened the partnership between corporate leaders and federal officials by relaxing the antitrust laws and encouraging coordination rather than competition among firms.[28]

Baruch's vision of a powerful corporate state that served business interests and forestalled radical challenges to corporate power meshed with the aspirations of farsighted corporate leaders. He shared with corporate leaders the recognition of "the tremendous advantages, both to themselves and to the general public, of combination, of cooperation and common action, with their natural competitors" that a corporate state could legitimize. Acknowledging the corporate capacity for "carrying out purposes of greatest public disadvantage," Baruch promised "strict Government supervision" to "increase production, eliminate waste ... promote efficiency in operation, and thus reduce costs to the ultimate consumer." His policies, nevertheless, led to wartime profits as high as 60 percent. Setting prices high enough to stimulate production in the least-efficient firms, the War Industries Board assured efficient firms disproportionate profits. "We are all," a steel executive admitted, "making more money out of this war than the average human being ought to."[29]

Labor's War

The war provided opportunities for labor as well. Syndicalist agitation began in a period of high unemployment, but with the coming of European war orders, labor's position improved. Beginning in the munitions industries in the summer of 1915, a wave of strikes for the eight-hour day and workplace control swept through cities over the next seven years. Workers' control of production became the watchword of a labor movement that more than doubled in size between 1910 and 1920. Mine and railway workers officially endorsed the nationalization of their respective industries. Machinists demanded "collective participation of the workers in the control of industry" and the "co-operative ownership and democratic management of industry."[30]

As long as unemployment remained low, federal officials on the War Labor Board and the President's Mediation Commission helped workers win union recognition and wage hikes. Consequently, no one proved a more patriotic defender of Wilson's war than Gompers. Long advocating a policy of voluntarism for labor, Gompers believed that only the economic power of an independent labor movement could secure permanent gains. But federal mediation encouraged Gompers to abandon voluntarism and enlist in the war for democracy. Rank-and-file workers, however, did not entrust their future to the paternalistic state. Despite the AFL's no-strike pledge, more than six thousand wartime strikes reinforced labor's demands.[31]

The strains of war, however, endangered labor's gains and venerable civil liberties alike. The "world must be made safe for democracy," Wilson explained in his war address in April 1917. But his private anxieties focused on a different prospect. "To fight you must be brutal and ruthless," he told a reporter on the day before his war address, "and the spirit of ruthless brutality will enter into the very fibre of our national life." Wilson doubted whether even the Constitution would survive the contest in which manpower would be conscripted, public opinion regimented, and dissent repressed. At Wilson's urging, Congress passed the Espionage Act of June 1917 to provide federal authorities with the power to fine and imprison opponents of the war and prohibit their use of the mails. When the Socialist Party urged "vigorous resistance" to conscription and censorship, Wilson's postmaster general banned from the mails Socialist and IWW publications or any others that "impugn the motives of the government and thus encourage insubordination."[32]

Federal repression and an atmosphere of intolerance smashed the radical wing of the labor movement. The IWW's aggressive organizing campaigns in the West generated an escalating level of violence that included the beating and murder of labor leaders. Wilson's Justice Department raided IWW offices and arrested its leaders in the fall of 1917. The Sedition Act of May 1918 strengthened the Espionage Act, outlawing criticism of the government and providing wide latitude for federal attorneys. More than eleven thousand Americans, many of them labor leaders, suffered arrest in 1918 for criticizing the government or the war. Eugene Debs received a sentence of ten years for a "treasonous" speech that declared it had become "extremely dangerous to exercise the right of free speech in a country fighting to make democracy safe for the world."[33]

But moderate labor organizations flourished during the war and turned militant in the postwar period. Seattle's general strike of 1919 exemplified the growing self-confidence of working people. *The Nation* called the strike the "most extraordinary phenomenon of the present time" and "the most alluring in its possibilities of ultimate good." "Labor will not only SHUT DOWN the industries," strike leaders announced, "but Labor will REOPEN, under the management of the appropriate trades, such activities as are needed to preserve public health and public peace." For several weeks, working people ran the city, serving thirty thousand meals a day and maintaining basic services.[34]

Nearly one in four workers, four million in total, went on strike in 1919. Working people believed they had earned the government's goodwill and support. But in the absence of war contracts, President Wilson had little leverage over corporate leaders. As strikes multiplied, antiradical hysteria escalated, and public opinion turned against the strikers, Wilson's commitment also waned. The great steel strike in the fall of 1919, which convulsed Chicago, Gary, Indiana, and cities and towns across the nation, provided a showdown over economic democracy. The steel industry, the foundation of the mass-production economy, aggressively mechanized during the war, undercutting the power of skilled labor. The remaining craft unions tried to hold together an unskilled and ethnically balkanized labor force in a last-ditch effort to maintain some semblance of workers' control. "We have established democracy in politics," Gompers explained, "now we must establish democracy in industry."[35]

With the war over and federal power in abeyance, the Industrial Conference that Wilson convened failed to even address the strike. Organized labor, determined to secure union recognition, stood alone in all-out combat with organized capital, determined to preserve managerial control. The strikers sensed their weakness. "The whole industrial world is in chaos," a syndicalist flyer put it, "and it is up to the Industrial Kings of America to grant their employees industrial democracy." The industrial kings, of course, granted no such thing, refusing even to meet with the union. U.S. Steel chairman Elbert Gary ignored Wilson's pleas to negotiate a strike settlement. "Our corporation and subsidiaries, although they do not combat labor unions as such," Gary explained, "decline to discuss business with them."[36]

The steel strike provided a test case for labor's ability to organize the emerging mass-production economy. While labor organizers tried to overcome divisions of ethnicity and skill, employers produced handbills warning of immigrants poised to take skilled jobs from strikers, hired detectives to stir up suspicions between ethnic groups, and paraded thousands of African American strikebreakers through the streets of steelmaking cities. In control of the press, the steelmakers turned public opinion against the strikers and secured the support of local and federal troops who clubbed strikers and broke up meetings.[37]

As the steel strikers headed for decisive defeat in January 1920, Attorney General A. Mitchell Palmer rounded up thousands of suspected radicals, roughing up and deporting hundreds. Although labor militancy continued into 1922, a sharp depression beginning in 1920 led to universal wage cuts and near 20 percent unemployment by the following summer. Sweeping federal injunctions under the Sherman Anti-Trust Act prohibited strikers from meeting and picketing, issuing public statements, and spending union funds. By 1924, conservative business unionists purged radicals and sought accommodation with employers.[38]

From Welfare Capitalism to Moral Capitalism

Corporate progressives still wanted an accommodation with labor. They hoped to establish stable labor relations through corporate initiatives, curtailing the role of the state and the union. Syndicalism appealed most strongly to skilled craft workers for whom the labor question remained a moral and civic issue. The unskilled immigrant factory workers who lacked the economic experiences and political ideals on which industrial democracy was built expressed a powerful interest in security. But the wartime strikes revealed the potential of fusing these two aspirations, of skilled workers for control and unskilled workers for security, in militant opposition to management autocracy. In 1920, the Amalgamated Clothing Workers, a union of unskilled immigrants, claimed the "responsibility to establish order in the industry in the place of the chaos created by the employers when they had things their own way."[39]

In the 1920s, corporate progressives provided the appearance of workers' participation in management while promoting a welfare capitalism that promised security. While scientific management continued to maximize management prerogatives, company unions and employee representative schemes, stock options and life insurance plans, lunchrooms and ball teams presented management's kinder face. By 1928, nearly six million employees enrolled in life insurance plans, almost four million in pension plans. Nearly one million workers owned stock in their firms. Workers' councils and company unions operated in four hundred firms. Support for social and religious institutions, parks, and playgrounds presented the corporation as a more appropriate guardian of public welfare than government.[40]

Corporate largess depended upon the success of scientific management. The effort to "make employment more secure, to pay fair wages," Swift & Company explained in 1923, depended upon "avoiding waste" and "improving the whole economic machine." Hoping to secure union recognition, labor leaders agreed that unions should "increasingly concern themselves to see that management policies are efficient." But management did not need union support, relying instead on techniques of personnel management and industrial psychology pioneered during the war. The Hawthorne experiments at the Western Electric plant outside Chicago showed how the creation and manipulation of work groups and conducting individual interviews to "find out what the worker thinks" could improve productivity and intensify supervision while defusing complaints about authoritarian management.[41]

As secretary of commerce in the 1920s, Herbert Hoover built a new associative state on a foundation of corporate benevolence. The wartime relaxation of antitrust laws continued as Hoover encouraged firms to cooperate in order to avoid "destructive" competition. Building on the closer communication within industry and between industry and government that began during the war, the associative state offered scientific management and social engineering as the voluntary means toward social harmony, economic productivity, and a humane industrial order. Fearful of government coercion, Hoover believed government-sponsored conferences, inquiries, and expert committees could produce new industrial leaders, more flexible and responsive than government bureaucrats but just as dedicated to public service and efficiency.[42]

Hoover saw the Department of Commerce as the government bureaucracy to end all bureaucracies, nurturing progressive leaders in private industry who would make the associative state unnecessary. The Department of Commerce provided public assistance to the "constructive" associations of a new, enlightened capitalism committed to "high public purposes." It subsidized shipping and air transport through the postal system; paid for federal highways to streamline the movement of goods; handed the public airways over to commercial, profit-oriented broadcasters; created specialized bureaus to promote business development; and spent lavishly on market studies, census investigations, and social surveys.[43]

The progressive scientific managers who restructured industrial production stood at the intersection of corporate benevolence and the associative state. In the 1920s, the Taylor Society became the meeting ground of progressive engineers and a group of powerful, consumption-oriented interests from department stores and appliance manufactures to real estate developers and investment bankers. Unlike the older industrial corporations scheming to prop up prices through artificial scarcity, progressive Taylorite Morris Cooke explained, the newer consumption-oriented corporations believed that "in itself any increase in the production of essential commodities is a desirable social end." Building an alliance with trade unionists willing to embrace scientific management, the Taylor Society advocated a democratic integration of labor and management in a constitutional order that resembled syndicalism. Scientifically determined production codes would be formulated and agreed to by labor and management.[44]

Cooke envisioned a future of expanding production and mild redistribution aimed at security and consumption, all sanctioned and promoted by the state with organized labor as a junior partner. "The interests of society—including those of the workers—suggest some measure of collective bargaining," Cooke explained in 1928. "Effective collective bargaining implies the organization of the workers on a basis extensive enough—say nation-wide—as to make this bargaining power effective." The integration of labor organizations into industrial governance would end violent conflicts, making the rise of responsible unionism "a deep social need." Strong labor organizations "ready to grapple with any group of employers guilty either of cupidity or industrial illiteracy," Cooke concluded, would secure abundance for all.[45]

But the Great Depression overwhelmed the ability and willingness of corporations to protect workers. Wage hikes and benefits disappeared, workers' councils and profit-sharing plans collapsed, and layoffs mounted. As working people looked to the federal government for security, they reshaped the corporate vision of a welfare capitalism into the political vision of a moral capitalism that informed the New Deal. Ultimately, working people found security in solidarity with one another in the new national unions of the Congress of Industrial Organizations (CIO). In building a more inclusive labor movement focused on the desire for job security, generous benefits, and high wages, the CIO also embraced the new vision of a moral capitalism. Moreover, the CIO's organizing successes depended on the common experiences workers shared through a consumer culture of chain stores and national brands, movies and radio programs.[46]

Democratic Unions, Labor Party

The labor movement's goals in the Great Depression owed much to the welfare capitalism of progressive employers and the New Deal policies of President Franklin D. Roosevelt, who came into office in 1933. But working people also mounted a determined effort to democratize the two most powerful institutions in American life, the corporation and the state. In building the industrial unions of the CIO, they demanded a voice in the policies of major corporations. Joining Roosevelt's New Deal coalition, they insisted that the Democratic Party be more responsive to labor's demands.[47]

The relief and labor policies of Roosevelt's First New Deal in 1933 brought workers into the Democratic Party. The New Deal transformed the federal government from an alien agency that shut down a key working-class institution during Prohibition into a source of relief, jobs, and support for unionization. But working people did not just substitute a paternalistic welfare state for paternalistic employers. In organizing radical movements of the unemployed, they demanded jobs or relief as an entitlement and just reward for their economic and civic contributions. Section 7 (a) of the National Recovery Act (NRA) of 1933 granted labor the right to "organize unions of their own choosing." Workers, however, launched the waves of strikes that turned a rhetorical commitment into an independent power base for labor.[48]

The NRA encouraged industrial leaders to cooperate to restrict production and thus maintain prices. The resulting codes of fair competition were supposed to include concessions to labor on wages and hours. But working people did not wait for these concessions, few of which were forthcoming. Under the leadership of John L. Lewis, the United Mine Workers began the struggle for industrial unionism before the ink had dried on Section 7 (a). Renewed organizing efforts in the textile, steel, and automobile industries quickly followed. Only the mine workers won significant gains in 1933, as the NRA failed to prevent the use of tear gas and company guards, labor spies and company unions. In 1934, labor conflict escalated, involving nearly a million and a half workers and general strikes in three major cities. With little help from the NRA or the AFL, industrial unionists stood up against a mounting wave of official and unofficial violence.[49]

In 1935, business intransigence, labor militancy, and a series of popular movements challenging the probusiness tenor of the First New Deal led Roosevelt to change course. As the nation's cities became the "smoldering and reddened arena of industrial conflict," as a federal study put it, Roosevelt reluctantly endorsed the Wagner National Labor Relations Act, which he signed in July 1935. A central part of the Second New Deal, the Wagner Act protected labor's right to organize from any interference by management, including the refusal to bargain collectively. But tied up in court challenges for two more years, the law still left working people to secure their own rights through direct action.[50]

At the end of 1935, Lewis, Sidney Hillman, and other industrial unionists formed a Committee on Industrial Organizations within the AFL. Seizing upon a new tactic, the CIO launched a series of sit-down strikes beginning in the rubber industry and spreading to steel, automobiles, and beyond. Local Democrats with prounion sympathies generally refrained from breaking up the sit-down strikes. But strikers needed military strategies to defeat company guards. Building interracial solidarity and mobilizing community resources, particularly women's auxiliaries, the sit-down strikes of the UAW won union recognition from the world's largest corporation, General Motors, in 1937. U.S. Steel signed a union contract in the same year.[51]

CIO leaders forswore any interest in wresting control of production away from management. Union contracts, including the one with General Motors, conceded control of production. A moral capitalism that stopped short of a restructuring of industrial relations still shaped the aspirations of many. But with rank-and-file militancy often outrunning that of union leadership, more radical changes appeared possible as union membership, dedication, and unity soared. Organization enabled workers to resist corporate dictates and elect shop stewards who managed the shop floor. Sit-down strikers defied the sanctity of private property. Rather than picket outside their factories where they were vulnerable to company guards, they sat down amid the expensive machinery inside the factory, thereby dramatizing their claim on the enterprise and frustrating efforts to replace them with strikebreakers. The CIO was "trying its utmost to control industry at the point of production," the National Association of Manufacturers complained.[52]

Working people changed the political landscape as well. Labor's interest in "economic planning" and "price, production and profit controls," Lewis argued during the 1936 presidential campaign, meant "that the labor movement must organize and exert itself not only in the economic field but in the political arena as well." Many workers agreed, but they failed to establish an independent national labor party committed to labor's agenda. Instead, labor remained one important constituency among many within the Democratic Party. Even the Communist Party joined the New Deal coalition, calling for a united popular front of all democratic forces against fascism. With both labor and the president condemning "economic royalists," the Democratic Party won a landslide victory in the fall elections.[53]

But the Democratic Party never committed itself wholeheartedly to the CIO organizing drives. Despite the victories over General Motors and U.S. Steel in 1937, employer intransigence intensified as propaganda campaigns warned that union victories would lead to plant closings. In the Little Steel campaign of 1937, when company guards and local police teargassed and shot strikers, Roosevelt refused to condemn the actions. The Roosevelt recession that began at the end of 1937, as the president scaled back public work projects, sent unemployment soaring. In 1939, the Supreme Court began to hedge in the Wagner Act, outlawing sit-down strikes and protecting employers' power to hire and fire and enforce contracts.[54]

Placed on the defensive, the CIO leadership prepared to rein in the rank and file. Struggling against national corporations intent on dividing their membership, CIO leaders undercut local prerogatives in favor of national goals. District leaders were often appointed rather than elected, fiscal independence was curtailed, and national staff members monitored local meetings. Staking their future on the Roosevelt administration rather than grassroots militance, CIO leaders promised responsible interest-group leadership. Shop floor actions and wildcat strikes had to be suppressed in favor of the businesslike routine of collective bargaining and subsequent enforcement of contract provisions.[55]

The Second New Deal: Consumerist Democracy and the End of Antimonopoly

Committed to a consumerist rather than a participatory democracy, the Roosevelt administration always focused more on economic recovery than economic reform. As Labor Secretary Frances Perkins explained in 1933, "programs long thought of as merely labor welfare such as shorter hours, higher wages, and a voice in the terms and conditions of work, are really essential economic factors for recovery." Even the Wagner Act appealed to the consumerist leaders of the Second New Deal primarily as a means of expanding "the purchasing power of wage earners" and stabilizing the mass-production–mass-consumption economy.[56]

The harsh antimonopoly rhetoric of the Roosevelt administration during the recession of 1937–1938 disguised, for a time, its consumerist intentions. "Organized wealth, which has controlled the Government so far, seizes this opportunity [the recession] to decide whether it is to continue to control the Government or not," Roosevelt told his cabinet in late 1937.[57] Renewed concerns about monopoly power briefly gave considerable influence to a younger group of New Dealers determined to strengthen public authority over the capitalist economy. An "irreconcilable conflict," New Dealer Harold Ickes told an NBC radio audience at the end of 1937, existed between "the power of money and the power of the democratic instinct." Early in 1938, Roosevelt addressed Congress on the troubles that "arise out of the concentration of economic control to the detriment of the body politic—control of other people's money, other people's labor, other people's lives."[58]

But even as New Deal liberals invoked the civic critique of monopoly as a threat to democracy, most still opposed monopoly, above all, for inflating prices and depressing demand. Without significant competition, monopolies charged administered prices rather than market prices. Economic concentration need not and could not be reversed, most New Deal liberals concluded, but government regulation could replace market competition in keeping prices low and stimulating demand. A permanent, welfare state staffed by managerial experts could not democratize the corporation or rescue small producers, but it might stabilize the economy and protect consumers.[59]

Public spending to counter recession and stimulate economic development had long appealed to New Deal liberals who saw underconsumption as the cause of the Great Depression. As British economist John Maynard Keynes theorized, the deficit spending that financed the Works Projects Administration jobs program in 1936 encouraged economic recovery. The consequences of Roosevelt's deflationary budget cuts in 1937, which appeared to be a major cause of recession in 1938, encouraged a coalition of liberals, trade unionists, and consumer activists to agitate in favor of countercyclical public spending.[60]

Public spending and antitrust initiatives might have grown in tandem. In April 1938, the Roosevelt administration sent to Congress a stimulus proposal for $3 billion in public spending and lending. "We suffer primarily from a lack of purchasing power," Roosevelt told the nation in a radio address, and public spending will "put idle money and idle men to work." Later the same month, he sent Congress a proposal for a broad investigation of monopoly. The monopoly investigation promised to curb the power of the great corporations and insure that public spending would not be absorbed in a hike of administered prices.[61]

The Antitrust Division appeared ready to put teeth into the antimonopoly crusade. Appointed to head the division in March 1938, Yale professor Thurman Arnold had ridiculed the antitrust laws in his study of the *Folklore of Capitalism* just a year earlier. But at his confirmation hearing, Arnold assured congressional progressives that he intended on "breaking up monopolies." Over the next five years, Arnold made vigorous use of an expanded Antitrust Division, increasing staff, budget, investigations, prosecutions, victories, and fines severalfold.[62]

But Arnold proved loyal to his professorial pronouncements. His prosecutions aimed not at breaking up monopolies, but at regulating them in the interest of lower prices for consumers. In doing so, Arnold abandoned the antitrust tradition's concern with the civic consequences of concentrated economic power. Far from seeing antitrust as a means of restoring the vitality of democracy, Arnold argued that the people's interest in corporate affairs had nothing to do with "the moral problem of the preservation of national character" and everything to do "the price of pork chops, bread, spectacles, drugs and plumbing."[63]

Arnold valued antitrust only as a myth to satisfy the public demand for a crusade while allowing managerial experts a free hand. Successful in the short run, he failed in the long run. Lower prices for consumers proved an insufficient motive to sustain even a regulatory battle against monopoly, particularly when consumers could be served by easier, less-controversial policies. The antimonopoly hearings of the congressional Temporary National Economic Committee (TNEC) that began in 1938 also failed to develop a politically viable policy. The TNEC, a journalist complained when its report appeared in 1941, "spent three years digging up the facts and then reinterred them with as much dispatch as possible."[64]

New Dealers saw the new war that broke out in Europe in 1939 as an opportunity to reshape the world economy along the lines of the Second New Deal. In August 1941, Roosevelt and British prime minister Winston Churchill met in the middle of the Atlantic Ocean to announce the Atlantic Charter, a joint declaration of the "common principles in the national policies of their respective countries on which they base their hopes for a better future for the world." The two leaders united in a common "desire to bring about the fullest collaboration between all nations in the economic field with the object of securing, for all, improved labor standards, economic advancement, and social security."[65]

From New Deal to New War: Liberals and Labor Abandon Reform

With the attack on Pearl Harbor at the end of 1941, a few New Deal liberals still hoped that the war might rally support around the president and allow for a democratic restructuring of the economy. But ten thousand business executives quickly took charge of the new war agencies and sought nonintrusive means of promoting full production. Totalitarian governments in Italy, Germany, and the Soviet Union added chilling examples of the dangers of state management of the economy. A new concern for individual liberty among New Deal liberals laid the groundwork for the assault on racial injustice and other forms of discrimination in years to come. But it also dampened their interest in using the state to democratize the economy. "National intervention to stimulate production is the method of the totalitarian state," explained New Dealer Leon Henderson. "National intervention to stimulate consumption is the democratic method" because it forced corporations to cater to consumer demands.[66]

The extraordinary performance of the economy during the war years reinforced the liberal abandonment of structural reform of the economy. Working together in the war mobilization, liberals and business leaders shed their suspicions of one another. The shared purpose of the war years and the liberal abandonment of reform facilitated postwar unity as liberals and business leaders pursued economic growth through the promotion of mass purchasing power. The failure of the War Production Board, the most important of the mobilization agencies, to establish civilian control over military procurement agencies and to direct war contracts to small businesses further eroded the liberal faith in the regulatory and planning powers of the state. In promoting closer ties between the armed forces, private industry, and federal agencies, the War Production Board also created the foundations of the military-industrial complex and the national security state, which promoted public spending, but shifted the emphasis from civilian to military purposes.[67]

As business and military interests grew closer during and after the war, labor radicals saw the issues of economic democracy pushed off the agenda. The National Labor Relations Board channeled labor disputes away from issues of control toward wages and benefit. Federal oversight placed labor mediators, more interested in industrial stability than industrial democracy, at the center of workplace conflicts. War mobilization also provided opportunities for labor, placing the industrial workforce at the center of the national purpose. But to realize those opportunities, labor needed to solidify its own independent base of power.[68]

Building on the suggestions of New Dealer Mordecai Ezekiel, CIO President Phillip Murray called for the creation of industrial councils in the spring of 1941. Condemning scientific management in its original form as "wrong and inhuman in regarding the worker simply as an unthinking set of arms," Ezekiel argued in 1939 that progressive scientific managers "find it is more effective to give the worker some responsibility, to leave him some intellectual part in planning and running the job." Murray agreed and urged that industrial councils with labor representation take over the work of mobilization.[69]

Murray's plan said little about maximizing production, the overriding concern of the Roosevelt administration. But Walter Reuther of the UAW supplied the missing ingredient. Reuther promised to quickly convert idle automobile plants to produce five thousand airplanes a day through a plan that included the industrial councils Murray advocated. Earning considerable support inside and outside the administration, the plan staked labor's claim to be more than "just a pressure group" and asserted its right "to participate in terms that have meaning to the participant." But corporate leaders resolutely opposed Reuther's plan. "To divide responsibility of management," the head of General Motors declared just months before Pearl Harbor, "would be to destroy the very foundations upon which America's unparalleled record of accomplishment is built." Former auto executives in the mobilization agencies quietly buried the plan.[70]

The attack on Pearl Harbor moved labor further from its militant stance. Through most of 1941, workers struck in near-record numbers, seeking long-delayed wage increases in a booming economy. In the fall, mine workers struck against operations controlled by steel corporations. Describing the strike as a fight between "a labor union and a ruthless corporation," Lewis insisted it involved neither patriotism nor national security. But once the United States entered the war, such defiance became more difficult. With the notable exception of Lewis's United Mine Workers, most of the major unions in the CIO and the AFL made "no-strike" pledges for the duration of the conflict.[71]

To stabilize wartime labor relations, Congress created a War Labor Board in January 1942. By July, the War Labor Board pegged wages to the cost of living, freezing labor's real income even as industry profits soared. In exchange, the labor movement won federal support for the "maintenance-of-membership" plan, whereby new hires in unionized plants were automatically enrolled in the union (with a rarely exercised fifteen-day escape clause). The plan helped raise organized labor's membership to nearly fifteen million by 1945, but it also made it dependent on a government-granted privilege.[72]

Most union leaders struggled to enforce the "no-strike" pledge among their members, widening the split between leadership and the rank and file. Frustrated with stagnant wages, three million workers engaged in wildcat strikes in 1943, pitting themselves against both their own leaders and the federal government. Compelled "to line up with management against workers," union officials feared their unions might collapse from within. But they also knew that the wildcat strikes intensified antilabor feeling inside Congress and out. Labor's "pivotal" task, *The Nation* warned, was "the winning of public opinion." The War Disputes Act (1943), curbing the right to strike, imposing criminal penalties, and making union political contributions illegal, showed labor losing that struggle.[73]

With its momentum halted, the labor movement looked to solidify its place in the New Deal state the best it could. The social movement of the great organizing drives, a product of militancy and solidarity on the shop floor and democratic participation in the union hall, gave way to a bureaucratized CIO determined to institutionalize the collective bargaining process and charged with the responsibility for maintaining discipline on the shop floor. Attempting to harness the volatile politicization of the depression era to the routines of interest-group negotiations, labor leaders abandoned the struggle for shop floor control and the broader syndicalist ambition of social leadership.[74]

Taming Labor in the Welfare/Warfare State

But even as labor gave up on the dream of industrial democracy, the new strategy held out the possibility of making labor a powerful force within the Democratic Party. When New Deal liberals argued that the postwar government must "ensure an adequate volume of purchasing power and effective demand," labor leaders agreed. Labor particularly supported public spending for "a national minimum of social service . . . improvement and development program of public works, regional resource development, urban redevelopment and public housing."[75]

In promoting full employment and public spending for civilian purposes, however, the labor-liberal alliance ran into opposition from the emerging military-industrial complex. "During the war, the Congress appropriated $400 billion for battleships and bombers to destroy homes and destroy life," Walter Reuther charged. "But when we call upon the Congress to help people, they don't appropriate billions and billions. They get out the Congressional eyedropper and give us a couple drops," Reuther continued. "We believe that a country that can spend $400 billion to destroy life can spend the same amount of money to improve life." An advocate of an expanded public spending and a generous welfare state, Reuther also hoped for greater public control of industry. "It is my determined belief that there can be no permanent prosperity," he argued, "so long as the controls of production remain in the hands of a privileged minority."[76]

As the war ended, Reuther advocated a "Peace Production Board" to set goals and coordinate resource allocation. In the UAW's 1946 strike against General Motors (GM), Reuther illustrated what he had in mind. Demanding a 30 percent wage hike for GM's 320,000 workers, Reuther argued that GM should freeze auto prices at their existing level. Reuther insisted that the labor movement would not "operate as a narrow economic pressure group." Autoworkers "want to make progress with the community and not at the expense of the community." GM protested that it could not possibly afford the raise nor would it surrender its power over pricing, which remained "the very heart of management judgment and discretion in industry." Reuther demanded that GM open its books to prove its poverty. GM refused, insisting that production decisions remained "the sole responsibility of the corporation." In the settlement that ended the strike, autoworkers won a limited pay raise and GM maintained exclusive control of production and pricing decisions. Although Reuther continued to pursue political goals at the bargaining table and in congressional lobbies, he never again challenged corporate control of production.[77]

As liberals abandoned the struggle for economic democracy, labor leaders faced a difficult situation at best. With the end of the war and the growing conflict with the Soviet Union, the rightward shift of politics left market controls less and less viable. Widespread strikes in 1946, involving more workers than 1919, proved to be a last hurrah. The Truman administration imposed settlements on labor and even threatened to draft strikers and issue injunctions. With wartime price controls lifted and inflation soaring, the unions' focus on wages and benefits helped protect working people. But it also neglected the workplace control issues that once energized the labor movement.[78]

The Taft-Hartley Act of 1947 completed the process of taming the labor movement. Labor leaders may have seen themselves as moderate leaders of a responsible and disciplined movement. But the postwar strike wave left employers determined to undercut the power of organized labor. Outlawing the closed shop and establishing complicated voting rules for the establishment of a union shop, Taft-Hartley also allowed states to mandate an open shop via "right-to-work" laws. Prohibiting union membership for foremen, the act also ensured management's right to express its views during an organizing campaign and facilitated court action against unions for "unfair labor practices."[79]

Authorizing employers to sue unions for breach of contract if they authorized a strike during the term of a collective-bargaining agreement, Taft-Hartley also established criminal penalties for union officials who refused to oppose wildcat strikes. By outlawing secondary boycotts, the act restricted the use of sympathy strikes and undercut the principle of solidarity. It also prohibited strikes by federal employees. Authorizing the president to convene a fact-finding board to investigate a strike's impact on national health and safety, Taft-Hartley empowered the president to order a strike ended, at the board's request, for a ninety-day "cooling off" period.[80]

Restricting the right of free speech for union members, Taft-Hartley prohibited unions from contributing to political campaigns for federal office. The law also instituted an anticommunist loyalty oath for all union officers, limiting union members' freedom to control their own organizations. President Harry Truman vetoed Taft-Hartley, although he supported many of its provisions. But enough Democrats joined Republicans to override the veto. A purge of communists from the CIO followed. By 1950, CIO membership fell to 3.7 million from its wartime high of 5.2 million.[81]

The growing fear of the Soviet Union and the spread of anticommunism also led to the passage of the National Security Act in 1947. Consolidating the armed forces under the Department of Defense and establishing the National Security Council and the Central Intelligence Agency as new and powerful executive agencies, the National Security Act established the warfare state as a permanent reality in the United States. Perceived as both immediate and long-term, the threat of the Soviet Union demanded an urgent and permanent program of preparedness of both civilian and military resources. As a new national security elite of corporate and financial leaders reshaped the agenda and the budget of federal government, defense spending escalated and social spending declined, confirming the triumph of the military-industrial complex.[82]

The emergence of the national security state generated a debate over the dangers of centralized power and the fate of the democratic traditions of the United States. Advocates might describe the struggle with the Soviet Union as an opportunity to rejuvenate civic virtue, "a test of national quality" and of "the over-all worth of the United States as a nation among nations," as George Kennan put it. But the centralization of government authority, the weakening of checks and balances within a representative system, the creation of a standing army, the growing prominence of military leaders in civilian affairs, the growing dominance of military research in institutions of higher education, and the spread of military training at the expense of the democratic virtues taught in the home, family, and school all threatened to undercut the republican traditions of the United States.[83]

New Deal liberals hoped that the war would legitimate an activist state, empowered to promote the general welfare as it provided for the common defense. Instead a military-industrial complex emerged that elevated guns over butter and corporate profits over the public good. Together, the Taft-Hartley Act and the National Security Act relegated organized labor to a role as a junior partner in what became more of a warfare than a welfare state. Military spending helped bring prosperity and middle-class status to organized workers in the mass-production industries. But the majority of working people gained little from the war economy and its funneling of funds away from the public realm.[84]

CHAPTER 10

Constructing a Consumer Culture

*Redirecting Leisure from Civic Engagement
to Insatiable Desire*

In 1902, Marshall Field's opened its new, twelve-story department store on State Street in Chicago. "We have built this great institution for the people," Field's announced, "to be their store, their downtown home, their buying headquarters." For opening day, Field's adorned its one million square feet of retail space with "cut flowers on every counter, shelf, showcase, and desk," six string orchestras, great "bulbs of electricity," as well as banners, streamers, and blooming plants. Although management permitted no purchases the first day, huge crowds swamped the store—not just "the swagger rich," but the "masses of shoppers" who flooded the new bargain basement. The "opening was one of the grandest events that has ever been known in Chicago," a young woman enthused, "in a word, simply Wonderland."[1]

The growth of productive capacity at the end of the nineteenth century set commercial leaders to work on the problem of distribution. New tools and assembly line techniques and new sources of energy produced an avalanche of goods awaiting buyers. The growth of the railroad network and the rise of a national market generated a merchandising web of wholesalers and retailers, hotels and restaurants, capped by the department store. With more than a hundred departments, the great retail palaces presented a world defined by goods. As "investment for gain" superseded "commitment to industry and workmanship," finance capitalists poured money into retailing. Encouraging a trend toward consolidation and national chains, they aimed to "get from the buyer all the buyer can be induced to pay."[2]

Commercial leaders described the rise of the consumer culture as natural and inevitable. The new culture "speaks to us," a merchant explained, "only of ourselves, our pleasures, our life.... It whispers, 'Amuse thyself, take care of yourself.' Is not this the natural and logical effect of an age of individualism?" But the architects of the consumer culture knew better. The consumer culture demanded a transformation of personal character from the Victorian emphasis on delayed gratification, prudence, and accumulation to a new focus on instant gratification, short-term thinking, and spending. Merchants and industrialists, investment bankers and retailers, advertisers and university professors, museum curators and government officials all helped craft new strategies of enticement—from advertising and decoration to fashion, design, and consumer service—that made the United States the land of desire.[3]

The consumer culture intersected with and depended on a popular demand for leisure that animated the most successful labor movements in the nineteenth century. "Eight hours for what we will" transcended divisions of craft, ethnicity, and gender and expressed working people's interest in self-improvement and civic engagement. Demanding for workers "more of the leisure that rightfully belongs to them," the Knights of Labor defined leisure as one of "those rights and privileges necessary to . . . enjoying appreciating, defending, and perpetuating the blessings of good government."[4]

Absorbing civic energies and values, the consumer culture redirected them and gave them new meanings. Democracy, once associated with political equality and participation, refocused on individual opportunities for amusement and luxury. Religious and civic meanings of service gave way to a rhetoric of customer satisfaction. Even the idea of the new, once linked to civic regeneration, became just another means of hyping the goods. The values of the consumer culture were neither "natural" nor "normal," sociologist Charles Cooley recognized, and "by no means the work of the whole people acting homogeneously." But as the consumer culture reshaped character, insatiable desire came to seem humanity's natural and normal condition.[5]

The Popular Demand for Leisure and the Rise of the Saloon

Toward the end of the nineteenth century, a new emphasis on consumption crept into the agitation for an eight-hour day. Workingmen began to see leisure as a separate sphere that compensated for the growing regimentation of the workplace. "A workingman wants something besides food and clothes in the country," a labor leader told a Senate committee in 1883. "He wants recreation. Why should not a workingman have it as well as other people?" Increased productivity also focused attention on consumption. Future employment, labor leaders argued, would "depend upon a more expensive style of living," for "wealth cannot be consumed sparingly by the masses and be produced rapidly."[6]

In combination with more disciplined workplaces, shorter hours and rising incomes made the saloon the preeminent commercial recreation for workingmen. The "modern methods in industry," an American Federation of Labor

(AFL) pamphlet explained, reduced "the social opportunities of the masses." The AFL demanded "more leisure, more physical and mental repose, more and larger periods of relief, from the strain which the specialized industrial life imposes." Even moral reformers recognized that the saloon catered "in a hundred ways to the social and political needs of men," providing food, warmth, meeting space, newspapers, check-cashing services, employment and political information, clean water, and toilets. The "absence of any time limit, some stimulus to self-expression, and a kind of personal feeling toward those into whose company one is thrown" made it the antithesis of the regimented workplace. Above all, the "craving for companionship" and the opportunity for "throwing off repression" brought workers to the saloon.[7]

Inhospitable to members of the wrong sex or ethnicity, the saloon absorbed precious resources and sometimes promoted dissipation and irresponsibility. At best, the saloon provided an alternative rather than an adversarial culture, providing little direct challenge to the loss of power in the workplace. But the saloon did have an important civic dimension. Encouraging conversation and debate in an atmosphere of equality, the saloon hosted "earnest discussions" of "political issues or social problems." The "names of Karl Marx and leaders of social and political thought are often heard" in the saloon, observed a reformer, who expressed astonishment at the "relatively small amount of drunkenness." The saloon served as the "official and unofficial meeting-place for the discussion of those interests ... uppermost in men's minds," another reformer wrote, and encouraged debates that provided "real insight into the causes of present evils."[8]

A concern with labor efficiency and good order led employers to oppose working-class drinking, first in the workplace and then in the saloon. The discouragement of drinking, employers reported in the 1880s, was "greatly increasing the efficiency" of wage earners. Manufacturers found "their employees are steadier and more industrious; men are not so often absent from their work." The labor movement acknowledged the value of temperance in contributing to self-discipline and group solidarity. The Knights of Labor's temperance pledge appealed to self-improvement, the protection of the family, and the collective interests of labor. Aimed at solidarity rather than upward mobility, labor temperance preached moderation. "If a man wants a glass of beer he should take it," one organizer advised, "but it is this going to extremes that is dangerous."[9]

Labor temperance sometimes took radical directions, at least until the antisaloon movement attacked a central institution of working-class life. In the 1870s, the Prohibition Party campaigned against the liquor trade and its corrupting influence on politics, uniting small proprietors and skilled artisans. Describing the drink trade as "a political wrong of unequaled enormity" in 1872, the Prohibition Party demanded an end to "all monopoly and class legislation." In 1876, the party advanced a broader agenda that demanded the suppression of speculation and the regulation of transportation corporations. But by 1881, a labor editor saw the emerging antisaloon campaign as itself an example of "class legislation." The "better element ... who believe in drink as a luxury" acted on the assumption "that the plebeians should not be allowed to degrade the habit by participation."[10]

For employers and antisaloon reformers, the saloon confirmed the failure of workers to adjust to the corporate transformation of society. The "masses have been left to themselves to work out the problems of industrial civilization and they are not equal to the task," the self-styled Sociological Group reported in 1890. A collection of religious, academic, and professional leaders, the Sociological group gave birth to the antisaloon movement and published a series of popular articles aimed at undermining the growing influence of the radical Prohibition Party in the 1880s. Divorcing the drink question from larger questions of political economy, the Sociological Group described workers' loss of control over the means of production and their vulnerability in "an uncertain and even capricious world market" as "definitive" developments.[11]

The difference between the Prohibition Party and antisaloonism thus hinged on attitudes to the emerging corporate order. Radical Prohibitionists defended small producers and opposed incorporation. The Knights of Labor explained that "one hundred thousand or fifty thousand sober, honest, earnest men . . . will wage the battle of labor more successfully than . . . twelve million . . . men who drink either moderately or drink to excess." In contrast, the antisaloon movement saw only a permanent, dependent, and degraded class of wage earners, incapable of self-reformation.[12]

The antisaloon movement sought to reshape workers' leisure to fit a rational, corporate order. The inevitable "irregularity of employment and income," the Sociological Group explained, led to "enforced idleness" in an urban environment "almost devoid of opportunities for innocent and wholesome recreation." The "liquor saloon presents never ending temptation to those who live in labor quarters, while the modern city is almost wholly devoid of opportunities for wholesome, life-giving recreation for the poor." Mass production promised a "golden age," but the popular demand for leisure must be given "the right direction," the Sociological Group concluded, for "increasing civilization means increasing wants of the most legitimate kind."[13]

The Leisure Question and Cheap Amusements

The question of legitimate wants spilled over into other recreational issues. The respectable classes favored large central parks, whose sedate recreations refined the manners of the unwashed. Working people demanded local, accessible parks that provided space for active recreations. While the competition between temperance and the saloon divided working people, the demand for neighborhood parks united them in defense of their equal rights. "We want more outside room, we want every inch of space the city can afford us," demanded an advocate for those "cooped up" and "huddled together."[14]

The demand for leisure on the part of workingwomen also focused on active recreations. For most of the nineteenth century, women remained tied to the household and enjoyed only limited access to the public world of trade unions, politics, and leisure. But the proliferation of new jobs in stores, offices, and factories at the turn of the century allowed young women to escape the confining world of domestic service and sweated labor. When regular wages and declining hours offered young women access to leisure, they gravitated to commercial recreations. In dance halls, movie theaters, and amusement parks, young women created a new heterosocial world of leisure centered on sexuality and fun. "The shorter work day brought me my first idea of there being such a thing as pleasure," recalled one young woman.[15]

The development of the new identity of wage earner, forged in the workplace with their peers, made young women impatient with the restrictions of family and ethnic cultures. To secure a portion of their wages for leisure-time pursuits, daughters living at home struggled against parental discipline. "Women adrift," about whom there was much anguished moralizing, lived independently or shared furnished rooms with other young women. Scrimping on essentials to purchase stylish clothing, young women explored their sexuality. Limited financial means meant that an evening's entertainment often required sexual negotiation with a young man.[16]

The spread of saloons, dance halls, peep shows, salacious films, and other cheap amusements raised concerns about the misuse of leisure and its impact on character. The decline of proprietorship and craftsmanship removed "the moral check from the competitive process," a civic reformer argued. With "the transformation of workers into machine-tenders, the real significance of work in the formation of character and the development of citizenship is becoming less." Routinized labor at a high-pressure pace tended to "make machines of men, to diminish their ethical responsibility." Serving only "to unnerve men and unfit them for serious attention to self-improvement," the civic reformer concluded, machine industry provided "a natural preparation for dissipation during long hours of leisure."[17]

With industrial democracy still nothing more than a dream, a wide range of opinion converged on the conclusion that the success or failure of democracy depended on the proper use of leisure time. The degradation of work meant that "the culture of life must be almost altogether undertaken in leisure hours." The "use of a nation's leisure" became "the test of its civilization." Only through the intelligent use of leisure could we produce "an educated people" and thereby "secure economic justice, responsible political freedom." Yet, leisure remained "disorganized, chaotic, utterly ignored and neglected by public support," left "to be organized by private speculation—the amusement business." The continued misuse of leisure would prove "fatal to democracy."[18]

City life reinforced machine industry in promoting dissipation. The "confining, nerve-racking, and tense" conditions in the city meant that "the insistence upon excitement and intense pleasure is more pronounced and more dangerous than anywhere else." Prostitution, drunkenness, and gambling were "ceaselessly preying upon the vitals of municipal democracy." Settlement house leaders condemned "the commercial enterprise which ministers to pleasure in order to drag it into excess because excess is more profitable." Other reformers agreed that if "the American city fails, it will fail not because of the work its people do or the places in which they live, but because of the pleasures which they seek."[19]

The leisure question also focused attention on the health of the family. Even as city life stimulated the sexual passion, industrialization made cities "unfit places for the birth and rearing of children." The tenement districts harbored "hordes of dirty and poorly clothed children swarming in the public ways," raised by adults "with few places for beneficial recreation to break the monotony of their lives, but with avenues of disastrous amusement on every side." The unusually high number of unmarried men and unusually low number of children in urban populations did not mean "less indulgence of the desires and passions of men," but signaled "the perversion of natural tendencies into the channels of vice." Lacking "the traditional line of domesticity," the sexual instinct acted "as a cancer in the very tissues of society and as a disrupter of the securest social bonds."[20]

Concern mounted that the family could no longer accomplish its traditional tasks of inculcating values and shaping character. Settlement reformers saw firsthand how commercial amusements tended "to tear the family to pieces." Where once "field sports, commemorative days, saints days, harvest festivals, folk dancing and pageantry" brought the family together, now the saloon and the dance hall broke it apart. The family retained "certain biological functions" and managed to pass on traditions of "warm human responsibility and loyalty." But the family was in "desperate need of social aid" if it was to continue "to provide the emotional, the ethical and broadly human side of education for its members." Since the family no longer could provide wholesome recreation, a settlement leader concluded, "the community itself must become the foster father and mother."[21]

Municipally sponsored recreations could, however, turn leisure into a potent force for civic renewal. Recognizing that the "deterioration of moral fibre more than anything else . . . . destroy cities and democracies," reformers argued that bringing "men's pleasures up to a higher ethical standard" represented nothing less than "the next great step in the development of human nature." A "leisure devoted to *social service*" and the "discussion of public affairs" might have "more to do with character building than any other influence." Reformers urged the municipality to extend "both its police power and its right of eminent domain" in addressing the leisure question. Reformers called for municipal dance halls, promoted folk dancing at settlement houses, organized chaperoned excursions to amusement parks, and encouraged the production and screening of wholesome films as a substitute for cheap amusements.[22]

Most of these efforts came to little as young women continued to join young men at commercial amusements where sexuality and consumerism promised autonomy and pleasure. Encouraging the growing association of leisure with consumption, cheap amusements weaned young men away from the saloon, lodge, and club that had linked male solidarity to economic and political issues. At commercial dance halls, young couples engaged in "tough dancing" that celebrated a loss of control and close physical contact. Outside nickelodeons, young women lingered "with a boy companion 'making dates' for a movie or affair," while inside, "the semi-darkness permits a 'steady's' arm to encircle a 'lady friend's' waist." The films themselves popularized the new culture of fun and sexuality, glamorizing scenes of sexual negotiation and titillation often set at places of amusement.[23]

The Discovery of Play

As working people pursued pleasure in public places, they eroded straitlaced decorum among the respectable. "It is a revelation to me to see these thousands of good, decent, ordinary people, just frankly enjoying themselves like human beings," remarked a Methodist minister of an immigrant picnic in a best-selling novel of the 1890s. A highbrow literary critic recalled that it was the "reality of passion freely expressed which fascinated us." Working people sensed the interest and took pride in their expressiveness. "The trouble is that these high people don't know how to dance," a young woman remarked. "I have to laugh when I see them at their balls and parties. If only I could get out on the floor and show them how—they would be astonished."[24]

The admiration and envy of working-class expressiveness contributed to the rise of a consumer ethic of immediate gratification. The movies spread the new culture of sexuality and fun upward on the social scale. The popularity of Mary Pickford and Douglas Fairbanks owed much to their transformation of the sexual culture of cheap amusements into wholesome athleticism and romantic companionship suitable for the respectable classes. Amusement parks served a similar purpose. The playful mixture of sexuality and comedy at Coney Island's Steeplechase Park focused on romance between couples, tamed the promiscuity of the cheap amusements, and rendered it harmless for a middle-class clientele. Mechanical rides jostled and tumbled patrons into each others' arms and sent skirts and limbs flying. In packaging sexuality as fun and romance, amusement parks pioneered a key technique of consumer culture and thus served "as laboratories of the new mass culture."[25]

The respectable classes' discovery of play as a solvent for Victorian restraint coincided with their discovery that play might provide the key to inculcating values and shaping character. A version of the celebration of the strenuous life as a means of rehabilitating the old middle class for national leadership, the new instrumental view of play shaped the movement for supervised playgrounds to reform working-class children. The most successful of leisure-oriented reforms, the playground movement grew out of the popular demand for neighborhood parks. From a worried beginning in the summer of Haymarket (1886), the park and playground movements gained momentum through the turbulent 1890s and then exploded in prestige as a new panacea in the Progressive Era. Settlement leaders, housing reformers, city planners, prohibitionists, educators, sociologists, social gospelers, and prominent industrialists all enthusiastically supported the movement. By 1917, more than five hundred cities built municipal playgrounds.[26]

Playground reformers expressed impeccable civic principles. The playground, the president of the Playground Association of America explained, is "our great ethical laboratory," where the child develops "those qualities which depend upon and which are developed only under conditions of freedom." Another reformer added that the "social virtues" and "social conscience" required of adults originated "in the early activities of the playground." Team sports promoted "the sheer experience of citizenship in its simplest and essential form—of the sharing in a public consciousness." In the team instinct, we find "final and conclusive proof of Aristotle's great saying . . . that man is by nature political and that as a consequence no man can be fully virtuous (or, as we might say, can fully live) unless he participates in government."[27]

Playground reformers argued that civic life depended on "the dedication of free, self-directed individuals to a common purpose," virtues developed in play as children learned to assert themselves within a group of equals. But in practice, the movement promoted professional expertise at the expense of self-government. Lauding the "intelligently equipped social worker," playground reformers aspired "to serve the public as experts." Supervised play, permits and regulations, and fenced and segregated play spaces discouraged the civic skills of imagination and self-organization. The proper playground, a manual on municipal parks explained, "should be fenced with a strong woven wire or iron picket fence," making it easier to "enforce discipline." "On the vacant lot we can do as we please," a playground reformer concluded, but "when we have a fenced playground it becomes an institution."[28]

Adding few parks to those created early in the Progressive Era, playground reformers focused more on inculcating industrial discipline. "The boy without a playground is the father to a man without a job" became a leading slogan of the movement. "In our playground we did not forget to teach children to work as well as to play," reported a supervisor. "As a child plays," added another, "so will he later work." The "efficiency test," the "classification of patrons," and elaborate schedules were all part of the "transition from 'free' to 'directed' play," adjusting working-class children to the rudiments of industrial discipline. At a model playground visited during their national conference in 1910, playground reformers proudly witnessed children who "at the stroke of the gong" engaged in the mass production of identical, symmetrical sand pies.[29]

In redirecting the "play instinct" and "team instinct" to socially acceptable channels, the playground movement joined other helping professions in encouraging adjustment to life in the city. But in reshaping character, playground reformers enjoyed only limited success. "I can't go to the playgrounds now," a young boy complained. "They get on me nerves with so many men and women around telling you what to do." The People's Institute estimated that less than 1 percent of the populace made use of supervised playgrounds, parks, and other structured recreations. But in the hands of more powerful agencies, the discovery of play provided the means of shaping a new working-class character in the interests of mass consumption and moving the goods off the shelves.[30]

Captains of Consciousness, Land of Desire

Merchants and advertisers had already discovered play as a means of stoking the fires of desire. "The selling departments," explained a retailer in 1902, "is the stage upon which the play is enacted." Mimicking French salons, Japanese gardens, or southern plantations, retail spaces associated goods with a "central idea" as far removed from the dreary details of production as possible. With an eye to "saloon architecture," retail experts advised that no "hindrance should be offered to people who may drift into the store." Revolving doors, escalators, elevators, wide aisles, and open spaces encouraged entry and circulation throughout the store. Glass enhanced the allure of goods. Mirrors directed consumers' imaginations to personal and intimate interaction with the goods.[31]

The department store display window stood at the pinnacle of a culture of desire that included magazine ads, billboards, posters, and electric signs. Marshaling color, glass, and light once reserved for religious or heroic imagery, the display window intensified desire by surrounding it with the aura of devotion. Edna Ferber called the display window a "breeder of anarchism, a destroyer of contentment." It "boasts of peaches, downy and golden, when peaches have no right to be," she wrote in the winter of 1911. Those who devoted their lives to creating the new commercial aesthetic, like advertiser Elbert Hubbard, were said to have "deified commerce." They built a $600 million industry that generated 4 percent of the national income by 1910.

The growth of the consumer culture transformed values. Bargain basements liquidated the commitment to social equality. One merchant felt the "experiment for separating the masses from the classes" to be "undemocratic and un-American—certainly alien to the New World ideas of equality." But he endorsed the experiment nonetheless. Tipping as a means of securing exemplary service from underpaid staffs introduced aristocratic manners among middle-class consumers. Hotels trained their staffs to behave in "servile" ways toward guests.

Retailers laid siege to Victorian restraint, encouraging impulsive purchasing. Even as immigration restrictions excluded Asians, "Oriental" ad campaigns promised safe and sanitized versions of impermissible luxuries and indulgences. An authority on display windows contrasted "stiff Americans" and "scheming" and "deceiving" Western merchants to Orientals who were "free and wild" and "children of impulse." Retailers worked in concert with museum curators who placed their exotic collections and exhibits at the service of contemporary design and fashion (and depicted ancient civilizations in terms of attractively displayed goods).

The intensification of desire weakened individual character, even on the mass retailers' own terms. Pampered treatment and liberal credit terms encouraged expectations of getting something for nothing. People "act as if a store were some sort of eleemosynary institution," a merchant complained, run "without regard to profit." An epidemic of returned goods and criminal charges for nonpayment beset department stores. The "malignant practice" of returning goods reached 15 percent of gross sales in major cities. Department store showrooms, arcades, and pavilions stirred up envy and fears of social inadequacy. Displays proved so effective that "kleptomaniacs,"—adolescent girls as well as older, well-educated genteel women—shoplifted jewelry, stockings, underwear, whatever they could carry away. "Furs is the most dangerous spot in the store at Christmas," reported a Field's manager, who placed "a detective right in the middle of the department." Trusting no one, the detective "always looked at everybody, looked into the eyes of all."

Many people objected to the department store on civic grounds. In the 1890s, small retailers deplored "the all-devouring monsters" that destroyed the "little man." The "big store" undercut "independence for men and women" and fostered "a dependence which, while it may give money to the fortunate ones, renders them subject to a central power which in time becomes a tyranny." The department store appeared as a "commercial vampire," sucking the lifeblood out of small proprietors. Small retailers demanded legislation to tax "the octopus which has stretched out its tentacles in every direction, grasping in its slimy folds the specialist or one-line man."[32]

In Chicago, Field's and other big firms clustered on State Street, driving up rents for small retailers and luring their customers away. Hundreds of small firms went bankrupt during the depression of the 1890s. Determined to eliminate the competition, Marshall Field drove down wages and crushed labor organizers with "professional toughs" or the National Guard he helped finance. Field symbolized for working people the power of "united capital" in the war against "organized labor." But reform-minded professionals, lawyers, doctors, and ministers, fearful of the mounting struggle between labor and capital, defended department stores as integrating agencies capable of creating a harmonious nation of contented consumers.[33]

A coalition of small retailers, the local women who patronized them, marginal real estate brokers, and labor leaders united against Chicago's department stores in 1897. The Democratic machine of Carter Harrison, charging that realty values were "unreasonably and enormously enhanced by the centralization," harassed the big stores by imposing restrictions and new license fees. In New York City and elsewhere, similar movements opposed "trusts and monopolies and the encroachments of the department stores upon all branches of business." But bowing to pressure from giant retailers, state legislatures and state courts defeated restrictive legislation or declared it unconstitutional.[34]

The civic opposition to the department store revealed the difficult tasks facing the architects of the consumer culture. "Mass production demands the education of the masses," merchant Edward A. Filene explained, "the masses must learn to behave like human beings in a mass production world." In part, this meant deflecting radical alternatives. When corporate leaders spoke of industrial democracy, they meant that workers should enjoy the consumer satisfactions their jobs made possible rather than "a larger share in the management of the enterprise which furnishes that job." But profitability also demanded ever-increasing consumption. We "have learned to create wealth," Wall Street banker Bernard Baruch explained, but "we have not learned to keep that wealth from choking us." The "future of business," an advertising journal added, "lay in its ability to manufacture customers as well as products."[35]

As captains of consciousness, the architects of the consumer culture took responsibility for the shaping of character and the inculcation of values once assigned to the family. They exploited every stage of the life cycle from birth through marriage to death, aspiring to "EDUCATE DESIRE," as one ad put it. But the apostles of shopping focused first and foremost on children. Toy departments created a lavish world, pressuring adults to supply the cost of admission. As Field's store manager lectured his staff, "children are the future customers of this store, and impression made now will be lasting." Win over "kids," a child market expert added, and "you will have them as customers for a lifetime." Santa Claus, holiday parades, and child experts served this effort. "Play is the child's business; toys the material with which he works," manufacturers instructed parents. "Failure," a child psychologist added, "is one of the most serious distractions" for children, "hence it is excellent that you have that graded series of toys."[36]

The character and values of the consumer also reshaped politics. "It is the increasing wealth of America," *New Republic* editor Walter Weyl wrote in 1912, "upon which the hope of a full democracy must be based." Two years later, Walter Lippmann agreed that the consumer would become "the real master of the political situation." But Lippmann could not contemplate the future with "unmixed joy." He deplored advertising as a "deceptive clamor that disfigures the scenery, covers fences, plasters the city, and blinks and winks at you through the night." A consumers' democracy would produce "a fickle and superstitious mob, incapable of any real judgment as to what it wants." Yet, Lippmann still bid good riddance to the small proprietor. "Six grocers in three blocks, dingy little butcher-shops, little retail businesses with the family living in the back room, the odor of cooking to greet you as you enter the door, fly-specks on the goods," Lippmann concluded, were conditions not worth saving.[37]

Exit the Saloon, Enter the Bijou

At the end of World War I, however, the saloon still offered conviviality, comradeship, and solidarity as alternatives to the values of the consumer culture. In joining the campaign against the saloon, reformers and business leaders assaulted the last obstacle to the full development of the consumer culture. Leisure "has become a reality for all classes," the National Municipal League declared in 1897. But we must realize that for parks, playgrounds, and other wholesome recreational facilities to produce "a new concept of personal responsibility," the saloon must be eliminated. National Prohibition, adopted in 1919, closed the saloon and paved the way for the newly incorporated movie industry to bring a new popularity and pervasiveness to the consumer culture.[38]

At the turn of the century, however, reformers and businessmen still preferred persuasion to legislation in fighting the saloon. Corporate welfare programs tried to wean workers from saloons. Enlisting "not only the personal interest of the individual employee, but the interest of his family as well," large urban employers found the most effective program was "that of taking the children of our workingmen and training them." But as the profitability of the saloon attracted new investors to the brewing industry, the liquor problem worsened. The industry's "ambition seemed to be to convert the rising generation of males into peripatetic tanks," complained a muckraker in 1907. As retailers competed for choice locations on "busy avenues" and "opposite great factories," and the largest brewers developed national chains of saloons, giant "glittering street-signs" and "highly expensive advertising campaigns" hawked beer from every corner. The "overcapitalization" of the industry benefited "the most irresponsible class of retailers."[39]

In the years just before World War I, therefore, corporate leaders embraced federal legislation and national Prohibition. With the rise of European war orders after 1914, employers complained, "it has become more difficult all the time to surround the employment of men with restrictions of any kind, particularly as may affect their leisure hours." The spread of sophisticated machinery, and new laws providing for workmen's compensation for workplace accidents, placed a premium on a stable and sober workforce. The "growth in complexity, high speed, and involved dangers of modern machinery absolutely bars the use of alcohol," an academic study reported. The saloon-going worker "will find himself more and more unable to fit into . . . industrial life." The role of saloons in the organization and maintenance of strikes clinched the corporate case for Prohibition.[40]

By 1919, most major transportation and manufacturing corporations lined up behind Prohibition. The Playground Association of America, the National Municipal League, the National Conference of Charities and Corrections, and other reform associations also endorsed Prohibition. The experience of the past few years, a prominent liquor reformer told the National Conference on Social Work in 1919, "has shown that no appreciable progress in the provision of saloon substitutes was possible as long as the saloon remained in any form whatso-ever." The hope "that the saloon might gradually be shorn of its social features . . . by private philanthropy or commercial enterprise, was proved to be without foundation." Worthy efforts of "providing the needed social opportunities furnished by the saloon can be successfully undertaken only when the saloon itself has ceased to exist."[41]

A part of the new political capitalism in which corporate progressives charged the federal government with creating conditions conducive to corporate profits, Prohibition aspired to transform the worker as both producer and consumer. We must "analyze the human mind and body carefully," a corporate progressive explained, with the purpose of bringing them "up to the highest state of productive ability." The "greatest of all" of Prohibition's social consequences, a reformer added, would be "the rise of those moral sentiments which give the home its essential value." Freed from the curse of drink, the worker would focus on the joys of automobiles, radios, washing machines, vacuum cleaners, and the other trappings of contented domesticity.[42]

Prohibition became national policy with the ratification of the Eighteenth Amendment in 1919. Its first ten years coincided with explosive growth in the leisure industry. Mass merchandisers—including dime-store magnate S. S. Kresge, department store merchant John Wanamaker, and soft-drink entrepreneur Asa Candler—made major financial contributions to the Prohibition movement. So did Henry Ford, whose consumption-oriented five-dollar day coexisted uneasily with the puritanical investigators of his Sociological Department. Entering workers' homes to stamp out "unwholesome living," the Sociological Department cut in half the pay of any worker who was "wasting his substance" on drink or spending "foolishly." But by the 1920s, with the saloon safely eradicated, Ford recognized that "the 'thrift' and 'economy' ideas have been overworked."[43]

Before Prohibition, the leisure industry suffered from a disreputable aura. The first challenges to Victorian strictures against sexuality and fun came from socially marginal and sometimes politically radical entrepreneurs. Few saloon keepers, amusement park entrepreneurs, and movie moguls hailed from the social register. A "keen shrewd businessman but not well regarded socially in some quarters," a credit agency reported of one entrepreneur, a "peculiar man of radical ideas in politics and religion." Defying bans against Sunday amusements, embracing sexuality as a commercial tool, and responding quickly to changing public tastes, renegade entrepreneurs built up an impressive industry.[44]

Increasing profits, however, lent an air of respectability to even the most suspect enterprise. Even the saloon underwent a transformation in the years before Prohibition. As saloon keepers amassed considerable wealth and brewers took greater control of saloons, large investments demanded greater attention to businesslike methods and a reputation for good order. Higher license fees and more stringent regulations crowded out marginal owners and suspect practices, including treating and free lunches. Shedding their association with gambling as well as political debate, saloon keepers prized their reputation as "real businessmen." One saloon featured a sign: "Nix on the conversation; this place is neutral."[45]

Eventually, the movie theater offered a respectable substitute for the saloon and an outpost of corporate power in city neighborhoods. But reformers did not initially see the nickelodeon, a locally controlled working-class amusement, as an improvement over the well-regulated saloon. When New York City's mayor closed all its nickelodeons in 1908 "in order to avert a public calamity," local papers noted with disapproval that the protesting proprietors were "chubby Irishmen as well as Hungarians, Italians, Greeks and just a handful of Germans, but the greater portion of the assembly were Jewish Americans." Most thought the "chief weakness of the moving picture lies in the conditions of presentation rather than in the picture itself. The halls and buildings are very dirty and poorly ventilated, and the audiences under no supervision or surveillance as to age or character."[46]

But after 1915, respectable investors transformed the movie industry. Determined to "kill the slum tradition" in movies, Adolph Zukor used Wall Street money to build the Paramount Studio and its nationwide chain of movie theaters during and after World War I. Other movie moguls followed suit. "Why so many 'Vaudettes,' 'Nickolet,' 'Dimes,' and 'Nickelodeons'?" asked a trade journal interested in upgrading the industry's image. The names of the industry's lavish new theaters—the Rialto, the Gem, the Bijou—reinforced the consumer fantasies appearing on their screens, as did the corps of ushers, clad in military attire, who assured respectable patrons of a well-ordered experience. Dubbed "the amusement octopus," the movie industry bought out live theaters or drove them to bankruptcy, narrowing the range of entertainment options. The "methods they are using," a theater owner complained in reference to the studios' development of nationwide chains, "are as near Bolshevism as anything I know of. They hope to gain a hold for each tentacle of their octopus by threats and financial force."[47]

Shaping Character, Inculcating Values

The popularity of the movies kindled new ambitions in reform-minded professionals. If only we could harness the "wonderful power" of movies, a school principal told the Chicago Motion Picture Commission in 1920, "the making over of this country would be greatly facilitated, indeed." Supervised playgrounds did much to combat "disorganization" and "degeneration" among children. But as reformers dreamed of what might be accomplished through the "control of the remaining 80 percent of the population during the sixty-four hours per week in which even the laboring element is at leisure," they embraced the logic and techniques of the consumer culture. "Too heavy a stress is laid on the duties of parents to children," consumer economist Simon Patten argued in 1913. In failing "to utilize the institutions of city life," we "rely on restraint to shape the character of boys when we should be thinking of their recreations."[48]

Reformers thus joined the architects of the consumer culture in supplanting the role of the family in shaping character and inculcating values. "In the social republic," a pioneer social worker explained, "the child as a future citizen is an asset of the state, not the property of its parents. Hence its welfare is a direct concern of the state." The specter of "the harm, often well-nigh irreparable, which the best intentioned parents may do to their children," drove the public schools and the helping professions to extend their jurisdiction at the expense of the family. Experts in social work, psychiatry, medicine, child development, juvenile justice, and public hygiene wrested much of the work of raising children away from parents. "Social, political, and industrial changes," prominent educators explained, "have forced upon the school responsibilities formerly laid upon the home. Once the school had mainly to teach the elements of knowledge, now it is charged with the physical, mental, and social training of the child as well."[49]

The reshaping of character and the inculcation of values reached beyond the young and beyond the school. There "is a sense in which all the people are the city's children," reformers argued. They urged municipalities to "reach out beyond the training of the youth" to reshape "the morals and amusements of adults as well." There "is a group of citizens who you might just as well classify with the child and you must legislate for that group of citizens," argued a juvenile court judge in defense of movie censorship. The reeducation of working people, he added, could prevent "social friction, class hatred, and class conflict." Reformers proceeded with the best of civic intentions. Advocates of the social gospel argued that "the school must find a way to cultivate the social temper, the habit of cooperation, the spirit of service, the consciousness of fraternity." Playground leaders promised to cultivate the "moral nature" of children and promote "civic unity." But in inculcating a "corporate conscience" and "new social notions, and a better standard of what is acceptable to those 'higher up,'" reformers worked in concert with more powerful agencies, more sure of their goals.[50]

As spending on entertainment, amusement, and recreation grew, the leisure industry, mass media, and advertising shaped personality and character more dramatically than reformers ever dreamed. Sweeping away the obsolete values of a producer's democracy, commercial agencies emphasized spending and consumption over saving and accumulation, and instant gratification over self-discipline. The new cultural appreciation of leisure offered the antidote to the drudgery of work and the decay of civic life. "The habits, instincts, and feelings we have inherited from our forefathers," Patten argued, "are no longer safe guides for us to follow." "Restraint, denial, and negation" were dysfunctional. The old system of values that "emphasized the repression of wants" made way for a new system of values centered on desire.[51]

Reformers found themselves working in harness with market agencies in ways that undercut civic purposes. Progressive educators hoped to make critical thought habitual, but advertisers studied "human instincts" to pinpoint the "psychological moment" in which the consumer's desire "is not criticized at all." Summarizing the literature on the mob mind, a psychologist of advertising noted that "We reason rarely, but act under suggestion constantly." Since the "actual effect of modern advertising is not so much to convince as to suggest," he concluded, the "advertiser should study human nature to discover these hidden springs of action."[52]

Advertisers needed little encouragement to mobilize the instincts in moving the goods. Promoting not so much self-indulgence as self-doubt, advertising undermined the self-reliance and independence of mind crucial to citizenship. Advertising made consumers "self-conscious about matter of course things such as enlarged nose pores, bad breath." Advertisers worked to "keep the masses dissatisfied with their mode of life, discontented with ugly things around them" because "satisfied customers are not as profitable as discontented ones." By generating desires not meant to be satisfied, advertising produced dissatisfaction and self-contempt. Seeking to make the consumer "emotionally uneasy, to bludgeon him with the fact that decent people don't live the way he does," advertising offered an endless litany of expert advice about how to overcome one's limitations: do you feel listless, is your job boring, is your life empty?[53]

The civic uses of leisure continued to haunt speculation about the consumer culture into the 1920s. "Politics, religion, and community welfare, like golf, bridge and other forms of recreation," sociologist Robert Park observed, "are leisure-time activities, and it is the leisure time of the community that we are seeking to organize." Consumer pleasures catered to "the desire to escape the dull routine of life at home and in the local community that drives us abroad in search of adventure," while civic life lost out in competition with these "livelier forms of recreation." In the "improvident use of our leisure," Park concluded, "the greatest wastes in American life occur."[54]

But the leisure question lost most of its civic content in the 1920s. Industrial civilization, a marketing analyst wrote, generated a "philosophy of futility," a pervasive fatigue, and a "disappointment with achievements." But, fortunately, it also provided an outlet in the "more superficial things in which fashion reigns." Increased wages and shorter hours, American Federation of Labor president William Green agreed, provided "recuperation" from drudgery and "readjustment" to the new industrial discipline. The reshaping of character thus reinforced the scientific management of labor in transforming democracy from a matter of participation into a matter of consumption. Just as scientific managers expropriated the technical knowledge of production, the helping professions and the leisure industry expropriated from parents the ability to define and satisfy their needs and those of their children. Relieved of "such onerous responsibilities," the working person won the freedom "to become a soldier in the army of production and a cipher in the process of decision."[55]

The Incorporation of the Consumer Culture

By the end of the 1920s, Prohibition had served its purpose. Although it paved the way for the triumph of the consumer culture, Prohibition exacerbated employer-employee conflicts over leisure. With Prohibition, an antisaloon leader observed in 1920, "the former would-be drinker turns against capital, employers and the industrial system, or at least is more ready to listen to advocates of radical views. . . . Deprived of the conviviality of the saloon he finds a proxy for it in strike meetings, where common cause brings him very close to his fellow men." President Herbert Hoover's National Commission on Law Observance and Enforcement learned that Prohibition bred anger and contempt for the law among working people. Conducting field interviews with workers and meeting with labor leaders in Washington, the commission discovered "strong and bitter resentment" over a law that was never intended "to be applied to any but the working man."[56]

Organized and dominated by corporate leaders, the Association Against the Prohibition Amendment (AAPA) monitored Prohibition almost from its inception. Corporate leaders worried that the controversy over Prohibition undercut the capacity of the "mild excitement of the movies, prize-fights, and our great national game" to provide "vents to compensate men for the long repressions that society and the mores always impose." Anxious to preserve respect for the state and its capacity to guide social development, the AAPA sought a more flexible and impartial approach to the drink problem. In working out a plan for repeal, President Franklin Roosevelt's administration followed the logic of Hoover's commission. While it remained "essential to the general welfare that our citizens do not drink to excess, and the State should put out a restraining hand in order to bring this about," a Democratic insider wrote in 1933, these efforts must avert "a nationwide disregard for law, with all the attendant abuses that follow in its train." Ratification of the Twenty-Second Amendment in 1933, repealing Prohibition but reasserting the legitimacy of state and national regulation of the liquor trade, accomplished those ends.[57]

Coming at the end of more than a decade of government support for the creation of the consumer culture, the repeal of Prohibition served to legitimate and preserve that legacy. More than any previous national leader, Hoover associated democracy with consumption. "America's high standard of living" is our most precious gift to "civilization," reported one of the countless studies Hoover commissioned while serving as the secretary of commerce. Hoover left the tasks of governing to experts and managerial elites. The people served democracy simply by purchasing "electrical appliances, radios, swings for the backyard, carpets, books and bookcases, or whatever," filling "one's own house with one's own arrangement of gadgets, rooms, and surroundings."[58]

Hoover knew, however, that consumption could not be taken for granted. "We are almost wholly lacking in the basic data of distribution," he explained, as expanding production, shifting populations, and new patterns of transportation created "blind markets." The Department of Commerce sponsored conferences, conducted surveys, and commissioned experts to help business speed the flow of goods. As "wants are almost insatiable," one survey explained, we need only "adjust our economic processes as to make dormant demands effective." In facilitating that adjustment, Hoover transformed the Department of Commerce from a small, disorganized, poorly funded bureaucracy into the most dynamic federal agency of the 1920s.[59]

By 1932, the Department of Commerce filled the largest office building in the world, sprawling across three full city blocks in Washington, D.C. At the center of Hoover's empire stood the Bureau of Foreign and Domestic Commerce, whose budget grew 8,000 percent over the decade as its staff expanded from 100 to 2,500. The bureau helped to locate and exploit overseas markets and target and develop domestic markets. Following Hoover's instructions to focus on "consumer wishes and desires," the bureau broke down "all barriers between the consumers and commodities." It sponsored census investigations to determine "what kind of goods offered the least resistance to sales promotion," recommended changes in urban design to facilitate sales, praised Hollywood for "starting a regular prairie-fire of enthusiasm for American specialities," and conducted a weekly radio show to promote business. "Lure the glance," one broadcast put it, "fire the imagination by means of brilliant primary colors, unusual composition and mastery of line."[60]

Under Hoover, the Department of Commerce and, after 1928, the presidency stood at the center of a network of institutions reshaping culture in the interests of corporate profitability. Popularizing the concepts of "mass leisure" and "mass consumption," Hoover emphasized the government's concern with the wants and desires of citizens over its concern for their rights and responsibilities. With the creation of the parcel post, for example, business became the largest user of the post office, shifting its focus from civic culture to consumer culture.[61]

The Radio Act of 1927 resulted in a similar transformation of broadcasting through the new Federal Radio Commission (FRC). Charged with allocating broadcasting licenses to stations that best served the "public interest, convenience or necessity," the FRC presided initially over a public utility. In 1925, more than two hundred nonprofit stations, often affiliated with educational and religious institutions, represented 40 percent of the total number of broadcasters. Even commercial broadcasters (only 4 percent of the total in 1925) presented themselves as public service corporations, more interested in providing high-quality programming than generating profits.[62]

Prior to 1927, most Americans agreed that nonprofit broadcasting should remain an important and perhaps dominant aspect of radio and that commercial advertising should be limited. In Great Britain, opposition to "pathetic or forcible appeals—in appropriate tones—on behalf of somebody's soap or tomato ketchup" led to a public broadcasting system underwritten by sales taxes and license fees. Similar concerns shaped debate in the United States. "The great feeling about radio in this country," an author of the 1927 legislation warned, "is that it will be monopolized by the few wealthy interests." In annual congressional debates over extending the life of the FRC, Congress instructed the commissioners to preserve nonprofit broadcasting and limit the power of commercial networks.[63]

But Hoover championed the "commercial emancipation" of radio against all opposition, and advocates of commercial broadcasting quickly dominated the FRC. In 1928, the FRC allocated fifty-thousand-watt clear channels to forty stations, all but three of them affiliated with one of the commercial networks (NBC and CBS). Some six hundred remaining stations shared channels on lower frequencies. Although some fought for access to a clear channel, most nonprofits went under. In 1929, only one hundred stations remained on the air. By 1931, NBC and CBS dominated 70 percent of U.S. broadcasting as measured by hours and level of power. Commercial advertising, barely existing in 1928, soared to an annual total of $72 million by 1934. In its *Third Annual Report* (1929), the FRC equated commercial broadcasting with "general public service" and classified nonprofits as "propaganda" stations.[64]

In 1930, *Education By Radio*, the journal of educational and nonprofit broadcasters, demanded new protective legislation. "There has never been in the entire history of the United States an example of mismanagement and lack of vision so colossal and far-reaching in its consequences as our turning of the radio channels almost exclusively into commercial hands," charged the populist director of the National Committee on Education for Radio. Chicago's nonprofit WCFL, the voice of the Chicago Federation of Labor, joined the fight against the "Radio Trust," charging that all the clear channels had been "given to capital and its friends and not even one channel to the millions that toil." Opponents of commercial broadcasting argued that the public airwaves should remain open to a diversity of voices and opinions as a contribution to a democratic culture. But they faced a powerful radio lobby of commercial broadcasters.[65]

The opposition had few weapons against the broadcasters' lobbying skills and public relations blitz, which depicted commercial broadcasting as the only American and democratic way. Newspaper publishers initially joined in the campaign against their rival for advertising dollars, but when newspaper owners began purchasing or affiliating with radio stations, they followed the radio lobby's lead. John Dewey joined the voices calling for public radio. Radio, he argued, "is the most powerful instrument of social education the world has ever seen." In "all social matters the mass of people are guided through hearing rather than sight," making the choice between radio for "propaganda or public interest" one "of the most crucial problems of the present."[66]

Despite some hope that the Roosevelt administration might reopen the debate, the Communications Act of 1934 created a permanent Federal Communications Commission to oversee the private industry. As the commercial future of radio appeared inevitable, Dewey expressed the frail hope that "radio even when in private hands is affected with a profound public interest." By the end of the 1930s, commercial broadcasting came to seem as American as apple pie. "No special laws had to be passed to bring these things about," the president of RCA told the nation. "They were already implicit in the American system, ready and waiting for broadcasting when it came about." Whoever "attacks the fundamentals of the American system" of broadcasting, the president of CBS added, "attacks democracy itself."[67]

Mass Culture, Mass Media, and the Consumerization of Politics

The president of CBS took for granted that democracy meant a homogeneous, mass culture of pleasures. In the 1920s, when Henry Ford and other corporate employers advocated higher wages and shorter hours to enable workers to "find out what is going on in the world," they meant consumer trends, not civic affairs. Advertisers rejoiced that through radio, movies, and other standardized commodities "we are fast getting to be a nation which lives to patterns everywhere." Mass culture served "all of the people all the time" and appeared to be erasing "lines of demarcation" to make us "a homogeneous people."[68]

Ethnic associations, enterprises, and neighborhoods once limited and mediated the reception of mass culture. But beginning in the Great Depression, chain stores, studio-controlled movie theaters, and national broadcasting and recording studios delivered a more standardized fare and encouraged a more homogenized audience. The spread of mass culture supported the Congress of Industrial Organizations' "culture of unity," facilitating unionization. Radio provided a foundation for conversation and reached workers in their homes when open meetings became impossible. The radio listener, two social psychologists wrote in 1935, "has an imaginative sense of participation in a common activity." Unlike the printed word, "radio fills us with a 'consciousness of kind' which at times grows into an impression of vast social unity. It is for this reason that radio is potentially more effective than print in bringing about concerted opinion and action."[69]

The Congress of Industrial Organizations used mass culture to encourage participation in the union movement. "So if you are beginning to be a doubter too," an organizer told his fellow workers in reference to company promises, "pack your lunch and 'Come up 'n see us' at the next meeting, and as Amos and Andy say, 'We'll talk the sichyation over.'" Hollywood movies also encouraged an inclusive culture organized around a producer's democracy. But without a culture of participation, mass culture could inflame unthinking prejudices, as did Father Charles Coughlin's anti-Semitic broadcasts during the Depression. Twenty million "often listen simultaneously to a single broadcast," social psychologists reported, making radio "an agency of incalculable power for controlling the action of men." Holding a "tenacious grip ... on the mental life" of the listening public, radio excelled at "forming a crowd mind" without actual "congregate crowds." The radio audience lacked the "direct give and take" of the "face-to-face group" and "derived little stimulation from one another." While the listener might wish "to ask a question or express an opinion ... he is unable to do so." Radio broadcasting, the psychologists concluded, could not promote the "emergence of new ideas based upon free discussion." During and after World War II, Hollywood movies similarly encouraged narrow, unthinking prejudices.[70]

In his best-selling study of *The Lonely Crowd* (1950), sociologist David Riesman summed up the consumerist transformation of the American character.

With the "shift from an age of production to an age of consumption," Riesman argued, the inner-directed character of the nineteenth century gave way to the other-directed character of the twentieth. The inner-directed character enjoyed an internalized set of values and goals, symbolized by the gyroscope, which kept the individual on an even keel as he or she responded to new opportunities and challenges. In contrast, the other-directed character deployed a hypersensitive apparatus for responding to the opinions and expectations of others, symbolized by radar.[71]

As Riesman examined how the mass media, advertising, public education, and the helping professions invaded intimate relations, he exposed the other-directed character as an empty vessel to be filled with socially determined beliefs, values, and behaviors. Subjected to a "bounteous flow of imagery from urban centers," the lives of the outer-directed were "mediated by the flow of mass communication." While parents turned "increasingly to books, magazines, government pamphlets, and radio programs" for lessons on child rearing, children quickly learned "what the norm of parental behavior is, and hold it over their parents' heads." Raised by "character-forming agencies outside the home," children learned the importance of "acquiring an unusual facility in one's duties as a consumer" and honed the skill with their peers.[72]

Inner-direction and other-direction produced fundamentally different sorts of citizens. Inner-directed citizens approached politics as "moralizers," committed to self-improvement and institutional reform. Riesman cited antebellum unions and labor associations as classic examples of the moralizing mode, "passionately concerned with questions of political, legal, and economic justice and only indirectly interested in wages and working conditions."[73] In contrast, other-direction made for apathetic citizens. Paralyzed by "the general lack of imaginative alternatives," they responded with "almost total passivity" to political affairs. Fearful of "looking and feeling like the uninformed outsider," the other-directed citizen approached politics "as a means of group conformity," scanning the mass media for the "acceptable opinions."[74]

As public opinion became a matter of what people thought other people thought, the mass media simultaneously emptied politics of content. Treating politics "in terms of consumer preferences," Riesman wrote, the mass media focused more on the politician's "manner and mode of doing things" than on "what is done." Acting "as a kind of a barker for the political show," the mass media taught spectators how to consume carefully packaged candidates. Riesman extracted the recipe for the perfect candidate from a study of the "subtle, psychological values" that a successful supermarket must possess. Like supermarkets, successful candidates required "the same traits that we like in our friends," specifically "cleanliness, up-to-date appearance, generosity, courtesy, honesty, patience, sincerity, sympathy, and good-naturedness."[75]

Examining the 1948 presidential campaign, Riesman identified Dwight Eisenhower as the exemplary candidate for the other-directed. As if on cue, the Republicans devoted themselves to "merchandising Eisenhower's frankness, honesty and integrity, his sincere and whole approach" in the 1952 campaign, the first in which television played an important role. After Ike's victory, Riesman wrote that the bland Eisenhower appealed to "a society-made generation who could not believe that society would let them down." Riesman assumed that the affluent United States faced few pressing issues and that the political torpidity of the other-directed hardly mattered. But if, as Eisenhower later warned, the preservation of the freedom in an age of centralization demanded "an alert and knowledgeable citizenry," the other-directed could not rise to the task.[76]

Riesman simply rejected the political realm as hopeless. The "political is devoid of substantial content," he wrote, and "the consumption of political vituperation may easily become more than ever an escape" from more serious matters. But he did hope to release the other-directed from the "fantastic fraud" promoted by advertisers and the mass media. The other-directed thought of themselves as excessively materialistic and pointed to advertising as proof. But Riesman reminded Americans of the scorn with which they greeted each new advertising campaign. Rather than passive subjects of a "coerced conformity" imposed by ruthless business interests, the other-directed suffered from a self-imposed conformity. The condemnation of business as "dull and disagreeable as well as morally suspect" only obscured the "genuine moral problem" of achieving some measure of personal autonomy and competence.[77]

But the means to autonomy and competence that Riesman recommended frustrated the end. We needed "rapidly to expand the tertiary trades that cater to leisure," Riesman argued, including the new profession of "avocational counselors." This "rather clinical term," he explained, stood for "travel agents, hotel men, resort directors, sports teachers and coaches, teachers of the arts" as well as interior decorators, even "the dude-ranch social director." Acknowledging the danger of increasing "the very dependence which keeps him other-directed rather than autonomous," Riesman thought the other-directed individual might be encouraged to "realize how very important for his own development toward autonomy play is." The process could begin with children. Given "script . . . allowing them to patronize some central store," they could be served by "market researchers, able and willing to help children make their selections."[78]

Riesman feared his "paltry suggestions" might be dismissed as utopian. But his "avocational counselors" were already hard at work, though not toward the ends he desired. Sluggish sales in the 1950s and fears of market saturation encouraged deep investigations of consumer motivation and psychology. Pouring over demographic and psychological traits to identify consumer insecurities and identities, retailers abandoned the mass market in favor of segmented markets. Describing some sixty-two clusters of buyers from "Blue Blood Estates" to "Shotguns and Pickups," market research showed that larger and more secure profits could come from the exploitation of segments. Spending billions on research to rethink the family as a disparate collection of individuals with discrete desires, marketing experts packaged television audiences to shrewd merchandisers eager to capture market segments (children on weekends, housewives during the day, and so forth).[79]

Market research and segmentation also reshaped politics. Political consultants searched for the same techniques for predicting and controlling human behavior that advertising agencies, efficiency engineers, educational psychologists, and other managers of complex social systems used. They found it in "attitude" psychology and survey research. Defined as "an enduring evaluative disposition," an attitude reflected a semirational combination of thoughts and feelings that directed behavior. Finding attitudes resistant to change (what they called the "law of minimal effects"), political consultants employed survey research and polling to identify and cater to existing attitudes. They then crafted candidates and campaigns that told voters what they wanted to hear.[80]

Resembling the radar of the other-directed, survey research endlessly recycled the socially determined attitudes of the lonely crowd, virtually precluding significant political change. Campaign specialists thought of "a man in a voting booth who hesitates between two levers as if he were pausing between competing tubes of toothpaste in a drug store" and acted accordingly. They also sold another commodity—prepackaged audiences—to political candidates. Political "spots" reached targeted demographics at specified times on broadcast television and, later, on narrowcast cable television. The growth of market segments also encouraged an identity politics based on age, gender, race, and ethnicity, redirecting even rebellious impulses toward consumer choices and away from questions of power and participation.[81]

The segmenting of voters into political markets discouraged any discussion of the greater public good, as candidates cobbled together winning coalitions by appealing to different sets of special interests. Campaign experts also legitimated the identity politics that further balkanized the public. In turn, voters identified their interests with membership in narrowly defined interest groups to the exclusion of any broader identification. The rising costs of campaigning placed a premium on fund-raising, empowering another group of direct-mail and lobbying experts and skewing politics further toward the concerns of special interests. Ultimately, voters judged both candidates and government programs as commodities. Ignoring any expansive conception of the public good, voters used market expectations to evaluate government programs in terms of private benefits. The consumer culture drained both leisure and politics of civic content.[82]

CHAPTER 11

Private Vision, Public Resources

◆

Mass Suburbanization and the Decline of the City

During World War II, with the cities of Europe under siege, the American city carried the hopes of democratic civilization. "In the great world drama involving the destiny of civilization which is moving toward a climax," a city planner wrote in 1943, "New York has become the center—the core—of the democratic system." But the city, he warned, carried both the "germs which may threaten social disintegration" as well as "the seeds of larger and better growth." Its future depended on the continuation of public investments that made the American city a center of democratic opportunity, providing "a wider, fuller, and more varied life" for all. Urban libraries, museums, concert halls, universities, amusements, and entertainments, all linked by public transit, kindled personal ambition and tied it to civic life.[1]

The Boston Public Library exemplified the generous public sphere that made the American city the hope of democracy. Founded in 1848 as the first publicly supported free municipal library in the world, the library moved to its present building in 1895. "Built by the People and Dedicated to the Advancement of Learning" reads its entablature, with "Free to All" emblazoned over its entrance. A turn-of-the-century Russian immigrant described the library as her "chamber of dreams," recalling that to "be set down in the midst of all the books that ever were written was a miracle as great as any on record." Another municipal project, New York City's subway opened in 1904. The distinguished architecture of its City Hall Station and the decorative embellishments throughout the system promoted civic pride. Frequent expansions and the system's five-cent fare provided affordable access to the entire city and its abundant opportunities. The subway enabled generations of New Yorkers, like the Ashcan school of painters who celebrated the energy found in subway crowds, to find their vocations and contribute to the life of the city.[2]

But during World War II, the suburban single-family home, replete with consumer durables, supplanted the city at the center of our democratic civilization. As a symbol of what Americans fought for, a private vision of domesticity and consumption filled wartime advertisements, government publications, and popular culture. The war was about "love and gettin' hitched, and havin' a home and some kids, and breathin' fresh air out in the suburbs," a federally sponsored radio drama put it in 1942. The suburban residence, the *Saturday Evening Post* explained, provided the foundation for "mass employment, mass production, mass advertising, mass distribution and mass ownership of the products of industry" and thus represented "the last bulwark of [democratic] civilization." In the thirty years following World War II, an unprecedented expenditure of public resources underwrote this private vision. Reversing its tradition of minimalist urban policy, the federal government reshaped the metropolis through home mortgage insurance, interstate highways, subsidies for suburban utilities, tax deductions for home owners, and the construction of public housing in the inner city.[3]

Mass suburbanization included a profoundly racial dimension, embedding prejudice in the built environment. The discriminatory policies of the Federal Housing Administration (FHA) reinforced the efforts of private realtors and white residents to police the boundaries of the ghetto. Meanwhile, urban redevelopment, urban renewal, and highway construction disrupted and destroyed black neighborhoods. Invariably located in the ghetto, public housing intensified segregation and concentrated poverty. Discrimination and segregation trapped African Americans in inner-city neighborhoods, just as declining employment and the deterioration of the public realm undercut the city's role as the center of democratic opportunity. In 1968, the federal *Report of the National Advisory Commission on Civil Disorders* warned that we were moving "toward two societies, one black, one white—separate and unequal." The concentration of "the most impoverished and dependent segments of the population into central-city ghettoes," the report concluded, meant that "within two decades, this division could be so deep that it would be almost impossible to unite."[4]

Reducing public investments in central cities, the liberal architects of postwar urban policy placed their hopes for a more democratic society in a massconsumption economy with the suburban home at its center. Citing an "increase in consumer spending" as "the basic and lasting solution to our economic future," the New Deal liberal Charles Bowles's best-selling *Tomorrow without Fear* (1946) described suburbanization as "perhaps our greatest single opportunity ... to increase the purchasing power of our people." In subsidizing major industries from construction to automobiles, federal mortgages and highways promoted prosperity. But they could not so easily secure public goals. "We can solve a housing problem, or we can try to solve a racial problem," the federally backed builder William Levitt explained in defense of his whites-only developments. "But we cannot combine the two."[5]

Postwar liberals defended their policies by arguing that they promoted economic growth and left people free to define the good life for themselves. Mass suburbanization, a senior FHA official argued in this vein, "is not a policy, it is a reality—and it is impossible for us to change this trend as it is to change the desire of birds to migrate to a more suitable location." Mass suburbanization did continue a century-old drift of residence to the urban periphery. But the postwar world of sprawling suburbs and decaying cities cannot be understood simply as a product of individual preferences. Public policies and resources made some choices more economically feasible than others. And even when federal subsidies gave officials significant leverage over the private market, they failed to use it. Echoing Levitt, FHA officials insisted their charge had been to stimulate the construction industry, not to shape sound metropolitan development.[6]

Postwar liberals did not explicitly intend to abandon public purposes. But their market-based initiatives could not provide the public goods—transit, education, recreation, affordable housing, integrated neighborhoods—essential to the more democratic society they desired. Even when public officials tried to revitalize cities through urban redevelopment and renewal legislation, they placed these powers at the disposal of private developers more interested in private profit than the public purpose. A different set of public policies and a bolder program of public investment could have produced a different future for American cities. Public funds for the maintenance and improvement of city neighborhoods might have undercut the vicious circle of racial prejudice undermining transitional neighborhoods and, in turn, reinforcing racial prejudice. Public investments in neighborhood schools, parks, libraries, and other urban amenities might have reversed the deterioration of central cities and slowed the flight to the suburbs. A more generous program of public housing might have provided a stabilizing force for the city rather than a stigmatized last resort.[7]

In the deterioration of central cities, Americans lost their best chance to revitalize democracy. In 1945, central cities still encouraged a shared public life. Municipal agencies and public schools served a broad range of socioeconomic groups who also depended on central-city police and firefighting forces, tax rates, and regulations. Businessmen and middle-class shoppers commuted to the city center, sharing streetcars and sidewalks with working people. Thirty years later, Americans commuted in private automobiles, shopped in exclusive malls, lived in gated communities, and insulated themselves from those unlike themselves. Supplanting the give-and-take of big-city politics that gave even marginal groups some voice, the multiplication of suburban jurisdictions fragmented political power and made much of metropolitan wealth unavailable for public investment in central cities.[8]

The automobile liberated many Americans from public transit and FHA mortgages allowed them to escape crowded neighborhoods. But the poor and the black enjoyed fewer choices, which were narrowed even further by the decay of public transit and private and public disinvestment in city neighborhoods. The affluent, a leading economist concluded in 1991, were "quietly seceding from the large and diverse publics of America into homogeneous enclaves, within which their earnings need not be redistributed to people less fortunate than them." Settling in communities of limited liability, the affluent allowed the city to deteriorate and thereby closed to the less affluent what municipal officials recognized as "the golden door to full participation in American life." The affluent themselves lost the joys of public life and all "those things which define a city's vitality," another economist added, including "the culture and ferment, material pleasures and comforts, exploration and invention" that "produce a flow of ideas and products for export."[9]

New Deal Urban Policy and the Suburban-Industrial Complex

The vision of mass-produced suburban housing originated with Secretary of Commerce Herbert Hoover during the 1920s. Home ownership provided "the foundation of a sound economy and social system," Hoover argued, and "permanent prosperity" would follow if the inefficiencies in the housing industry could be eliminated. He therefore encouraged industry leaders to adopt national standards for building materials and a uniform building code. The housing industry set construction records between 1922 and 1928, but ground to a halt during the Great Depression just as Hoover assumed the presidency. Committed to voluntary actions by private interests, President Hoover resisted calls for direct public intervention into the housing market.[10]

President Franklin Roosevelt's New Deal provided the first sustained federal support for the housing industry. Determined to produce the maximum of private investment with a minimum expenditure of public funds, Roosevelt supported a mortgage insurance program. With half of all residential mortgages in default in 1933, the newly created federal Home Owners Loan Corporation (HOLC) spent $3 billion to help refinance one-tenth of all nonfarm residences. The HOLC enlisted the aid of realtors and lenders to compile a series of Residential Security Maps and Surveys, ranking neighborhoods according to financial risk. The age and condition of housing, the quality of public amenities and infrastructure, the prevalence of "a lower grade population," and, above all, the degree of racial and ethnic homogeneity determined the classifications.[11]

The HOLC assumed that when neighborhoods began to go black, their physical and social decline could not be reversed. It thus gave neighborhoods with even a small black population the lowest rating (D or red, hence "redlining"). The HOLC nevertheless issued mortgages impartially and enjoyed greater success in getting mortgages repaid in red-lined areas than in higher-rated districts. But the Federal Housing Administration (FHA), created by the 1934 National Housing Act, adopted the HOLC's classification system and systematically denied loans to red-lined districts. The FHA's 1939 *Underwriting Manual* cited high densities, older properties, as well as shops, stores, and rental units as dangerous signs, designating city neighborhoods as high-risk areas. New suburban developments avoided all these dangers and received the vast majority of FHA assistance.[12]

The FHA also adopted the HOLC's assumptions about race. Citing "inharmonious racial groups" as a key indicator of financial risk, the FHA denied mortgage insurance to neighborhoods with even a tiny black population. Less than 2 percent of three million mortgages the FHA insured through 1952 went to African Americans. A Detroit developer could not get FHA support until he built a foot-thick, six-foot-high wall protecting his subdivision from an adjacent black enclave. Until the Supreme Court declared them unconstitutional in 1948, the FHA recommended restrictive covenants that prohibited owners from selling to specified minorities. Legitimizing the racial prejudices of developers, lenders, realtors, and home owners, the FHA policy of red-lining became a self-fulfilling prophecy as the denial of loans for maintenance and repair spread urban blight throughout black districts.[13]

The FHA nonetheless stimulated the housing industry and underwrote postwar prosperity. In popularizing the self-amortizing mortgage (which extended payments over thirty years, at which point the loan would be fully repaid), the FHA also brought home ownership within reach of middle-income families. Covering as much as 93 percent of purchase, FHA insurance reduced the typical down payment from 30 percent or more to below 10 percent. Attracting investment capital into the residential mortgage market, FHA insurance reduced interest payments by two or three percentage points. In 1944, the Servicemen's Readjustment Act—the "G.I. bill"—committed the Veteran's Administration (VA) to a similar policy. Almost half of all suburban residences in the postwar era benefited from FHA or VA mortgage insurance. By 1972, the national rate of home ownership increased from 44 to 63 percent.[14]

Federally funded expressways represented the New Deal's second major contribution to postwar urban policy. Like FHA mortgages, the promotion of the automobile over public transit fit the preference for private, market-based solutions to urban problems. The Public Works Administration and other federal agencies put hundreds of thousands of the unemployed to work building streets and highways, accounting for more than one-third of all New Deal work-relief jobs. The New Deal also protected gasoline taxes from "diversion" to nonhighway purposes. By 1940, surfaced road mileage doubled to nearly 1.4 million miles. Faced with subsidized competition in the thirty years after the war (when only 1 percent of federal transportation funds went to public transit), streetcars, subways, and interurban trains retrenched or went bankrupt. Others fell prey to a consortium of oil, rubber, and highway interests organized by General Motors (GM) to buy out and shut down streetcar systems, their rights-of-way disappearing with them.[15]

Federal expressways funneled population out of the city and required the razing of city neighborhoods for their construction. The GM-led American Road Builders Association, a coalition of auto-related businesses and labor unions, lobbied hard for the highway program. "We must dream of gashing our way ruthlessly through built-up sections of overcrowded cities, in order to create traffic ways," an industry leader mused. In 1942, the Federal National Resources Planning Board recommended the creation of "a modern interregional highway system and urban express routes to accommodate the automobile of the future." The 1944 Federal-Aid Highway Act proposed a national network of highways piercing major cities. The 1956 Interstate Highway Act set federal bulldozers to work, ripping up city neighborhoods to make way for new highways.[16]

President Roosevelt envisioned federal mortgages and highways primarily as the means "to utilize productively some of the manpower and industrial capacity" idled by the Depression. The third component of New Deal urban policy, public housing, also served first and foremost as an economic stimulus. Accordingly, the early New Deal supported low-income housing through loans to private, limited-dividend corporations rather than public construction. Roosevelt's landslide victory in 1936, and his second inaugural pledge to help "one-third of a nation ill-housed, ill-clad, ill-nourished," led to the passage of a potentially far-reaching measure. The U.S. Housing Act of 1937 offered loans to local governments for up to 90 percent of capital costs for public housing and grants to assist construction and maintenance. But starved for funds, the program provided only 130,000 units in 300 projects by 1941. Barely touching a need measured in the millions of units, new public housing did not even replace a third of the dwelling units demolished in the 1930s.[17]

The postwar housing shortage revived interest in public housing. In 1946, *Fortune* reported that "nearly half of those who were polled went so far as advocating government construction of homes on a large scale." Describing the housing shortage as a "failure of capitalism" that "will do more to undermine free institutions than ten thousand Union Square orators," *Fortune* endorsed a limited public housing program. But unlike the federal mortgages and highways (that subsidized private industry), public housing competed with private industry. With the postwar housing boom, public housing lost its rationale as an economic stimulus and faced charges of "creeping socialism." By 1980, public housing accounted for only 1 percent of the U.S. housing market (contrasted with 46 percent in England and 37 percent in France). Meanwhile, President Harry Truman pledged "every encouragement and assistance" to private industry. By the late 1950s and for the rest of the century, "housing starts" became a key indicator of economic and social health.[18]

New Deal urban policy gave rise to a suburban-industrial complex of public and private agencies devoted to the mass production of suburban housing. Between 1947 and 1951, at Levittown on Long Island, New York, an "army of trucks" dropped "identical bundles of lumber, pipes, bricks, shingles and copper tubing," as "giant machines" and two- and three-man work crews completed a new house every fifteen minutes. At Lakewood, south of Los Angeles, the developers commissioned a dramatic series of aerial photographs, documenting the industry's new assembly-line methods. "This is planning as businessmen can do it," they boasted to *Time* magazine.[19]

Suburbanization promised profits beyond the construction and real estate industries. During the war, General Electric launched an advertising campaign promoting the "home of tomorrow," a detached, single-family suburban residence sketched in the dirt by a GI about to go overseas. The GI would return to his bride and their "victory home," the ad read, with "*better living built in . . .* electrical living with new comforts, new conveniences, new economies to make every day an adventure in happiness." Urging builders to equip suburban housing with air conditioning and electric heat, electrical utilities generated profits and extinguished the wartime interest in solar power. The manufacturers of electric appliances successfully lobbied to have built-in refrigerators, ranges, washing machines, and dishwashers—even vacuum cleaners—covered by FHA mortgages. In the first five postwar years, consumer spending jumped 60 percent. Spending on appliances rose 240 percent.[20]

Concerned about declining downtown retail sales in the 1950s, department stores built suburban shopping malls and added their weight to the suburban-industrial complex. "The movement to the suburbs means more automobiles, more mileage per car and more multiple-car families," a sales manager observed in 1954. "I leave it to your imagination to think what it means in terms of automotive home workshops, sporting goods, lawnmowers, garden tools, casual goods." Hudson's, Detroit's largest department store, financed the Northland Shopping Center in 1954, with one hundred stores, wide pedestrian malls, and plenty of parking. Its $78 million in sales the first year doubled predictions. Southdale Mall, outside Minneapolis and also financed by the city's largest department store, initiated a trend toward enclosed, climate-controlled malls with garden courts and sidewalk cafes. By the early 1960s, suburban shopping malls accounted for 60 percent of metropolitan retail trade. By 1976, developers built more than seventeen thousand shopping centers (a nineteenfold increase since 1957).[21]

Suburban shopping malls provided a perfect landscape of consumption. With store-lined walkways, benches, and landscaping, security and ample parking, shopping malls offered a safe and sanitized version of urban downtowns. Designed as stage sets for consumption, suburban malls eliminated the distractions of the city. No older buildings or alternative institutions reminded consumers of priorities and values other than consumer ones. Central ownership insured a controlled and soothing experience. Everything about the mall—trees and flowers, fountains and music, graphic art and colorful awnings—focused attention on the goods. Malls dropped both bargain basements and high-style shops, catering to a middle-income, socially homogenous, white world. Merchants, mindful that "segregated suburban centers" appealed to whites troubled by "low-income, Negro shoppers" in downtown stores, discouraged both public transit and black job applicants.[22]

THE ORIGINS OF THE URBAN CRISIS I: ERODING THE TAX AND EMPLOYMENT BASE

As wealth and population moved out to the suburbs after 1945, central cities faced mounting challenges. The municipal tax base eroded as the suburban percentage of metropolitan residences rose from 32 percent in 1940 to 41.5 percent in 1950 and 48.5 percent in 1960. The closing of big-city department stores in the late 1950s and early 1960s proved another heavy blow, undercutting the downtown property values that provided between 12 and 20 percent of municipal revenues. The erosion of the city's employment base also weakened municipal finances as manufacturing fled the city in the 1940s and 1950s, followed by office employment in the 1960s and 1970s.[23]

In 1945, however, the deterioration of the urban core appeared anything but inevitable. During the Depression, an exodus of people out of the city undermined municipal finances and spread blight. But the war produced a boom for downtown offices, hotels, and department stores. Heavy use and postponed investments wore down public infrastructure, particularly public transit, which served 23 billion riders in 1945. But city officials and business leaders compiled their wish lists of public projects during the war years, passing bond issues and redevelopment legislation in preparation for postwar Reconstruction. In the decade after the war, municipal governments spent billions to improve sewer, water, and mass-transit systems, and reduce pollution. Private investment followed in the wake of public munificence, as slum clearance, centripetal freeways, and subsidized parking facilities led to new and expanded department stores, office buildings, universities, and hospitals.[24]

Hopeful signs could be found in the field of race relations as well. The busy factories of industrial cities served as the "arsenals of democracy" during World War II, providing full employment. A tight labor market, interracial union organizing, and the federal Fair Employment Practices Commission combined to break down a segregated labor market and doubled the number of blacks in skilled and semiskilled occupations. "You could get a job anywhere you went," a black worker recalled of Detroit. Obstacles remained, but the fight against fascism and the African American campaign for a double victory over racism at home and abroad pushed racial equality toward the top of the national agenda. As liberal and labor activists fought for racial integration, not even the clashes between whites and blacks in parks, schools, and workplaces that sometimes escalated into ugly wartime riots dampened expectations.[25]

Building an interracial movement, organized labor advanced a social democratic agenda that included full employment, civil rights, and public investments in transportation, housing, and health. Activists dreamed of replacing "dirty, bad-smelling, germ-ridden structures, abutting upon crowded, ugly, barren streets" with "cheery, comfortable, healthful homes" amid "playgrounds, municipal health centers, domestic science classes, musical organizations, cultural clubs, forums, and classes." In the postwar wave of strikes in 1945–1946, labor joined women and African Americans in placing the continuation of wartime price controls at the center of the struggle for a broad public agenda and an activist state.[26]

But business leaders delivered labor a series of defeats and passed on modest wage hikes to consumers. As inflation rose through the spring and summer of 1946, a timid Democratic Congress failed to extend price controls. In the elections of 1946, ten million disillusioned Democratic voters stayed home and conservatives regained control of Congress, ensuring the defeat of labor's agenda, the reduction of the federal role in postwar economic adjustment, and the dismantling of the wartime federal Fair Employment Practices Commission. Labor activists found themselves defending public housing, racial integration, and other public initiatives against the charge of "creeping socialism."[27]

Despite its defeat, labor's aggressive political agenda led manufacturers to rethink their commitment to the big industrial cities. Warning that the "militant and venomous attitude toward industry has and will continue to limit job opportunity," a Detroit employer concluded that there is "something seriously wrong with our business climate." Across the industrial Midwest, labor militance meant that future expansion would "take place elsewhere at a faster rate than in the corporate limits of Detroit and its sister cities in the automobile belt." Manufacturers decentralized production as the means to create a contented, nonunion working class in the suburbs. The suburbanization of industry, employers argued, allowed working families to "find happiness in their garden-set homes."[28]

With manufacturers joining the suburban-industrial complex, industrial decentralization devastated central cities. Detroit lost 134,000 manufacturing jobs between 1947 and 1963. New York lost 175,000 between 1947 and 1967 and then another 286,000 over the next decade. Virtually every other major city lost between 20 and 40 percent of all manufacturing jobs in the two decades after the war. Tax incentives and the absence of unions attracted industrial corporations to suburban and rural jurisdictions. Automobile manufacturers invested billions of dollars in twenty-five new plants in the Detroit metropolitan area between 1947 and 1958, every one of them in the suburbs. Small- and medium-sized cities from the Midwest to California attracted even more new plants. Federal spending on highways sped the movement of manufacturing to the suburbs and the Sunbelt. So did the federal policy of decentralizing defense production to reduce vulnerability to nuclear attack.[29]

Manufacturers cited the need for sprawling, one-story plants as the reason for leaving the city. But shop-floor struggles over work rules and wages reinforced those decisions and quickened interest in automation to reduce the need for skilled labor. As a Ford manager in a Cleveland plant remarked to United

Auto Workers (UAW) president Walter Reuther, "you are going to have trouble collecting union dues from all these machines." The shift of production from Detroit's River Rouge plant to an automated plant in Cleveland decimated the militant UAW Local 600, cutting Rouge jobs from 85,000 to 30,000 between 1945 and 1960.[30]

Some union locals questioned the prerogatives of corporations. The 60,000-member, interracial UAW Local 600 fought against automation and runaway plants. As the Ford Corporation hauled machines out of its River Rouge plant under cover of darkness, Local 600 also staged dozens of wildcat strikes and shop floor actions and asserted the worker's "inalienable right to a job." "Where is your gratitude to your men, your city?" the unionists asked Henry Ford II, asserting the corporation's responsibility to the people and the communities that had enriched it. Local 600 demanded that the city of Detroit investigate the "migration of industrial operations and jobs from this area and to seek ways and means of ending such migration."[31]

But even in blue-collar suburbs like Dearborn, Michigan, local governments enjoyed little leverage against multinational corporations. Municipal officials cleared blighted residential districts in a policy of "industrial renewal" to attract new industrial enterprise. But major corporations preferred lower labor costs and taxes in the suburbs and the Sunbelt. Smaller manufacturers without the capital resources to automate fled to the suburbs, small towns, and the Sunbelt even faster than the corporate giants, or else went under taking jobs with them. Job retraining became the preferred response to the flight of jobs from the city, absolving corporations of responsibility.[32]

African Americans suffered most from industrial decentralization, experiencing unemployment rates two and three times that of whites. Automation eliminated unskilled and dangerous jobs once reserved for blacks, while decentralization removed entry-level hires just as the number of young black workers rose. Racial prejudice made it difficult to follow employment into the suburbs and small towns. The last hired and first fired, black workers in segregated neighborhoods lacked both access to the personal networks that filled many jobs and public transportation to jobs in the suburbs. Declining employment devastated black commercial districts and bankrupted black home owners. Stranded in cities with inadequate tax bases, black home owners struggled to maintain infrastructure, schools, and social welfare services.[33]

The Origins of the Urban Crisis II: Homeowner Populism and the Fragmentation of Metropolitan Government

In contrast to hard-pressed central cities, suburban jurisdictions enjoyed both lower tax rates and higher levels of public services. By making home ownership cheaper than renting in the city, FHA policies stripped the city of much of its white, taxpaying middle class and provided a solid tax base for suburbs. The chief beneficiaries of public policy, suburban home owners nevertheless came to see themselves as the backbone of the virtuous, self-reliant, taxpaying public and believed they paid more than their fair share of taxes. But the high property values and low taxes enjoyed by white home owners in rigidly segregated neighborhoods depended upon federal subsidies. The FHA, a 1961 report of the U.S. Civil Rights Commission explained, "created the machinery through which housing discrimination operates." There "is no nondefense segment of American economic life," the report concluded, "so dependent on the federal government."[34]

Suburban home owners refashioned the populist rhetoric radical unionists used to assert the public responsibilities of corporations into a defense of small taxpayers against tax-shirking corporations and, later, tax-gobbling cities. In 1947, the city council of the Oakland suburb San Leandro cut a deal with Chrysler Motor Parts that allowed the industry to escape the suburb's tax rolls while still securing municipal services. Angry home owners demanded that "industries, sharing in the benefits which the community has to offer them... must be made to realize their responsibility." In local elections the following year, insurgent home owners put forward a reform slate pledged to "let the people decide and know where their tax dollar is spent." A populist fury defeated the incumbent council members who "forgot to remember that there are thousands of little property owners who were not impressed with the desirability of underwriting the manufacturing costs of such enterprises as the Chrysler corporation."[35]

Over the next three decades, San Leandro drove its property tax rate to the lowest level in the state, routing Oakland in the competition for industry and middle-income residents. By 1966, balanced development turned San Leandro into an industrial garden of homes and factories, good schools and generous public services, praised by the *Wall Street Journal* as a "model municipality." But San Leandro's strategy depended upon the barriers it erected against prospective black home owners from Oakland. Reinforcing the discriminatory policies of private realtors and federal underwriters, San Lenadrans blanketed their community with restrictive covenants while collecting more than $3 million in federal mortgage subsidies denied to the adjacent black neighborhoods of Oakland. In cities across the nation, residential segregation similarly limited the housing and employment options of African Americans. "For an unemployed Atlantan without a car," the *New York Times* reported, "jobs in Cobb and Gwinnett counties might as well be in China."[36]

The Oakland suburb of Milpitas illustrated how home owner populism and a progrowth, low-tax consensus trumped other forms of social activism. In 1954, the Ford Motor Company prepared to build a new plant on property it owned near San Jose. Eager to avoid annexation of the property by the high-tax city of San Jose, Ford officials encouraged five civic activists to orchestrate the incorporation of Milpitas. But a "problem in absorbing Negroes" threatened the project, as black workers from the outdated Richmond plant north of Oakland could not find housing in segregated Milpitas. Racial liberals in Richmond UAW Local 560 thus planned to build a private, interracial, cooperative housing development so that "those brothers and sisters who work side by side with us in our plants" would not "be forced to live in the least desirable areas, in the slums and ghettos."[37]

Fearful that black residents would threaten FHA and VA funds for surrounding subdivisions, private developers mobilized to block the UAW project. They announced plans for a segregated development across the railroad tracks from the plant. Condemning the developers' "high wall of prejudice, bigotry, and intolerance," the UAW conducted a successful boycott of the developers' projects and managed to open its interracial cooperative in 1955. But the project never became a wedge for open housing. Adjoining real estate developments remained exclusively white, and most black workers at the Ford plant commuted from segregated neighborhoods. In 1960, San Jose, with its declining infrastructure and multiracial, low-income population, attempted to annex Milpitas to beef up its tax base. Even UAW activists joined the low-tax home owner populism that defeated annexation three to one to avoid San Jose's "tax and financial pains."[38]

The sprawling Oakland suburb of Fremont further illustrated how suburbs tried to appropriate the social benefits of postwar economic growth without sharing its costs. Long wary of "runaway development," Fremont recognized in the late 1950s that it needed to "aggressively seek industrial development" to "cut the tax rate for the homeowner." In 1960, General Motors decided to locate northern California's largest automobile plant in Fremont and to close its Oakland factory. Welcoming the factory, Fremont did nothing to provide affordable housing for GM workers. Across the nation, as suburbs captured the center city's industrial tax base but excluded its low-income residents, suburbanites learned to justify their prejudices. Suburbanites say to themselves, a suburban Atlanta legislator said of his constituents, "the reason I worked for so many years was to get away from the pollution, bad schools and crime, and I'll be damned if I'll see it all follow me."[39]

The fragmentation of metropolitan government made suburban wealth unavailable to address urban needs. A 1959 study reported that "suburban legal independence" and the "cult of localism" provided opportunities for "escaping the greater community" that never existed before. Where the black and the poor once negotiated for concessions within municipal politics, they now lacked leverage over the hundreds of suburban jurisdictions to which the affluent fled. For their part, the affluent judged governmental expenditures in market terms, gauging individual benefit rather than social consequences. But the differing quality of public services in suburb and city added to the market-based gap between rich and poor and extended inequality into future generations, particularly in the case of education.[40]

CENTRAL CITY HOUSING: THE RACIAL TIME BOMB

The growing importance of home ownership also reshaped politics within the city. Declining economic conditions left working people to hang even more of their hopes for social stability and status on house and neighborhood. At the same time, deteriorating conditions within the ghetto reinforced racist attitudes toward blacks and the determination to maintain segregation. Thus, in the wake of failed populist campaigns against deindustrialization, white working-class anger refocused on the defense of property values and threatened neighborhoods. Detroit's Thomas Poindexter epitomized the trend. An angry critic of plant closings and automation-related layoffs in the 1950s, the Democratic activist became a racist opponent of open housing and high taxes in the 1960s. Opposing proposed federal civil rights legislation in 1963 before a congressional committee, Poindexter charged that "when integration strikes a previously all-white neighborhood" there "will be an immediate rise in crime and violence ... of vice, of prostitution, of gambling and dope."[41]

The private housing market set the fuse to this racial "time bomb." While public housing languished, segregation restricted access to home ownership for African Americans, inflating rents and forcing severe overcrowding. Lax enforcement of building and health codes, an overtaxed sanitation system, a plague of rats, and the constant threat of fire created horrible conditions in the ghetto. Even as a postwar building boom began to ease conditions for whites, segregation forced blacks to squeeze into cellars, attics, garages, and stables. The ghetto still contained its share of "brains and organization and business," an official for the National Association for the Advancement of Colored People said of Detroit's Paradise Valley in 1946, its "social uplift organizations ... , militant protest groups," blues and jazz clubs, and other small businesses. But overcrowding and the denial of loans for maintenance and improvement left ghetto neighborhoods the vulnerable targets for urban redevelopment, highway construction, and public housing projects.[42]

As whites left city neighborhoods for the suburbs and more black migrants arrived in the city, African Americans sought vacancies in neighborhoods surrounding the ghetto. Pressuring both federal agencies and the real estate industry to end discriminatory practices, civil rights organizations called for open housing and championed the virtues of integrated neighborhoods. But even as open housing advocates tried to educate home owners on the financial benefits of racial transition (eager black buyers raised property values), unscrupulous "blockbusting" realtors ratcheted up fears in the quest of fast profits. Charging inflated prices, blockbusters forced black home owners to defer maintenance and rent out rooms. The persistence of discriminatory lending practices added to the blight taking over transitional neighborhoods and caused whites to fear black "invasion."[43]

Home owners' associations led the battle against open housing. Organized in "civic" and "improvement" associations, home owners embraced the values of local government and participatory democracy, self-help, and individual achievement. In alliance with real estate interests who profited from segregated markets, home owners' associations countered the rhetoric of the civil rights movement by asserting the right to protect their property, control their neighborhoods, and choose their associates. Citywide organizations of home owners' associations pressured municipal officials to legislate apartheid or buy back homes sold by blockbusting realtors. Detroit's home owners' associations secured passage of a Homeowners' Rights Ordinance in 1964, asserting the individual's "right to freedom from interference with his property by public authorities attempting to give special privileges to any group." Oakland's home owners' associations helped pass California's Proposition 14, repealing the state's open housing law. "A property owner has an inherent right to rent or sell—or to refuse to rent or sell—to whomever he sees fit," an Oakland councilman proclaimed.[44]

Hard-pressed, working-class home owners on the edge of the expanding ghetto, who stood to lose their biggest investment, saw open housing as a cynical ploy of suburban whites protected by FHA regulations, municipal boundaries, and zoning regulations. "The hypocrites ... who advocate open housing," a Detroit woman charged in 1965, "are the very ones who live in ultraexclusive neighborhoods." With little power to control the larger social and economic changes in the city, working-class home owners intimidated and cajoled white sellers, posted warnings to black buyers, threatened realtors, protested, picketed, and vandalized. Ultimately, they resorted to violence against those who crossed racial boundaries, ranging from thousands of individualized hit-and-run assaults to large-scale riots involving thousands of men, women, and children and lasting for days. In transitional neighborhoods, the struggle shifted to control of public parks, playgrounds, schools, beaches and commercial recreations.[45]

The dominance of home owner interests in city politics also slowed the construction of public housing and confined it to sites within the ghetto. The wartime controversy over the Sojourner Truth housing project on Detroit's northwest side set the precedent for that city and many others. Although the chosen site lay near an existing concentration of blacks, white home owners deluged municipal officials with protests when the city opened the project to black war workers, particularly after the FHA withdrew mortgage support from adjacent neighborhoods because of the planned project. When the first black families moved in, more than a thousand people took to the streets in fighting that injured at least forty. Nearby suburbs also refused public housing. "Housing the Negroes is Detroit's problem," Dearborn's mayor proclaimed during the war. "When you remove garbage from your backyard, you don't dump it in your neighbor's."[46]

In response to the Sojourner Truth incident, the Detroit Housing Commission promised that future projects would "not change the racial pattern of a neighborhood." Sporadic efforts to construct public housing in white neighborhoods succumbed to grassroots mobilization until passage of the 1949 Federal Housing Act, when the Detroit Housing Commission announced plans for eight new housing projects in predominately white neighborhoods. The 1949 mayoral campaign hinged on the issue as a conservative Republican, pledging to block public housing, defeated a progressive Democrat. Racking up majorities even in the most blue-collar, prounion neighborhoods, the new Republican mayor quickly dismantled the public housing program in favor of market-driven urban redevelopment projects. In Detroit, as in other cities, the housing crisis worsened and the few public housing projects erected remained segregated and concentrated in the ghetto.[47]

As white anger replaced racial injustice as the greatest threat to urban order, agencies once concerned with racial justice became architects of racial segregation. The fate of the integrationist Chicago Housing Authority (CHA) illustrated the process. In 1948, Chicago's city council, keenly aware of its white constituents' opposition to integration, secured the power to approve the sites of new public housing. Rejecting CHA recommendations, the council located the vast majority of public housing inside the ghetto, uprooting twelve thousand more families in the process. The city council also compelled the CHA to abandon its efforts to integrate existing public housing projects.[48]

Between 1950 and the mid-1960s, Chicago built thirty-three public housing projects. With one exception (a project for the elderly), all the projects arose in areas that were at least 84 percent black, most in areas at least 95 percent black. "The hate mongers are determined to confine the Negro population of Chicago within a walled city," the *Chicago Defender* charged. But black representatives on the city council, benefiting from the ghetto's concentration of the black vote, did little to challenge segregation. The "pyramiding of existing ghettos" culminated in 1962, when Chicago completed the infamous Robert Taylor Homes—twenty-eight sixteen-story buildings, each an exact copy of the other, in a space two miles long and a quarter of a mile wide. Isolated from the city by railroad tracks and an expressway, the project housed a poor, black population of 27,000, all but 7,000 of them children.[49]

Forfeiting the opportunity to dismantle the inheritance of segregation, federal policy helped create the enlarged, second ghetto of the postwar period. A product of both private prejudice and public policy, the second ghetto encoded racial prejudice into urban space, giving it a physical implacability and permanence. Critics charged that the second ghetto would "determine the physical framework and . . . greatly influence the socio-psychological atmosphere in which that antidiscrimination struggle must take place for decades to come." That sociopsychological atmosphere included both white prejudice and the "deep-felt resentments, hostilities, and bitterness" of ghetto residents. The civil disturbances of the 1960s originated in a pattern of racial segregation that "spawned and cultivated the spirit of rebellion."[50]

Dispossession: Urban Redevelopment and Urban Renewal

As the expansion of the ghetto eroded downtown property values, business interests sought enlarged public powers to revitalize central-city real estate. Providing a model for national legislation, Illinois' Blighted Areas Redevelopment Act of 1947 established slum clearance as a public purpose for which property could be taken by eminent domain. The law empowered a municipal commission to acquire and clear land and then resell it to private housing developers at below market cost. Supported by Chicago merchants and bankers committed to a "complete rehabilitation of the center of the city," the Illinois law promised to restore "deteriorating areas to profitable uses" and stem "decentralization with further loss of jobs, business, families and tax revenues." Business leaders in cities across the nation embraced urban redevelopment and prepared to show that "slum conditions can be eliminated through private enterprise," reducing "the pressure for a large-scale public housing program."[51]

Urban redevelopment nevertheless required a limited program of public housing to relocate those displaced by slum clearance. When Illinois state legislators balked at supporting public housing, Chicago's business leaders insisted that a "hard core of low-income families" could not be relocated without public housing. Failure would "only cause further claims that private enterprise cannot do the job." The legislature acquiesced, but the companion Relocation Act of 1947 stipulated that no more than 15 percent of acquired land be turned over to local housing authorities. The 15 percent proviso turned public housing from a program intended to house "one-third of a nation" into "the critical key to freeing land for redevelopment by private enterprise." As the pace of redevelopment picked up in the early 1950s, redevelopment and relocation projects displaced more and more people who were moved from one temporary residence to another "as though they were checkers."[52]

Redevelopment thus exacerbated the low-income housing shortage, particularly for African Americans. The framers of Illinois' redevelopment legislation assumed that the private housing market would accommodate those not eligible for public housing. But limited resources and racial discrimination left displaced residents of the ghetto few choices other than crowding into adjacent neighborhoods. Redevelopment thus caused "new slums to develop in place of those it cleared," by compelling the displaced to "double up in areas of transition." Sometimes private developers also demanded the clearance of stable neighborhoods. To afford lake views for its residents, Chicago's Lake Meadows project required the condemnation of "a well-kept Negro area where the bulk of the property is resident owned, its taxes paid, and its maintenance above par."

By increasing the pressure on stable neighborhoods to absorb displaced African Americans, urban redevelopment led to a shift in postwar policy from slum clearance to neighborhood conservation. Crafting a new policy which became known as urban *renewal*, Chicago leaders sought new legislation to make slum *prevention* a public purpose justifying the use of eminent domain. The story unfolded in the South Side neighborhood of Hyde Park, site of the University of Chicago. Established in 1949, the Hyde Park-Kenwood Community Conference (HPKCC) hoped to avoid the "type of disorder and violence which has disgraced other communities" and to establish an "interracial community of high standards." Less visibly, the University of Chicago continued a generation-long struggle to prevent racial transition in its neighborhood. Working together, the two agencies slowed the out-migration of whites.

In order to avoid a mass exodus of whites as blacks moved into Hyde Park, the HPKCC organized block by block to counter rumors and monitor building and health regulations. But the HPKCC recognized that the strains of racial transition could only be relieved through a "comprehensive planning program for Chicago and its region," particularly the open housing policy that most whites emphatically rejected. By 1956, facing a steady exodus of whites in the face of continued black migration, the HPKCC screened all applicants for apartments in the neighborhood while continuing to plead for "massive resources, public as well as private, and an imaginative and long-term planning program."

Meanwhile, the South East Chicago Commission (SECC), a coalition of local agencies headed by the University of Chicago, conducted long-term planning. Having long backed restrictive covenants and raised funds to "buy, control, and rebuild our neighborhood," the university explored the use of eminent domain in the late 1940s. To overcome the limitations of Illinois' Redevelopment Act of 1947, the university financed a report that argued in favor of the use of eminent domain to "eliminate standard as well as substandard structures" to protect districts that while not yet blighted threatened to become so. Critics feared that the proposal, which laid the basis for Illinois' Urban Community Conservation Act of 1953, gave "technicians wide power that could only be checked by the public with great difficulty."

The Urban Community Conservation Act empowered the University of Chicago to stabilize its neighborhood without regard to larger metropolitan issues of race and housing. The new legislation extended the power of eminent domain to the SECC and the university, which used it to condemn a predominantly black section, despite the excellent condition of the buildings themselves, by asserting that overcrowding "inevitably led to slum and blight." Speaking for neighboring communities that now faced even greater pressure for racial transition, thanks to the "conservation" of Hyde Park, the Archdiocese of Chicago delivered a stinging critique. Hundreds of thousands of poorly housed Chicagoans became "irrelevant" to urban renewal, the Archdiocese charged, leaving "the city all slum but for one section, the one with those 'high standards.'"

Shifting the emphasis from slum clearance (redevelopment) to neighborhood conservation (renewal), the Federal Housing Acts of 1949 and 1954 applied Chicago's experience nationally. As the 1954 law eased the acquisition and clearance of property in stable neighborhoods and made federal funds available for purposes other than housing, urban renewal earned the name "negro removal."

Condemned black neighborhoods gave way to upscale residential and commercial developments and expansions of universities and hospitals. Nearly two-thirds of all families displaced by urban redevelopment and renewal between 1949 and 1963 were nonwhite. A "keystone of the reverse welfare state," urban renewal also squeezed small manufacturers out of central cities, dimming the employment prospects of ghetto residents.[53]

One of the nation's first and largest urban renewal programs decimated Cincinnati's West End, the center of the city's African American community. Combined with expressway construction, urban renewal destroyed upwards of twenty thousand dwellings and displaced fifty thousand residents in the 1950s and 1960s. Urban renewal eliminated much substandard housing, but it made little provision for those replaced, constructing barely one thousand new housing units in the area, virtually none for low-income residents. Renewal provided new sites for light industry, but as one black activist complained, "we're not working there." With the social, cultural, and political center of black Cincinnati gone, displaced residents crowded into other neighborhoods, exacerbating racial tensions in the city.[54]

In cities across the nation, urban redevelopment and renewal redistributed jobs and capital, shifting public resources (the tax base) to the suburbs and concentrating social costs (poverty) in the city. Having already missed out on the FHA-supported capital investment in housing, African Americans in West Oakland initially welcomed the Oakland Planning Commission's declaration of a "war" on "slum conditions." Residents agreed that inadequate sidewalks, playgrounds, and parks, as well as overcrowding, crime, and physical deterioration blighted their neighborhoods. But residents insisted that blight reflected public neglect rather than irreversible economic and physical decline. Most of them wanted to remain in the area if public funds made renewal possible.[55]

The Oakland Planning Commission initially emphasized the need to revitalize inner-city Oakland with new jobs and a stronger tax base which would provide funds for new parks and public health initiatives. But when the Oakland Redevelopment Agency announced its plans for West Oakland in 1959, they reflected the view that the black neighborhood dragged down the city's economy and needed to make way for middle-income housing and new industry. Faced with bulldozers rather than public investments and low-interest loans they had hoped for, residents appealed unsuccessfully to the courts which failed even to insure the relocation of displaced residents on a racially open basis. Nor did many West Oaklanders find jobs in the developments that supplanted their neighborhoods. "What really are we telling these people?" a member of the U.S. Commission on Civil Rights asked the chair of the redevelopment agency in 1967. "We are taking your home and you are not getting a job either?"[56]

The construction of three major interstate highways and the Bay Area Rapid Transit (BART) line completed the destruction of West Oakland in the 1960s. Connecting the suburbs to downtown San Francisco, the new transportation arteries sent San Francisco real estate prices soaring and provided suburban commuters access to good jobs. But their construction leveled large parts of West Oakland, isolating neighborhoods from one another and cordoning others off behind a mass of concrete. Construction of the BART line destroyed a vital black commercial district of small stores and restaurants, jazz clubs, and barber shops. Unlike the railroad yards that provided good-paying jobs to black residents, the new systems employed few and, even as a transportation system, bypassed West Oakland's densest neighborhoods.[57]

Urban planners argued that highway construction would give "shape and definition" to neighborhoods, creating self-contained and focused communities. But in building "white men's highways through black men's bedrooms," urban planners treated highway construction as "a handy device for razing slums" and destroyed black businesses, institutions, and housing. Expressways created toxic "hot spots," turning some inner-city neighborhoods into Environmental Protection Agency (EPA) Superfund sites. Construction scars, ugly structures, and accumulating refuse blighted poor neighborhoods and lessened property values. Repair shops and car washes, muffler and spray paint services, and used car lots and parking garages arose disproportionately in poor neighborhoods. Six of Manhattan's seven diesel bus depots spewed carcinogens into the streets of Harlem.[58]

African Americans experienced urban redevelopment and urban renewal as dispossession. Black neighborhoods of home owners, good-paying jobs, convenient streetcars, and the lively street life of the immediate postwar period disappeared, replaced with shabby streets, aggressive policing, and either "eerie quiet" or rushing traffic. Redevelopment and renewal evicted more than twenty thousand small businesses, most of which never reopened, gutting the heart and soul of many black communities. In some cities, black residents complained that the location of highways was "racially motivated to uproot a neighborhood of Negro leaders." Long delays between the announcement of urban renewal plans and actual construction left many neighborhoods to decay as landlords refused to maintain buildings slated for destruction. Despite legislative guarantees, only 0.5 percent of redevelopment and renewal funds between 1949 and 1964 went to aid the relocation of displaced residents; most ended up paying higher rents in overcrowded neighborhoods.[59]

Confronting the Reverse Welfare State: From Civil Rights to Black Power

The expansion of the ghetto strengthened political leaders within the black community who acquiesced in segregation in exchange for patronage. But the concentration of black votes also raised the potential for an alternative, interracial politics based on black electoral power. Struggling to redirect the priorities of a welfare state that benefited suburban whites at the expense of urban blacks, the northern civil rights movement focused on economic issues earlier and to a greater extent than the southern movement. Civil rights and, later, black power advocates demanded fair employment and fair housing legislation, the desegregation of unions, adequate provision of public housing, an unbiased implementation of urban renewal, and antipoverty and other public investment in central cities.[60]

Initially working within the framework of liberalism, civil rights activists focused on legal remedies to remove obstacles to individual advancement. They placed hope in fair employment legislation such as Michigan's 1954 and California's 1959 law. But activists soon recognized that the "case-by-case method alone falls far short of solving the massive problem," as the executive officer of California's Fair Employment Practices Commission told the U.S. Senate in 1963. Painstaking research might result in a judgment against a single union or employer, but the judgment relied on voluntary compliance and did little to dismantle systemic discrimination. Abandoning legal, punitive remedies for affirmative action, the Fair Employment Practices Commission (FEPC) proposed instead to "stimulate recruiting, hiring, and promoting of the best-qualified personnel, inclusive of all groups in the population."[61]

Affirmative action strategies achieved some success. In 1964, when the Congress on Racial Equality launched protests against the Bank of America, the bank pledged to hire a multiracial workforce. But such agreements still relied on voluntary compliance. Eliminating overt signs of discrimination and incorporating affirmative action pledges into contracts, employers and unions made it virtually impossible to prove discrimination. White liberals nevertheless judged affirmative action a success in terms of process. But black activists, evaluating affirmative action in terms of outcomes, found it wanting. Impatient with liberal remedies, they moved toward collective, community-based solutions.[62]

The 1962 strike at Beth-El Hospital in the Brownsville section of Brooklyn demonstrated the potential of community action, particularly when it could rally a larger liberal coalition. Joining Local 1199 of the Hospital Workers of America in 1962, black and Puerto Rican workers at Beth-El struck for higher wages and union recognition. The entire community mobilized behind them as friends, family, and neighbors picketed and donated food. Linking their demands to the southern civil rights struggle, the strikers charged that the hospital treated its "workers as if this were Mississippi not New York." Civil rights organizations, the city's unions, elected officials, and the media all lined up behind the strikers, as did local college students fresh from the "freedom rides and sit-ins in the North and South." Fearing civil disorder, New York governor Nelson Rockefeller intervened, supporting legislation to provide collective bargaining rights for hospital workers.[63]

West Oakland's struggle to secure its fair share of jobs on the Bay Area Rapid Transit project (BART) in 1966 also illustrated the potential of community action. As BART threatened to transform yet another black neighborhood into a slum, black activists created Justice on BART (JOBART). When BART displaced residents and businesses while refusing to employ local workers, JOBART demanded jobs and economic development for West Oakland. "We've been bull dozed one time too many," residents protested. BART acted as if "property owners should not expect very much money for their property because their neighborhood is run down." When union discrimination turned the destruction of black neighborhoods into jobs for white unionists, JOBART protested that "our tax money will solve the unemployment problem of other areas," but not West Oakland's.[64]

BART officials replied that the new transit system provided individual residents of West Oakland access to the entire region. "The non-white clearly needs mobility," they argued, "the freedom to move out of ghetto life on a daily basis; for others, on a lifetime basis." BART allowed "a person to live where he chooses and work where he chooses anywhere in the metropolitan area." But West Oaklanders knew that racial discrimination undercut the promise of physical and social mobility. They instead looked to JOBART to defend their collective interest in the fate of a specific place. To redirect the public resources that fueled private enterprise, JOBART inserted itself into the political and contractual processes. "No BART contracts are valid," JOBART's 1966 manifesto held, "which do not include the negotiated conditions of the JOBART proposals." With an eye to endangered federal grants, Oakland's mayor pressured BART to adopt an affirmative action plan in 1967.[65]

The community action strategy also shaped a part of President Lyndon Johnson's War on Poverty. Treating inadequate education and pathological behaviors as the causes of urban poverty, most War on Poverty programs focused on education and social services. Rather than tackle racial discrimination and industrial decentralization, the War on Poverty spent its limited funds on local bureaucracies and social workers. Reflecting a postwar liberalism that contemplated neither a democratization of the economy nor a redistribution of wealth, the War on Poverty never contemplated the aggressive assault on discrimination or the massive public investment in central cities that national black leaders demanded. But the War on Poverty did include a mandate for "maximum feasible participation" and a provision for community action projects designed to redistribute political power.[66]

Fresh from their success in the Beth-El strike, Brownsville activists organized one of the War on Poverty's first community action projects. The Brownsville Community Council (BCC) mobilized black voting power to demand better schools, sanitation, and other municipal services. When Brownsville changed from a white to a black neighborhood, an activist explained, "the city services went down." Therefore, the BCC focused on "maintaining or recouping city services." Wresting control of the antipoverty effort from established politicians, the BCC demanded "socially useful jobs" and "the know-how needed in solving day to day problems of city life." Administering a $2 million program with a full-time staff of more than one hundred, the BCC improved municipal services, made government bureaucracies more responsive, and secured jobs for many residents in public agencies.[67]

One of the most successful of the community action projects, the Brownsville Community Council focused on social transformation rather than individual uplift. Anticipating the black power movement, the BCC promoted adult education and cultural initiatives to mobilize the poor politically. The BCC also articulated a strategy of community control of public and private institutions, starting with the schools. Its Brownsville Cadet Corp provided troubled youth with the combination of black pride and conservative discipline that later characterized the Black Panther Party. In securing opportunities for the most highly educated, the BCC provided some leaders with a route out of neighborhood and left the poorest behind. But the BCC also created a more engaged, hopeful, and effective political community.[68]

In Oakland, which secured some of the largest War on Poverty grants, the mayor and city council hoped to funnel the money through the municipal bureaucracy. But black activists took control of the Oakland Economic Development Council (OEDC) and turned it into a neighborhood-based vehicle of political mobilization. Redirecting the War on Poverty's emphasis from unblocking exits to empowering the ghetto, the OEDC demanded jobs rather than more social services. Toward that end, activists turned their attention to a federal grant to modernize the Port of Oakland. The federal grant, nearly ten times the size of the entire OEDC budget, came in the wake of the explosive Watts Riot of 1965 and offered what critics called "riot insurance." Under OEDC pressure, the port modernization project promised three thousand jobs, a third for minorities and "hard-core unemployed."[69]

But the OEDC could not guarantee the cooperation of unions, the Port of Oakland, or the private employers operating out of it. By the early 1970s, the project provided fewer than three hundred new jobs for West Oaklanders. "The present problem isn't lack of jobs," the OEDC director charged in 1968. "The problem is the way jobs are distributed across the community." While Oakland's regional economy boomed, segregation trapped West Oakland residents in a downward spiral. "The only thing that will be understood by business is the same thing as with unions," a disillusioned black liberal argued, "a power base." Railing against "the people who come here and make the money and take it back to the suburbs," he told the Federal Commission on Civil Rights in 1967 that "they are the ones that have us enslaved. We are their colonies." Oakland found itself, he concluded, "ringed by a white noose of suburbia."[70]

Nationwide, community activists struggled with local officials to redirect federal poverty funds from skills training and social services to jobs and political power. One-time liberal poverty warriors now demanded "massive employment programs" and "massive rehabilitation of our cities." In 1967, Oakland's poverty board demanded control of all local jobs through neighborhood councils and hiring halls. "If black folks don't work in Oakland," the head of the poverty board asserted, "we can say nobody works in Oakland." When local and state officials blocked the plan, the board published a scathing critique of metropolitan development, lambasting the destruction of West Oakland and subsidies for high-profile projects that did nothing for city residents.[71]

The same logic of community control that shaped West Oakland's struggle over jobs led to a struggle over schools in Brownsville. Frustrated by failed efforts to integrate Brooklyn's schools, Brownsville activists demanded that local parents be allowed to control their children's education. In 1964, activists orchestrated a citywide boycott of New York City's segregated schools. Ninety percent of Brownsville's students joined the boycott, attending alternative "Freedom Schools" with diverse faculties teaching African American and Latino history and culture. But the city's Board of Education still refused to move forward on integration. When a token busing plan in 1965 ended in violence, Brownsville activists turned to community control. "The outside folks were not going to protect us," an activist recalled, "so you turn inward."[72]

Brownsville's experiment in community control of public schools reflected the logic of the black power movement. When existing institutions proved unresponsive, black power theorists argued, black communities "must devise new structures, new institutions to replace those forms or make them responsive." The Brownsville Community Council provided a model of just that, encouraging local activists to stage a sit-in at the Board of Education in 1966. Creating an "Ad Hoc People's Board of Education," they demanded a local school board that could make teachers and administrators treat Brownsville's children as "educable beings, endowed with creative capabilities and potential." A local board could also involve parents in their children's education, encouraging them to volunteer and battle the city bureaucracy to provide more resources.[73]

During the 1967-1968 school year, New York City's Board of Education grudgingly authorized a pilot community control project in the Ocean Hill-Brownsville district. The local governing board revamped the curriculum, implemented new literacy efforts, trained parent aides, and launched extracurricular and after-school programs, including a student-run community newspaper. The governing board also replaced incompetent and unsympathetic teachers and principals. Outside agencies found positive changes in the school and community. Student and parental involvement in education soared.[74]

But the United Federation of Teachers opposed the experiment, worried that community control endangered newly won pay increases and job security. In a series of strikes in the spring and fall of 1968, the teacher's union accused the governing board of anti-Semitism (even though 50 percent of the replacement teachers were Jewish). Citywide, the strikes divided liberals between allegiance to the union and the neighborhood. Amid escalating tensions and police presence at the schools, state agencies intervened to end the experiment in November 1968. The strike inflicted lasting damage on New York City's liberal coalition, calling into question the values of pluralism and integration. But for the Brownsville activists, community control simply meant the effort to improve education for their children. They understood community control not as Afrocentric separatism, but as an effort to build stronger schools and neighborhoods that would provide citywide "support for integration when it is tried."[75]

Two Societies, Separate and Unequal

For all the potential of the War on Poverty, community action, and black power initiatives, they did little to alter the deindustrialization, segregation, and dispossession that left central cities beset by poverty, crime, and other social ills. As the successes of the southern civil rights movement highlighted failures in the North, the frustration that activists tried to turn into political mobilization found other outlets in civil disturbances. As African Americans protested the hardening walls of the ghetto, four major riots occurred in the summer of 1964. In the following summer, the vast Watts Riot in Los Angeles focused national attention on central cities as never before. Violence continued sporadically during the summer of 1966. In 1967, major upheavals convulsed Cincinnati, Newark, and Detroit, the greatest civil disorder since the draft riots of 1863. Young black males, suffering from unemployment and police harassment, made up a disproportionate percentage of the rioters. Defined as the enemy by white authorities, they lashed out at occupying authorities (especially the police) and exploiting agents (especially retail outlets).[76]

As political protest, the riots proved a colossal failure. No matter how frightening, the riots did little to disrupt life in the suburbs and only confirmed the isolation of the ghetto from the mainstreams of metropolitan life. The War on Poverty, the community action program, maximum feasible participation, and the riots all merged in the minds of suburban whites, who wrote off central cities as the turf of violent, rebellious blacks. White municipal officials also confused the political mobilization of black neighborhoods with civil disorder. The mayor of Los Angeles condemned the community action projects as "fostering class struggle," while the mayor of Newark blamed his city's riots on the local community action project. In 1971, a distinguished forum, "Is the Inner City Doomed?" described the city as "an Indian reservation made up of inmates and keepers, economically dependent on transfer payments from the outside society made in consideration of custodial services rendered."[77]

Ceding central cities to African Americans, suburban whites redoubled their opposition to open housing. Eager to escape the ghetto, African Americans appealed to the moral sensibilities of the "responsible white community." But in California's campaign for Proposition 14, white suburbanites deployed their own moral language of rights. Open housing law, they argued, "forced" home owners to sell to blacks, infringing upon the sacred "freedom of choice" and the "right to acquire and protect property." Such language defended an apartheid-like segregation. San Leandro, for example, benefited from more than $3 million in federal mortgage guarantees, but its population was less than one-tenth of 1 percent black. Just across the city line, the adjoining black-majority Oakland neighborhoods enjoyed no such subsidies.[78]

Opposition to open housing intensified home owner populism in suburban areas across the country in the mid-1960s. Shifting from denunciations of communist conspiracies to a defense of the rights of suburban home owners, the conservative movement dramatically expanded its base. Suburban Orange County, south of Los Angeles, provided a prototype. A prime beneficiary of billions of dollars in FHA mortgages, interstate highways, and defense contracts, Orange County nonetheless nurtured a virulent antistatism. Pitting property rights against civil rights in the struggle to defeat open housing, the most privileged beneficiaries of metropolitan development imagined themselves as victims of an overzealous state. "The philosophical fallacy" of open housing, the *Los Angeles Times* editorialized, "lies in seeking to correct such a social evil while simultaneously destroying what we deem a basic right in a free society."[79]

The civil disturbances added fuel to the conservative fire. The Watts Riot reinforced the determination of Orange County residents to keep the city's "lawlessness," "immorality," and "social decay" at arm's length. In California's gubernatorial campaign of 1966, first the Democrat Samuel Yorty and then the Republican Ronald Reagan stoked the resentments of middle-class suburban whites frustrated with what Yorty called the "leftist takeover of the Democratic Party." Appealing to suburban whites secure in their subsidized communities, Reagan campaigned against welfare, high taxes, and central city criminality. "For the law abiding," the Reagan administration later explained, "the policeman is our friend. For all our science and sophistication, for all our justified pride in intellectual accomplishment, the jungle is waiting to take over. The man with the badge helps to hold it back." Such rhetoric established a close correlation between opposition to open housing in 1964 and support for Reagan in 1966.[80]

Suburbanites mobilized to keep the black and the poor, and all the social problems and financial burdens they associated with them, out of their communities. As a nationwide series of lawsuits challenged residential segregation and developers pushed for more opportunities to build profitable apartment complexes, aggrieved home owners felt themselves under siege. "It is against the public interest to zone for apartments in this predominantly single-family area," the head of a California home owners' association complained, conflating the public interest with that of white home owners. New Jersey's Supreme Court thought otherwise. In 1975, the Court ruled that the general welfare required that affluent suburbs plan and provide for a diverse population. In 1985, the New Jersey legislature endorsed the decision but allowed suburbs to set less-strict guidelines on the basis of "the established pattern of development in the community" and to buy their way out by contributing to low-income housing in nearby cities.[81]

Having declined to address segregation and affordable housing, suburban home owners displayed no more willingness to shoulder the other costs of uneven metropolitan development. As a means of implementing the 1954 *Brown v. Board of Education* decision declaring racial segregation in the public schools unconstitutional, federal courts ordered the busing of children long distances to equalize racial representation in central city schools. White working-class parents often resisted, sent their children to private schools, or simply moved out of the city to the suburbs. Some federal judges thus mandated interdistrict busing between cities and suburbs. In 1972, federal district judge Stephen Roth ordered the busing of three hundred thousand students across a three-county area including Detroit to achieve racial balance. In *Miliken v. Bradley* (1974), the U.S. Supreme Court rejected the argument that city and suburbs "are bound together by economic interests, recreational interests, social concerns and interests, governmental interests of various sorts, and a transportation network." The Court ruled (5–4) in favor of the tradition of local control of schools, placing its imprimatur on the fragmentation of the metropolis.[82]

The growing trend of black electoral successes accelerated white flight from central cities. In 1973 alone, 48 black mayors won election, with 268 more winning office over the next decade and a half. Winning with racially oriented campaigns and through racially skewed voting patterns, black mayors increased the black share in municipal jobs and municipal contracts and helped build up a black middle class. But municipal coffers were no longer the rich prizes they once were, squeezed even tighter by the demands of public-service unions for higher wages. Efforts to squeeze more revenue out of the remaining tax base only encouraged the flight of business to more accommodating suburban locales. Working with white liberals and moderates, black leaders often secured payroll taxes on suburban commuters. But the burden of a declining tax base still fell heaviest on the black middle class.[83]

Cast off on their own, central cities declined more rapidly. The sale or transfer of sewer and transit systems, as well as power plants, museums, and zoos to regional authorities covered fiscal shortfalls for a time, but left the city with fewer assets. By the mid-1970s, central cities faced impending bankruptcy. When New York City's municipal government went broke in 1975 and the state of New York took over its finances, President Gerald Ford refused federal assistance. The infamous *New York Daily News* headline, "Ford to City: Drop Dead," captured the mood of an increasingly suburban nation. Municipal governments retrenched, cutting back on fire protection, building inspections, and sanitation. Absentee landlords began abandoning buildings they could not remortgage and defaulting on municipal taxes. An epidemic of arson swept through inner-city neighborhoods while the emergence of crack cocaine provided an employer of last resort for ghetto youth. "Block after block has been left vacant for years," a study of Brownsville in 1973 reported, "forming a wasteland of gutted carcasses of buildings and rat-filled rubble." Such neighborhoods, the mayor of Boston remarked, provide "the first tangible sign of the collapse of our civilization."[84]

Declining conditions in central cities fueled the tax revolt among suburban home owners in the late 1970s. Beginning in California, increased spending on education and health, transit and environmental protection, and public services and utilities combined with rising property value assessments to dramatically raise the tax burden on suburban home owners. As early as 1968, a California ballot initiative called for property taxes to be used exclusively for "property-related services" (fire, police, water, streets) and not "people-related services" (welfare, health, education). It also placed a 1 percent of market value cap on property taxes. Although the measure failed, it provided the foundation for the nationwide tax revolt that drastically cut spending on cities.[85]

Suburban Secession and Farewell to the Public Realm

In 1978, California's Proposition 13 initiated a nationwide surge of tax revolts. Proposition 13 limited property taxes to 1 percent of assessed value and required a two-thirds vote for all future state and local tax increases (the measure could only be overturned by another referendum). Populist anger fueled the tax revolt, as tax burdens fell heaviest on home owners rather than on corporations. But a well-organized movement led by realty interests wrested tax reform from leftists who condemned the regressive nature of the tax system and redirected home owner anger toward feckless inner-city residents and wasteful bureaucrats. The movement also misrepresented the connection between rising property taxes and wasteful state government. As opponents pointed out, federal mandates protected much of welfare spending while property-related services (fire, police, water, sewer, parks, and streets) and education suffered the deepest cuts. Moreover, Proposition 13 delivered the lion's share of tax relief to businesses and landlords.[86]

Twenty states followed California in passing tax relief measures in 1979 and as many passed income tax reductions as well. Proponents of Proposition 13 and other measures denied any racial animus. But black commentators rightly described the tax revolt as a declaration of white suburbanites' "unwillingness to pay for public facilities and services that are needed for central cities." Even suburbanites without a reflexive antistatist orientation or racist attitudes found it easy to think first and foremost about local, property-centered concerns, not about the social needs of distant—and black—cities.[87]

Racial animosities and the struggle over integration fueled an abandonment of public institutions and the flight to the suburbs. Across the South, whites left big-city public schools for private academies or the suburbs. In Atlanta during the 1950s and 1960s, the desegregation of public parks, golf courses, and pools led to calls for privatization of those facilities and a local tax revolt. Bond issues in 1962 and 1963 for investments in Atlanta's schools, streets, and sewers, as well as a new civic auditorium and cultural center all failed. The "vote went heaviest," the *Atlanta Journal* reported, "against projects where integration or benefits for Negroes might appear to be involved." The equation of public works and "benefits for Negroes" was not confined to the South. "As of today, Detroit, Chicago, Cleveland public transportation systems are mere shells of their former place in public utility," a northerner warned an Atlanta official who contemplated the desegregation of the city's buses. "They are almost abandoned to the private car—bumper to bumper, one man to a vehicle—definitely to avoid

Integration." In New Jersey, the demand for equal treatment in public accommodations led many commercial establishments to avoid integration by claiming status as private clubs, further shrinking the public realm.[88]

The suburban secession also reshaped national politics. Richard Nixon's famed "southern strategy" appealed to white, middle-class suburbanites, regardless of region. Promising law and order and opposing affirmative action and busing, Nixon delivered on his assurances that the suburbs would not be integrated. Initiating the trend toward federal cutbacks in urban spending, President Nixon told his attorney general that the ideal Supreme Court nominee would be "against busing and against forced housing integration." The new "Nixon Court" (Nixon appointed four judges in two years) handed down the 1974 *Miliken* decision and a year earlier ruled that suburban school districts bore no responsibility to share their property taxes with poor school districts.[89]

Yet, even after years of neglect, central cities still generated much of the wealth that fueled federal largess. Regional economies still depended upon their dense infrastructure of physical, educational, and human capital. But while central-city officials complained that "the taxpayer of the central city is subsidizing the suburban dweller," suburbanites acknowledged no debt to the cities. A report of Chicago's mayor in 1947 revealed that although "the City of Chicago supplies the bulk of all tax revenues collected by the State of Illinois, it receives back only a tiny fraction of these millions." Twenty-five years later, Boston's mayor expressed the same frustration; "for every $25 Boston contributes to the state and federal governments, we receive back in aid only $1." In 1980, the federal government still collected as much as $11 billion more from New York City than it returned in expenditures.[90]

The election of President Ronald Reagan in 1980, with tax relief and cuts in urban spending at the center of his campaign, strengthened the suburban secession. Federal aid to cities fell approximately by half between 1977 and 1985, reinforcing the state tax revolts. No community could long prosper, a federal report predicted in 1937, if those "who gain the greatest benefits from it, escape from most of the obligations communal life imposes, and if those who obtain the least . . . amenities of life are left to bear the brunt of civic responsibility and taxation." Even as they added to the burden of local taxpayers, cities slashed payrolls, curtailed services, and privatized or divested themselves of as many responsibilities as possible. The era of an expansive public sector came decisively to an end as municipal officials preached austerity and sacrifice.[91]

The only signs of life came from glitzy new private developments that treated the city as a niche in the market. Convention centers, festival marketplaces, and sports stadia attracted visitors and tourists, while young urban professionals capitalized on the romance and history of the city, renovating buildings in deteriorating neighborhoods. But neither childless, affluent yuppies nor visitors and tourists provided the motivation to maintain the bedrock institutions of the day-to-day public realm, the schools and hospitals, parks and libraries, public utilities and transit systems. The city became a place of social and economic polarization, "the glint of glass-sheathed downtown office structures" and "blocks of abandoned houses and apartment buildings with hollow windows." Soaring office towers and gentrified neighborhoods testified to "the faith of private capital" in the city's future. But behind the gleam lay "a world of continuing decay and distress," of homelessness and devastated neighborhoods.[92]

Private redevelopment remade the city in the image of the suburbs. "It's like a suburban mall in an urban area," the public relations director of a Philadelphia development remarked. Security enticed the affluent into the city, as municipal governments subsidized upscale shopping areas and office complexes with privately owned and enclosed enclaves. They "are all built like fortresses, with their lobbies up on the second floor and retail space in atriums and courts," explained a critic of Newark's post-riot redevelopment. The new spatial arrangements shrank the public realm to virtually nothing. "It would not be surprising in the future to see cities rely more and more on private businesses to perform functions once performed by governmental agencies," Justice Thurgood Marshall predicted in a dissenting opinion in a 1972 case involving free speech. As "governments rely on private enterprise, public property decreases in favor of privately owned property," he concluded, and "it becomes harder for citizens to communicate with other citizens. Only the wealthy may find effective communication possible."[93]

The suburbs never provided a substitute for the downtown sidewalks and public transit that once brought together a diverse population. But many hailed the shopping mall as the new downtown. To be sure, by the early 1960s, the suburban shopping mall became a central institution in economic and social life. In 1976, recognizing that mall managers eliminated or restricted the community rooms and public galleries they once ballyhooed, the progressive developer James Rouse asked department store merchants why they could not "plan the centers and their public spaces so as to provide the most resourceful and productive possible relationships between the center and public agencies, educational and cultural institutions." But even Rouse's own company showed little interest in developing links to the larger public world.[94]

With few alternatives, activists treated shopping malls as civic spaces. Blood drives, petition drives, labor picketing, and political campaigning all took place at malls. When mall owners tried to prevent such activities, court cases followed. In *Amalgamated Food Employee Union Local 590 v. Logan Valley Plaza, Inc.* (1968), the Supreme Court ruled that unions could picket legitimately in the public thoroughfares of private malls. Picketing and leafleting on "streets, sidewalks, parks and other similar public places," Justice Marshall wrote in *Logan Valley Plaza*, "are so historically associated with First Amendment rights" that those rights applied even in privately owned developments. But subsequent cases eroded the decision. In *Lloyd v. Tanner* (1972), Justice Lewis F. Powell wrote for the majority in holding that antiwar leafleting infringed on property rights. The reigning decision is *Pruneyard Shopping Center v. Robbins* (1980), in which the Court upheld a ruling that California's state constitution secured high school students the right to petition against a United Nations resolution. But *Pruneyard* also held that the First Amendment did not guarantee access to malls, leaving it to the states themselves to decide.[95]

Even in states that protect free speech, mall managers can still set times for leafleting, require liability insurance for activists, and prohibit demonstrations, soliciting funds, pickets, parades, speeches, and bullhorns. More than fifty years of market-based urban policies have made both the city and its suburbs inhospitable to activities other than the commercial transaction. A reporter covering the 1994 election campaign observed that there "are no rallies. There are no neighborhood walks. There are no encounters with the public." Labor Secretary Robert Reich added that the "wealthiest 20 or 30 percent of Americans are 'seceding'" into exclusive suburbs, luxury automobiles, and upscale marketplaces. They rarely interact with "members of non-wealthy classes, except in the latter's role as receptionists or repairmen."[96]

The 1994 congressional election confirmed the suburban secession. Railing against big government, Georgia congressman Newt Gingrich united Republican candidates behind a "Contract with America," centered on five major tax relief measures. The contract, a conservative columnist explained, would "limit the power, resources, and reach of government," even "in some areas, delegitimizing government." The quintessential representative of suburban secession, Gingrich rejected the sharing of suburban resources with urban areas. "What people worry about," Gingrich explained to a journalist during the campaign, "is the bus line . . . bringing people out for public housing who have no middle-class values and whose kids as they become teenagers often are centers of robbery and where the schools collapse because the parents who live in the apartment complexes don't care that the kids don't do well in school." Once symbols of urban opportunity, public education, public transit, and public housing had become the nightmares of suburban voters.[97]

Conclusion

*The Future of the City: Civic Renewal
and Environmental Politics*

The results of the 2008 elections suggested we might be on the verge of dramatic political changes. During the campaign, political commentators described a stalemate between "the irresistible force of secular belief in public investment set against the immovable object of faith-based laissez-fairism." But polls showed that since 1999, more than 60 percent of Americans acknowledged a broad range of necessary functions for government, and the number continued to rise. The election of President Barack Obama showed that leaders willing to "speak to people as citizens, asking them to participate in something that has a larger national purpose," might produce a political realignment on the basis of civic renewal.[1]

But commentators also noted that the case for public action suffered from the failure to make a persuasive case. Scholars agreed that we possessed a rich language of individual rights, but our language of civic engagement remained weak and abstract. We may simply not know what civic means, which would explain why our civic history is so often filled with grand rhetorical pronouncements followed by disappointing results. As recently as 1992, Bill Clinton campaigned for the presidency on a pledge to spend fifty billion dollars on public works in each of the following four years. Nothing of the sort happened. By 1998, federal outlays for public construction hit a fifty-year low. If we want to take full advantage of the opportunities that are again before us, we should briefly review a debate between "civic" liberals and "money" liberals that shaped the Clinton campaign.[2]

In 1990, an insurgent group of civic liberals called on money liberals to abandon their fixation with economic equality. Money liberals really wanted social equality, an "equality in the way we treat each other in everyday life." But their efforts to promote social equality through a redistribution of wealth proved ineffective and politically unpopular. The reconstruction of the public realm, civic liberals maintained, provided a better means of promoting social equality. They advocated for a shared set of civic obligations and opportunities indifferent to wealth, including a national draft and universal health care, improved public schools and parks, a public jobs program to replace welfare, and a political system sealed off from the influence of private wealth.[3]

Money liberals did not buy the argument. Refusing to treat "the causes of inequality [as] deep economic facts essentially beyond our control," money liberals charged civic liberals with failing to recognize the market as a creation of civic life, a product of the law of contract and incorporation, public spending on infrastructure, the internal revenue code, the Federal Reserve Act, the Wagner Labor Relations Act, and a thousand other political choices. "We can have a more equal distribution of wealth and income, if we want," money liberals insisted, because different political choices created different markets. When money liberals suggested that we could "choose to pay schoolteachers and nurses more, and lawyers and bond traders less," civic liberals were incredulous. "How? By direct regulation of incomes? Without sacrificing economic efficiency?" Civic liberals dismissed the whole proposition as nonsense.

Money liberals should have pointed out that local governments already established the incomes of public school teachers and could decide to pay them more. Stockbrokers, they should have added, operated in a highly regulated industry dependent upon public policies that were just then disastrously promoting speculation. By setting the market aside as an autonomous realm that resists political control, civic liberals crippled the public realm in its relation to its most important creation. They also left their program open to the charge that it amounted to nothing more than a set of unexamined prescriptions, imposed from above, to reshape character and values.

Recognizing this vulnerability, money liberals charged civic liberals with forcing "a particular view of the good life on people." Rejecting "social engineering," money liberals favored addressing economic inequality and then letting "people live their own lives." But money liberals admitted that any set of laws and regulations always imposed some view of the good life. In removing constraints on financial speculation, slashing social spending, and undercutting the power of trade unions in the 1980s, we made political choices that rewarded certain types of activities over others, sometimes in morally dubious ways. These policies supposedly rewarded a skills-based meritocracy. But what "possible conception of merit," money liberals asked, "would require a society in which the boss earned a thousand times the wage of his workers?"

Civic liberals wanted a restored public realm precisely to counterbalance the morally dubious outcomes of the market. In the face of a growing inequality of wealth, social equality prevented the rich "from thinking they're better than the rest of us." Drafting Donald Trump's son, civic liberals argued, made the point better than raising his taxes. Civic liberals also criticized the money liberals' "check-cashing mentality" for promoting "individualistic consumerism." They intended to expand the civic sphere and also to set "clear bounds of acceptable behavior within it." Far from an elitist program, civic liberals argued, their proposals could win broad public support. The "vast majority of American voters aren't instinctively anti-government," civic liberals concluded, and the party that campaigned on "billions for workers, not a penny for welfare" would "sweep the nation."

The Great Unfinished Tasks of American Civilization

Clinton's victory supported the civic liberals' reading of the political landscape. But then Clinton, scrapping his plans for public spending in subservience to a jittery bond market, underscored the civic liberals' blind spot. Treating the market as something beyond our political control is a faulty foundation for civic renewal. Market liberals, however, also suffered from a blind spot. Civic renewal will fail unless we set high standards for one another and apply them impartially. The great unfinished tasks of American civilization remain the construction of an economy and a culture that complement our civic aspirations. Civic renewal must include taking responsibility for economic arrangements and promoting the fullest development of the mind and character of every citizen.

The program of civic renewal that shaped Bill Clinton's 1992 campaign depended upon the revitalization of our cities. Civic liberals imagined cities relieved of homelessness and crime and enjoying public facilities that attracted rather than repelled. They wanted a city where "richer and poorer Americans bump into each other as equals with increasing frequency," on sidewalks and in parks, in post offices, public libraries, and schools, and above all, in heterogeneous neighborhoods. "Is there any doubt that if all this happened," they asked, "the country would in an important sense be transformed?"[4]

The city still provides the essential starting point for a politics that transforms our economy and our culture. Our most pressing public questions, social inequality and the deterioration of the environment, also point us toward the city. The wellspring of our most taxing demands on the environment, the city is also where our social inequalities are most acute. But the city is also our best hope to address these challenges. The most promising venue for a multicultural society, resource-efficient cities also lessen our dependence on foreign oil, slow global warming, and preserve agricultural land and open space. In supporting public life and cultural institutions, the city offers an alternative vision of the good life in place of restless consumption. The city's public spaces and institutions can also generate the trust, solidarity, and willingness to compromise on which democratic politics depends.[5]

Private City, Public Crisis

Los Angeles offers the best guide to the tasks before us. A collective effort to live the private life, Los Angeles could never have existed without colossal public projects from aqueducts and harbors to railways and freeways. But private land speculation endangered the natural beauty on which the city's future depended. As riverbeds became industrial sewers and private developments arose on flood plains, the city forfeited the chance to provide recreational parks and a natural drainage system. Public investments in roads, sanitation, fire protection, and flood control underwrote private profit. But the underproduction of public space left just over one-half of 1 percent of the metropolis as parkland and provided only one-half inch of oceanfront per citizen. An affluent society built on cheap oil and the "vast consumption of handsomely packaged products" overwhelmed public efforts to control pollution, resulting in "the agony of a city without useable air."[6]

Already suffering an imbalance between private interests and public goods, Los Angeles soon faced a ferocious assault on the public realm. In 1954, the private development of Lakewood, California (twice the size of the more famous Levittowns of the East), resisted annexation by the city of Long Beach and incorporated as an independent municipality. But Lakewood also contracted to secure its public services (fire, police, water, sewers) from Los Angeles County at rates that reflected metropolitan economies of scale. State legislation also allowed Lakewood to capture for its own use a 1 percent sales tax from the shopping center located within its jurisdiction. Dozens of suburban developments rushed to claim this same "exit privilege," avoiding the burden of city taxes while still enjoying metropolitan services.[7]

In 1978, California's Proposition 13 reduced property taxes and forced state budget cuts just as demands escalated on public institutions to avert environmental breakdown. In 1987, Los Angeles's Hyperion Water Treatment Plant, on which three million people depended, backed up waste into Santa Monica Bay. The *Los Angeles Times* reported that "planning procedures have been so slack that nobody made that most basic connection between population growth and the carrying capacity of a sewage system." Reports of groundwater contamination carried cleanup bills estimated between $2 billion and $40 billion, money that public officials did not have. Los Angeles also asked for a twenty-five-year extension to comply with the 1970 Clean Air Act, while a new study estimated the need for $100 billion in new highways simply to maintain traffic congestion at current levels.[8]

Looming environmental disaster intensified fears of social disorder and prompted new innovations in security. Los Angeles developers, fearful that public transit compromised the security of the historic downtown, constructed a new downtown nearby, isolated from the old core by a moat of highways and palisades. Promising to be "the type of place that 'respectable people' . . . tend to frequent," the multibillion-dollar Bunker Hill development offered affluent shoppers privatized malls and underground concourses. The proximity of the homeless required an official plan for their "containment" along a dangerous Skid Row. Barrel-shaped, "bum-proof" bus benches, outdoor sprinklers that soaked at random, and fortified garbage dumpsters kept the homeless out of Bunker Hill, while high-security parking garages with direct access to offices and shops protected the affluent from unwanted public encounters on the streets. Electronically sealed by steel doors, stopped escalators, and locked pedestrian passageways, Bunker Hill escaped damage during the Rodney King Riot in 1992.[9]

Outside the fortified scanscape of downtown, low-rise tenement districts offered a first stopping point for the immigrants. The 1992 riot, the most violent civil disorder since the Civil War draft riots, exposed the despair of Los Angeles's multicultural slums. In the 1990 recession, the metropolis accounted for 27 percent of all jobs lost nationally. Cutbacks in welfare threw tens of thousands of families and their children deeper into poverty. Twenty thousand people lined up for five hours for a Christmas handout of food in 1991. The riots provided a chance to seize needed items. City officials responded with more repression, deporting illegal immigrants, recovering stolen goods, and jailing violators. Capital flight left these neighborhoods without jobs or retail, their main corridor a high-rise ghost town.[10]

The 1992 riots cemented the connection between security and urban design. Celebrity architect Frank Gehry designed a defensive architecture for affluent pioneers braving the urban frontier. Featuring blank walls "introverted and fortress-like," Gehry's buildings centered on luxurious interiors open to the sky. His branch library in Hollywood—the "most menacing library ever built"—featured a fifteen-foot security wall and a sunken entrance. While Gehry established beachheads for future gentrification, developer Alexander Haagen built fortified malls for inner-city residents abandoned by other retailers. A typical Haagen mall, surrounded by an eight-foot high security fence, equipped with video cameras, floodlights, and infrared motion detectors, included a substation of the Los Angeles Police Department (LAPD) atop a panopticon observatory.[11]

The LAPD ceded labor-intensive tasks to the private sector. But it remained bullish on the macrosystems of security, including crime databases, aerial surveillance, a system of jails, and paramilitary actions against gangs, rioters, and terrorists. Battling an evil city, the LAPD embraced every technological innovation from radio cars and helicopters to a computerized communications system and a proposal for a space satellite. The LAPD operated on the principle of "good citizens, off the streets, enclaved in their high-security private consumption spheres; bad citizens, on the streets (and therefore not engaged in legitimate business)" subjected to a relentless scrutiny.[12]

While the well-to-do retreated to gated developments, the demand for security moved down the social scale. With support from home owners, the LAPD barricaded middle-income neighborhoods and restricted access in the hopes of keeping out crime. "Armed Response" signs sprouted on lawns as the private security industry tripled in size during the 1980s. Surveillance cameras and sentient buildings—retinal scanners, voice keys, and thermal facial imagers—testified to a pervasive fear.[13]

In neighborhoods without the political clout to demand public safety, residents armed themselves and landlords hired thugs to deter drug dealers. Private housing, retail outlets, and public agencies, including schools, all adopted a "Brinks aesthetic" of bars, partitions, and limited access. Affluent neighborhoods secured additional law enforcement resources or enhanced sanctions and punishments. Containment districts quarantined social problems and social types (especially the homeless). Meanwhile, a growing race war victimized African Americans and other minorities in Los Angeles's deteriorating inner-ring of suburbs.[14]

Race-based and drug-related warfare also raged in Los Angeles's gulag rim of prisons. Housing more than one hundred thousand new inmates since 1980, prisons crammed two inmates into a single six- by ten-foot cell (rats similarly confined went berserk and ate one another). While California's colleges and universities retrenched, the Department of Corrections hired 26,000 new employees (it cost twice as much to send an eighteen-year-old to prison than to college). As the real streets got meaner, tightly controlled theme park simulations like Universal City's CityWalk (where stray candy wrappers are embedded in sidewalks as part of design) offered city life in "easy, bite-sized pieces." Designed for tourists who "don't need the excitement of dodging bullets," CityWalk offered a junk food version of city life. "Have we so lost L.A. as a real city," California's leading historian asked, that "we need this level of social control for anything resembling the urban experience?"[15]

Visions of Fear and Hope

Los Angeles faces a mounting set of troubles. Class war and racial hatred compete with fire, flood, and drought to bring the city of sunshine to its knees. Having risen to world city status during a historically unusual period of high rainfall and low seismic activity, Los Angeles is unprepared to pay the piper. The Northridge earthquake of 1994, the costliest natural disaster in our history before Hurricane Katrina, barely began to repay the seismic debt. But its cleanup forced the postriot "Rebuild L.A." program off the public agenda, sharpening inequality and social tensions.[16]

Countless novels, short stories, and movies depict the violent destruction of Los Angeles, revealing our deepest fears about the future. The earliest of these nightmare scenarios featured invading hordes of ethnic outsiders, but increasingly the ethnic threat came from inside the multiracial city. After World War II, visions of ecological disaster became more prominent. In one, a huckster peddles a superfertilizer, developed by a woman to end world hunger, to "imbeciles" who want to "grow grass in the desert." The Bermuda grass spreads uncontrollably despite flamethrowers, tanks, and an atomic bomb, swallowing Los Angeles whole. In another, suburbanites gripped with a death wish water their lawns during a drought while "the police powers of fifty 'sovereign' cities" are powerless to stop them. After 1970, a rash of novels and films combined race war and environmental deterioration, exploiting the fear "that natural disaster might destroy the increasingly precarious firewall that separated the suburban 'us' from the inner city 'them.' "[17]

The ugly underside of our belief in progress, these literary nightmares raise the troubling question of whether we have any faith in the future at all. They are the imaginative counterpart to our neglect of mounting social and environmental challenges. Reeking with racism and antipathy to the city, the ritual sacrifice of Los Angeles speaks to our worst impulses. Unlike previous disaster fiction that signaled the collapse of civilization, the destruction of multicultural Los Angeles is celebrated as a victory for civilization. It also suggests how the neglect of the public realm can lead to social and environmental disaster.[18]

There is, of course, another and more hopeful Los Angeles, a city of successful multiethnic neighborhoods and public spaces—like the enduring Los Angeles Plaza—that bring citizens together for the purposes of celebration and collective action. These most admirable aspects of our urban inheritance represent our best chance of avoiding the nightmare scenarios. In depicting the logical culmination of our dominant social values and environmental practices, the literary destruction of Los Angeles should underscore for us the need to reinvest in our cities with an eye to social and environmental responsibility.[19]

We also need a political movement that is both democratic and participatory, for both entrenched interests and popular attitudes are responsible for social inequality and environmental deterioration. The modern environmental movement provides a useful foundation and can encourage the widest possible distribution of responsibility, which remains the key to creating good citizens. In contrast with the top-down, expert-dominated conservation movement of the early twentieth century, post–World War II environmentalism depended on grassroots organizations and changing cultural values. Where once technocrats sought to manage the productive use of natural resources, postwar citizens demanded protection of environmental amenities—health, beauty, permanence—as essential parts of the good life.[20]

The concern with pollution and the destruction of places of natural beauty gave rise to dramatic new forms of state intervention into the economy. At its most radical, the environmental movement focused attention on how the decisions of corporate interests and government regulators reshaped our environment and infiltrated our bodies. But for all its potential, the environmental movement revolved too exclusively around the concerns of middle-class consumers.[21]

Environmentalism's relationship to the mass production of housing illustrates both the movement's potential and its limitations. Living amid a dramatic environmental transformation in the postwar decades, middle-class suburbanites developed a powerful critique of the housing industry. When builders relied on septic tanks for waste disposal in tracts of thousands of houses, home owners complained of contaminated drinking water and demanded stricter regulations. Bulldozed landscapes and the construction of housing in wetlands, on hillsides, and in flood plains led suburban home owners to protest the disappearance of open space and the "rape of the land." The erosion of soil, the deterioration of rivers and lakes, and the destruction of wildlife habitat brought a new "urban consciousness" to federal conservation agencies and provided suburban home owners with new allies.[22]

The Water Quality Act of 1965, the National Environmental Policy Act of 1970, and other legislation reflected a quiet revolution in the law prompted by mass suburbanization. The courts long held that land-use regulations that severely decreased the value of property represented a taking, requiring just compensation. But in the 1960s, legal scholars caught up to the public in rethinking land-use regulation and the rights of property. "Although land is still mainly thought of as a commodity in the free market," jurists noted, "the public is beginning to think of land as a basic community resource." The laissez-faire philosophy must give way, they concluded, to "regulation of land as a social asset" that took the "social costs" of development into account.

The new legal thinking reflected the influence of the central insight of ecology, that everything is connected. "Property does not exist in isolation," wrote one legal scholar. "Particular plots are tied to one another in complex ways, and property is more accurately described as being inextricably part of a network of relationships." A "parcel of land is inextricably intertwined with other parcels," another scholar added, so that "causes and effects flow across artificially imposed divisions in the land without regard for legal boundaries. The land simply cannot be neatly divided into mine and yours." The "ecological facts of life," these scholars concluded, left the traditional view of property rights untenable.

In the 1970s, state courts handed down decisions reflecting the new legal thinking. "An owner of land," the Wisconsin Supreme Court held in a 1972 case, "had no absolute and unlimited right to change the essential natural character of his land." The widely discussed decision held that property rights must be balanced with "the public interest in stopping the despoliation of natural resources." The Wisconsin decision and other state cases prompted a national debate on the need for a land ethic. But when a land-use bill came before Congress in 1973, opponents mobilized in defense of property rights and against the "centralization of all power over land in state—and ultimately federal—regulatory agencies." A combination of small property owners and organized interests defeated the bill.

Toward an Ecology of the City

Despite successes in securing legislation for clean air and water, the environmental movement failed to transform the mass production of housing. The oil shocks of the 1970s brought economic hard times, especially in the housing industry, and made regulation less affordable. Environmentalists also underestimated the difficulty of their task, treating land use as just another pollution issue. Corporate polluters offered an easier target than vast numbers of small property owners for whom a house represented their single biggest investment.

Above all, the environmental movement never resolved the contradiction between private profit and the public good. Good environmental practice required either private developers or private home buyers to pay for a public good enjoyed by all. Neither developers nor middle-class consumers proved willing to pay the bill for benefits they shared with anonymous others. The environmental movement needed a compelling public vision of the green house and the green city to overcome both organized opposition and individual self-interest. But the environmental movement's antiurban bias, its idea of nature as something apart from the city, frustrated the effort to develop such visions. The "proponents of nature emphasize preservation," environmental planner Ian McHarg wrote in 1966, "a negative position ... which excludes the positive participation in the real and difficult tasks of creating noble and ennobling cities in fair landscapes."

The environmental movement needs an ecology of the city. In seeking to uncover the totality and pattern of relations between and among humans and their environment, an ecological approach to the city focuses attention on both our productive and consumptive practices. It encourages us to ask how—and based on what values and assumptions—natural resources and labor are appropriated. An ecology of the city also challenges our "let them eat bytes" economic policy. We rhapsodize about a globalized information economy while the basic foundations of human life—clean water and air, fertile soil, and moderate temperatures—deteriorate. We live in a world where sunshine causes cancer, rain kills trees, and food poisons us. All of us, from Wall Street on down, have forgotten that the "larger purpose of the economic order ... is to support the material conditions for human existence" and "not to undermine and destabilize them."[23]

An ecology of the city also underscores the importance of settlement. In 1980, the Presidential Commission for a National Agenda described the decay of our central cities as the result of forces "potent and enduring" and "persistent and immutable" trends. The commission urged acceptance of the "long-term inevitability and desirability of this transformation" and the liquidation of investments in "outdated urban structures and functions." "Public policy," the commission concluded, "should seek to loosen the tie between distressed people and distressed places just as a variety of technological developments have loosened the ties between industry and its traditional and urban location." Nothing in the report suggested the role of corporate and federal policies in urban decay, the human costs of abandonment, or the possibility that a different set of policies might reverse current trends.[24]

More than economic engines, cities are settlements, places, and cultures. But economic decisions are crucial and cities as settlements cannot be protected without making economic decisions part of political debate. A reintegration of economic and political life is what social ecologists mean when they urge us to "municipalize the economy." In contrast to a corporate or nationalized economy controlled by an economic or political elite, a municipalized economy depends upon a new citizenship that brings "the economy as a whole into the orbit of the public sphere." Economic decisions become political decisions and management of the economy becomes a collective responsibility. Instead of the market determining what shape the city may take, citizens dictate what forms the market shall take.[25]

An ecologically informed discussion of city planning and city building offers us the best chance to create a just and sustainable civilization. Civic reformers in the Progressive Era tried to turn city planning and city building into democratic movements. The city represented the ultimate test, an architect wrote, of the public's "ability to translate our analysis of our social ideals into physical expressions." From its public squares and civic monuments down to its sewers, he argued, the city "constitutes the real, vital art of a people" and "the physical expression of social and democratic ideals." Popular engagement with issues of planning generated an "urban conversation," a recent historian of city planning argued, which served to "justify public action to a society that is deeply individualistic."[26]

The most successful urban environmental planning in American cities resulted from just such urban conversations. One such conversation resulted in Boston's Back Bay, Emerald Necklace, and the Fens, massive nineteenth-century public projects that improved public health, provided building space, and served as a storm drainage system. An urban conversation also shaped the regional planning successes of Portland, Oregon, since 1970, including its urban growth boundary that halted sprawl, preserved open space, increased the viability of public transit, and revitalized downtown neighborhoods. But much of professional city planning failed precisely because it "has forsaken the language and strategies of the urban conversation for the technical discourse of the academy and the bureaucracy."[27]

In reviving an urban conversation, we might find inspiration in the urban populists of the Progressive Era. Henry George and his followers developed both a land ethic and a compelling public vision of the good city. The growth of the city, George explained, brought out "a superior power in labor, which is localized in land." The resulting rise in land values represented a socially created form of wealth that should be used for public benefit. George designed his single tax, a confiscatory tax on the speculative value of land, to secure rising land values for public purposes. The "enormous value which the presence of a million and a half of people gives to the land of this city," George declared during his mayoral campaign in New York City in 1886, "belongs properly to the whole community" and should be "applied to the improvement and beautifying of the city, to the promotion of the health, comfort, education, and recreation of its people."[28]

George envisioned the single tax as a means of rationalizing patterns of settlement in environmentally and socially responsible ways. Land speculation encouraged a destructive pattern of land use. "We are cutting down forests which we do not replant," George warned, "we are shipping abroad, in wheat and cotton and tobacco and meat, or flushing into the sea through the sewers of our great cities, the elements of fertility that have been embedded in the soil by the slow processes of nature, acting for long ages." Speculative values also produced a concentration of population that "impoverishes social life at the extremities, as well as poisons it at the center." The single tax promoted a responsible and rational use of land, George concluded, securing "breathing room and neighborhood" for all.[29]

Elements of George's vision reappeared in the 20th century, even amid Los Angeles's orgy of land speculation. Early in the century, City Beautiful activists advocated a comprehensive park plan and civic acropolis along the Los Angeles River to be paid for through excess condemnation and the sale of "property on the edge of a public improvement." During and after World War II, the architects Richard Neutra and Robert Alexander advocated a regional plan for Los Angeles centered on agricultural greenbelts and residential nodes, creating a virtuous circle of clustered housing, reduced cost of schools and utilities, greater density to sustain rapid transit, neighborhood identity, and democratic participation. As late as the 1950s, ecologist and architect Garrett Eckbo argued that to resolve "the contradiction between social relations and individual land use" land speculation had to be placed under "proper public control." Eckbo's argument informed the Urban Metropolitan Open Space Study, delivered to California governor Jerry Brown in 1965, that called for new tax and zoning policies to protect LA's remaining foothills and valley spaces and discourage sprawl. The report also recommended a dramatic expansion of public space, in part by rebuilding inner city neighborhoods around denser, pedestrian-based nodes and attractive public parks and squares.[30]

The central element of George's vision—land values as socially created wealth—reappeared as recently as the congressional debate on a land ethic in the 1970s. A report on *The Uses of Land* (1973), commissioned by the Rockefeller Brothers Fund, concluded that we needed "to change the view that land is little more than a commodity to be exploited and traded." Americans believed that land values came from the efforts of the landowner, the report explained, but land values actually came from the growth of settlements, which provided opportunities for economic development. In isolation, a parcel of land could never produce more than subsistence value; only settlement gave land greater value. Society, the report concluded, should therefore define the obligations of property owners.[31]

For all their troubles, our cities still generate high land values that testify to their continuing vitality. A tax on speculative land values (a form of wealth that cannot flee our shores) would restore the city's declining tax base and provide revenues for a rebuilding of the public realm. Such a tax would also underscore the obligations of property owners to the settlements that enrich them. As we turn back to our cities to address environmental deterioration and social inequality, we can find in our past not only inspiration and encouragement but concrete proposals of considerable merit.

ACKNOWLEDGMENTS

This work is immeasurably indebted to the painstaking labors of historians over the past fifty years. There are a hundred monographs I have read that should have found their way into this narrative and hundreds more I have not read that I should have. But I could not even have begun this book without the stubborn devotion of historians to their craft. They recovered the rich history of civic aspiration and public experience examined in these pages. By and large, I do not know the historians whose work I synthesize and I have not heard them talk about what they thought they were doing in their work. I have simply read their work with a fresh eye and tried to interpret it for other Americans, sometimes finding different arguments than the authors intended.

I am thankful for the advice I received from David Stradling, a coeditor of the series who read an earlier and much longer version of this study. He made many useful suggestions essential to turning an ungainly manuscript into a book. I am particularly grateful for his expertise and encouragement in helping me to expand the treatment of post-1945 cities, which resulted in the final chapter. At Temple University Press, the senior acquisitions editor, Mick Gusinde-Duffy, offered steadfast support and steered the project adeptly through the publication process. Despite the manuscript's unusual length and form, he believed in its potential to reach a wide audience. If it reaches such an audience, it is in large part because of his suggestions on reducing its length and sharpening its argument. The anonymous readers for Temple University Press also made a host of valuable suggestions that greatly improved this work. Two research sabbaticals from Xavier University, and the support and stimulation of my many friends and colleagues there, have enabled me to complete this study. I am also grateful for the hard work of a remarkable research assistant, Linda Dehner, who provided me with the intelligent and discerning eye usually available only to historians at major research universities.

The mistakes and limitations are, of course, my own. My greatest debt in this project, far and away, is to Zane L. Miller, who shepherded it through many rocky times over the past decade. An exemplary editor, Zane always knew the right thing to say when my confidence or energy began to flag. Most remarkable, he has the stunning ability to cut out huge swaths of unnecessary prose (pages and pages at times), leaving the remaining pieces to fit together better than ever. He is an author's dream come true. But more than that, in teaching me to think and to write over the past twenty years, Zane made me a better historian and shared with me the many joys of the life of the mind. I am deeply grateful to him as a mentor and a friend.

As a young college student, I met the late Christopher Lasch in Rochester, New York, "by blue Ontario's shore," and he changed my life. I miss him terribly and think about him every day. I think he is somewhere reading this book, no doubt making incisive editorial comments, but also, I hope, thinking that the time and energy and care he gave me have been in some small measure repaid. I also met my wife Mary McPartland in Rochester, in one of Lasch's classes. This book began many years ago in spirited conversations with her about "bourgeois domesticity" and "promiscuous sociability." I hope she will see it as partial repayment for those wonderful conversations. She knows that this book is also for our children, Sally, Tom, Fran, and Polly, and the world they are helping to make.

NOTES

PREFACE

1. Carl Degler, *Out of Our Past: The Forces That Shaped Modern America* (New York: Harper 1959), 2, 291; Richard Hofstadter, *The American Political Tradition* (New York: Vintage Books 1974), xxxvi–xxxvii.

2. Robert Fishman, ed., *The American Planning Tradition: Culture and Policy* (Washington, DC: Woodrow Wilson Center Press, 2000), 2; John D. Fairfield, "Private City, Public City: Power and Vision in American Cities," 29 *Journal of Urban History* (May 2003): 437–462.

3. Thomas Frank, "The Rise of Market Populism: America's New Secular Religion," *The Nation* 271 (October 30, 2000); Fishman, *The American Planning Tradition*, 1ff.; Peter Calthrope, *The Next American Metropolis* (New York: Princeton Architectural Press, 1993), 13–38.

4. Russell Jacoby, *The Last Intellectuals; American Culture in an Age of Academe* (New York: Basic Books, 1987); Thomas Bender, *New York Intellect: A History of Intellectual Life in New York City, from 1750 to the Beginnings of Our Own Time* (New York: Knopf, 1987).

5. Benjamin Barber, *Strong Democracy: Participatory Politics for a New Age* (Berkeley: University of California Press, 1984), 243; Jurgen Habermas, *The Structural Transformation of the Public Sphere* (Cambridge, MA: MIT Press 1989); Hannah Arendt, *The Human Condition* (Chicago: University of Chicago Press, 1958); John Dewey, *The Public and Its Problems* (New York: Holt & Company, 1927); J. G. A. Pocock, *The Machiavellian Moment: Florentine Political Thought and Atlantic Republican Tradition* (Princeton, NJ: Princeton University Press, 1975); Michael J. Sandel, *Democracy's Discontent: America in Search of a Public Philosophy* (Cambridge, MA: The Belknap Press of Harvard University Press, 1996).

6. Thomas Bender, "Wholes and Parts: The Need for Synthesis in American History," *Journal of American History* 73 (June 1986): 120–134.

7. John Dewey, *Art as Experience* (New York: Minton, Balch & Company, 1934), 348–350.

8. This paragraph is indebted to a series of exchanges with Vincent Colapietro. Dewey, *The Public and Its Problems*, 252; John Dewey, "Socialization of Ground Rent" (1935), in

John Dewey: The Later Works, 1925–1953, ed. Jo Ann Boydston (Carbondale, IL: Southern Illinois University Press, 1984), 11: 256–257.

9. William Gaddis, *The Recognitions* (New York: Avon, 1955).

INTRODUCTION

1. Perry Miller, *Errand into the Wilderness* (Cambridge, MA: The Belknap Press of Harvard University Press, 1984), vii–15; Robert Griffith, ed., *Major Problems in American History since 1945* (Lexington, MA: D.C. Heath, 1992), Eisenhower on 166–167.

2. Michael J. Sandel, *Democracy's Discontent: America in Search of a Public Philosophy* (Cambridge, MA: 1996); Christopher Lasch, "Liberalism and Civic Virtue," *Telos* (Summer 1991), 57–68.

3. Robert Bellah et al., *The Good Society* (New York: Knopf, 1991); Mary Ann Glendon, *Rights Talk* (New York: Maxwell Macmillan, 1991); Christopher Lasch, *The True and Only Heaven: Progress and Its Critics* (New York: Norton, 1991); John Patrick Diggins, *The Lost Soul of American Politics: Virtue, Self-Interest, and the Foundations of Liberalism* (New York: Basic Books, 1984); Sandel, *Democracy's Discontent*.

4. Christopher Lasch, *The Revolt of the Elites and the Betrayal of Democracy* (New York: W.W Norton &Company, 1995), 80–91, 129–133; Sandel, *Democracy's Discontent*; Louis Hartz, *The Liberal Tradition in America* (San Diego: Harcourt Brace Jovanovich, 1991); Kenneth Jackson, *Crabgrass Frontier: The Suburbanization of the United States* (New York: Oxford University Press, 1985), especially chapter 3; David Potter, *People of Plenty: Economic Abundance and the American Character* (Chicago: University of Chicago Press, 1954).

5. Frederick Jackson Turner's frontier thesis, as amended by William Appleman Williams, remains persuasive. Frederick Jackson Turner, *The Frontier in American History* (New York: Henry Holt & Company, 1958); William Appleman Williams, *The Tragedy of American Diplomacy* (New York: Dell Publishing, 1962); William Appleman Williams, *The Contours of American History* (Chicago: Quadrangle Books, 1966); Kevin Phillips, *American Dynasty* (New York: Penguin Books, 2004); Bernard Bailyn, *The Ideological Origins of the American Revolution* (Cambridge, MA: The Belknap Press of Harvard University Press, 1992), 378–379.

6. Arthur M. Schlesinger, "The City in American History," *Mississippi Valley Historical Review* 27 (June 1940): 43–66.

7. Modern urban historians, then, can trace their roots to a century of thought about the ideal of a great city. Warren I. Susman, "The City in American Culture," in Warren I. Susman, *Culture as History: The Transformation of American Society in the Twentieth Century* (New York: Pantheon Books, 1984), 237–251; see also Robert Fishman, ed., *The American Planning Tradition: Culture and Policy* (Washington, DC; Woodrow Wilson Center Press, 2000), 6–7; John D. Fairfield, "Democracy in Cincinnati: Civic Virtue and Three Generations of Urban Historians," *Urban History* 24 (1997): 200–220.

8. Susman, *Culture as History*, 237–251; Daniel Bluestone, *Constructing Chicago* (New Haven, CT: Yale University Press, 1991).

9. Susman, *Culture as History*, 237–251; the progressive is Delos F. Wilcox, *The American City* (New York: The Macmillan Company, 1904), 168–169; the settlement leader is John Collier, "Leisure Time: The Last Problem of Conservation," *Recreation* 6 (June 1912): 93–106.

10. William McNeil, *The Rise of the West* (New York: University of Chicago Press, 1961), 36; Murray Bookchin, *From Urbanization to Cities: Toward a New Politics of Citizenship* (New York: Cassell, 1995); Jean Bethke Elshtain, "Catholic Social Thought, the City, and Liberal America," in *Catholicism and Liberalism: Contributions to American Public Philosophy*, ed. R. Bruce Douglass and David Hollenbach (New York: Cambridge University Press, 1994), 97–114.

11. Zane L. Miller and Patricia M. Melvin, *The Urbanization of Modern America* (San Diego: Harcourt Brace Jovanovich, 1987), 5ff.; Richard C. Wade, *The Urban Frontier* (Urbana,

IL: University of Illinois Press, 1996); Stephen L. Elkin, *City and Regime in the American Republic* (Chicago: University of Chicago Press, 1987), 1–17, 105–119, 147.

12. The term "overlapping" deliberately invokes the postmodernist concept of "imbrication." Overlapping narratives and analyses offer us the best means of avoiding totalizing narratives that marginalize certain ideas, values, groups, and practices. Nell Irvin Painter, "Bias and Synthesis in History," *Journal of American History* 74 (June 1987): 109–112; Richard Wightman Fox, "Public Culture and the Problem of Synthesis," *Journal of American History* 74 (June 1987): 113–116.

PART I

1. Eric Hobsbawm, *The Age of Revolution* (New York: New American Library, 1962); Eric Hobsbawm, *The Age of Capital* (New York: New American Library, 1979).

2. Steven J. Ross, *Workers on the Edge: Work, Leisure and Politics in Industrializing Cincinnati, 1788–1890* (New York: Columbia University Press, 1985), xv–xx; David Montgomery, *Citizen Worker* (New York: Cambridge Press, 1993), 1–12; Gordon S. Wood, *The Radicalism of the American Revolution* (New York: Vintage Books, 1991), Ramsay on 169; other quotations in Christopher Lasch, *The Revolt of the Elites and the Betrayal of Democracy*,(New York: W.W. Norton & Company, 1995), 58; see also Nathan O. Hatch, *The Democratization of American Christianity* (New Haven, CT: Yale University Press, 1989), 3–16ff.

3. This paragraph and the next four are based on Alexis de Tocqueville, *Democracy in America*, ed. Richard D. Heffner (New York: New American Library, 1984), 67–68, 108–111, 162.

4. Hannah Arendt, *On Revolution* (New York: Viking Press, 1963), 111–137.

5. An "asylum for mankind" is Thomas Paine, *Common Sense* (1776), quoted in Bernard Bailyn, *The Ideological Origins of the American Revolution* (Cambridge, MA: The Belknap Press of Harvard University Press, 1992), 143; "last, best hope on earth" is from Abraham Lincoln's annual message to Congress (December 1, 1862); "government by the people" is from Lincoln's Gettysburg Address: Roy P. Basler, ed., *The Collected Works of Abraham Lincoln* (Washington: authorized by Lincoln Sesquicentennial Commission 1959, 1974, 1990), 5: 537, 7: 23.

CHAPTER 1

1. T. H. Breen, *The Marketplace of Revolution: How Consumer Politics Shaped American Independence* (New York: Oxford University Press, 2004), 1–29: "forego" is Christopher Gadsden, quoted on 24, and "A Consistent Patriot" is quoted on 26; Bernard Bailyn, *The Ideological Origins of the American Revolution* (Cambridge, MA: The Belknap Press of Harvard University Press, 1992); Gordon S. Wood, *The Creation of the American Republic, 1776–1787* (Chapel Hill, NC: University of North Carolina Press, 1969); Gordon S. Wood, *The Radicalism of the American Revolution* (New York, Vintage Books, 1991); Drew McCoy, *The Elusive Republic: Political Economy in Jeffersonian America* (Chapel Hill, NC: University of North Carolina Press, 1980); J. G. A. Pocock, *The Machiavellian Moment: Florentine Political Thought and Atlantic Republican Tradition* (Princeton, NJ: Princeton University Press, 1975); Gary B. Nash, *The Urban Crucible: The Northern Seaports and the Origins of the American Revolution* (Cambridge, MA: Harvard University Press, 1986).

2. McCoy, *The Elusive Republic*, 48–75: Franklin quoted on 65; Lance Banning, *The Jeffersonian Persuasion: Evolution of a Party Ideology* (Ithaca, NY: Cornell University Press, 1978); Joyce Appleby, *Capitalism and a New Social Order: The Republican Vision of the 1790s* (New York: New York University Press, 1984).

3. Wood, *The Radicalism of the American Revolution*, 256–260; Wood calls the Pennsylvania debate "maybe the crucial moment" in the history of American politics.

4. Smith quoted in Ralph Ketcham, ed., *The Anti-Federalist Papers and the Constitutional Convention Debates* (New York: New American Library, 1986), 342–347; Edwin G. Burrows

and Mike Wallace, *Gotham: A History of New York City to 1898* (New York: Oxford University Press, 1999), 319–321; Wood, *The Radicalism of the American Revolution*, 271–286.

5. Nash, *The Urban Crucible*; Benjamin L. Carp, *Rebels Rising: Cities and the American Revolution* (New York: Oxford University Press, 2007), 3–22; Breen, *The Marketplace of Revolution*.

6. Nash, *The Urban Crucible*, 14–32, "rabble" on 28; Burrows and Wallace, *Gotham*, 91–102; Michael Schudson, *The Good Citizen: A History of American Civic Life* (New York: Martin Kessler Books, 1998), 11–13; Carp, *Rebels Rising*, 3–22.

7. Thomas Bender, *New York Intellect: A History of Intellectual Life in New York City, from 1750 to the Beginnings of Our Own Time* (Baltimore: Johns Hopkins University Press, 1988), 9–45; Carp, *Rebels Rising*; compare to Jurgen Habermas, *The Structural Transformation of the Public Sphere: An Inquiry into a Category of Bourgeois Society* (Cambridge, MA: MIT Press, 1989).

8. Schudson, *The Good Citizen*, 11–13; Jim Cullen, *The Art of Democracy: A Concise History of Popular Culture in the United States* (New York: Monthly Review Press, 1996), 23–29.

9. Nash, *The Urban Crucible*, quotations on 123–127; Schudson, *The Good Citizen*, 16–40; Wood, *The Radicalism of the American Revolution*, 169–174; Alan Brinkley, *The Unfinished Nation* (Boston: McGraw-Hill, 2000), 86–87; "Deference or Defiance in Eighteenth-Century America? A Round Table," *Journal of American History* (June 1998): 13–97.

10. Schudson, *The Good Citizen*, 32–40.

11. Nash, *The Urban Crucible*, 46–54, 82–89, 92–98.

12. Nash, *The Urban Crucible*, 99–146, Mather on 101; Burrows and Wallace, *Gotham*, 150–190; Kevin Phillips, *Wealth and Democracy* (New York: Broadway Books, 2003), 3–31.

13. Nash, *The Urban Crucible*, 99–146, quotations on 134–136; Burrows and Wallace, *Gotham*, 150–190.

14. Nash, *The Urban Crucible*, 99–194; quotations on 140, 108.

15. Nash, *The Urban Crucible*, 147–199: "rage" on 187, "level'd" on 194; Burrows and Wallace, *Gotham*, 196–200, "cram" on 199; Wood, *The Creation of the American Republic*, 319–328.

16. Sam Bass Warner, Jr., *The Private City: Philadelphia in Three Periods of Its Growth* (Philadelphia: University of Pennsylvania Press, 1968), 16–21; Stuart M. Blumin, *The Emergence of the Middle Class: Social Experience in the American City, 1760–1900* (New York: Cambridge University Press, 1989), 17–65.

17. Carp, *Rebels Rising*, 23–61, quotations on 27, 44.

18. This paragraph and the next are based on Carp, *Rebels Rising*, 62–98, quotations on 78 (italics in the original), 84, and 95.

19. Carp, *Rebels Rising*, 172–184.

20. Nash, *The Urban Crucible*, 240–246: "Rabble on 240, "Tyrannical" on 241; Carp, *Rebels Rising*, 172–212: "Doors" on 194–195, "determine" on 199; Eric Foner, *Tom Paine and Revolutionary America* (New York: Oxford University Press, 1976), 107–144.

21. This paragraph and the next are based on Carp, *Rebels Rising*, 198–212.

22. Breen, *The Marketplace of Revolution*, 1–29, 235–331; Edward Countryman, *The American Revolution* (New York: Hill and Wang, 1985), 87–113.

23. Breen, *The Marketplace of Revolution*, xiv–29; 235–331: "self-denial" on 264, "rotten" on 299.

24. Mary Beth Norton, *Liberty's Daughters: The Revolutionary Experience of American Women, 1750–1800* (Boston: Little, Brown, 1980), 155–194, quoted passages on 157–170; Linda Kerber, *Women of the Republic: Intellect and Ideology in Revolutionary America* (Chapel Hill, NC: University of North Carolina Press, 1980), 33–114; Carp, *Rebels Rising*, 143–171.

25. Norton, *Liberty's Daughters*, 154–177.

26. This paragraph and the three that follow are based on Carp, *Rebels Rising*, 136–171 (italics in the original).

27. Carp, *Rebels Rising*, 195–212, quotations on 201, 210–211; Nash, *The Urban Crucible*, 219–247; Breen, *The Marketplace of Revolution*, 1–29, 234–331; Edmund S. Morgan, "The Puritan Ethic and the American Revolution," *William and Mary Quarterly* 24 (1967): 3–43; Bailyn, *The Ideological Origins of the American Revolution*, 32–33; Robert Shalhope, "Republicanism and Early American Historiography," *William and Mary Quarterly* 39 (1982): 334–356; Pocock, *The Machiavellian Moment*, 506–509.

28. Bailyn, *The Ideological Origins of the American Revolution*; Wood, *The Radicalism of the American Revolution*, 95–96ff.; Nash, *The Urban Crucible*, 217–233; McCoy, *The Elusive Republic*, 13–75; Isaac Kramnick, "Republican Revisionism Revisited," *American Historical Review* 87 (June 1982): 629–664; Appleby, *Capitalism and a New Social Order*, 16–23; Morgan, "The Puritan Ethic and the American Revolution," 10–13; Banning, *The Jeffersonian Persuasion*.

29. Carp, *Rebels Rising*, Gadsden on 167; Nash, *The Urban Crucible*, 217–233; Isaac Kramnick, "Republican Revisionism Revisited," *American Historical Review* 87 (June 1982): 629–664; Appleby, *Capitalism and a New Social Order*, 16–23 passim; Morgan, "The Puritan Ethic and the American Revolution," 10–13.

30. Nash, *The Urban Crucible*, 217–233: "mow down" on 226, "burthens" on 225; Shalhope, "Republicanism and Early American Historiography," 334–356.

31. Bailyn, *The Ideological Origins of the American Revolution*, 17–20; McCoy, *The Elusive Republic*, 13–47; Wood, *The Creation of the American Republic*, 91–93ff.; Pocock, *The Machiavellian Moment*, 506–552; Breen, *The Marketplace of Revolution*, 1–29. In using the term "myth," I do not mean to dismiss the intellectual seriousness of civic republicanism. People "can and should see their citizenships as forms of participation in enormously important collective historical enterprises that in fact do transcend their individual lives in time and space." Rogers M. Smith, *Civic Ideals: Conflicting Visions of Citizenship in U.S. History* (New Haven, CT: Yale University Press, 1997), 11.

32. Bailyn, *Ideological Origins of the American Revolution*, 77–93, "rising on every hill" on 83–84; Wood, *Creation of the American Republic*, 3–49, 60–63, 97–101; Wood, *The Radicalism of the American Revolution*, 95–109 passim; McCoy, *The Elusive Republic*, 62–75; Appleby, *Capitalism and a New Social Order*, 16ff., and Schudson, *The Good Citizen*, 18; Countryman, *The American Revolution*, 16–18.

33. Bailyn, *The Ideological Origins of the American Revolution*, 32–54, "critical juncture" on 33; Wood, *The Creation of the American Republic*, 60–61, 114–122; Morgan, "The Puritan Ethic and the American Revolution," 6; Pocock, *The Machiavellian Moment*, 511–513; Foner, *Tom Paine and Revolutionary America*, 81; James T. Kloppenberg, "The Virtues of Liberalism: Christianity, Republicanism, and Ethics in Early American Discourse," *Journal of American History* 74 (June 1987): 9–33.

34. Bailyn, *Ideological Origins of the American Revolution*, 93–138, Eliot quoted on 93; Breen, *The Marketplace of Revolution*, 294–331; Wood, *Creation of the American Republic*, 3–47.

35. Bailyn, *Ideological Origins of the American Revolution*, 94–149: Adams on 135, "cause" on 139–140 (italics in original). The conclusion of modern historians that there was no British conspiracy reinforces the interpretation of civic republicanism as a revolutionary myth, but as it shaped colonial perceptions and actions, the myth was also an important part of reality; Bailyn, "A Note on Conspiracy," in *Ideological Origins of the American Revolution*, especially 148–149; Breen, *The Marketplace of Revolution*, 294–331; Wood, *Creation of the American Republic*, 42–52.

36. Bailyn, *The Ideological Origins of the American Revolution*, 101–140: Adams on 101–102 and 140, a "world regenerative creed" is Bailyn's phrase, 138; Morgan, "The Puritan Ethic and the American Revolution," 19.

37. Adams quoted in Wood, *The Creation of the American Republic*, 119–120, and Ralph Lerner, *The Thinking Revolutionary* (Ithaca, NY: Cornell University Press, 1987), 21–28.

38. Wood, *The Creation of the American Republic*, 91–124, quotations on 108–109; Breen, *The Marketplace of Revolution*, 148–192, 294–331; see also Wood, *The Radicalism of the American Revolution*, 124–225.

39. This paragraph and the next are based on Wood, *The Creation of the American Republic*, 101–118.

40. Charles Royster, "'The Nature of Treason': Revolutionary Virtue and American Reactions to Benedict Arnold," *William and Mary Quarterly* 36 (1979): 163–193; Charles Royster, *A Revolutionary People at War: The Continental Army and the American Character, 1775–1783* (Chapel Hill, NC: University of North Carolina Press, 1979); Wood, *The Radicalism of the American Revolution*, 247–252.

41. Royster, "'The Nature of Treason,'" 163–193; Royster, *A Revolutionary People at War*; Wood, *The Radicalism of the American Revolution*, 247–252.

42. Barbara Clark Smith, "Food Rioters and the American Revolution," *William and Mary Quarterly* 51 (January 1994): 3–38; Foner, *Tom Paine and Revolutionary America*, 145–163, Smith quoted on 153; Wood, *The Creation of the American Republic*, 95–97, Jay quoted on 96.

43. Foner, *Tom Paine and Revolutionary America*, 145–163, "harangued upon" on 163; Sam Bass Warner, Jr., *The Private City: Philadelphia in Three Periods of Its Growth* (Philadelphia: University of Pennsylvania Press, 1968), 32–45.

44. Foner, *Tom Paine and Revolutionary America*, 163–182, quotations on 165 and 169; Wood, *The Creation of the American Republic*, 319–327.

45. Royster, "'The Nature of Treason'"; Royster, *A Revolutionary People at War*.

46. Wood, *The Creation of the American Republic*, 65–95, 118–122, 362–366: "annihilate" on 362, "co-legislator" on 366; McCoy, *The Elusive Republic*, 76–104; Breen, *The Marketplace of Revolution*, 148–192; Wood, *The Radicalism of the American Revolution*, 169–178, 189–225, Bailyn, *The Ideological Origins of the American Revolution*, 198–229.

47. Foner, *Tom Paine and Revolutionary America*, 81–87, 120: "silly clown" on 120, "mysterious" on 85; Bailyn, *The Ideological Origins of the American Revolution*, 282–288, "tailors and cobblers" on 284; Wood, *Creation of the American Republic*, 52–61, 91–114, 228–249.

48. Wood, *The Creation of the American Republic*, 328–344, 409–413, quotation on 343; Wood, *The Radicalism of the American Revolution*, 180–189.

49. Wood, *The Creation of the American Republic*, 413–425 (italics in original).

50. Wood, *The Creation of the American Republic*, 397–398, 410–472; Wood, *The Radicalism of the American Revolution*, 248–254; McCoy, *The Elusive Republic*, 95–104; W. W. Abbot et al., eds., *The Papers of George Washington*, Confederation Series, vol. 4, April 1786–January 1787 (Charlottesville, VA: University Press of Virginia, 1992), 318–320; Clinton Rossiter, ed., *The Federalist Papers* (New York: Penguin, 1961), 71, Federalist No. 9.

51. Isaac Kramnick, "The 'Great National Discussion,'" *William and Mary Quarterly* 45 (January 1988): 1–32; Rossiter, *The Federalist Papers*, Madison's Federalist No. 10; Bailyn, *The Ideological Origins of the American Revolution*, 351–372, "study and pursue" on 364; Pocock, *The Machiavellian Moment*, 520–523.

52. Rossiter, *The Federalist Papers*, Federalist Nos. 10 and 51; Bailyn, *The Ideological Origins of the American Revolution*, 351–372; Wood, *The Creation of the American Republic*, 543–593, 610–615.

53. Rossiter, *The Federalist Papers*, Federalist No. 10; Wood, *The Creation of the American Republic*, 588–593, 610–616; Christopher Lasch, "Liberalism and Civic Virtue," *Telos* (Summer 1991): 57–68.

54. Hannah Arendt, *On Revolution* (New York: Penguin Books, 1977), 115–132; Jefferson's "where every man is a sharer"—a part of which Arendt quotes—is from a letter of 1816, in Thomas Jefferson, *Writings* (New York: Viking Press, 1984), 1380; Bailyn, *Ideological Origins of the American Revolution*, 379; Schudson, *The Good Citizen*, 48–55.

55. Kramnick, "The 'Great National Discussion,'" "private vices," and "refinement" on 11; Bailyn, *The Ideological Origins of the American Revolution*, 331–351; Ketcham, *The Anti-Federalist Papers*, "Speeches of Patrick Henry," 200.

56. Wood, *The Radicalism of the American Revolution*, 255–260; Ketcham, *The Anti-Federalist Papers*: "Farmers" on 248, Smith on 342–346; see also Ralph Ketcham,

"Anti-Federalist Political Thought," introduction in *The Anti-Federalist Papers*, 16–20; and Herbert J. Storing, ed., *The Complete Anti-Federalist* (Chicago: University of Chicago Press, 1981).

57. Appleby, *Capitalism and a New Social Order*, 1–15; "Moving beyond Beard: A Symposium," *Radical History Review* 42 (1988): 7–47, especially Alfred F. Young, "The Framers of the Constitution and the 'Genius' of the People," 8–18; Kloppenberg, "The Virtues of Liberalism," 23–29.

58. Wood, *The Radicalism of the American Revolution*, 68–69, 282–283, 338–339, "fickleness" and "proprietary" on 68; Appleby, *Capitalism and a New Social Order*, 1–50, Paine on 50; Breen, *The Marketplace of Revolution*, 148–192; Bailyn, *The Ideological Origins of the American Revolution*; Pocock, *The Machiavellian Moment*, 532–534; Shalhope, "Republicanism and Early American Historiography," 346; McCoy, *The Elusive Republic*, 68.

59. Wood, *The Radicalism of the American Revolution*, 261–266; Lance Banning, "Jeffersonian Ideology Revisited: Liberal and Classical Ideas in the New American Republic," *William and Mary Quarterly* 43 (January 1986): 3–19; Appleby, *Capitalism and a New Social Order*, 38; Kramnick, "The 'Great National Discussion,'" 23–32.

60. Appleby, *Capitalism and a New Social Order*, 51–55; Christopher Lasch, *The True and Only Heaven:Progress and Its Critics* (New York: Norton, 1991), footnote on 195–196; Bailyn, *The Ideological Origins of the American Revolution*, 379.

61. Schudson, *The Good Citizen*, 48–89, quotations on 57–60; Appleby, *Capitalism and a New Social Order*, 54–70.

62. Appleby, *Capitalism and a New Social Order*, 54–70; John Patrick Diggins, *The Lost Soul of American Politics* (New York: Basic Books, 1984), Jefferson on 104; Schudson, *The Good Citizen*, "echo" on 62.

63. Appleby, *Capitalism and a New Social Order*, 54–70, "favorite" on 65; Thomas Slaughter, *The Whiskey Rebellion* (New York: Oxford University Press, 1986).

64. This paragraph and the three that follow are based on Appleby, *Capitalism and a New Social Order*, 65–90.

65. Appleby, *Capitalism and a New Social Order*, 89–105, "blessed" on 91; Blumin, *The Emergence of the Middle Class*, Philadelphia artisans on 37; Bruce Laurie, *Artisans into Workers: Labor in Nineteenth-Century America* (New York: Hill and Wang, 1989), mechanic on 47; McCoy, *The Elusive Republic*, 152–161.

66. Appleby, *Capitalism and a New Social Order*, 89–105; Wood, *The Radicalism of the American Revolution*, 271–286.

67. Ellen Carol DuBois, *Feminism and Suffrage: The Emergence of an Independent Women's Movement in America, 1848–1869* (Ithaca, NY: Cornell University Press, 1978), trade unionist on 43; Michael J. Sandel, *Democracy's Discontent: America in Search of a Public Philosophy* (Cambridge, MA: The Belknap Press of Harvard University Press, 1996), Sylvis on 185–186.

68. Wood, *The Radicalism of the American Revolution*, 7, 51, 172–173; Gary Nash, *Race and Revolution* (Madison, WI: Madison House, 1990); Douglas R. Egerton, *Rebels, Reformers, and Revolutionaries* (New York: Routledge, 2002), 3–19; Kenneth S. Greenberg, *Masters and Statesmen* (Baltimore, MD: Johns Hopkins University Press, 1985).

69. Countryman, *The American Revolution*, quoted passages on 233–238; Norton, *Liberty's Daughters*, 154–194; Kerber, *Women of the Republic*; Linda Kerber, "The Republican Mother: Women and the Enlightenment—An American Perspective," *American Quarterly* 28 (Summer 1976): 187–205, "The Female Advocate" quoted on 200; Mary Ryan, *Women in Public* (Baltimore, MD: Johns Hopkins University Press, 1990).

70. Kerber, "The Republican Mother," 187–205; Kerber, *Women of the Republic*, 265–288.

71. Kerber, *Women of the Republic*, 282–288; Kerber, "The Republican Mother," 203–205; orator quoted in Wood, *The Radicalism of the American Revolution*, 356–357; DuBois, *Feminism and Suffrage*, 15–24; Linda Kerber, "The Republican Ideology of the Revolutionary Generation," *American Quarterly* 37 (1985): 482–485.

72. DuBois, *Feminism and Suffrage*, 15–24; Kerber, *Women of the Republic*, Stanton quoted on 287–288.

73. DuBois, *Feminism and Suffrage*, 15–37; Ellen DuBois, "The Radicalism of the Woman Suffrage Movement: Notes toward the Reconstruction of Nineteenth-Century Feminism," *Feminist Studies* 3 (1975): 63–71; Carl Degler, *At Odds: Women and the Family in America from the Revolution to the Present* (New York: Oxford University Press, 1980), 328–361; Linda Kerber, "A Constitutional Right to Be Treated Like American Ladies: Women and the Obligations of Citizenship," in *U.S. History as Women's History: New Feminist Essays*, ed. Linda Kerber, Alice Kessler-Harris, and Kathryn Kish Sklar (Chapel Hill, NC: University of North Carolina Press, 1995), 21–26.

74. Richard C. Wade, *Slavery in the Cities: The South 1820–1860* (New York: Oxford University Press, 1964); Nash, *Race and Revolution*, 2–87; Egerton, *Rebels, Reformers, and Revolutionaries*, 13–19; Ira Berlin and Ronald Hoffman, eds., *Slavery and Freedom in the Age of the American Revolution* (Urbana, IL: University of Illinois Press, 1983); Eugene D. Genovese, *From Rebellion to Revolution: Afro-American Slave Revolts in the Making of the New World* (New York: Vintage Books, 1981), 82–137.

75. Wade, *Slavery in the Cities*, quotations on 245 and 239, on civic experience, 278–281; Louis P. Masur, *1831: Year of Eclipse* (New York: Hill and Wang, 2001), "march" on 22.

76. Nash, *Race and Revolution*, Forten on 81–82; Genovese, *From Rebellion to Revolution*, Douglass on 132–133; John Hope Franklin, *From Slavery to Freedom: A History of African Americans* (New York: Alfred A. Knopf, 1994), 172.

77. John W. Blassingame and John R. McKivigan, eds., *The Frederick Douglass Papers—Series One: Speeches, Debates, and Interviews*, vol. 4 (New Haven, CT: Yale University Press, 1991), 62–68; David W. Blight, *Frederick Douglass' Civil War: Keeping Faith in Jubilee* (Baton Rouge, LA: Louisiana State University Press, 1989), 1–25.

78. Wood, *The Radicalism of the American Revolution*, "consequence" on 276.

CHAPTER 2

1. Alexis de Tocqueville, *Democracy in America*, ed. Richard D. Heffner, (New York: New American Library, 1984) 108–111, 192–197, 209–213, 293–294, 301–313; Tocqueville, *Democracy in America*, ed. J. P. Mayer and Max Lerner (New York: Harper & Row, 1966), 511–513.

2. Tocqueville, *Democracy in America*, ed. Heffner, 58–61, 192–197, 293, 303; Tocqueville, *Democracy in America*, ed. Mayer and Lerner, 497–499; Stephen L. Elkin, *City and Regime in the American Republic*, (Chicago: University of Chicago Press, 1987), 1–17, 147.

3. Carol Sheriff, *The Artificial River: The Erie Canal and the Paradox of Progress, 1817–1862* (New York: Hill and Wang, 1996), 1–51, capstone quoted on 35 (italics in original); Michael J. Sandel, *Democracy's Discontent: America in Search of a Public Philosophy* (Cambridge, MA: The Belknap Press of Harvard University Press, 1996), 123–200.

4. Sheriff, *The Artificial River*, 1–51, 138–171, quotation on 170.

5. Sheriff, *The Artificial River*, 1–51, quotations on 47 and 49.

6. Sean Wilentz, *Chants Democratic: New York City and the Rise of the American Working Class* (New York: Oxford University Press, 1984), "Less" quoted on 71, "Suffer" on 92; Steven J. Ross, *Workers on the Edge: Work, Leisure and Politics in Industrializing Cincinnati, 1788-1890* (New York: Columbia University Press, 1985), "bone" on 23; Bruce Laurie, *Artisans into Workers: Labor in Nineteenth-Century America* (New York: Hill and Wang, 1989); Charles Sellers, *The Market Revolution: Jacksonian America, 1815–1846* (New York: Oxford University Press, 1991); Eric Foner, *Free Soil, Free Labor, Free Men: The Ideology of the Republican Party before the Civil War* (New York: Oxford University Press, 1970).

7. Ross, *Workers on the Edge*, 67–93, quotation on 85; Wilentz, *Chants Democratic*, 35–42, 97–103.

8. Wilentz, *Chants Democratic*, 107–167, "products" on 165; Laurie, *Artisans into Workers*, 47–73; Christopher Lasch, *The True and Only Heaven: Progress and Its Critics* (New York: Norton, 1991), "universal" on 205; Sellers, *The Market Revolution*, 284–289.

9. Wilentz, *Chants Democratic*, 61–103, journeyman-master exchange on 62; Ross, *Workers on the Edge*, 3–93, artisan on 28; Lasch, *The True and Only Heaven*, 168–225.

10. Sellers, *The Market Revolution*, 34–48.

11. Andrew M. Schocket, *Funding Corporate Power in Early National Philadelphia* (DeKalb, IL: Northern Illnois University Press, 2007), 3–76, "moneyed" on 7; Sellers, *The Market Revolution*, 34–48.

12. Sellers, *The Market Revolution*, 85–87; Schocket, *Funding Corporate Power*, 3–48, 203–216; Daniel Walker Howe, *The Political Culture of American Whigs* (Chicago: University of Chicago Press, 1979), 98–99.

13. Schocket, *Funding Corporate Power*, 3–76, 203–216, quotation on 78; Sellers, *The Market Revolution*, 44–55.

14. Sellers, *The Market Revolution*, 44–55; Sheriff, *The Artificial River*, 79–171; Foster Rhea Dulles and Melvin Dubofsky, *Labor in America* (Arlington Heights, IL: Harlan Davidson, 1984), 29–31, 62–64; Wilentz, *Chants Democratic*, 284–294; Glenn C. Althschuler and Stuart M. Blumin, "Limits of Political Engagement in Antebellum America: A New Look at the Golden Age of Participatory Democracy," *Journal of American History* 84 (December 1997): 855–885.

15. Sellers, *The Market Revolution*, 40–42, 52–55, "broadened" is Sellers's judgment, 53; Stanley Schultz, *Constructing Urban Culture: American Cities and City Planning, 1800–1920* (Philadelphia: Temple University Press, 1989), "reasonable" on 53.

16. Quotations taken from Sandel, *Democracy's Discontent*, 150–154; Sellers, *The Market Revolution*; Daniel Walker Howe, *The Political Culture of the American Whigs*,(Chicago: University of Chicago Press, 1979), 96–108.

17. Adams quoted in Michael J. Lacey, "Federalism and National Planning: The Nineteenth-Century Legacy," in *The American Planning Tradition: Culture and Policy*, ed. Robert Fishman (Washington, D.C.: Woodrow Wilson Center Press, 2000), 108–111; Howe, *The Political Culture of the American Whigs*, passim, but especially 16, 21, 29–30, 48, and 73–75.

18. David Montgomery, *Citizen Worker*, (New York: Cambridge Press, 1993), 1–12ff.; Laurie, *Artisans into Workers*, 47–73, on Heighton, 66–72; Wilentz, *Chants Democratic*, 172–216, on Skidmore, 182–190; Sellers, *The Market Revolution*, 285–289.

19. Wilentz, *Chants Democratic*, 184–216, quotation on 184; Laurie, *Artisans into Workers*, 66–73. Sellers, *The Market Revolution*, 301–363.

20. Wilentz, *Chants Democratic*, 211–254: "obliged" on 229, "propriety" on 233; Laurie, *Artisans into Workers*, 74–91: "The combination of radicalism and unionism ... nudged worker and politician further apart since unions were only for workers and most political figures were critics of unions" (84). See also Dulles and Dubofsky, *Labor in America*, 56–57.

21. Wilentz, *Chants Democratic*, 211–254, quotations on 219, 237, 245; Arthur M. Schlesinger, Jr., *The Age of Jackson* (Boston: Little, Brown and Company, 1945), GTU president quoted on 192; Laurie, *Artisans into Workers*, 74–91; Dulles and Dubofsky, *Labor in America*, 56–57.

22. Dulles and Dubofsky, *Labor in America*, 61–64, "hellish appetites" on 63; Wilentz, *Chants Democratic*, 284–294, "at variance" on 292; David P.. Roediger, *The Wages of Whiteness: Race and the Making of the American Working Class* (New York: Verso, 1991), 65–87.

23. Dulles and Dubofsky, *Labor in America*, 70–89, Lynn shoemakers quoted on 74; Laurie, *Artisans into Workers*, 47–73: "daughters of freemen," and "Factory slaves" and National Trades Union quoted on 63; Lasch, *The True and Only Heaven*, 203–216; Sandel, *Democracy's Discontent*, 150–154, "vassalage" on 153; Sellers, *The Market Revolution*, 288–289.

24. Roediger, *The Wages of Whiteness*, 43–92, quotations on 65 and 83–84.

25. Roediger, *The Wages of Whiteness*, 43–92, "unworthy" on 84, Dubois on 55.

26. Roediger, *The Wages of Whiteness*, 43–92; Wilentz, *Chants Democratic*, "species" and "price" on 242; Sellers, *The Market Revolution*, 133–135, 332–334.

27. Sellers, *The Market Revolution*, 321–326; Marvin Meyers, "The Jacksonian Persuasion," *American Quarterly* (Spring 1953): 8–9.

28. Sellers, *The Market Revolution*, 341–363, quoted passages on 347–348; Meyers, "The Jacksonian Persuasion," 14–15; Sean Wilentz, "On Class and Politics in Jacksonian America," *Reviews in American History* 10 (December 1982): 52–56.

29. Meyers, "The Jacksonian Persuasion," Jackson quoted on 8–13; Sellers, *The Market Revolution*, 316–363, the *Washington Globe* masthead on 318.

30. Meyers, "The Jacksonian Persuasion," 8–13; Sellers, *The Market Revolution*, 316–363; Richard Hofstadter, *The American Political Tradition* (New York: Vintage Books, 1989), 82–86; Daniel Walker Howe, *The Political Culture of American Whigs* (Chicago: University of Chicago Press, 1979), 98–99.

31. Sellers, *The Market Revolution*, 289–354, Jackson quoted on 347; William Freehling, *The Reintegration of American History* (New York: Oxford University Press, 1994), 195–196; William Freehling, *The Road to Disunion* (New York: Oxford University Press, 1990), 146–148, 153–156; 410–411; Wilentz, *Chants Democratic*, 326–333.

32. The democratization of competence gave way to the effort to "democratize capital." Sellers, *The Market Revolution*, 316–363, quotations on 351–353 and 363; Howe, *The Political Culture of American Whigs*, Emerson on 19.

33. Sandel, *Democracy's Discontent*, "evil" on 156; Lacey, "Federalism and National Planning," "competition" and ICC quoted on 111–115; Marvin Meyers, *The Jacksonian Persuasion: Politics and Belief* (Stanford, CA: Stanford University Press, 1957), 185–188.

34. Howe, *The Political Culture of American Whigs*, "mind and heart" on 101; Sandel, *Democracy's Discontent*, 154–167: Clay on 163, "great increase," "redeem," and "no mere" on 155.

35. Howe, *The Political Culture of American Whigs*; Tocqueville, *Democracy in America*, ed. Heffner, 301–313.

36. Howe, *The Political Culture of American Whigs*, 23–37, 102–105, 130–131, "papspoon" on 37. See also David Rothman, *The Discovery of the Asylum* (Boston: Little Brown, 1971).

37. Wilentz, *Chants Democratic*, Mike Walsh quoted on 333.

38. Christopher Lasch, *The Revolt of the Elites and the Betrayal of Democracy* (New York: W.W.Norton & Company, 1995), 50–79, quotations on 58–61; Thomas Bender, *New York Intellect* (Baltimore: Johns Hopkins University Press, 1988), 78–88; Sandel, *Democracy's Discontent*, 168–184.

39. Howe, *The Political Culture of American Whigs*, 108–115.

40. The middle landscape, a balanced mixture of urban and rural, industry and agriculture, represented Carey's ideal. Abraham Lincoln came of age in the area around Springfield, Illinois, that approximated the middle landscape. Lincoln's response to the mudsill theory is quoted in Lasch, *The Revolt of the Elites*, 66–70; Foner, *Free Soil, Free Labor, Free Men*, 30–37; Howe, *The Political Culture of American Whigs*, 115–122.

41. Foner, *Free Soil, Free Labor, Free Men*, 11–39; Mark E. Neely, Jr., *The Last Best Hope of Earth: Abraham Lincoln and the Promise of America* (Cambridge, MA: Harvard University Press, 1995), "intelligent" on 44.

42. Foner, *Free Soil, Free Labor, Free Men*, 11–39; Sandel, *Democracy's Discontent*, 182: "In Lincoln's hands," writes Sandel, "the conception of freedom deriving from the artisan republican tradition became the rallying point for the northern cause in the Civil War."

43. Howe, *The Political Culture of American Whigs*, 263–291, "calculated" on 291; Neely, *The Last Best Hope of Earth*, 18–20, "falls" on 20; Gabor S. Boritt, *Lincoln and the Economics of the American Dream* (Memphis, TN: Memphis State University Press, 1978), 155–193, "superior" and "Working" on 176.

44. Boritt, *Lincoln and the Economics of the American Dream*, 155–193: "right" on 172, "relation," "total," and "ancient" on 159; Sandel, *Democracy's Discontent*, 168–184, "better state" on 174; Lasch, *The Revolt of the Elites*, 66–72, "basis" on 71; Foner, *Free Soil, Free Labor, Free Men*, 261–300.

45. Philip Shaw Paludan, *A People's Contest: The Union and Civil War, 1861–1865*, (Lawrence, KS: University Press of Kansas, 1996), 105–197, Greeley on 128; James M.

McPherson, *Abraham Lincoln and the Second American Revolution* (New York: Oxford University Press, 1991), 43–64, 131–152.

46. Paludan, *A People's Contest*, 105–197; McPherson, *Abraham Lincoln and the Second American Revolution*, 43–64, 131–152; Howe, *The Political Culture of American Whigs*, "constantly" on 291; "Gettysburg Address," in John H. Clifford and Marion M. Miller eds., *The Works of Abraham Lincoln* (New York: C.S. Hammond & Company, 1907), vol. 5, 183; McPherson, *Abraham Lincoln and the Second American Revolution*, 43–64, 131–152.

47. McPherson, *Abraham Lincoln and the Second American Revolution*, 43–64, 131–152, quotations on 43–44; the final sentence of the Fourteenth Amendment is worded slightly differently, but to the same purpose. The long-delayed Nineteenth Amendment granting women the vote in 1919, satisfying a demand from the Civil War era, concludes with the same words as the Thirteenth and Fifteenth Amendments.

48. McPherson, *Abraham Lincoln and the Second American Revolution*, 131–139, quotations on 138–139; see also Michael Les Benedict, "Preserving the Constitution: The Conservative Basis of Radical Reconstruction," *Journal of American History* 61 (June 1974) and Robert J. Kaczorowski, "To Begin the Nation Anew: Congress, Citizenship and Civil Rights after the Civil War," *American Historical Review* 92 (February 1987).

49. McPherson, *Abraham Lincoln and the Second American Revolution*, 131–139, quoted passages on 138–139; Eric Foner, *Reconstruction: America's Unfinished Revolution, 1863–1877* (New York: Harper & Row, 1988), 110–119; Elsa Barkley Brown, "Negotiating and Transforming the Public Sphere: African American Political Life in the Transition from Slavery to Freedom," *Public Culture* 7 (1994): 107–146.

50. David Montgomery, *Beyond Equality: Labor and Radical Republicans, 1862–1872* (Urbana, IL: University of Illinois Press, 1981), Grant on 85; C. Vann Woodward, "The International Context of Emancipation," in *Major Problems in the Civil War and Reconstruction*, ed. Michael Perman (Lexington, MA: D.C. Heath, 1991), 365–376; Foner, *Reconstruction*, 364–379.

51. Woodward, "The International Context of Emancipation," 365–376; Leon Litwack, "Back to Work: The New Dependency," in *Major Problems in the Civil War and Reconstruction*, ed. Perman, 387–398, "ought" on 390; Eric Foner, *Nothing but Freedom: Emancipation and Its Legacy* (Baton Rouge, LA: Louisiana State University Press, 1983), 39–73, "sweat" on 56; "South Carolina Blacks Assert Their Demands" (November 1865), in *Major Problems in the Civil War and Reconstruction*, ed. Perman, "consent," "onerous," and "three" on 477–478.

52. In 1862, as Northern investors flocked to Union-occupied South Carolina to employ slaves as wage workers, the land-hungry slaves "were beginning to plant corn in their patches but were disinclined to plant cotton, regarding it as a badge of servitude." Willie Lee Rose, *Rehearsals for Reconstruction: The Port Royal Experiment* (Indianapolis: Bobbs-Merrill, 1964); Foner, *Reconstruction*, 50–60; Gerald David Jaynes, *Branches without Roots: Genesis of the Black Working Class in the American South, 1862–1882* (New York: Oxford University Press, 1986), 3–23, "plant" on 13. "Richard M. Cain of South Carolina Stresses the Importance of Land," in *Major Problems in the Civil War and Reconstruction*, ed. Perman, 478–479; Leon Litwack, "Back to Work: The New Dependency," 387–398, "stuffed" and "democratization" on 387–389; Eric Foner, *Politics and Ideology in the Age of the Civil War* (New York: Oxford University Press, 1980), 97–127, "wild" and ""hirelings" on 106–107.

53. McPherson, *Abraham Lincoln and the Second American Revolution*, 131–152; Foner, *Politics and Ideology in the Age of the Civil War*, 97–149, Stevens on 135; Foner, *Reconstruction*, 228–280, especially 235–236; Hofstadter, *The American Political Tradition*, Phillips on 200; William L. Barney, *Battleground for the Union* (Englewood Cliffs, NJ: Prentice-Hall, Inc., 1990), 239–249; Hans Louis Trefousse, *The Radical Republicans* (Baton Rouge, LA: Louisiana State University Press, 1975).

54. Foner, *Politics and Ideology in the Age of the Civil War*, 97–149, Stevens on 134; Foner, *Reconstruction*, 228–280; Barney, *Battleground for the Union*, 239–249, Julian on 240.

55. Foner, *Politics and Ideology in the Age of the Civil War*, 128–149.

56. The Republicans never mustered more than a minority in favor of confiscation. Thirty-seven of 133 voting Republicans (about 28 percent) supported Stevens's confiscation amendment in February 1866. Foner, *Politics and Ideology in the Age of the Civil War*, 97–149; Foner, *Reconstruction*, 228–280; Barney, *Battleground for the Union*, 239–279, army officer on 279; Jaynes, *Branches without Roots*, 3–53.

57. Foner, *Reconstruction*, 228–280 passim, "If" on 239; McPherson, *Abraham Lincoln and the Second American Revolution*, 131–152, Sumner and "aristocracy" on 141.

58. W.E.B. Dubois, *Black Reconstruction* (New York: Harcourt, Brace & Company, 1935); Foner, *Reconstruction*, 346–379; Barney, *Battleground for the Union*, 239–249; Foner, *Nothing but Freedom*, 56–110; Thomas C. Holt, "Black State Legislators in South Carolina during Reconstruction," in *Major Problems in the Civil War and Reconstruction*, ed. Perman, 485–496.

59. Montgomery, *Beyond Equality*, 73, 228–229, Stevens on 73; Foner, *Politics and Ideology in the Age of the Civil War*, Wade on 144; Hofstadter, *The American Political Tradition*, 205; on Sylvis and the National Labor Union, see Alan Trachtenberg, *The Incorporation of America: Culture and Society in the Gilded Age* (New York: Hill and Wang, 1982), 93–96.

60. The Fourteenth Amendment provided that if the vote be "denied to any of the male inhabitants" of a state, then that state's representation in Congress would be reduced proportionately. Ellen C. DuBois, *Feminism and Suffrage: The Emergence of an Independent Women's Movement in America, 1848-1869* (Ithaca, NY: Cornell University Press, 1978), 53–62 passim, Stanton on 53.

61. DuBois, *Feminism and Suffrage*, 31–40, Grimke on 36; Aileen S. Kraditor, *Means and Ends in American Abolitionism: Garrison and His Critics on Strategy and Tactics, 1834–1850* (Chicago: I.R.Dee, 1989).

62. DuBois, *Feminism and Suffrage*, 37–41.

63. DuBois, *Feminism and Suffrage*, 40–52; 135–140.

64. DuBois, *Feminism and Suffrage*, 46–52; Carl Degler, *At Odds: Women and the Family in America from the Revolution to the Present* (New York: Oxford University Press, 1980), 328–361; Foner, *Reconstruction*, Child on 473.

65. Sandel, *Democracy's Discontent*, 174–176: Fitzhugh on 176, "must" on 175 is Wendell Phillips who, unlike most abolitionists, later became a strong champion of the labor movement; Hofstadter, *The American Political Tradition*, 175–210. Although he embraced the civic critique of wage labor, Lincoln also hesitated to apply it to slaves, consistently defending their natural right to the fruit of their labor, but wavering on the issue of full social and political equality. Lincoln's wavering is discussed in countless works, but see especially Rogers M. Smith, *Civic Ideals: Conflicting Visions of Citizenship in U.S. History* (New Haven, CT: Yale University Press, 1997), 246–253.

66. DuBois, *Feminism and Suffrage*, 54–57; Hofstadter, *The American Political Tradition*, 195–210.

67. Democratic iron manufacturer Abram Hewitt put it more bluntly: "It is for the master to do the thinking." Montgomery, *Beyond Equality*, quotations on 231–238; Roediger, *The Wages of Whiteness*, 167–184, Steward on 176 (italics in original); Trachtenberg, *The Incorporation of America*, 70–100.

68. Montgomery, *Beyond Equality*, quoted passages on 231–238; David R. Roediger and Philip S. Foner, *Our Own Time: A History of American Labor and the Working Day* (New York: Greenwood Press, 1989).

69. A California Republican added: "Give them time to think." Montgomery, *Beyond Equality*, 238–248.

70. Montgomery, *Beyond Equality*, 238–248.

71. Montgomery, *Beyond Equality*, quotations on 248–260; Sandel, *Democracy's Discontent*, 190–192.

72. On Steward, see Stuart Ewen, *Captains of Consciousness: Advertising and the Social Roots of the Consumer Culture* (New York: McGraw-Hill, 1976), 9 and 222n11; on cooperatives,

see Sandel, *Democracy's Discontent*, 190–192; Montgomery, *Beyond Equality*, 248–260; Roediger and Foner, *Our Own Time*, 95.

73. Trachtenberg, *The Incorporation of America*, Whitman on 70; Foner, *Reconstruction*, 492; Nick Salvatore, *Eugene V. Debs: Citizen and Socialist* (Urbana, IL: University of Illinois Press, 1982).

CHAPTER 3

1. Eric Foner, *Reconstruction: America's Unfinished Revolution, 1863–1877* (New York: Harper & Row, 1988), 488–563, "by nature" on 492; George M. Fredrickson, *The Inner Civil War: Northern Intellectuals and the Crisis of the Union* (New York: Harper & Row, 1965), 183–216; Thomas Bender, *New York Intellect* (Baltimore: Johns Hopkins University Press, 1988), 169–191; William L. Barney, *Battleground for the Union* (Englewood Cliffs, NJ: Prentice-Hall Inc., 1990), 297–337; Andrew Carnegie, "The Road to Business Success: A Talk to Young Men" (1885), in Andrew Carnegie, *The Empire of Business* (New York: Doubleday, Page &Company, 1902), 3–18; William Graham Sumner, "The Absurd Effort to Make the World Over" (1894), in *War and Other Essays*, ed. Albert Galloway Keller (New York: AMS Press, 1970), 195–210.

2. Privately, Schurz described the Ku Klux Klan Act as "insane." Foner, *Reconstruction*, 454–459, 488–511: "disorders" on 499, "insane" on 456; William S. McFeely, *Grant* (New York: Norton, 1981), 332–385; Barney, *Battleground for the Union*, 291–301; David W. Blight, *Race and Reunion: The Civil War in American Memory* (Cambridge, MA: Belknap Press of Harvard University Press, 2001), 108–123.

3. Foner, *Reconstruction*, 488–511, quotations on 499; Barney, *Battleground for the Union*, 292–301.

4. Foner, *Reconstruction*, 488–511: "burden" on 498, Greeley on 503–504; Blight, *Race and Reunion*, 59–63, 124–127.

5. Foner, *Reconstruction*, 488–563, "incapable" on 508; Barney, *Battleground for the Union*, 262–335; Fredrickson, *The Inner Civil War*, 199–216; Michael E. McGerr, *The Decline of Popular Politics* (New York: Oxford University Press, 1986); John G. Sproat, *"The Best Men": Liberal Reformers in the Gilded Age* (New York: Oxford University Press, 1968).

6. Blight, *Race and Reunion*, 221–231.

7. Andrew Carnegie, *The Gospel of Wealth and Other Timely Essays*, ed. Edward C. Kirkland (Cambridge, MA: Belknap Press of Harvard University, 1962), 15; Richard Hofstadter, *Social Darwinism in American Thought* (Boston: Beacon Press, 1955), Sumner quoted on 57.

8. Charles Sellers, *The Market Revolution: Jacksonian America, 1815–1846* (New York: Oxford University Press, 1991), "pitilessly" on 54–55; Sproat, *"The Best Men"*; Bender, *New York Intellect*, 169–205; Lawrence W. Levine, *Highbrow/Lowbrow: The Emergence of Cultural Hierarchy in America* (Cambridge, MA: Harvard University Press, 1988), 171–231: Distinguishing themselves from the masses "less by pedigree than by their life style, manners, and cultural artifacts," the "old genteel classes" and the "newly rich" used culture as "a carapace impervious to assault from above or below" (227); John F. Kasson, *Rudeness and Civility: Manners in Nineteenth-Century Urban America* (New York: Hill and Wang, 1990), 243–245.

9. Bender, *New York Intellect*, 176–191: "These literary men," Bender writes, "perhaps in a fitting exercise of their special skills, deserve considerable credit—or blame—for setting new and rather constricting boundaries on the language of American politics. By separating the discourse of politics from that of economics—at a crucial moment in the history of American capitalism—they immunized the market economy from the challenge of politics, whether in theory or in practice" (190–191); Blight, *Race and Reunion* passim, "bad taste" on 189; Ann Douglas, *The Feminization of American Culture* (New York: Knopf, 1977).

10. Richard Hofstadter, *The American Political Tradition* (New York: Vintage Press, 1989), 213–238, quotations on 218–221; Sproat, *"The Best Men,"* 94–118, 275–280 passim.

11. Hofstadter, *The American Political Tradition*, "desire" on 219; Foner, *Reconstruction*, 484–499; Sproat, *"The Best Men,"* 7–28, "better" on 94; Barney, *Battleground for the Union*, 297–300, 327–335; David Montgomery, *Beyond Equality: Labor and Radical Republicans, 1862–1872* (Urbana, IL: University of Illinois Press, 1981), 335–386.

12. Foner, *Reconstruction*, 488–499, "dishonesty" on 489; Montgomery, *Beyond Equality*, 335–386; Sproat, *"The Best Men,"* 7–118, 275–280, "determined" and "drunk" on 82; Barney, *Battleground for the Union*, 297–300, 327–335; Matthew Josephson, *The Politicos* (New York: Harcourt, Brace and Company, 1966), "nothing" on 374.

13. Thomas Bender, *New York Intellect*, 169–191; Montgomery, *Beyond Equality*, 382–385; Foner, *Reconstruction*, 488–499, "eternal" on 490; Sproat, *The Best Men*," 143–154; Karl Polanyi, *The Great Transformation: The Political and Economic Origins of Our Time* (Boston: Beacon Press, 1944), 45–89, "harmony" is Polanyi's assessment on 85.

14. Sproat, *"The Best Men,"* 48–49, "transfer" on 49; Bender, *New York Intellect*, 169–205, "tone" and "short" on 188–189; Foner, *Reconstruction*, 488–499, "Universal" on 497.

15. Sproat, *"The Best Men,"* 48–49; Montgomery, *Beyond Equality*, 230–260, 335–386, "nullify" on 248; Bender, *New York Intellect*, 169–205, "gravity" on 185.

16. Hofstadter, *The American Political Tradition*, 211–238; Josephson, *The Politicos*; Matthew Josephson, *The Robber Barons* (New York: Harcourt, Brace & World, 1962); Alfred Chandler, *The Visible Hand: The Managerial Revolution in Business* (Cambridge, MA: Belknap Press of Harvard University Press,1977); Geoffrey Blodgett, "Reform Thought and the Genteel Tradition," in H. Wayne Morgan, *The Gilded Age* (Syracuse, NY: Syracuse University Press, 1970), 55–76.

17. Bender, *New York Intellect*, 169–205; Montgomery, *Beyond Equality*, "highest" on 339; Sproat, *The Best Men*," 51, 275–280, "loss" on 51; Fredrickson, *The Inner Civil War*, 32; Carl Smith, *Urban Disorder and the Shape of Belief*, (Chicago: University of Chicago Press, 1995), 81–87, "monster" on 84; Daniel Bluestone, *Constructing Chicago* (New Haven, CT: Yale University Press, 1991), 164–181, "best" on 166.

18. Sproat, *"The Best Men,"* 48–82, "gutter" on 48; Montgomery, *Beyond Equality*, "perfect" on 379.

19. Van Wyck Brooks, *America's Coming-of-Age* (New York: Huebsch, 1915), "orgy" on 17–18; George Santayana, "The Genteel Tradition" (1913), in *The American Intellectual Tradition*, ed. David A. Hollinger and Charles Capper (New York: Oxford University Press, 1993), 97–109; Polanyi, *The Great Transformation*, 45–89; Christopher Lasch, *The True and Only Heaven: Progress and Its Critics* (New York: Norton, 1991), 58–63, the "higher" phrase is Lasch's, on 59; Douglas, *The Feminization of American Culture*.

20. Kasson, *Rudeness and Civility*, 195–200; Mary Ryan, *Civic Wars: Democracy and Public Life in the American City during the Nineteenth Century* (Berkeley: California University Press, 1997), 277, the "gargantuan" phrase is Ryan's, on 277; Sproat, *"The Best Men,"* 45–69; Josephson, *The Robber Barons*, 332–340.

21. Both sides understood the contest, Trachtenberg writes, as "the realm of the feminine against the realm of the aggressive masculine." Sproat, *"The Best Men,"* 45–69; Hofstadter, *The American Political Tradition*, quotations on 228–229; Trachtenberg, *The Incorporation of America*, 163; Bender, *New York Intellect*, 208.

22. Sproat, *"The Best Men,"* on Atkinson's cookbook, 216–217; Edward Atkinson, *The Science of Nutrition* (Boston: Darnell & Upham, 1895), 3, 21. The book is strangely fascinating and, as Sproat suggests, if offered as an alternative to political agitation, it might have found an audience among working people. It includes essays by the pioneer ecologist Ellen Richards and a compendium of charts such as one comparing the diets of "Under-fed laborers, Lombardy, Italy," "Trappist monk in cloister," "Miners at very severe work, Germany," "German soldiers, war footing," "College football team," and so forth. The recipes do tend to feature the shinbone.

23. Sproat, *"The Best Men,"* 7–28, "morality" and "Virtue" are Sproat's judgments on 274–275; J. G. A. Pocock, *Virtue, Commerce, and History* (New York: Cambridge University

Press, 1985); Kasson, *Rudeness and Civility*, 34–69: "smiles" on 69 (italics in original), "Plain" on 46; "Manners and Etiquette," *Encyclopedia of American Social History*, ed. Mary Kupiec, Elliot J. Gorn, and Peter W. Williams, vol. 2 (New York: Scribner, 1995), "You may be" on 1349.

24. Kasson, *Rudeness and Civility*, 60–69.

25. Kasson, *Rudeness and Civility*, 60–69, 157–165, quotation on 160; Pocock, *Virtue, Commerce, and History*, 42–50, 103–116.

26. Kasson, *Rudeness and Civility*, 80–117.

27. *The Nation* was conceived in 1863 as a vehicle for grafting the authority of New York's metropolitan gentry onto the national state. *Harper's Weekly* billed itself as a "Journal of Civilization." Bender, *New York Intellect*, 176–185.

28. Bender, *New York Intellect*, 176–191.

29. Theodore Roosevelt rightly charged that the liberal reformers "shrink from contact with the rough people who do the world's work." Bender, *New York Intellect*, 176–191.

30. Carl Smith, *Urban Disorder and the Shape of Belief*, 34–63.

31. Smith, *Urban Disorder and the Shape of Belief*, 64–81.

32. Smith, *Urban Disorder and the Shape of Belief*, 103–105; Iver Bernstein, *The New York City Draft Riots* (New York: Oxford University Press, 1990).

33. Bender, *New York Intellect*, 185–191, "debarred" on 186; Montgomery, *Beyond Equality*, "entitled" on 372.

34. In 1878, the Citizens' Association presented two Gatling guns to the city of Chicago. Montgomery, *Beyond Equality*, 25–26; Bernstein, *The New York City Draft Riots*, 237–264; Foner, *Reconstruction*, 460–524; Smith, *Urban Disorder and the Shape of Belief*, "lamp-post" on 106; Paul Avrich, *The Haymarket Tragedy* (Princeton, NJ: Princeton University Press, 1984), 16–18, 26–38, "content" on 28, "Gatling" on 35.

35. Alan Trachtenberg, *The Incorporation of America* (New York: Hill and Wang, 1982), 166–168, George's platform quoted on 166–167; Bender, *New York Intellect*, 191–194.

36. Smith, *Urban Disorder and the Shape of Belief*, 166–168.

37. Smith, *Urban Disorder and the Shape of Belief*, 102–118, quotation on 114; Avrich, *The Haymarket Tragedy*, 15–67.

38. Smith, *Urban Disorder and the Shape of Belief*, 111–146 (italics in original).

39. Smith, *Urban Disorder and the Shape of Belief*, 102–118; Avrich, *The Haymarket Tragedy*, 197–214, "Goaded" on 207.

40. Sproat, *"The Best Men,"* 232–235.

41. Bender, *New York Intellect*, 191–194, "smiling" and "freest" on 192 (Howell's italics); Alfred Kazin, *On Native Grounds* (New York: Harcourt Brace Jovanovich, 1970), 3–12, "five" on 6, "fifty" on 5, "astonished" is Kazin's judgment, on 6.

42. Bender, *New York Intellect*, 191–194, quotations on 193; Kazin, *On Native Grounds*, 3–50.

43. Trachtenberg, *The Incorporation of America*, 140–145.

44. Trachtenberg, *The Incorporation of America*, 140–145.

45. Bender, *New York Intellect*, 206–209, Whitman on 152–156; Trachtenberg, *The Incorporation of America*, 156–161; Levine, *Highbrow/Lowbrow*, 225.

46. Smith, *Urban Disorder and the Shape of Belief*, 177–208; Avrich, *The Haymarket Tragedy*, 33.

47. Smith, *Urban Disorder and the Shape of Belief*, 177–208.

48. Smith, *Urban Disorder and the Shape of Belief*, 203–208 (italics in original).

49. Smith, *Urban Disorder and the Shape of Belief*, 233–238, Addams on 200–201, "destitution" on 234; Trachtenberg, *The Incorporation of America*, 232–234; Nick Salvatore, *Eugene V. Debs: Citizen and Socialist* (Urbana, IL: University of Illinois Press, 1982), 114–146; Louis Menand, *The Metaphysical Club* (New York: Farrar, Straus and Giroux, 2001), 285–316.

50. Smith, *Urban Disorder and the Shape of Belief*, 233–238; Menand, *The Metaphysical Club*, 291–298.

51. Smith, *Urban Disorder and the Shape of Belief*, 238–246, "natural" on 239; Menand, *The Metaphysical Club*, 299–306, Taft on 300.
52. Smith, *Urban Disorder and the Shape of Belief*, 238–246, "pretty" on 204; Menand, *The Metaphysical Club*, 297–306, "combat" on 303, "organism" on 297.
53. Smith, *Urban Disorder and the Shape of Belief*, 203–208, 238–246, Ely on 205; Menand, *The Metaphysical Club*, 306–316, Addams on 314.
54. Menand, *The Metaphysical Club*, 306–316.
55. Menand, *The Metaphysical Club*, 315–316; James R. Green, *The World of the Worker: Labor in Twentieth-Century America* (New York: Hill and Wang, 1980), 32–65; James Weinstein, *The Corporate Ideal in the Liberal State, 1900–1918* (Boston: Beacon Press, 1968), 3–39.
56. Smith, *Urban Disorder and the Shape of Belief*, 233–246, *Times* on 234, Commission on 244; Trachtenberg, *The Incorporation of America*, 232–234, Debs on 234.

PART II

1. "Editor's Easy Chair," *Harper's New Monthly Magazine*, December 1863, 129–133; Lawrence W. Levine, *Highbrow/Lowbrow: The Emergence of Cultural Hierarchy in America* (Cambridge, MA: Harvard University Press, 1988), 57–58.
2. "Editor's Easy Chair," 129–133; Thomas Bender, *New York Intellect: A History of Intellectual Life in New York City, from 1750 to the Beginnings of Our Own Time* (Baltimore: Johns Hopkins University Press, 1988), 46–116, Cooper Union discussed on 114–116; Philip Shaw Paludan, *"A People's Contest": The Union and Civil War, 1861–1865* (Lawrence, KS: University Press of Kansas, 1996), 10–15 passim.
3. "Editor's Easy Chair," 129–133.
4. Edwin G. Burrows and Mike Wallace, *Gotham: A History of New York City to 1898* (New York: Oxford University Press, 1999), 995.
5. "Editor's Easy Chair," *Harper's New Monthly Magazine*, March 1870, 605–610.
6. Levine, *Highbrow/Lowbrow*, 227–228.

CHAPTER 4

1. Michael Schudson, *The Good Citizen: A History of American Civic Life* (New York; Martin Kessler Books, 1998), 48–89; "Moving beyond Beard: A Symposium," *Radical History Review* 42 (1988): 7–47; Alfred F. Young, "The Framers of the Constitution and the 'Genius' of the People," *Radical History Review* 42 (1988), 8–18; Michael Sandel, *Democracy's Discontent: America in Search of a Public Philosophy* (Cambridge: Belknap Press of Harvard University Press, 1996), 123–142; Richard R. John, *Spreading the News: The American Postal System from Franklin to Morse* (Cambridge, MA: Harvard University Press, 1995), Rush on 30.
2. John, *Spreading the News*, 1–40. Merchant letter writers who used the postal system to lay the groundwork for a national market subsidized the postal system.
3. Johns, *Spreading the News*, 1–63, 112–168, 206–256; "comers" on 155.
4. Mary Ryan, *Civic Wars: Democracy and Public Life in the American City during the Nineteenth Century* (Berkeley: University of California Press, 1997), 21–43; Mary P. Ryan, *Women in Public: Between Banners and Ballots, 1825–1880* (Baltimore: Johns Hopkins University Press, 1990), 60–61, "beggars" on 61; Stuart M. Blumin, *The Emergence of the Middle Class: Social Experience in the American City, 1760–1900* (New York: Cambridge University Press, 1989), 163–179; Kevin Lynch, *The Image of the City* (Cambridge: MIT Press, 1960).
5. Ryan, *Civic Wars*, 21–43; Ryan, *Women in Public*, 60–61.
6. Ryan, *Civic Wars*, 43–57; Christine Stansell, *City of Women: Sex and Class in New York 1789–1860* (New York: Knopf, 1986), 42–56; compare with Nancy Cott, *The Bonds of Womanhood: "Women's Sphere" in New England* (New Haven, CT: Yale University Press, 1977); Blumin, *The Emergence of the Middle Class*, 179–191.

7. Ryan, *Civic Wars*, 43–57, quoted passages on 49, 52, and 54; David R. Johnson, "Police Reform: A Comparative View," in *Major Problems in American Urban History*, ed. Howard P. Chudacoff (Lexington, MA: D.C. Heath, 1994), "nature" on 104.

8. Ryan, *Civic Wars*, 57–77.

9. Ryan, *Civic Wars*, 96–129, quotations on charity, 105.

10. Stanley K. Schultz, *Constructing Urban Culture: American Cities and City Planning, 1800–1920* (Philadelphia: Temple University Press, 1989), 35–57, "literally arose from city streets" on 35; William Novak, *The People's Welfare: Law and Regulation in Nineteenth-Century America* (Chapel Hill, NC: University of North Carolina Press, 1996); Mary Ann Glendon, *Rights Talk* (New York: Maxwell Macmillen, 1991), 18–46.

11. Schultz, *Constructing Urban Culture*, 35–57.

12. Ryan, *Civic Wars*, 40–41; Schultz, *Constructing Urban Culture*, 112–128.

13. Schultz, *Constructing Urban Culture*, 35–57.

14. Schultz, *Constructing Urban Culture*, 35–57; Novak, *The People's Welfare*; Morton J. Horwitz, "The History of the Public/Private Distinction," *University of Pennsylvania Law Review* 130 (1982): 1423–1428.

15. Schultz, *Constructing Urban Culture*, 35–57.

16. Schultz, *Constructing Urban Culture*, 47–53.

17. Schultz, *Constructing Urban Culture*, 47–53.

18. Schultz, *Constructing Urban Culture*, 35–57; Novak, *The People's Welfare*, 19–25.

19. Jon C. Teaford, *The Unheralded Triumph: City Government in America, 1870–1900* (Baltimore: Johns Hopkins University Press, 1984); Ryan, *Civic Wars*, 77–114.

20. The few women present at civic ceremonies were generally silent consorts of elite men. Ryan, *Civic Wars*, 77–93; Ryan, *Women in Public*, 19–57.

21. Ryan, *Civic Wars*, 91; Shane White, "It Was a Proud Day: African-American Festivals, and Parades in the North, 1741–1834," *Journal of American History* 81 (1994): 13–50; Johns, *Spreading the News*, 138–143, Douglass on 143; Robert Wiebe, *Self-Rule: A Cultural History of American Democracy* (Chicago: University of Chicago Press, 1995), 61–111.

22. Ryan, *Civic Wars*, 94–108; "speechifying" on 96.

23. Ryan, *Civic Wars*, 108–114; on the Loco-Focos, see Arthur Schlesinger, Jr., *The Age of Jackson* (Boston: Little, Brown & Company, 1946), 191–200.

24. Whigs scurried to abandon the pose of "natural aristocrats," organizing as merchants or manufacturers while appealing to a constituency of strivers and improvers. Ryan, *Civic Wars*, 114–129; on female abolitionists and the public realm, see Aileen S. Kraditor, *Means and Ends in American Abolitionism: Garrison and His Critics on Strategy and Tactics, 1834–1850* (Chicago: I.R. Dee, 1989), 39–77 passim.

25. Ironically, as a painter, Morse contributed to the development of the idea of "Culture" as divorced from the life of the city and its people. Thomas Bender, *New York Intellect: A History of Intellectual Life in New York City, from 1750 to the Beginnings of Our Own Time* (Baltimore: Johns Hopkins University Press, 1988), 122–126ff.; Daniel J. Czitrom, *Media and the American Mind from Morse to McLuhan* (Chapel Hill, NC: University of North Carolina Press, 1982), 3–29, "affinity" on 12; Jim Cullen, *The Art of Democracy* (New York: Monthly Review Press, 1996), 49–50.

26. Czitrom, *Media and the American Mind*, 3–29: "universal" on 12, "evil" on 22, "exacting" on 29; Cullen, *The Art of Democracy*, 49–50; Alan I. Marcus and Howard P. Segal, *Technology in America: A Brief History* (San Diego: Harcourt Brace Jovanovich, 1989), 98–101. There is no definitive answer as to why the federal government decided not to build a public telegraph system, but the Jacksonian philosophy of laissez-faire is a logical explanation. See Johns, *Spreading the News*, 206–256, especially 255–256.

27. Ryan, *Civic Wars*, 94–96, 124–131; Edwin G. Burrows and Mike Wallace, *Gotham: A History of New York City to 1898* (New York: Oxford University Press, 1999), 822–826.

28. Ryan, *Civic Wars*, 124–131; see also Jean Harvey Baker, "Politics, Paradigms, and Public Culture," *Journal of American History* 84 (December 1997): 894–899.

29. Horace Bushnell, "City Plans," in Horace Bushnell, *Work and Play: Or Literary Varieties* (New York: Charles Scribner, 1864), 308–336, quoted passages on 309 and 311; Cullen, *The Art of Democracy*, 20–22; Lawrence W. Levine, *The Unpredictable Past* (New York: Oxford University Press, 1993), 291–319, the phrase "folklore of industrial society" is Levine's; Warren Susman, *Culture as History* (New York: Pantheon Books, 1984), 237–241.

30. Cullen, *The Art of Democracy*, 30–53; Cathy Davidson, *Revolution and the Word: The Rise of the Novel in America* (New York: Oxford University Press, 1986); Edwin G. Burrows and Mike Wallace, *Gotham: A History of New York City to 1898*, 509–512, the phrase "think, speak, and legislate for themselves" is Burrows and Wallace's.

31. David M. Henkin, *City Reading* (New York: Columbia University Press, 1998), 101–135; Robert H. Wiebe, *Self-Rule*, 67–68; Kenneth Cmiel, *Democratic Eloquence* (New York: W. Morrow, 1990), 12–13; Cullen, *The Art of Democracy*, 42–90, "daily" on 48.

32. Czitrom, *Media and the American Mind*, 13–29; Neal Gabler, *Life: The Movie* (New York: Knopf, 1998), 29; Levine, *Highbrow/Lowbrow*, 11–40.

33. "I should have no chance of success while public taste is occupied with their trash," Nathaniel Hawthorne complained of popular novelists, "and I should be ashamed of myself if I did." Gabler, *Life: The Movie*, 11–31: Emerson on 28, Hawthorne on 14.

34. Gabler, *Life: The Movie*, 28–33; Edward Pessen, *Jacksonian America: Society, Personality, Politics* (Urbana: University of Illinois Press, 1985); Czitrom, *Media and the American Mind*, 14–21, "newspaperism" on 1–20.

35. Gabler, *Life: The Movie*, 28–30; Czitrom, *Media and the American Mind*, 11–21: "mind" on 16, Thoreau on 11.

36. Edward L. Widmer, *Young America: The Flowering of Democracy in New York City* (New York: Oxford University Press, 1999), 3–26, quotations on 9; Bender, *New York Intellect*, xiii–xix.

37. Widmer, *Young America*, 27–39.

38. The Whigs noticed the power of the *Review* and responded with their own *American Review*. Widmer, *Young America*, 27–39: Adams on 37, "pernicious" on 38; Bender, *New York Intellect*, 140–156.

39. Bender, *New York Intellect*, 140–156; Daniel Walker Howe, *The Political Culture of the American Whigs* (Chicago: University of Chicago Press, 1979), 7–8; Sean Wilentz, "1840" in *Running for President: The Candidates and Their Images*, ed. Arthur Schlesinger, Jr., and Fred Israel (New York: Simon & Schuster, 1994), 145–153, "carnivalization" on 145.

40. Widmer, *Young America*, 40–63.

41. Widmer, *Young America*, 40–63; Michael Heiman, "Civilization over Nature," in *Major Problems in American Environmental History*, ed. Carolyn Merchant (Lexington, MA: D.C. Heath, 1993), 191–198.

42. Widmer, *Young America*, 125–184.

43. Widmer, *Young America*, 125–184.

44. Levine, *Highbrow/Lowbrow*, 11–115, Whitman on 25.

45. Levine, *Highbrow/Lowbrow*, 11–115: Lind tour on 96–97; musical culture on 104–107.

46. Levine, *Highbrow/Lowbrow*, 11–45.

47. Gabler, *Life: The Movie*, 32–36, "music," "contempt," and Whitman on 32; Blumin, *The Emergence of the Middle Class*, 108–137, "operative" on 123.

48. Gabler, *Life: The Movie*, 32–36; Michael Chevalier, *Society, Manners, and Politics in the United States: Letters on North America* (Ithaca, NY: Cornell University Press, 1969), 428–431; Wiebe, *Self-Rule*, "art" on 65; Neil Harris, *Humbug: The Art of P. T. Barnum* (Boston: Little, Brown, 1973), 61–89. Modern historians agree that antebellum politics approximated the ideal of participatory democracy. Education and participation, Wiebe writes, "created a far more assertive, self-confident electorate" than we have in the twentieth century (7). "Not only did *everybody* participate," he adds, "but everybody *participated*" (61, italics in original). Even in challenging that dominant view, Glenn Althschuler and Stuart Blumin endorse participatory democracy as an organizing principle of early American history: Glenn C. Althschuler and

Stuart M. Blumin, "Limits of Political Engagement in Antebellum America: A New Look at the Golden Age of Participatory Democracy," and "Politics, Society, and the Narrative of American Democracy," *Journal of American History* 84 (December 1997): 855–885, 904–909.

49. Edward K. Spann, *The New Metropolis: New York City, 1840–1857* (New York: Columbia University Press, 1981), 342–343; Sean Wilentz, *Chants Democratic: New York City and the Rise of the American Working Class* (New York: Oxford University Press, 1984), 257–271.

50. Spann, *The New Metropolis*, 342–347; Stansell, *City of Women*, 89–101; Wilentz, *Chants Democratic*, 257–271.

51. Wilentz, *Chants Democratic*, 257–271, "clink" on 257; Spann, *The New Metropolis*, 254–255, 347; Burrows and Wallace, *Gotham*, 822–824.

52. Michael Feldberg, *The Turbulent Era: Riot and Disorder in Jacksonian America* (New York: Oxford University Press, 1980), 55–61; Herbert Gutman, *Work, Culture, and Society in Industrializing America* (New York: Knopf, 1976), Walsh on 56–57; Wilentz, *Chants Democratic*, 257–271. On the intersection of play and politics (and the connection to risk and daring), see Johan Huizinga, *Homo Ludens* (Boston: Beacon Press, 1950), 206 passim; Christopher Lasch, *The Culture of Narcissism* (New York: Norton, 1979), 184–187; Benjamin Barber, *Strong Democracy* (Berkeley: University of California Press, 1984); Norbert Elias and Eric Dunning, *Quest for Excitement* (New York: B. Blackwell, 1986). For an explication of modern political culture where only insiders are called "players," see Robert Westbrook, "Politics as Consumption: Managing the Modern American Election," in *The Culture of Consumption*, ed. Richard Wightman Fox and T. J. Jackson Lears (New York: Pantheon Books, 1983).

53. Adult baseball games were officially banned in Central Park until the 1920s. Teams often played at Hoboken's Elysian Fields, which also hosted firemen's parades and chowder dinners, as well as union meetings. Roy Rosenzwieg and Elizabeth Blackmar, *The Park and the People: a History of Central Park* (Ithaca, NY: Cornell University Press, 1992) 247–249, 307–339, "out-lying" on 249; Schultz, *Constructing Urban Culture*, "grievous" on 124; Michael Gershman, *Diamonds: The Evolution of the Ballpark* (Boston: Houghton Mifflin, 1993), "within" on 11–12; Benjamin G. Rader, *Baseball: A History of America's Game* (Urbana, IL: University of Illinois Press, 1992), 1–2; Melvin L. Adelman, *A Sporting Time: New York City and the Rise of Modern Athletics, 1820–1870* (Urbana, IL: University of Illinois Press, 1986); John D. Fairfield, "The Park in the City: Baseball Landscapes Civically Considered," *Material History Review* 54 (Fall 2001): 21–39. On the enclosure of urban activities, see Lyn Lofland, *The Public Realm* (New York: Aldine de Gruyter, 1998), 17ff.

54. Warren Goldstein, *Playing for Keeps: A History of Early Baseball* (Ithaca, NY: Cornell University Press, 1989), 27–31, 77–80; Rader, *Baseball*, 1–2; "Germany in New York," *Atlantic Monthly* 19 (1867): 563–564; Wilentz, *Chants Democratic*, 259–262, "pride" on 260.

55. Spann, *The New Metropolis*, chaps. 12–13, especially 335.

56. John F. Kasson, *Rudeness and Civility: Manners in Nineteenth-Century America* (New York: Hill and Wang, 1990), 218–228; Levine, *Highbrow/Lowbrow*, 23–27, 56–69.

57. Kasson, *Rudeness and Civility*, 218–228; Levine, *Highbrow/Lowbrow*, 23–27, 56–69: Irving quoted on 61, Trollope on 25, and Melville on 68.

58. Kasson, *Rudeness and Civility*, 220–222; Levine, *Highbrow/Lowbrow*, 23–29, 60–63: "send" on 62, "public" on 29.

59. Kasson, *Rudeness and Civility*, 218–228; Iver Bernstein, *The New York City Draft Riots* (New York: Oxford University Press, 1990), 148–155: Bellows, *The Relation of Public Amusements to Public Morality* (1857) quoted on 154, Olmsted quoted on 153; Jim Cullen, *The Art of Democracy*, 56–60; Edward Pessen, *Jacksonian America*; Widmer, *Young America*, 26; Gabler, *Life: The Movie*, 29–33.

60. Kasson, *Rudeness and Civility*, Astor Place Opera House described on 225–226; Bernstein, *The New York City Draft Riots*, 148–151; Gabler, *Life: The Movie*, 29–33, "air" on 33.

61. Levine, *Highbrow/Lowbrow*, quotations on 62–69; Bernstein, *The New York City Draft Riots*, 148–151; Cullen, *The Art of Democracy*, 59.

62. Levine, *Highbrow/Lowbrow*, quotations on 62–69; Bernstein, *The New York City Draft Riots*, 148–151; Cullen, *The Art of Democracy*, 59.

63. Levine, *Highbrow/Lowbrow*, quotations on 62–69; Kasson, *Rudeness and Civility*, 227–228.

64. For good reason, the Astor Place Riot has played the central role for historians of early nineteenth-century culture that Chicago's 1893 World's Columbian Exposition has played for historians of the late nineteenth century. The Columbian Exposition used culture as a legitimation for a hierarchical, corporate order. The Astor Place Riot revealed an earlier struggle to preserve a democratic culture. Bernstein, *The New York City Draft Riots*, 149; Levine, *Highbrow/Lowbrow*, 66–69, "citizens" on 68; Mary P. Ryan, *Civic Wars*, "warfare" on 137; Gabler, *Life: The Movie*, "indisputable" on 36. On Chicago's 1893 fair, see Alan Trachtenberg, *The Incorporation of America* (New York: Hill and Wang, 1982), 208–234.

65. Howe, *The Political Culture of the American Whigs*, "war" on 162; "thirty-years' war" is from an 1863 issue of the evangelical journal *Home Missionary*.

66. John L. O'Sullivan, "Annexation," *Democratic Review* 17 (July 1845): 5–10; Widmer, *Young America*, 185–209 passim.

67. Bernstein, *The New York City Draft Riots*, 132–148, quotation on 134; Widmer, *Young America*, 185–209.

68. Widmer, *Young America*, 185–209, "East" on 194 (italics in original).

69. Widmer, *Young America*, 185–209 (italics in original).

70. Burrows and Wallace, *Gotham*, 487–490, 642–643; Wilentz, *Chants Democratic*, 258–259; Cullen, *The Art of Democracy*, 60–69; David R. Roediger, *The Wages of Whiteness: Race and the Making of the American Working Class* (New York: Verso, 1991), 95–163.

71. Burrows and Wallace, *Gotham*, 487–490, 642–643; Wilentz, *Chants Democratic*, 258–259; Roediger, *The Wages of Whiteness*, 95–163; Cullen, *The Art of Democracy*, 60–69, quotations on 66. In one skit, a black man endured the criticism of a white man (if you don't know phrenology, grammar, or spelling, then "tree quarters of your life is gone") until the ferry they are riding on capsized. "I axed him if he knowed how to swim. He said no. Den, says I, de whole four quarters of your life am gone—shure" (66). Such moments could not redeem the overarching racism of the minstrel shows, but they gave African Americans a small share in the elevation of practical knowledge over impractical intellectualism.

72. Warner, *The Private City*, 89–98; Bernstein, *The New York City Draft Riots*, 132–148; Amy Bridges, *A City in the Republic: Origins of Machine Politics in Antebellum New York* (New York: Cambridge University Press, 1984).

73. David Black, *The King of Fifth Avenue* (New York: Dial Press, 1981), 32–41.

74. Steven A. Riess, *City Games* (Urbana, IL: University of Illinois Press, 1989), 25, 181; Melvin L. Adelman, *A Sporting Time*, 83–88.

75. As a member of the sporting crowd, Belmont lent authority to the rants of rabble-rousers like Walsh and earned the enmity of evangelical reformers. "So long as it is looked upon as indecent, if not criminal for persons to run, sing, dance, and skylark in the public streets and squares," Walsh asserted, "so long will the greater mass of the poorer portion of people, who have scarcely the room enough to turn around in, continue to seek excitement and amusement in public places." Riess, *City Games*, 11–31; Bernstein, *The New York City Draft Riots*, 148–152; Spann, *The New Metropolis*, Walsh on 348; Benjamin Quarles, *Black Abolitionists* (New York: Oxford University Press, 1969).

76. Quarles, *Black Abolitionists*; the *Appeal* is excerpted in Elizabeth Cobbs Hoffman and Jon Gjerda, eds., *Major Problems in American History*, vol. 1 (Boston: Houghton Mifflin, 2002), 266–268.

77. Sellers, *The Market Revolution*, 202–236; Kasson, *Rudeness and Civility*, 34–69; Schudson, *The Good Citizen*, 98–126; Wilentz, *Chants Democratic*, 146; Bertram Wyatt-Brown, *Lewis Tappan and the Evangelical War against Slavery* (Cleveland: Press of Case Western Reserve University, 1969), 52–55 passim.

78. Sellers, *The Market Revolution*, 202–217, Beecher on 210; Paul E. Johnson, *A Shopkeeper's Millennium* (New York: Hill and Wang, 1979); Howe, *The Political Culture of the*

American Whigs, 150–167; Charles I. Foster, *An Errand of Mercy: The Evangelical United Front, 1790–1837* (Chapel Hill, NC: University of North Carolina Press, 1960); Ronald G. Walters, *The Antislavery Appeal: American Abolitionism after 1830* (New York: Norton, 1978), 37–53.

79. Sellers, *The Market Revolution*, 208–217: Beecher quoted on 213, Channing quoted on 217; Howe, *The Political Culture of the American Whigs*, 150–167; Charles I. Foster, *An Errand of Mercy*.

80. Sellers, *The Market Revolution*, 231–236, Lewis Tappan on 231; Sydney E. Ahlstrom, *A Religious History of the American People* (New Haven, CT: Yale University Press, 1972), 458–461; Wilentz, *Chants Democratic*, 145–146, 263–266.

81. Sellers, *The Market Revolution*, 231–236, Finney quoted on 234 (italics in original); Ahlstrom, *A Religious History of the American People*, 458–461; Wilentz, *Chants Democratic*, 145–146, 263–266.

82. Sellers, *The Market Revolution*, 232–236, Finney quoted 233–234; Wilentz, *Chants Democratic*, 265–266; Leonard L. Richards, *"Gentlemen of Property and Standing": Anti-Abolition Mobs in Jacksonian America* (New York: Oxford University Press, 1970), 28–29, 38.

83. Gutman, *Work, Culture, and Society*; John J. Rumbarger, *Profits, Power, and Prohibition* (Albany, NY: State University of New York Press, 1989), part I.

84. Richards, *"Gentlemen of Property and Standing,"* 47–81; Johns, *Spreading the News*, 60–63, 169–205, 257–280: Madison on 63, minister on 184.

85. Richards, *"Gentlemen of Property and Standing,"* 47–81, 134–150.

86. Richards, *"Gentlemen of Property and Standing,"* 47–100: resolutions of the public meeting quoted in Birney's *Narrative of the Late Riotous Proceedings against the Liberty of the Press, in Cincinnati* (Cincinnati, OH: Ohio Anti-Slavery Society, 1836), copy in the Cincinnati Historical Society; Daniel Aaron, *Cincinnati: Queen City of the West, 1819–1838* (Columbus, OH: Ohio State University Press, 1992), 300–314; David Grimsted, "Rioting in Its Jacksonian Setting," *American Historical Review* 77 (April 1972): 361–397.

87. Johns, *Spreading the News*, 257–283; Richards, *"Gentlemen of Property and Standing,"* 49–62, Jackson on 51.

88. Johns, *Spreading the News*, 257–283, "shield" and "stirred" on 279.

89. Richards, *"Gentlemen of Property and Standing,"* 10–19; Grimsted, "Rioting in Its Jacksonian Setting," publicist quoted on 364–365 (italics in original); Howe, *The Political Culture of American Whigs*, 81–85, 225–237; Abraham Lincoln, "Address before the Young Men's Lyceum of Springfield, Illinois" (January 27, 1838), in *The Collected Works of Abraham Lincoln*, ed. Roy P. Basler, vol. 1 (Washington: authorized by Lincoln Sesquicentennial Commission, 1959, 1974, 1990), 108–115.

90. An antiabolitionist complained that abolitionists taught "little children when they meet to eat sugar plums or at the Sunday schools," even using spellers that taught "A B stands for abolition." Lincoln, "Address before the Young Men's Lyceum of Springfield, Illinois"; Howe, *The Political Culture of American Whigs*, 270ff.; Richards, *"Gentlemen of Property and Standing."*

91. "The democratic sermo humilis," wrote Kenneth Cmiel in reference to Lincoln's humble style, "draws on the commonest culture, not to pander or flatter, but to call us back to our best possibilities as human beings and citizens." Lincoln, "Temperance Address" (February 22, 1842), in *The Collected Works of Abraham Lincoln*, 271–279; Howe, *The Political Culture of the American Whigs*, 270–298; James M. McPherson, *Abraham Lincoln and the Second American Revolution* (New York: Oxford University Press, 1991), 97–98; Kenneth Cmiel, *Democratic Eloquence*, 94–122, "sermo" on 120.

92. Howe, *The Political Culture of American Whigs*, 276–298; John Patrick Diggins, *The Lost Soul of American Politics* (Chicago: University of Chicago Press, 1984), "scarce" on 19; Mark E. Neely, Jr., *The Last Best Hope of Earth: Abraham Lincoln and the Promise of America* (Cambridge, MA: Harvard University Press, 1993), "judgment" on 31.

93. In stopping the spread of slavery, Lincoln told Northerners, we "shall not only have saved the Union; but we shall have so saved it, as to make and to keep it forever worth saving." Howe, *The Political Culture of the American Whigs*, 270–290.

94. In the broad sense of conspiracy as a "union or combination for one end or purpose," the Democratic Party designed its doctrine of popular sovereignty (allowing settlers themselves to vote whether slavery would be allowed in a territory) to overcome Constitutional objections to the expansion of slavery. The *Dred Scott* decision (1857) satisfied a more precise definition of conspiracy. The decision resulted from a concealed and illegitimate transaction, as Republican Senator William Seward put it, between "the executive and judicial departments to undermine the national legislature and the liberties of the people." William L. Barney, *Battleground for the Union* (Englewood Cliffs, NJ: Prentice-Hall Inc., 1990), 84–92, Seward on 86; Howe, *The Political Culture of the American Whigs*, 79–81, 276–290. For skeptical views of Lincoln's conspiracy theory, see Michael Schudson, *The Good Citizen*, 133–143; Neely, *The Last Best Hope of Earth*, 48–54. Boritt adds that if slaves were to be treated just like any other property, then a demand for its federal protection (in a new *Dred Scott* decision) would seem a just demand to an ex-Whig like Lincoln. Hence Lincoln's concern to show that slavery was not just another form of property but one that had to be examined in light of civic concerns. Garbor S. Boritt, *Lincoln and the Economics of the American Dream* (Memphis, TN: Memphis State University Press, 1978), 169–171.

95. Howe, *The Political Culture of the American Whigs*, 288–290, "difficult" is Roy Basler, quoted on 289.

96. Schudson, *The Good Citizen*, 133–143; Howe, *The Political Culture of the American Whigs*, 281–285; Boritt, *Lincoln and the Economics of the American Dream*, "magnifying" on 175; Eric Foner, *Free Soil, Free Labor, Free Men: The Ideology of the Republican Party before the Civil War* (New York: Oxford University Press, 1970), 301–316, especially 305; Sandel, *Democracy's Discontent*, "false" on 23. On the distinction between action and behavior, see Hannah Arendt, *The Human Condition* (Chicago: University of Chicago Press, 1958); Christopher Lasch, *The True and Only Heaven: Progress and Its Critics* (New York: Norton, 1991), 133–135, footnote on Lincoln on 376.

97. William E. Gienapp, *Abraham Lincoln and Civil War America* (New York: Oxford University Press, 2002), 67–68; Neely, *The Last Best Hope of Earth*, 54; Howe, *The Political Culture of the American Whigs*, 281–285; Widmer, *Young America*, 182.

98. Lincoln, "Address at Cooper Institute" (February 27, 1860), *The Collected Works of Abraham Lincoln*, vol. 3, 523–550.

99. Widmer, *Young America*, 214–215.

100. Bender, *New York Intellect*, 163–168; Godwin's articles for *Putnam's* are collected in Parke Godwin, *Political Essays* (New York: Dix, Edward & Co., 1856).

101. Godwin, *Political Essays*, 250–279; Bender, *New York Intellect*, 163–168; George Haven Putnam, *Memoirs of a Publisher, 1865–1915* (New York: G.P. Putnam's Sons, 1916), 12–13.

102. Foner, *Free Soil, Free Labor, Free Men*, 301–316 (italics in original).

103. Foner, *Free Soil, Free Labor, Free Men*, 261–319: Curtis on 309, Douglass on 262; Bernstein, *The New York City Draft Riots*, 148–161, Bellows on 156.

104. Philip Shaw Paludan, *"A People's Contest": The Union and Civil War, 1861–1865* (Lawrence, KS: University Press of Kansas, 1996), 194–195; Bernstein, *The New York City Draft Riots*, 148–161, Bellows on 149; George Fredrickson, *The Inner Civil War* (New York: Harpers & Row, 1965), 26–27, 136–144, "Providential" on 141.

CHAPTER 5

1. Sean Wilentz, *Chants Democratic: New York City and the Rise of the American Working Class, 1788–1850* (New York: Oxford University Press, 1984), 363–389, Whitman on 389.

2. Iver Bernstein, *The New York City Draft Riots: Their Significance for American Society and Politics in the Age of the Civil War* (New York: Oxford University Press, 1990), 75–124, "anything" on 89; Edwin G. Burrows and Mike Wallace, *Gotham: A History of New York City to 1898* (New York: Oxford University Press, 1999), 768–773.

3. Eric Foner, *Free Soil, Free Labor, Free Men* (New York: Oxford University Press, 1970), 21–23 passim.

4. George Fredrickson, *The Inner Civil War: Northern Intellectuals and the Crisis of the Union* (New York: Harpers & Row, 1965); Bernstein, *The New York City Draft Riots*; David W. Blight, *Race and Reunion: The Civil War in American Memory* (Cambridge, MA: Belknap Press of Harvard University Press, 2001).

5. Fredrickson, *The Inner Civil War*, 7–129: "vital" on 49, Phillips quoted on 128.

6. Fredrickson, *The Inner Civil War*, 23–150: "strong" on 55–56, "unconditional" on 136–137.

7. Fredrickson, *The Inner Civil War*, 113–150, "thought" on 120.

8. William L. Barney, *Battleground for the Union* (Englewood Cliffs, NJ: Prentice-Hall Inc., 1990), 253.

9. Fredrickson, *The Inner Civil War* passim, "hold" on 73; David Quigley, *Second Founding: New York City, Reconstruction, and the Making of American Democracy* (New York: Hill and Wang, 2004), 71–78 passim; Eric Foner, *Reconstruction: America's Unfinished Revolution, 1863–1877* (New York: Harper & Row, 1988), 460–511, esp. 492; Bernstein, *The New York City Draft Riots*, 148–190, "hostilities" on 156 (italics in original); Burrows and Wallace, *Gotham*, 649–1038.

10. Bernstein, *The New York City Draft Riots*, 251–264; the phrase "authentic popular rule" (77) is Bernstein's; Foner, *Reconstruction*, 512–524.

11. Refugees from the failed European revolutions of 1848 helped organize the Industrial Congress. Bernstein, *New York City Draft Riots*, 75–92; Wilentz, *Chants Democratic*, 363–389; Burrows and Wallace, *Gotham*, 768–773.

12. Bernstein, *New York City Draft Riots*, 75–92; Wilentz, *Chants Democratic*, 363–389; Burrows and Wallace, *Gotham*, 768–773.

13. Bernstein, *New York City Draft Riots*, 75–92: "people turning their own lawyers" on 89, "practical laboring man" on 87; Wilentz, *Chants Democratic*, 363–389, "those in favor" quoted on 384.

14. Bernstein, *The New York City Draft Riots*, 90–94 (italics added for readability).

15. Bernstein, *The New York City Draft Riots*, 90–101.

16. Nativists thus advanced the municipal revolution. Treating the city as a residential community rather than a republican commonwealth, the municipal revolution deemphasized questions of economic justice and focused on enhancing the health and safety of the urban environment. Barney, *Battleground for the Union*, 54–61, 73–76; Mary Ryan, *Civic Wars: Democracy and Public Life in the American City during the Nineteenth Century* (Berkeley: University of California Press, 1997), 139–158; Jon C. Teaford, *The Municipal Revolution in America* (Chicago: University of Chicago Press, 1975); Zane L. Miller, "Scarcity, Abundance, and American Urban History," *Journal of Urban History* 4 (February 1978): 131–156; Alan I Marcus, *A Plague of Strangers* (Columbus, OH: Ohio State University Press, 1991).

17. Burrows and Wallace, *Gotham*, 821–829; Ryan, *Civic Wars*, 139–158.

18. Burrows and Wallace, *Gotham*, 821–835, quotations on 830; Ryan, *Civic Wars*, 151–157.

19. Ryan, *Civic Wars*, 151–157; Burrows and Wallace, *Gotham*, 835–837.

20. Ryan, *Civic Wars*, 151–157; Burrows and Wallace, *Gotham*, 837–841, quoted passages on 838.

21. Ryan, *Civic Wars*, 151–157; "Burly" on 153; Burrows and Wallace, *Gotham*, 837–841, "scene" on 839.

22. Ryan, *Civic Wars*, 157–167, Wood on 164; Bernstein, *The New York City Draft Riots*, 184–190.

23. Bernstein, *The New York City Draft Riots*, 100–104, "forbidden" on 100; Burrows and Wallace, *Gotham*, 864–868.

24. Ryan, *Civic Wars*, 165–170, Wood on 168; Philip Shaw Paludan, *A People's Contest: The Union and Civil War, 1861–1865* (Lawrence, KS: University Press of Kansas, 1996), 170–197; Bernstein, *The New York City Draft Riots*, 3–72; Burrows and Wallace, *Gotham*, 883–905.

25. Paludan, *A People's Contest*, 70–197; Bernstein, *The New York City Draft Riots*, 3–72; Burrows and Wallace, *Gotham*, 883–905, "hoards" on 884.

26. Burrows and Wallace, *Gotham*, 883–889, Seymour on 888; Bernstein, *The New York City Draft Riots*, 3–42.
27. Burrows and Wallace, *Gotham*, 888–892; Bernstein, *The New York City Draft Riots*, 17–42.
28. Burrows and Wallace, *Gotham*, 892–895; Bernstein, *The New York City Draft Riots*, 17–72, "subject" on 19.
29. Burrows and Wallace, *Gotham*, 892–895, quotations on 894; Bernstein, *The New York City Draft Riots*, 17–72.
30. Frederick Law Olmsted privately wrote E. L. Godkin to urge that Belmont, Seymour, and others be hanged: "Stir the gov't up to it." Bernstein, *The New York City Draft Riots*, 43–72: "era" on 54, Olmsted on 56; Burrows and Wallace, *Gotham*, 895–899.
31. Bernstein, *The New York City Draft Riots*, 43–72; Burrows and Wallace, *Gotham*, 895–899.
32. Bernstein, *The New York City Draft Riots*, 43–72, 162–192, AICP on 68.
33. Bernstein, *The New York City Draft Riots*, 43–72, 162–192, AICP on 68–69.
34. Bernstein, *The New York City Draft Riots*, 43–72, 125–161, 195–236, "perilous" on 141.
35. Bernstein, *The New York City Draft Riots*, 43–72 passim.
36. These categories—plebiscitary, paternalistic, and so forth—are mine, but they arise from my reading of Bernstein, *The New York City Draft Riots*. For example, Bernstein writes of the Union Leaguers: "the patrician fraternity sought both to regain contact with the poor and to veil their authority through the new communal settings" (154).
37. Paludan, *A People's Contest*, 189–197, Melville on 194.
38. Burrows and Wallace, *Gotham*, 896–897; Bernstein, *The New York City Draft Riots*, 75–124, "usurping" on 84–85.
39. Bernstein, *The New York City Draft Riots*, 18–25, "concourse" on 19.
40. Bernstein, *The New York City Draft Riots*, 17–42, 104–124, quotations on 22.
41. In the 1864 election, Lincoln increased his percentage of the vote over 1860 in many of the cities of the North (although slipping 1.5 percent in New York City). Paludan, *A People's Contest*, 189–197; David Montgomery, *Beyond Equality: Labor and the Radical Republicans, 1862–1872* (Urbana, IL: University of Illinois Press, 1981), 101–113.
42. Montgomery, *Beyond Equality*, 101–113: "stake" on 107, other quotations on 113; Paludan, *A People's Contest*, 189–197.
43. Harold M. Hyman, *A More Perfect Union* (New York: Knopf, 1973), 326–346, "dynasty" on 328–329; Barney, *Battleground for the Union*, 252–254; Bernstein, *The New York City Draft Riots*, 184–190; Stanley Schultz, *Constructing Urban Culture: American Cities and City Planning, 1800–1920* (Philadelphia: Temple University Press, 1989), 109–149.
44. Burrows and Wallace, *Gotham*, 917–928, "control" on 918; Barney, *Battleground for the Union*, 252–253; Bernstein, *The New York City Draft Riots*, 184–190.
45. Bernstein, *The New York City Draft Riots*, 184–190, "closely-packed" on 187; Burrows and Wallace, *Gotham*, 917–928, "sway" on 919; Quigley, *Second Founding*, 27–44.
46. Burrows and Wallace, *Gotham*, 926–928, "WHITE" on 926; Quigley, *Second Founding*, 15–69.
47. Quigley, *Second Founding*, 57–69; Burrows and Wallace, *Gotham*, 926–928.
48. Quigley, *Second Founding*, 71–89; Burrows and Wallace, *Gotham*, 927–928.
49. Quigley, *Second Founding*, 71–89, Tweed on 85; Burrows and Wallace, *Gotham*, 926–928.
50. Bernstein, *The New York City Draft Riots*, 195–236; Burrows and Wallace, *Gotham*, 917–928.
51. Burrows and Wallace, *Gotham*, 927–931; Bernstein, *The New York City Draft Riots*, 195–236; Quigley, *Second Founding*, 94–95.
52. Burrows and Wallace, *Gotham*, 929–931, quotation on 931; Bernstein, *The New York City Draft Riots*, 195–236.
53. Burrows and Wallace, *Gotham*, 931–950.

54. Burrows and Wallace, *Gotham*, 931–950.

55. Bernstein, *The New York City Draft Riots*, 195–210, "avowed" on 207. Tweed might have become New York's version of Paris's Baron von Haussmann who, with the blessing of Louis Napoleon, transformed the face of Paris in the wake of the failed revolution of 1848.

56. Bernstein, *The New York City Draft Riots*, 206–228; Burrows and Wallace, *Gotham*, 986–988.

57. Bernstein, *The New York City Draft Riots*, 206–228.

58. In 1690, William of Orange defeated King James II at the Battle of the Boyne and established Protestant rule in Ireland. Bernstein, *The New York City Draft Riots*, 228–236; Burrows and Wallace, *Gotham*, 1005–1008, "mud" on 1008.

59. Bernstein, *The New York City Draft Riots*, 228–236, "once" on 235; Burrows and Wallace, *Gotham*, 1005–1008, "Dangerous" on 1008; Ryan, *Civic Wars*, 229–234.

60. Ryan, *Civic Wars*, 229–234, descriptions of violence on 232–233; Bernstein, *New York City Draft Riots*, "commune" on 230; Quigley, *Second Founding*, 95–100.

61. Bernstein, *The New York City Draft Riots*, 228–236: "criminal" on 231, "fraternization" on 234, "throw" on 234; Burrows and Wallace, *Gotham*, 1005–1008, "higher" on 1008.

62. Burrows and Wallace, *Gotham*, 1008–1012.

63. This is not to deny the role of Northern racism in the collapse of Reconstruction and the transformation of the Republican Party. Foner, *Reconstruction*, 460–499; Montgomery, *Beyond Equality*, 230–386; Bernstein, *The New York City Draft Riots*, 195–257; Quigley, *Second Founding*, 50, 100–101 passim.

64. Burrows and Wallace, *Gotham*, 1012–1013, manufacturers on 1013; Bernstein, *The New York City Draft Riots*, 237–257; Montgomery, *Beyond Equality*, 296–334.

65. Burrows and Wallace, *Gotham*, 1012–1013, quotations on 1013; Bernstein, *The New York City Draft Riots*, 237–257.

66. Bernstein, *The New York City Draft Riots*, 237–247, "enemies" on 243.

67. Bernstein, *The New York City Draft Riots*, 243–250, two employers quoted on 248.

68. Bernstein, *The New York City Draft Riots*, 243–250.

69. Bernstein, *The New York City Draft Riots*, 248–253, banner on 252.

70. Bernstein, *The New York City Draft Riots*, 252–257, "although" on 253.

71. Bernstein, *The New York City Draft Riots*, 251–257, AICP report quoted on 255.

72. Foner, *Reconstruction*, 512–524; Bernstein, *The New York City Draft Riots*, 251–264, the editor is *The Nation*'s E. L. Godkin, quoted on 256. Bernstein writes: the "more recognizably modern city of the late nineteenth century was a place where social debate was not so sweeping nor fundamentally critical, where justice as denied by 'the best men' had far greater power and legitimacy, and where popular democracy, for all its vitality, was vitiated from its former self" (262). "Because the world of July 1863 was short-lived, the riots' ugliest and most sanguinary forms of violence disappeared from the political repertoire of succeeding generations of workers. Sadly, something of the draft rioters' audacity—their readiness to solve, all at once, the problems of an industrializing city and a divided nation—may have been lost as well" (264).

73. Burrows and Wallace, *Gotham*, 1020–1027.

74. Burrows and Wallace, *Gotham*, 1020–1027; see also Herbert G. Gutman, "The Tompkins Square 'Riot' in New York City on January 13, 1874: A Re-examination of Its Causes and Its Aftermath," *Labor History* 6 (1965): 44–70.

75. On positive and negative conceptions of liberty, see Quigley, *Second Founding*, 93–95; 104–108; Burrows and Wallace, *Gotham*, 1027–1038, "soup" on 1031; Foner, *Reconstruction*, 512–563, "proletariat" on 519; Ryan, *Civic Wars*, 159–180.

76. Quigley, *Second Founding*, 111–121, "consequences" on 118; Burrows and Wallace, *Gotham*, 1032–1033.

77. Quigley, *Second Founding*, 121–130; Burrows and Wallace, *Gotham*, 1027–1038; Bernstein, *The New York City Draft Riots*, 219–222; Michael McGerr, *The Decline of Popular Politics: The American North, 1865–1928* (New York: Oxford University Press, 1986), 42–52.

78. Burrows and Wallace, *Gotham*, 1032–1033, "preposterous" on 1033; Quigley, *Second Founding*, 137–160: "protect" on 146, "failure" on 147.

79. Quigley, *Second Founding*, 137–160, "public" on 137; Burrows and Wallace, *Gotham*, 1032–1033.

80. Quigley, *Second Founding*, 152–160: Swinton on 155, "franchise" on 160.

81. The new educational politics discussed in the next chapter represented one of the most important efforts of the New York reformers. Tilden and fellow New Yorkers Abram Hewitt and William Whitney took the lead in promoting educational politics within the Democratic Party. Senator William Evarts, chairman of the Tilden Commission, brought the educational campaign to the Republican Party. Grover Cleveland, reform-minded governor of New York, rode the new educational politics into the White House. New York journalists, not only Godkin and Curtis but also Whitelaw Reid, William Cullen Bryant, and others also spread the new style. Quigley, *Second Founding*, 161–174, "serious" on 164; Thomas Bender, *New York Intellect* (Baltimore, MD: Johns Hopkins University Press, 1988), 169–205; McGerr, *The Decline of Popular Politics*, 42–106 passim.

CHAPTER 6

1. Lawrence W. Levine, *Highbrow/Lowbrow: The Emergence of Cultural Hierarchy in America* (Cambridge: Harvard University Press, 1988); John F. Kasson, *Rudeness and Civility: Manners in Nineteenth-Century Urban America* (New York: Hill and Wang, 1990); Jim Cullen, *The Art of Democracy* (New York: Monthly Review Press, 1996), 91–134; Edwin G. Burrows and Mike Wallace, *Gotham: A History of New York City to 1898* (New York: Oxford University Press, 1999), 951–965; 1013–1016.

2. Levine, *Highbrow/Lowbrow*, 155–160, quotations on 155; Edward L. Widmer, *Young America: The Flowering of Democracy in New York City* (New York: Oxford University Press, 1999).

3. Ellen C. DuBois, *Feminism and Suffrage: The Emergence of an Independent Women's Movement in America, 1848–1869* (Ithaca, NY: Cornell University Press, 1978), passim, "triple" on 125, "Muscle" on 95.

4. Privately, Stanton wrote: "Think of Patrick and Sambo and Hans and Ung Tung, who do not know the difference between a Monarchy and a Republic . . . making laws for Lydia Maria Child, Lucretia Mott, or Fanny Kemble." DuBois, *Feminism and Suffrage*, 162–202: "insult" on 173, "wealth" on 178; Eric Foner, *Reconstruction: America's Unfinished Revolution, 1863–1877* (New York: Harper & Row, 1988), "Think" on 448.

5. Levine, *Highbrow/Lowbrow*; Michael McGerr, *The Decline of Popular Politics: The American North, 1865–1928* (New York: Oxford University Press, 1986), "restrict" on 72, "dry" on 78; David Quigley, *Second Founding: New York City, Reconstruction, and the Making of American Democracy* (New York: Hill and Wang, 2004), 129–130, 149–150, 168–170.

6. Levine, *Highbrow/Lowbrow*, 69–81.

7. Levine, *Highbrow/Lowbrow*, 85–104.

8. Levine, *Highbrow/Lowbrow*, 104–116: "extravagances" on 114, "have only done" on 115; Kasson, *Rudeness and Civility*, 230–239; Thomas Bender, *New York Intellect* (Baltimore, MD: Johns Hopkins University Press, 1988), 217–219.

9. Levine, *Highbrow/Lowbrow*, 108–132, quotations on 115; Kasson, *Rudeness and Civility*, 230–239.

10. Levine, *Highbrow/Lowbrow*, 116–132; Alan Trachtenberg, *The Incorporation of America* (New York: Hill and Wang, 1982), 144–145; Bender, *New York Intellect*, 169–176; Kasson, *Rudeness and Civility*, 230–239.

11. Levine, *Highbrow/Lowbrow*, 132–155; Trachtenberg, *The Incorporation of America*, 144–145; Kasson, *Rudeness and Civility*, 247–248; Casey Nelson Blake, *Beloved Community: The Cultural Criticism of Randolph Bourne, Van Wyck Brooks, Waldo Frank and Lewis Mumford* (Chapel Hill, NC: University of North Carolina Press, 1990); John Dewey, *Art as Experience* (New York: Minton, Balch & Company, 1934).

12. Both Boston's and Chicago's libraries nevertheless circulated more than a million books a year. Jon C. Teaford, *The Unheralded Triumph: City Government in America, 1870–1900* (Baltimore: Johns Hopkins University Press, 1984), 72–75, 146–150, 258–262; Levine, *Highbrow/Lowbrow*, 155–160.

13. Levine, *Highbrow/Lowbrow*, 219–231, *Times-Picayune* quoted on 221; Kasson, *Rudeness and Civility*, 230. "Highbrow" came into use in the 1880s and "lowbrow" soon after 1900. The phrenological terms "highbrowed" and "lowbrowed" had become common earlier in the nineteenth century.

14. Levine, *Highbrow/Lowbrow*, 177–185, quotations on 183 and 186; Kasson, *Rudeness and Civility*, 243–244.

15. Levine, *Highbrow/Lowbrow*, 177–195, *Dial* on 189; Kasson, *Rudeness and Civility*, 245–246. Defending himself from the charge of nostalgia, Levine writes: "I do not want my audiences to shout me down when they disagree, or make me repeat sentences they find particularly stirring, or indulge in riots when they find the conditions in the auditorium not to their liking" (9). One tends to agree with Levine. But what college teacher has not, at times, wished for a bit more spunk in his or her somnolent classroom? And what role does the fear of being judged by the people they profess to speak for play in the tendency of many would-be radicals to write in impenetrable prose? Russell Jacoby, *The Last Intellectuals: American Culture in the Age of Academe* (New York: Basic Books, 1987).

16. Levine, *Highbrow/Lowbrow*, 200–218.

17. Levine, *Highbrow/Lowbrow*, 195–199: "cleanliness" and "vulgarisms" on 195–196, "homelike" on 196; Kasson, *Rudeness and Civility*, 239–252, "circuit" on 249; Robert Sklar, *Movie-Made America* (New York: Random House, 1975), 3–12.

18. John G. Sproat, *"The Best Men": Liberal Reformers in the Gilded Age* (New York: Oxford University Press, 1968), 244–257, "No" on 255; McGerr, *The Decline of Popular Politics*, 42–48, the *Times* on 47; Bernstein, *The New York City Draft Riots*, 219–220; Sproat, *"The Best Men,"* 254.

19. McGerr, *The Decline of Popular Politics*, 46–52, quotations on 48; Burrows and Wallace, *Gotham*, 1032–1033.

20. McGerr, *The Decline of Popular Politics*, 3–41.

21. McGerr, *The Decline of Popular Politics*, 12–51, "activity" on 51.

22. McGerr, *The Decline of Popular Politics*, 52–58: "organized" on 53, *Harper's Weekly* on 58; Sproat, *"The Best Men,"* 112–141, 250.

23. McGerr, *The Decline of Popular Politics*, 36–62, Greeley on 38.

24. McGerr, *The Decline of Popular Politics*, 60–68; Michael Schudson, *The Good Citizen: A History of American Civic Life* (New York: Martin-Kessler Books, 1998), 144–187; Schudson argues that the reformers helped "transform voting from a social to a civic act" (147) and encouraged the parties to "to take policy seriously" (187). Elections, once a community event and expression, became "more nearly an aggregation of individual preferences" (173).

25. McGerr, *The Decline of Popular Politics*, 70–78: "quiet" is McGerr's judgment, 70, "cold" on 71, "*carefully*" on 73 (italics in original).

26. McGerr, *The Decline of Popular Politics*, 76–92; Mary Ryan, *Civic Wars: Democracy and Public Life in the American City during the Nineteenth Century* (Berkeley: University of California Press, 1997), 276.

27. McGerr, *The Decline of Popular Politics*, 84–106, 142.

28. McGerr, *The Decline of Popular Politics*, 84–106.

29. McGerr, *The Decline of Popular Politics*, 84–106.

30. McGerr, *The Decline of Popular Politics*, 64–65, 81, "party" on 65.

31. Stanley K. Schultz, *Constructing Urban Culture: American Cities and City Planning, 1800–1920* (Philadelphia: Temple University Press, 1989), 57–66, Kent on 61; the New York legislature did infringe on municipal autonomy in the 1850s, as discussed in Chapter 5; see Burrows and Wallace, *Gotham*, 836.

32. Strict application of the minority opinion in the 1850s would have prevented the municipality from constructing sewers and horsecar lines, cleaning streets and repairing docks

and wharves, providing fresh water to poorer neighborhoods, or any other realm in which private enterprise continued to operate. Schultz, *Constructing Urban Culture*, 62–66 (italics in original).

33. The United States Supreme Court adopted Dillon's Rule in 1907. Schultz, *Constructing Urban Culture*, 65–75.

34. Schultz, *Constructing Urban Culture*, 66–70.

35. Schultz, *Constructing Urban Culture*, 66–75.

36. Schultz, *Constructing Urban Culture*, quotations on 78–81; Teaford, *The Unheralded Triumph*, 83–102; 217–282.

37. Teaford, *The Unheralded Triumph*, passim, figures on Chicago, 217.

38. Burrows and Wallace, *Gotham*, 966–985; Schultz, *Constructing Urban Culture*, 183–205; Teaford, *The Unheralded Triumph*, 15–82, 132–173, 281; George Fredrickson, *The Inner Civil War* (New York: Harpers & Row, 1965), traces the emergence of a modernizing elite, dedicated to professionalism and scientific and technical expertise, skeptical of popular abilities and the democratic state, impervious to humanitarian appeals, and stoic in the face of the sufferings of others.

39. Teaford, *The Unheralded Triumph*, 15–82, 132–173; Burrows and Wallace, *Gotham*, 966–985, Roebling on 967; Schultz, *Constructing Urban Culture*, 183–205; Fredrickson, *The Inner Civil War*.

40. Teaford, *The Unheralded Triumph*, 283–313, on Bird Coler, 57–58; Bird Sim Coler, *Municipal Government* (New York: D. Appleton, 1900), 186–200; Lincoln Steffens, *The Shame of the Cities* (New York: Hill and Wang, 1963).

41. Schultz, *Constructing Urban Culture*, 129–181, quotation on 148.

42. Paul Boyer, *Urban Masses and Moral Order in America, 1820–1920* (Cambridge: Harvard University Press, 1978), "slimy" on 171; Schultz, *Constructing Urban Culture*, 129–181, "outside" on 176; Carl Smith, *Urban Disorder and the Shape of Belief* (Chicago: University of Chicago Press, 1995), 151, 186–193, "sewage" on 191.

43. Teaford, *The Unheralded Triumph*, 217–250; Schultz, *Constructing Urban Culture*, 111–219; on street pavements, see Clay McShane, *Down the Asphalt Path: The Automobile and the American City* (New York: Columbia University Press, 1994); John D. Fairfield, "Rapid Transit: Automobility and Settlement in Urban America," *Reviews in American History* (March 1995): 80–85; Peter C. Baldwin, *Domesticating the Street: The Reform of Public Space in Hartford, 1850–1930* (Columbus, OH: Ohio State University Press, 1999); Ryan, *Civic Wars*, 203–209.

44. In affluent districts, public utilities rarely reached servants' quarters on the top floors. Teaford, *The Unheralded Triumph*; 217–250, 272–274, "meager" on 274; Burrows and Wallace, *Gotham*, 991–992; Marilyn Thornton Williams, *Washing "The Great Unwashed": Public Baths in Urban America* (Columbus, OH: Ohio State University Press, 1991).

45. Max Page, *The Creative Destruction of Manhattan, 1900–1940* (Chicago: University of Chicago Press, 1999), 69–109, "estimate" on 76, Riis on 79.

46. Ryan, *Civic Wars*, 203–209; Teaford, *The Unheralded Triumph*, 233 on the Brooklyn Bridge.

47. Olmsted's partner Calvert Vaux also "disliked discussion" and "wrangling of any kind." Roy Rosenzweig and Elizabeth Blackmar, *The Park and the People: A History of Central Park* (Ithaca, NY: Cornell University Press, 1992),15–205; Burrows and Wallace, *Gotham*, 790–795; Ryan, *Civic Wars*, 203–209; Teaford, *The Unheralded Triumph*, on Vaux, 142–143; Levine, *Highbrow/Lowbrow*, Olmsted on 183 and 186.

48. Ryan, *Civic Wars*, 203–209: "rush" and "potent" on 206, "arid" on 207; Baldwin, *Domesticating the Street*: 20–29, 261–266 passim, Bushnell on 25. What Nancy Cott calls the "canon of domesticity" profoundly shaped the design of parks and the larger city planning tradition in the United States. "The canon of domesticity," Cott argues, "expressed the dominance of what may be designated a middle-class ideal, a cultural preference for domestic retirement and conjugal family intimacy over both the 'vain' and fashionable sociability of the rich

and the promiscuous sociability of the poor." Nancy Cott, *The Bonds of Womanhood: Women's Sphere in New England, 1780–1835* (New Haven, CT: Yale University Press, 1977), 92.

49. Ryan, *Civic Wars*, 203–209; Burrows and Wallace, *Gotham*, "vacant" on 792, 951–953ff.; Daniel M. Bluestone, "From Promenade to Park: The Gregarious Origins of Brooklyn's Park Movement," *American Quarterly* 39 (Winter 1987), 529–549; Bluestone, *Constructing Chicago* (New Haven, CT: Yale University Press, 1991), 3–4, 36–61; Rosenzweig and Blackmar, *The Park and the People*, 211–233; Teaford, *The Unheralded Triumph*, 252–258, Whitman on 257.

50. Ryan, *Civic Wars*, 203–209; Rosenzweig and Blackmar, *The Park and the People*, 315, 391–392, 489–490; Baldwin, *Domesticating the Street*, 116–146, especially 119.

51. Frederick Law Olmsted, *Public Parks and the Enlargement of Towns* (New York: Arno Press, 1970), 19–22.

52. Ryan, *Civic Wars*, 183–203, "boudoir view" is a photographer's technical term, but it invokes the domestication of city life; on legibility, see Kevin Lynch, *The Image of the City* (Cambridge, MA: MIT Press, 1960).

53. Lumping large percentages of urbanites into the generic categories of "laborer" and "clerk," the census also revealed the demise of proprietorship and self-directed work. Ryan, *Civic Wars*, 185–194, "civic vertigo" is Ryan's phrase; Robert H. Wiebe, *Self-Rule: A Cultural History of American Democracy* (Chicago: University of Chicago Press, 1995), 113–137.

54. Ryan, *Civic Wars*, 185–196; Sam Bass Warner, Jr., "The Management of Multiple Urban Images," in *The Pursuit of Urban History*, ed. Derek Fraser and Anthony Sutcliffe (London: Edward Arnold, 1983), 383–394, the phrase "smoke, or bricks, or saloons" is Warner's.

55. Ryan, *Civic Wars*, 185–196; Gunthur Barth, *City People: The Rise of Modern City Culture in Nineteenth-Century America* (New York: Oxford University Press, 1980), 45–57, "moral" on 51, "excessive" on 47.

56. Ryan, *Civic Wars*, 194–203: "grass" on 198, "Saints" on 199; Barth, *City People*, 110–147.

57. Bluestone, *Constructing Chicago*, 104–151: "impart" and "occupy" on 143, "clouds" on 149, "culture" on 140.

58. Bluestone, *Constructing Chicago*, 143–151, "pigmies" on 149.

59. Ryan, *Civic Wars*, 209–217, "links" on 212; Barth, *City People*, "weakness" on 28; Olmsted, *Public Parks and the Enlargement of Towns*.

60. Smith, *Urban Disorder and the Shape of Belief*, 147–155, "civilization" on 149; Ryan, *Civic Wars*, other quotations on 209–217.

61. Jane Addams, *Twenty Years at Hull House* (New York: The Macmillan Co., 1910); Ryan, *Civic Wars*, 214–217, "absolutely" and "Whenever" on 215.

62. Trachtenberg, *The Incorporation of America*, 70–100, "lazy" on 71; Ryan, *Civic Wars*, 214–217, "kill" on 215; Quigley, *Second Founding*, 129–130, 149–151, 168–169.

63. This paragraph is based on a list compiled by historian Philip Foner, which includes twenty-one more epithets from the July 1877 issues of the *New York Times*; Trachtenberg, *The Incorporation of America*, 70–100, Foner's list on 71; Ryan, *Civic Wars*, 214–217; Roy Rozenzweig, *Eight Hours for What We Will* (New York: Cambridge University Press, 1983), "dirty" on 136–138.

64. Ryan, *Civic Wars*, 200, 217–222; Teaford, *The Unheralded Triumph*, 275–279.

65. Robert M. Fogelson, *America's Armories* (Cambridge: Harvard University Press, 1989); Ryan, *Civic Wars*, 200–222, "club" quoted on 219; Teaford, *The Unheralded Triumph*, 275–279; Quigley, *Second Founding*, 129–130, 149–151, 168–169, "heavy" on 129; Smith, *Urban Disorder and the Shape of Belief*; Jeremy Brecher, *Strike!* (Boston: MA South End Press, 1972), 1–100; Fredrickson, *The Inner Civil War*, 211–216; Boyer, *Urban Masses and Moral Order*, 143–161.

66. Quigley, *Second Founding*, 129–130, 149–151, 168–169; McGerr, *The Decline of Popular Politics*, 90–100; Trachtenberg, *The Incorporation of America*, 171.

67. McGerr, *The Decline of Popular Politics*, 90–100.

68. McGerr, *The Decline of Popular Politics*, 107–113: "great" on 108, "dissemination" on 111.

69. McGerr, *Decline of Popular Politics*, 107–122, Curtis on 115; Schudson, *The Good Citizen*, 174–182.

70. Quotations from Daniel T. Peirce, "Does the Press Reflect Public Opinion?" *Gunton Magazine* 19 (November 1900): 418–425; Lasch, *The Revolt of the Elites*, 172–175. Nor was "non-partisanship synonymous with moral superiority," for the independent journals perpetrated some of the "worst cases of misrepresentation and perversion of facts," a charge documented with a detailed examination of the distortions in two stories from the *Boston Herald* and the *New York Times*. See "Integrity of Newspaper Discussion," *Gunton Magazine* 19 (December 1900): 509–521.

71. McGerr, *The Decline of Popular Politics*, 107–134: "bewilder" on 122, "passionless" on 133, Greeley on 115; Lasch, *The Revolt of the Elites*, 161–175; the defense of a partisan press is from "Integrity of Newspaper Discussion," *Gunton Magazine* 19 (December 1900): 509–521.

72. Language also reflects the parting of the ways. The inclusive, popular civil rhetoric of the nineteenth century gave way to the technical, jargon-heavy language of reformers and professionals on the one hand, and the emotional but shallow rhetoric of sensational journalism and mass advertising on the other. McGerr, *The Decline of Popular Politics*, 100–106, 134–137, 145–151; Michael Schudson, *The Good Citizen: A History of American Civic Life* (New York: Martin-Kessler Books, 1998), 177; Christopher Lasch, *The Revolt of the Elites and the Betrayal of Democracy* (New York: W.W. Norton, 1995), 173–175; Kenneth Cmiel, *Democratic Eloquence* (New York: W. Morrow, 1990).

73. McGerr, *The Decline of Popular Politics*, 122–128; on the interview, see Schudson, *The Good Citizen*, 179–180.

74. The important issues of the day, complained a critic of Hearst, "drew half-columns of condensation. But if Taft puts on a sweater and walks around the Washington Monument, *that's* worth a half-column" (italics in original). McGerr, *The Decline of Popular Politics*, 127–129.

75. McGerr, *The Decline of Popular Politics*, 129–151, Steffins on 129; Lippmann, *Drift and Mastery* (New York: Mitchell Kennerley, 1914); Frank Luther Mott, *A History of American Magazines, 1885–1905*. vol.5 (Cambridge: Harvard University Press, 1938), 207–209, 395ff.

76. McGerr, *The Decline of Popular Politics*, 129–151, Roosevelt on 145.

77. McGerr, *The Decline of Popular Politics*, 129–151; Lawrence Goodwyn, *The Populist Moment: A Short History of the Agrarian Revolt in America* (New York: Oxford University Press, 1978), especially 45–54, 69–80, 206–212, 293–310.

78. "The Real American Ruler," *The Nation* 57 (August 24, 1893): 130–131; "Mob Violence," *The Nation* 63 (October 29, 1896): 322.

79. Daniel J. Czitrom, *Media and the American Mind from Morse to McLuhan* (Chapel Hill, NC: University of North Carolina Press, 1982), 20–29.

80. Czitrom, *Media and the American Mind*, 20–29.

81. Boyer, *Urban Masses and Moral Order*, 123–131; "imbecility" and "obstruction" in "Mobs," *Living Age* 196 (February 1893): 451–464; on Russia, see Boris Sidis, "A Study of the Mob," *Atlantic Monthly* 75 (February 1895): 188–197.

82. Gustave Le Bon, "The Work of Ideas in Human Evolution," *Popular Science Monthly* 47 (August 1895): 541–548.

83. Le Bon, "The Work of Ideas in Human Evolution," 541–548.

84. Edward A. Ross, "The Mob Mind," *Popular Science Monthly* 51 (July 1897): 390–398.

85. Ross, "The Mob Mind," 390–398.

86. Ross, "The Mob Mind," 390–398; see also Franklin Smith, "The Despotism of Democracy," *Popular Science Monthly* 51 (August 1897): 489–507.

87. Gerald Stanley Lee, "The Dominance of the Crowd," *Atlantic Monthly* 86 (December 1900): 754–761; Gregory W. Bush, *Lord of Attention: Gerald Stanley Lee and the Crowd Metaphor in Industrializing America* (Amherst, MA: University of Massachusetts Press, 1991); on Opper, see Michael Kazin, *The Populist Persuasion* (Ithaca, NY: Cornell University Press, 1998), 52.

PART III

1. Glenn Porter, *The Rise of Big Business* (Arlington Heights, IL: Harlan Davidson, 1992), 41–90; Mansel G. Blackford and K. Austin Kerr, *Business Enterprise in American History* (Boston: Houghton Mifflin, 1986), 152–225.

2. Alfred D. Chandler, *The Visible Hand: The Managerial Revolution in American Business* (Cambridge: Belknap Press, 1977); David F. Noble, *America by Design: Science, Technology, and the Rise of Corporate Capitalism* (New York: Knopf, 1977); Nick Salvatore, *Eugene V. Debs: Citizen and Socialist* (Urbana, IL: University of Illinois Press, 1982), 4–22ff.; Graham R. Taylor, *Satellite Cities: A Study of Industrial Suburbs* (New York: D. Appleton and Company, 1915); Jon C. Teaford, *Cities of the Heartland: The Rise and Fall of the Industrial Midwest* (Bloomington, IN: Indiana University Press, 1993), 109–110 on Gary; Herbert N. Casson, *The History of the Telephone* (Chicago: A.C. McClurg, 1910), 173–233, 289–299.

3. Theodore Roosevelt, *The New Nationalism, with an Introduction by Ernest Hamlin Abbott* (New York: The Outlook Company, 1910), 3–33; Richard L. McCormick, "The Discovery that Business Corrupts Politics: A Reappraisal of the Origins of Progressivism," *American Historical Review* 86 (April 1981): 247–274; Kevin Mattson, *Creating a Democratic Public: The Struggle for Urban Participatory Democracy during the Progressive Era* (University Park, PA: Pennsylvania State University Press, 1998), 7; Michael J. Sandel, *Democracy's Discontent: America in Search of a Public Philosophy* (Cambridge, MA: The Belknap Press of Harvard University Press, 1996), 201–249; James Weinstein, *The Corporate Ideal in the Liberal State, 1900–1918* (Boston: Beacon Press, 1968), 3–39, Perkins on 10.

4. Weinstein, *The Corporate Ideal in the Liberal State*, 3–39; William Leach, *Land of Desire: Merchants, Power, and the Rise of a New American Culture* (New York: Pantheon Books, 1993), 3–12 passim.

5. Benjamin Parke DeWitt, *The Progressive Movement: A Non-Partisan, Comprehensive Discussion of Current Tendencies in American Politics* (New York: Macmillian, 1915), 3–5; Charles Forcey, *The Crossroads of Liberalism* (New York: Oxford University Press, 1961), xviii–xix; Arthur S. Link and Richard L. McCormick, *Progressivism* (Arlington Heights, IL: Harlan Davidson, Inc., 1983), 21–25.

6. DeWitt, *The Progressive Movement*, 3–5; W.E.B. Dubois, *The Souls of the Black Folk* (New York: Vintage, 1996), 127; Walter Lippmann, *Drift and Mastery* (New York: Mitchell Kennerley, 1914), 14–18.

7. Mattson, *Creating a Democratic Public*, 77–85, "Good" on 77; Delos F. Wilcox, *The American City: A Problem in Democracy* (New York: The Macmillan Company, 1904),10–12, "kind" on 11; Christopher Lasch, *The True and Only Heaven: Progress and Its Critics* (New York: Norton, 1991), 340–352.

8. Herbert Croly, *Progressive Democracy* (1914; repr., New Brunswick, NJ: Transaction Publishers, 1998), 25–28, 424–430; Lasch, *The True and Only Heaven*, 168–170, 329–368.

CHAPTER 7

1. It was "absolutely essential for Americans at this time to grasp the debilitating effects of centralized control, both in the workplace and in politics," Christopher Lasch argues. The great need was "to reformulate a participatory conception of democracy, and to encourage a revival of active citizenship." But "few of them managed to confront this issue in any sustained way, in spite of all the talk about 'civic spirit,' in which prewar progressives liked to indulge."

Anxiety about the decay of civic life might "have led to a reassertion of republican principles in politics, education, and social thought—a rededication to the idea of citizenship that had played such an important part in the nation's founding." But "the republican idiom" had "begun to decay from disuse," Lasch concludes, "and those who tried to revive it found themselves ridiculed as cranks and visionaries." Christopher Lasch, *The True and Only Heaven: Progress and Its Critics* (New York: Norton, 1991), "absolutely" on 343, "reassertion" on 68, "republican idiom" on 64. John Patrick Diggins adds that the Progressive Era "political thinker felt it necessary to return to the foundations of his Republic," even if only to expose their inadequacy. Progressives, Diggins continues, "would have found in classical political thought an answer to the moral and political problems facing America at the turn of the century," except that "the idea of political virtue had ceased to have relevance and meaning in America." John P. Diggins, *The Lost Soul of American Politics: Virtue, Self-Interest, and the Foundations of Liberalism* (Chicago: University of Chicago Press, 1984), 126–130. Although Americans failed to effectively readapt republican ideals to the challenges they faced, Lasch and Diggins underestimate the extent to which progressives recognized and grappled with the importance of their republican inheritance and with the questions of corruption and civic virtue central to republicanism. "No concept, after all, had been more central to the Progressive vision of social reform than that of 'the public,'" writes Wilfred M. McClay in his "Introduction," to Walter Lippmann, *The Phantom Public* (1927; repr., New Brunswick, NJ: Transaction Publishers, 1993), xix–xx. "The progressives' favorite synonym for 'the people,'" writes Michael Kazin in distinguishing progressivism from nineteenth-century populism, "was 'citizens' or 'the public' rather than 'producers.' A desire to serve the interest of the whole was the coveted virtue, not whether one made a living performing manual work." Michael Kazin, *The Populist Persuasion* (Ithaca, NY: Cornell University Press, 1995), 51. On "moment," see J. G. A. Pocock, *The Machiavellian Moment: Florentine Political Thought and Atlantic Republican Tradition* (Princeton, NJ: Princeton University Press, 1975). Pocock's Machiavellian moment refers to a historical period (from the Renaissance to the American Revolution) when republican principles shaped political debate, but also to a moment in the life of every republic when its survival required that citizens reassert first principles.

2. Theodore Roosevelt, *The New Nationalism, with an Introduction by Ernest Hamlin Abbott* (New York: Outlook Company, 1910), 3; Michael J. Sandel, *Democracy's Discontent: America in Search of a Public Philosophy* (Cambridge, MA: The Belknap Press of Harvard University Press, 1996), 201–221, "free" on 215; Richard Hofstadter, *The American Political Tradition* (New York: Vintage Books, 1989), 327–336, "machinery" on 328.

3. James Weinstein, *The Corporate Ideal in the Liberal State, 1900–1918* (Boston: Beacon Press, 1968); Lasch, *The True and Only Heaven*, 312–353.

4. Herbert Croly, *Progressive Democracy* (1914; repr., New Brunswick, NJ: Transaction Publishers, 1998), 406; Delos F. Wilcox, *The American City: A Problem in Democracy* (New York: The Macmillan Company, 1904), 3–9, 27.

5. Michael J. Lacey, "Federalism and National Planning: The Nineteenth-Century Legacy," in *The American Planning Tradition: Culture and Policy*, ed. Robert Fishman (Washington, DC: Woodrow Wilson Center Press, 2000), 111–118; Jon C. Teaford, *Cities of the Heartland: The Rise and Fall of the Industrial Midwest* (Bloomington, IN: Indiana University Press, 1993), "chief" on 114; Roosevelt, *The New Nationalism*, 12–15; Kevin Mattson, *Creating a Democratic Public: The Struggle for Urban Participatory Democracy during the Progressive Era* (University Park, PA: Pennsylvania State University Press, 1998), 8–9; Thomas Bender, *New York Intellect* (Baltimore: Johns Hopkins University Press, 1987), xvi, 3–6; Thomas Bender, "Metropolitan Life and the Making of Public Culture," in *Power, Culture, and Place*, ed. John Mollenkompf (New York: Russell Sage Foundation, 1988), 261–269.

6. Paul Boyer, *Urban Masses and Moral Order in America, 1820–1920* (Cambridge: Harvard University Press, 1978), 123–131; Mike Davis, *The Ecology of Fear* (New York: Metropolitan Books, 1998), 273–293; Stanley K. Schultz, *Constructing Urban Culture: American Cities and City Planning, 1800–1920* (Philadelphia: Temple University Press, 1989), 3–32, quotation on 3.

7. Robert Westbrook, *John Dewey and American Democracy* (Ithaca, NY: Cornell University Press, 1991), 83–113, Dewey on 84; Louis Menand, *The Metaphysical Club* (New York: Farrar, Straus and Giroux, 2001), 285–333; John D. Fairfield, "A Populism for the Cities: John Dewey, Henry George and the City Planning Movement," *Urban Design Studies* 8 (2002): 19–27; Katherine Kish Sklar, "Hull House in the 1890s," *Signs* 10 (1985): 658–677.

8. Mattson, *Creating a Democratic Public*, 1–86, "improvement" on 1; Jean Quandt, *From the Small Town to the Great Community* (New Brunswick, NJ: Rutgers University Press, 1970); Stanley K. Schultz, "The Morality of Politics: The Muckrakers' Vision of Democracy," *Journal of American History* 52 (December 1965): 527–547.

9. Mattson, *Creating a Democratic Public*, 14–22, "soothe" on 17; William Wilson, *The City Beautiful Movement* (Baltimore: Johns Hopkins University Press, 1989); Charles Zueblin, "The Making of the City," *Chautauquan* 38 (November 1903): 275; Daniel Burnham, *The Plan of Chicago* (Chicago: The Commercial Club, 1909), 120–123; Boyer, *Urban Masses and Moral Order*, 261–276; Charles Mulford Robinson, *Modern Civic Art: Or the City Made Beautiful* (New York: G.P. Putnam's Sons, 1903), 81–91. On "pleasing prospects," see Raymond Williams, *The Country and the City* (New York: Oxford University Press, 1973), 120–126 passim; Alan Trachtenberg, *The Incorporation of America* (New York: Hill and Wang, 1982), 208–234.

10. Mattson, *Creating a Democratic Public*, 14–24.

11. Jane Addams, *Twenty Years at Hull House* (New York: The Macmillan Co., 1910), 115–127; Jane Addams, "A Modern Lear," in *The Social Thought of Jane Addams*, ed. Christopher Lasch (Indianapolis: Bobbs-Merrill, 1965), 114–123; Mattson, *Creating a Democratic Public*, 22–30; Christopher Lasch, *The New Radicalism in America* (New York: Knopf, 1965), 3–37.

12. Mattson, *Creating a Democratic Public*, quoted passages on 23–30; M. Christine Boyer, *Dreaming the Rational City: The Myth of American City Planning* (Cambridge: MIT Press, 1983), 1–56.

13. On Zueblin, see Mattson, *Creating a Democratic Public*, 24–30; on Columbia, see Bender, *New York Intellect*, 265–293.

14. Mattson, *Creating a Democratic Public*, quotations on 25–30; Peter Novick, *That Noble Dream: The "Objectivity Question" and the American Historical Profession* (New York: Cambridge University Press, 1988), 61–85.

15. Mattson, *Creating a Democratic Public*, 25–30; Novick, *That Noble Dream:* "partisan" was the reason offered by the chair of the Department of Political Economy for the dismissal of the public lecturer Edward Bemis who supported the Pullman strikers, 68, "sympathize" on 64; Westbrook, *John Dewey and American Democracy*, 59–113, especially 83–92.

16. Mattson, *Creating a Democratic Public*, 31–36, "intelligent" and "city" on 32; Frederic C. Howe, *The City: The Hope of Democracy* (New York: C. Scribner's Sons, 1905), 114–123 passim; Teaford, *Cities of the Heartland*, 111–123; Jon Teaford, "Home Rule," in *Encyclopedia of Urban America*, ed. Neil Larry Shumsky (Santa Barbara, CA: ABC-CLIO, 1998), 345–346; John D. Fairfield, *The Mysteries of the Great City: The Politics of Urban Design, 1877–1937* (Columbus, OH: Ohio State University Press, 1993), 83–95.

17. Mattson, *Creating a Democratic Public*, 31–36: "self-government" and "republic" on 34, "Home" quoted on 35, "real" on 36; Frederic C. Howe, *The City: The Hope of Democracy*, 114–123 passim; Teaford, *Cities of the Heartland*, 111–123; Fairfield, *Mysteries of the Great City*, 83–95.

18. Frederic C. Howe, "The City as a Socializing Agency," *American Journal of Sociology* 17 (March 1912): 590–601; Frederic C. Howe, "City Building in Germany," *Scribner's Magazine* 47 (May 1910): 601–614.

19. Henry George, *Progress and Poverty* (New York: H. George, 1887), on "improvement" and "decay," 427–439, quoted passages on 432 and 437; Henry George, *Social Problems* (New York: Doubleday, Page & Company, 1883), passim, "social intelligence" and "public opinion" on 2–3, "virtue enough" on 213, "moral and intellectual" on 216; Lasch, *The True and Only Heaven*, 63–67; John L. Thomas, *Alternative America: Henry George, Edward*

Bellamy, Henry Demarest Lloyd and the Adversary Tradition (Cambridge: Belknap Press, 1983), 102–131; Fairfield, *Mysteries of the Great City*, 21–41.

20. George, *Progress and Poverty*, 207–219, 410. The "enormous value which the presence of a million and a half of people gives to the land of this city," George declared during his mayoral campaign in New York City in 1886, "belongs properly to the whole community" and should be "applied to the improvement and beautifying of the city, to the promotion of the health, comfort, education, and recreation of its people." Louis F. Post and Fred C. Luebuscher, *Henry George's 1886 Campaign* (Westport, CT: Hyperion Press, 1976), 14. Dewey recognized that George condemned monopoly and privilege not only because it generated poverty, "but especially because it renders one-sided and inequitable the people's share in these higher values." John Dewey, "Socialization of Ground Rent" (1935), in *John Dewey: The Later Works, 1925–1953*, ed. Jo Ann Boydston (Carbondale, IL: Southern Illinois University Press, 1990), 11: 256–257.

21. The Georgists were an important component of the "urban liberalism" examined in John Buenker, *Urban Liberalism and Progressive Reform* (New York: Scribner, 1973); "Editorial Confidences," *The Public* 14 (January 6, 1911): 3; Fairfield, "A Populism for the Cities."

22. All these articles and quotations are taken from a sampling of volume 13 of *The Public*, February 11, 1910 through December 9, 1910.

23. Mattson, *Creating a Democratic Public*, 36–40.

24. Mattson, *Creating a Democratic Public*, 36–40: "indifference" on 38, "learn" on 39; the tent meeting resembled the political culture of rural populism; see Lawrence Goodwyn, *The Populist Moment: A Short History of the Agrarian Revolt in America* (New York: Oxford University Press, 1978) 20–54 passim. "The people need to 'see themselves' experimenting in democratic forms," Goodwyn writes on the opening page of his study (facing xxviii).

25. Mattson, *Creating a Democratic Public*, 39–43.

26. Mattson, *Creating a Democratic Public*, 39–43.

27. Mattson, *Creating a Democratic Public*, 42–45; Croly, *Progressive Democracy*, 305–310; Charles Forcey, *The Crossroads of Liberalism: Croly, Weyl, Lippmann, and the Progressive Era, 1900–1925* (New York: Oxford University Press, 1961), 155–160.

28. Mattson, *Creating a Democratic Public*, 43–47 (italics in original). Expertise became political knowledge, Dewey argued, only through "that common understanding and thorough communication which is the precondition of the existence of a genuine and effective public." Experts should be understood as experts in inquiry, not "in framing and executing policies." Only the public could "judge of the bearing of the knowledge supplied by others upon common concerns." John Dewey, *The Public and Its Problems* (1927) in *John Dewey: The Later Works, 1925–1953*, ed. Jo Ann Boydston (Carbondale, IL, 1984), 364–366; Timothy V. Kaufman-Osborne, "Pragmatism, Policy Science, and the State," *American Journal of Political Science* 29 (1985): 840–867.

29. The next eight paragraphs are based on Mattson, *Creating a Democratic Public*, 46–92.

30. Thus, Follett attempted to reconcile pragmatism (the collective search for a contingent truth always open to question) with idealism (unity and certainty based on transcendent truth). She accepted pragmatism's emphasis on pluralism and difference, but saw interpenetration as generating a synthesis of opinion that represented a higher unity—though an always changing unity rather than a transcendent, static unity. Mattson, *Creating a Democratic Public*, 91–102; Westbrook, *John Dewey and American Democracy*, 117–194.

31. Mattson, *Creating a Democratic Public*, 94–104.

32. Croly, *Progressive Democracy*, 260–270, 280–285, 320–329; Lasch, *The True and Only Heaven*, 342–345.

33. Daniel J. Czitrom, *Media and the American Mind: From Morse to McLuhan* (Chapel Hill, NC: University of North Carolina Press, 1982), 91–100.

34. Czitrom, *Media and the American Mind*, 102–108, Ford and Park on 105; Westbrook, *John Dewey and American Democracy*, 51–58: "extends" on 58, "dead" and "untried" on 53.

35. Czitrom, *Media and the American Mind*, 91–100, Cooley quoted on 99–100. The movies heightened the vicarious and irresponsible enjoyment of extreme situations that trou-

bled Cooley. One of the great appeals of the movies was their "ability to give viewers access to events that happened when they were not there, to the dangerous, the fantastic, the grotesque, the impossible, at a close but safe remove." Robert Sklar, *Movie-Made America: A Social History of American Movies* (New York: Random House, 1975), 21.

36. Czitrom, *Media and the American Mind*, 100–119: Cooley on 101, Park on 118–119; Robert E. Park, *The Crowd and the Public and Other Essays* (Chicago: University of Chicago Press, 1972).

37. John Collier, "Leisure Time: The Last Problem of Conservation," *Recreation* 6 (June 1912): 93–106; Czitrom, *Media and the American Mind*, 100–102, 115–119; Jim Cullen, *The Art of Democracy* (New York: Monthly Review Press, 1996), chap. 4 passim; Lary May, *Screening Out the Past: The Birth of Mass Culture and the Motion Picture Industry* (Chicago: University of Chicago Press, 1980), 3–146.

38. Collier, "Leisure Time," 93–106; Benjamin Parke DeWitt, *The Progressive Movement: A Non-Partisan, Comprehensive Discussion of Current Tendencies in American Politics* (New York: Macmillan, 1915), 362. Percy MacKaye added that a civic theater "implies the conscious awakening of a people to self-government in the activities of its leisure." MacKaye referred to live drama rather than movies. Percy MacKaye, *The Civic Theatre: In Relation to the Redemption of Leisure* (New York: M. Kennerly, 1912), 15.

39. Sklar, *Movie-Made America*, 3–17; Steven J. Ross, *Working-Class Hollywood: Silent Film and the Shaping of Class in America* (Princeton, NJ: Princeton University Press, 1998), 3–16; Cullen, *The Art of Democracy*, 115; Lawrence W. Levine, *Highbrow/Lowbrow: The Emergence of Cultural Hierarchy in America* (Cambridge: Harvard University Press, 1988), 231–235. In his famous essay, "The Work of Art in an Age of Mechanical Reproduction," Walter Benjamin argued that the mass production of cultural artifacts destroyed the aura of elite cultural artifacts and resulted in "the liquidation of the traditional value of the cultural heritage." In the American context, what Benjamin described was the assault on a cultural hierarchy of quite recent invention. Walter Benjamin, *Illuminations* (New York: Harcourt Brace & World, 1968), 221. What might be called "Habermasian doubt"—the concern for the deteriorating quality of public discourse that accompanied the quantitative expansion of the public—is inseparable from the growing importance of images in public discourse. But Collier and others thought that visual literacy might be taught. Jurgen Habermas, *The Structural Transformation of the Public Sphere* (Cambridge, MA: MIT Press, 1989). For a popular and engaging version of "Habermasian doubt," see Neal Gabler, *Life: The Movie* (New York: Knopf, 1998).

40. Ross, *Working-Class Hollywood*, 5–8, 34–111, "joy" on 13; Czitrom, *Media and the American Mind*, 41–50; Sklar, *Movie-Made America*, 33–47; May, *Screening Out the Past*, 36, and Czitrom, *Media and the American Mind*, 49–50; William R. Taylor, *Inventing Times Square: Commerce and Culture at the Crossroads of the World* (Baltimore: Johns Hopkins University Press, 1991), 16–50 passim; Neal Gabler, *An Empire of Their Own: How the Jews Created Hollywood* (New York: Crown Publishers, 1988).

41. Barton W. Currie, "The Nickel Madness," *Harper's Weekly* 51 (August 24, 1907): 1246; Czitrom, *Media and the American Mind*, 43–59: "blow" on 45, "weariness" on 44, "cruel" on 56; May, *Screening Out the Past*, 38–42; Sklar, *Movie-Made America*, 18–32; Ross, *Working-Class Hollywood*, 24–30; Kathy Peiss, *Cheap Amusements: Working Women and Leisure in Turn-of-the-Century New York* (Philadelphia: Temple University Press, 1986), 148–158.

42. May, *Screening Out the Past*, 38–42, "biggest" on 39; Sklar, *Movie-Made America*, 125–126, "laws," "soul," and "alone" on 126; Czitrom, *Media and the American Mind*, 56–59, "field" on 57.

43. Sklar, *Movie-Made America*, 125–126, "intensify," "suggestibility," and "incomparable" on 126; Czitrom, *Media and the American Mind*, 56–59, "enthusiasm" on 58.

44. Czitrom, *Media and the American Mind*, "learn" on 58; May, *Screening Out the Past*, 35–42, "something" on 36; Ross, *Working-Class Hollywood*, 5–24; Peiss, *Cheap Amusements*, 139–162.

45. Ross, *Working-Class Hollywood*, 5–24: "twinkling" on 18, "wasted" on 6; Peiss, *Cheap Amusements*, 139–162; May, *Screening Out the Past*, 35–42; John Collier, "Censorship and the National Board," *Survey* 34 (October 2, 1915): 9–14, 31–33, "agent" on 31.

46. Walter Prichard Eaton, "Class-Consciousness and the 'Movies,'" *Atlantic Monthly* 115 (January 1915): 49–51; Ross, *Working-Class Hollywood*, 24–30; May, *Screening Out the Past*, 38–42; Judith Mayne, "Immigrants and Spectators," *Wide Angle* 5 (1982): 33; Miriam Hansen, "Early Silent Cinema: Whose Public Sphere?" *New German Critique* 29 (Spring/Summer 1983): 158.

47. Ross, *Working-Class Hollywood*, 34–35, 73–74, 81–85, 98–99.

48. Ross, *Working-Class Hollywood*, 34–35, 73–74, 81–85, 98–99.

49. Ross, *Working-Class Hollywood*, 5–35, 73–74, 81–99: "Far" on 5, "crowds" on 91; Kay Sloan, *The Loud Silents: Origins of the Social Problem Film* (Urbana, IL: Universsity of Illinois Press, 1988).

50. Ross, *Working-Class Hollywood*, 34–55; for a brief, useful discussion of "Easy Street," see Sklar, *Movie-Made America*, 113, but there is no substitute for viewing the widely available film *Easy Street* (1917) in *Charlie Chaplin: The Early Years*, vol. 2, VHS, directed by Charlie Chaplin (Los Angeles: Republic Pictures Home Video, 1989); May, *Screening Out the Past*, 43–59. Although he does not discuss "Easy Street," May's discussion of "Rescuing the Family: Urban Progressivism and Modern Leisure" links the issues Chaplin's film raises to the Progressive Era concern that the rise of large-scale enterprise and a consumer culture undermined both individual character and family cohesion.

51. Ross, *Working-Class Hollywood*, 36–42, "moral" on 38; May, *Screening Out the Past*, 80–85; Michael McGerr, *The Decline of Popular Politics: The American North, 1865–1928* (New York: Oxford University Press, 1986), 165.

52. Ross, *Working-Class Hollywood*, 34–111.

53. Ross, *Working-Class Hollywood*, 34–111: "insanity" on 92, "breaking" on 102.

54. May, *Screening Out the Past*, 54–60; Czitrom, *Media and the American Mind*, 46–54; Sklar, *Movie-Made America*, 30–32; Nancy Rosenbloom, "Between Reform and Regulation: The Struggle over Film Censorship in Progressive America, 1909–1922," *Film History* 1 (1987): 307–308.

55. May, *Screening Out the Past*, 54–60; Czitrom, *Media and the American Mind*, 46–54, "public" on 53; Sklar, *Movie-Made America*, 30–32; Garth S. Jowett, "'A Capacity for Evil': The 1915 Supreme Court *Mutual* Decision," *Historical Journal of Film, Radio, and Television* 9 (1989): 59–78; Rosenbloom, "Between Reform and Regulation," 307–308. The following discussion is indebted to Linda Dehner, "The *Mutual* Decision of 1915: Legalized Censorship and Its Effect on the Democratic Potential of the Motion Picture," undergraduate thesis, Xavier University, Cincinnati, Ohio, 1998.

56. Collier, "Leisure Time," "sociability" and "consciousness" on 99; Collier, "Censorship and the National Board," "civic" on 32; Jowett, "'A Capacity for Evil'"; John Collier, "The Learned Judges and the Films," *Survey* 34 (September 4, 1915): 513–516.

57. Eaton, "Class Consciousness and the 'Movies,'" 50–53; Ross, *Working-Class Hollywood*, 86–111; Czitrom, *Media and the American Mind*, 43–48: Edward Ross quoted on 43, Patten quoted on 45.

58. Czitrom, *Media and the American Mind*, 43–59: "recreation" on 44, Pittsburgh study on 49; Jane Addams, *The Spirit of Youth and the City Streets* (New York: Macmillan, 1909), 98.

59. Frederic Howe, "What to Do with the Motion-Picture Show: Shall It Be Censored?" *Outlook* 107 (June 20, 1914): 412–416; Rosenbloom, "Between Reform and Regulation," 315–317.

60. Jowett, "A Capacity for Evil," "youngest" on 71; John Collier, "Before the Footlights: The School-Keeping of the Motion-Picture Showmen," *Survey* 34 (July 3, 1915): "proof" on 315; May, *Screening Out the Past*, 54–58; for the various activities of the National Board of Review, see the Papers of the National Board of Review of Motion Pictures, Special Collections, New York Public Library; Nancy J. Rosenbloom, "From Regulation to Censorship: Film

and Political Culture in New York in the Early Twentieth Century," *Journal of the Gilded Age and Progressive Era* 3 (October 2004), 369–406.

61. Gilbert Montague, "Censorship of Motion Pictures before the Supreme Court," *Survey* 34 (April 24, 1915), "extra-legal" on 83; censorship as political as well as moral is the judgment of Richard Randall, *Censorship of the Movies: The Social and Political Control of a Mass Medium* (Madison: University of Wisconsin Press, 1968), 23; Sklar, *Movie-Made America*, 127–128. The decision was overturned in *Burstyn v. Wilson* (1952).

62. *Mutual Film Corp. v. Industrial Commission*, 236 U.S. 230; Randall, *Censorship of the Movies*, 18–25; Ira Carmen, *Movies, Censorship, and the Law* (Ann Arbor, MI: University of Michigan Press, 1966), 10–15; John Wertheimer, "*Mutual Film* Reviewed: The Movies, Censorship, and Free Speech in Progressive America," *American Journal of Legal History* 37 (1993): 158–161.

63. Collier, "The Learned Judges and the Films," 513–516: "guaranty" on 513, "in those" and "fundamentally" on 516; Collier, "Before the Footlights," "star-chambered" on 320; on *The Strike at Coaldale*, see John Collier, "Censorship in Action," *Survey* 34 (August 7, 1915): 424.

64. "Censorship of Motion Pictures," *Yale Law Journal* 49 (November 1939): 94–95; "Motion Pictures and the First Amendment," *Yale Law Journal* 60 (1951): 699–705; Ross, *Working-Class Hollywood*, 108–110, 215, 235; *Times Film Corp. v. Chicago*, 365 U.S. 43 (1961), 69–72; May, *Screening Out the Past*, 82–95, "malignant" on 83; Ross, *Working-Class Hollywood*, 108 and 310n54; *Intolerance* (1916) VHS, directed by D. W. Griffith (Los Angeles: Kino Video, 1990).

65. May, *Screening Out the Past*, 82–93; *Intolerance*; Foster Rhea Dulles and Melvin Dubofsky, *Labor in America* (Arlington Heights, IL: Harlan Davidson, 1984), 207–211.

66. May, *Screening Out the Past*, 82–93; the defense of *Intolerance* from an unsigned typescript, Box 105, National Board of Review of Motion Pictures.

67. As major corporations with labor problems of their own, the studios encouraged films that condemned labor radicalism. Ross, *Working-Class Hollywood*, 115–142, 173–211, "United" on 120; Sklar, *Movie-Made America*, 82–85, 127–157; May, *Screening Out the Past*, 200–236, on the "Big Eight" firms of Hollywood, see table IIIa, 253.

68. Ross, *Working-Class Hollywood*, 143–172.

69. Ross, *Working-Class Hollywood*, 212–239.

70. Ross, *Working-Class Hollywood*, 212–239.

71. Sklar, *Movie-Made America*, 3–157ff.; Ross, *Working-Class Hollywood*, 168–239, "insidious" on 177–178; May, *Screening Out the Past*, 147–236.

72. Ross, *Working-Class Hollywood*, 203–211; Lizabeth Cohen, *Making a New Deal: Industrial Workers in Chicago, 1919–1939* (New York: Cambridge University Press, 1990), 120–147; Walter Lippmann, *Public Opinion* (New York: Harcourt, Brace and Company, 1922), 90–91; Habermas, *The Structural Transformation of the Public Sphere*, 181–210; McGerr, *The Decline of Popular Politics*, 107–183; Gabler, *Life: The Movie*. For a discussion of an ultimately failed effort to revive the democratic potential of movies in the 1930s, see Lary May, *The Big Tomorrow* (Chicago: University of Chicago Press, 2002).

73. Ross, *Working-Class Hollywood*, 203–211; Lippmann, *Public Opinion*, 91 and 254.

74. Howe, "What to Do with the Motion-Picture Show: Shall It Be Censored?"; Collier, "The Learned Judges and the Films," "field" on 513; Ross, *Working-Class Hollywood*, 86–111; Wilton A. Barrett, "The Work of the National Board of Review," *The Annals of the Academy of Political and Social Sciences* 128 (November 1926): 176–184.

CHAPTER 8

1. Walter F. Weyl, "The Sovereign Crowd," *The New Republic* 4 (October 9, 1915): 266–267.

2. Robert W. Bruere, "Can Democracy Be Efficient?" *Harpers' Magazine* 134 (May 1917): 821–826; Kevin Mattson, *Creating a Democratic Public: The Struggle for Urban Participatory*

Democracy during the Progressive Era (University Park, PA: Pennsylvania State University Press, 1998), 105–127.

3. Mattson, *Creating a Democratic Public*, 106–109; David M. Kennedy, *Over Here: The First World War and American Society* (New York: Oxford University Press, 1980), 48–92, 231–295.

4. Kennedy, *Over Here*, 269–291; James R. Green, *The World of the Worker: Labor in Twentieth-Century America* (New York: Hill and Wang, 1980), 93–99.

5. Henry Adams Bellows, "The Crowd in Action," *The Bellman* 26 (June 28, 1919): 721–723; Everett Dean Martin, *The Behavior of Crowds: A Psychological Study* (New York: Harper & Brothers, 1920), 1–13. Martin served as the director of the Cooper Union Forum of the People's Institute; Charles Forcey, *The Crossroads of Liberalism* (New York: Oxford University Press, 1961), 281.

6. Christopher Lasch, *The New Radicalism in America* (New York: Knopf, 1965), 182–185; Thomas Bender, *New York Intellect* (Baltimore:Johns Hopkins University Press, 1987), 241–249; Casey Nelson Blake, *Beloved Community: The Cultural Criticism of Randolph Bourne, Van Wyck Brooks, Waldo Frank, and Lewis Mumford* (Chapel Hill, NC: University of NorthCalolina Press, 1990), 157–180.

7. Walter Lippmann, *Public Opinion* (New York: Harcourt, Brace and Company, 1922), "too" on 16; Walter Lippmann, *The Phantom Public* (New York: New York University Press, 1925); Robert Westbrook, *John Dewey and American Democracy* (Ithaca, NY: Cornell University Press, 1991), 275–286; Kennedy, *Over Here*, 91–92.

8. Westbrook, *John Dewey and American Democracy*, 195–318: "shown" on 202, Bourne on 208; Blake, *Beloved Community*, 157–180.

9. Lippmann, *Public Opinion*, "failure" on 365; John Dewey, *The Public and Its Problems* (1927) in *John Dewey: The Later Works, 1925–1953*, ed. Jo Ann Boydston (Carbondale, IL: Southern Illinois University Press, 1984); John Dewey, "Review of *Public Opinion*," *New Republic* 30 (May 1922): 286–288; John Dewey, "Practical Democracy," review of Lippmann, *The Phantom Public*, in *The New Republic* 45 (December 2, 1925): 52–54; Robert E. Park, "Review of *Public Opinion*," *American Journal of Sociology* 28 (September 1922): 232–234; "essential" is from Dewey, *The Public and Its Problems*, quoted in Mattson, *Creating a Democratic Public*, 1. For a discussion of the Dewey-Lippmann debate that reflects the long, pessimistic shadow it cast, see Michael Schudson, *The Good Citizen: A History of American Civic Life* (New York: Martin-Kessler, 1998), 211–219; Michael Schudson, "The 'Lippmann-Dewey Debate' and the Invention of Walter Lippmann as an Anti-Democrat 1986–1996," *International Journal of Communication* 2 (2008): 1031–1042; for an effort to build on Dewey's side of the argument, see Benjamin Barber, *Strong Democracy: Participatory Politics for a New Age* (Berkeley: University of California Press, 1984).

10. Ronald Steel, *Walter Lippmann and the American Century* (Boston: Little, Brown, 1980), 12–44.

11. Steel, *Walter Lippmann and the American Century*, 33–87.

12. Westbrook, *John Dewey and American Democracy*; Louis Menand, *The Metaphysical Club* (New York: Farrar, Straus and Giroux, 2001), 285–316, "Chicago" on 318; Mattson, *Creating a Democratic Public*, "socialism" on 50.

13. Mattson, *Creating a Democratic Public*, "public" on 50; Westbrook, *John Dewey and American Democracy*, "agencies" on 192.

14. Westbrook, *John Dewey and American Democracy*, 113; Bender, *New York Intellect*.

15. Forcey, *The Crossroads of Liberalism*, 3–5, 223–272; Westbrook, *John Dewey and American Democracy*, 193–194; Steel, *Walter Lippmann and the American Century*, 59–62; Bender, *New York Intellect*, 222–245.

16. Bender, *New York Intellect*, 222–245: "inclusive" on 224, "terrifying" on 243; Westbrook, *John Dewey and American Democracy*, 193–194.

17. Kennedy, *Over Here*, 14–19, 30–38, 99–113, Howe on 34; Forcey, *The Crossroads of Liberalism*, 225–234; Arthur S. Link, *Woodrow Wilson and the Progressive Era* (New York: Harper, 1954), 174–196; Lasch, *The New Radicalism in America*, 184–188.

18. Kennedy estimates that 95 percent of federal taxes were shifted to those with incomes over $20,000 (16). Kennedy, *Over Here*, 3–44, 99–113; Forcey, *The Crossroads of Liberalism*, 241–263, "associating" on 252; Link, *Woodrow Wilson and the Progressive Era*, 174–251.

19. Steel, *Walter Lippmann and the American Century*, 71–115.

20. Steel, *Walter Lippmann and the American Century*, 110–115: "believed" on 107, "Decision" on 113; Lasch, *The New Radicalism*, 223; Kennedy, *Over Here*, 39–44, 91–92, "Colorado" on 39; James Weinstein, *The Corporate Ideal in the Liberal State, 1900–1918* (Boston: Beacon Press, 1968), 214–216.

21. Westbrook, *John Dewey and American Democracy*, 195–202.

22. Westbrook, *John Dewey and American Democracy*, 195–202.

23. Westbrook, *John Dewey and American Democracy*, 196–212, 275–278: "depth" on 197, "fruitful" on 198, "sensed" on 275; Blake, *Beloved Community*, 157–169; Kennedy, *Over Here*, 45–53.

24. Westbrook, *John Dewey and American Democracy*, 196–212, 233–235, 275–278, "Failure" on 206; Blake, *Beloved Community*, 157–169, "plastic" on 159; Kennedy, *Over Here*, 45–53.

25. Westbrook, *John Dewey and American Democracy*, 202–212; 275–278: "glamour" on 205, "competency" on 276, "consciousness" on 277; Kennedy, *Over Here*, 45–53.

26. Kennedy, *Over Here*, 45–49ff.; Lasch, *The New Radicalism in America*, 141–250; Westbrook, *John Dewey and American Democracy*, 150–318; Mattson, *Creating a Democratic Public*, 105–115, "train" on 106.

27. Kennedy, *Over Here*, 42–92; Mattson, *Creating a Democratic Public*, 105–115, "white-hot" on 107; Lasch, *The New Radicalism in America*, 141–250; Richard Hofstadter, *The American Political Tradition* (New York: Vintage Books, 1989), 307–365.

28. Forcey, *The Crossroads of Liberalism*, 3–11, 174–185, 223–272; Lasch, *The New Radicalism in America*, 182–185, 205–213: "malleable" on 206, "absolute" on 208, "coercion" on 209; Link, *Woodrow Wilson and the Progressive Era*, 174–196; Kennedy, *Over Here*, 3–44; Bender, *New York Intellect*, 241–249; Blake, *Beloved Community*, 157–180.

29. Kennedy, *Over Here*, 45–59, "primarily" on 55; Lasch, *The New Radicalism in America*, 199–213.

30. Kennedy, *Over Here*, 59–61 (italics in original).

31. Steven J. Ross, *Working-Class Hollywood: Silent Film and the Shaping of Class in America* (Princeton, NJ: Princeton University Press, 1998), 123–126, "sell" on 123, "bring" on 124; Kennedy, *Over Here*, 60–63, "spreads" and "singing" on 62.

32. Mattson, *Creating a Democratic Public*, 106–115, "School" and "piece" on 108; Kennedy, *Over Here*, 48–66.

33. Mattson, *Creating a Democratic Public*, 109–115.

34. Kennedy, *Over Here*, 63–75.

35. Kennedy, *Over Here*, 67–73.

36. Kennedy, *Over Here*, 75–88.

37. Steel, *Walter Lippmann and the American Century*, 45–57, 77–80, 100–124: Wilson on 124, Bourne on 114; Lasch, *The New Radicalism*, 162–163, 205–213, Dewey on 213; Blake, *Beloved Community*, 157–169; Westbrook, *John Dewey and American Democracy*, 196–197, 203–212.

38. Steel, *Walter Lippmann and the American Century*, 116–132.

39. Steel, *Walter Lippmann and the American Century*, 131–140.

40. Steel, *Walter Lippmann and the American Century*, 140–151, "away" on 142; Lasch, *The New Radicalism*, 221.

41. Steel, *Walter Lippmann and the American Century*, 149–154.

42. Westbrook, *John Dewey and American Democracy*, 223–227.

43. Westbrook, *John Dewey and American Democracy*, 223–227.

44. Westbrook, *John Dewey and American Democracy*, 147–149, 202–204, 367–373, "unanalyzed term" and "Workmen" on 204; Kennedy, *Over Here*, 45–53, "least" on 51; Blake, *Beloved Community*, 157–169, Bourne's critique of pragmatism on 158–161.

45. Kennedy, *Over Here*, 51–53, "peculiar" and "If" on 52; Westbrook, *John Dewey and American Democracy*, 204–212.

46. Lippmann even fed information to the Senate committee orchestrating the treaty's defeat. Steel, *Walter Lippmann and the American Century*, 153–170.

47. Steel, *Walter Lippmann and the American Century*, 153–170.

48. Steel, *Walter Lippmann and the American Century*, 171–180: "reexamine" on 170, "premium" and "basic" on 172; Lasch, *The True and Only Heaven*, 363–366, 412–416, "steady" on 364.

49. Lippmann, *Public Opinion*, "picture" on 29–30; Westbrook, *John Dewey and American Democracy*, 293–300.

50. Lippmann, *Public Opinion*, "picked" on 81, "common" on 206; Westbrook, *John Dewey and American Democracy*, 293–300.

51. Unlike Lippmann, Robert Park recognized that the crucial function of the news was to "make people talk and think, for most people do not think until they begin to talk." Lippmann, *Public Opinion*, "like" on 364, "hidden" on 358; Steel, *Walter Lippmann and the American Century*, 171–185; Lasch, *The True and Only Heaven*, 363–366, "remedy" on 364–365 is Lasch's gloss on Lippmann; Christopher Lasch, *The Revolt of the Elites and the Betrayal of Democracy* (New York: W. W. Norton & Company, 1995), 161–175; Robert E. Park, "Review of *Public Opinion*," *American Journal of Sociology* 28 (September 1922): 232–234.

52. Lippmann, *The Phantom Public*, "theory" on 101–102, "false" on 28–29; Steel, *Walter Lippmann and the American Century*, 211–216; Lasch, *The True and Only Heaven*, 363–366.

53. Lippmann, *The Phantom Public*, 93–145: "law" on 93, "support" on 114, "place" on 145; Steel, *Walter Lippmann and the American Century*; Lasch, *The True and Only Heaven*, 363–366; for a fuller history of the "procedural republic," see Michael J. Sandel, *Democracy's Discontent: America in Search of a Public Philosophy* (Cambridge, MA: The Belknap Press of Harvard University Press, 1996).

54. This and the next two paragraphs are based on Westbrook, *John Dewey and American Democracy*, 231–274.

55. Lasch, *The True and Only Heaven*, 412–416.

56. Westbrook, *John Dewey and American Democracy*, 275–280.

57. Westbrook, *John Dewey and American Democracy*, 275–286; David M. Ricci, *The Tragedy of Political Science: Politics, Scholarship, and Democracy* (New Haven, CT: Yale University Press, 1984); Lasch, *The True and Only Heaven*, 412–421; Kennedy, *Over Here*, 45–92; Lasch, *The New Radicalism in America*, 181–224; Mattson, *Creating a Democratic Public*, 115–120.

58. Westbrook, *John Dewey and American Democracy*, 281–285.

59. Mattson, *Creating a Democratic Public*, 115–127; Robert E. Park, "Community Organization and the Romantic Temper," in Robert E. Park and Ernest W. Burgess, *The City* (Chicago: University of Chicago Press, 1925), 113–122, "incompetent" on 113, "busy" on 117; Westbrook, *John Dewey and American Democracy*, 282–286.

60. Park, "Community Organization and the Romantic Temper," "restless" on 117, "seeking" on 118; Mattson, *Creating a Democratic Public*, 123–127, "foreground" on 123–124.

61. This and the following two paragraphs are based on Westbrook, *John Dewey and American Democracy*, 288–300.

62. Westbrook, *John Dewey and American Democracy*, 298–313; Dewey, *The Public and Its Problems*.

63. Westbrook, *John Dewey and American Democracy*, 298–313; Dewey, *The Public and Its Problems*.

64. Westbrook, *John Dewey and American Democracy*, 309–312; Dewey, *The Public and Its Problems*; Timothy V. Kaufman-Osborne, "Pragmatism, Policy Science, and the State," *American Journal of Political Science* 29 (1985), 827–849.

65. Westbrook, *John Dewey and American Democracy*, 313–315; Dewey, *The Public and Its Problems*; James W. Carey, *Communication as Culture: Essays on Media and Society* (Boston: Unwin Hyman, 1989); Lasch, *The Revolt of the Elites*, 161–175.

66. Dewey, *The Public and Its Problems*, 371.

67. Dewey did play a leading role in launching the city-oriented New School for Social Research in 1919. Dewey, *The Public and Its Problems*, 322–323, 367–372; Westbrook, *John Dewey and American Democracy*, 278, 314–316; Timothy V. Kaufmann-Osborne, "John Dewey and the Liberal Science of Community," *Journal of Politics* 46 (1984): 1153–1159.

68. Ross, *Working-Class Hollywood*, 115–142, 173–211: "presented" on 124, "essential" on 125.

69. Ross, *Working-Class Hollywood*, 127–142, 173–211.

70. Dewey, *The Public and Its Problems*, 214, 368–371; Westbrook, *John Dewey and American Democracy*, 298–300; Lasch, *The True and Only Heaven*, 366–368.

71. Dewey, *The Public and Its Problems*, 368–371; Lippmann, *Public Opinion*, "assumption" on 311–313; Lippmann, *The Phantom Public*, the tasks of the public on 61–64, 101–104; Westbrook, *John Dewey and American Democracy*, 298–300; Lasch, *The True and Only Heaven*, 366–368.

72. William Leach, *Land of Desire: Merchants, Power, and the Rise of a New American Culture* (New York: Pantheon Books, 1993), 39–70, 104–111, 134–138, 173–176, 319–348.

73. "Are We Victims of Propaganda? A Debate," *The Forum* 81 (March 1929): 142–149; Bernays debated Edward Dean Martin of the People's Institute. See also Edward L. Bernays, *Crystallizing Public Opinion* (1923; repr., New York: Liveright Pub. Corp., 1961), 96–97; Kennedy, *Over Here*, 90–91; Stephen Vaughn, *Holding Fast the Inner Lines: Democracy, Nationalism, and the Committee on Public Information* (Chapel Hill, NC: University of North Carolina Press, 1980), 191 passim; Mattson, *Creating a Democratic Public*, 116–117.

74. Bernays, *Crystallizing Public Opinion*, 17–19 on bacon, "scrutiny" on 215; Larry Tye, *The Father of Spin: Edward L. Bernays and the Birth of Public Relations* (New York: Crown Publishers, 1998).

75. Lasch, *The Revolt of the Elites*, 166–175; Walter Lippmann, "The Basic Problem of Democracy," *Atlantic Monthly* 124 (November 1919): 616–627; John Dewey, "Practical Democracy," *The New Republic* 45 (December 2, 1925): 52–54; Kennedy, *Over Here*, 90.

76. Bernays, *Crystallizing Public Opinion*, "purveyor" on 182, "basic" on 150, "instincts" on 171–172, "future" on 216–218.

77. Bernays' *Crystallizing Public Opinion*, 217–218; Herman J. Mankiewitz, review of Bernays, *Crystallizing Public Opinion*, *New York Times*, April 6, 1924, Book Review section, 3; Ernest Gruening, "The Higher Hokum," review of Bernays, *Crystallizing Public Opinion*, *The Nation* 118 (April 16, 1924): 450.

PART IV

1. On democratic culture, see Van Wyck Brooks, *America's Coming of Age* (New York: B.W. Huebsch, 1915); Herbert Croly, *Progressive Democracy* (1914; repr., New Brunswick, NJ: Transaction Publishers, 1998), 8–28; Casey Nelson Blake, *Beloved Community: The Cultural Criticism of Randolph Bourne, Van Wyck Brooks, Waldo Frank, and Lewis Mumford* (Chapel Hill, NC: Univercity of North Carolina Press, 1990); Christopher Lasch, *The True and Only Heaven: Progress and Its Critics* (New York: Norton, 1991), 345–348; on the consumerist vision of democracy, see Lasch, *The True and Only Heaven*, 329–368; Alan Brinkley, *The End of Reform: New Deal Liberalism in Recession and War* (New York: Alfred A. Knopf, 1995), 268–271 passim; Michael J. Sandel, *Democracy's Discontent: America in Search of a Public Philosophy* (Cambridge, MA: The Belknap Press of Harvard University Press, 1996), 250–273; Kevin Mattson, *Creating a Democratic Public: The Struggle for Urban Participatory Democracy during the Progressive Era* (University Park, PA: Pennsylvania State University Press, 1998), 77–85.

2. This "moving sign," Edward Bernays said of a giant Dodge Brothers' sign he helped place, is "half a city block in length" and seen "by a million people passing through Times Square in a day." William R. Taylor, *Inventing Times Square: Commerce and Culture at the Crossroads of the World* (Baltimore: Johns Hopkins University Press, 1991), 16–50 passim;

William Leach, *Land of Desire: Merchants, Power, and the Rise of a New American Culture* (New York: Pantheon Books, 1993), 338–348, Bernays on 341–342.

3. We filled museums with European art, Randolph Bourne charged before the war, but neglected the "nausea at Main Street," doing nothing about the city's "disheveled and barbaric streets" and shabby "civic clothing." Leach, *Land of Desire*, 323–348, Mumford on 345–346; Randolph Bourne, "Our Unplanned Cities," and "The Architect," in Randolph Bourne, *The Radical Will: Selected Writings 1911–1918* (New York: Urizen Books, 1977), 275–281; Blake, *Beloved Community*.

4. Leach, *Land of Desire*, 323–348, Chesterton on 347.

5. The spread of the commercial aesthetic, William James feared, extinguished "the power even of imagining what the ancient idealization of poverty could have meant: the liberation from material attachments, the unbridled soul." Leach, *Land of Desire*, 279–285, 344–348: "largest" and MacDonald on 281, Chesterton on 347–348, James on 260; "symbol of force" is A. N. Rebori, "The Straus Building, Chicago," *Architectural Record* 56 (May 1925): 387–392.

CHAPTER 9

1. The "trust" was an early form of corporate consolidation in which a legal entity (a "trust") held the decision-making power of a group of nominally independent firms. The Sherman Anti-Trust Law of 1890, which outlawed such arrangements, led to a wave of corporate mergers at the turn of the century. The term "anti-trust" survived as a term for opposition to concentrated economic power. Nelson Lichtenstein, *State of the Union* (Princeton, NJ: Princeton University Press, 2002), 1–19ff.; David Montgomery, "The 'New Unionism' and the Transformation of Workers' Consciousness in America, 1909–22," *Journal of Social History* 7 (Summer 1974): 509–529; Nelson Lichtenstein and Howell John Harris, eds., *Industrial Democracy in America: The Ambiguous Promise* (New York: Cambridge University Press, 1993); Ellis W. Hawley, *The New Deal and the Problem of Monopoly* (Princeton, NJ: Princeton University Press, 1966), especially 3–16, 472–473; Michael J. Sandel, *Democracy's Discontent; America in Search of a Public Philosophy* (Cambridge, MA: The Belknap Press of Harvard University Press, 1996), 231–249; Alan Brinkley, *The End of Reform: New Deal Liberalism in Recession and War* (New York: Alfred A. Knopf, 1995), 55–61; Herbert Croly, *Progressive Democracy* (1914; repr., New Brunswick, NJ: Transaction Publishers, 1998), 8–28.

2. James Weinstein, *The Corporate Ideal in the Liberal State, 1900–1918* (Boston: Beacon Press, 1968), 172–213; Steve Fraser, "The 'Labor Question,'" in *The Rise and Fall of the New Deal Order, 1930–1980*, ed. Steve Fraser and Gary Gerstle (Princeton, NJ: Princeton University Press, 1989), 55–84; Nelson Lichtenstein, "From Corporatism to Collective Bargaining: Organized Labor and the Eclipse of Social Democracy in the Postwar Era," in *The Rise and Fall of the New Deal Order*, 122–152, Murray quoted on 126; Brinkley, *The End of Reform*, 106–136, 201–226.

3. Steve Fraser, "The 'Labor Question'"; Nelson Lichtenstein, "From Corporatism to Collective Bargaining"; Brinkley, *The End of Reform*, 201–226 passim; Irving Bernstein, *The Turbulent Years: A History of the American Worker, 1933–1941* (Boston: Houghton Mifflin, 1969); Nelson Lichtenstein, *Walter Reuther: The Most Dangerous Man in Detroit* (Urbana, IL: University of Illinois Press, 1997); Lizabeth Cohen, *Making a New Deal: Industrial Workers in Chicago, 1919–1939* (New York: Cambridge University Press, 1990), 329–368; Christopher Lasch, *The True and Only Heaven: Progress and Its Critics* (New York: Norton, 1991); Michael Kazin, *The Populist Persuasion* (Ithaca, NY: Cornell University Press, 1995), 49–77, especially 51–53, 76–77; Bennett Harrison and Barry Bluestone, *The Great U-Turn: Corporate Restructuring and the Polarizing of America* (New York: Basic Books, 1988), "one-sided" on 10; Joyce Kolko and Gabriel Kolko, *The Limits of Power: The World and the United States Foreign Policy, 1945–1954* (New York: Harper & Row, 1972); William Appleman Williams, *The Tragedy of American Diplomacy* (New York: Dell Pub. Co., 1972); Athan Theoharis, ed., *The Truman Presidency: The Origins of the Imperial Presidency and the*

National Security State (Stanfordville, NY: E. M. Coleman Enterprises, 1979); Thomas Byrne Edsall, "The 'Reagan Revolution' as a Revolution from Above," in *The Reagan Legacy*, ed. Sidney Blumenthal and Thomas Byrne Edsall (New York: Pantheon Books, 1988); Kevin Boyle, *The UAW and the Heyday of American Liberalism, 1945–1968* (Ithaca, NY: Cornell University Press, 1995).

4. Alan Trachtenberg, *The Incorporation of America: Culture and Society in the Gilded Age* (New York: Hill and Wang, 1982), 91–100, 232–234; Nick Salvatore, *Eugene V. Debs: Citizen and Socialist* (Urbana, IL: University of Illinois Press, 1982), 114–146; Louis Menand, *The Metaphysical Club* (New York: Farrar, Straus, Giroux, 2001), 285–316; James R. Green, *The World of the Worker: Labor in Twentieth-Century America* (New York: Hill and Wang, 1980), 32–65; James Weinstein, *The Corporate Ideal in the Liberal State*, 3–39.

5. Green, *The World of the Worker*, 32–38, 50–51, 60–66, "educate" on 38; Weinstein, *The Corporate Ideal in the Liberal State, 1900–1918*, 3–39; Mickey Kaus, *The End of Equality* (New York: Basic Books, 1992), "nothing" on 19; Montgomery, "The 'New Unionism' and the Transformation of Workers' Consciousness in America, 1909–22."

6. Green, *The World of the Worker*, 37–65, quotations on 59–60; Foster Rhea Dulles and Melvin Dubofsky, *Labor in America* (Arlington Heights, IL: Harlan Davidson, 1984), 200–207; Weinstein, *The Corporate Ideal in the Liberal State, 1900–1918*, 3–39; Melvyn Dubofsky, *We Shall Be All: A History of the Industrial Workers of the World* (New York: Quadrangle/New York Times Book Co., 1969); Montgomery, "The 'New Unionism' and the Transformation of Workers' Consciousness in America, 1909–22."

7. Green, *The World of the Worker*, 67–84, "craft" on 71; Montgomery, "The 'New Unionism' and the Transformation of Workers' Consciousness in America, 1909–22," "until" on 518; Keith Sward, *The Legend of Henry Ford* (New York: Russell & Russell, 1968), passim, 32–33; Upton Sinclair, *The Flivver King: A Story of Ford-America* (1937; repr., Chicago: Charles H. Kerr Publishing Co., 1984); Harry Braverman, *Labor and Monopoly Capital: The Degradation of Work in the Twentieth Century* (New York: Monthly Review Press, 1975); James J. Flink, *The Car Culture* (Cambridge, MA: MIT Press, 1975), 67–112.

8. Weinstein, *The Corporate Ideal in the Liberal State*, 92–116, especially 107; Green, *The World of the Worker*, 68–84; Martin Schiesl, *The Politics of Efficiency* (Berkeley: University of California Press, 1977); Richard W. Judd, *Socialist Cities: Municipal Politics and the Grass Roots of American Socialism* (Albany, NY: State University of New York Press, 1989).

9. Green, *The World of the Worker*, 68–77.

10. Dubofsky, *We Shall Be All*, 146–170, "Whenever" on 167; Green, *The World of the Worker*, 84–91; Weinstein, *The Corporate Ideal in the Liberal State*, 172–182; Lasch, *The True and Only Heaven*, 296–342, the phrase "syndicalist moment" is Lasch's.

11. Dubofsky, *We Shall Be All*, 227–290; Green, *The World of the Worker*, 84–91; Dulles and Dubofsky, *Labor in America*, 207–211; Weinstein, *The Corporate Ideal in the Liberal State*, 172–182; Lasch, *The True and Only Heaven*, 296–342.

12. Dubofsky, *We Shall Be All*, 227–290; Green, *The World of the Worker*, 84–91; Dulles and Dubofsky, *Labor in America*, 207–211; Weinstein, *The Corporate Ideal in the Liberal State*, 172–182; Lasch, *The True and Only Heaven*, 296–342.

13. Dubofsky, *We Shall Be All*, 19–87; Lasch, *The True and Only Heaven*, 332–340.

14. Dubofsky, *We Shall Be All*, 166–170: "brain" on 167, "Our" on 169; Lasch, *The True and Only Heaven*, 332–340, "executive" on 333.

15. The odd alliance of Industrial Workers of the World (IWW) and Village intellectuals led to the Paterson Strike Pageant, a dramatization of the workers' cause in the 1913 strike staged at Madison Square Garden in New York City. An artistic triumph, the pageant may have helped to defeat the strike as strikebreakers entered the plant while strike leaders were away staging the pageant. The pageant distracted "the workers' minds from the actual struggle to the pictured struggle," fumed organizer Elizabeth Gurley Flynn. Green, *The World of the Worker*, 88–91; Weinstein, *The Corporate Ideal in the Liberal State*, 191–198; Montgomery, "The 'New Unionism' and the Transformation of Workers' Consciousness in America, 1909–22," 514–524. Dubofsky, *We Shall Be All*, 263–290; Lasch, *The True and Only Heaven*, 332–340; William

Leach, *Land of Desire: Merchants, Power, and the Rise of a New American Culture* (New York: Pantheon Books, 1994), 185–190, Flynn on 189.

16. Sandel, *Democracy's Discontent*, 211–216, Brandeis on 212; Osmond K. Fraenkel, ed., *The Curse of Bigness: The Miscellaneous Papers of Louis D. Brandeis* (New York: The Viking Press, 1934); Arthur S. Link, *Woodrow Wilson and the Progressive Era, 1910–1917* (New York: Harper, 1954), 20ff.

17. Croly, *Progressive Democracy*, 378–392, 421–423; see also Link, *Woodrow Wilson and the Progressive Era*, 18–19.

18. Croly, *Progressive Democracy*, 386–405.

19. Croly, *Progressive Democracy*, 395–405; Samual Haber, *Efficiency and Uplift: Scientific Management in the Progressive Era* (Chicago: University of Chicago Press, 1964); Schiesl, *The Politics of Efficiency*; Daniel T. Rodgers, "In Search of Progressivism," *Reviews in American History* 10 (1982): 122–127; Ellis W. Hawley, *The New Deal and the Problem of Monopoly*, 283–292ff.

20. Gompers quoted in Sean Wilentz, "Speedy Fred's Revolution" (a review of Robert Kanigel, *The One Best Way*), *New York Review of Books*, November 20, 1997, 32–37; Croly, *Progressive Democracy*, 395–405; Fraenkel, *The Curse of Bigness*; Fraser, "The 'Labor Question,'" 55–84.

21. Link, *Woodrow Wilson and the Progressive Era*, Roosevelt on 18–20; Weinstein, *The Corporate Ideal in the Liberal State*, 139–171; Gabriel Kolko, *The Triumph of Conservatism: A Reinterpretation of American History, 1900–1916* (Chicago: Quadrangle Books, 1963), 57–78, 159–216; Richard Hofstadter, *The American Political Tradition* (New York: Vintage Books, 1976), 286–303; Sandel, *Democracy's Discontent*, 231–234.

22. Hofstadter, *The American Political Tradition*, 286–298, "remedy" on 292; Link, *Woodrow Wilson and the Progressive Era*, 1–24, "new" on 21; Weinstein, *The Corporate Ideal in the Liberal State*, 16–171; Sandel, *Democracy's Discontent*, 216–219; Salvatore, *Eugene V. Debs*, 244–266.

23. Link, *Woodrow Wilson and the Progressive Era*, 1–24; Sandel, *Democracy's Discontent*, "centralized" and "loomed" quoted on 214–216; Hofstadter, *The American Political Tradition*, 322–351, "for big business" and "illicit competition" on 331; Louis D. Brandeis, "Competition," (1913) in Fraenkel, *The Curse of Bigness*, 112–124; Link, *Woodrow Wilson and the Progressive Era*, 1–24; Weinstein, *The Corporate Ideal in the Liberal State*, 16–171; on the civic basis of Brandeis's support for industrial democracy and proprietorship, see Sandel, *Democracy's Discontent*, 214–216, 235–239.

24. Link, *Woodrow Wilson and the Progressive Era*, 68–80, "tabby" on 72–73; Hofstadter, *The American Political Tradition*, 322–336; Dulles and Dubofsky, *Labor in America*, 194–195; Green, *The World of the Worker*, 83–84.

25. Weinstein, *The Corporate Ideal in the Liberal State*, 62–91, "responsible" on 84; Link, *Woodrow Wilson and the Progressive Era*, 68–80, "counselor" on 74; Kolko, *The Triumph of Conservatism*, 172–181, 255–278.

26. Williams, *The Tragedy of American Diplomacy*, "Business" on 63; Sandel, *Democracy's Discontent*, 216–219; Hofstadter, *The American Political Tradition*, 267–305, "No" on 270–276.

27. Williams, *The Tragedy of American Diplomacy*, 58–90, "Our" on 90; Link, *Woodrow Wilson and the Progressive Era*, 81–144; David M. Kennedy, *Over Here: The First World War and American Society* (New York: Oxford University Press, 1980), 45–53; John Milton Cooper, Jr., *The Warrior and the Priest: Woodrow Wilson and Theodore Roosevelt* (Cambridge, MA: Belknap Press of Harvard University Press, 1983).

28. Kennedy, *Over Here*, 113–140, 299–347; Weinstein, *the Corporate Ideal in the Liberal State*, 214–226, "relations" on 218; Williams, *the Tragedy of American Diplomacy*, 90–161.

29. Kennedy, *Over Here*, 128–139, Baruch and steel executive on 135; Weinstein, *The Corporate Ideal in the Liberal State*, 214–226.

30. Jeremy Brecher, *Strike!* (Boston, MA: South End Press, 1972), 101–143; Montgomery, "The 'New Unionism' and the Transformation of Workers' Consciousness in America, 1909–22," 511–524: "collective participation" on 523, "co-operative" on 520; Green, *The World of the Worker*, 90–99; Kennedy, *Over Here*, 258–279.

31. Green, *The World of the Worker*, 90–93; Montgomery, "The 'New Unionism' and the Transformation of Workers' Consciousness in America, 1909–22," 517–521; Kennedy, *Over Here*, 114–115; Dulles and Dubofsky, *Labor in America*, 191–220; Weinstein, *The Corporate Ideal in the Liberal State*, 214.

32. Kennedy, *Over Here*, 3–44, 75–78: "safe" on 42, "vigorous" on 26, "impugn" on 76; Link, *Woodrow Wilson and the Progressive Era*, 274–282, "To" on 277.

33. Kennedy, *Over Here*, 75–88, 262–267; Green, *The World of the Worker*, 90–92, Debs on 92; Montgomery, "The 'New Unionism' and the Transformation of Workers' Consciousness in America, 1909–22," 521; Weinstein, *The Corporate Ideal in the Liberal State*, 227–228; Salvatore, *Eugene V. Debs*, 288–296.

34. Brecher, *Strike!* 101–143.

35. Kennedy, *Over Here*, 258–279, Gompers on 270; Green, *The World of the Worker*, 90–99; Montgomery, "The 'New Unionism' and the Transformation of Workers' Consciousness in America, 1909–22," 514–524.

36. Kennedy, *Over Here*, 258–279; Green, *The World of the Worker*, 90–99, "whole" on 94; Dulles and Dubofsky, *Labor in America*, 220–227, Gary on 225; Montgomery, "The 'New Unionism' and the Transformation of Workers' Consciousness in America, 1909–22," 514–524.

37. Brecher, *Strike!* 118–128; Kennedy, *Over Here*, 270–279; Dulles and Dubofsky, *Labor in America*, 224–227; Cohen, *Making a New Deal*, 38–52.

38. Kennedy, *Over Here*, 289–293; Brecher, *Strike!* 128–140; Dulles and Dubofsky, *Labor in America*, 227–232; Green, *The World of the Worker*, 100–132.

39. Fraser, "The Labor Question," 62–67; Montgomery, "The 'New Unionism' and the Transformation of Workers' Consciousness in America," 519–524, "responsibility" on 524; Cohen, *Making a New Deal*, 160–183.

40. Green, *The World of the Worker*, 100–132; Dulles and Dubofsky, *Labor in America*, 233–254; Cohen, *Making a New Deal*, 159–211.

41. Cohen, *Making a New Deal*, 160–183: "make" on 161, "find" on 173; Green, *The World of the Worker*, 100–132, "concern" on 104; Kennedy, *Over Here*, 261–262; Braverman, *Labor and Monopoly Capital*.

42. Ellis W. Hawley, "Herbert Hoover, the Commerce Secretariat, and the Vision of an 'Associative State,' 1921–1928," *Journal of American History* 61 (June 1974): 117–140; Leach, *Land of Desire*, 349–378; Ellis W. Hawley, *The Great War and the Search for a Modern Order* (New York: St. Martin's Press, 1979); Kennedy, *Over Here*, 140–141; Green, *The World of the Worker*, 100–132.

43. Hoover quoted in Hawley, "Herbert Hoover, the Commerce Secretariat, and the Vision of an 'Associative State,' 1921–1928." Hawley uses the phrase "bureaucratic empire to end future bureaucratic empires." Leach, *Land of Desire*, 349–378; Hawley, *The Great War and the Search for a Modern Order*; Kennedy, *Over Here*, 140–141; Green, *The World of the Worker*, 100–132.

44. Fraser, "The Labor Question," 59–61.

45. Fraser, "The Labor Question," 61–62.

46. Cohen, *Making a New Deal*, 208–249; Green, *The World of the Worker*, 133–173; Fraser, "The Labor Question," 67–70.

47. Cohen, *Making a New Deal*, 292–293 passim; Green, *The World of the Worker*, 133–134ff.

48. Cohen, *Making a New Deal*, 251–304; Paul Kleppner, *Who Voted? The Dynamics of Electoral Turnout, 1870–1980* (New York: Praeger Publishers, 1982), 55–111; Brecher, *Strike!* 144–177; Green, *The World of the Worker*, 133–151, NRA on 140; Fraser, "The Labor Question," 67–70.

49. Hawley, *The New Deal and the Problem of Monopoly*, 19–146; Green, *The World of the Worker*, 133–151; Dulles and Dubofsky, *Labor in America*, 255–265; Brecher, *Strike!* 150–177; Cohen, *Making a New Deal*, 293–301.

50. National Resources Planning Board, *Our Cities: Their Role in the National Economy* (Washington, DC: U.S. Govt. Print. Off., 1937), "smoldering" on vi–vii; Green, *The World of the Worker*, 146–153; Dulles and Dubofsky, *Labor in America*, 260–267; Fraser, "The Labor Question," 67–71; William E. Leuchtenburg, *Franklin D. Roosevelt and the New Deal, 1932–1940* (New York: Harpers & Row, 1963), 63–166.

51. The Committee on Industrial Organization broke with the AFL in 1938 and adopted the name Congress of Industrial Organizations. Green, *The World of the Worker*, 150–158; Dulles and Dubofsky, *Labor in America*, 267–300; Brecher, *Strike!* 177–220.

52. Green, *The World of the Worker*, 150–158, NAM on 158; Dulles and Dubofsky, *Labor in America*, 267–300; Cohen, *Making a New Deal*, 301–321; Brinkley, *The End of Reform*, 201–203.

53. Green, *The World of the Worker*, 148–160; Dulles and Dubofsky, *Labor in America*, 301–307, Lewis on 302; Brecher, *Strike!* 177–220.

54. Green, *The World of the Worker*, 164–173; Dulles and Dubofsky, *Labor in America*, 298–309; Brinkley, *The End of Reform*, 23–30.

55. Green, *The World of the Worker*, 165–173; Cohen, *Making a New Deal*, 357–368; Fraser, "The Labor Question," 76–78.

56. Cohen, *Making a New Deal*, 251–289; Fraser, "The Labor Question," 67–72, Perkins on 68–69; Lasch, *The True and Only Heaven*, 67–72; "purchasing" is from the National Labor Relations Act (1935) at http://www.ourdocuments.gov/doc.

57. Brinkley, *The End of Reform*, 31–49, Roosevelt on 48; Hawley, *The New Deal and the Problem of Monopoly*, 130–146.

58. Brinkley, *The End of Reform*, 48–64, quotations on 57–58; Hawley, *The New Deal and the Problem of Monopoly*, 149–280.

59. Brinkley, *The End of Reform*, 48–64; Hawley, *The New Deal and the Problem of Monopoly*, 283–379.

60. Brinkley, *The End of Reform*, 65–85; Hawley, *The New Deal and the Problem of Monopoly*, 383–456; Lasch, *The True and Only Heaven*, 67–72; Leach, *Land of Desire*, 3–38.

61. Brinkley, *The End of Reform*, 86–105, Roosevelt on 104; Hawley, *The New Deal and the Problem of Monopoly*, 404–419.

62. Brinkley, *The End of Reform*, 106–136, "breaking up monopolies" is Senator William Borah, quoted on 111; Hawley, *The New Deal and the Problem of Monopoly*, 420–455; Lasch, *The True and Only Heaven*, 429–439.

63. Hawley, *The New Deal and the Problem of Monopoly*, 420–455; Sandel, *Democracy's Discontent*, 239–243, quotations on 241–242; Brinkley, *The End of Reform*, 106–136; Lasch, *The True and Only Heaven*, 429–439.

64. Brinkley, *The End of Reform*, 106–136, "three" on 128; Hawley, *The New Deal and the Problem of Monopoly*, 404–419; Lasch, *The True and Only Heaven*, 429–439.

65. Brinkley, *The End of Reform*, 137–174; Richard Hofstadter, *Great Issues in American History*, vol. 3 (New York: Vintage Books, 1982), Atlantic Charter on 399–401.

66. Brinkley, *The End of Reform*, 137–170, Henderson on 164; on the "rights" reorientation of postwar liberalism, see Michael J. Sandel, *Democracy's Discontent: America in Search of a Public Philosophy*; Michael Schudson, *The Good Citizen: A History of American Civic Life* (New York: Martin-Kessler Books, 1998), 240–294.

67. Brinkley, *The End of Reform*, 170–200.

68. Brinkley, *The End of Reform*, 201–203ff.

69. Brinkley, *The End of Reform*, 203–205.

70. Brinkley, *The End of Reform*, 205–209.

71. Green, *The World of the Worker*, 174–190, Lewis on 181; Brinkley, *The End of Reform*, 209–212.

72. Brinkley, *The End of Reform*, 209–212; Green, *The World of the Worker*, 174–190.

73. Brinkley, *The End of Reform*, 212–217, "winning" on 215; Fraser, "The Labor Question," 72–78; Green, *The World of the Worker*, 174–190, "line" on 184.

74. Green, *The World of the Worker*, 174–190; Fraser, "The Labor Question," 72–78; Brinkley, *The End of Reform*, 217–226; Boyle, *The UAW and the Heyday of American Liberalism*, 10–60.

75. Brinkley, *The End of Reform*, 217–235, quotations on 233. The labor movement did play an important role in postwar liberalism, particularly in promoting civil rights and in supporting the early New Left. Boyle, *The UAW and the Heyday of American Liberalism*, passim. Boyle argues that the UAW never abandoned the broader ambitions of economic democracy, but was hampered by the larger constellation of political forces in the post–World War II era. Boyle admits, however, that Walter Reuther's vision for the labor movement "was not inherently democratic. . . . It assumed, rather, that a select group of institutional elites . . . could and should speak for 'the people.'" In the wake of the UAW's failed 1946 strike, Boyle adds, Reuther "would never again try to use the UAW's bargaining power to redefine the position of the corporations in the political economy" (31).

76. Brinkley, *The End of Reform*, 235–245; Boyle, *The UAW and the Heyday of American Liberalism*, 10–34, "determined" on 24; "Congressional" is from *Sit Down and Fight* (1992) VHS, Charlotte Zwerin Films, Inc. production for the PBS series, American Experience.

77. Boyle, *The UAW and the Heyday of American Liberalism*, 22–31, Reuther quoted on 30; Green, *The World of the Worker*, 193–209.

78. Boyle, *The UAW and the Heyday of American Liberalism*, 22–31 passim; Green, *The World of the Worker*, 193–209; Robert O. Self, *American Babylon: Race and the Struggle for Postwar Oakland* (Princeton, NJ: Princeton University Press, 2005), 34–46.

79. A closed shop meant that employers could only hire union members; a union shop meant that new hires had to join the union within a specified period; an open shop allowed union and nonunion employees, even where the union had been designated as sole bargaining agent. Dulles and Dubofsky, *Labor in America*, 343–356; Green, *The World of the Worker*, 193–209.

80. Dulles and Dubofsky, *Labor in America*, 343–356; Green, *the World of the Worker*, 193–209.

81. Dulles and Dubofsky, *Labor in America*, 343–356; Green, *the World of the Worker*, 193–209.

82. Michael J. Hogan, *A Cross of Iron: Harry S. Truman and the Origins of the National Security State, 1945–1954* (New York: Cambridge University Press, 1998), 1–68 passim; John Kenneth Galbraith, *The Affluent Society* (New York: New American Library, 1958).

83. Hogan, *A Cross of Iron*, 1–22, Kennan on 16.

84. Hogan, *A Cross of Iron*, 22; Brinkley, *The End of Reform*, 175ff.; Green, *The World of the Worker*, 203–209.

CHAPTER 10

1. William Leach, *Land of Desire: Merchants, Power, and the Rise of a New American Culture* (New York: Pantheon Books, 1993), 30–32.

2. Leach, *Land of Desire*, 15–26, quotations on 17–18; Alan Trachtenberg, *The Incorporation of America* (New York: Hill and Wang, 1982), 130–136.

3. Leach, *The Land of Desire*, 3–12, 35–43, "speaks" on 3.

4. "Preamble to the Constitution of the Knights of Labor," in Terrence V. Powderly, *Thirty Years of Labor: 1859 to 1889* (New York: A.M. Kelley, 1967). The Knights of Labor updated the equation of the health of the crafts with that of the republic that stretched back to the American Revolution. A leader of the Jacksonian-era struggle for the ten-hour day demanded for workers "sufficient time in each day for the cultivation of the mind and for self-improvement." Anything less would result in such "servility as must necessarily . . . render the benefits of our liberal institutions to us inaccessible and useless." David R. Roediger and Philip

S. Foner, *Our Own Time: A History of American Labor and the Working Day* (New York: Greenwood Press, 1989), 7, 14–15.

5. Leach, *Land of Desire*, 3–12, Cooley on 8.

6. Roediger and Foner, *Our Own Time*, 19ff., 83, "depends" on 85; Roy Rosenzweig, *Eight Hours for What We Will* (New York: Cambridge University Press, 1983), passim, "wants" on 1; E. P. Thompson, "Time, Work-Discipline and Industrial Capitalism," *Past and Present* 38 (1967): 56–97.

7. The average work week for nonagricultural employees fell to fifty hours by 1910. Manufacturing wages increased by 25 percent over the first two decades of the century. Rosenzweig, *Eight Hours for What We Will*, 35–64, 179–180: "modern" and "more" on 39, "hundred" and "craving" on 53; Raymond Calkins, *Substitutes for the Saloon* (Boston: Houghton, Mifflin and Co., 1901), 2–3, 10–11, "absence" on 2; Felix Adler, "The Social Function of the Saloon," *Municipal Affairs* 5 (December 1901): 876–880, "repression" on 878; George Ade, *The Old-Time Saloon* (New York: R. Long & R,R. Smith, 1931).

8. Rosenzweig, *Eight Hours for What We Will*, 35–64; John J. Rumbarger, *Profits, Power, and Prohibition* (Albany, NY: State University of New York Press, 1989), "Marx" on 117; Calkins, *Substitutes for the Saloon*, "official and unofficial" on 10–11; Ade, *The Old-Time Saloon*, "earnest" on 91; Delos F. Wilcox, *The American City: A Problem in Democracy* (New York: The Macmillan Company, 1904) also acknowledged the usefulness of the saloon, 150–154; on the civic dimension of the saloon and other "third places" (i.e., neither work nor home), see Ray Oldenburg, *The Great Good Place* (New York: Paragon House, 1989) and Christopher Lasch's review of Oldenburg, "Preserving the Mild Life," *Pittsburgh History* (Summer 1991), which appears in revived form in Christopher Lasch, *The Revolt of the Elites and the Betrayal of Democracy* (New York: W.W. Norton & Company, 1995), 117–128.

9. Rosenzweig, *Eight Hours for What We Will*, 93–126, employers on 102; Leon Fink, *Workingmen's Democracy: The Knights of Labor and American Politics* (Urbana, IL: University of Illinois Press, 1983), 3–37; Sean Wilentz, *Chants Democratic: New York City and the Rise of the American Working Class* (New York: Oxford University Press, 1984), 307–314.

10. Rumbarger, *Profits, Power, and Prohibition*, on Prohibition Party, 57–62; Rosenzweig, *Eight Hours for What We Will*, 93–126, editor on 93.

11. Rumbarger, *Profits, Power, and Prohibition*, 66–80.

12. Rosenzweig, *Eight Hours for What We Will*, 35–64, 93–126, quotation on 109–110; Rumbarger, *Profits, Power, and Prohibition*, 65–80; Perry Duis, *The Saloon: Public Drinking in Chicago and Boston, 1880–1920* (Urbana, IL: University of Illinois Press, 1983). Paul Johnson, *A Shopkeeper's Millennium: Society and Revivals in Rochester, New York, 1815–1837* (New York: Hill and Wang, 1978) examines an early struggle over recreations in the workplace.

13. Rumbarger, *Profits, Power, and Prohibition*, 66–108, quotations on 76–77.

14. Rosenzweig, *Eight Hours for What We Will*, 127–152, "outside" on 132; Steven A. Riess, *City Games: The Evolution of American Urban Society and the Rise of Sports* (Urbana, IL: University of Illinois Press, 1989), 127–168; Roy Rosenzweig and Elizabeth Blackmar, *The Park and the People: A History of Central Park* (Ithaca, NY: Cornell University Press, 1992), chapters 8–9, 12.

15. Kathy Peiss, *Cheap Amusements: Working Women and Leisure in Turn-of-the-Century New York* (Philadelphia: Temple University Press, 1986), 3–33 passim, "brought" on 43.

16. Peiss, *Cheap Amusements*, 34–76 passim; Joanne Meyerowitz, *Women Adrift: Independent Wage-Earners in Chicago, 1880–1930* (Chicago: University of Chicago Press, 1988).

17. Wilcox, *The American City*, passim: "make" on 10–11, "transformation," "unnerve," and "natural" on 120–122, "moral" on 146; see also John Collier, "Leisure Time: The Last Problem of Conservation," *Recreation* 6 (June 1912): 93–106.

18. Wilcox, *The American City*, "fatal" on 10–11, "culture" and "principally" on 120–122; "educated" is Collier, "Leisure Time"; Percy MacKaye, *The Civic Theater: In Relation to the Redemption of Leisure* (New York: M. Kennerly, 1912), "nation's," "disorganized," and "private" on 30–31.

19. Benjamin Parke DeWitt, *The Progressive Movement* (New York: Macmillan, 1915), "city fails," "confining," and "insistence," 361–363; Wilcox, *The American City*, 149–172, 229–243, "ceaselessly" on 149; Jane Addams, *The Spirit of Youth and the City Streets* (New York: Macmillan, 1909), "commercial" on 98.

20. Lary May, *Screening Out the Past: The Birth of Mass Culture and the Motion Picture Industry* (Chicago: University of Chicago Press, 1980, 43–59, "traditional" on 49; other quotations from Wilcox, *The American City*, 121–172.

21. May, *Screening Out the Past*, 43–59; Peiss, *Cheap Amusements*, 1–33, 163–184, "foster" on 179; other quotations from Collier, "Leisure Time." See also Paul S. Boyer, *Urban Masses and Moral Order, 1820–1920* (Cambridge: Harvard University Press, 1978), 162–251.

22. DeWitt, *The Progressive Movement*, "deterioration" on 363; Lary May, *Screening Out the Past*, 43–59; Wilcox, *The American City*, 162–172: "*social service*" and "*discussion*" on 169 (italics in original), "ethical" and "next" on 170; "police" is Collier, "Leisure Time"; Boyer, *Urban Masses and Moral Order*, 220–251; Peiss, *Cheap Amusements*, 160–184.

23. Peiss, *Cheap Amusements*, 88–162, quotations on 151; Rosenzweig, *Eight Hours for What We Will*, 188.

24. A similar glimpse of working-class culture in city parks and commercial streets encouraged the development of consumer economics. Walking the streets of an eastern city, economist Simon Patten noticed the "wrong" side of the street was dark, where "the very Institutions of Civilization itself" (the church, school, and library) were closed and locked. On the "right" side of the street, soda fountains and popcorn wagons, penny shows and nickel theaters filled the streets with noise and life and enthusiastic people. Leach, *Land of Desire*, 240–242, "wrong" and "right" are Patten's terms, on 241; Rosenzweig, *Eight Hours for What We Will*, 140–152, "revelation" and "reality" on 140; May, *Screening Out the Past*, 3–42; Peiss, *Cheap Amusements*, 101–104, 183–186, "trouble" on 116; see also John Kasson, *Amusing the Million: Coney Island at the Turn of the Century* (New York: Hill and Wang, 1978).

25. Rosenzweig, *Eight Hours for What We Will*, 140–152; May, *Screening Out the Past*, 96–241; Robert Sklar, *Movie-Made America: A Social History of American Movies* (New York: Random Books, 1975), 67–103; Peiss, *Cheap Amusements*, 115–138; Leach, *The Land of Desire*, 104–111; Kasson, *Amusing the Million*, "laboratories" on 8; David Riesman, *The Lonely Crowd* (1950, abridged ed. 1969; repr., New Haven, CT: Yale University Press, 1989). "From the 1880s to the 1920s," Riesman writes, the "white Protestant majority waged an increasingly unsuccessful war to maintain its dominance not only in the sphere of work . . . but in the sphere of play, where it was constantly having to fight for a precarious competence" (284).

26. Rosenzweig, *Eight Hours for What We Will*, 140–152; on the "strenuous life," see Christopher Lasch, *The World of Nations* (New York: Knopf, 1973), 80–99; George Fredrickson, *The Inner Civil War: Northern Intellectuals and the Crisis of the Union* (New York: Harper & Row, 1965), 166–180; Boyer, *Urban Masses and Moral Order*, 242–251; Rosenzweig, *Eight Hours for What We Will*, 140–152; Reiss, *City Games*, 127–168. Johan Huizinga, *Homo Ludens: A Study of the Play Element in Culture* (Boston: Beacon Press, 1955) and Christopher Lasch, *The Culture of Narcissism* (New York: Warner Books, 1979), 181–219, suggest the way in which a utilitarian view of play undercuts its cultural creativity.

27. The team instinct must be broadened, Lee added, so that it promoted what Josiah Royce had praised as "not loyalty to the immediate object alone but loyalty to the loyalty of others, including your opponents; loyalty to the spirit of loyalty wherever found." Luther Halsey Gulick, "Play and Democracy," *Charities and the Commons* 18 (August 3, 1907): 481–486; Joseph Lee, "Play as a School of the Citizen," *Charities and the Commons* 18 (August 3, 1907): 486–491; Rosenzweig, *Eight Hours for What We Will*, 140–152; Boyer, *Urban Masses and Moral Order*, 242–251.

28. On "self-direction," see Lee, "Play as a School of the Citizen"; Boyer, *Urban Masses and Moral Order*, 246–251, "equipped" and "serve" on 249–250; L. H. Weir, *A Manual of*

Municipal and County Parks (New York: A.S. Barnes, 1928), 4, 125, 398; Rosenzweig, *Eight Hours for What We Will*, 140–152, "vacant" on 146.

29. Rosenzweig, *Eight Hours for What We Will*, 140–152, "forget," "child," and "boy" on 148; on the "transition from 'free' to 'directed' play," see Rainwater, *The Play Movement in the United States*, 250–253, 303–328; Boyer, *Urban Masses and Moral Order*, 243–244, "identical" is Boyer's description.

30. Boyer, *Urban Masses and Moral Order*, 245–249; Stuart Ewen, *Captains of Consciousness: Advertising and the Social Roots of the Consumer Culture* (New York: McGraw-Hill, 1976), 31–39; Lasch, *The Culture of Narcissism*, 267–280 passim; Rosenzweig, *Eight Hours for What We Will*, 127–152, 168–171, "can't" on 151; People's Institute, *Twelfth Annual Report* (New York, 1909), cited in Peiss, *Cheap Amusements*, 183.

31. The next five paragraphs are based on Leach, *The Land of Desire*, 35–46, 71–84, 104–111, 130–134, 164–173, 344–348.

32. Leach, *The Land of Desire*, 26–32, "monsters" and "octopus" on 27; Sandel, *Democracy's Discontent*, 201–249 places the "retail wars" in a civic context; see the 1898 editorial cartoon "The Commercial Vampire" (originally published in *Vim*) in Amon Carter Museum of Western Art, *The Image of America in Caricature and Cartoon* (Fort Worth, TX: Amon Carter Museum of Western Art, 1975), 88.

33. Leach, *The Land of Desire*, 26–32.

34. Leach, *The Land of Desire*, 26–32.

35. Ewen, *Captains of Consciousness*, 1–56ff.: Filene on 54, "larger" on 27, Baruch on 52; Lasch, *The Culture of Narcissism*, 135–140; Leach, *Land of Desire*, passim.

36. Leach, *The Land of Desire*, 85–90, 127, 328–330. Merchants thus pioneered the reshaping of character and the inculcation of values, what Lasch calls "the socialization of reproduction." Christopher Lasch, *The Culture of Narcissism*, 267–317, 369–397. The socialization of reproduction has become much more sophisticated in our own day. See, for example, Eric Schlosser, *Fast Food Nation* (New York: HarperCollins, 2002), 31–57; The Project on Disney, *Inside the Mouse: Work and Play at Disney World* (Durham, NC: Duke University Press, 1995); Lizabeth Cohen, *A Consumers' Republic* (New York: Knopf, 2003), 292–344.

37. Michael J. Sandel, *Democracy's Discontent: America in Search of a Public Philosophy* (Cambridge MA: Belknap Press of Harvard University Press, 1996), 221–249.

38. Rumbarger, *Profits, Power, and Prohibition*, 83–122, 184–190; Francis Peabody, "Substitutes for the Saloon," *The Forum* 21 (March 1896): 595–606, "social" on 595; Leo S. Rowe, "American Ideas and Institutions in Their Relation to the Problem of City Government," *Proceedings, National Municipal League* (Louisville, KY, 1897), 317–318; Boyer, *Urban Masses and Moral Order*, 189–251; Neal Gabler, *Life: The Movie* (New York: Knopf, 1998), 46–52.

39. Rumbarger, *Profits, Power, and Prohibition*, 123–151, "personal" and "taking" on 132–133; James Weinstein, *The Corporate Ideal in the Liberal State, 1900–1918* (Boston: Beacon, 1968), 18–22; the muckraking account is George Kibbe Turner, "Beer and the City Liquor Problem," *McClure's* 33 (September 1909): 528–533; Edward A. Ross, "Prohibition as the Sociologist Sees It," *Harper's Monthly* 142 (January 1921): 187; Rosenzweig, *Eight Hours for What We Will*, 184–186; Duis, *The Saloon*.

40. Rumbarger, *Profits, Power, and Prohibition*; 123–183, "become" on 139; Elton Raymond Shaw, *Prohibition Coming or Going?* (Berwyn IL: Shaw Pub. Co., 1924), "growth" and "will" on 203, 213–214; Lewis Edwin Theiss, "Industry Versus Alcohol," *Outlook* 107 (August 8, 1914): 856–858; John S. Gregory, "A Saloonless Nation by 1920," *World's Work* 30 (June 1915): 202; "No 'Booze' for Big Business," *Literary Digest* 52 (March 4, 1916): 569–570; "Exit the American Saloon," *World's Work* 37 (March 1919): 492.

41. Rumbarger, *Profits, Power, and Prohibition*, 184–188, quotations on 185; Boyer, *Urban Masses and Moral Order*, 195–219.

42. Rumbarger, *Profits, Power, and Prohibition*, 155–198, "analyze" on 171; Robert A. Woods, "Prohibition and Its Social Consequences," National Conference on Social Work, *Pro-*

ceedings,1919 (Chicago, 1920), "greatest" on 763; Martin Sklar, *The Corporate Reconstruction of American Capitalism, 1890–1916: The Market, the Law, and Politics* (New York: Cambridge University Press, 1988); Weinstein, *The Corporate Ideal in the Liberal State*; Gabriel Kolko, *The Triumph of Conservatism: A Reinterpretation of American History, 1900–1916* (Chicago: Quadrangle Books, 1963).

43. Rumbarger, *Profits, Power, and Prohibition*, 189–190; Ade, *The Old-Time Saloon*, 171; Keith Sward, *The Legend of Henry Ford* (New York: Russell & Russell, 1968), 50–63, "unwholesome" on 58–60; James J. Flink, *The Car Culture* (Cambridge: MIT Press, 1975), 79–92, "thrift" on 83.

44. Rosenzweig, *Eight Hours for What We Will*, 46–53, 172–183, "keen" on 178; Peiss, *Cheap Amusements*, 124–136; May, *Screening Out the Past*, 167–199; Neal Gabler, *An Empire of Their Own: How the Jews Created Hollywood* (New York: Crown Publishers, 1988).

45. Rosenzweig, *Eight Hours for What We Will*, 183–190, "Nix" on 186; Duis, *The Saloon*.

46. May, *Screening Out the Past*, 43–59, "avert" on 44; Rosenzweig, *Eight Hours for What We Will*, 191–221, "chief" on 207.

47. Rosenzweig, *Eight Hours for What We Will*, 191–221; Sklar, *Movie-Made America*, 40–46, 141–157, "kill" on 46; Peiss, *Cheap Amusements*, trade journal quoted on 161; Don Carle Gillette, "The Amusement Octopus," *American Mercury* 11 (May 1927): 91–99; Steven J. Ross, *Working-Class Hollywood: Silent Film and the Shaping of Class in America* (Princeton, NJ: Princeton University Press, 1998), 118–123, "methods" on 120; Gabler, *An Empire of Their Own*.

48. Sklar, *Movie-Made America*, "wonderful" on 131; Clarence E. Rainwater, *The Play Movement in the United States* (Chicago: University of Chicago Press, 1922); Boyer, *Urban Masses and Moral Order*, "control" on 251; Leach, *Land of Desire*, Patten on 239–240.

49. Lasch, *The Culture of Narcissism*, 267–317, 369–397, quotations on 268–269.

50. Wilcox, *The American City*, 121–173, "sense," "reach," and "morals" on 121; Lasch, *The Culture of Narcissism*, 269–271: "social" on 270, "school" on 276; May, *Screening Out the Past*, juvenile court judge on 58; Boyer, *Urban Masses and Moral Order*, playground leaders on 243–244.

51. William R. Taylor, *Inventing Times Square: Commerce and Culture at the Crossroads of the World* (Baltimore: Johns Hopkins University Press, 1991), 16–50 passim; Leach, *The Land of Desire*, Patten on 235.

52. Walter Dill Scott, *The Psychology of Advertising* (Boston: Small, Maynard, 1913), 47–115 passim, quotations on 79–83. Scott defined instinct as "the faculty of acting in such a way as to produce certain ends, without foresight of the ends" (52); compare with John Dewey's effort to promote habits of thought that subjected uninterrogated desire to critical scrutiny in terms of origins and consequences; Robert Westbrook, *John Dewey and American Democracy* (Ithaca, NY: Cornell University Press, 1991), 402–418, especially 409–410; Loren Baritz, *The Servants of Power: A History of the Use of Social Science in American Industry* (New York: John Wiley & Sons, 1965), 26–27 passim; Ewen, *Captains of Consciousness*, 31–39; Lasch, *The Culture of Narcissism*, 283–284.

53. Lasch, *The Culture of Narcissism*, 308–312; 135–141; Ewen, *Captains of Consciousness*, 31–39, "enlarged," "keep," and "profitable" on 39, "bludgeon" on 37.

54. Robert E. Park, "Community Organization and the Romantic Temper," in Robert E. Park and Ernest Burgess, *The City* (Chicago: University of Chicago Press, 1925), 113–122.

55. Lasch, *The Culture of Narcissism*, 135–140, 221–229, 288–291: "philosophy" on 138, "onerous" on 288; Roediger and Foner, *Our Own Time*, Green on 237.

56. "That way lay Bolshevism," argued New York's mayor in reference to impartial enforcement of Prohibition. "You took away our beer, now take away the snow," read the protest of a snow removal gang. Rosenzweig, *Eight Hours for What We Will*, 208–228, "former" on 189–190; Rumbarger, *Profits, Power, and Prohibition*, 189–198, National Commission on 196; Stanley Walker, *The Night Club Era* (New York: Blue Ribbon Books, 1933), "Bolshevism" and "snow" on 51–54, 89, 133.

57. Having spent most of the decade as secretary of commerce building an activist state committed to business expansion, Hoover shared the AAPA's concern. Rosenzweig, *Eight Hours for What We Will*, 183–198: "mild" on 190, "essential" on 198; Rumbarger, *Profits, Power, and Prohibition*, 189–198; Ellis W. Hawley, "Herbert Hoover, the Commerce Secretariat, and the Vision of an "Associative State,' 1921–1928," *Journal of American History* 61 (June 1974): 117–140; Leach, *Land of Desire*, 349–378; Ellis W. Hawley, *The Great War and the Search for a Modern Order* (New York: St. Martin's Press, 1979).

58. Leach, *Land of Desire*, 349–378.

59. Leach, *Land of Desire*, quotations on 349–358; Hawley, "Herbert Hoover, the Commerce Secretariat, and the Vision of an "Associative State,' 1921–1928."

60. Leach, *Land of Desire*, 358–368.

61. Leach, *Land of Desire*, 183–185, 349–378.

62. Lizabeth Cohen, *Making a New Deal: Industrial Workers in Chicago, 1919–1939* (New York: Cambridge University Press, 1990), 129–144; Robert W. McChesney, "The Battle for the U.S. Airwaves, 1928–1935," *Journal of Communications* 40 (1990): 29–57; the Radio Act of 1927 and related documents are reproduced in Frank J. Kahn, ed., *Documents of American Broadcasting* (New York, 1968).

63. McChesney, "The Battle for the U.S. Airwaves, 1928–1935," 29–34, "feeling" on 32; Asa Briggs, *Mass Entertainment: The Origins of a Modern Industry* (Adelaide: Griffin Press, 1960), "pathetic" on 25–27.

64. Gleason L. Archer, *The History of Radio* (New York: The American Historical Society, Inc., 1938), "emancipation," 267–276, 397–399; McChesney, "The Battle for the U.S. Airwaves, 1928–1935," 29–34; Cohen, *Making a New Deal*, 129–144.

65. McChesney, "The Battle for the U.S. Airwaves, 1928–1935," 34–40, "given" on 36; Cohen, *Making a New Deal*, 141.

66. McChesney, "The Battle for the U.S. Airwaves, 1928–1935," 39–49; John Dewey, "Our Un-Free Press," *Common Sense* 4 (November 1935): 6–7; John Dewey, "Radio—for Propaganda or Public Interest?" *Education by Radio* (February 28, 1935): 11.

67. McChesney, "The Battle for the U.S. Airwaves, 1928–1935," 39–49, RCA and CBS executives quoted on 47; Dewey, "Our Un-Free Press"; Dewey, "Radio—for Propaganda or Public Interest?"

68. Cohen, *Making a New Deal*, 99–158, quotations on 100.

69. Cohen, *Making a New Deal*, 99–158, 323–360; Lary May, *The Big Tomorrow: Hollywood and the Politics of the American Way* (Chicago: University of Chicago Press, 2002); Hadley Cantril and Gordon W. Allport, *The Psychology of Radio* (New York: Harper & Brothers, 1935), "imaginative" on 331.

70. Cohen, *Making a New Deal*, 323–360, "sichyation" on 329; May, *The Big Tomorrow*; Cantril and Allport, *The Psychology of Radio*, 11–12, 21; Alan Brinkley, *Voices of Protest* (New York: Vintage Books, 1983).

71. Updating Alexis de Tocqueville, Riesman asked why "one kind of social character, which dominated America in the nineteenth century, is gradually being replaced by a social character of quite a different sort." David Riesman, *The Lonely Crowd*, 3–36, 83–116, 126–160, quotations on 3 and 5. Riesman repeatedly invoked Tocqueville in his study. For a complementary account of another twentieth-century Tocqueville, see Richard H. Millington, "Hitchcock and American Character: The Comedy of Self-Construction in *North by Northwest*," in *Hitchcock's America*, ed. Jonathan Freedman and Richard H. Millington (New York: Oxford University Press, 1999), 135–154.

72. Riesman, *The Lonely Crowd*, 3–85.

73. Riesman, *The Lonely Crowd*, 163–187.

74. Riesman, *The Lonely Crowd*, 3–36, 83–108, 163–187.

75. Riesman, *The Lonely Crowd*, 188–205.

76. Riesman, *The Lonely Crowd*, 190–197; Robert Westbrook, "Politics as Consumption: Managing the Modern American Election," in *The Culture of Consumption*, ed. Richard Wightman Fox and T. J. Jackson Lears (New York: Pantheon Books, 1983), 145–173, "mer-

chandising" on 155; Douglas T. Miller, *On Our Own: Americans in the Sixties* (Lexington, MA: D.C. Heath, 1996), "society-made" on 30; Eisenhower's warning from his Farewell Address in Robert Griffith, ed., *Major Problems in American History since 1945* (Lexington, MA: D.C. Heath, 1992), 166–167; Lasch, *The Culture of Narcissism*, 124.

77. Riesman, *The Lonely Crowd*, 188–235.

78. Riesman, *The Lonely Crowd*, 276–303.

79. Riesman, *The Lonely Crowd*, 304–307; Cohen, *A Consumers' Republic*, 292–331; Westbrook, "Politics as Consumption," 145–173.

80. The "polity," Westbrook writes, "has become a caricature of the social world of the lonely crowd." Westbrook, "Politics as Consumption," 145–173; Cohen, *A Consumers' Republic*, 309–397.

81. The radar analogy is Westbrook's. Westbrook, "Politics as Consumption," 145–173, "voting" on 155; Cohen, *A Consumers' Republic*, 309–397.

82. Cohen, *A Consumers' Republic*, 345–397; Thomas Byrne Edsall, "The 'Reagan Revolution' as a Revolution from Above," in *The Reagan Legacy*, ed. Sidney Blumenthal and Thomas Byrne Edsall (New York: Pantheon Books, 1988).

CHAPTER 11

1. Jon C. Teaford, *The Metropolitan Revolution* (New York: Columbia University Press, 2006), 8–9, city planner Cleveland Rodgers quoted on 8; Henry George, *Progress and Poverty* (New York: H. George, 1879), "wider" on 213; Christopher Lasch, *The Revolt of the Elites and the Betrayal of Democracy* (New York: W. W. Norton & Company, 1995), 129–133; Jon C. Teaford, *The Unheralded Triumph: City Government in America, 1870–1900* (Baltimore: Johns Hopkins University Press, 1984); Robert Fishman, ed., *The American Planning Tradition: Culture and Policy* (Washington, DC: Woodrow Wilson Center Press, 2000); Thomas Bender, *New York Intellect* (Baltimore: Johns Hopkins University Press, 1988), 3–6.

2. Christopher Lasch, *Women and the Common Life* (New York: W. W. Norton, 1997), Antin on 98; Clifton Hood, *722 Miles: The Building of the Subways and How They Transformed New York* (New York: Simon & Schuster, 1993), 11–132.

3. Adam Rome, *The Bulldozer in the Countryside* (New York: Cambridge University Press, 2001), 1–118, "fresh" on 40; Lizabeth Cohen, *A Consumers' Republic* (New York: Knopf, 2003), 62–165, "mass" on 102; Alan Brinkley, *The End of Reform: New Deal Liberalism in Recession and War* (New York: Alfred A. Knopf, 1995); Robert O. Self, *American Babylon: Race and the Struggle for Postwar Oakland* (Princeton, NJ: Princeton University Press, 2003), 3 passim; Jon C. Teaford, *The Metropolitan Revolution*, 72–73; Kevin M. Kruse, *White Flight: Atlanta and the Making of Modern Conservatism* (Princeton, NJ: Princeton University Press, 2005), 234–266.

4. *Report of the National Advisory Commission on Civil Disorders* (Washington, D.C.: U.S. Govt. Print. Off., 1968), quotations on 1, 28; Arnold R. Hirsch, *Making the Second Ghetto: Race and Housing in Chicago, 1940–1960* (New York: Cambridge University Press, 1983); Self, *American Babylon*; Thomas J. Sugrue, *The Origins of the Urban Crisis: Race and Inequality in Postwar Detroit* (Princeton, NJ: Princeton University Press, 1996); Teaford, *Metropolitan Revolution*; Douglas S. Massey and Nancy Denton, *American Apartheid* (Cambridge: Harvard University Press, 1993); Raymond A. Mohl, "Race and Space in the Modern City: Interstate-95 and the Black Community in Miami," in *Urban Policy in Twentieth-Century America*, ed. Arnold R. Hirsch and Raymond A. Mohl (New Brunswick, NJ: Rutgers University Press, 1993).

5. Rome, *The Bulldozer in the Countryside*, Bowles on 32–33; Cohen, *Consumers' Republic*, 112–289; Kenneth T. Jackson, *Crabgrass Frontier: The Suburbanization of the United States* (New York: Oxford University Press, 1985), 190–230; Teaford, *Metropolitan Revolution*, Levitt on 79; Cohen, *A Consumers' Republic*, 62–165; Nicholas Dagen Bloom, *Merchant of Illusion: James Rouse, America's Salesman of the Businessman's Utopia* (Columbus, OH: Ohio State University Press, 2004).

6. Alan Wolfe, *America's Impasse: The Rise and Fall of the Politics of Growth* (New York: Pantheon Books, 1981); Brinkley, *The End of Reform*; Michael J. Sandel, *Democracy's Discontent: America in Search of a Public Philosophy* (Cambridge, MA: Belknap Press of Harvard University Press, 1996); Jackson, *Crabgrass Frontier*, 190–230, FHA official quoted on 190; Self, *American Babylon*, 10–12 passim; Cohen, *A Consumers' Republic*, 62–165, 204–205.

7. Jackson, *Crabgrass Frontier*, 219–230; Bloom, *Merchant of Illusion*. For an example of the potential of even modest public investments, see Wendell Pritchett, *Brownsville, Brooklyn: Blacks, Jews, and the Changing Face of the Ghetto* (Chicago: University of Chicago Press, 2002), 256ff.

8. Teaford, *Metropolitan Revolution*, 1–7; Self, *American Babylon*; Kruse, *White Flight*.

9. Jon C. Teaford, *Rough Road to Renaissance: Urban Revitalization in America, 1940-1985* (Baltimore: Johns Hopkins University Press, 1990), 253–307; Kruse, *White Flight*, 234–258, "seceding" on 246; Teaford, *Metropolitan Revolution*, "golden" and "vitality" on 137–138.

10. Rome, *The Bulldozer in the Countryside*, 1–43: Hoover on 20–21, the phrase "suburban-industrial complex" is journalist Godfrey Hodgson's, on 43; Jackson, *Crabgrass Frontier*, 190–218; Teaford, *Metropolitan Revolution*, 62–72.

11. Jackson, *Crabgrass Frontier*, 190–218; Teaford, *Metropolitan Revolution*, 62–72.

12. By standardizing mortgage arrangements, Fannie Mae (Federal National Mortgage Association) also encouraged local capital to flow out of cities into suburbs. Jackson, *Crabgrass Frontier*, 190–218; Teaford, *Metropolitan Revolution*, 62–72; Hirsch, *Making the Second Ghetto*, 10; Sugrue, *Origins of the Urban Crisis*, 41–47.

13. Jackson, *Crabgrass Frontier*, 190–218; Sugrue, *Origins of the Urban Crisis*, 63–72; Teaford, *Metropolitan Revolution*, 62–72.

14. Traditional mortgages extended over shorter periods and required a balloon payment at the end. Jackson, *Crabgrass Frontier*, 190–218; Teaford, *Metropolitan Revolution*, 72–89; Rome, *The Bulldozer in the Countryside*, 34–43.

15. Owen D. Gutfreund, *20th-Century Sprawl; Highways and the Reshaping of the American Landscape* (New York: Oxford University Press, 2005), 19–59; Jane Holtz Kay, *Asphalt Nation: How the Automobile Took Over America, and How We Can Take It Back* (Berkeley: University of California Press, 1997), 35–53, 195–245; Jackson, *Crabgrass Frontier*, 248–251; Teaford, *Rough Road to Renaissance*, 93–105.

16. Kay, *Asphalt Nation*, 214–245; Teaford, *Rough Road to Renaissance*, 93–105; Jackson, *Crabgrass Frontier*, 248–251.

17. Jackson, *Crabgrass Frontier*, 219–230; Bloom, *Merchant of Illusion*, 56–106; *Historical Statistics of the United States* (Washington, DC: U.S Govt. Print. Off., 1960), 394–395.

18. Jackson, *Crabgrass Frontier*, 219–230; Bloom, *Merchant of Illusion*, ix–xxii, 1–106, *Fortune* quoted on 10; Roger Biles, "Public Housing and the Postwar Urban Renaissance," in *From Tenements to the Taylor Homes*, ed. John F. Bauman, Roger Biles, and Krisin M. Szylvian (University Park, PA: Pennsylvania State University, 2000), 144–159; Sugrue, *Origins of the Urban Crisis*, 33–55; Cohen, *A Consumers' Republic*, 62–165, Truman quoted on 122; Rome, *The Bulldozer in the Countryside*, 1–43.

19. Rome, *The Bulldozer in the Countryside*, 1–43: "identical" on 15, "planning" on 1; Teaford, *Metropolitan Revolution*, 72–85; Self, *American Babylon*, 255–265.

20. Rome, *The Bulldozer in the Countryside*, 1–86, "victory" on 36 (italics in original); Cohen, *A Consumers' Republic*, 62–165; Teaford, *Metropolitan Revolution*, 72–107.

21. Teaford, *Metropolitan Revolution*, 72–107, "imagination" on 74; Cohen, *A Consumers' Republic*, 257–289.

22. Cohen, *A Consumers' Republic*, 257–289; Bloom, *Merchant of Illusion*, 107–125; Teaford, *Metropolitan Revolution*, 91–107, quotations on 96; Sugrue, *Origins of the Urban Crisis*, 112–113.

23. Cohen, *A Consumers' Republic*, 257–289; Teaford, *Metropolitan Revolution*, 8–204, on municipal revenues, 19; Teaford, *Rough Road to Renaissance*, 200–252 passim; Self,

American Babylon, 135–214; Sugrue, *Origins of the Urban Crisis*; Jon C. Teaford, *Cities of the Heartland* (Bloomington, IN: Indiana University Press, 1994), 211–252.

24. Teaford, *Metropolitan Revolution*, 8–89; Jon C. Teaford, *Rough Road to Renaissance*, 1–121; Kay, *Asphalt Nation*, 195–226.

25. Teaford, *Metropolitan Revolution*, 8–89; Jon C. Teaford, *Rough Road to Renaissance*, 1–121; Self, *American Babylon*, 23–60; Sugrue, *Origins of the Urban Crisis*, 1–33, "You" on 27; Hirsch, *Making the Second Ghetto*, 1–37; Pritchett, *Brownsville*, 51–103; Nicholas Lemann, *The Promised Land: The Great Black Migration and How It Changed America* (New York: A. A. Knopf, 1991).

26. Cohen, *A Consumers' Republic*, 100–129; James R. Green, *The World of the Worker* (New York: Hill and Wang, 1980), 193–195; Self, *American Babylon*, 1–95; Sugrue, *Origins of the Urban Crisis*, 1–33; 125–164; Pritchett, *Brownsville*, 62–145, "dirty" on 64–65.

27. Cohen, *A Consumers' Republic*, 100–129; Green, *The Word of the Worker*, 193–195; Pritchett, *Brownsville*, 62–145.

28. Sugrue, *Origins of the Urban Crisis*, 125–152, "militant" on 138; Teaford, *Cities of the Heartland*, 184–187, "take" on 185; Self, *American Babylon*, 23–60, "happiness" on 29; Cohen, *A Consumers' Republic*, 112–129.

29. Sugrue, *Origins of the Urban Crisis*, 125–152; Teaford, *Metropolitan Revolution*, 126–139; Self, *American Babylon*, 96–214; Roger Lotchin, *The Martial Metropolis* (New York: Praeger, 1984); Ann Markusen, *The Rise of the Gunbelt* (New York: Oxford University Press, 1991).

30. Sugrue, *Origins of the Urban Crisis*, 125–152.

31. Sugrue, *Origins of the Urban Crisis*, 143–177.

32. Sugrue, *Origins of the Urban Crisis*, 143–177.

33. Sugrue, *Origins of the Urban Crisis*, 143–177; Self, *American Babylon*, 96–131; Cohen, *A Consumers' Republic*, 194–289; Kruse, *White Flight*, 242–251.

34. Jackson's sample of 241 mortgages in St. Louis showed 220 in suburbs—half to former urbanites from B classification (i.e., stable, middle-income) neighborhoods. Jackson, *Crabgrass Frontier*, 190–218; Self, *American Babylon*, 96–100, quotations on 97 and 99; Kruse, *White Flight*, 242–251; Pritchett, *Brownsville*, 48, 53; Mike Davis, *City of Quartz; Excavating the Future in Los Angeles* (New York: Verso, 1990), 165–169.

35. Self, *American Babylon*, 61–111; Teaford, *Metropolitan Revolution*, 72–89.

36. Self, *American Babylon*, 100–111; Kruse, *White Flight*, 242–251, quoted passage on 249.

37. Self, *American Babylon*, 109–119.

38. Self, *American Babylon*, 109–119.

39. Self, *American Babylon*, 109–131; Kruse, *White Flight*, 242–251, quotation on 247.

40. Self, *American Babylon*, 157–176, 256–272; Cohen, *A Consumers' Republic*, 194–256, 331–344, quotations on 229; Kruse, *White Flight*, 234–258.

41. Sugrue, *Origins of the Urban Crisis*, 125–164, 209–229; Self, *American Babylon*, 34–46, 76–95.

42. Sugrue, *Origins of the Urban Crisis*, 33–88: "time" on 33, "brains" on 36; Hirsch, *Making the Second Ghetto*, 1–67; Bloom, *Merchant of Illusion*, 56–106; Teaford, *Metropolitan Revolution*, 8–9; Self, *American Babylon*, 46–95; Jackson, *Crabgrass Frontier*, 190–230; Cohen, *Consumers' Republic*, 200–227; Teaford, *Rough Road to Renaissance*, 44–121; Roger Biles, "Public Housing and the Postwar Urban Renaissance," 144–159.

43. Sugrue, *Origins of the Urban Crisis*, 1–35, 81–207, 231–258; Hirsch, *Making the Second Ghetto*, 1–99; Kruse, *White Flight*, 42–130.

44. Sugrue, *Origins of the Urban Crisis*, 125–164, 209–258, "right" on 227; Kruse, *White Flight*, 42–130; Self, *American Babylon*, 34–46, 76–95, 159–170, "property" on 167.

45. Sugrue, *Origins of the Urban Crisis*, 1–35, 81–258, "hypocrites" on 227; Hirsch, *The Making of the Second Ghetto*, 1–99, 171–211; Kruse, *White Flight*, 42–130.

46. Sugrue, *Origins of the Urban Crisis*, 57–88, "Housing" on 76; Hirsch, *Making the Second Ghetto*, 212–258 passim; Self, *American Babylon*, 62–76.

47. Sugrue, *Origins of the Urban Crisis*, 57–88; Pritchett, *Brownsville*, 147–173.

48. Hirsch, *Making the Second Ghetto*, 36–99, 127–134, 212–228, 248–253; Sugrue, *Origins of the Urban Crisis*, 231–258.

49. Hirsch, *Making the Second Ghetto*, 220–263: "hate" on 227, "pyramiding" on 243; Teaford, *Metropolitan Revolution*, 62–72, 139–142.

50. Hirsch, *Making the Second Ghetto*, 253–258, "determine" and "deep-felt" on 254–255; Sugrue, *Origins of the Urban Crisis*, 57–88, 231–258, "spawned" on 258; Teaford, *Metropolitan Revolution*, 139–149.

51. Hirsch, *Making the Second Ghetto*, 100–108: "rehabilitation," "restore," and "loss" on 101, "only way" on 108; Teaford, *Metropolitan Revolution*, 49–62; Teaford, *Rough Road to Renaissance*, 44–81; Teaford, *Cities of the Heartland*, 213–216; Bloom, *Merchant of Illusion*, 56–106, "slum" on 64.

52. The following six paragraphs are based on Hirsch, *Making the Second Ghetto*, 103–174; see also Teaford, *Rough Road to Renaissance*, 105–120, 145–162.

53. Hirsch, *Making the Second Ghetto*, 259–275; Self, *American Babylon*, 135–149; June Manning Thomas, "Urban Renewal," in Neil Larry Shumsky, *Encyclopedia of Urban America: The Cities and Suburbs*, vol. 2 (Santa Barbara, CA: ABC-CLIO, 1998), 826–829; the Housing Acts of 1959 and 1961 authorized assistance to, respectively, universities and hospitals. Bernard J. Friden and Lynne B. Sagalayn, *Downtown, Inc.: How America Rebuilds Cities* (Cambridge, MA: MIT Press, 1989), 17; Bloom, *Merchant of Illusion*, 16–55, "reverse welfare state" is the judgment of historian Roy Lubove, quoted on 53; Teaford, *Rough Road to Renaissance*, 105–121, 145–162; Joel Schwartz, *The New York Approach: Robert Moses, Urban Liberals, and the Redevelopment of the Inner City* (Columbus, OH: Ohio State University Press, 1993); John Emmeus Davis, *Contested Ground: Collective Action and the Urban Neighborhood* (Ithaca, NY: Cornell University Press, 1991), 99–140.

54. Davis, *Contested Ground*, 128–149, quotation on 146.

55. Self, *American Babylon*, 135–149.

56. Self, *American Babylon*, 135–149.

57. Self, *American Babylon*, 149–155.

58. Kay, *Asphalt Nation*, 44–48; Bloom, *Merchant of Illusion*, 58–61, "shape and definition" is James Rouse, quoted on 61; Robert A. Caro, *The Power Broker: Robert Moses and the Fall of New York* (New York: Knopf, 1974), 520–525 passim; Sugrue, *Origins of the Urban Crisis*, 47–48, "handy" quoted on 47; Raymond Mohl, "Planned Destruction: The Interstates and Central City Housing," in *From Tenements to Taylor Homes*, ed. Bauman, Biles, and Szylvian; Raymond A. Mohl, "Stop the Road: Freeway Revolts in American Cities," *Journal of Urban History* 30 (July 2004): 674–706.

59. Self, *American Babylon*, 155–159, "eerie" on 157; Pritchett, *Brownsville*, 243–250; Hirsch, *Making of the Second Ghetto*, 202–203, 230, 273–274; Sugrue, *Origins of the Urban Crisis*, 36, 47–51, 294–295; Mohl, "Stop the Road"; Mohl, "Planned Destruction"; Teaford, *Metropolitan Revolution*, 112–122, "racially" on 115.

60. Hirsch, *Making the Second Ghetto*, 15, 129–133, 248–250; Sugrue, *Origins of the Urban Crisis*; Self, *American Babylon*.

61. Self, *American Babylon*, 82–87; 177–214, quotations on 188; Sugrue, *Origins of the Urban Crisis*, 170–177.

62. Self, *American Babylon*, 177–214.

63. Pritchett, *Brownsville*, 175–189.

64. Self, *American Babylon*, 182–196: "property owners" on 193, "bull dozed," and "tax money" on 195.

65. Self, *American Babylon*, 195–198.

66. Allen J. Matusow, *Unraveling of America: The History of Liberalism* (New York: Harper & Row, 1984), 97–127, 217–271; Self, *American Babylon*, 198–205, "talk" on 203; Sugrue, *Origins of the Urban Crisis*, 170–177; Teaford, *Metropolitan Revolution*, 147–148; Pritchett, *Brownsville*, 191–197.

67. Pritchett, *Brownsville*, 191–219.

68. Pritchett, *Brownsville*, 191–219.
69. Self, *American Babylon*, 149–155, 204–210.
70. Self, *American Babylon*, 209–214.
71. Self, *American Babylon*, 233–242.
72. Pritchett, *Brownsville*, 221–227.
73. Pritchett, *Brownsville*, 226–229.
74. Pritchett, *Brownsville*, 228–233.
75. Pritchett, *Brownsville*, 228–237.
76. Self, *American Babylon*, 217–233; Teaford, *Metropolitan Revolution*, 125–164; *Report of the National Advisory Commission on Civil Disorders*; Robert M. Fogelson, *Violence as Protest: A Study of Riots and Ghettos* (Garden City, NY: Doubleday, 1971).
77. Cohen, *Consumers' Republic*, 355–376; Teaford, *Metropolitan Revolution*, 125–164; Teaford, *Rough Road to Renaissance*, 200–203, "Indian" on 202.
78. The San Leandro precincts bordering Oakland voted over 80 percent in favor of Proposition 14; the adjoining Oakland precincts voted over 92 percent against. Self, *American Babylon*, 157–176, 256–272, "responsible" on 266; Cohen, *A Consumers' Republic*, 194–256.
79. Self, *American Babylon*, 256–272; Lisa McGirr, *Suburban Warriors: The Origins of the New Right* (Princeton, NJ: Princeton University Press, 2001), 3–53, 182–186, "philosophy" on 185; Kruse, *White Flight*, passim.
80. McGirr, *Suburban Warriors*, 187–210, quotations on 188, 199, and 204; Self, *American Babylon*, 256–290.
81. Cohen, *A Consumers' Republic*, 194–256, 235–238, "established" on 237; Self, *American Babylon*, 272–281, "It" on 279.
82. Teaford, *Metropolitan Revolution*, 151–156, "bound" on 154; Sugrue, *Origins of the Urban Crisis*, 259–271.
83. Self, *American Babylon*, 155–176, 312–314; Teaford, *Metropolitan Revolution*, 125–164; Teaford, *Rough Road to Renaissance*, 200–252; Heather Ann Thompson, "Rethinking the Collapse of Postwar Liberalism: The Rise of Mayor Coleman Young and the Politics of Race in Detroit," in *African-American Mayors: Race, Politics and the American City* (Urbana, IL: University of Illinois Press, 2001), ed. Colburn and Adler, 227–248.
84. Pritchett, *Brownsville*, 239–255: "Block" on 245, "tangible" on 242; Self, *American Babylon*, 155–176, 312–314; Teaford, *Rough Road to Renaissance*, 200–252; Teaford, *Metropolitan Revolution*, 125–164; Davis, *City of Quartz*, 284–316.
85. Self, *American Babylon*, 281–290; McGirr, *Suburban Warriors*, 182–216, 237–240.
86. Self, *American Babylon*, 316–327; McGirr, *Suburban Warriors*, 147–240; Kruse, *White Flight*, 234–266.
87. Self, *American Babylon*, 316–327; McGirr, *Suburban Warriors*, 147–240; Kruse, *White Flight*, 234–266.
88. Kruse, *White Flight*, 105–179, 234–266: quotations on 115 and 130, "vote" on 130, "abandoned" on 11; Cohen, *A Consumers' Republic*, 173–191.
89. Kruse, *White Flight*, 234–266, Nixon on 255; McGirr, *Suburban Warriors*, 210–216; Self, *American Babylon*, 309–327.
90. Kruse, *White Flight*, 234–266; McGirr, *Suburban Warriors*, 259–274; Teaford, *Rough Road to Renaissance*, 12–18, 44–121, 218–231: Chicago report quoted on 79, Boston's mayor quoted on 225, "taxpayer" quoted on 17; Jackson, *Crabgrass Frontier*, on New York City's revenues, 191.
91. Teaford, *Rough Road to Renaissance*, 12–18, 218–231, "who" on 17.
92. Cohen, *A Consumers' Republic*, 173–191; Kruse, *White Flight*, 105–179, 234–266; Teaford, *Rough Road to Renaissance*, quotations on 1, 287 and 306; Michael Sorkin, ed., *Variations on a Theme Park: The New American City and the End of Public Space* (New York: Noonday Press, 1992); Sharon Zukin, *Landscapes of Power: From Detroit to Disney World* (Berkeley: University of California Press, 1991).
93. Teaford, *Rough Road to Renaissance*, 253–307, "mall" on 272; Cohen, *A Consumers' Republic*, 274–278, 286–289: "surprising" on 277, "fortresses" on 289.

340 • NOTES TO CHAPTER 11

94. Cohen, *A Consumers' Republic*, 257–289; Bloom, *Merchant of Illusion*, 107–125, Rouse on 121.
95. Cohen, *A Consumes' Republic*, 274–278, "streets" on 275; Bloom, *Merchant of Illusion*, 120–125.
96. Kay, *Asphalt Nation*, quotations on 50; Davis, *City of Quartz*, 221–263; Davis, *The Ecology of Fear*; Sorkin, *Variations on a Theme Park*.
97. Kruse, *White Flight*, 259–266.

CONCLUSION

1. Michael Tomasky, "The Democrats," *New York Review of Books* (March 15, 2007): 16–18; Robert L. Borosage, "Where's the Idea Primary?" *The Nation* (March 19, 2007): 4–5.
2. Michael Tomasky, "How Democrats Should Talk," *New York Review of Books* (May 31, 2007): 26–28; Daniel Rodgers, *Contested Truths* (New York: Basic Books, 1987); Mary Ann Glendon, *Rights Talk* (New York: Maxwell Macmillan, 1991); Louis Menand, "Inside the Billway," *New York Review of Books* (August 14, 1997): 4; Tom Ichinowski, "Federal Outlays Hit 50-Year Low," *Engineering News Record* (February 16, 1998): 10.
3. This paragraph and the next five are based on "On Civic Liberalism: A Symposium," *New Republic* (June 18, 1990): 26–29; "The End of Equality," *New Republic* (August 10, 1992): 24–25; Mickey Kaus, *The End of Equality* (New York: Basic Books, 1995).
4. Kaus, *The End of Equality*, 149.
5. Samuel P. Hays, "From the History of the City to the History of the Urbanized Society," *Journal of Urban History* 19 (August 1993): 3–24; Andrew Hurley, *Environmental Inequalities: Class, Race, and Industrial Pollution in Gary, Indiana, 1945–1980* (Chapel Hill, NC: University of North Carolina Press, 1995); Julie Sze, *Noxious New York: The Racial Politics of Urban Health and Environmental Justice* (Cambridge, MA: MIT Press, 2007); Mike Davis, *The Ecology of Fear* (New York: Metropolitan Books, 1998), 93–147; Murray Bookchin, *From Urbanization to Cities: Toward a New Politics of Citizenship* (New York: Cassell, 1995); Richard Register, *Ecocities: Building Cities in Balance with Nature* (Gabriola, BC: New Society Publishers, 2006).
6. Davis, *Ecology of Fear*, 57–91; John Kenneth Galbraith, *The Affluent Society* (New York: New American Library, 1958), 186–199, quotations on 190; Robert Fishman, *Bourgeois Utopias: The Rise and Fall of Suburbia* (New York: Basic Books, 1987), x, 155–181, the phrase "collective effort to live a private life" is Lewis Mumford's, quoted on x.
7. Mike Davis, *City of Quartz; Excavating the Future in Los Angeles* (New York: Verso, 1990), 153–219, "exit" on 166; Lizabeth Cohen, *A Consumers' Republic* (New York: Knopf, 2003), 193–289.
8. Davis, *City of Quartz*, 153–219, "planning" on 198.
9. Davis, *City of Quartz*, 223–263, "type" on 231, "containment" on 232; Davis, *Ecology of Fear*, 336, 359–422; Michael Sorkin, ed., *Variations on a Theme Park: The New American City and the End of Public Space* (New York: Noonday Press, 1992), 123–153; Cohen, *A Consumers' Republic*, 286–289.
10. Davis, *City of Quartz*, 369–377.
11. Davis, *City of Quartz*, 236–244, quotations on 238–239; Sorkin, *Variations on a Theme Park*, 61–93.
12. Davis, *City of Quartz*, 250–253, "good" is Davis's summary.
13. Davis, *City of Quartz*, 244–250; Davis, *Ecology of Fear*, 366–368.
14. Davis, *Ecology of Fear*, 359–422, "Brinks" on 380.
15. Davis, *Ecology of Fear*, 392–418.
16. Davis, *Ecology of Fear*, 3–55, 95–147.
17. Davis, *Ecology of Fear*, 273–355; Christopher Lasch, *The True and Only Heaven: Progress and Its Critics* (New York: Norton, 1991), 168–170.
18. Davis, *Ecology of Fear*, 273–355; Christopher Lasch, *The Minimal Self* (New York: W. W. Norton, 1984).

19. Mark Wild, *Street Meeting: Multiethnic Neighborhoods in Early Twentieth-Century Los Angeles* (Berkeley, CA: University of California Press, 2005); Mary P. Ryan, "A Durable Centre of Urban Space: The Los Angeles Plaza, *Urban History* 33 (2006): 457–483.

20. Samuel P. Hays, "From Conservation to Environment: Environmental Politics in the United States since World War II," *Environmental Review* 6 (Fall 1982): 14–29; Samuel P. Hays, *Beauty, Health, and Permanence: Environmental Politics in the United States, 1955–1985* (New York: Cambridge University Press, 1987); Adam Rome, *The Bulldozer in the Countryside* (New York: Cambridge University Press, 2001); Samuel P. Hays, *Conservation and the Gospel of Efficiency* (Cambridge, MA: Harvard University Press, 1959).

21. Rome, *Bulldozer in the Countryside*; Samuel P. Hays, *Explorations in Environmental History* (Pittsburgh: University of Pittsburgh Press, 1998); Christopher C. Sellers, "Environmentalists by Nature: The Postwar America of Samuel Hays," *Reviews in American History* (March 2000): 112–119; Nathan Hare, "Black Ecology," in *Major Problems in American Environmental History*, ed. Carolyn Merchant (Lexington, MA: D.C. Heath, 1993), 479–482.

22. This paragraph and the next five are based on Rome, *Bulldozer in the Countryside*, 181–188, 221–253, 248–270 passim.

23. "Bubble Capitalism," *The Nation* (August 19/26, 2002): 3–5; Henry Glassie, "Vernacular Architecture and Society," *Material Culture* 16 (1984): 7–22.

24. Thomas Bender, "The End of the City," *Democracy* 13 (Winter 1983): 8–20.

25. Bookchin, *From Urbanization to Cities*, quotations on 231–236; Bender, "End of the City"; Karl Polanyi, *The Great Transformation* (Boston: Beacon Press, 1944); Ira Katznelson, *City Trenches* (New York: Pantheon Books, 1981); Jean Bethke Elshtain, "Catholic Social Thought, the City, and Liberal America," in *Catholicism and Liberalism: Contributions to American Public Philosophy*, ed. R. Bruce Douglass and David Hollenbach (New York: Cambridge University Press, 1994), 97–114.

26. Frederick L. Ackerman, "The Battle With Chaos," *Journal of the American Institute of Architects* 3 (1915), 444-447; Frederick L. Ackerman, "The Relation of Art to Education," *Journal of the American Institute of Architects* 4 (1916): 234–238; Robert Fishman, ed., *The American Planning Tradition: Culture and Policy* (Washington, DC: Woodrow Wilson Center Press, 2000), 4–7.

27. Fishman, *The American Planning Tradition*, 5, 241–261, 297–313.

28. Henry George, *Progress and Poverty* (New York: H. George, 1887), "localized" on 211; Louis F. Post and Fred C. Luebuscher, *Henry George's 1886 Campaign* (Westport, CT: Hyperion Press, 1976), "enormous" on 14; John D. Fairfield, "A Populism for the Cities: John Dewey, Henry George and the City Planning Movement," *Urban Design Studies* 8 (2002): 19–27.

29. Henry George, *Social Problems* (New York: Doubleday, Page & Company, 1883), 20–30, 234–240: "forests" on 27, "impoverishes" and "breathing room" on 238.

30. Davis, *Ecology of Fear*, 59–91

31. William K. Reilly, ed., *The Uses of Land: A Citizen's Policy Guide to Urban Growth* (New York: Crowell, 1973), quoted in Rome, *Bulldozer in the Countryside*, 137–138; Sharon Zukin, *Landscapes of Power: From Detroit to Disney World* (BerkeleyL University of California Press, 1991), 271–275. Zukin describes an "innate populism" that makes Americans receptive to "a politics that emphasizes local continuity, a social return on investment to citizens . . . and obligations on businesses to put down roots."

INDEX

Addams, Jane, 146, 155, 164; influence on John Dewey, 173; and labor movement, 149–150; on Pullman, 65, 66–67; and settlement house movement, 135, 149–150

advertising: and domesticity, 239, 244; and independent journalism, 137; and market segmentation, 236–237; and politics, 139, 177, 225, 230, 235–236, 312n72; psychology of, 229–230, 333n52; and radio, 232–233; reshaping character and personality, 223, 228–230, 234–236; strategies of enticement, 144, 215–216, 223; and transformation of city, 166, 188–189, 191–192, 226

African Americans, xi, 120, 133, 246; in abolitionist movement, 90; and affirmative action, 257–258; black power movement, 256, 259–260; as central-city homeowners, 247, 250–251; and community action/control, 258–260; and demand for citizenship, 31, 46, 48, 49, 50–51, 60, 109, 110; and democratic legacy of the Revolution, 31–32; depicted in minstrel shows, 89, 302n71; dispossessed of vital neighborhoods, 253–256; electoral success in cities, 263; excluded from or segregated in antebellum cities, 31; and free labor ideal, 45–48; and housing discrimination, 242, 248–249, 250, 252, 253; and industrial decentralization, 247; in Jacksonian cities, 31, 39, 40, 77; judged as unprepared for citizenship, 39–40, 49, 54, 56, 121; limits of Revolution for, 29–32; as model working class, 105, 106, 109; and movies, 163; and open/fair housing, 249, 250–251, 254, 256–257, 261–262; political implications of segregation, pro and con, 252, 256–257; and the post-1945 second ghetto, 252; preparation for and use of citizenship in Civil War era, 46–48; and racial liberalism in 1940s, 245; in revolutionary era, 17, 30–31; and rioting in 1960s, 261; segregated in cities of declining opportunity, 239; as strikebreakers, 104, 171, 203; victims of violent mobs, 39, 53, 93, 104–105, 107, 171, 273. *See also* civil rights movement; emancipation (of slaves)

American Revolution, xi, 5–7, 9–10, 287n31, 287n35; democratic legacy of, 24–25, 29–32, 34, 36, 39, 46, 96, 313n1; limits of, 22–23, 29; nonimportation and nonconsumption agreements, 13, 15–17, 18, 19, 21; origins in imperial crisis, 13–15; role of civic virtue in, 17–20

antislavery movement, 43, 45, 50, 93–94, 99; African-American abolitionists, 90; and democratic public, 70–71, 97; early antislavery sentiment, 17, 29, 31; and evangelical religion, 89–92, 103–104; and

antislavery movement (*continued*)
  labor movement, 39–40, 70, 71, 88, 89, 98, 103–104; limits of, 70, 71, 97, 98–99; and Lincoln, 93–96, 97, 99; use of postal system, 92–93; and women's rights movement, 49–50
antitrust movement, 200, 204, 208; and consumerist democracy, 209; and economic democracy, 193, 198–199
artisans (and skilled labor), 98; belief in cooperation, 52, 62, 67, 85, 98, 100–101, 115, 122, 139, 194, 249; in colonial era, 9, 13; defining free labor, 34–35, 43–44, 292n42; effect of citizenship on, 5–6, 69, 98–101, 106, 107–108, 152, 194, 217; entrepreneurial and radical, 34–35; as heirs of the Revolution, xi, 9–10, 25, 29, 31–32, 34, 35, 39; and Jacksonian democracy, 37–40; and Jeffersonian Republicanism, 25–29; and New York City draft riots, 104–105, 107–108; and popular culture, 82–85; in revolutionary crisis, 14–15, 16–17, 23; shaping municipal debate in antebellum New York City, 100–101; struggle for industrial democracy, 194–195, 197–198, 202–203, 217, 246–247; suspicion of activist government, 26, 28, 37–38, 40–41, 67, 89–90, 194, 201, 231
Astor Place Riot (1849), 85–87, 97, 302n64
Atlanta, 248, 249, 264, 267
automobiles, 206, 210–211, 239, 240–241, 242, 243, 244, 246, 249

banking: reformed in Progressive Era, 199; Bank of America, 257; Bank of North America, 10; Bank of the United States, 37; early republican suspicion of, 36, 38; in Hamilton's financial plans, 26; investment banking, 143, 144, 204, 216, 225; Jackson's war upon the Bank of the United States, 40, 41; and Tweed machine, 111, 113; and urban redevelopment and renewal, 253
Belmont, August, 90, 104, 111, 302n75, 306n30
Bernays, Edward, 188–190, 323n2
big government, xii–xiii, 2, 7, 26, 28, 37–38, 40, 41–42, 45–46, 47, 48–49, 62, 78, 156, 170, 211, 267, 268, 270; as counterweight to corporate power, 144–145, 147–148, 198–199, 208; and environmental regulation, 274–275; and fear of totalitarianism, 209–210; Hamilton's vision of a fiscal-military state, 26; and labor movement, 199, 201–202, 205, 211, 212–214; and moral capitalism, 205; national security state, 210, 213–214; as partner to big business, 199–201, 204, 216, 227, 231–233; and projection of American power abroad, 200; and regulatory state, 198–199, 208–209, 210; and reshaping of post-1945 metropolis, 239, 247–248; and reverse welfare state, 254–255, 256–257; as threat to self-government, 53, 148, 157, 177–178, 214; and warfare state, 2, 200–201, 210, 213–214; and welfare state, 208, 212, 214, 262, 264, 267, 269–270
Boston, 11–12, 19, 20, 22, 37, 41, 82, 90, 108, 122, 148, 154, 156, 172, 263, 265; and civic republicanism's conservative implications, 18; environmental planning in, 277; public library, 238; waterfront in the revolutionary crisis, 13, 16
Bourne, Randolph, 172, 174, 176–177, 179, 180–181, 183, 324n3
Brooklyn (including Brownsville district), 84, 257, 258–259, 260, 263
Brooklyn Bridge, 111, 114, 129, 131

Charleston (South Carolina), 5, 16–17, 18, 23, 31
Chicago, 3, 36, 57, 59, 64–65, 108, 122, 123, 150–151, 164, 188, 195, 202, 204, 228, 233, 264, 265, 297n34, 302n64, 309n12; and development of urban redevelopment and renewal legislation, 253–254; fire, 60–61; Gilded Age labor conflicts, 61–64; Haymarket incident, 62–64; Hull House, 66, 135, 149, 173; and John Dewey, 66, 148, 173; and Marshall Field's department store, 215, 224; public housing in, 252; public services in, 129; Pullman strike, 65–67; race riots, 1919, 171; skyscrapers, 134
Cincinnati, 36, 93, 122, 153, 255, 261
citizen-proprietorship (and small producers), 7, 38, 40, 56, 114, 311n53; and antitrust movement, 193; and Chautauqua, 64; and City Beautiful movement, 149; and civic critique of department store, 224; decline of, as factor in decay of personal character, 219–220; and early movie culture, 161; former slaves' interest in, 47–48; and free labor ideal, 34–35, 37–40, 43–45; and ideal of labor and learning, 43–44; and the Industrial Workers of the World, 196; Jackson's defense of,

40–41; as limiting revolutionary legacy, 29–32, 50; Lippmann's farewell to, 225; and Prohibition Party, 217; and Radical Republicans during Reconstruction, 47–48; and Republican program of industrialization, 43–44; as revolutionary ideal, 9–10, 25–29; syndicalist version of, 195–196

citizenship, 1–2, 72, 115, 117, 145, 147, 178, 192, 228, 266, 268, 272, 274, 277, 287n31, 303n91, 313n1; as democracy's highest ideal, 3–4, 156–157; efforts to revive, in Progressive Era, 150, 151, 153, 156, 157, 159; focused on individual rights and desires, xii–xiii, 33, 232, 237; and fullest development of the mind and character of all, 5–7, 20, 29–32, 35, 37, 38, 42, 43–44, 67, 69–70, 71, 72, 82, 83, 125, 144, 148, 154–155, 170, 270; habits as key to shaping, 139, 185; and other-directed personality, 235–236, 237; and playground movement, 222; promoted in cities, 2–3, 4, 13, 15, 33, 148–150, 151–152; racist and sexist assumptions about, 29–31, 45, 50, 53–54, 77; skepticism about popular capacity for, 53–54, 60, 113–114, 120–121, 129–130, 136, 168–169, 171–172, 181–182, 188, 229; small proprietors and, 7, 9–10, 25–29, 34–35, 37–40; undermined by advertising, 229–230; undermined by economic hierarchy and inequality, 34–35, 38–39, 44, 45, 47, 51–52, 144, 145, 147, 148, 197, 219; and unfinished tasks of American civilization, 2, 3–4, 270; and union of labor and learning, 27, 37–38, 43, 64, 79; and widest distribution of political and economic responsibility, 145, 274

city: as basis of democratic civilization, 3–4, 69, 145, 149–150, 151–152, 184, 219, 238–239, 240, 263, 270, 274, 277, 331n24; as center of mass media and mass culture, 157–159, 221, 234–235; and consumer culture, 168, 187–188, 191–192, 205, 216, 221, 223–224, 228, 230, 244–245, 331n24; as crucible of public and market, 10–13; and deindustrialization, 246–247; deterioration of public realm in, xii, 192, 239, 240, 241, 245, 255, 262–264, 265–267, 268–269, 270, 273; disruption of family life, 219–221; as focus of political corruption, 42, 44, 113–114, 116, 131, 148, 151, 172; incompatibility with slavery, 17, 31; as incubator of Jacksonian democracy, 72–73, 77–78, 79–82; inspiring vision of, xii–xiii, 2–4, 129, 149–150, 151–152, 238, 270, 276, 277–278; as key to addressing environmental degradation, 270, 274, 276–270; liberal reformers retreat from, 59–60, 61–64; and literature of urban pathology and dystopia, 135, 148, 273–274; plagued by arson, 263; revitalization of, as key to civic renewal, 270; and rise of popular culture, 79–80; as seedbed of civic virtue, 2–3, 4, 13, 15, 33, 148–150, 151–152; as settlement, 276–278; and shared public life, 72–73, 77–78, 120, 240; as site of civic renewal in Progressive Era, 148–150, 151–152, 153, 156, 157, 159; as social product, 152, 277–279; as source of temptation and dissipation, 219–220; as stage for Revolution, 13–15; suburban abandonment of, in 1960s, 261–263

City Beautiful movement, 3, 149–150, 151, 165, 174, 278

city planning, xii, 74–76, 79, 127–133, 149, 151–152, 277, 310n48. *See also* urban redevelopment and renewal

civic ceremonies (and parades), 34–35, 46, 73, 76, 77, 105, 113, 115, 125, 126, 132, 134, 267, 299n20, 301n53

civic republicanism: eclipse of, in Gilded Age, 56, 57–59; as factor in 19th century labor movement, 32, 34–35, 38–40, 44–45, 51–52; as factor in Revolutionary era, 9–10, 16, 17–22, 23–24, 25–26, 27–28; in recent historical writing, xii; rediscovery of, in Progressive era, 144, 145, 149, 152, 156, 313n1. *See also* civic virtue

civic virtue, 2–3, 6, 13, 16, 64, 74, 84, 94, 106, 130, 172, 200; cold war as opportunity to revive, 214; in commercial republic, 7, 33–35; as demanding ethic, 29; democratized in revolutionary crisis, 9–10; and playground movement, 222; and proprietary wealth, 10, 26; role in revolutionary ideology, 17–20; role of, in Constitution, 1–2, 23–25; small proprietors and, xi, 9–10, 32, 34–35, 40, 80–81; transformed into manners, 57–59; and vice in revolutionary era, 20–22; Walter Lippmann's farewell to, 182; and women, 30, 76, 121. *See also* civic republicanism

civil rights movement, 144, 245–246, 248, 250–251, 255, 256–257, 259, 261–262, 329n75

Civil War, 7, 45–46, 47–48, 50, 54, 69–70, 71, 97, 99–100, 137, 162; draft riots, 103–109, 272

Cleveland, 151, 153, 171, 246–247, 264

coffeehouses and taverns, 10, 11, 13–14, 17, 30, 74, 84, 89

Collier, John, 158–159, 161, 164–165, 166, 169, 317n39

colonial seaports, 7, 10–13; and imperial war, 12; and revolutionary agitation, 13–22; and Stamp Act, 13–14, 16–17, 18, 20

commerce: colonial expansion of, 10–11; and consumer culture, 134, 164, 204, 215–216, 231–233, 331n24; courts encouragement of, 36–37; reconciling with republicanism, 9–10, 25–29, 33–35; threat to republic, 9–10, 20–22, 23–24, 25, 42, 57, 80, 81–82, 138, 144–145, 149, 150, 158–159, 188, 219–220, 224, 229, 267, 324n5. *See also* advertising; consumer culture; corporations

community action programs, 257–260, 261

competence (and incompetence), 31, 43, 52, 68, 161, 236, 292n32, 331n25; democratization of, 6, 28–29, 43, 158; skepticism about popular competence, 70, 120–121, 122–123, 124–125, 181–183

conscription: in Civil War, 105; lack of, in revolutionary war, 22; in World War I, 201. *See also* Civil War

conspiracy, 162, 196, 261; of British to corrupt colonial virtue, 9, 18–20, 287n35; of employers to enslave Jacksonian workers, 37–38, 39; fear of, in Progressive Era, 139, 149; of Republicans to make slaves of white workers, 103; of slaveholders to make slavery national, 95–96, 304n94; unions and union officials charged with, 37, 39, 66

Constitution, U.S., 9, 10, 26, 29, 31, 96, 97, 166, 178, 201, 242, 262, 304n94; Antifederalists, 10, 25; Civil War amendments, 45–46, 48, 49, 110; and corporations, 36; guarantee of republican form of government, 46; as historical innovation, 1–2; three-fifths compromise, 41; writing of, 23–25, 29

consumer culture: avocational counselors, 236–237; and cheap amusements, 83, 135, 138, 158–161, 162, 163, 164, 165, 191, 219–221, 227–228, 229, 238, 331n24; and children, 225, 228–229, 332n36; civic opposition to, 158–159, 164–165, 191–192, 220, 224–225; and civic passivity, 134, 138, 150–151, 159, 219–220, 235–236; corporate investments in, 191, 215–216, 221, 223–224, 226, 228, 229; department stores, 134, 188, 192, 204, 215, 223–225, 227, 244, 245, 266; disreputable aura surrounding, 219–221, 226, 227–228; as factor in rise of Congress of Industrial Organizations, 234; federal promotion of, 204, 231–233; immigrant and working-class contribution to, 216, 219, 221; as imposed from above, 192, 215–216; and museums, 216, 223–224; origins, 215–217, 218–219; and redefinition of democracy, 191, 216; shopping malls, 244, 266; stimulated by mass suburbanization, 239, 244; Times Square as headquarters of, 191–191, 323n2; and transformation of personal character, 224–225, 228–230, 234–235; transformation of social values, 191; use of color, glass, and light, 192, 223, 232, 244; use of mass media, 188, 229, 232, 235; use of play, 221, 223, 225, 236; use of sexuality, 221. *See also* advertising; leisure; movies

Continental Congress, 5, 15–16, 21–22

Cooper Union, 69, 95, 113–114, 154, 320n5

corporations: and administered prices, 199, 201, 204, 206, 208; corrupting the political process, 36, 42, 55–57, 78, 112, 116, 139, 144–145, 148, 162, 217; decentralization of production, 246–247; defense of management prerogatives, 211, 212, 213, 247, 329n75; interest in industrial psychology, 204; interest in temperance and prohibition, 218, 226–227, 230–231; liberalization of the law of, 36, 41; New Deal liberals accommodation to, 209–210; as object of antitrust efforts, 193, 198–199, 208–209, 324n1; and public relations, 188–190, 233; and regulatory state, 198, 199, 208–209, 210, 231; rise of oligopoly, 143; shielded from public power in early republic, 36–37, 41; and Taft-Hartley Act (1947), 213; threat of, to democracy, 7, 36, 40, 41, 44, 205, 206, 208, 213–214, 247, 277, 302n64; and welfare capitalism, 203–205. *See also* antitrust movement

corruption, 3, 9, 26, 39, 40, 44, 53, 65, 78, 102, 112, 125, 149, 151, 155, 187, 313n1; and British colonial policy, 18–20; and business, 36, 42, 55–57, 78, 112, 116, 139, 144–145, 148, 162, 217; cities as center of, 42, 44, 113–114, 116, 131, 148, 151, 172; consequence of laissez-faire policy, 42; and frustration with municipal politics, 130; Hamilton's financial plans and, 26–27; liberal reformers and, 55–57, 58; of Tweed's Tammany Hall, 100, 103, 112, 113, 131

Croly, Herbert: and city beautiful, 174; and industrial democracy, 197–198; and *The New Republic*, 174; on participatory democracy, 145, 148, 154, 157, 184; as war intellectual, 174

crowds: antiabolitionist, 93; and Astor Place riot (1849), 85–87; in colonial cities, 10, 13–15, 29; disciplining of, 123–124; in draft riots, 104–105, 106, 108, 109; in Gilded Age cities, 59, 60, 62, 112–113, 122, 124, 133, 134, 136; at Haymarket (1886), 62–64; as irrational and foolish, 138, 140–142, 158, 160, 170–171, 188, 229; in Jacksonian and antebellum cities, 39, 72–73, 83, 85–86, 95, 103; *The Lonely Crowd* (1950), 234–236, 237, 335n80; in museums, 123; as passive audiences, 123–124, 154, 158–159, 160, 309n15; in Progressive Era cities, 154, 187, 215, 239; and radio, 234; in Revolution, 16–17; the sporting crowd, 90, 302n75; in theaters (including movie), 69–70, 83, 86–87, 89, 121, 138, 159, 160, 161, 164, 167, 168, 170–171, 188, 228; and television, 236–237; in Tompkins Square (1874), 61, 117, 118; World War I era, 171, 172

Curtis, George William, 60, 61, 63–64, 69–70, 86, 97, 137, 308n81

Debs, Eugene V., 58, 66, 67, 202

democracy: and capitalism, 5; and competence, 28–29, 34, 43, 52, 158, 161; competing conceptions of, 98–99, 106–107, 147–148, 191–192, 216, 229, 230, 238–239, 307n72, 313n1; and concept of the public, xiii; consumerist conception of, 138, 144, 188, 191–192, 207–209, 219, 223, 224, 225, 229, 230, 231, 232, 233, 235–237; and conversation, xii, 14, 16, 70, 186, 187, 217, 234, 277; dependent on socialization of intelligence, 158, 165, 181; as despotism, 23; and efficiency, 154, 170, 198; and environmental movement, 274, 276, 277; expansion of, in Civil War, 48–50, 69–70, 98; expansion of, in Jacksonian Era, 38–43, 76–78, 79–85; expansion of, in Reconstruction, 46–50, 112; failures of, as matter of social conditions, 185; as irrepressible demand, 3–4; as moral ideal, xiii; as most educational form of politics, 153–154; participatory conception of, 7, 9, 11, 13–15, 16, 19, 24–25, 26–29, 30–32, 38, 42, 67, 69–70, 72, 82, 98, 107–108, 117, 125, 145, 147–157, 159–161, 171–175, 180, 183–187, 191–192, 193–198, 201, 207, 211, 216, 222, 230, 237, 250–251, 258, 274, 300n48, 313n1; racist perversion of, 30–31, 48, 77, 88–89, 97; realist theory of, 171–172, 183–185; revolutionary origins of, 9–10, 11–16, 25–29, 31–32; skepticism about, 53–55, 56, 60, 64, 81, 99–100, 108–109, 117–119, 120–124, 140–142, 170, 172, 181–183, 184–185; Tocqueville on, 6, 33. *See also* labor movement, and industrial democracy; public space

Democratic Party: abandonment of reform after 1945, 209–210, 258; co-opting workingmen's movements, 38; criticism of economic and political privilege, 40–42; defense of popular culture, 89–90; during draft riots, 105, 106–107; encouraging enterprise, 41; faith in the people, 42–44; laissez-faire policy of, 41–42, 77–78, 102; and New Deal, 205–209, 212, 241–243; and post office, 72; and price controls in 1940s, 213; as proslavery party, 40–41, 43, 88–89, 93, 100, 103; racial divisions in, 262, 267

Detroit, 152, 196, 242, 244, 245, 246–247, 250, 251–252, 261, 263, 264

Dewey, John: abandonment of engagement with cities, 173, 187–188, 323n67; belief that World War I provided opportunity for democratic reform, 175–176, 180; cities as stimulus to his thought, 148, 173; and cooperative inquiry, 148–149; critic of public relations, 189; on habits as key to promoting citizenship, 185, 333n52; and Lippmann, 186, 187, 188; and movement to outlaw war, 183; opposition to US entry into World War I, 172, 175; on possibility, xiii; *The Public and Its Problems* (1927), 186–188, 316n28; on Pullman strike, 66; on radio as public utility, 233; relationship to Henry George, 316n20; relationship with Jane Addams, 173; second thoughts about support for US entry into World War I, 172, 177, 180, 181, 183–184; support for US entry into World War I,

Dewey, John (*continued*)
172, 173–176, 179; as theorist of public, xii, 155, 158; *Thought News* project, 158
domestic realm: in census of 1880, 133; domesticity as ideology and value, xii, 2, 54, 64, 65, 76, 83, 84, 90, 105, 116, 124, 133, 135, 220, 227, 310n48, 311n52; and genteel culture, 54–55, 57; and liberal reformers, 57–58, 60, 126; politicized during Revolution, 15–17; and public parks and services, 130, 132; and republican motherhood, 29–30; and suburbanization, 192, 239, 244, 246; women confined to or escaping from, 16, 49, 219. *See also* homeownership; suburbanization
Douglass, Frederick, 31, 46, 77, 97

eight-hour-day movement, 61, 100; and civic conception of free labor, 50–52; connection of consumer culture, 216; during World War I, 201; and Haymarket incident, 62–64; liberal reformers opposition to, 56, 58, 61; as means to self-improvement and civic engagement, 51–52, 114–115, 216; and postwar transformation of Republican party, 114–116
emancipation (of slaves), 37, 45, 46, 48–49, 50–51, 99, 104
environmental movement, 256, 263, 270, 271, 274–279
equality, 18, 19, 35, 63–64, 84; civic and political, 29–31, 46–48, 80, 96, 101, 216, 294n67; cultural, 80–83, 87; economic, 268–270; lack of, 7; opposition to, 57, 99; racial, 45–50, 245, 294n67; role of government in promoting, 38–40, 45–50; sexual, 49–50, 76; social, 14, 23, 64, 149, 194, 217, 223, 268–270; de Tocqueville on, 6
evangelical religion and reform: in antebellum New York City, 91–92, 102, 103, 106–107; and antislavery, 71, 81, 90, 92; in Great Awakening, 12–13; opposition to popular culture, 90–91, 302n75; and Second Great Awakening, 91; use of new means of communication, 91–92
experts (in government), 128–130, 132, 154–155, 169, 170, 171, 182, 186, 204, 208, 209, 231

Federal Housing Administration, 239–240, 241, 242, 244, 247–248, 249, 251, 255, 262

Federalists: during constitutional debates, 22–25; in 1790s, 25–29
Follett, Mary Parker, 156–157, 316n30
Founding Fathers, 1–2, 23–25, 72, 94; Adams, John, 6, 20, 24, 50; Franklin, Benjamin, 9–10, 11–12, 21; Hamilton, Alexander, 24, 25, 26–28; Jefferson, Thomas, 6–7, 24–25, 27; Madison, James, 24, 92; Washington, George, 21, 22, 23–24, 26–27
free labor ideal, 7, 34–35, 71, 108; civic and contractual definitions of, 43–45, 47–52; and contrast with slavery, 39–40, 43, 44; and the freed people, 45–48; origins, 34–35; and transformation of Northern Whiggery, 43–45

genteel culture, 69, 84, 89, 90, 120, 121–122, 123–124, 135, 295n8; and Chautauqua, 64; and domestic realm, 55, 57–59; and liberal reform, 54–55, 57; and market, 54–55, 57; and public space, 59–60, 85–87, 132–133, 134, 160; and Pullman, 64–65; settlement house as rejection of, 66, 150
George, Henry, 62, 140, 151–154, 162, 277–279, 316n21
Gilded Age: cultural hierarchy in, 120–121, 122–124; decay of civic life in, 133–135; degeneration of popular politics in, 136–139; economic determinism in, 7, 53–55; fear of mob mind in, 140–142; and genteel culture, 54–55; and good government reform, 124–130; origins of, 53–54, 114–119; political corruption in, 55–57; public projects in, 131–133; and women's rights movement, 120–121
good government reform, 70, 124–127, 129, 137, 139; and cultural hierarchy, 120–121, 124; educational campaigning, 125, 126–127, 308n81; franchise restrictions, 118, 121, 124–125, 127, 136; and municipal politics, 124, 127–130; opposition to partisanship, 125–127

highbrow/lowbrow (cultural hierarchy), 69–70, 120–124; challenged by movies, 158; and good government reform, 120–121
homeownership: as central to democratic aspirations, 239, 244, 246; homeowner populism, 247–249, 250, 261–262, 264–265; homeowners associations,

250–251, 262; and race, 247, 248, 250–251, 256, 261–262
Hoover, Herbert, 204, 231–232, 241, 334n57

immigrants: anti-immigrant attitudes, 34, 54, 60, 76, 96, 101–102, 121, 135, 171, 178, 203, 272, 273; and consumer culture, 159, 161, 221, 223, 331n24; integration into republic, 77, 85, 96, 100, 104, 105, 113, 178, 203, 216
individualism: alternatives and antidotes to, 1, 2–3, 17–18, 33, 66, 98, 100, 152, 158, 276–277; as dominant American value, xi–xiii, 1, 2, 6, 12, 116, 168, 186, 199, 210, 215–216, 249, 251, 268; in tension with other values, 10, 24, 45, 46, 74, 75, 98, 106, 194, 216, 270, 276, 278

Jackson, Andrew, 40–41, 72, 80, 93
Jacksonian era: labor politics in, 37–40; market development in, 34–37; popular culture in, 79–87; struggle against privilege, 40–42, 76–78; urban development in, 72–76
Jeffersonian Republicans: democratic vision of, 25–29; and election of 1800, 27–28; fear of energetic government, 28

labor movement: American Federation of Labor, 140, 163, 167–168, 194–195, 197, 201, 206, 211, 216–217, 230, 328n51; business unionism, 194–195; in Civil War era, 50–52; Congress of Industrial Organizations, 193, 205–207, 210, 211–212, 213, 234, 328n51; in Depression and New Deal eras, 205–207, 209–212; in Gilded Age, 60–61; and industrial democracy, 145, 180, 184, 191–193, 195–197, 202–203, 225; Industrial Workers of the World, 194–197, 325n15; in Jacksonian era, 37–40; Knights of Labor, 140, 216, 217, 218, 329n4; losing faith in political action, 67; and movies, 167–168; production plans during World War II, 210–211; in Progressive Era, 194–197; in Reconstruction era, 50–52, 112–114; resistance to scientific management, 195, 197; Taft-Hartley Act (1947), 213; and Wagner Labor Relations Act (1935), 206–207; in World War I era, 201–202. *See also* eight-hour-day movement; leisure

law: and private enterprise, 35–42; effort to democratize, 82; and public realm, 74–76, 127–129; relation to civic virtue, 59
leisure: and civic virtue, 3, 26, 28; commercialization of, dividing the family, 220, 236–237; debate over proper use of, 51, 61, 219, 226; as key to future of democracy, 219; as means to self-improvement, 192, 216; as opportunity for shaping character, 218, 220–221, 228–229; popular demand for, 192, 216–219; redirected to insatiable desire, 216, 223–224, 225, 227, 229–230, 232
liberalism: abandonment of reform, 209–210, 258; civic and money varieties of, 268–279; and civil rights movement, 210; as element in revolutionary ideology, 7, 9–10, 12–13, 18, 19–20, 21, 23–24, 25–26, 28; emphasis on private life, 1–2; faith in market-based policies, 239–240; and Keynesian economic policy, 208. *See also* liberal reformers (of Gilded Age)
liberal reformers (of Gilded Age): allegiance to laissez-faire and natural law, 53–55, 56–57; and the city, 59–61, 297n29; constricting public debate, 55, 56, 61–64; and domestic realm, 57–59; and Haymarket incident, 62–64; origins in Liberal Republicanism, 53–54; relation to corporate order, 56–57; view of democracy, 56; view of political corruption, 55–56. *See also* genteel culture
liberal rights, 77, 78, 188, 202, 213, 268; and African-Americans, 31, 39, 46, 47, 48, 49, 144, 245, 248, 250–251, 256–257, 259, 261–262; in Civil War era, 45–47, 48, 49–50, 51, 53, 110, 115, 116, 294n65; circumscribed, 71, 74–76, 140, 275; and Constitution, 23–24; as insufficient basis for democratic government, 1–2; as natural, 19, 28, 51, 56, 62, 294n65; renewed emphasis on in face of totalitarian threat, 210; in revolutionary crisis, 9–10, 18, 19, 23; and women, 30, 49–50, 189
liberty, 9, 16, 18, 22, 29, 197, 210; African-American demand for, 46; American defense of, in Revolution, 19–20; artisans' defense of, 26–29, 38–40, 62, 117; Republicans' positive conception of, 45–48, 99; women's demand for, 29, 49
Lincoln, Abraham, 44–45, 88, 94–96, 97, 99
Lippmann, Walter, 139, 144–145, 168–169, 189, 225, 322n46; move away from urban politics, 171–172; postwar skepticism

Lippmann, Walter (*continued*)
about the public, 169, 171–172, 181–183, 186, 188; role at *The New Republic*, 173–175; service in Wilson administration, 179
Los Angeles, 164, 244, 261, 274; dependent on public projects, 271; environmental degradation in, 271; and homeowner populism, 262, 271; literary destruction of, 273–274; neglected environmental plans for, 278; and neglect of public realm, 271, 272–273; urban redevelopment in, 271–272, 273

machine politics, 59–60, 70, 89–90, 100, 102–103, 109–110, 111, 112, 113–114, 155, 184, 224; and good government reformers, 60–61, 100, 103, 113–114, 125, 127–128; and mediating conflicts, 106–107; as object of Dillon's Rule, 127–128
market, the: development of, after War of 1812, 33–37; disputes over expansion of, in revolutionary era, 16, 20–22, 23–24; Jeffersonian Republicans and, 25–29; liberal faith in, as vehicle of reform, 239–242, 267; as natural and self-directing, 26, 28, 56–57, 66; origins of, in colonial seaports, 9–13; as product of law and civic life, 35–37, 269; public realm as counterbalance to, 268–270; relation to law and manners, 59; and reorganization of the crafts, 35; role of, disguised by genteel culture, 55, 57–59; and visible hand of management, 56–57, 143–144, 208. *See also* consumer culture; corporations
mass media, 168, 188, 229; as basis for a participatory democracy, 157, 158; effects on popular culture, 157–159; and public opinion, 177, 235. *See also* movies; radio
military-industrial complex, 2, 210, 213–214
movies: censorship of, 163–164, 165–167; corporate consolidation of industry, 167–168; and degradation of popular culture, effects on mind, 160, 168–169, 234, 316n35; and labor movement, 161, 163–168; National Board of Review of Motion Pictures, 163–167, 169; as part of civic and political culture, 158–159, 160, 161, 162–169, 228, 234; as part of consumer culture, 124, 158–159, 161, 164–165, 167–169, 205, 221, 231, 234; role of working people in early history of, 159–160, 161; supplanting the saloon, 227–228; and World War I, 167, 169, 177, 187–188, 228
municipal corporation: autonomy limited by state government, 100, 102–103, 109, 117–118, 127–129, 309n32; and black elected officials, 263; and corruption, 42, 102, 113, 130, 148; Dillon's Rule, 128–129; and economic responsibility, 276–277; efforts at industrial renewal, 247; and eminent domain, 74–75, 128, 220, 253–254; eroding tax base, 245, 263; expanded powers of public planning in antebellum period, 74–76; financial retrenchment and selloff of assets, 117, 263, 265; home rule, 151; municipal ownership, 131, 151, 153, 158; and police power, 75–76, 128–129, 220, 274; post-1945 spending, 245, 266; and professional experts, 129, 195; proposals for expanding responsibilities of, 100, 106, 135, 151–153, 158–159, 164, 173, 220, 245–246; and public services and utilities, 75, 129, 130–131, 135, 151–153, 158–159, 164, 220, 222, 238, 240, 258; reshaping character, 152, 220, 222, 229; Tweed machine's expansive use of, 110–112, 127; as vehicle for disciplining working class, 106; and the War on Poverty, 259, 261. *See also* public services and utilities

New Deal: accommodation to concentrated economic power, 207, 208–210, 213; and consumerist conception of democracy, 207–209, 239; National Recovery Act (1933), 206; opposition to concentrated economic power, 208; relation to labor movement, 205–207, 210–212; shaped by vision of moral capitalism, 205; urban policy, 241–244; Wagner Labor Relations Act (1935), 206, 207, 208
newspapers (and journalism), xiii, 71, 79, 80, 83, 93, 98, 104, 148, 153, 154, 158, 186, 203, 217, 260; Associated Press and Western Union, 80, 140; circulation through post offices, 72; colonial origins, 11–12; compared to movies, 159, 162, 166, 168; *Democratic Review*, 80–81; and evangelical reform, 91–93; and independent journalism, 54, 58, 60, 137–138; Lippmann's critique of role in democracy, 181–182; muckraking, 67, 139, 158, 162, 172, 177, 226; *The New Republic*,

173–174, 179, 181; partisan press, 72, 125, 137–139; the penny press, 79–80; *The Public*, 152–153; *Putnam's*, 96–97; and radio, 233; and revolutionary agitation, 13, 14, 15, 16, 20; sensational journalism, 138–139, 158; suppressed in 1790s, 27; suppressed in World War I, 178; *Thought News*, 158; using new technologies, 79, 91, 92

New York City: antebellum labor movement in, 98, 100–101; antislavery in, 91–93, 95–96, 97, 98; Astor Place riot (1849), 85–87, 97; bankruptcy, 263; Boss Tweed in, 59–60, 100, 105, 109–112, 113–114, 307n55; Bowery neighborhood, 83–84; Central Park, 132; and Civil War era Republican Party, 95–96, 98–100, 101–109, 114–116, 117, 306n41; and democratic culture, 72, 73, 77–78, 79, 81, 90, 122; draft riots, 97, 100, 103–107, 131, 306n36; and emergence of public, 11; evangelical reformers in, 91–93; franchise restrictions in, 74, 77, 109–110, 117–118, 124; highbrow culture in, 123–124; Jacksonian labor movement in, 34, 35, 38–39, 43; labor conflicts in, 1870s, 61, 107–109, 112–114, 115–117, 118, 136; and liberal reformers, 58, 59–60, 62, 64, 69–70, 116–119, 297n27, 308n81; loss of industrial jobs, 246; mayoral campaign, 1886, 62, 277–278; metropolitan capital in, 100, 114–116; movie theaters closed in, 163, 227–228; nativist politics in, 101–103; Progressive Era reforms in, 150, 174, 195, 224, 325n15, 333n56; pro-slavery politics in, 78, 88, 92; public space in, 72–73, 134; in revolutionary era, 10, 13, 14, 18, 25, 26, 32; sensational journalism in, 138; slum conditions in, 131; subway, 238–239; tax revenues, 265; teachers' strike, 260; Times Square, 191–192

Oakland, 248–249, 251, 255–256, 257–258, 259, 261, 339n78

Philadelphia, 14–15, 21, 22, 27, 37, 79, 83, 90, 128, 153, 266
Phillips, Wendell, 46, 47, 50, 51, 99, 294n65
police (and militias): and Astor riot (1849), 87; and demonstrations in Tompkins Square (1874), 61, 117; and draft riots, 104–105, 108; and elections, 102, 110; and Haymarket (1886), 62–63; intimidation of public, 62, 66, 78, 100–101, 110, 114, 117, 124, 136, 163, 166, 167, 196, 197, 203, 207, 261; and Orange Riot (1871), 112–113; professionalization of, eclipsing public, 73, 102, 109, 136, 262; in revolutionary era, 15, 22; and security in Los Angeles, 272–273; state control of, in New York City, 100, 102–103

political campaigning: and advertising, 139, 235–236, 237; educational, 121, 125–127, 137; loss of public dimension, 267; and popular culture, 81; spectacular, 62, 95, 125–127

political parties: and partisanship, 80, 90, 103, 109, 116, 125–126, 127, 137–139; and postal system, 72, 77; similar to giant corporations, 136–37. *See also names of individual parties*

political science, 156, 184

popular culture, 79–85, 88–90, 121–122; connection to political culture severed, 121–122, 123–124, 138, 165–166, 168; and cultural hierarchy, 120–124; effort to elevate, 80–82, 158–159, 164–165; effort to suppress, 71, 85, 86, 87, 88, 90, 99, 109, 123, 158; and election of 1840, 81; evangelical imitation of, 91–92; intersection with political culture in nineteenth century, 64, 67, 69–70, 79–87, 89, 90, 96; Jacksonian origins of, 71, 79–80; minstrel shows, 89; as political issue, 83, 84, 85–87; as product and possession of all, 79, 82, 83; reunited with political culture in Progressive Era, 150, 155, 157, 158–159, 161–162; role of images in, 58, 93, 139, 141, 142, 158, 160, 168–169, 187; Shakespeare as, 82, 121; transformation of, as factor in democratic decline, 169, 187–188; ugly aspects of, 80, 83, 88, 89, 158. *See also* consumer culture; genteel culture; highbrow/lowbrow (cultural hierarchy)

popular sovereignty: and civic buildings and spaces, 73, 79; emergence during Revolution, 22–23; and municipal politics, 128, 151; rioting as expression of, 93; skepticism about, 23, 99, 109, 182–183

postal system: abolitionists' use of, 92–93; colonial origins, 11–12; as component of consumer culture, 204, 232; expansion of in early 19th century, 71, 72, 77; in 1790s, 27; and telegraph, 78; in World War I, 201

private interests: central to American politics, xi, xii, 1–2, 10, 27, 41, 48, 54, 55, 75, 84, 112, 144, 156, 158, 174, 194, 198, 200,

352 · INDEX

private interests (*continued*)
207, 211–212, 274; as substitute for public good, 12, 21, 24, 26, 42, 237, 240; in tension with civic aspirations, 4, 6, 9–10, 12, 17–18, 26, 33, 36, 66, 78, 103, 125, 144, 148, 188, 276

Prohibition, 205, 226–227, 333n56; antisaloon movement, 217–218; corporate support for, 226–227; corporate support for repeal of, 231; Prohibition Party, 217–218; Sociological Group, 218; stimulation to the consumer culture, 227, 230; temperance movement, 89, 94, 217–218

public, the (as noun): as alternative vision of democracy, xii–xiii; biological metaphors for, 133, 135–136; colonial origins of, 9–13; as counterweight to corporate power, 145, 147–149; cultural infrastructure for, 71–72; decline of faith in, after World War I, 145, 170–172, 181–185, 187–188; and deliberation, 15, 28, 58, 69, 141, 145, 150, 153, 154, 155, 156–158, 169, 170–171, 172, 173–174, 177–178, 180, 184, 187, 193; as different from community, 156; eclipsed by cultural hierarchy, 120–124; eclipsed by good government reforms, 121, 124–130; on eve of World War I, 170; in everyday language, xii; expansion of in Jacksonian era, 42, 76–78; expansion of in Revolution, 15–17, 23; and intersubjectivity and interpenetration, 156–157; and Jeffersonian Republicans, 26–28; legal infrastructure for, 71–72, 74–75; and mass media, 157–159, 168, 177, 234–236; and origins of Revolution, 13–15; physical infrastructure for, 71–73; post-WWII neglect of, 238–241; rediscovery of, in Progressive era, 144–145, 147–154; scholarly interest in, xii–xiii; sensational journalism and, 138–140, 158; and support for land-use regulations, 274–275

public good: ceded to market agencies, 36, 41–42, 218, 232–233, 239–241; cities as focusing attention on, 4, 151–152; conflated with interests of white homeowners, 262; eclipsed by market segmentation, 237; emergence in colonial politics, 10–13; and environmental movement, 274–276; and paternalistic elites, 74, 77, 78, 184; private vices as substitute for, 2, 24–25; in recent historical writing and popular usage, xi–xiii; rediscovery of, 66, 157; and regulatory authority, 75–76, 127, 198; and Republican program during the Civil War and Reconstruction, 48–49, 51; in revolutionary ideology, 9–10, 14, 18, 25, 30; skepticism about, 75, 76, 78, 182

public housing, 212, 239, 240, 243, 246, 250, 251–252, 253, 257, 267

public interest: *See* public good

public meetings, xii, 711, 98, 149, 217; and City Beautiful movement, 149; during Civil War and Reconstruction, 46, 69–70, 90, 101, 103, 104, 113–114, 115–117, 118; and educational politics, 125, 127, 138; forum movement, 155; and Gilded Age, 63; and Jacksonian era, 39, 71, 77–78, 86, 91, 93; in Progressive Era, 153, 155–157, 163, 194; prohibited, 132, 153, 203; and revolutionary era, 11, 14, 15. *See also* social centers movement

public opinion, xii, 4, 112, 140, 158, 181, 183–184, 196, 202–203, 211; and antislavery movement, 90–91, 92–97; and conversation, xii, 11, 14, 16, 70, 186–187, 217, 234, 277; defer to expertise, 170; faith in, Progressive Era, 148, 152, 153, 154, 155, 176, 177; and images, 93; and independent journalism, 137–139; and liberal reformers, 60, 61–64; loss of faith in, 171, 179, 181–182; as manufactured consent, 145, 170–171, 181, 184, 188–189; and mass media, 157, 169, 233, 234–235; and movie culture, 159, 162, 165–166; as product of mob mind, 141–142; restrictions on, 63, 140, 148, 201; and social centers movement, 156–157, 316n30

public purpose: and charters of incorporation, 36–37, 127; and eminent domain, 37, 74–75, 128, 220, 253–254; expansive definition of, in relation to private enterprise, 37; expansive definition of, in relation to public regulation, 75–76; and Hoover's associative state, 204; included under public use, 75; and post-WWII liberalism, 240; and slum clearance, 253; and slum prevention, 253–254; and socially-created forms of wealth, 152, 277–279

public relations, 4, 162, 171, 186, 188–190, 233

public services and utilities, xii, 72, 129, 151–152; as crucial to democratic civilization, 238–239, 240, 270; deterioration of, 239, 263–265, 267,

271; as element in American standard of living, 129; as focus of community action projects, 258; lack of, contributing to slum conditions, 135, 239, 240, 255, 263–265; and middle-class domesticity, 130–131; and monopoly, 37, 41, 78, 80, 140, 151–152, 232; parks and playgrounds, 71, 73, 76–78, 86, 87, 100–101, 103, 111, 132–133, 135, 136, 149, 152, 218, 221–223, 245, 251, 266, 269, 271, 278, 301n53, 310n48, 331n24; as part of a city republic, 151–153; as part of suburban subsidy, 230; source of corruption, 148, 151; transportation, 35–36, 131, 151, 242–243, 245–246, 247, 255–256, 263, 264. *See also* municipal corporation; public welfare; streets

public space: and City Beautiful movement, 149–150; and consumer culture, 188, 191–192; as crucial to democracy, 11, 71, 145, 153, 267; erosion of, in wake of 1960s rioting, 266; and genteel culture, 59–60, 85–87, 132–133, 134, 160; and the Georgists, 153–154; in Jacksonian cities, 72–73, 74, 77, 78, 79; and liberal reformers, 60; and middle-class domesticity, 132–133; neglect of, 120, 131, 133–134, 149; nickelodeon as, 160–161; post office as, 11–12, 72; and Pullman, Illinois, 65; in revolutionary crisis, 11–12, 13–15; shopping malls as, 266–267. *See also* public services and utilities

public spending, 210, 214, 246, 263, 269; and Clinton administration, 270; and Keynesian economics, 208, 239; labor support for, 38, 212; and market transformation in early republic, 35–37, 38; opposition to, 114, 117, 263–264, 265

public welfare, 33, 66, 71, 75, 101, 198, 203. *See also* public good

Pullman, Illinois, 65–67, 130. *See also* strikes

radio, 158, 205, 208, 227, 231, 232–233, 234, 235, 239

Reconstruction era: collapse of, 48–51, 53–55, 60; in New York City, 109–119; role of eight-hour strikes in ending, 51–52; turning slaves into citizens, 46–48

red-lining, 241–242

Republican Party: abandonment of Reconstruction, 53–55, 60; antebellum economic program, 43–44; anti-slavery elements of, 45–46, 93–96, 97, 99; confiscation issue, 47–48; conservative wing of, 48, 103; defining American nationalism, 96–97; and free labor ideal, 43–48; and good government reform, 125–126; as intrusive minority in New York City, 99, 100–102, 103–106; and labor movement, 50–52; Liberal Republicans, 7, 53–54, 61, 114; origins, 93–95; post-Civil War transformation of, 51–52, 54–55, 100, 114, 116–117; and post-Civil War urban reconstruction, 108–112, 114, 116; radical wing of, 47–52, 54, 60, 62, 114; relation to labor movement, 50–52, 101, 103–104, 105–106, 108, 109, 114–116; relation to women's movement, 49–50; and suffrage, 48; view of large cities, 98–99, 100

rioting (and mobs), 39, 83, 93, 97, 124, 136, 225; antiabolitionist mobs, 92, 93; Astor Place Riot (1849), 85–87, 97, 302n64; draft riots (1863), 97, 100, 103–107, 131, 307n72; during World War II, 245; election, 78; enforcing residential segregation, 245; as expression of popular sovereignty, 78, 93; in Los Angeles (1992), 272, 273; against Metropolitan police in New York City (1857), 103; and mob mind, 140–142, 158, 160, 170, 171, 188, 229; Orange riot in New York City (1871), 112–113; police, at Haymarket (1886), 63; post World War I, 171; race, 1960s, 251, 259, 261, 262, 266; in revolutionary crisis, 13, 21; secession described as, 99

Rochester, New York, 155

Roosevelt, Franklin, 205, 206, 207–208, 209, 210, 231, 233, 241, 243

Roosevelt, Theodore, 139, 144, 147, 156, 173–174, 197, 198–199, 200, 297n29

saloons, 57, 65, 83, 102, 133, 173, 216–218, 219, 220–221, 223, 225–226, 227, 230–231

schools, 153, 248, 269, 278; and civic life, 28, 42, 46, 47, 48, 85, 164, 165, 214, 240, 269, 270, 273; community control of, 258–259, 260; controversial curriculum in, 92, 94, 177; decay of, 247, 265, 267, 273; social centers movement in, 155; struggle over integration of, 166, 245, 249, 251, 262, 263, 264, 265; vehicle for transforming working-class culture, 106, 109, 228–229

Seattle, 202

settlement house movement, 3, 66, 135, 145, 149–150, 164, 171, 173; and debates over urban recreations, 164, 166, 220, 222; during World War I, 178; post World War I transformation of, 184, 187

single-family home, 131, 262; at center of American dream, 2, 239, 244; as object of federal subsidies, 192, 239–244, 248

slavery (and slaves), xi, 7, 34, 43, 49, 65, 70, 71, 77, 90, 108, 121, 133, 259, 293n52, 294n65, 303n93, 304n94; and city life, 17, 31; and Democratic party, 40–41, 43, 88–89, 104; disrupted by Revolution, 13, 16–17, 30–31; fears of British conspiracy to enslave colonists, 9, 16, 17–18, 19, 20, 23; growth in opposition to, in antebellum period, 90–97, 98; as issue of modern industrial life, 162, 194, 195–197; and legacy of revolution, 29–32; making slaves into citizens, 4, 7, 45–48, 50–51; plantation romanticized, 54; proslavery argument, 40, 43, 44, 50, 93; support for, uniting whites, 17, 18, 29, 39–40, 50, 54, 88–89, 98–99, 103; and wage or white slavery, 35, 37, 39–40, 51–52, 162, 194, 195–197. *See also* emancipation (of slaves)

slums, 57, 109, 133, 175, 228, 249, 272; clearance and prevention, 245, 253–254, 255, 256; contrast with affluent areas, 135; fatalism about, 131, 133; result of unequal public benefits, 135, 173, 257–258; as tangle of pathology, 135, 258

social centers movement, 145, 155–157, 173, 187; and early movie culture, 159, 164; post World War I transformation of, 184–185; role in World War I, 171, 177–178

social science, 52, 137, 186; democratic, 176, 186; development in opposition to laissez-faire, 66; expert, 184; and fatalism, 109, 133

Stanton, Elizabeth Cady, 30, 31, 49, 120–121, 308n4

Stevens, Thaddeus, 46, 47–48, 49, 294n56

streets, 56, 61, 64, 90–91, 101, 111, 114, 128, 129, 130, 131, 135, 149, 152–153, 203, 242, 256, 264; advertising in, 188, 191–192, 226; crowding and rushing in, 59, 74, 134; ferment of Revolution in, 10, 13, 17, 18, 21, 22, 30; highways, 111, 204, 239, 242–243, 246, 250, 252, 255–256, 262, 271; and Jacksonian democracy, 73, 77, 78, 79; and legal creation of public realm, 74–76; negative attitudes to, 116, 132, 135, 246, 272, 273, 324n3; promenading, 73, 83–84; and public life, xii, 77, 84–85, 108, 134, 148, 162, 240, 256, 266, 302n75, 331n24; speeding vehicles in, 131, 256; violence in, 105, 108, 112–113, 251; and visual order and disorder, 73, 133–134

strikes, 64, 100–101, 141, 167, 194, 201, 211, 226, 231, 247; armories as response to, 136; at Brooklyn's Beth-El Hospital (1962), 257; courts outlawing, 37; during Reconstruction, 51, 61, 100, 112–113, 114–116; during World War I, 171, 201, 202–203; during World War II, 211; for eight hour day, 63, 114–116, 201; in Gilded Age, 61, 63, 64, 140; Lawrence, Massachusetts (1912), 166, 196; in Progressive Era, 163, 166, 194–196, 325n15; Pullman (1894), 65–67, 140, 173, 194, 315n15; against railroads in 1877, 61, 118, 136; sit-down strikes, 206–207; teachers' strike in New York City (1968), 260; use of court injunctions to defeat, 66, 197, 199, 203; use of troops to defeat, 55, 67, 194, 203; wave of, 1945–1946, 212–213, 246, 329n75; wave of, 1919, 171, 202–203; wave of, 1930s, 206–207;

suburbanization, 64, 131, 135, 160, 192, 239–241; and decentralization of industry, 246–247; and environmental movement, 274–275; and fragmentation of metropolitan government, 247–249, 263; and homeowner populism, 247–249, 250, 261–262, 264–265; and opposition to open housing, 249, 250–251, 254, 256–257, 261–262; and public services, 239, 245, 263–265, 267, 271; suburban-industrial complex, 243–245; supplanting city at center of democratic aspirations, 239–240; and tax revolts, 248, 249, 262, 263–264, 265, 267, 271; and white flight from the city, 247–248, 263, 264–265, 267

taxpayers, 15, 109–110, 117–118, 135, 247–248, 265

Tocqueville, Alexis de, 5–6, 33, 42

Tweed, William, 58, 59–60, 90, 100, 105, 109–114, 119, 127, 131

urban redevelopment and renewal, 212, 239–240, 250, 252, 253–256

Whig party: civic ideals, 41–42, 43–44; co-opting workmen's movements, 38; effort to suppress popular culture, 71; moral reform and paternalism, 42–43; and post office, 72; program of improvement, 41–42; transformation of Northern wing of, 43–44

Whitman, Walt, 52, 64, 67, 81, 82, 83, 98, 132

Wilson, Woodrow: and Progressive era, 144, 147, 156, 163, 197, 199; and World War I, 145, 170–171, 174–175, 176–178, 179, 181, 200, 201, 202

women, xi, 7, 11, 57, 69, 79, 105, 113, 156, 161, 219, 246, 251; in abolition movement, 49–50; as audience for abolitionist agitation, 93; and civic imagery, 76, 229n20; demand for leisure, 219, 220–221; and democratic legacy of Revolution, 29–30, 31–32; as factory workers, 37, 39, 150–151, 161, 164, 195, 196, 219; and genteel culture, 84, 85, 120, 224; limits of Revolution for, 29–32; in public spaces of pre-Civil War cities, 73, 77, 84, 85; in public spaces of post-Civil War cities, 132, 134, 135, 160–161; role in Congress of Industrial Organizations, 206; role in Revolution, 16–17, 21, 29; unthinking exclusion of, 50, 77. *See also* domestic realm; settlement house movement; women's rights movement

women's rights movement, 30, 49–50, 189; and abolition movement, 49–50, 120; demand for suffrage, 49–50, 120–121, 161; revolutionary origins of, 30–32

World War I, 4, 145, 170–172, 173–181, 183, 200–203; Committee on Public Information, 170–171, 176–178, 179, 187, 188–189; debate over preparedness, 176, 200; effects on movie industry, 167, 169, 177, 187–188, 228; federal repression of dissent, 171, 176, 201–202; and mobilization of economy, 147, 175–176, 180, 200–201; as opportunity for democratic reform, 174–176, 180, 183; policy of peace without victory, 174; and Prohibition, 226; propaganda, 170–171, 172, 176–177, 178, 179–180, 183–184, 187, 188–189; strikes, 171, 201, 202–203; U.S. decision to intervene, 172, 173, 174, 175, 176, 181; vigilante suppression of dissent, 171; War Industries Board, 200–201; war intellectuals, 171, 173, 174–177, 178–179, 180–181

World War II, 234, 209–211, 238–239, 244, 245; and dream of single-family home, 238–239, 244; as opportunity for global New Deal, 209–211; War Production Board, 210

John D. Fairfield is Professor of History and Academic Director of the Institute for Politics and Public Life at Xavier University and the author of *The Mysteries of the Great City: The Politics of Urban Design, 1877–1937*.

6482366